Quilting
from little things...

Sarah Fielke

Quilting
from little things...

Krause Publications
Cincinnati, Ohio

Contents

Introduction

Writing this book and designing and making the quilts that are in it has been the biggest adventure I have ever had.

They say that from little things, big things grow. When I started my new little business at the beginning of 2010, I wondered just what I would be able to grow from it. It was a leap of faith to leave my previous business partnership, Material Obsession, and begin again on my own... but things are growing and putting down roots everywhere I look, and life is very exciting!

I have written two quilt books before this one and also written articles for magazines. But writing this book has meant deciding on what my own personal style really is, distilling it, and applying it liberally to anything that came into contact with the creation of *Quilting*.

To find just what that style is, I needed a huge amount of self-examination, and also examination of my quilts: what I like and don't like about them; why I made them; and what I think works and doesn't work about them. Doing all this and sticking with what I found has required a lot of discipline and focus.

Why am I telling you all this? Because every quilt you make should be an adventure, and every new project should be a project in self-awareness and discovery.

Let's not get too highbrow here, though. I don't expect that all of you are going to go out and reinvent your quilting lives because I tell you to. What I do hope you take from this book, however, is the courage to try something different, to experiment with techniques, colors or textures that you may not have tried before, and discover what inspires, fulfills, and delights you about the quilts that you make.

The pairs of quilts in this book are designed to be like little lessons, although you certainly don't have to use them that way. Each pair is a dolly (or small) quilt, and a larger quilt to go with it. The pair of quilts uses the same technique to arrive at a finished product. The idea is that if you have not tried a technique before, you can make the small quilt first as a tester, to see whether the style of working suits you. That way, you can

Every new project you start should be a project in self-awareness and discovery

expand your skill base without committing to a big bed quilt every time. From little things—your dollies—you can grow a large quilt, or use the skills you have learned to grow your own design.

You could also make all the dolly quilts as a collection. There are loads of websites on the Net, showing off dolly quilt collections, both antique and modern. They look wonderful displayed on a wall, framed, or even made into a clutch of cushions to brighten up a sofa.

Try to use the quilts in this book to find out more about growing your own quilting. Why do you choose the fabrics you do? Do your quilts look "the same" every time, or is every one different? Do you usually choose the same style of fabrics for every quilt? Do you often make quilts with only three or four fabrics in them, or do you cram so many fabrics in that you can't see the wood for the trees? Do you love your quilts, do they make you happy—and why do you make them in the first place?

I make my quilts because if I didn't, I would be a very cross girl indeed! I need to make them to feel happy and useful. They are something that is entirely mine but, at the same time, something that I share with others. All my life, I have had a creative outlet of some kind, but until I came to quilt designing, I didn't realize how unfulfilling those other outlets were to me. I love to make my quilts; I love to design them and to use them,

From little things— your dollies—you can grow a large quilt, or use the skills you have learned to grow your own design

and I love others to use them. Whether or not other people think they are good or worthy is to me a bonus—I would still make quilts even if no one but my children saw them. They make me feel energized and excited and full of possibilities.

I design from my stash, and I encourage you to do the same. If you don't have a large stash, I encourage you to start growing one! You don't need huge amounts of fabric: even 8-inch pieces can be the seeds of a diverse quilt, somewhere down the line.

My stash is large, but it's never large enough. I don't ever feel bad about how much fabric I have—the fabric is as essential to my inspiration as the actual construction of the quilts.

Buy fabrics because you love them and because they make your heart sing, not because they have a specific purpose. One day, the perfect fabric will jump right into your hands from your stash, without your ever knowing the reason for which it was bought! These random discoveries are what make your fabric choices interesting and exciting rather than pre-determined.

Get excited, get passionate! Nothing is "wrong" if you love the finished product. Go on, get growing—I mean, sewing.

Yes, I meant now! What are you waiting for?

Sarah Fielke

Choosing fabrics

*t*he question I am asked most often is how I choose my fabrics, and what makes me use certain fabrics together. I'm sorry to say that I don't have a definite answer for you. All I can do is tell you what kind of fabrics I buy and how I know that they are right together.

My stash is full of fabrics in different-size graphics. This is just as important as having a good range of colors. My fabrics are divided by color, but also often by tone and print size. I try to make sure that I have a good range of lights, mediums, and darks in all the colors in my stash: for example, my blues range from a very pale powder blue through aqua and cerulean right through to a very dark navy. Within those colors, there will be small, medium, and large prints, and always, always, dots and stripes.

I have lots of small graphics—little flowers, small checks, and dots, tiny motifs and pin stripes. Reproduction ranges and shirtings and 1930s prints are great places to find smaller prints.

Then there are the medium-size prints, the ones that would be the most present in most people's stashes. These prints include florals, tone-on-tones, stripes, checks, and dots. Modern fabric ranges lean mainly into the medium range in both graphics and tone. That's all fine, but you need to make sure that you have variations in color, graphic, and tone if you want to create movement and interest in your quilts.

Many quilters shy away from large-scale prints, not knowing how to use them except in large pieces. I always have a good range of large prints in my stash—I love that when you cut a large print into small pieces, you get so much more diversity and interest into your quilt than you do with a smaller print, in conveniently coordinating colors! And, of course, a large print always makes a striking border.

There are three things I cannot live without. I have a huge stash of predominantly white fabrics that I love and hoard with a passion. They are indispensable when I make the kinds of quilts I love to make most. These fabrics have dots, stripes, floral prints, checks...but they are predominantly white. I also have a real passion for fabrics with little animals on them—I have literally hundreds and nearly all my quilts

You need to make sure that you have variations in color, graphic, and tone if you want to create movement and interest in your quilts

have an animal in them somewhere. And I never met a dot I didn't like! Dots are my neutrals—I use them as basics and backgrounds. A dot with an irregular spread becomes a neutral and recedes, whereas a regular print dot comes forward.

You will notice that I don't list solids as essential in my stash. That's because, as a rule, I don't use them. Even though, in this book, you will see a few quilts with "plain" fabrics included in them, these fabrics are shot cottons or linens that have texture and layered color rather than being a flat, solid fabric. I particularly like to use Kaffe Fassett's shot cottons, Oakshott fabrics, and Essex linen.

OK, now you've planted the seeds of your stash, you want to know why I use fabrics together, and this is where it gets hard. Essentially, the answer is this.

When I start a new project, I go to my stash and pull out a few fabrics that I think would be a good start. Then I go through all my piles of fabric with those fabrics in mind. I don't have the original fabrics in sight, as the temptation then is to match everything up, and that takes all the surprise out of the color combinations.

When I have a good pile of things that are making me smack my lips together, I put everything in one pile and start holding things up against each other. Sometimes, there are little piles "brewing" all over the place in the studio, for days or weeks on end. The bonus of this is that sometimes when I clean up, things are put together that never were intended to go together, and then there's magic! The unexpected joy of two very different fabrics playing harmoniously together can be the highlight of my day. As a Gee's Bend quilter once said: "Let chance be your creative director."

When I am relatively happy with a pile (and often the original fabrics don't make the grade!), I start to cut pieces and put them on the design wall. I always work with a design wall so that I can stand back from pieces I have arranged, have a good long look, and let them "steep" a while longer. Sometimes, a piece I think is perfect looks totally different when it is cut up and on the wall.

Keep changing, keep moving things around. Try something different if you're not convinced. My fabric choice philosophy boils down to this— if it makes your heart sing, it's perfect.

As a Gee's Bend quilter once said: "Let chance be your creative director."

Before you begin...

Using this book

The quilts in this book are grouped into 10 pairs, with each pair consisting of a dolly quilt and a full-size quilt that was inspired, in some way, by the dolly.

My suggestion would be—especially if you are a less experienced quilter—that you should make the dolly quilt before you attempt the larger version. The dolly quilts give you the opportunity to perfect a particular piecing technique or experiment with colors and fabrics before spending considerable time and money on a large project. Of course, you don't have to take my advice—you may want to get stuck right into the larger version without attempting the dolly. Or you may, indeed, plan to make only dolly-size quilts and none of the large ones. It's entirely up to you, but whatever you choose to do, check out the basic information below before you begin and, when you get to the projects themselves, do take a few minutes to read through all the steps before you start.

A note on cutting

Apart from your fabric, of course, the most essential thing you are going to need for your quilting adventure is a rotary cutter. If you have already used one, then you know just how indispensable this little gadget is. It enables you to cut multiple layers of fabric so much more quickly and accurately than using scissors.

If you haven't used one before, ask advice from your quilting store about which one to buy—but do use one. It will change your life!

Degree of difficulty *

*
Straightforward piecing

**
More complex techniques

***
Complex techniques such as inset piecing

****
More than one complex technique required

Fabrics and preparation

All fabric requirements listed under Materials and Tools are based on fabric that is 44 inches wide, unless specified otherwise. I recommend that all your fabrics be 100 percent cotton or linen, and be ironed before you cut them.

Many quilters prefer to wash, dry, and iron cotton quilting fabrics before use, and this is an especially good idea with dark fabrics. Wash each fabric separately in warm water with a scrap of white cotton fabric to test if the color runs. If it does, the fabric should be discarded or used for another purpose. Otherwise, when the quilt is washed, the color may run and ruin the quilt.

Washing pre-shrinks fabric and removes all finishes added by the manufacturer. Such finishes can make the fabric stiffer and easier to sew; if you wish to restore the stiffness, spray the fabric lightly with spray starch before sewing.

Before sewing, remove the tightly woven edges (selvages) from all fabrics. These shrink at a different rate from the rest of the fabric, so if they are left on and included in seams, they may cause the fabric to pucker and bunch when it is laundered.

Unless otherwise stated, all seam allowances are $1/4$ inch throughout.

The dolly quilts give you the opportunity to perfect a particular piecing technique or experiment with colors and fabrics

{*note*}

ROTARY CUTTER SAFETY
Safety should be a priority when using the rotary cutter. The blade should be exposed only when a cut is to be made (by retracting the cover with the thumb) and the protective sheath should be replaced as soon as the cut is finished to protect you and to prevent the blade from being damaged. Never leave rotary cutters lying about where they can be found by children or pets.

A rotary cutter is essentially a circular razor blade, so treat it accordingly.

Fat quarters

A "fat quarter" is made by cutting one yard of fabric in half, first vertically, then horizontally. The resultant squarish piece, approximately 18 x 22 inches, is sometimes a more useful size than a "standard" quarter-yard that is simply cut across the width of the fabric. Fat quarters are a good size for backing a dolly quilt.

General sewing and patchwork supplies

Rather than repeating this list under Materials and Tools for every project, I am assuming that you will have the following basic requirements before you begin:

- Sewing machine (unless you are a very patient hand-sewer!)
- $1/4$-inch sewing machine foot, for accurate sewing of seams
- Machine thread to match your chosen fabrics—see note on choosing threads, opposite
- Dress-making scissors—to be used only for cutting fabric
- Thread snippers, or small sharp scissors
- Scissors that can be used for cutting paper or template plastic
- Seam ripper
- Pins
- Tape measure
- Quilter's ruler—it is handy to have two rulers of the same size to assist in cutting strips without having to turn the cutting mat around
- Rotary cutter—buy the best one you can afford
- Self-healing cutting mat
- Masking tape, for securing backing fabric to a flat surface and marking quilting lines
- Chalk pencil and gel pen, for marking quilting and appliqué lines
- Quilter's safety pins (if you are pinning quilt layers, rather than basting—see page 193)
- Quilter's hoop, for hand-quilting
- Quilter's thimble

{note}

CHOOSING THREADS

Match the thread to the fabric when piecing: for example, when using cotton fabric, use cotton thread. Avoid using polyester thread with a cotton fabric; over time it will cut through the fibers of the cotton.

In most situations, cream, white, or gray threads are appropriate for piecing. If using a multicolor fabric, use a neutral thread, such as gray or beige, to match the tone of the background.

Using a design wall

If you're making a quilt that has a lot of blocks of different colors or tones, I really recommend laying them all out on a flat surface, such as the floor or a wall or, better still, on a design wall, made with batting or felt, which helps the cut shapes to stay in place. If you don't have space, you can even use a piece of flannel or an old sheet to lay your pieces out on to view, then fold it up and put it away when you are not working on the quilt.

By using a design wall, it is possible to "audition" or sample colors or shapes before committing to sewing them together. You can move the blocks about until you get a pleasing arrangement, and check that the same fabrics aren't too close to each other, and that the eye is not drawn to particular blocks or areas at the expense of the rest of the design. Squinting at the quilt or looking at it through the lens of a camera can help you discern "holes" or unbalanced areas. It is always a good idea to lay out the blocks and step back. However, if this isn't possible, cover a piece of cardboard with batting scraps and keep it next to the sewing machine. Lay out each block on the batting before sewing it together.

Special rulers

All of the quilts in this book can be made using a standard 24-inch quilter's ruler and the templates provided. However, occasionally I have included an optional specialized ruler in the Materials and Tools list. These rulers can make accurate cutting much quicker and easier, and if you wish to use them, then by all means do so. They are usually sold with detailed instructions for their use.

Half-square triangle ruler

A half-square ruler, also called a 45-degree triangle ruler, is useful, but not strictly necessary, for cutting half-square triangles. You can, of course, cut these triangles with your standard quilter's ruler by cross-cutting strips into squares, then cutting each square diagonally in half, giving two half-square triangles. (The size of the square that you cut when cutting half-square triangles in this way should always be $7/8$ inch larger than the desired finished size of the triangle.)

Specialized half-square triangle rulers, however, have already made allowance for the seam allowance at the point of the triangle, thus eliminating the "ears" on the seam. This means that if you are using a

By using a design wall, it is possible to "audition" or sample colors or shapes before committing to sewing them together

half-square triangle ruler, the size of your cut square should only be $1/2$ inch larger than the desired finished size of the triangle, not $7/8$ inch. The half-square triangles that you cut with this type of ruler will all have a blunt point.

Wedge ruler

Wedge rulers, also called circle segment, fan, or Dresden plate rulers, are used for cutting accurate segments of a circle—or wedges—and come in a variety of brands and sizes. In this book, I have used an 18-degree wedge ruler to cut the wedges in *Hanging Lanterns*.

60-degree triangle ruler

This ruler is primarily used to cut equilateral triangles (each internal angle is 60 degrees and all three sides are the same length), but it is also useful for accurately cutting diamonds, half-diamonds, and 30-degree triangles. I have used this ruler for *Peaks and Troughs* and *Stars in Your Eyes*.

Specialized rulers can make accurate cutting much quicker and easier.

Finishing your quilt

Each of the projects takes you step-by-step through the construction of the quilt top. When you are ready to combine your completed top with the batting, backing, and binding, turn to the Quilt layout and assembly section on page 190 for detailed instructions.

The projects

Row by row construction

Diamond Chips
Dolly quilt, 12$^1/_2$ inches square

Botanical Gardens
Throw, 74$^1/_2$ inches square

The secret to making both these quilts is simple—understanding that the blocks are constructed in rows of squares across the quilt, rather than in constructed blocks that are then sewn together, is the key. Practice by sewing together a smaller, more controlled number of squares and colors before you challenge yourself with the more complex color layouts of *Botanical Gardens*. Using a design wall and a reducing glass or camera to check the placement and value of the fabrics in *Botanical Gardens* will make your job so much easier!

Diamond Chips

The blue and white fabrics in this quilt are what create the diamond sparkle in the pattern. The fabric used for the diamonds is a triangular graphic, which makes the diamond shape of the block seem more faceted.

Finished quilt size
Dolly quilt, 12½ inches square

MATERIALS AND TOOLS

- 4 inches dot white fabric
- 4 inches blue-pattern fabric with a strong graphic
- 4 inches dot yellow fabric, or scrap
- 6 inches striped fabric for binding
- 1 fat quarter for backing
- 16 inches square cotton batting
- Half-square triangle ruler (optional, see page 24)
- White and blue perle cotton No 8 for quilting
- No 9 crewel embroidery needles for quilting
- General sewing and patchwork supplies (see page 22)

CUTTING

All fabrics are strip-cut across the width of the fabric from fold to selvage unless otherwise specified or unless you are using a directional print.

FROM DOT WHITE FABRIC, CUT:
- Two strips, 1½ inches wide. Cross-cut these strips to yield 48 squares, each 1½ inches.
- One strip, 1⅞ inches wide. Cross-cut this strip to yield 16 squares, each 1⅞ inches. Cross-cut these squares across one diagonal to yield 32 half-square triangles. Alternatively, cut your strip 1½ inches wide and use a half-square triangle ruler to cut these triangles.

FROM BLUE-PATTERN FABRIC, CUT:
- Two strips, 1½ inches wide. Cross-cut these strips to yield 48 squares, each 1½ inches.
- One strip, 1⅞ inches wide. Cross-cut this strip to yield 16 squares, each 1⅞ inches. Cross-cut these squares on one diagonal to yield 32 half-square triangles. Alternatively, cut your strip 1½ inches wide and use a half-square triangle ruler to cut these triangles.

FROM DOT YELLOW FABRIC, CUT:
- One strip, 1½ inches wide. Cross-cut to yield 16 squares, each 1½ inches.

FROM STRIPED BINDING FABRIC, CUT:
- Two strips, 3 inches wide. Set aside for binding.

Block diagram

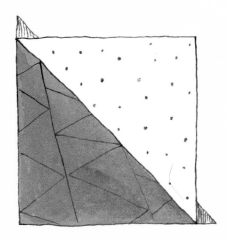

Diagram 1

Constructing the quilt top

1 Begin laying out the pieces for each block according to the Block diagram and the photograph of the quilt. The quilt is put together in rows (rather than in complete blocks), so lay out all of the squares in their rows until the whole quilt is spread in front of you on a table or a piece of batting. Your quilt should be 12 squares across each row and 12 rows down.

2 Sew the first row together into a strip. When you reach the half-square triangles, sew the triangles together into a square across the diagonal (Diagram 1). Press the seam towards the darker fabric, trim the "ears," and then sew the square to the strip, and continue. Press all the seams toward the dark fabrics.

3 Sew the second row. Press the seams toward the dark fabrics.

4 Continue until you have completed 12 rows. Now sew the first row to the second row, being careful to match the seams when the squares meet. Continue until you have sewn 12 rows together. Press the top carefully and make sure it is square. Your quilt top is complete.

Backing, quilting, and binding

Using masking tape, tape the backing fabric, face down, onto a table, smoothing out any creases as you go. Lay the batting piece onto the backing, and then the quilt top on top. Smooth any creases and hand-baste the three layers together using large stitches and working from the center out. As this is only a small quilt, it does not need a lot of basting. The backing and batting should be larger than the top for ease of quilting; don't be tempted to trim them back.

Refer to pages 190–199 for instructions on finishing.

{note on quilting}

I hand-quilted *Diamond Chips* using white perle cotton No 8 in a criss-cross fashion over the whole quilt, except the yellow squares. Where the grid crosses the blue-pattern squares, I changed to blue cotton thread.

Botanical Gardens

Flowers bloom and leaves sway in the lush botanical gardens of this quilt. Large–scale floral prints and coordinating graphics are the secret to making your own Botanical Garden bloom. Be sure to include a wide variety of prints, but make certain that the pairs of fabrics you choose are complementing each other, not contrasting, and you will create a blended garden bed just like the one shown here.

Finished quilt size

Throw, 74½ inches square

Degree of difficulty
*

MATERIALS AND TOOLS

- 4 inches each of 8 different light-blue and 8 different dark-blue fabrics

- 4 inches each of 8 different light-green and 8 different dark-green fabrics

- 4 inches each of 8 different light-orange or light-yellow and 8 different dark-orange or dark-yellow fabrics

- 4 inches each of 8 different light-pink or light-red and 8 different dark-pink or dark-red fabrics

- 20 inches dark-brown fabric for accent squares

- 4 inches medium floral fabric for border inserts

- 1 yard large floral fabric for border

- 27 inches striped fabric for binding

- 4⅝ yards backing fabric

- 83 inches square cotton batting

- General sewing and patchwork supplies (see page 22)

CUTTING

All fabrics are strip-cut across the width of the fabric from fold to selvage unless otherwise specified or unless you are using a directional print.

FROM EACH OF THE 4-INCH PIECES OF LIGHT AND DARK FABRICS, CUT:

- One strip, 3⅞ inches wide, across the width of the fabric, giving a total of 64 strips. Separate the fabrics into 32 pairs, each containing a light and a dark strip from the same colorway (eight pairs of each colorway).

{note}

I recommend using a design wall for this quilt. You can also use a half-square triangle ruler to cut your triangles, if you prefer (see page 24).

FROM EACH COLORWAY PAIR, CUT:

- Two pairs of squares, each 3⅞ inches (four squares in total). Cross-cut these pairs of squares on one diagonal into four pairs of half-square triangles (eight half-square triangles in total). Trim the remaining section of each colorway pair to be 3½ inches wide.

FROM EACH TRIMMED PAIR, CUT:

- Six pairs of squares, each 3½ inches (12 squares in total). Set the eight half-square triangles and 12 squares from each colorway pair aside in their pairs (zippered plastic bags are handy here for keeping things in order) and continue with the remaining fabric pairs until you have cut all the squares and triangles for 32 pairs.

FROM DARK-BROWN FABRIC, CUT:

- Five strips, 3½ inches wide. Cross-cut these strips into 3½-inch squares—you will need 49 squares in all.

FROM BORDER INSERT FABRIC, CUT:

- One strip, 3½ inches wide. From this strip, cross-cut seven pieces, each 6 x 3½ inches.

FROM BORDER FLORAL, CUT:

- Six strips, 6 inches wide.

FROM RED BINDING FABRIC, CUT:

- Nine strips, 3 inches wide. Set aside for binding.

Constructing the quilt top

1 Using the photograph of the finished quilt and the Block diagram, begin by laying out the pieces for each row. Your quilt should be 21 squares across each row and 21 rows down.

Each "block" of the quilt contains the four pairs of half-triangles and the six pairs of squares that you cut from a light/dark colorway pair, as well as four brown accent squares. However, the quilt top is constructed square by square, and row by row, rather than a block at a time. As you lay out the rows, you will see how the blocks in each colorway are formed and it helps to visualize the design in terms of blocks.

(Using a design wall is a great way to lay out your pieces, as you can see your colors clearly. Follow the layout of alternating colors as in the picture, but don't be too worried about where each fabric goes yet. It is much better to lay the fabric down, and then move the colors around until you are happy with the layout.)

2 You will also see from the photograph that the edges of the patchwork quilt top are composed of half-blocks and, in the upper left- and lower right-hand corners, of quarter-blocks. For these rows, you will need to divide some of your sets of square and triangle pairs into the appropriate number.

3 When you are happy with the arrangement of your squares, sew the first row together into a strip. When you come to the half-square triangles, sew the triangles together into a square (Diagram 1). Press the seam allowance toward the darker fabric, trim off the "ears" at each corner, and then sew the completed square to the strip, and continue. Press all the seams toward the dark fabrics.

4 Sew the second row. Press the seams toward the dark fabrics.

Block diagram

Diagram 1

5 Continue in this way until you have completed all 21 rows of the quilt top. Now sew the first row to the second row, being careful to match the seams when the squares meet. Continue until you have sewn all 21 rows together. Press the top carefully and make sure it is square.

Border

6 Beginning and ending with a 6-inch border insert piece, sew the seven inset pieces and six floral border strips together, end to end, into one long strip.

7 Measure your quilt through the center in both directions to get the true width. It should measure 63½ inches. (If it does not, you should adjust the following border measurements.)

8 Cut two strips from the assembled border fabric, each 63½ inches long. Find the center of one edge of the quilt and the center of one border strip and pin, then pin the ends together. Pin in between, easing if needed. Sew and repeat with the opposite border. Press.

9 Measure the quilt across the center again with the borders attached. Cut the remaining two borders to this measurement. Attach the remaining two borders as above. Your quilt top is complete.

Backing, quilting, and binding

Cut the backing fabric in half crosswise, giving two pieces, each 83 inches long. Trim the selvages and sew the pieces together along the length to form one backing piece. Press the seam allowance open.

Refer to pages 190–199 for instructions on finishing.

{note on quilting}

I had *Botanical Gardens* machine-quilted by Kim Bradley in an all-over floral pattern.

Strip piecing

Rebel with a Rotary
Dolly quilt, 16 inches square

Sandwich Short of a Picnic
Twin, 60 x 87½ inches

Both these quilts are strip-pieced. Strip piecing is a way to create your own "fabric" from which to cut another shape. In both of these quilts, triangles are cut from strips sewn together into yardage, to create striped triangles.

There are so many applications of this technique. Try out the dolly quilt or *Picnic* quilt for practice, and then try making other shapes—diamonds, rectangles, squares. You can even strip piece and cut circles to appliqué. Just be sure to sew onto a cloth or paper foundation if you are going to have too many bias edges!

Rebel with a Rotary

Unintentionally, this little quilt came out looking like some kind of rebel flag! In red, white, and blue, it could be an American flag, an English flag, an Australian flag, a French flag—why not make it in red, white, and green for Italy? Or dive into your stash and create your own flag of the Patchwork Nation.

Finished quilt size
Dolly quilt, 16 inches square

Degree of difficulty
*

MATERIALS AND TOOLS

- 6 inches red-and-white stripe fabric

- 4 inches white fabric

- 6 inches dark-blue star fabric

- 6 inches dark-blue fabric for binding

- 1 fat quarter for backing

- 20 inches square cotton batting

- 2B pencil

- Template plastic

- Red perle cotton No 8 for hand-quilting and tying

- No 9 crewel embroidery needles for quilting

- General sewing and patchwork supplies (see page 22)

TEMPLATES

Trace Rebel with a Rotary Template 1 triangle (on pattern sheet) onto template plastic with a sharp 2B pencil and cut out accurately using sharp scissors (but not your fabric scissors).

CUTTING

All fabrics are strip-cut across the width of the fabric from fold to selvage unless otherwise specified or unless you are using a directional print.

FROM RED-AND-WHITE STRIPE FABRIC, CUT:
- Four strips, 1½ inches wide.

FROM WHITE FABRIC, CUT:
- Two strips, 1½ inches wide.

FROM DARK-BLUE STAR FABRIC, CUT:
- Three strips, 2 inches wide. Cross-cut these strips to yield eight strips, each 2 x 5½ inches, and four strips, each 2 x 12½ inches.

FROM BINDING FABRIC, CUT:
- Two strips, 3 inches wide. Set aside for binding.

Constructing the quilt top

1 Sew together two sets of three strips, each set consisting of two red-and-white stripe strips with a white strip in between (Diagram 1). Press the seams toward the striped fabric.

2 Using Template A, cut 16 triangles total from the two pieced strips. Alternatively, using the 45-degree angle on your patchwork ruler, cut a 45-degree bias line from your strip set. Re-align the ruler and cut a 45-degree angle at the top of the strip. Cut 16 triangles total (Diagram 2).

3 Following Diagram 3, join one shorter side of a triangle to one edge of a 5½ x 2-inch star fabric strip. Sew a second triangle to the other edge of the strip to form a half-block. Make sure to line up the end of the strip with the 90-degree corner of the triangles so that the other end sticks out for trimming later. Repeat with all eight pairs of triangles to make eight half-blocks total.

4 Sew two half-blocks together with a 12½-inch star strip in between. To do this, fold the star strip in half and finger-press the center crease. Do the same with the triangle strip and match the creases before sewing, so that the strip is sticking out the same amount at each end for trimming later. Make four blocks in this way.

Diagram 1

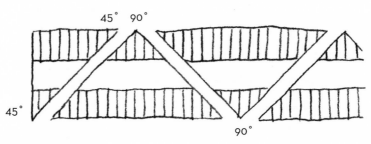

45°   90°

45°

90°

Diagram 2

Quilting from little things...

5 Using your patchwork ruler, trim the blocks to measure 8¼ inches square (Diagram 4).

6 Sew two pairs of blocks together, taking care to match the seams on the diagonals. Now, sew the pairs together across the middle seam of the quilt. Press. Your quilt top is complete.

Backing, quilting, and binding

Using masking tape, tape the backing fabric, face down, onto a table, smoothing out any creases as you go. Lay the batting piece onto the backing, and then the quilt top on top. Smooth any creases and hand-baste the three layers together using large stitches and working from the center out. As this is only a small quilt, it does not need a lot of basting. The backing and batting should be larger than the top for ease of quilting; don't be tempted to trim them back.

Refer to pages 190–199 for instructions on finishing.

Diagram 3

Diagram 4

{note on quilting}

I hand-quilted *Rebel with a Rotary* using red perle cotton No 8 along the "down" sides of the strip-pieced seams and around the outside of each square. I also tied a knot of perle cotton in the center of the Xs made by the star fabric.

Sandwich Short of a Picnic

There's a beautiful memory behind this simple quilt. When I was a tiny little girl, about two or three years old, I would go to my grandma's house for the day, so my mom could have a break and look after my baby brother. We did all sorts of different things together, but my favorite thing was rowing our boats.

Grandma would announce that it was "a nice day to row our boats to Bobbin Head," and we would go straight to the kitchen and spend the morning making ribbon sandwiches and baking a sultana slice for the journey. I was allowed to help with everything but the knives.

At lunchtime, we would collect my grandpa from the study with his hat and his pipe, and head out to the picnic blanket on the front lawn and eat our picnic.

After lunch, my marvelous grandma would get out two battered cardboard cartons, we would each climb into one—with grandma's floral skirts hitched up around her knees—and proceed to row our "boats" and have an adventure.

This quilt is about my trips to Bobbin Head with my grandma and her beautiful ribbon sandwiches.

Finished quilt size
Twin, 60 x 87 ½ inches

Degree of difficulty
*

MATERIALS AND TOOLS

- 6 inches each of eight different fabrics for outer sandwich fillings (see Note page 55)

- 4 inches each of eight different fabrics for inner sandwich fillings

- 1⅛ yards plain white fabric for bread

- 2¾ yards "picnic blanket" fabric for triangles and binding

- 27 inches green check fabric for binding

- 5½ yards backing fabric

- 72 x 90 inches cotton batting

- General sewing and patchwork supplies (see page 22)

CUTTING

All fabrics are strip-cut across the width of the fabric from fold to selvage unless otherwise specified or unless you are using a directional print.

FROM EACH OF THE EIGHT DIFFERENT OUTER SANDWICH FILLINGS FABRICS, CUT:
- Two strips, 2½ inches wide (16 strips total).

FROM EACH OF THE EIGHT DIFFERENT INNER SANDWICH FILLINGS FABRICS, CUT:
- One strip, 2½ inches wide (8 strips total).

FROM WHITE FABRIC, CUT:
- 16 strips, 2½ inches wide.

FROM THE PICNIC BLANKET FABRIC, CUT:
- Three strips, 21 inches wide. Cross-cut these strips into six squares, each 21 inches. Cross-cut these squares on both diagonals to yield four quarter-square triangles from each square, for a total of 24 quarter-square triangles. (You will actually only need 22.)
- Three strips, 10½ inches wide. Cross-cut these strips into six squares, each 10½ inches. Cross-cut these squares on one diagonal to give 12 half-square triangles. (You will actually only need 10.)

FROM THE GREEN CHECK FABRIC, CUT:
- Nine strips, 3 inches wide. Set aside for binding.

Diagram 1

Diagram 2

Diagram 3

Constructing the quilt top

Making the sandwiches

1 To make your sandwiches, sew together eight sets of "fillings" and "bread" along the length of the strips (Diagram 1). Each 5-strip set should read:

- Outer filling strip
- Bread strip
- Inner filling strip
- Bread strip
- Outer filling strip

(I realize that sandwiches usually have the bread on the outside not the fillings, but the fillings are brighter and provide more contrast! You will have to use your imagination.) When you have sewn a 5-strip set together, press the seams away from the white bread fabric.

2 Using the 45-degree angle on your patchwork ruler, cut a 45-degree bias line across your strip set. Re-align the ruler and cut at a 45-degree angle from the top of the strip, giving a triangle. (The internal angle at the top of this triangle will be 90 degrees, as shown.) Cut three triangles from each of the eight fabric sets (Diagram 2)—24 triangles total.

3 From the remaining piece at the end of each strip set, cut one half-square triangle. Using the 45-degree angle already cut in the strip, measure along ¾ inch from the top of the angle and cut down at a 90-degree angle (Diagram 3)—eight half-triangles total.

Piecing the rows

4 Using a design wall or a bed for color balancing, lay the sandwich blocks and "picnic rug" triangles out according to the photograph of the quilt. Move the sandwich blocks around until you are happy with their positions. Refer to the photograph for placement of the half-square triangles.

5 Beginning with the top row, sew the triangles together in rows across the quilt. Make sure to clip the "ears" off the triangles, and then press the seams toward the sandwiches.

6 When you have pieced all the rows, join the rows together down the quilt. An easy way to make sure that the points meet is to insert a pin through the point of both seam allowances as you sew, and remove it just as you sew up to it. Make sure that the needle goes right into the place where the pin was (Diagram 4). Press. Your quilt top is complete.

Backing, quilting, and binding

Cut the backing fabric crosswise in half into two pieces, each 99 inches long. Remove the selvages and stitch the pieces together up the long sides. Press the seam allowance open and press the backing piece carefully.

Refer to pages 190–199 for instructions on finishing.

{note}

If you are intending your triangles to represent the sandwiches in the picnic, as mine do, think about your fillings before you choose the colors. My fillings include some of my grandma's favorites, such as tuna and celery, cheese and tomato, and chicken and asparagus. You could also use whole wheat or multigrain bread if you like! My grandma always used soft white "bunny bread" with the crusts cut off, so that's what I have used here.

Diagram 4

{note on quilting}

I had *Sandwich Short of a Picnic* machine-quilted by Kim Bradley in a pattern of butterflies, using white thread.

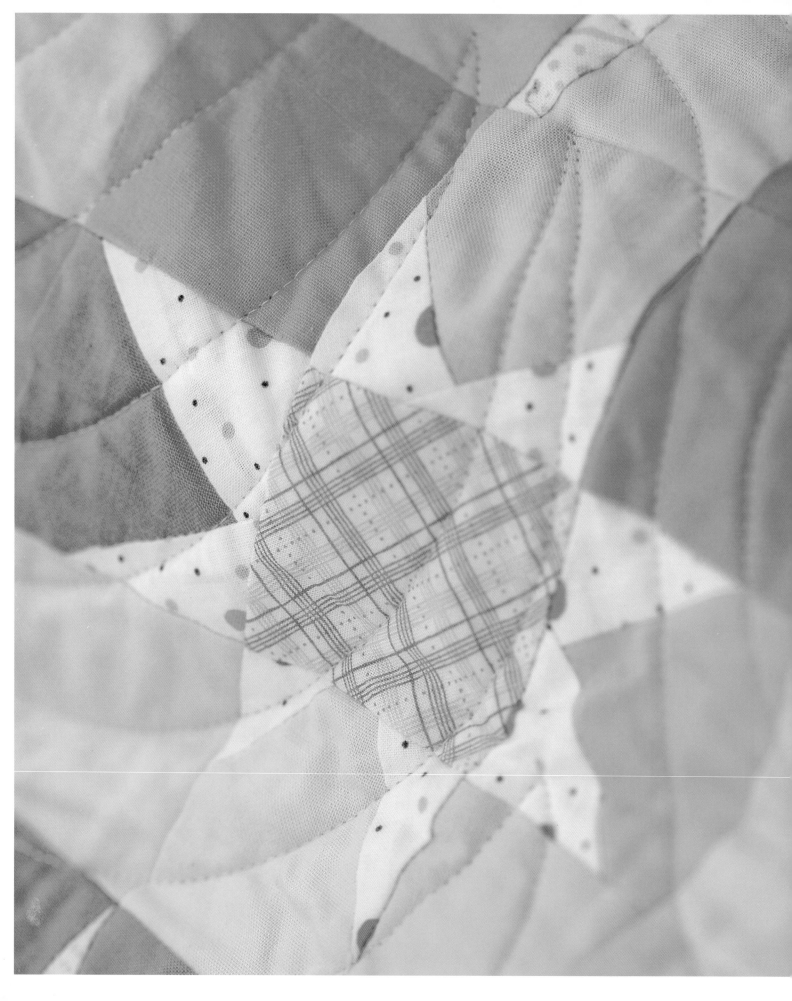

Deconstructed piecing

The Woodpile

Dolly quilt, 11½ x 10½ inches

Dandelions

Twin, 59 x 83 inches

Uneven piecing can be daunting if you have never attempted it before. The concept of cutting pieces without a ruler when every patchwork pattern has urged you to be so careful can be scary! To master this technique, you need to let go of your worries about points that meet and straight seams, and do what feels right. Everything can be trimmed straight when the block is finished and then everything goes together smoothly.

I recommend trying out the technique on *The Woodpile* dolly before launching into the *Dandelions* quilt—there are a lot of little flowers in there!

The Woodpile

These little uneven log cabin blocks are sure to whet your appetite for deconstructed piecing. I decided they wouldn't really be log cabins and had to be woodpiles—whoever lived in those crazy little cabins would be banging their head on the roof much too often!

Degree of difficulty **

Finished quilt size

Dolly quilt, 11½ x 10½ inches

MATERIALS AND TOOLS

- Scrap fabrics of different blues, greens, pinks, purples, and oranges, cut roughly into strips, at least 1½ inches wide x 5 inches long

- 4 inches dark-brown fabric for border triangles

- 4 inches pink-pattern fabric for border triangles

- 6 inches multicolor-stripe fabric for binding

- 1 fat quarter for backing

- 12 inches square cotton batting

- Purple and green silk or cotton for hand-quilting

- Quilting needles ('betweens')

- General sewing and patchwork supplies (see page 22)

CUTTING

Do not use a ruler to cut your scrap pieces if you can help it—you don't want the seams to be straight or the block will look too symmetrical.

FROM SCRAP FABRICS, CUT:

- Rough strips, approximately 1½ inches wide— do not use a ruler to cut these.

FROM DARK-BROWN FABRIC, CUT:

- Two strips, 1½ inches wide. Cross-cut these strips into 38 squares, each 1½ inches.

FROM PINK-PATTERN FABRIC, CUT:

- Two strips, roughly 1½ inches wide.

FROM BINDING FABRIC, CUT:

- Two strips, 3 inches wide. Set aside for binding.

Diagram 1

Diagram 2

Diagram 3

Diagram 4

Constructing the quilt top

1 Begin by cutting a small piece for the center of each block. Decide what color the "logs" are going to be. Each block has two colorways for the logs, one for each side. If the block is blue and green, for instance, I have used a different color for the center. Sew a strip of one color to the side of the center piece and trim off the end of the strip (Diagram 1). Finger-press the seam open. It is fine to angle the fabrics on top of each other so that the seams are not straight.

2 Sew a strip of the same color to the next side of the center block, trim and finger-press the seam open (Diagram 2).

3 Sew a strip of the second color to the next side of the block (Diagram 3).

4 Complete a round of logs by sewing another strip of the second color to the last side of the center block and trim (Diagram 4).

5 Keep sewing around the block in this manner until the block is at least 5 inches square. Take the block to the ironing board, press all the seams flat, and then trim the block to be 5 x 4½ inches.

6 Repeat to make four blocks: two that are predominantly blue and green and two that are pink and yellow, or purple and orange.

7 Arrange the blocks according to the photograph, or in an order that pleases you. Sew two blocks together along the 5-inch side to make a pair, and repeat with the other two blocks. Sew the blocks together to form the quilt center. Press.

Pink/brown border

8 Take a brown square and lay the pink strip over the top of it at an angle, right sides together (Diagram 5). This angle is not critical—in fact each of your finished squares will be slightly different. Sew, and then trim the brown fabric away from the seam allowance. Press and trim the piece to 1½ inches square (Diagram 6). Repeat to make 38 squares.

9 Sew the squares together into two strips of eight squares and two strips of 11 squares, with all the pink diagonals pointing in the same direction (see the photograph of the quilt for guidance).

10 Sew the two strips of eight squares to the top and bottom of the quilt, and the two strips of 11 squares to either side. Press. Your quilt top is complete.

Backing, quilting, and binding

Using masking tape, tape the backing fabric, face down, onto a table, smoothing out any creases as you go. Lay the batting piece onto the backing, and then the quilt top on top. Smooth any creases and hand-baste the three layers together using large stitches and working from the center out. As this is only a small quilt, it does not need a lot of basting. The backing and batting should be larger than the top for ease of quilting; don't be tempted to trim them back.

Refer to pages 190–199 for instructions on finishing.

Diagram 5

Diagram 6

{note on quilting}

I hand-quilted *The Woodpile* using silk thread, quilting along the logs on one side of the block, ⅛ inch apart, and in the ditch on the other side of the logs.

Dandelions

I wandered lonely as a cloud,
That floats on high o'er vales and hills
When all at once I saw a crowd
A host of...
(from the poem "Daffodils" by William Wordsworth)

OK, well they're not golden daffodils, they're white dandelions, but I think these fluffy little flowers remind me of my childhood more than any other flower. Our local park certainly had a host of them, and we used to pick them and blow all the seeds away into the park gardens to make fairy wishes. I'm sure the gardeners didn't love us much. Our blowing must have been creating dandelions faster than they could pull them out. You can make your own childhood fairy wishes with this quilt, or piece all the flowers in different colors for a field of wildflowers instead.

Finished quilt size

Twin, 59 x 83 inches

Degree of difficulty ******

MATERIALS AND TOOLS

- 24 inches each of seven different plain green fabrics for the background

- 4 inches each of eight different yellow fabrics for the dandelion centers

- White or pale print fabrics (or scraps), totaling about 2⅞ yards, for dandelion petals

- 26 inches lime-green fabric for setting triangles and corners

- 28 inches spotted yellow fabric for binding

- 5 yards backing fabric

- 71 x 91 inches cotton batting

- General sewing and patchwork supplies (see page 22)

CUTTING

All fabrics are strip-cut across the width of the fabric from fold to selvage unless otherwise specified or unless you are using a directional print.

FROM EACH OF THE SEVEN GREEN FABRICS, CUT:

- Nine strips, 2½ inches wide. Cross-cut these nine strips into 142 squares (total), each 2½ inches. There will be a few extra. From the seven fabrics, you need a total of 992 green 2½-inch squares.

FROM EACH OF THE EIGHT YELLOW FABRICS, CUT:

- One strip, 2½ inches wide. Cross-cut each strip into 16 squares, each 2½ inches. From the eight fabrics, you need a total of 124 yellow 2½-inch squares. (There will be a few extra.)

FROM THE WHITE FABRICS, CUT:

- Strips of any length, 2½ inches wide. If you are using fabric lengths, cut all of your fabrics up into 2½-inch strips. If using scraps, make sure that your pieces are at least 2½ inches square.

FROM LIME-GREEN FABRIC, CUT:

- Two strips, 10¼ inches wide. Cross-cut these strips into eight squares, each 10¼ inches. Cross-cut these squares on both diagonals to yield 32 quarter-square triangles for the setting triangles (you only need 30). From the remaining piece of fabric, cut two squares, each 5⅞ inches, and cross-cut on one diagonal to yield two half-square triangles for the corners.

FROM SPOTTED YELLOW BINDING FABRIC, CUT:

- Nine strips, 3 inches wide. Set aside for binding.

Constructing the quilt top

Making a dandelion "star"

1 Each dandelion star begins with eight random green squares and one yellow square (Diagram 1). Take four of these green squares to be the background of the petals.

2 From your 2½-inch wide strips of white fabric, cut a strip that is longer than the angle you are going to sew. Lay the white strip over one of the four green squares, right sides together, overlapping the pieces at odd angles. Remembering to allow for seams in your angle, sew the white strip onto the green square (Diagram 2). Trim the excess green away from the seam, as shown. Fold the white fabric over and press flat (Diagram 3). Trim the edges of the white strip to be square with the original green fabric square—that is, 2½ inches square (Diagram 4).

3 Using a scrap of the same white fabric, repeat Step 2 on the other side of the green square, being sure to use a different angle for the petal point (Diagram 5). Trim, as before, into a 2½-inch square (Diagram 6).

4 Repeat Steps 2 and 3 with the three remaining green squares. This makes the units for one complete dandelion.

5 Sew the dandelion squares into rows and then sew the rows together (Diagram 7). You have now completed one dandelion.

6 Repeat the process until you have 124 dandelions, mixing the greens and whites well as you go (noting, however, that each individual flower is made from a single white fabric). Press the blocks.

Diagram 1

Diagram 2

{*tip*}

For a quick method of sewing the star-point squares, see Diagram 9 on page 67.

Diagram 3   Diagram 4

Diagram 5

Diagram 6

Diagram 7

Assembling the blocks

7 Using a design wall or a bed for color balancing, lay the dandelion blocks out in 10 rows of seven blocks on point. There will be nine rows of six blocks on point in between. Move the blocks around until you are happy with their positions.

8 Beginning at one corner, sew the blocks together in diagonal rows across the quilt, beginning and ending each row with a setting triangle (Diagram 8). Please note that the setting triangles are too large for the blocks of the quilt. This is so that when you have finished sewing the top together, you can trim the triangles and ensure that the quilt is square.

9 When you have sewn all the rows of blocks, sew the rows together in strips, matching the seams as you go, until you have sewn all the rows together. Press. Your quilt top is complete.

Backing, quilting, and binding

Cut the backing fabric in half crosswise, giving two pieces, each 90 inches long. Trim the selvages and sew the pieces together along the length to form one backing piece. Press the seam allowance open.

Refer to pages 190–199 for instructions on finishing.

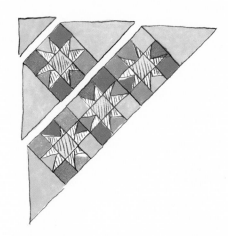

Diagram 8

Diagram 9: Quick method for star-point squares

a. sew to strip

b. trim excess

c. trim cut squares

{note on quilting}

I had *Dandelions* machine-quilted by Kim Bradley in a swirling pattern, using green thread.

Appliqué *with bias strips*

Spring

Dolly quilt, 21 x 20 inches

Whirligig

Throw, 63½ inches square

The techniques here are simple but excellent ones to add to your patchwork arsenal. If you have never tried my method of needle-turn appliqué before, *Spring* is a great place to do it. I use this method because I find it quick and easy, while still allowing me to achieve accurate shapes and placement.

Making and shaping bias vines for quilts can be a tedious job, but using pre-made bias tape or a bias tape maker can give you great results in half the time.

You will find that the placement of the leaves in both quilts is a rather fluid thing. Having the leaves placed irregularly on both quilts adds to the whimsical feel.

Spring

"Spring has sprung, the grass is riz..." This joyful dolly quilt would make an excellent cushion to brighten up a dark corner.

Finished quilt size
Dolly quilt, 21 x 20 inches

MATERIALS AND TOOLS

- 1 deep-purple fat quarter for background
- Wide variety of scraps for leaves and butterfly
- 1²/₃ yards x ½ inch-wide pre-made polka dot green bias tape
- 10 inches fabric for binding
- 24 inches backing fabric
- 24 inches square cotton batting
- Cotton threads to match appliqué fabrics
- 2B pencil
- Template plastic
- Appliqué glue
- Straw needles for appliqué
- Silver gel pen

- Perle cotton No 8 in orange and gray for hand-quilting (optional)
- No 9 crewel embroidery needles for quilting
- General sewing and patchwork supplies (see page 22)

TEMPLATES

Trace Spring Leaf and Butterfly templates (on pattern sheet) onto template plastic with a sharp 2B pencil and cut out accurately using sharp scissors (but not your fabric scissors).

CUTTING

All fabrics are strip-cut across the width of the fabric from fold to selvage unless otherwise specified or unless you are using a directional print.

FROM THE DEEP-PURPLE FAT QUARTER, CUT:
- One piece, 20 x 21 inches, for background.

Constructing the quilt top

Appliqué

Read the instructions for Appliqué on page 186 before proceeding.

1 Place the plastic Leaf template onto the right side of one of the scrap fabrics and trace around it using the gel pen. Using small, sharp scissors, cut the shape out, a scant ¼ inch outside the gel pen line.

2 Repeat this process with the other appliqué scraps until you have cut 39 Leaves and one Butterfly shape.

3 Fold the purple background square into quarters to find the center and finger-press the crease. Fold again on the diagonals and finger-press the crease. Using the photograph as a guide, take the gel pen and draw a large, widely spaced spiral onto the background, starting at the center point of the square and radiating out.

4 Take the square to the ironing board and place one end of the green bias tape onto the beginning of the gel line, in the center of the piece. Working slowly, iron the bias tape along the gel line, stretching it around the curves until you have pressed the tape into the shape of your spiral.

5 Lift the edges of the tape, put a drop of appliqué glue onto the back and press it down. It will take a few moments to dry.

6 Using the photograph as a guide, glue the leaves into place around the vine in a spiral. Take care not to glue too close to the edge of the fabric. If the spirals of your vine are too close together in some places to fit a leaf, don't worry—just overlap the leaves onto the next spiral. Glue the butterfly in the center of the quilt.

7 When the glue is dry and the shapes are fused to the background, begin by sewing on the spiral vine. Start in the center of the quilt, on the inside curve. Sew all the way along the inside of the vine until you reach the other end, then go back to the middle and sew around the outside of the vine. Sewing in the same direction will prevent puckering.

8 Next, sew the leaves and butterfly. Thread a straw needle with cotton to match the fabric you are appliquéing. Finger-press along the silver gel line all around the edge of the shape, turn the edge under along the pressed line, and sew the shape to the background, using small stitches. You will need to clip into the inside curves to turn them under. Press. Your quilt top is complete.

Backing, quilting, and binding

Using masking tape, tape the backing fabric, face down, onto a table, smoothing out any creases as you go. Lay the batting piece onto the backing, and then the quilt top on top. Smooth any creases and hand-baste the three layers together using large stitches and working from the center out. As this is only a small quilt, it does not need a lot of basting. The backing and batting should be larger than the top for ease of quilting; don't be tempted to trim them back.

Refer to pages 190–199 for instructions on finishing.

{*note on quilting*}

I hand-quilted *Spring* using orange perle cotton No 8. I outline-quilted all the leaves and the vine, using orange, then outline-quilted around the butterfly in gray and, finally, quilted the butterfly's antennae.

Whirligig

I think that I enjoyed making this quilt the most of any
in this book. I love to hand-appliqué, and the combination
of the bright scraps and Anna Maria Horner's beautiful
rose print in the large triangles made hand-quilting a joy.
The added dimension of the free tabs in the outer border
gives the quilt a fluttery feeling that complements the
windmill of flowers in the center.

Finished quilt size

Throw, 63½ inches square

MATERIALS AND TOOLS

- 1⅞ yards yellow-and-blue-dot fabric for Medallion and Outer Border

- 1¾ yards blue floral fabric for Setting Triangles

- 1⅛ yards dot blue fabric for Narrow Borders and binding

- 1 pink fat quarter for Pollen

- 8 inches dot brown fabric for Flowers

- 4⅜ yards x ½ inch-wide spotted green bias tape for vines

- Wide variety of scraps for Leaves and Border Tabs (you will need about 1⅞ yards fabric in total; scraps need to be at least 3 inches wide)

- 4⅛ yards backing fabric

- 74 inches square cotton batting

- Cotton threads to match appliqué fabrics

- 2B pencil

- Template plastic

- Appliqué glue

- Straw needles for appliqué

- Silver gel pen

- Perle cotton No 8 in blue and yellow for hand-quilting

- No 9 crewel embroidery needles for quilting

- General sewing and patchwork supplies (see page 22)

TEMPLATES

Trace Whirligig Leaf, Flower, and Pollen templates (on pattern sheet) onto template plastic with a sharp 2B pencil and cut out accurately using sharp scissors (but not your fabric scissors).

CUTTING

All fabrics are strip-cut across the width of the fabric from fold to selvage unless otherwise specified or unless you are using a directional print.

FROM YELLOW-AND-BLUE DOT FABRIC, CUT:
- One square, 41 inches, for Center Medallion.
- Seven strips, 3½ inches wide, for Outer Border.

FROM BLUE FLORAL FABRIC, CUT:
- Two squares, each 30 inches. Cross-cut these squares on one diagonal to yield a total of 4 half-square triangles for the Setting Triangles.

FROM POLKA DOT BLUE FABRIC, CUT:
- 11 strips, 1½ inches wide, for inner and outer Narrow Borders.
- Seven strips, 3 inches wide, for binding.

FROM ASSORTED SCRAPS, CUT:
- 240 squares, each 3 inches, for the Border Tabs.

Constructing the quilt top

Appliqué

Read the instructions for Appliqué on page 186 before proceeding.

1 Place the Flower template onto the right side of the dot brown fabric and trace around it using the gel pen. Using small, sharp scissors, cut the shape out, a scant ¼ inch outside the gel pen line. Repeat to cut a total of eight Flowers.

2 Repeat this process with the other appliqué templates. Cut eight Pollen shapes from the pink fabric and a total of 112 Leaves from scrap fabric.

3 Fold the Medallion square into quarters to find the center and finger-press the creases. Fold again on the diagonals and finger-press the creases. Using the photograph as a guide, cut and arrange the bias tape vines onto the background until you are happy with the placement. They should begin near the center of the medallion, run up along the creases, and then curve over as they reach the top. Remember that your medallion square is cut two inches too large and will be trimmed back after completing the appliqué, so don't take the vines right to the edge.

4 Lift the edges of the vines and put a drop of glue onto the fabrics and press them down. Take care not to glue too close to the edge of the fabric. You only need a small spot of glue to make the pieces stick. They will take a few moments to dry.

5 Glue a brown-dot Flower to the end of each vine and a Pollen shape above each Flower. Following Diagram 1, glue eight Leaves onto the background in a spiral flower pattern for the center of the quilt.

Diagram 1

6 When the glue is dry and the shapes are fused to the background, select a shape on which to begin sewing. Thread a straw needle with cotton to match the fabric you are appliquéing. Finger-press along the silver line all around the edge of the shape, turn the edge under along the pressed line, and sew the shape to the background, using small stitches. You will need to clip into the inside curves to turn them under. The bias will not need turning under, as it already has a folded edge. When you sew the center flower, turn under each petal edge until you get to where it is overlapped by the next one.

7 When you have appliquéd these shapes, arrange the Leaves along the vines in six pairs of Leaves along each stem, and one Leaf in the "v" shape where the vines meet the central flower. These leaves are not supposed to be perfectly symmetrical—place them in a way that is pleasing to your eye and not measured. Glue in place and stitch.

8 When you have completed the appliqué, trim the Medallion square to be 39 inches.

Narrow inner borders

9 Trim two of the dot blue 1½-inch strips to 39 inches long. Find the center of one strip and the center of the quilt top and pin. Pin the ends, then pin in between, easing as you go if needed. Sew. Repeat with the opposite side of the square.

10 Trim two more dot blue strips to 41 inches long. Repeat Step 9 and sew the borders to the remaining sides of the quilt top. Press the seams toward the Center Medallion.

Diagram 2

Diagram 3

Diagram 4

Setting triangles

11 Find the center of one side of the quilt and the center of the diagonal side of one blue floral setting triangle and pin. Pin the ends, then pin in between and ease. Sew. Repeat with the opposite side of the quilt.

12 Sew the two remaining triangles to the remaining sides of the quilt, as above. Trim the quilt top to be square, trimming the triangles to a ¼-inch seam above the point of the center square on point. Press the seams toward the blue triangles.

Narrow outer borders

13 Sew the remaining seven dot blue 1½-inch strips together, end to end, into one long strip. Measure the quilt through the center. Cut a piece from the strip to this measurement. Pin and sew the blue strip to one side of the quilt, as for Step 9, and then sew another border to the opposite side in the same way.

14 Measure the quilt through the center in the opposite direction and cut and sew border strips, as before. Press the seams toward the blue triangles.

Border tabs

15 Place the 3-inch scrap squares together in random pairs, right sides facing each other. Randomly cut a tab-shaped piece with a curved end at one end and a straight end at the other (Diagram 2). Sew from the straight end along the edge and around the curve, leaving the straight end open (Diagram 3). Clip along the curves, turn the Tab right side out, and press flat (Diagram 4). Make approximately 120 tabs of different sizes and shapes.

16 Arrange approximately 30 Tabs along one side of the quilt, right sides together, with the curved edge of the Tabs facing inward, and the straight edges level with the edge of the quilt. Pin into place. Depending on the width of your Tabs, you may want more or fewer than 30 to achieve a look you like.

17 Sew the Tabs to the quilt ¼ inch from the edge of the quilt. Repeat for the remaining three sides.

Outer border

18 Sew all the 3½-inch yellow-and-blue-dot Outer Border strips together, end to end, into one strip.

19 Measure your quilt through the center in both directions to get the true width. Cut two Outer Border strips to be the measurement of the quilt in one direction. Find the center of a side of the quilt top and the center of one of the Outer Borders. Pin the center together, then pin the ends. Pin in between, easing if needed. Sew, catching the edges of the tabs as you go. Repeat with the opposite border. Press.

20 Measure the quilt across the center again, from Outer Border to Outer Border. Cut the remaining two Outer Borders to this measurement and attach them as for Step 19. Press the border toward the center of the quilt, carefully pressing the tabs flat to the border. Your quilt top is complete.

Backing, quilting, and binding

Cut the backing fabric crosswise in half into two 74-inch long pieces. Remove the selvages and stitch the pieces together up the long seams. Press the seam allowance open and press the backing piece carefully.

Refer to pages 190–199 for instructions on finishing.

{note on quilting}

I hand-quilted *Whirligig* using blue and yellow perle cotton No 8. I outline-quilted all the appliqué, using blue, and cross-hatched the Medallion background and the Outer Border in a 1½-inch grid, using yellow. I then outline-quilted the flowers in the blue setting triangles, using blue cotton. Finally, I outline-quilted each of the Tabs in blue.

Flying geese and foundation piecing

Geese Around the World
Dolly quilt, 13½ inches square

North by North East
Queen size, 91 inches square

A Flying Geese block is not hard to make after you have made one or two accurately, so I have given you two different techniques with these two quilts: traditional Flying Geese in *North By North East* and foundation piecing for *Geese Around the World.*

The trick to foundation piecing is to take care with how large you cut your fabric pieces. Be sure to be generous when cutting, so that you can overlap the paper foundations with room to spare, and you won't find yourself unpicking all your hard work.

Both quilts use bright triangles and white contrast to effect, and both create their own flying patterns.

Geese Around the World

The geese here are flying in a circle, creating a whirling pattern. If you try this and like foundation piecing, this pattern would make a wonderful bed-size quilt.

Finished quilt size
Dolly quilt, 13½ inches square

Degree of difficulty **✳✳**

MATERIALS AND TOOLS

- 16 scraps, at least 6 x 3½ inches, or 3½ inches of 8 pink, orange, and green fabrics for "geese"

- 14 inches white fabric for background

- 6 inches check fabric for binding

- 1 fat quarter for backing

- 20 inches square cotton batting

- 4 sheets of foundation paper, or any thin letter-size paper

- Aqua perle cotton No 8 for quilting

- No 9 crewel embroidery needles for quilting

- General sewing and patchwork supplies (page 22)

TEMPLATES

Trace or photocopy the foundation pieces for Geese Around the World Templates A, B, C, and D (on pattern sheet) onto letter paper. You need four copies of each template to make the circle of geese. Roughly cut out the templates from the paper, NOT on the ¼-inch seam allowance line, but outside it.

CUTTING

All fabrics are strip-cut across the width of the fabric from fold to selvage unless otherwise specified or unless you are using a directional print.

FROM THE COLORED SCRAP FABRICS, CUT:
- 16 pieces, about 3½ x 6 inches, for the "geese."

FROM WHITE FABRIC, CUT:
- Four strips, 3½ inches wide.

FROM CHECK FABRIC, CUT:
- Two strips, 3 inches wide, for the binding.

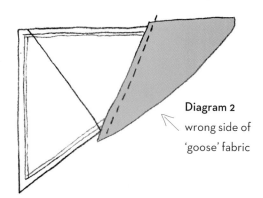

Diagram 1
wrong side of
white fabric

Diagram 2
wrong side of
'goose' fabric

Diagram 3

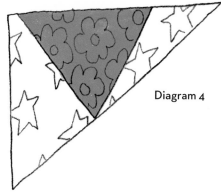

Diagram 4

Constructing the quilt top

Foundation piecing

Read the instructions for Foundation piecing on page 184 before proceeding.

1 Begin sewing with a Template A piece. Place a white background piece and a colored goose piece right sides together with white background uppermost and place the foundation paper on top (Diagram 1). The white piece should be positioned so that it covers piece 1 on the template. Check to make sure that the colored piece will also cover piece 2 when the seam is opened after sewing.

2 Adjust the stitch length on your sewing machine to be quite small, about 1.8 or 2, depending on the make of your machine. Position the fabrics so that they are approximately ¼ inch out from the sewing line and sew along the line on the paper. Trim away any excess fabric ¼ inch from the seam line (Diagram 2).

3 Turn the paper over and iron the fabric open (Diagram 3). Cut another piece of white background fabric to fit piece 3. Position the white fabric, right sides together, against the goose fabric. Check that it will cover Piece 3 when it is open, then turn to the paper side and stitch along the sewing line. Turn to the fabric side and press the fabric open.

4 Turn the piece over to the paper side again and trim the shape along the outer ¼-inch line using a rotary cutter (Diagram 4). Set aside without removing the paper, and repeat with all the other template shapes, alternating the patterned fabrics as you go so that they are well mixed.

Constructing the blocks

5 When you have pieced together all the foundation shapes take one each of Template A, B, C, and D. Lay them out in order (Diagram 5).

6 Take Template A and Template B and put a pin through the corners of the ¼-inch seam to line them up. Make sure the pieces are well matched. Sew along the seam line on the paper side. Repeat to join Template C and Template D to the row of geese, forming a square.

7 Make four squares in this way and press all the seams away from the geese points.

8 When you have completed four squares, remove the paper backing by carefully tearing it away from the seams. Use tweezers or a pin to get any small pieces out that are stuck in the stitches.

Joining the blocks

9 Referring to the photograph for placement, lay the four squares out so that the geese form a circle. Stitch the top two squares together into a pair and repeat with the bottom two. Join the pairs, taking care to match the center seam. Press. Your quilt top is complete.

Backing, quilting, and binding

Using masking tape, tape the backing fabric, face down, onto a table, smoothing out any creases as you go. Lay the batting piece onto the backing, and then the quilt top on top. Smooth any creases and hand-baste the three layers together using large stitches and working from the center out. The backing and batting should be larger than the top for ease of quilting; don't be tempted to trim them back.

Refer to pages 190–199 for instructions on finishing.

Diagram 5

{note on quilting}

I hand-quilted *Geese Around the World* using using aqua perle cotton No 8, quilting along the down side of all the foundation seams on the white fabric.

North by North East

All those geese, flying south for the winter! Or in the southern hemisphere, flying north. Or perhaps they are flying north after winter, and coming home to all those spring colors. Whatever you decide, these geese will fly into an amazing formation to form the center of this quilt.

Degree of difficulty **

Finished quilt size

Queen size, 91 inches square

MATERIALS AND TOOLS

- 20 inches each of 10 different prints with white backgrounds

- $5\frac{5}{8}$ yards total of a wide range of different color prints, or 12 inches each of 15 different prints

- $4\frac{1}{8}$ yards cherry-print fabric for setting triangles

- $1\frac{1}{2}$ yards tone-on-tone white fabric for setting triangles

- 30 inches green fabric for binding

- $8\frac{1}{3}$ yards backing fabric

- 98 inches square cotton batting

- General sewing and patchwork supplies (page 22)

CUTTING

All fabrics are strip-cut across the width of the fabric from fold to selvage unless otherwise specified or unless you are using a directional print.

FROM EACH OF THE **10** WHITE BACKGROUND FABRICS, CUT:

- Seven strips, $2\frac{1}{4}$ inches wide. Cross-cut these strips into rectangles, 4 x $2\frac{1}{4}$ inches, yielding a total of 696 pieces.

FROM ONLY ONE OF THE WHITE BACKGROUND FABRICS, CUT:

- One strip, $2\frac{5}{8}$ inches wide. Cross-cut this strip into 16 squares, each $2\frac{5}{8}$ inches. Cut these squares in half along one diagonal to yield 32 half-square triangles. (You could also cut a total of 16 squares from scraps of several white fabrics, rather than just one, if you prefer.)

FROM THE COLORED FABRICS, CUT:

- Enough strips, $2\frac{1}{4}$ inches wide, to cross-cut into a total (from all the fabrics) of 1,392 squares.

- Enough strips, 2⅝ inches wide, to cross-cut into 16 squares (total). Cut these squares in half along one diagonal to yield 32 half-square triangles.

FROM THE CHERRY-PRINT FABRIC, CUT:
- Six squares, each 23 inches. Cut these squares in half on one diagonal to yield 12 half-square triangles.

FROM TONE-ON-TONE WHITE FABRIC, CUT:
- Two squares, each 23 inches. Cut these squares in half on one diagonal to yield four half-square triangles.

FROM GREEN BINDING FABRIC, CUT:
- Ten strips, 3 inches wide. Set aside for binding.

Constructing the quilt top

Flying geese panel

1 Matching the corners, lay a colored 2¼-inch square on one end of a white rectangle, right sides together, and sew diagonally across the square (Diagram 1).

2 Trim the seam allowance (Diagram 2) and press the triangle open. Repeat with another square of a different fabric on the other end of the white rectangle (Diagram 3). Trim the seam allowance again. Press open (Diagram 4). This is one Flying Geese unit.

3 Repeat Steps 1 and 2 to make 696 Flying Geese units.

4 Join a white half-square triangle and a colored half-square triangle together along the diagonal edge and press open. Trim the "ears" from the triangles to make a square unit. Make 32.

{note}

I recommend using a design wall for this quilt (see page 24).

Diagram 1

Diagram 2

Diagram 3

Diagram 4

5 On the design wall, lay out your Flying Geese in rows, as follows, mixing the colors well. Row A begins and ends with a square unit. There are 15 Flying Geese units in this row and the point of the white triangle should point downward. Row B consists entirely of Flying Geese units (no squares). There are 16 Flying Geese in this row and the points on the white triangles should point upward. Starting with a Row A and alternating with a Row B, lay out 32 rows, referring to the photograph for guidance. Move the Geese around within the rows until you are happy with the color placement, taking care to keep the orientation of the white triangle points correct.

6 Sew the Geese together into their rows until you have pieced 32 rows.

7 Join the rows, beginning at the top of the panel and working down. Take care to match the ends together and pin each point carefully. Press the panel.

Setting triangles

8 Referring to the photograph of the quilt for placement, join a cherry-print triangle to either side of a white solid triangle and press the seams toward the cherry fabric. Join a cherry triangle to the remaining side of the white triangle (Diagram 5). Make four of these units for the corners of the quilt.

9 Find the center of the long edge of the corner unit and the center of one side of the center panel and pin. Sew the corner unit to the quilt, matching the centers.

Diagram 5

{note}

The setting triangles are too large for the center panel, but they will be trimmed back.

10 Next, sew a corner unit in the same manner to the opposite corner of the quilt.

11 Join the other two corners to the quilt top in the same way and press.

12 Measuring through the center in both directions, trim the quilt to 84½ inches square.

Border

13 Take the remaining 200 Flying Geese units and, mixing the colors well, sew them together along their long edge into two strips of 48 geese and two strips of 52 geese.

14 Find the center of the top edge of the quilt and the center of a strip of 48 geese and pin. Pin the ends and pin in between, easing if needed. Sew and repeat with the bottom edge of the quilt. Press the seams toward the setting triangles.

15 Attach the longer borders to the sides of the quilt in the same manner. Press. Your quilt top is complete.

Backing, quilting, and binding

Cut the backing fabric crosswise into three pieces, each 100 inches long. Trim the selvages and sew the pieces together along the length to form one backing piece. Press the seam allowance open.

Refer to pages 190–199 for instructions on finishing.

{note on quilting}

I had *North by North East* machine-quilted by Kim Bradley in an all-over floral pattern.

Inset piecing

Peaks and Troughs
Dolly quilt, 18³/₄ x 21¹/₄ inches

Stars in Your Eyes
Twin, 64¹/₂ x 82 inches

Inset piecing is the technique of setting a piece of fabric into an L- or Y-shape seam. It doesn't have to be as mysterious as it sounds—careful marking of the ¹/₄-inch point and accurate sewing will get you there. Practicing on the *Peaks and Troughs* dolly is also very helpful, before tackling the more difficult seams of *Stars in Your Eyes.*

Peaks and Troughs

Diamonds go up and diamonds go down, forming the zigzags
in this quilt. Enlarging this quilt to a twin or double bed size
with zigzags all the way across would be spectacular.

Finished quilt size
Dolly quilt, 18³⁄₄ x 21¹⁄₄ inches

*Degree
of difficulty*
***

MATERIALS AND TOOLS

- 2 inches each of 9 different blue-
  and-green fabrics, or scrap

- 10 inches natural linen for
  background

- 6 inches blue-stripe fabric for
  binding

- 22 x 25 inches backing fabric

- 22 x 25 inches cotton batting

- Variegated blue perle cotton
  No 8 for hand-quilting

- No 9 crewel embroidery needles,
  for quilting

- 60-degree triangle ruler
  (optional, see page 29)

- Template plastic and 2B pencil
  (optional)

- General sewing and patchwork
  supplies (see page 22)

TEMPLATES

If you are not using the 60-degree triangle ruler, trace
Peaks and Troughs Templates A, B, C, and D (on
pattern sheet) onto template plastic with a sharp
2B pencil. Cut out accurately using sharp scissors.

CUTTING

All fabrics are strip-cut across the width of the
fabric from fold to selvage unless otherwise
specified or unless you are using a directional print.

FROM EACH OF THE NINE BLUE-AND-GREEN
FABRICS, CUT:

- One strip, 1¹⁄₂ inches wide.

FROM THE LINEN, CUT:

- One strip, 3¹⁄₂ inches wide. Using the 60-degree
  ruler or Templates A, B, and D, cross-cut this
  strip into five 60-degree diamonds with 4-inch
  sides (Template A), two half-square triangles
  (Template B), and two 60-degree triangles
  (Template D).
- One strip, 2¹⁄₂ inches wide. Using the 60-degree
  ruler or Template C, cut five half-diamonds from
  this strip, with 8³⁄₄-inch bottom edges. (Note that
  these triangles are slightly too large, but the extra
  can be trimmed back when piecing.)

• Two strips, 2 inches wide, for the Outer Border.

FROM THE BLUE-STRIPE FABRIC, CUT:
• Two strips, 3 inches wide. Set aside for binding.

Constructing the quilt top

Diamonds

1 Take a set of three blue/green strips. Sew them together along the length of the strip in the order you have chosen until you have a piece of patchwork that is 3½ inches wide x the width of the fabric (Diagram 1). Press all the seams to one side.

2 Repeat Step 1 until you have made three pieces like this.

3 Using the 60-degree ruler or Template A, from each patchwork strip cut six diamonds with 4-inch long sides (Diagram 2). You need to cut 18 diamonds in all.

4 Using the photograph as a guide, lay the quilt out, taking care that the strips of fabrics in the diamonds lie in alternating positions to form the pattern.

5 Begin by piecing together Row 1 of the pieced diamonds in their zigzag pattern. Begin and end each seam ¼ inch from the end of each seam so that you can set the other pieces into the Y-shape space of the blocks.

Diagram 1

Diagram 2

Diagram 3

Row 1

6 Sew a Template B linen half-square triangle to either end of the strip as shown (Diagram 3). Press all the seams toward the pieced diamonds.

7 Next, piece a Template C linen half-diamond into the Y seam. (Because the C triangles are too large, you should match the inner points first and allow the excess to extend beyond the outer edge.) Begin sewing at the outer end of the seam and sew the pieces together until you are ¼ inch from the trough of the Y at the inner point. When you reach this point, leave your needle in the fabric, lift the presser foot, pivot the fabric on the needle, and lower the presser foot again. Continue sewing to the end of the next seam, first making sure that the fabrics are lying flat (Diagram 4).

8 Piece in the next Template C linen half-diamond in the same way. Trim the upper edge square, remembering to leave ¼-inch seam allowance.

9 Next, piece a Template A linen diamond into the Y seam of the first and third pair of pieced diamonds (Diagram 5).

10 Sew together Row 2 of the pieced diamonds. Piece a linen diamond into the middle Y seam of this row, and then join the two rows together (Diagram 6).

Diagram 4

Row 1

Pivot at the
Y seam

Row 1

Diagram 5

11 Sew a Template D linen 60-degree triangle to the first diamond piece and a linen diamond into the second Y seam of Row 2 (Diagram 7).

12 Piece together Row 3 of diamonds and sew a linen diamond A into the first Y seam, and a Template D triangle onto the last diamond. Join this row to the quilt top (Diagram 8).

13 Inset-piece three Template C linen half-diamonds into the last three Y seams (Diagram 9), noting again, that the Template C triangles are too large—see Step 7, above. Press, trim the excess seam allowance and check that your quilt is square.

Row 1

Row 2

Diagram 6

Row 1

Row 2

Diagram 7

Row 1

Row 2

Row 3

Diagram 8

Row 1

Row 2

Row 3

Diagram 9

Border

14 Sew the two border strips together into one long strip. Measure your quilt through the center across the shorter measurement to get the width. Cut two border strips to this measurement.

15 Find the center of a short side of the quilt top and the center of one of the borders. Pin the centers together, pin the ends, then pin in between, easing if needed. Sew and repeat with the other short border. Press.

16 Now measure the quilt through the center along the longer measurement. Cut and attach the long borders, as before. Press. Your quilt top is complete.

Backing, quilting, and binding

Using masking tape, tape the backing fabric, face down, onto a table, smoothing out any creases as you go. Lay the batting piece onto the backing, and then the quilt top on top. Smooth any creases and hand-baste the three layers together using large stitches and working from the center out. As this is only a small quilt, it does not need a lot of basting. The backing and batting should be larger than the top for ease of quilting; don't be tempted to trim them back.

Refer to pages 190–199 for instructions on finishing.

{note on quilting}

I hand-quilted *Peaks and Troughs* by outlining the diagonal lines in the diamonds using variegated perle cotton No 8. I also quilted along the down side of the seams in the pieced diamonds.

Stars in Your Eyes

All your favorite fabrics can sparkle and pop in this quilt. Pick your bright and happy colors to spark against the white fabric, add a wonderful large floral border, and this is a recipe for success. You could also use a black background fabric and make this a fantastic boys' quilt.

Degree of difficulty
***

Finished quilt size
Twin, 63¹/₂ x 82 inches

MATERIALS AND TOOLS

- 1¹/₄ yards aqua-and-white dot fabric for setting diamonds

- 6 inches each of 6 sets of 5 fabrics for stars, or 60 strips of scrap at least 2¹/₂ inches wide (fabrics should be bright and in a range of different colors and patterns)

- 12 inches deep-pink fabric for Inner Border

- 1⁷/₈ yards cream-and-pink floral fabric for Outer Border

- 24 inches multicolor-stripe fabric for binding

- 4 yards backing fabric

- 70 x 88 inches cotton batting

- Perle cotton No 8 in aqua, deep-pink, candy-pink, lime-green and orange for hand-quilting

- 1-inch wide masking tape for marking quilting lines

- No 9 crewel embroidery needles for quilting

- 60-degree triangle ruler (optional, see page 29)

- General sewing and patchwork supplies (see page 22)

TEMPLATE

If you are not using the 60-degree triangle ruler, trace Stars in Your Eyes Template A (on pattern sheet), onto template plastic with a sharp 2B pencil. Cut out accurately using sharp scissors.

CUTTING

All fabrics are strip-cut across the width of the fabric from fold to selvage unless otherwise specified or unless you are using a directional print.

FROM AQUA-AND-WHITE DOT FABRIC, CUT:

- Seven strips, 5³⁄₈ inches wide. From these strips, cut 42 diamonds with a 6¼-inch long side, using the 60-degree line on your patchwork ruler or the 60-degree triangle ruler. For greater accuracy, you can use Template A as a guide.
- One strip, 3¹⁄₈ inches wide, for the half-diamonds. Using the 60-degree line on your ruler and Template A as a guide, cut four half-diamonds from the strip.

FROM EACH OF THE STAR FABRICS, CUT:

- Two strips, 2½ inches wide. You should have a total of 60 strips. Separate these strips into 12 sets of five fabrics, coordinating the colors as you go.

FROM DEEP-PINK FABRIC, CUT:

- Seven strips, 1½ inches wide. Set aside for Inner Border.

FROM CREAM-AND-PINK FLORAL FABRIC, CUT:

- Eight strips, 8½ inches wide. Set aside for Outer Border.

FROM MULTICOLOR-STRIPE FABRIC, CUT:

- Eight strips, 3 inches wide. Set aside for binding.

{note}

I recommend using a design wall for balancing the colors in this quilt (see page 24).

Constructing the quilt top

Stars (make 11 + two half-stars)

1 Take a set of five fabrics. Sew them together along the length of the strip in the order you have chosen, until you have a piece of patchwork that is 10½ inches wide x the width of the fabric. Press all the seams to one side (Diagram 1). Repeat with the remaining sets of fabrics until you have 12 patchwork strips.

2 Iron a pieced strip in half along the length, wrong sides together (Diagram 2). Take care not to distort the strips as you press.

3 Using the 60-degree ruler or Template A, cut six diamonds from each strip by placing the wide end of the ruler (or template) along the fold of the fabric and the squared-off tip at the raw edge (Diagram 3). Cut along the edges on each side, moving the ruler along the strip until you have cut six diamonds. When the diamonds are opened out, they should look like the one in Diagram 4.

4 From the remaining fabric in some of the strips, use the triangle template to cut six half-diamonds for the edges and four quarter-diamonds for the corners of the top. (Remember to allow for ¼-inch seam allowance on the straight edges of these half- and quarter-diamonds.)

5 When you have cut all the pieced diamonds, take the six diamonds from one set and piece three of them together to form a half-star (Diagram 5). Begin piecing ¼ inch in from the "corner" join to make setting the background diamonds easier. Take care to press the seams in opposite directions to make a neat join. Make a matching half-star in the same way.

6 Join the two half-stars together across the center to form a star, again leaving ¼ inch open at the corners (Diagram 6). Press.

Diagram 1

Diagram 2

ruler

Diagram 3

{*tip*}

If you have cut carefully, the remaining scrap triangles from each strip can be pieced together to make a beautiful border, or into hexagons to use in another project.

Diagram 4

Diagram 5

Diagram 6

7 Repeat Steps 5 and 6 until you have made 11 full stars and 2 half-stars.

Background diamonds

8 Lay the stars out on a design wall (or the floor) and balance the colors until you are happy with their arrangement. This is also a good way to keep track of the piecing together of the rows, which can be confusing if you don't have everything in front of you.

9 You can see from the Assembly diagram, that only one star is pieced into a complete hexagon, while the others are constructed in a different order. To inset-piece the diamonds on the whole hexagon star, begin at the outside point of the star and sew in to the inner corner of the star. Leave the needle in the fabric when you get ¼ inch from the corner. Raise the presser foot and pivot the diamond around on the needle so that it lies flat against the other point of the star, lower the presser foot, raise the needle, and adjust the fabric beneath so that it lies flat and even. Put the needle back into the fabric at the same point it came out and continue sewing to the point of the star. Press the seam under the star. Repeat this process until you have added all six diamonds (Diagram 7). Set the whole star aside while you construct the rest of the quilt top.

10 Following the Assembly diagram, row by row, inset-piece the background diamonds to the stars in the order shown, using the same technique as for the whole star.

11 When you have pieced all the rows, join the rows together until you have completed the quilt top. Sew the corner quarter-diamonds in last. Press and check to make sure the quilt top is square before continuing.

Diagram 7

Inner border

12 Sew all the strips for the Inner Border together into one long strip and press the seams to one side.

13 Measure your quilt through the center across the width. Cut two pieces from the border strip to exactly this measurement.

14 Find the center of a short side of the quilt top and the center of one of the borders. Pin the centers together, then pin the ends together, and pin in between. Sew as pinned. Repeat with the other short border. Press the seams toward the border.

15 Measure your quilt top through the center again to get the long measurement. Cut the two border strips to your measurement. Attach the remaining borders as before. Press the seams toward the border.

Outer border

16 Sew the Outer Border strips together, end to end, into four pairs.

17 Measure your quilt through the center to get the width. Cut two border strips to this measurement, plus 16 inches, to allow for mitered corners.

18 Find the center of a short side of the quilt top and the center of one of the Outer Borders. Pin the centers together. Mark the border at 8½ inches in from the ends of the border strip, and pin this mark to the end of the quilt top at both ends. Pin in between, easing if needed. Begin sewing ¼ inch in from the edge of the quilt top, and finish the seam ¼ inch in from the opposite edge. Sew and repeat with the other short border. Press.

Assembly diagram

19 Measure and attach the long borders in the same way. (Remember to add the extra 16 inches to allow for mitered corners.)

20 Using the 45-degree angle on your patchwork ruler, rule a 45-degree angle across the corners of the borders. Sew the corners together along the 45-degree angle and check that the border will lie flat before trimming the excess fabric. Press the mitered seam open or to one side, and the border seam toward the border. Repeat with the other three corners. Your quilt top is complete.

Backing, quilting, and binding

Cut the backing fabric in half crosswise, giving two pieces, each 72 inches long. Trim the selvages and sew the pieces together along the length to form one backing piece. Press the seam allowance open.

Refer to pages 190–199 for instructions on finishing.

{note on quilting}

I hand-quilted *Stars in Your Eyes* by outlining the diagonal lines in the diamonds using aqua perle cotton No 8. I then used 1-inch masking tape as a guide to quilt 1 inch inside the seam of all the diamonds. Finally, I outline-quilted all the seams in the stars using different color perle cotton No 8.

Needle-turn appliqué

A Little Silhouette

Dolly quilt, 16½ inches square

A Wing and a Prayer

Queen size, 88½ inches square

A Wing and a Prayer is a four-block quilt, which is one traditional arrangement of antique American quilts. Making this quilt will give you the experience of working with large appliqué pieces and backgrounds. If you haven't used my appliqué technique before, making A Little Silhouette will try your skills at needle-turn appliqué, with inside and outside curves and points.

A Little Silhouette

Here is a little eagle: there's no mistaking his silhouette.
His shadowy outline reminds me of a Pennsylvania Dutch
Scherenschnitte, or paper cutting, although a very simple one.

The art of silhouette cutting was brought to America in the
eighteenth century from central Europe. Although in its original
European form it was very intricate, it was often simplified
in American folk art. I think the positive and negative shapes
created by silhouette cutting make wonderful graphic quilts.
Why not try cutting your own silhouettes to appliqué?

Finished quilt size
Dolly quilt, 16½ inches square

Degree
of difficulty
**

MATERIALS AND TOOLS

- 36 scraps, at least 2½ inches
  square, in different pastels for
  background

- 12 inches polka dot black fabric
  for Eagle and Border

- 10 inches green fabric
  for binding

- 1 fat quarter for backing

- 20 inches square cotton batting

- Black cotton thread for appliqué
  and hand-quilting

- Template plastic

- 2B pencil

- Appliqué glue

- Straw needles for appliqué

- Silver gel pen

- Quilting needles ("betweens")

- General sewing and patchwork
  supplies (see page 22)

TEMPLATE

Trace the Eagle template (on pattern sheet) onto template plastic with a sharp 2B pencil and cut out accurately using sharp scissors (but not your fabric scissors).

CUTTING

All fabrics are strip-cut across the width of the fabric from fold to selvage unless otherwise specified or unless you are using a directional print.

FROM SCRAP FABRICS, CUT:

- 36 squares, each 2½ inches, for the background.

FROM POLKA DOT BLACK FABRIC, CUT:

- One Eagle shape. Place the Eagle template onto the right side of the black fabric and trace around it, using the gel pen. Cut the shape out using small, sharp scissors a scant ¼ inch from the gel pen line. Make sure to cut this first, so that you have a piece wide enough for the template.
- Three strips, 2½ inches wide x the remaining length of the fabric, for the Border. (You may, as I did, need to piece these strips to get enough length for your borders.)

FROM GREEN FABRIC, CUT:

- Three strips, 3 inches wide, for the binding.

Constructing the quilt top

Background

Make yourself a little design board by covering a piece of cardboard or similar with a leftover scrap of batting. This is very useful when you are piecing a block together and you don't want to lose track of your layout.

1 Lay the 2½-inch background squares out on the design board, or on a table, in six rows of six, to make a larger square containing 36 squares. Move the squares around until you are happy with the placement.

2 Pick the squares in the first row up in order and sew them into a strip of six squares. Put the strip back in the place it came from, so you don't lose track. Repeat with the other six strips of squares. Press the seams in each row in opposite directions, that is, Row 1 to the left, Row 2 to the right, Row 3 to the left, and so on (Diagram 1).

3 Using the pressed seams as a guide to get your points perfect, sew the rows together in order until your background is pieced. Press.

Appliqué

Read the instructions for Appliqué on page 186 before proceeding.

4 Fold your pieced background square into quarters to find the center and finger-press the creases. Fold again on the diagonals and finger-press the creases. Using the wings and the tail of the eagle as a guide, center the silhouette onto the background until you are happy with the placement (Diagram 2).

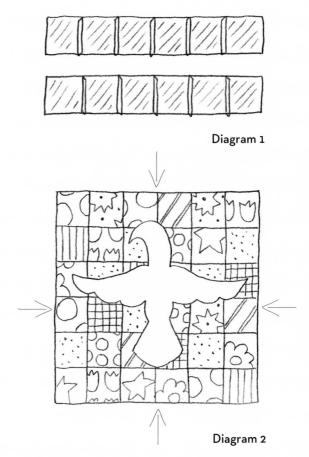

Diagram 1

Diagram 2

5 Lift the edges of the Eagle and put a drop of glue onto the fabric and press it down. Take care not to glue too close to the edge of the fabric or you will not be able to turn the edges under to appliqué. You only need a small spot of glue to make the piece stick. It will take a few moments to dry.

6 When the glue is dry and the shape is fused to the background, select a place on the shape on which to begin sewing. Do not begin on an inside curve or a point. Thread a straw needle with cotton to match the fabric you are appliquéing. Finger-press along the silver line all around the edge of the shape. Turn the edge under along the pressed line and sew the shape to the background using small stitches. You will need to clip into the inside curves to turn them under.

7 When you have completed the appliqué, press your block.

Border

8 From the 2½-inch border strips of black fabric, cut two pieces, each 12½ inches, and two pieces, each 16½ inches long. (If your fabric strips are not long enough to cut these strips from one piece, simply join them end to end until you have the required length.)

9 Find the center of one side edge of the appliquéd square and the center of one of the 12½-inch borders. Pin the centers together, then pin the ends. Pin in between, easing if needed. Sew, and repeat with the opposite border. Press.

10 Attach the two 16½-inch borders to the top and bottom edges of the quilt, as above. Press. Your quilt top is complete.

Backing, quilting, and binding

Using masking tape, tape the backing fabric, face down, onto a table, smoothing out any creases as you go. Lay the batting piece onto the backing, and then the quilt top on top. Smooth any creases and hand-baste the three layers together using large stitches and working from the center out. As this is only a small quilt, it does not need a lot of basting. The backing and batting should be larger than the top for ease of quilting; don't be tempted to trim them back.

Refer to pages 190–199 for instructions on finishing.

{note on quilting}

I hand-quilted *A Little Silhouette* using black sewing cotton. I echo-quilted around the eagle, in lines approximately ¼ inch apart, all over the background, and quilted lines, ¼ inch apart, in the border.

A Wing and a Prayer

The symbol of an eagle is often found in American antique quilts. I have always loved these quilts and wanted to make one, although my colorful eagle looks more like a fantasy bird of paradise! This quilt is fun to make and the large appliqué shapes and bright fabrics make the sewing go quickly.

When choosing backgrounds, don't be afraid to choose fabrics with bolder, more interesting graphics. I feel that the newsprint fabric really makes this quilt more interesting.

Finished quilt size

Queen size, 88½ inches square

Degree
of difficulty
***

MATERIALS AND TOOLS

- 1⅛ yards each of 4 different white fabrics for backgrounds, sashing and Borders 1 and 3

- 10 inches each of pink and tangerine linen for birds' Heads

- 20 inches each of aqua-pattern fabric and yellow-pattern fabric for birds' Wings and Bodies

- 8 inches turquoise-pattern fabric for birds' Eyes and Feet

- 8 inches each of 8 different plain red, pink, and orange fabrics for birds' Tails and Border 2

- 4 inches each of 8 different pink, yellow, and aqua print fabrics for birds' Tails and Border 2

- 8 inches pink-and-yellow dot fabric for Stars

- 8 inches teal-and-pink floral fabric for Circles

- Scrap of pink fabric for Inner Circle

- 26 inches blue-and-green dot fabric for Border 4 and Outer Star

- 16 inches red-stripe or dark-pink-stripe fabric for Border 4

- 1⅞ yards multicolor-spot fabric for Border 5

- 30 inches bright-pink-stripe fabric for binding

- 6 yards backing fabric
- 92 inches square cotton batting
- Cotton threads to match appliqué fabrics
- Several large sheets of template plastic
- 2B pencil
- Appliqué glue
- Straw needles for appliqué
- Silver gel pen
- Perle cotton No 8 in white, pink, orange, and variegated for hand-quilting
- No 9 crewel embroidery needles for quilting
- General sewing and patchwork supplies (see page 22)

TEMPLATES

Trace A Wing and a Prayer Templates A (Head), B (Body), C (Wing), D (Foot), E (Eye), F (Wedge Tail), G (Outer Star), H (Outer Circle), I (Inner Star), J (Inner Circle), K (Half-Circle), and L (Half-Star) (on pattern sheets), onto template plastic with a sharp 2B pencil and cut out accurately using sharp scissors (but not your fabric scissors). Label all the pieces and be sure to label Templates C and D "right side up."

CUTTING

All fabrics are strip-cut across the width of the fabric from fold to selvage unless otherwise specified or unless you are using a directional print. When cutting the appliqué shapes, place the template on the right side of the fabric and trace around it with the gel pen. Cut the shapes out using small, sharp scissors, a scant ¼ inch from the gel pen line. Use a ruler to rule a ¼-inch seam along the top edge only of each Wedge Tail shape.

FROM EACH OF THE FOUR WHITE BACKGROUND FABRICS, CUT:

- Four squares, each 12½ inches, for appliqué backgrounds (16 squares total).

Cut all of the remaining fabric into 4½-inch wide strips, for the sashing and Borders 1 and 3, and set aside.

FROM EACH OF THE PINK AND TANGERINE LINENS, CUT:

- Two Template A Eagle Head (four Heads total).

FROM EACH OF THE YELLOW-PATTERN AND AQUA-PATTERN FABRICS, CUT:

- Two Template B Body (four Bodies total).
- Two Template C Wing, right side up (four Wings total).
- Two Template C Wing, right side down (four Wings total).

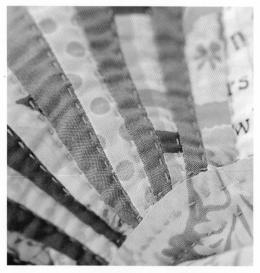

FROM THE TURQUOISE-PATTERN FABRIC, CUT:
- Four Template D Foot, right side up.
- Four Template D Foot, right side down.
- Four Template E Eye.

FROM EACH OF THE PLAIN RED, ORANGE, AND PINK FABRICS, CUT:
- Four Template F Wedge Tail (32 Wedge Tails total). Cut all the remaining fabric into $1\frac{1}{2}$-inch strips for Border 2 and set aside.

FROM EACH OF THE ASSORTED PINK, YELLOW, AND AQUA PRINT FABRICS, CUT:
- Four Template F Wedge Tail (32 Wedge Tails total). Cut all the remaining fabric into $1\frac{1}{2}$-inch strips for Border 2 and set aside.

FROM PINK-AND-YELLOW DOT, CUT:
- One Template I Inner Star.
- Four Template L Half-Star.

FROM TEAL-AND-PINK FLORAL FABRIC, CUT:
- One Template H Outer Circle.
- Four Template K Half-Circle.

FROM PINK SCRAP, CUT:
- One Template J Inner Circle.

FROM BLUE-AND-GREEN DOT FABRIC, CUT:
- One Template G Outer Star.
- 10 strips, $1\frac{1}{2}$ inches wide, for Border 4.

FROM RED-STRIPE FABRIC, CUT:
- 10 strips, $1\frac{1}{2}$ inches wide, for Border 4.

FROM MULTICOLOR-DOT FABRIC, CUT:
- Eight strips, $6\frac{1}{2}$ inches wide, for Border 5.

FROM BRIGHT-PINK-STRIPE BINDING FABRIC, CUT:

- 10 strips, 3 inches wide, for binding.

Constructing the quilt top

Background blocks (make 4)

1 Sew the 16 white background 12½-inch squares into pairs, making sure to mix the patterns. Press the seams to one side.

2 Join two of the pairs along the length to make a four-patch block. Repeat to make four blocks in this manner. Press.

Diagram 1

Wedge tails (make 4)

3 Arrange the 64 Wedge Tail shapes into four sets of 16, alternating eight plain and eight patterned fabrics until you are happy with the arrangement. Sew the Wedges together along the long side in order (Diagram 1), and press the seams under the plain fabrics. Make four Wedge Tails.

Appliqué

Read the instructions for Appliqué on page 186 before proceeding. The birds are appliquéd first, and the Star and Half-Stars are appliquéd in place when the sashing and Border 1 have been added.

4 Fold one of your four-patch background squares in half on the diagonal and finger-press the crease. Repeat across the other diagonal. Using the photograph and the seams and diagonal creases as a guide, arrange the pieces of a bird onto the background until you are happy with the positioning. Remember that the edges of the Wings, Tail, and Feet will go under the Body.

5 Lift the edges of the fabrics, put a drop of glue onto the fabrics, and press them down. Take care not to glue too close to the edge of the fabrics or you will not be able to turn the edges under to appliqué. You only need a small spot of glue to make the pieces stick. They will take a few moments to dry.

6 When the glue is dry and the shapes are fused to the background, select a shape on which to begin sewing. Thread a straw needle with cotton to match the fabric you are appliquéing. Finger-press along the silver line all around the edge of the shape. Turn the edge under along the pressed line and sew the shape to the background, using small stitches. You will need to clip into the inside curves to turn them under.

7 When you have appliquéd these shapes, turn the block over to the back. Select a shape and carefully pinch the background fabric away from the appliqué fabric on the front. Make a small cut, using small scissors, and carefully cut the background away from behind the appliqué, approximately ¼ inch from the seam lines (Diagram 2). I do not usually cut my backgrounds away, but due to the large size of these shapes, I have done so to make quilting on the appliqué easier.

8 Press the block, and trim to square it up, if necessary, to be 24½ inches square. Repeat until you have completed four blocks.

Sashing (white)

9 From the 4½-inch wide strips of white fabric for sashing and Borders 1 and 3, cut each long piece into two random lengths. For example, if the strip is 44 inches long, you might remove the selvages, then cut a 20-inch strip and a 23-inch strip. Repeat with all of the fabrics, so that there are several different lengths. You do not need

{tip}

This glue is designed to be removable. If you put something in the wrong place you can peel it back and reposition it, and after your appliqué is finished, it washes out.

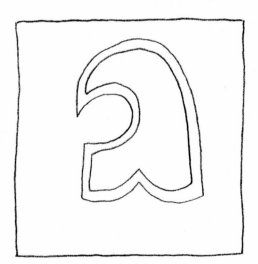

Diagram 2

to measure, just cut. Next, sew all the 4½-inch border strips together, end to end, into one long strip. This makes your sashing and borders appear random. Press.

10 Arrange your Bird blocks on a design wall or the floor, in their correct positions with their heads toward the center, so that you do not get confused when piecing them together.

11 Cut two pieces from the border strip, each 24½ inches long, for sashing. Sew a sashing strip between the two upper Bird blocks (Diagram 3), then repeat for the two lower Bird blocks. Press the seams under the appliqué squares.

12 Cut another sashing piece, 52½ inches long. Find the center of the top strip of birds and the center of the sashing strip. Pin the centers together, then pin the ends. Pin in between, easing if needed. Sew. Repeat this process to add the bottom strip of birds to the lower edge of the sashing. Press.

Diagram 3

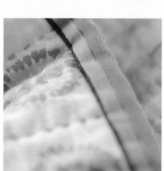

Center star appliqué

13 Center Template G (Outer Star) into the space between the blocks and glue. The shape will overlap the sashing and the corners of the blocks. Sew, then add, in layers, Template H (Outer Circle), then Template I (Inner Star), then Template J (Inner Circle) at the center of the star. After you sew each layer, turn the block over and cut the fabric away from behind the shape you just sewed, using small sharp scissors, about ¼ inch away from the sewing line. This will stop the appliqué from becoming too bulky.

Border 1 (white)

14 From the long white border strip, cut two more strips, each 52½ inches long. Pin one to the top of the quilt as for Step 12, and sew. Repeat with the bottom edge.

15 For the side borders, cut two pieces, each 60½ inches long. Sew these borders to either side of the quilt top, as above. Press the seams under the appliquéd blocks.

Outer star appliqué

16 When you have sewn the border pieces on, find and mark the center of each border. Finger-press each Template K (Half-Circle) in half to find the center, match this point to the halfway point on the border and glue the four Half-Circles in place. Appliqué the Half-Circles in position, cut away the excess fabric from the back, then add the four Template L (Half-Stars) on top.

Border 2 (pieced)

17 Take all the 1½-inch strips you cut from the remaining eagle Tail fabrics. Sew them together lengthwise in rows of eight, alternating a plain fabric with a patterned fabric (Diagram 4). Press all the seams to one side. Repeat with all the fabrics until you have sewn them into 8-strip sets, alternating and mixing the groupings of fabrics. Press.

18 Trim the end of one 8-strip set to be square, and cross-cut into strips, 2½ inches wide. Repeat until you have cut all of the 8-strip sets into 2½-inch pieces (Diagram 5).

19 When you have cut all the pieces, sew them together along the short edge to make long strips, 2½ inches wide. You will need two strips, 60½ inches long, and two strips, 64½ inches long.

20 Repeating the steps to attach borders, detailed in Step 12 above, pin the 60½-inch strips to the top and bottom of the quilt, and sew. Repeat with the 64½-inch strips on either side of the quilt top. Press the seams under the white borders.

Diagram 4

Diagram 5

Border 3 (white)

21 Take the remaining white 4½-inch strip and cut two pieces, each 64½ inches long. Sew these to the top and bottom of the quilt. Cut another two pieces, each 72½ inches long, and sew these to the sides of the quilt top. Press the seams under the white borders.

Border 4 (pieced)

22 Sew together lengthwise the red-stripe and blue-and-green dot fabrics into sets of 6 strips, alternating the fabrics as you go. You should have three sets of six strips each, and one set of only two strips.

23 Cross-cut the sets into 2½-inch strips, as for Border 2. Join the strips, end to end, to make two strips, 72½ inches long, and two strips, 76½ inches long. Attach the shorter strips to the top and bottom of the quilt and the longer strips to the sides. Press the seams under the white borders.

Border 5 (multicolor spots)

24 Remove the selvages and sew all of the Border 5 strips together, end to end, into one long strip. From this strip, cut two pieces, 76½ inches long, and two pieces, 88½ inches long. Sew to the top and bottom and sides of the quilt, as above. Press the seams under the white borders. Your quilt top is complete.

Backing, quilting, and binding

From the backing fabric, cut two pieces 96 inches long, and three pieces, 8 inches wide. Sew the 8-inch pieces together, end to end, into one long strip. From this strip, cut a piece 96 inches long. Remove the selvages and stitch the pieces together up the long seams. Press the seam allowance open and press the backing piece carefully.

Refer to pages 190–199 for instructions on finishing.

{note on quilting}

I hand-quilted *A Wing and a Prayer* using perle cotton No 8. I outline-quilted all the appliqué using pink or orange, and quilted a grid pattern in the backgrounds, 2 inches apart, using white. I then quilted the outer borders, using variegated perle cotton.

Using wedges

Fanfare
Dolly quilt, 18½ inches square

Hanging Lanterns
Queen size, 87½ x 95½ inches

A wedge ruler is one of the most exciting patchwork tools I own. Just when I think I know everything it can do, it surprises me again. Here, you can use wedge shapes to make the little fans in the fanfare quilt, and also try out some needle-turn appliqué if you haven't tried it before.

Hanging Lanterns is a more complex use of a Dresden Plate wedge. There is a lot of piecing and appliqué in this quilt, but the results are spectacular.

Although the sewing in these quilts can be a little tricky, if you are careful and keep your seams accurate you should be fine. The magic of both these blocks is that if you do have to make your lanterns or fans a little flatter, you can pleat them slightly at the center and then cover the pleat with the appliqué, but shhh...don't tell anyone I told you!

Fanfare

Fans are a fantastic graphic shape in quilts. Different placement of them can create a quilt full of movement and interest. You may like to make all your fan blocks and then play with different configurations of them before you sew them together.

Finished quilt size

Dolly quilt, 18½ inches square

Degree
of difficulty
***

MATERIALS AND TOOLS

- 8 inches each of two different contrasting purple fabrics for fans

- 10 inches pink/green/white check fabric for background

- 4 inches polka dot green fabric for fan centers

- 10 inches dark-purple fabric for binding

- 24 inches for backing

- 24 inches square cotton batting

- Purple cotton thread for appliqué

- Template plastic

- Sharp 2B pencil and silver gel pen

- Appliqué glue

- Straw needles for appliqué

- Silver gel pen

- White perle cotton No 8 for hand-quilting

- No 9 crewel embroidery needles for quilting

- General sewing and patchwork supplies (see page 22)

TEMPLATES

Trace Fanfare Templates A, B, and C (on pattern sheet) onto template plastic with a sharp 2B pencil and cut out using sharp scissors (but not your fabric scissors).

CUTTING

All fabrics are strip-cut across the width of the fabric from fold to selvage unless otherwise specified or unless you are using a directional print.

FROM PINK/GREEN/WHITE CHECK FABRIC, CUT:
- Two strips, 5 inches wide. Cross-cut these strips into 16 squares, each 5 inches, for the background.

FROM EACH OF THE TWO PURPLE FABRICS, CUT:
- Two strips, 3 inches wide, for the fans. Cross-cut these strips into 80 fan blades (from each fabric), using Template A (160 fan blades in total).

Diagram 1

Diagram 2

Diagram 3

FROM POLKA DOT GREEN FABRIC, CUT:

• 16 fan centers, using Template B.

FROM DARK-PURPLE FABRIC, CUT:

• Three strips, 3 inches wide, and set aside for binding.

Constructing the quilt top

Fans

1 Sew together a set of 10 fan blades, five of each fabric, along the long side of the blades. Begin at the left-hand side of the fan and start with a light-purple blade (Diagram 1). Make sure that all your blades are sewn in the same order. Press all the seams to one side. Continue in this manner until you have made 16 fans.

Appliqué

Read the instructions for Appliqué on page 186 before proceeding.

2 Using a patchwork ruler and silver gel pen, draw a line ¼ inch from the outside edge of the fan (Diagram 2).

3 Place a fan onto a pink/green/white background square by lining up the long edges of the fan with the edges of the square (Diagram 3).

4 Lift the edges of the fan and put a drop of appliqué glue onto the back of the fabric and press it down. Take care not to glue too close to the edge of the fabric or you will not be able to turn the edges under to appliqué. You only need a small spot of glue to make the piece stick. It will take a few moments to dry.

5 When all the fans are fused to the backgrounds, begin sewing along the outside edge of the fan to appliqué the fan to the background. Finger-press along the silver line around the edge of the shape, then turn the edge under, and sew along the pressed line using small stitches. Repeat with all 16 fans.

6 Place Template C in the corner of the Template B fan center shapes and draw the seam allowance on, using the gel pen (Diagram 4).

7 Glue the fan centers into the corner of the background squares and appliqué the curved edge, as above. Complete all 16 blocks in this way.

8 Press your blocks and ensure they are 5 inches square. Trim if necessary.

Assembling the quilt top

9 Lay all the blocks out onto a table or design board, referring to the photograph for placement.

10 Sew the blocks together into rows of four, then sew the four rows together. Take care to match the seams and the edges of the fans and fan corners. Press. Your quilt top is complete.

Backing, quilting, and binding

Using masking tape, tape the backing fabric, face down, onto a table, smoothing out any creases as you go. Lay the batting piece onto the backing, and then the quilt top on top. Smooth any creases and hand-baste the three layers together using large stitches and working from the center out. The backing and batting should be larger than the top for ease of quilting; don't be tempted to trim them back.

Refer to pages 190–199 for instructions on finishing.

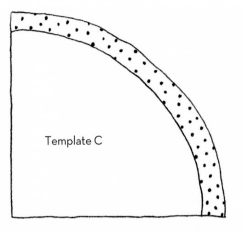

Template C

Diagram 4

{note on quilting}

I hand-quilted *Fanfare* using white perle cotton No 8, echo-quilting around the fans and the fan centers.

Hanging Lanterns

Designing this quilt, I had an image of a Chinese garden at dusk, the sun going down, making soft shadows, and pastel colors in the plants. Bunches of red paper lanterns hang in the trees, glowing pink and orange, and inviting you to come for a walk.

When I was choosing backgrounds I was very careful to choose fabrics that would not jump out and spoil the effect of the red lanterns. All the lantern fabrics are strong and able to hold their own against the backgrounds.

Finished quilt size
Queen size 87½ x 95½ inches

Degree
of difficulty
****

MATERIALS AND TOOLS

- 1 yard each of six different gray and pale-blue fabrics for backgrounds

- 1⅝ yards dark-gray fabric for sashing strips and binding

- 4 inches each of a wide selection of red and dark-pink fabrics for lanterns, totalling 5¾ yards, OR use half-yards of 11 different fabrics for simplicity

- 3 yards brown fabric for "eyes" and setting squares

- 26 inches gray-pattern fabric for top and bottom borders

- 8⅔ yards backing fabric

- 98 x 104 inches cotton batting

- 18-degree wedge ruler (optional, see page 29)

- 2B pencil

- Template plastic

- Silver gel pen

- Appliqué glue

- Straw needles for appliqué

- Medium-pink and brown cotton thread to match appliqué fabrics

- Perle cotton No 8 in brown and red for hand-quilting

- No 9 crewel embroidery needles for quilting

- General sewing and patchwork supplies (see page 22)

TEMPLATES

Trace Templates A and B (on pattern sheet) onto template plastic with a sharp 2B pencil and cut out accurately using sharp scissors (but not your fabric scissors). If you are using an 18-degree wedge ruler, you will not need Template B.

CUTTING

All fabrics are strip-cut across the width of the fabric from fold to selvage unless otherwise specified or unless you are using a directional print.

FROM EACH OF THE GRAY AND PALE-BLUE BACKGROUND FABRICS, CUT:

- Two strips, 6½ inches wide. Cross-cut these strips into 12 squares, each 6½ inches (72 squares total).
- Five strips, 4½ inches wide. Cross-cut three of these strips into 10½-inch pieces, to yield 12 rectangles, each 4½ x 10½ inches (72 rectangles total). Cross-cut remaining two strips into 6½-inch pieces, to yield 12 rectangles, each 4½ x 6½ inches (72 rectangles total).

FROM DARK-GRAY FABRIC, CUT:

- 14 strips, 1½ inches wide, for sashing.
- 11 strips, 3 inches wide, for binding.

FROM THE RED AND DARK-PINK FABRICS, CUT:

- 50 strips, 4 inches wide. Using either Template B or the 2-inch line on the 18-degree ruler, cut a total of 800 plate blades. (You can cut approximately 16 blades from each fabric.)

FROM BROWN FABRIC, CUT:

- Nine strips, 4½ inches wide. Cross-cut these strips into 80 squares, each 4½ inches. Set remaining fabric aside for appliqué.

FROM GRAY-PATTERN FABRIC, CUT:

- Five strips, 5 inches wide, for the Top and Bottom Borders.

Constructing the quilt top

Background blocks
(make 64 blocks + 8 half–blocks)

The background is made up of vertical rows of blocks. Each full block contains a $6\frac{1}{2}$-inch square, a $4\frac{1}{2}$ x $6\frac{1}{2}$-inch rectangle and a $4\frac{1}{2}$ x $10\frac{1}{2}$-inch rectangle. Choose the pieces for a block, taking care not to choose two fabrics the same.

Diagram 1
Full block

1 Sew the $4\frac{1}{2}$ x $6\frac{1}{2}$-inch rectangle to the side of the $6\frac{1}{2}$-inch square. Finger-press the seam toward the $4\frac{1}{2}$-inch piece. Sew the $10\frac{1}{2}$ x $4\frac{1}{2}$-inch rectangle to the long side of this unit (Diagram 1). Press and repeat to make 64 full blocks.

Diagram 2
Half block

2 Make eight half-blocks by sewing the remaining $6\frac{1}{2}$-inch squares to the remaining $4\frac{1}{2}$ x $6\frac{1}{2}$-inch rectangles (Diagram 2).

3 Lay out all of the blocks on your design wall in eight vertical rows of nine blocks. Each vertical row should contain eight full blocks and one half-block. You can alternate where you place the half-block within each row.

4 Turn the blocks a half-turn around as you move down the rows, so that they look random. Mix the blocks until you are happy with the placement, and then sew the blocks into vertical rows. Each finished row should be $86\frac{1}{2}$ inches long (including seam allowance).

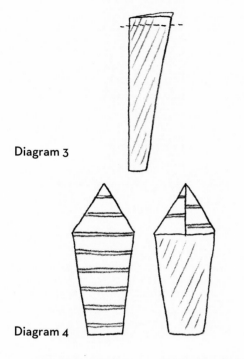

Diagram 3

Diagram 4

Hanging lanterns

5 First, sew the lantern "blades." Fold each of the wedges in half lengthwise, with right sides together, and sew along the top (longer) edge using a ¼-inch seam (Diagram 3). This is an excellent time to chain piece—there are a lot of wedges!

6 Turn the edges right side out, taking care to poke the point out so it is nice and sharp. Press the wedges flat, with the seam at the back aligning with the center line of the wedge (Diagram 4).

7 Sew the wedges together along the long raw edges into sets of five wedges, forming an arc (Diagram 5), mixing the fabrics well. Repeat until you have sewn together 160 arcs.

8 Place an arc face down onto the right side of a 4½-inch brown square, ¼ inch from the corner (Diagram 6). Sew. Place another arc on the other side of the square in a similar manner and sew (Diagram 7). Press the seams toward the arcs.

Diagram 5   **Diagram 6**

Diagram 7

Diagram 8

9 Repeat this step at the opposite end of the arc. Depending on how accurate your cutting and piecing has been at the wedge stage, you may find that the arc does not lie perfectly flat—this can easily be fixed at the appliqué stage so don't worry too much!

10 Next join an arc to either side of the second square. The corner of the square will be visible at the point where the arc meets (Diagram 8). Press.

11 Repeat in this manner until you have created a chain of 10 hanging lanterns, beginning and ending with a square. Make eight chains of 10 hanging lanterns like this.

Appliqué

Read the instructions for Appliqué on page 186 before proceeding.

12 Place the Template A shape onto the right side of the reserved brown fabric and trace around it with the silver gel pen. Cut out the shape, approximately ¼ inch outside the gel pen line. Repeat to cut a total of 80 Template A shapes.

13 Take a vertical background row and press it in half along the length to make a line down the center. Lay it out on the floor or a large table. Using the ironed crease as a guide, center a strip of lanterns down the background strip, making sure that the corners of the squares on the ends of the strip are touching the top and bottom edges of the backgrounds.

14 Lift the edges of the lantern shapes and put a drop of appliqué glue onto the appliqué fabrics and press them down. You only need a small amount of glue to make the pieces stick. They will take a few moments to dry.

15 When the glue is dry and the arcs are stuck to the background, take an eye-shape Template A piece and place it over the center hole in the first lantern. Position the eye by using a pin through the point of the eye at the gel pen line and lining it up with the seams on the lanterns. When the eye is in position, glue it in place, taking care not to glue too close to the edge, so that you can turn the edges of the shape under.

16 Thread your straw needle with a medium-pink cotton. Sew along the edges of the arcs using small stitches. When you reach the point where the brown square is showing between the arcs, tuck it underneath the seams using your needle to hide it and keep sewing. Continue sewing around all the arcs.

17 Thread your needle with brown cotton. Finger-press along the silver line all around the edge of the first eye shape. Turn the edge under along the pressed line and sew the eye to the lantern using small stitches.

18 Repeat until you have sewed all the arcs and eyes to the background strips. Press.

Sashing

19 Piece all the 1½-inch strips of dark gray fabric together into one long strip, first removing the selvages, if you have not already done so. Press. From this strip, cut seven strips, 1½ inches wide x 86½ inches long. (Adjust this measurement if your lantern strips are not 86½ inches long.)

20 Sew all of the lantern strips together with gray sashing strips in between, beginning and ending with a lantern strip. Be sure to find the center of a lantern strip, the center of a gray sashing strip and pin; then pin the ends and pin in between, easing as you go, before you sew. This will prevent any waves in your long strips. Press.

Borders

21 Sew together all of the 5-inch gray-pattern strips, end to end, to make one long strip. Measure your quilt top through the center to get the true width. It should measure 87½ inches. Cut a Top and Bottom border strip to this length.

22 Find the center of the top of the quilt top and the center of one strip and pin. Pin the ends, then pin in between, easing as you go, if needed. Sew and repeat with the bottom border. Press. Your quilt top is complete.

Backing, quilting, and binding

Cut the backing fabric into three pieces, each 104 inches long. Remove the selvages and stitch the pieces together up the long seams. Press the seam allowance open and press the backing piece carefully.

Refer to pages 190–199 for instructions on finishing.

{note on quilting}
I hand-quilted *Hanging Lanterns* using perle cotton No 8. I outline-quilted around the lanterns using red, and outlined the squares using dark-brown.

Step-down piecing

A Step Down
Dolly quilt, 15½ inches square

The Night Garden
Throw or twin bed topper,
54 x 64 inches

If you have never done this kind of piecing before, I strongly recommend that you make the dolly quilt before you attempt *The Night Garden.* It's not that the sewing in the quilt is difficult as such, only that the idea of leaving the seams open and working out where each piece goes next can be quite confusing. Making the dolly quilt will give you the confidence to set your pieced tulips into your night garden with ease.

A Step Down

I used a square of some of my favorite novelty fabrics for this quilt. Anyone who has ever had a peek in my stash knows my fondness for fabrics with little animals on them, so this quilt has only used a very tiny part of a big load of fabric. It's hard to know which is my favorite, but I am very fond of elephants!

This pattern makes a wonderful larger quilt too. Double the size of your squares and sew until the quilt seems large enough, then add the border rectangles. Sometimes simple is wonderful.

Finished quilt size

Dolly quilt, 15½ inches square

Degree of difficulty
**

MATERIALS AND TOOLS

- 4-inch square of 24 different novelty prints with light backgrounds, or scrap

- 4 inches dark-brown fabric for accent squares

- 6 inches dark-blue pattern fabric for binding

- 1 fat quarter for backing

- 20 inches square cotton batting

- White and dark-brown perle cotton No 8 for hand-quilting

- No 9 crewel embroidery needles for quilting

- General sewing and patchwork supplies (see page 22)

CUTTING

All fabrics are strip-cut across the width of the fabric from fold to selvage unless otherwise specified or unless you are using a directional print.

FROM THE 24 SQUARES OF NOVELTY FABRIC, CUT:
- 16 squares, each 3½ inches.
- 8 rectangles, 3½ x 2 inches, for edges.

FROM DARK-BROWN FABRIC, CUT:
- One strip, 2 inches wide. Cross-cut into 20 squares, each 2 inches.

FROM DARK-BLUE BINDING FABRIC, CUT:
- Two strips, 3 inches wide. Set aside for binding.

Diagram 1 • • • = seam left open

Diagram 2 • • • = seam left open

Diagram 3

• • • = seam left open

{tip}

Piecing a quilt top together in this way may seem very confusing at first, but the best way to learn is simply to do it. You will find that after you have done a few open and closed seams in this way, you will be just fine. As long as you remember that the quilt cannot be put together in the usual rows, everything will be OK!

Constructing the quilt top

This quilt is put together in an interesting manner. Due to the step-downs in the pattern, it cannot be sewn together in a straight line, or in rows. You will need a design board or similar flat surface to lay out the quilt on, so that you do not get mixed up.

1 Referring to the photograph, lay the large and small squares out according to the pattern. Don't worry too much about positioning until you have them all laid out, and then you can rearrange them until you are happy with the color placement.

2 When you are pleased with the layout, begin sewing at the top left-hand corner. Sew brown square A to the bottom edge of rectangle B as shown in Diagram 1. Leave the end of the seam open by ½ inch. Turn the seam toward piece A.

Diagram 4

• • • = seam left open

Diagram 5

• • • = seam left open

3 Sew the unit you have just created to the right-hand side of large square C in the top left-hand corner (Diagram 2). Finger-press the seam toward the brown square.

4 Sew brown square D to the left-hand top edge of large square E, again leaving the seam open at the lower end (Diagram 3). Turn the seam toward the brown fabric and sew this unit to the unit above (Diagram 4).

5 Next, sew brown square F to the bottom of large square E, leaving the end of the seam open, as shown (Diagram 5).

6 Sew edge piece G to the bottom of brown square D (Diagram 6), then close the open seam all the way from part-way down D to the bottom of G (Diagram 7).

7 Continue in this manner, until you have pieced all the squares together according to the photograph. Your quilt top is complete.

Backing, quilting, and binding

Using masking tape, tape the backing fabric, face down, onto a table, smoothing out any creases as you go. Lay the batting piece onto the backing, and then the quilt top on top. Smooth any creases and hand-baste the three layers together using large stitches and working from the center out. As this is only a small quilt, it does not need a lot of basting. The backing and batting should be larger than the top for ease of quilting; don't be tempted to trim them back.

Refer to pages 190–199 for instructions on finishing.

Diagram 6

••• = seam left open

Diagram 7

••• = seam left open

{note on quilting}

I hand-quilted *A Step Down*. I quilted a diamond shape into each large square using white perle cotton No 8 and an "X" onto each brown square using dark-brown.

The Night Garden

The scattering of bright flowers against the night–time backdrop makes the tulips seem like little jewels. The flowers are not hard to construct, but you must square them up carefully before you piece, or everything will go wrong! Fabrics for this quilt need brightness, interest, and pattern in the leaves for the flowers, or they won't stand out against the plain, dark backgrounds.

Finished quilt size

Throw or twin bed topper
54 x 64 inches

Degree of difficulty
****

MATERIALS AND TOOLS

- 2½ yards plain dark-blue fabric for background

- 14 inches each of six plain dark-blue and dark-green fabrics for background

- 12 inches dark-blue-pattern fabric for setting rectangles

- 22 inches green-pattern fabric for setting rectangles and outer border

- Pink, orange, blue, and yellow scraps totalling 34 inches for tulip flowers

- 4 inches each of five different lime-green fabrics for tulip leaves

- 22 inches stripe fabric for binding

- 3½ yards backing fabric

- 64 x 70 inches cotton batting

- Template plastic (optional)

- 2B pencil

- The Night Garden template set available at www.sarahfielke.com (optional, see page 210)

- General sewing and patchwork supplies (see page 22)

TEMPLATES

If you are not using the template set, trace Night Garden Templates A, B, and C (on pattern sheet) onto template plastic with a sharp 2B pencil and cut out accurately using sharp scissors (but not your fabric scissors). Mark the right side up on each template.

{tip}

**I recommend using a design
wall for this quilt (see page 24).**

CUTTING

All fabrics are strip-cut across the width of the fabric from fold to selvage unless otherwise specified or unless you are using a directional print.

FROM DARK-BLUE BACKGROUND FABRIC, CUT:

- Three strips, 5 inches wide. Cross-cut these strips into 24 rectangles, 4¼ x 5 inches, for plain blocks.
- 186 Template A shapes.
- 93 Template C triangles.
- 93 Template C Reverse triangles.

FROM EACH OF THE OTHER DARK-BLUE AND DARK-GREEN FABRICS, CUT:

- Three strips, 5 inches wide. Cross-cut these strips into 18 rectangles, 4¼ x 5 inches, for the plain blocks (you should have a total of 90 plain blocks from these fabrics). It is a good idea not to cut these blocks until you have completed your Tulip blocks. They need to be the same size.

FROM DARK-BLUE SETTING RECTANGLE FABRIC, CUT:

- Four strips, 2¾ inches wide. Cross-cut into 100 rectangles, 1¾ x 2¾ inches.

FROM DARK-GREEN-PATTERN SETTING RECTANGLE FABRIC, CUT:

- Four strips, 2¾ inches wide. Cross-cut into 100 pieces, 1¾ x 2¾ inches.
- Six strips, 1½ inches wide, for the Borders.

FROM EACH OF THE LIME-GREEN FABRICS, CUT:

- 18 pairs of Template B triangles (180 triangles).
- From just three of the fabrics, cut an extra pair of B triangles (186 triangles or 93 pairs of "tulip leaves" in total).

FROM THE SCRAP FABRICS, CUT:
- 93 Template A shapes, for the tulip tops.

FROM THE STRIPE BINDING FABRIC, CUT:
- Seven strips, 3 inches wide. Set aside for binding.

Diagram 1

Constructing the quilt top

Tulip blocks (make 93)

1 To make one Tulip block, sew a dark blue Template A piece to either side of a colored scrap Template A piece (Diagram 1). Trim the "ear" from the top of the points and finger-press the seams under the colored center piece.

2 Sew a Template B triangle to one side of the Template A unit (Diagram 2). Stop sewing ¼ inch from the end of the seam, as shown.

3 Sew a matching Template B triangle to the other side of the Template A unit. When you reach the Y junction of the seam, pivot on your needle and continue sewing out to the stem of the Y (Diagram 3). Press the seams under the green fabric.

4 Sew a Template C triangle to one side of the tulip and a matching Template C Reverse triangle to the other side (Diagram 4). Press the seams under the green fabric.

5 The finished blocks should measure 4¼ inches wide x 5 inches high. Trim your blocks if necessary.

6 Repeat Steps 1 to 5 to make a total of 93 Tulip blocks.

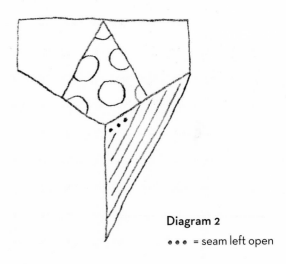

Diagram 2

• • • = seam left open

Diagram 3

Assembling the blocks

If you did not try your hand at the *A Step Down* Dolly quilt before attempting this quilt, you will find that it is put together in an interesting manner. Due to the step-downs in the pattern, it cannot be sewn together in a straight line, or in rows. The easiest way to keep track of where you are up to is to lay the whole quilt out on a design wall or sheet so that you can pick up the pieces in order as you sew.

7 Referring to the photograph of the finished quilt, lay the Tulips and setting rectangles out according to the pattern. Don't worry too much about positioning until you have them all laid out, and then you can rearrange them until you are happy with the color placement.

8 When you are pleased with the layout, begin sewing at the top left-hand corner. Sew setting rectangle A to the top edge of rectangle B (Diagram 5). Leave the end of the seam open by ½ inch, as shown. Turn the seam toward the setting rectangle.

9 Sew a setting rectangle D to the bottom of a Tulip block C, leaving the end of the seam open, as shown (Diagram 6). Now sew the first unit you created to the right-hand side of the Tulip C unit. Fold the seam toward the setting rectangle D.

10 Sew setting rectangle F to the side of Tulip block E, again leaving the seam open (Diagram 7). Turn the seam toward the setting rectangle and sew this unit to the unit above (Diagram 8).

11 Continue in this manner to expand the quilt. When you come to edges, trim the pieces to fit the space required and attach as above. This may seem a bit confusing, but the best way to understand it is to do it. You will find that after you have done a few open and

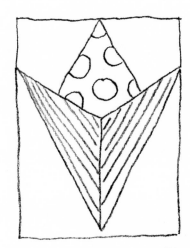

Diagram 4

••• = seam left open

B (plain)

Diagram 5

C (tulip)

B (plain)

A

D

Diagram 6

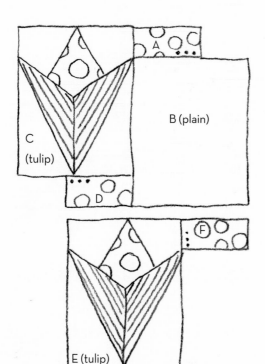

Diagram 7

• • • = seam left open

closed seams this way, you will be just fine. As long as you remember that the quilt cannot be put together in the usual rows, everything will be OK!

12 Continue until you have pieced all the Tulip blocks and rectangles together according to the photograph.

Borders

13 Sew all the 1½-inch border strips together, end to end, into one long strip. Press.

14 Ensure your quilt top is square and trim if it is not. Measure the quilt top through the center across the middle of the quilt. Cut two pieces from the long strip to this measurement.

15 Find the center of the top edge of the quilt top and the center of one Border strip and pin. Pin the ends, then pin in between, easing if needed. Sew. Repeat with the bottom Border of the quilt.

16 Measure your quilt through the center again, this time from top to bottom, and cut two strips to this measurement. Repeat Step 15 to attach the side Borders, as above. Press the border seams toward the border fabric. Your quilt top is complete.

{note on quilting}

I hand-quilted *The Night Garden* using a variety of different variegated perle cottons No 8. I outline-quilted all the tulips and quilted a tulip shape into the plain blocks. I then quilted a cross into the setting rectangles.

Backing, quilting, and binding

Cut the backing fabric crosswise in half into two pieces, each 63 inches long. Remove the selvages and stitch the pieces together up the long seams. Press the seam allowance open and press the backing piece carefully.

Refer to pages 190–199 for instructions on finishing.

Feathered blocks

Reflections in a Lake
Dolly quilt, 15 x 17 inches

Flock Together
Queen size, 92 inches square

Feathered Star quilts are notoriously difficult to put together, but piecing them is much easier if you first master the art of accurate half-square triangles on a small scale. Piecing the small units in the dolly quilt will help to train your eye and get your accuracy levels up. Take care to carefully study the diagrams of the feathered stars before you begin. You might also find that making the *A Step Down* dolly quilt (on page 150) will also help you to practice piecing this quilt together, as there is an open seam technique there as well.

Reflections in a Lake

The Delectable Mountains blocks in this quilt seem to be reflected in the water. To achieve this effect, you need to make sure that you choose your fabrics carefully, so that the mountains are a deeper shade than the reflections. This quilt would make a beautiful bed-size quilt as well; you need only expand the blocks across and down until the quilt is the right width and length.

These mountains are being reflected at sunset—you might want to try a green mountain in a blue summer lake, or snowy mountains in the winter. It would be interesting to make this quilt a night time scene also—imagine white mountains reflected in the moonlight on an ice-blue lake. The possibilities are endless.

Finished quilt size

Dolly quilt, 15 x 17 inches

Degree of difficulty ***

MATERIALS AND TOOLS

- 6 inches medium-pink fabric
- 6 inches light-pink fabric
- 2 inches blue-pattern fabric for water
- 8 inches light-blue fabric for background
- 6 inches dark-pink fabric for binding
- 1 fat quarter for backing fabric
- 18 x 20 inches cotton batting

- Sharp 2B pencil
- Template plastic
- Half-square triangle ruler (optional, see page 24)
- General sewing and patchwork supplies (see page 22)

TEMPLATES

Trace Reflections in a Lake Templates A, B , C, and D (on pattern sheet) onto template plastic with a sharp 2B pencil and cut out accurately using sharp scissors.

CUTTING

All fabrics are strip-cut across the width of the fabric from fold to selvage unless otherwise specified or unless you are using a directional print.

FROM MEDIUM-PINK FABRIC, CUT:

- One strip, 1½ inches wide. Cross-cut this strip into 32 half-square triangles, using Template A, or your half-square ruler.
- One strip, 2¾ inches wide. Cut this strip into four quarter-square triangles using Template B.

FROM LIGHT-PINK FABRIC, CUT:

- One strip 1½ inches wide. Cross-cut this strip into 32 half-square triangles, using Template A, or your half-square ruler.
- One strip, 2¾ inches wide. Cut this strip into four quarter-square triangles using Template B.

FROM LIGHT-BLUE FABRIC, CUT:

- Two strips, 1½ inches wide. Cross-cut these strips into 48 half-square triangles using Template A, or your half-square ruler. From the remaining fabric in the strips, cut four squares, each 1½ inches.
- One strip, 4¼ inches wide. Cut this strip into four Template C quarter-square triangles and eight Template D half-square triangles.

FROM BLUE-PATTERN "WATER" FABRIC, CUT:

- One strip, 1½ inches wide. (Strip will be trimmed to length during construction.)

FROM DARK-PINK FABRIC, CUT:

- Two strips, 3 inches wide. Set aside for binding.

Constructing the quilt top

1 Sew 24 of each of the medium-pink and light-pink Template A half-square triangles to a light blue Template A half-square triangle to make 48 squares total (Diagram 1). Trim off the ears and finger-press the seam toward the pink fabrics.

2 Using the photograph as a guide, sew three of the medium-pink/blue squares together, with the pink diagonals all pointing in the direction shown (Diagram 2). Make four of these units. Make another four medium-pink/blue units with the diagonals pointing in the opposite direction (eight units in total).

3 Repeat Step 2 with the light-pink/blue squares to make another eight units.

4 Sew a pink half-square triangle (in the appropriate colorway) to the end of each strip (Diagram 3).

5 Sew a medium-pink triangle strip to the left-hand side of a medium-pink Template B quarter-square triangle (Diagram 4). Repeat with the remaining three medium-pink Template B quarter-square triangles.

6 Repeat Step 5 for the light-pink triangle strips and Template B quarter-square triangles.

Diagram 1

Diagram 2

Diagram 3

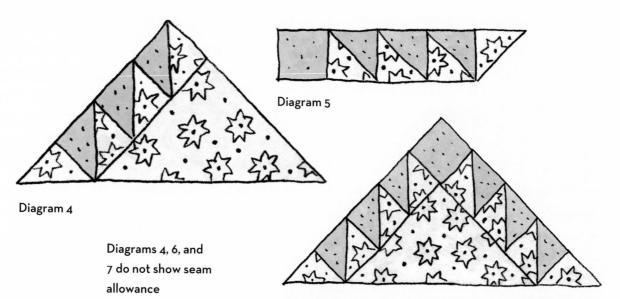

Diagram 5

Diagram 4

Diagrams 4, 6, and
7 do not show seam
allowance

Diagram 6

Diagram 7

7 Sew a blue 1½-inch square to the end of the remaining pink triangle strips in each colorway (Diagram 5).

8 Keeping the colorway sequence correct, sew these triangle strips to the right-hand side of the Template B quarter-square triangles (Diagram 6). Press.

9 Using the photograph of the quilt and Diagram 7 as a guide, sew a Template D half-square triangle to a medium-pink triangle unit, then a Template C quarter-square triangle, then another medium-pink triangle unit, and finally, another Template D half-square triangle. Press. Make another row identical to this one.

10 Repeat Step 9 for the light-pink triangle units, taking note of the positioning of the half-square and quarter-square triangles in each row. Press.

11 Measure your triangle rows through the center and make sure they are straight. Trim if they are not. Cut two strips from the piece of blue water fabric to the length of your triangle row measurement.

12 Find the center of Row 1 and the center of a water strip. Pin the centers together, pin the ends, then pin in between, easing as you go if needed. Sew as pinned. Sew the next row to the lower edge of the water strip in the same way.

13 Sew a second water strip between Rows 3 and 4 in the same way, then sew the two sections together to assemble the quilt top. Your quilt top is complete.

Backing, quilting, and binding

Using masking tape, tape the backing fabric, face down, onto a table, smoothing out any creases as you go. Lay the batting piece onto the backing, and then the quilt top on top. Smooth any creases and hand-baste the three layers together using large stitches and working from the center out. As this is only a small quilt, it does not need a lot of basting. The backing and batting should be larger than the top for ease of quilting; don't be tempted to trim them back.

Refer to pages 190–199 for instructions on finishing.

{note on quilting}
I machine-quilted *Reflections in a Lake* in the ditch, using white cotton.

Flock Together

It's funny how things come together sometimes. I had been given a wonderful piece of red Vietnamese floral fabric by a friend, and I wanted it to become something spectacular as it was so beautiful. It was sitting on my bench in the studio to "percolate" (I often leave things I want to work with lying around so I can see them), when a package arrived from South Africa. It had in it some amazing hand-stamped fabric that had caught my eye on Etsy. The two fell together, and when I added a box of Kaffe Fassett fat eighths I had been given at a show some months previously, I was in love!

Finished quilt size

Queen size, 92 inches square

Degree of difficulty ✳✳✳✳

MATERIALS AND TOOLS

- 1 yard each of nine different white fabrics for backgrounds (see Note (a), opposite)

- 20 inches each of nine different bold red fabrics for stars

- 4 inches each of 45 different bright-color fabrics for star points (see Note (b), opposite)

- 4 inches polka dot blue fabric for the cornerstones

- 1 yard black-stripe fabric for binding

- 8¾ yards backing fabric

- 3 yards square cotton batting

- Half-square triangle ruler (optional, see page 24)

- General sewing and patchwork supplies (see page 22)

{note}

(a) All my fabrics had either a red or a blue print on a white background. Be sure that the fabrics have enough contrast with the star points.

(b) I used a fat eighth pack of a Kaffe Fassett range—each pattern is a different group of star points. There are five different colorways of the same print in each star, 45 different fabrics in all. You can use larger amounts of fewer prints than this if you wish.

TEMPLATE

Trace Flock Together Template A (on pattern sheet) onto template plastic with a sharp 2B pencil and cut out accurately using sharp scissors. (If you prefer, you can also use the 45-degree line on your patchwork ruler instead of a template to cut the diamonds.)

CUTTING

All fabrics are strip-cut across the width of the fabric from fold to selvage unless otherwise specified or unless you are using a directional print.

FROM EACH OF THE NINE WHITE BACKGROUND FABRICS, CUT:

- One strip, 15½ inches wide. From this strip, cross-cut one square 15½ inches. Cut this square on both diagonals to yield four quarter-square triangles (36 quarter-square triangles total).
- One strip, 8½ inches wide. From this strip, cross-cut four squares, each 8½ inches (36 squares total).
- Six strips, 1⅞ inches wide. From these strips, cross-cut 60 squares, each 1⅞ inches. Cross-cut these squares on one diagonal to yield 120 half-square triangles per star (1,080 half-square triangles total). Alternatively, you can cut your strips 1½ inches wide and use the half-square triangle ruler to cut 120 half-square triangles per star.

FROM EACH OF THE NINE RED STAR FABRICS, CUT:

- One strip, 11⅞ inches wide. From this strip, cut one square, 11⅞ inches (nine squares total).
- One strip, 7⅜ inches wide. Cross-cut this strip into four squares, each 7⅜ inches. Cross-cut these squares on one diagonal to yield eight half-square triangles (72 half-square triangles total). Alternatively, cut your strip 7 inches wide and use the half-square triangle ruler to cut these triangles.

FROM EACH OF THE BRIGHT FABRICS, CUT:

- One strip, 1⅞ inches wide. Cross-cut these strips to yield 11 squares, each 1⅞ inches. Cross-cut these squares on one diagonal to yield 22 half-square triangles from each strip (990 triangles total). You will need 104 triangles per star, or 936 triangles total. Alternatively, cut your strips 1½ inches wide and use the half-square triangle ruler to cut 936 half-square triangles.
- One strip, 2 inches wide. Cross-cut these strips into 2-inch squares. You will need a total of 456 squares for the sashing and border (or 10 squares from each fabric, plus six extra).

From the remaining fabric, using Template A or the 45-degree line on your patchwork ruler, cut eight different patterned diamonds for each star, each 1½ inches wide with 2-inch long sides (a total of 72 diamonds).

FROM POLKA DOT BLUE FABRIC, CUT:

- One strip, 2 inches wide. Cross-cut this strip to yield 16 squares, each 2 inches, for the cornerstones.

FROM BLACK-STRIPE FABRIC, CUT:

- 11 strips, 3 inches wide, for binding.

Constructing the quilt top

Feathered star blocks (make nine)

Before you start, it is a good idea to separate out all the pieces that you need for each of the nine complete star blocks. For each star block, you will need: one red square and eight red half-square triangles (all from the same fabric); four white background squares, four quarter-square triangles, and 120 small half-square triangles (all from the same fabric); eight Template A diamonds (from random brights); and 104 small half-

square triangles (from random brights). Work on one block at a time, as follows:

1 Begin by sewing a white half-square triangle to each of the 104 colored half-square triangles to form 104 squares. Carefully press the seams toward the colored triangles. These are very small pieces, so make sure to simply press them, rather than moving the iron back and forth.

2 Lay all the pieces for one star out on a design wall or large piece of flannel or batting. Each star takes quite a while to make and it is easy to get confused about what goes where. Taking careful note of the direction of each triangle and diamond when you are laying out will save you the heartache of unpicking later on! Use Diagram 16 on page 179 as a guide: this will be simpler than trying to pick out all the little pieces in the photograph of the quilt.

3 Referring to Diagram 1, sew together a strip of five squares, with the triangles all facing in the correct direction. Add a white half-square triangle at the top of the strip, as shown. This is unit A1. Make four of these units. Press and return to the design wall.

4 Referring to Diagram 2, sew together a strip of five squares with the triangles all facing in the other direction. Add another square at the bottom (note the direction of the triangles) and a white half-square triangle at the top, as shown. This is unit A2. Make four of these units. Press and return to the design wall.

5 Referring to Diagram 3, sew together a strip of seven squares, with the triangles all facing the correct direction. Add a white half-square triangle and a Template A diamond at the top, as shown. This is unit A3. Make four of these units. Press and return to the design wall.

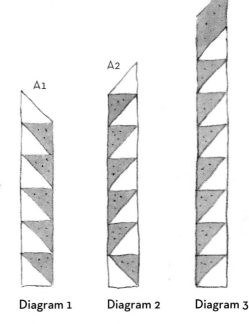

Diagram 1   **Diagram 2**   **Diagram 3**

Diagram 4

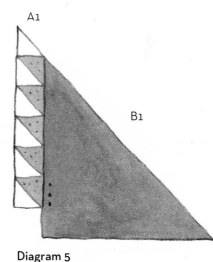

Diagram 5

••• = seam left open

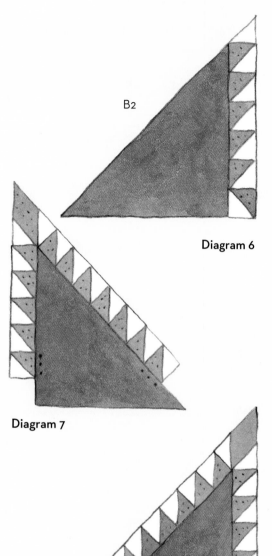

B2

Diagram 6

Diagram 7

Diagram 8

••• = seam left open

6 Referring to Diagram 4, sew together a strip of seven squares, with the triangles all facing in the other direction. Add a white half-square triangle and a Template A diamond at the top and another square at the bottom (note the direction of the triangles). This is unit A4. Make four of these units. Press and return to the design wall.

7 Next, sew an A1 unit to the straight side of a red half-square triangle with a left-facing diagonal (Diagram 5). Leave at least 1 inch of the seam open at the bottom, as indicated. This is unit B1. Press.

8 Now sew an A2 unit to the straight side of a red half-square triangle with a right-facing diagonal (Diagram 6). The A2 unit is longer and will reach all the way to the bottom of the triangle. Sew to the end of the seam. This is unit B2. Press.

9 Referring to Diagram 7, sew an A3 unit to the diagonal edge of the B1 unit, taking care to match the seams at the point of the diamond. This strip will not reach the end of the large triangle, and you should again leave the seam open by at least 1 inch at the lower edge, as shown. Press.

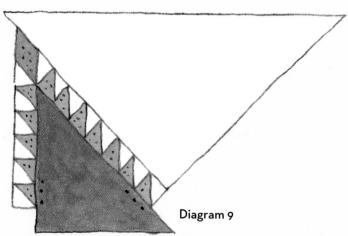

Diagram 9

Quilting from little things...

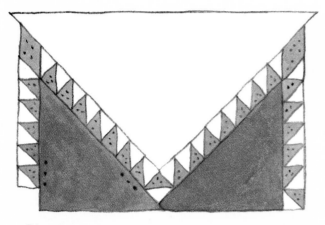

Diagram 10

... = seam left open

Diagram 11

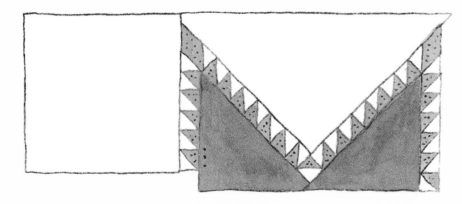

Diagram 12

10 Referring to Diagram 8, sew an A4 unit to the diagonal edge of the B2 unit, taking care to match the seams at the point of the diamond. Sew the seam all the way along. Press.

11 Referring to Diagram 9, take a large white background quarter-square triangle and sew the B1 unit to one of the short sides, as shown. Press.

12 Sew the B2 unit to the other side of the triangle. The B2 unit will reach all the way along the triangle and match with the end of the B1 unit (Diagram 10).

13 Close the seam on the B1 unit (Diagram 11). Press.

Diagram 13

Diagram 14

Diagram 15

• • • = seam left open

14 Next, sew an 8½-inch white background square to the short side of all four B1 units to make four star-point strips (Diagram 12). Press.

15 Find the center of one edge of the center red square and finger-press a crease. Match this crease with the center of one star-point strip and sew the two together (Diagram 13). Leave the end of the seam open at the B2 unit end of the seam by at least 1 inch. Do not press at this stage, until you have finished the whole block.

Diagram 16

16 If you have not already done so, return all the pieces to the design wall to check placement and orientation. Referring to Diagram 14, sew another star-point strip to the next side of the red square. First, join the seam of the B2 unit to the white background square, then sew the triangles along the center square, closing the seam on the B1 unit as you do so.

17 Turn the unit to the next side and join another star-point strip as before, closing the seam again as shown in Diagram 15.

18 Join the last star-point strip to the center square, closing all the seams as you do so, as shown in Diagram 16. Press the block and check that it is square, trimming if it is not.

Sashing

19 Take the 2-inch bright sashing squares and sew them randomly together into 24 strips of 19 squares each. Press. Set aside 12 strips.

20 Take the remaining 12 sashing strips and sew together four long rows of sashing, beginning and ending with a polka dot blue square cornerstone. Each row should have three sashing strips with a polka dot blue square in between, and at each end. Press.

{note on quilting}

I had *Flock Together* machine-quilted by Kim Bradley in a large all-over floral pattern, in white cotton.

Assembling the quilt top

21 Using the photograph of the quilt as a guide, sew together three rows of Feathered Star blocks, beginning and ending with a 19-square sashing strip, and with a sashing strip in between each block. Press.

22 Starting and finishing with a long row of sashing, assemble the quilt in rows, with a long row of sashing between each row. Take care to match all the seams and pin where needed. Press. Your quilt top is complete.

Backing, quilting, and binding

Cut the backing fabric crosswise, giving three pieces, each 105 inches long. Remove the selvages and stitch the pieces together up the middle seams. Press the seam allowance open and press the backing piece carefully.

Refer to pages 190–199 for instructions on finishing.

Basics, layout, and assembly

Quilt basics

Sewing techniques

Foundation piecing

Foundation piecing is a clever technique, used to make blocks of exactly the same size, to achieve accurate designs with sharp points or to stabilize scraps, and control bias stretching.

It involves, as the name implies, the use of paper or fabric as a base, or foundation, for piecing. Lines drawn on the underside of the foundation allow straight accurate seams that make even the most advanced blocks able to be sewn perfectly.

Foundation papers can be purchased in quilt or craft stores. The block designs need to be traced or copied onto the papers, so you will need at least one page per block. Be sure to choose a paper that feeds into your printer or photocopier. In some cases, it is possible to use standard copier paper. However, if seams intersect, this is not such a good option. The paper gets removed once the blocks are sewn and this task can be tedious if the paper cannot be removed easily.

The first step is to trace or copy the pattern for the desired number of blocks onto the foundation paper (Picture 1). Set your sewing machine to a small stitch, say 1.5, which helps when the time comes to remove the papers later. Sewing through the paper will dull your needle, so remember to change to a fresh needle when doing other sewing.

The fabrics need to be placed right sides together with the paper, right side up, on top (Picture 2). Hold the paper up to a light to be sure that the fabric covers the necessary area. Be aware of where the fabric will be sewn and make

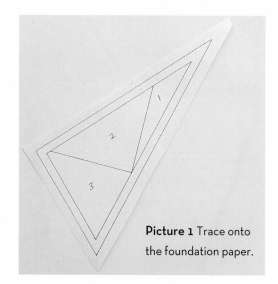

Picture 1 Trace onto the foundation paper.

Picture 2 Place the fabric, wrong side up, under the paper.

Picture 3 To complete your block, use a seam ripper to gently remove the foundation paper.

sure that it covers the next seam line when pressed flat. Sew the line, trim off the excess seam allowance, then flip the strip and press in place. Be sure to leave a $1/4$-inch seam allowance on the last strip.

When the block is completely stitched, fold over the first strip at the seam, and finger-press along the sewing line. Use a seam ripper to gently help loosen the paper. Do not rip out the paper or the stitches will loosen (Picture 3).

Appliqué

There are various appliqué techniques, but my favorite is the needle-turn method, described below. Whatever appliqué method you choose, complete all the appliqué before piecing the blocks together, unless otherwise instructed.

Before beginning the appliqué, decide where you want your shapes to sit on the background block. Use a sharp 2B pencil or other marker to lightly trace the shapes onto the background fabric. A light box is useful when tracing; if you don't have one, tape the design to be traced onto a sunny window, lightly tape the fabric over it, then trace the design.

Remember that some designs will need to have their various elements sewn down in a particular order. For example, when sewing a flower, the stem will need to be sewn first so that it sits under the flower petals, then the petals added, and lastly the flower center and the leaves. If you are working on a complicated appliqué design and you think you might get confused, draw or photocopy a diagram of the complete design, determine the order in which the pieces need to be laid down, and then number the shapes on the diagram so you can keep track.

Needle-turn appliqué

Trace the template shapes onto template plastic or card, using a sharp 2B pencil. Using paper scissors (not your fabric scissors), cut out along the traced line.

Place the template on the right side of the fabric and trace around it. I use a silver gel pen for marking my sewing lines, firstly, because it's reflective and shows up on any fabric, and secondly, because it's really easy to see whether or not you have turned your shape under neatly or not. If you can still see silver, you haven't got the shape right! However, gel pen does not wash off. Once you have traced your shape onto the fabric, you're married to it, so be careful with that tracing!

Trace the shape you are going to appliqué onto the right side of the fabric with the gel pen, taking care to leave space between the pieces for a seam allowance. Cut the shapes out a scant $1/4$ inch from the gel line. Finger-press along the line all around the shape, including into any curves or points. Do not be tempted to iron the press in. A finger-pressed line is easy to manipulate, whereas an ironed line is difficult to change if you iron a point into a crease or a line in the wrong spot. You will also be very likely to burn your fingers!

Position the pieces on the background block using the traced outline or photograph supplied with the pattern as a guide. Note which parts of the pieces may go under others; dotted lines on the template pieces indicate which parts of each piece should be placed under adjacent pieces.

Instead of pins, I use appliqué glue to fix the pieces temporarily onto the background. You can glue all the appliqué shapes onto a quilt and carry it around with you, without worrying that the pins have come out. You only need a few dots of glue on each shape to make them stick. Leave for a few minutes for the glue to dry. Don't worry if the glue smudges, as it is easily peeled back later or washed off.

Thread your appliqué needle with thread to match the appliqué fabric. You should always match your appliqué thread to the color of the fabric shape that you are

Tracing the outlines lightly onto the background fabric will help to position the shapes.

Picture 1 Run your needle along underneath the background and come up again right on the edge of the appliqué shape.

Picture 2 Your stitches should just catch the edge of the fabric and be quite small and close together.

appliquéing, not to the background. I use very long, fine straw needles for appliqué: the finer the needle, the smaller you can make your stitches for invisible appliqué. You can start anywhere, but try never to start on an inside curve.

Tie a knot in the thread and come up from the back to the front of the quilt, catching the very edge of the fabric with your needle. Go down into the background fabric right next to where you came up, run your needle along underneath the background and come up again right on the edge of the appliqué shape (Picture 1). Don't try to turn the whole edge under before you sew it; just turn under the small section you are working on. This makes it easier to keep track of the gel pen line and make sure that you turn it all under.

Sew all around the cut edge in this manner. Your stitches should just catch the edge of the fabric and be quite small and close together, which will make the appliqué strong and avoid its being torn or looking puckered (Picture 2).

The best way to get a sharp point is this: sew all the way up to the point on one side. Fold the fabric down 90 degrees under the point, then sweep the remaining fabric downward and underneath the main part of the point. Take

Picture 3 You will need to clip in all the way to the seam line on an inside point.

a stitch right at the point again and give it a sharp tug, then continue sewing down the other side of the point.

When you get to an inside curve, you've reached your next challenge! You can sew all around the outside curves without clipping, but inside curves needs clipping (Picture 3). Using very sharp, small scissors, carefully clip in to the silver line, about 1/4 inch apart, all around the inner curve.

I never clip anything until I am ready to sew it. If you do, it can fray and get messy. Sew all the way up to the curve before you clip, and then sew the curve right away.

Continue until you have sewn all around the outside of the shape and tie the thread off at the back with a small knot.

Turn the block over and make a small cut at the back of the shape, taking care not to cut the appliqué. Cut the background away underneath the appliqué. Be sure not to cut closer than 1/4 inch away from the seam lines. Although it is not necessary, removing the fabric in this way makes the appliqué sit nicely and creates fewer layers to quilt through, especially where appliqué pieces overlap.Repeat this process with each shape. Remove the background from under each piece before applying the next one (Picture 4).

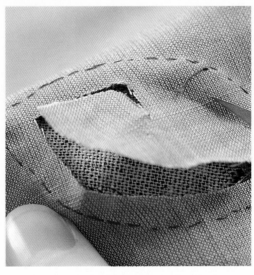

Picture 4 To reduce bulk, cut the background away beneath the appliqué.

Quilt layout and assembly

Constructing your quilt

If a layout diagram is given, be sure to refer to it as well as the photograph. Many quilt designs, especially complex ones using more than one type of block, feature optical illusions caused by the way in which the various components are combined. Sometimes the logic of the quilt's construction will not become clear until you look at a layout diagram.

Adding borders

Borders may be added for decorative effect, to increase the quilt's size, or both. They may have squared-off or mitered corners. The quilt pattern will tell you what length to cut the borders, but you should always measure your quilt before cutting the border fabric, then adjust the length of the border strips if necessary.

Measure in both directions through the center of the quilt rather than along the edges. This is because the edges may have distorted a little during the making of the quilt, especially if any of the edge pieces are bias cut. Use these measurements to calculate the length of each border.

If adding squared-off borders, the side borders will be the length of the quilt top. The top and bottom borders will be the width of the quilt top with the side borders added. Unless a pattern indicates otherwise, sew the side borders on first, press the seams toward the border, then add the top and bottom borders.

If adding borders with mitered corners, each border will need to be the width or length of the quilt, plus twice the width of the border, to allow enough fabric for mitering, plus seam allowance. Sew each border to the edge of the

quilt, beginning and ending the seam a precise $^1/4$ inch
from the edge of the quilt. Fold the quilt so that the side and
the top are flush and the two border strips extend to the side.
Use your ruler and a 45-degree-angle line to mark a line
from the $^1/4$-inch point to the edge of the strip. Sew along
this line and check before cutting—it must lie flat. When
confident, trim off the extra, and repeat for all four corners.

Layering the quilt

Once you have added all the borders, and before you can
begin quilting, you need to assemble or sandwich all three
layers of the quilt.

The batting and backing should both be at least 4 inches
larger all round than the quilt top. You may need to join two
widths of fabric, or add a strip of scraps or leftover blocks,
to obtain a large enough piece for the backing.

Press the quilt top and backing. Lay the backing right side
down on a large, flat, clean surface (preferably one that is
not carpeted), smooth it out carefully, then tape it to the
surface using masking tape. Tape it at intervals along all

Sandwich the batting between
the quilt top and the backing.

sides, but do not tape the corners, as this will cause the bias to stretch out of shape.

Place the batting atop the backing and smooth it out. If you need to join two pieces of batting, abutt them together and machine-zigzag a seam.

Atop the batting, place the well-pressed quilt top, right side up, ensuring that the top and backing are square to each other. Smooth it out.

The three layers must now be basted together ready for quilting.

Basting

Basting can be done with safety pins or long hand-stitches.

If using safety pins, start from the center of the quilt, and pin through all three layers at intervals of about 8 inches. If you are intending to machine-quilt, make sure the pins are kept away from the lines to be quilted. Once the whole quilt is safety-pinned, it can be moved.

If you are intending to hand-quilt, baste the whole quilt both horizontally and vertically, always working from the center out, using long hand-stitches at intervals of about 6 inches. Using a curved needle is a good idea, as this makes the task easier on the wrists.

Do not baste using hand-stitches if you intend to machine-quilt, as the basting threads will get caught under the presser foot. Do not use safety pins if you are hand-quilting as the pins prevent the hoop from sitting evenly.

Some quilting stores offer a machine-basting service. This can be a worthwhile investment, especially if you are going to be doing fine hand-quilting in the traditional manner, a task that can take months or even years.

Remove the basting stitches or safety pins only once all the quilting is complete.

{note}

TYPES OF BATTING

Some battings need to be quilted closer together than others to stop them from drifting around within the quilt or fragmenting when washed. Polyester batting requires less quilting than cotton or wool batting. However, some polyester battings have a tendency to "fight" the sewing machine.

Wool battings (usually actually a wool/polyester or a wool/cotton blend) provide more warmth and comfort than polyester battings. However, they require more quilting, and those that are not needle-punched tend to pill. Needle-punched wool blends are more stable and require less quilting. Traditional cotton battings require a lot of quilting, as much as every $1/2$–3 inches. Needle-punched cotton battings are more stable and can be quilted up to 10 inches apart. Ask your quilt store for advice if you are unsure of what to choose.

Hold the thread out to the side with your left hand, and loop a one-loop knot using the needle (Picture A, page 196). Slide the loose knot down the thread until it lies directly on the quilt top, and tighten the knot (Picture B, page 196). Take the needle back down through the hole the thread is coming out of and slide it away through the batting. Bring the needle back up to the top of the quilt and give the thread a tug. The knot will follow down into the hole and lodge in the batting. Cut the thread close to the surface (Picture C, page 197).

Picture 1 Use a thimble to push the needle through the three layers of the quilt.

Quilting

Quilting can be fairly rudimentary, its main purpose being to hold together the layers of the quilt, or it can be decorative, and sometimes extremely elaborate. Machine-quilting is quick, but nothing beats hand-quilting for sheer heirloom beauty.

Designs for hand-quilting, or elaborate designs for machine-quilting, are generally marked on the quilt top before the quilt's layers are sandwiched together. On pale fabrics, the marking is done lightly in pencil; on dark fabrics, use a special quilter's silver pencil. Pencil lines can be erased later.

If you intend to quilt straight lines or a cross-hatch design, masking tape can be used to mark out the lines on the quilt top. Such tape comes in various widths, from 1/4 inch upwards. Free-flowing lines can be drawn on with a chalk pencil.

If you intend to outline-quilt by machine, you may be able to sew straight enough lines by eye; if not, you will need to mark the quilt top first.

Hand-quilting

Quilting by hand produces a softer line than machine-quilting and will give an heirloom quality to quilts. Most of the quilts in this book are quilted using perle cotton, since it is often easier for beginners to work with and stands out vividly against the fabric's surface, although traditional quilting thread can be used if you prefer.

To quilt by hand, the fabric needs to be held in a frame (also known as a quilting hoop). Free-standing frames are available, but hand-held ones are cheaper, more portable, and just as effective. One edge of a hand-held frame can be leaned against a table or bench to enable you to keep both hands free.

Hand-quilting, like machine-quilting, should commence in the center of the quilt and proceed outward. To commence hand-quilting, place the plain (inner) ring of the frame under the center of the quilt. Position the other

Picture 2 Put your thumb in front of the needle while pushing from the back.

ring, with the screw, over the top of the quilt to align with the inner ring. Tighten the screw so that the fabric in the frame becomes firm, but not drum-tight.

For traditional quilting, choose the smallest needle that you feel comfortable with. (These needles are known as "betweens.") For quilting with perle cotton, use a good-quality crewel embroidery needle (I use a No 9). Thread the needle with about 18 inches of thread. Knot the end of the thread with a one-loop knot and take the needle down through the quilt top into the batting, a short distance from where you want to start quilting. Tug the thread slightly so that the knot pulls through into the batting, making the starting point invisible. Proceed as follows.

The hand-quilting action With your dominant hand above the quilt and the other beneath, insert the needle through all three layers at a time, with the middle or index finger of your dominant hand (use a metal thimble to make this easier) until you can feel the tip of the needle resting on your finger at the back (Picture 1). Without pushing the needle

Picture A (top) Hold the thread out to the side and loop a one-loop knot using the needle.

Picture B (bottom) Slide the loose knot down the thread until it lies directly on the quilt top, and tighten the knot.

through, rock the needle back to the top of the quilt and use your underneath finger to push the tip of the needle up. Put your upper thumb down in front of the needle tip while pushing up from the back (Picture 2). This will make a small "hill" in the fabric. Push the needle through the fabric. This makes one stitch. To take several stitches at once, push the needle along to the required stitch length then dip the tip into the fabric and repeat the above technique. Gently pull the stitches to indent the stitch line evenly. You should always quilt toward yourself, as this reduces hand and shoulder strain, so turn the quilt in the required direction. You can protect your underneath finger using a stick-on plastic shield such as a Thimble-It. You can also use a leather thimble: however, this does make it more difficult to feel how far the needle has come through, and thus more difficult to keep your stitches even.

To move a short distance from one part of the quilting design to another, push the tip of the needle through the batting and up at the new starting point. Take care not to drag a dark thread under a light fabric, as the line will show.

When you come to the edge of the hoop, leave the thread dangling so that you can pick it up and continue working with it once you have repositioned the hoop. Work all the quilting design within the hoop before repositioning the hoop and beginning to quilt another area. If you need to quilt right up to the border edge, baste lengths of spare cotton fabric to the edge of the quilt, thus giving you enough fabric area to position the edges of the quilt under the quilting hoop.

To fasten off a length of thread, see page 194.

Machine-quilting

You may want to machine-quilt your quilt yourself, but I use and recommend a professional quilting service for a couple of good reasons.

Firstly, finished quilts are usually quite large and, consequently, rather cumbersome. It really is a fairly tricky job to manipulate the bulk of the quilt on a domestic sewing machine, even using a specialized walking foot. Having pieced your precious quilt so carefully, it would be a shame to spoil it now with puckers and distortions.

Secondly, professional machine-quilters offer a large range of quilting patterns to suit every need and taste and can also advise you on a design that will enhance all your careful work.

Binding

From the width of the binding fabric, cut enough strips of fabric to equal the outside edge of your quilt, plus about 6 inches to allow for mitered corners and for the ends to be folded under. I cut my binding strips 3 inches wide and use a $1/2$-inch seam when attaching them to the quilt.

Seam the strips into a continuous length, making the joins at 45-degree angles as shown on page 199. To do this, fold under one end at a 45-degree angle and finger-press a crease. Unfold. The crease line will become the seam line. Mark this line lightly with a pencil. With right sides together and the two fabric pieces at 90 degrees, align the angled cut end with another strip of binding fabric. Align the $1/4$-inch measurement on a quilter's ruler with this line and trim off the corner. Sew the two strips together along the marked line. Press all seams to one side and trim off the "ears."

Press the entire strip in half along its length. Doubling the fabric like this makes the binding more durable.

Trim the backing and the batting so that they are even with the edge of the quilt top. Beginning at one end of the binding strip, pin the binding to one edge of the quilt, starting about 4 inches in from a corner, and having raw edges even. Attach a walking foot to your machine and machine-sew in place through all the layers of the quilt, using a $1/2$-inch seam allowance, and mitering the corners. To miter corners, end the seam $1/2$ inch from the corner and fasten off. Fold the binding fabric up at a 45-degree angle, then fold it down so that the fold is level with the

Picture C Cut the thread close to the surface.

To create your binding, join the strips (left), trim the corners (below), and tuck the end of the binding under itself using a diagonal fold (bottom), which will become the seam line.

edge of the binding just sewn. Begin the next seam at the edge of the quilt and proceed as before. Repeat this process to miter all the corners.

When you approach the point at which the binding started, trim the excess, tuck the end of the binding under itself using a diagonal fold, and stitch the rest of the seam.

Press the binding away from the quilt. Turn the binding to the back of the quilt and blind hem-stitch in place by hand to finish. Your quilt is now complete!

Glossary

APPLIQUÉ A technique in which small pieces of fabric are stitched to a background fabric.

BACKING The undermost layer of a quilt.

BASTING A method of holding together several layers of fabric during quilting, so that they do not move around. Basting may be done using a long hand-stitch, or with safety pins. The stitches or pins are removed once the quilting is complete.

BATTING The middle layer of a quilt.

BIAS The diagonal of a woven fabric, at a 45-degree angle to the straight grain (the warp and weft). Fabric cut on the bias stretches, so care must be taken when handling and sewing bias-cut pieces.

BINDING The narrow strips of fabric (usually made of a double thickness) that enclose the raw edges and batting of a quilt.

BLOCK The basic unit of a quilt top. Blocks are usually square, but may be rectangular, hexagonal, or other shapes. They may be plain (of one fabric only), appliquéd, or pieced.

BORDER A strip of fabric (plain, appliquéd, or pieced) joined to the central panel of a quilt and used to frame it and also to add extra size.

CHAIN-PIECING A method of joining fabric pieces by machine in an assembly-line fashion, which speeds up the process, and uses less thread. Pairs or sets of block pieces are fed into the machine, one after the other, without snipping the threads between them.

CROSS-HATCHING A quilting pattern of parallel equidistant lines that run in two directions to form a grid of squares or diamonds.

DIRECTIONAL PRINT Printed fabric in which there is a distinct direction to the pattern, whether straight or at an angle; for example, stripes, human or animal figures, or some florals.

EASE To make two pieces of fabric of different sizes fit together in the one seam. One piece may have to be stretched or gathered slightly to bring it to the required length. To ease, first pin the pieces at intervals until they fit, then sew them.

FAT QUARTER A piece of fabric that is made by cutting a yard of fabric in half, first vertically, then horizontally. The quarter-of-a-yard piece of fabric thus cut is approximately 18 x 22 inches.

FEED DOGS The teeth under the sewing plate of a sewing machine, which move to pull the fabric through the machine. The feed dogs must be lowered to allow for free-motion quilting.

FINGER-PRESSING A way of pressing a temporary crease in a piece of fabric, for example when finding the center of two pieces so that they can be matched before being joined. Running a fingernail along a crease will make it lie flat.

GRAIN The direction of the fabric, along the warp (vertical threads) or the weft (horizontal threads). These are both straight grains, along which woven fabrics do not stretch. Compare with Bias.

HALF-SQUARE TRIANGLE A triangle that is made from a square cut across one diagonal. Half-square triangles have the bias along the hypotenuse (or longest side). Compare with Quarter-square triangle.

MITERED CORNER A corner that is joined at a 45-degree angle.

NOVELTY PRINT A fabric printed with themed designs, such as toys, cartoon characters, or animals.

ON POINT An arrangement in which the quilt blocks are placed diamond-fashion, with their corners at the 12, 3, 6, and 9 o'clock positions, rather than in a square fashion.

OUTLINE-QUILT To make one or more outlines of a motif or block design, radiating outwards.

PATCHWORK A generic term for the process of sewing together many small pieces of fabric to make a quilt. Also known as piecework.

PIECE An individual fabric shape that may be joined to other fabric shapes to make a quilt block, or used on its own (in which case it is known as a one-patch). Also known as a patch.

PIECING The process of joining together pieces of fabric to make a quilt top, a quilt block, or a border.

PIN-BASTE To pin through the layers of a quilt "sandwich," using safety pins, to hold them together during quilting. The pins are removed once the quilting is complete.

QUARTER-SQUARE TRIANGLE A triangle that is made from a square, cut across both diagonals. Quarter-square triangles have the bias along the two short sides.

QUILT TOP The uppermost, decorative layer of a quilt. It may be pieced, appliquéd, or a combination of both, with or without borders.

QUILTER'S RULERS Precision-cut, straight-edge plastic rulers in various sizes, used with rotary cutters and rotary-cutting (self-healing) mats. They make it easy to cut accurate shapes, and to cut through several layers of fabric at once. They come in straight varieties and also those designed for cutting at various angles or for creating triangles.

QUILTING In general, the process of making a quilt; more specifically, the process of stitching patterns by hand or machine into the quilt layers to decorate the quilt, add strength, and anchor the batting inside the quilt.

QUILTING FRAME A free-standing floor apparatus, made of wood or plastic tubing, in which a quilt is held while it is being quilted.

QUILTING HOOP A hand-held circular wooden device in which a quilt is held while being quilted.

RAW EDGE The cut edge of a fabric.

ROTARY CUTTER A cutting device similar in appearance to a pizza cutter, with a razor-sharp circular blade. Used in conjunction with a quilter's ruler and quilting mat, it allows several layers of fabric to be cut at once, easily, and with great accuracy.

ROTARY-CUTTING MAT A self-healing plastic mat on which rotary cutters are used. It protects both the blade of the cutter and the work surface beneath the mat.

SASHING Strips of fabric that separate blocks in a quilt, to frame them, and/or make the quilt larger.

SEAM ALLOWANCE The margin of fabric between the cut edge and seam line. For quilting and most appliqué, it is ¼ inch.

SEAM LINE The guideline that is followed while sewing.

SELVAGES The woven finished edges along the length of the fabric.

SETTING The way in which blocks are arranged in a quilt top, for example, square or on point.

SETTING SQUARE A plain block or square used with pieced or appliquéd blocks in a quilt top.

SETTING TRIANGLE A triangle placed between blocks along the side of a quilt set on point, to straighten up the edges.

STASH A quilter's hoard of fabrics.

TEMPLATE Plastic, card, or paper shape used for tracing and cutting fabric pieces for piecing or appliqué, or to transfer quilting designs to a quilt top.

WALKING FOOT A special sewing-machine foot that feeds the top layer of a quilt sandwich evenly through the machine, while the feed dogs control the bottom layer.

WARP The lengthwise threads in a woven fabric, which interlock with the weft threads. See also Weft.

WEFT The widthwise threads in a woven fabric, which interlock with the warp threads. See also Warp.

{acknowledgments}

Who to thank, who to thank…the list is long and distinguished, but as usual I will start with my wonderful, supportive, and long suffering husband Damian, and my home-based fan club of Charlie and Oscar. My three boys make everything in life worthwhile. Thanks also to my Dad for his support through a crazy, crazy year.

Thank you to Kay, and to the marketing team at Murdoch Books for having the faith in me to go forward in a new venture. Your support means everything! Also at Murdoch, thank you to Diana Hill, Vivien Valk, and the team behind the scenes. Extra thanks to lovely Sophia Oravecz for putting up with my millions of emails and organizing everything so wonderfully. Working with Murdoch Books is a fantastic experience, I always feel so involved with every aspect of the production of the book, and I am so very grateful for that.

Huge thanks to my editor, Georgina Bitcon, for her incredible mathematical brain and her endless patience! Without Georgina you would all be making very strangely shaped quilts indeed.

I was very lucky to have the amaaaaaazing photography of Sue Stubbs, which has shown the quilts off so beautifully. Thanks Sue, for being able to take such great pictures, even in my tiny little sewing room!

Thanks and kisses to Flo, Erica, Amy, and Bee for champagne and chocolates, listening to my ramblings, and giving me your fantastic friendships and your strong opinions. To my Wednesday Night Girls for sticking with me, even when I've been so tired I'm not much of a teacher!

To all my online friends near and far who read my blog, tweet me, read Sewn, buy my books, and send me chatty, friendly emails. I love to hear from you all and enjoy seeing your quilts so much. Don't stop!

And lastly, to my delicious little white dog, Madam, for being such a perfect cover girl. Well done Muttie, chicken for you.

{resources}

I'm aware that many people who buy my books are just starting out on their quilting journey, so here are a few bits and pieces, interesting places to go, and sites to shop at.

There are many wonderful bricks-and-mortar quilt shops in the world, and where possible I encourage you to shop at your local patchwork store rather than buy online. I'm aware that this isn't always possible, but a local quilt store will help you select your fabric, give you recommendations and hints, and offer great classes to help you along the way. Your local quilt store can't survive to have your classes unless you also shop with them.

Websites for quilting information and industry news

- **Craft Gossip** www.craftgossip.com
- **Fat Quarterly** www.fatquarterly.com
- **Sewn** www.sewn.net.au
- **True Up** www.trueup.net
- **Whip Up** www.whipup.net

Inspirational blogs for quilts, fabrics, and fun

- **A Quilt is Nice**
  www.aquiltisnice.blogspot.com
- **Bemused** www.bemused.typepad.com
- **Glorious Applique**
  www.gloriousapplique.blogspot.com
- **I'm a Ginger Monkey**
  www.imagingermonkey.blogspot.com
- **Inspired by Antique Quilts**
  www.inspiredbyantiquequilts.blogspot.com
- **Mrs Schmenkman Quilts**
  www.mrsschmenkmanquilts.wordpress.com
- **One Flew Over**
  www.oneflewover-oneflewover.com
- **Pam Kitty Morning**
  www.pamkittymorning.blogspot.com
- **Red Pepper Quilts**
  www.redpepperquilts.com
- **The Happy Zombie**
  www.thehappyzombie.com
- **Wee Wonderfuls**
  www.weewonderfuls.com

Sarah Fielke patterns, books, ruler sets, and kits

- **Sarah's blog** www.thelastpiece.net
- **Sarah's website** www.sarahfielke.com
  or Google your nearest quilt store!

{index}

Published in 2011 by Murdoch Books Pty Limited
Published in the United States by Krause Publications, F+W Media, Inc.,
4700 East Galbraith Road, Cincinnati, Ohio, 45236. (800) 289-0963. First Edition.

F+W PUBLICATIONS, INC.

www.fwmedia.com

Murdoch Books Australia
Pier 8/9
23 Hickson Road
Millers Point NSW 2000
Phone: +61 (0) 2 8220 2000
Fax: +61 (0) 2 8220 2558
www.murdochbooks.com.au

Murdoch Books UK Limited
Erico House, 6th Floor
93–99 Upper Richmond Road
Putney, London SW15 2TG
Phone: +44 (0) 20 8785 5995
Fax: +44 (0) 20 8785 5985
www.murdochbooks.co.uk

Publisher: Diana Hill
Photographer: Sue Stubbs
Editor: Georgina Bitcon
Project editor: Sophia Oravecz
Designer: Clare O'Loughlin

Printed by 1010 Printing International Limited, China

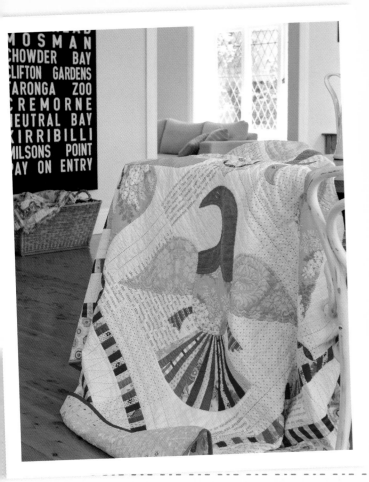

Needle?
Thread?
Fabric?

You're ready to go at
Store.MarthaPullen.com!
Find inspiration and
instruction for all
stitchers, whether you
sew by machine or hand!

A Community of Crafters

 Visit us on Facebook: *www.facebook.com/fwcraft*

 Join us on Twitter: *@fwcraft*

flickr *Share with us on Flickr:*
www.flickr.com/northlightcrafts

Check out these other great sewing titles by Krause Publications!

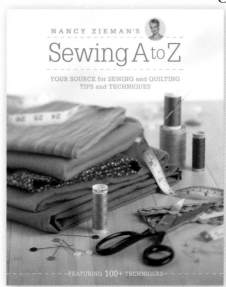

The answer to all your sewing and quilting questions!
Set aside your sewing fears and let Nancy Zieman guide you step-by-step through 100+ basic to advanced sewing methods and techniques.

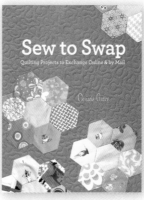

Connect! Sew! Swap!
From fabric to block to project exchanges, Chrissie Grace and her team of popular contributors show you the best way to organize and run your very own swap while making 12 beautiful projects.

Quick quilts as easy as 1-2-3!
No need to stress about choosing lots of coordinating fabrics. With a few tricks and tips, choose three fabrics and one of twelve fabulous designs, and you'll be on your way to a gorgeous finished quilt!

Inclusion in Early Childhood Settings

Children with Special Needs in Canada

Inclusion in Early Childhood Settings
Children with Special Needs in Canada

160801

Ingrid Crowther

Athabasca University

PEARSON
Prentice
Hall

Toronto

National Library of Canada Cataloguing in Publication

Crowther, Ingrid, 1944–
    Inclusion in early childhood settings: Children with special needs in Canada / Ingrid Crowther.

Includes index.
ISBN 0-13-127376-0

1. Inclusive education. 2. Early childhood education. 3. Special education. I. Title.

LC4019.2.C76 2006   371.9'046   C2005-907329-2

ISBN 0-13-127376-0

Vice President, Editorial Director: Michael J. Young
Acquisitions Editor: Dave Ward
Marketing Manager: Toivo Pajo
Developmental Editor: Patti Altridge
Production Editor: Richard di Santo
Copy Editor: Martin Townsend
Proofreader: Dana Kahan
Production Coordinator: Peggy Brown
Permissions Manager: Susan Wallace-Cox
Composition: Phyllis Seto
Art Director: Julia Hall
Cover and Interior Design: Anthony Leung
Cover Image: PhotoEdit Inc.

1 2 3 4 5   10 09 08 07 06

Printed and bound in the United States of America

PEARSON
Prentice
Hall

Brief Contents

Contents

Chapter 11   **Issues Concerning Inclusive Care in Canada   358**

Preface

This text has been written to introduce the early childhood educator to working with children with special needs. Many students lack expertise in this area and may have had limited experiences with children with special needs. Therefore this text endeavours to:

- Dispel biases by presenting real children with real problems through photographs, interviews and scenarios
- Create excitement about working with children with special needs in inclusive settings, through identification of real success stories with children, practitioners and students in the field
- Portray introductory concepts that are critical to interacting with children and families with special needs
- Instill understanding that all of us have strengths and weaknesses
- Provide relevance to what students are learning about children with special needs
- Provide an active approach that looks at child care in the context of inclusiveness, avoiding classifying children by their needs but rather dealing with them as individuals

Many of the current texts in the field of children with special needs provide information about dealing with identification, discussion of causes and theoretical intervention strategies. That sort of approach is not inclusive. It does not give individuals knowledge about how children should be treated or what strategies could be implemented. In contrast, this text aims to help in other ways:

- Promoting a change of attitude about working with children with special needs
- Providing individuals with information and references in practical, accessible formats such as charts, lists, photographs, graphs and diagrams
- Involving learners in active participation through such strategies as an interactive CD-ROM, student exercises, class participation exercises and community-based exercises
- Involving learners in realistic and meaningful experiences to gain new understanding about inclusive settings
- Linking learners to relevant internet references to help them find pertinent up-to-date information
- Creating a forum for discussion

Organization

The information in this text is presented in a user-friendly way. The flow of information starts with the child and family through the use of photos, scenarios, individual education plans or portfolios, and interviews. The theoretical components are woven around the interaction patterns of children and adults, the inclusive program and the learning environment. Thus the focus is on the child, the family and the practitioner, but the broader focus of the community at large is also included.

Typical aspects of the book's content include discussion of every child's right to learn through play; an overview of the types of programs for children with special needs in Canada; identification of the major disabilities from a Canadian perspective; information on how to organize an inclusive child care environment; specific guidelines for setting up inclusive environments to foster communication, play, positive interactions, motor activities, social, emotional and cognitive growth; and a discussion of Canadian issues related to the care of children with special needs.

Special Features

- **Interactive CD-ROM** featuring additional student exercises in an interactive format and including:
  - Presentations of scenarios with photographs—Students receive immediate feedback to their responses.
  - Weblinks from the text for easy access
  - Forms, charts and observational tools for convenient replication
- **IPPs and individual portfolios**—Actual individual program plans are provided, with instructions on how to develop them. Also included are samples of individual portfolios, another strategy to develop individualized programming for children with special needs (see Chapter 5).
- **Voices**—Final chapter, devoted to issues concerning inclusive care in Canada, features comments from all of those involved: staff members, parents, directors, consultants and children.
- **Reflections**—These recurring features present relevant personal insights from the author and other professionals in the field, and direct students toward their own insights.
- **Floor plans** of successful inclusive learning environments
- **Appendices**
  - Appendix A—SpeciaLink Child Care Inclusion Practices Profile, Principles Scale, and Recommendations for Inclusive Care
  - Appendix B—Excerpts from *Early Childhood Education and Care in Canada 2004* produced by the Childcare Resource and Research Unit, listing provincial and territorial profiles on regulated child care particular to special needs children

ACKNOWLEDGMENTS

I would like to acknowledge the children and families across Canada who helped in the creation of this text, especially Jordan, Susan, Gabriella and Christopher. In addition I would like to acknowledge the help of the following individuals: Sharon Hope Irwin, executive director of SpeciaLink; Dr. Arlene Young, psychologist; and the following for their invaluable insight during the review process: Shirley Bainbridge, Karla Baxter-Vincent, Janet Berezowecki, Cindy Brandon, Karen Chandler, Lana-Lee Hardacre, Susan Hartwell, Dawn Loran, Ann McDonald, Margaret H. Patten, Jane Proudlove, Janice Quade, Dawna Wojkowski, and Christine Wojcik.

I would also like to include special thanks to the staffs of the following inclusive centres: Capilano College Child Care Centre, Vancouver; Child Development Centre, Whitehorse; Cedar Road Aboriginal Head Start Program, Prince Rupert, British Columbia; Loyalist College Curriculum Lab Preschool, Belleville, Ontario; Berwick Child Development Centre, Vancouver; and Brite Beginnings, Edmonton. I would like to extend my appreciation to both SpeciaLink and the Childcare Resource and Research Unit for their permission to include the valuable information on special needs children contained in the appendices.

DEDICATION

I would like to dedicate this text to:

Dr. Harold Goldsman, who has spent a lifetime selflessly working to improve the quality of life for the children and families of his communities; and

Ross Smithrim, who, with the help of his family, overcame a number of handicapping conditions to successfully complete a college diploma program and used his creative talents to support the children and families in his community.

1

CHAPTER

Setting the Stage

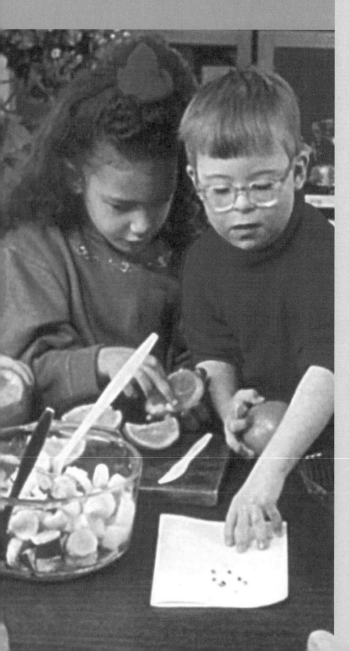

"Inclusion, as a value, supports the rights of all children, regardless of their diverse abilities, to participate actively in natural settings within their communities. A natural setting is one in which the child would spend time had he or she not had a disability. Such settings include but are not limited to home, family, play groups, child care, nursery schools, Head Start programs, kindergartens, and neighbourhood school classrooms" (Hope Irwin, Lero & Brophy, 2000: 5).

Learning Outcomes

After studying this chapter, you will be able to:

1. Identify the importance of the right to play for all children.
2. Discuss causes of bias and appropriate strategies to mitigate bias.
3. Describe the main reasons for individual differences.
4. Describe the strategies needed to set up an inclusive environment.
5. Explain the importance of forming collaborative partnerships.

Photo 1.1

Photo 1.2

Children's Right to Play

Play is the most powerful means of learning for young children. When children actively explore the environment, using all of their senses, they gain skills to:

- Communicate with each other (Photo 1.1)
- Learn about the world around them (Photo 1.2)
- Develop physically, emotionally, socially and mentally (Photo 1.3)
- Learn to solve problems (Photo 1.4)
- Make meaningful decisions (Photo 1.5)
- Build upon what they already know (Photo 1.6)
- Gain self-confidence in their ability to act (Photo 1.7)
  (Crowther, 2003; IPA World, 2004)

Photo 1.3

Photo 1.5

Photo 1.7

Photo 1.4

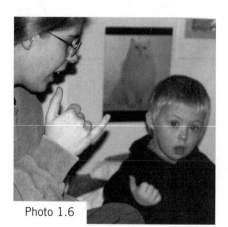

Photo 1.6

The right to play has long been supported by international organizations such as the United Nations. Article 31 of the UN Convention on the Rights of the Child identifies the critical role of play in every child's life:

1. Parties recognize the right of the child to rest and leisure, to engage in play and recreational activities appropriate to the age of the child and to participate freely in cultural life and arts.

2. Parties shall respect and promote the right of the child to participate fully in cultural and artistic life and shall encourage the provision of appropriate and equal opportunities for cultural, artistic, recreational and leisure activity (Covell, 2001: 176).

Photo 1.8

Further, in Article 13 the charter defines the child's right to freedom of expression: "... this right shall include freedom to seek, receive and impart information and ideas of all kinds, regardless of frontiers, either orally, in writing or in print, in the form of art, or through any other media of the child's choic." (Covell, 2001: 168).

The right of children to learn through play is supported by most of the relevant legislation. However, what constitutes play for young children, especially children with special needs, is often interpreted differentially (see Reflection). Children with special needs must have the same rights as all other children. Therefore, the focus of care for should be on:

• Equal opportunities to participate in all learning activities (Photo 1.8)
• Facilitation of equal opportunities by organizing learning spaces effectively in a way that provides opportunities to solve problems and engage in active choices
• Accessibility of materials and equipment to all children (Photo 1.9)
• Observation in order to identify where adaptations may be needed
• Active participation in indoor and outdoor activities (Photo 1.10)

Photo 1.9

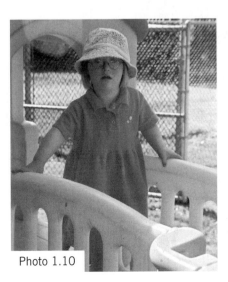

Photo 1.10

- Development of schedules that support regularly-occurring indoor and outdoor play, and monitoring and adapting all learning areas to provide maximum opportunities for active involvement of all children
- Provision of opportunities to make personal choices and decisions (Photo 1.11)
- Organization of the learning environments to set up learning experiences that foster independent interactions with peers, materials and equipment.
- Provision of learning experiences and materials that are developmentally appropriate and age appropriate (Photo 1.12)
- Awareness of the developmental abilities of all children in order to provide appropriate learning materials and experiences

Photo 1.11

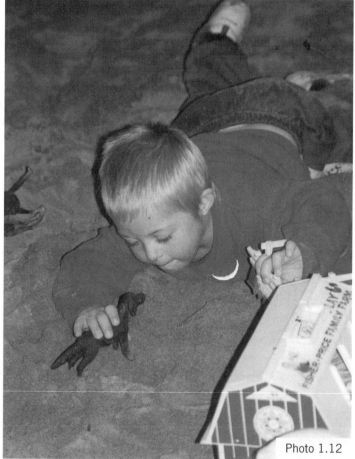

Photo 1.12

From the Author

In centres across Canada I have often observed children with special needs engaged in structured, teacher-directed activities. Here is a relevant example of an observed interaction:

During free play activities, Nancy, a four-year-old, was sitting at a table with one of the early childhood educators. Under the guidance of the adult, Nancy was encouraged to trace letters on a piece of paper. This activity was provided because Nancy needed to improve her fin- motor skills.

Careful observation of the activity identified a number of developmentally inappropriate practices. Nancy was trying to trace letters with her left hand. This process obscured much of what she was tracing because her arm and hand covered most of the area she was working on. She was also holding her pencil with a palmar grasp, which made it very difficult for her to follow the printed example. Nancy used a full-arm movement to try to accomplish her task, which further inhibited her ability to trace the letters appropriately. The result of her attempts was poor. She did not produce clear, recognizable letters. The letters extended beyond the area of the page. Nevertheless, she was rewarded with a "Good job!" at the end of the activity.

This activity was totally inappropriate for Nancy. If the intent was to improve her fine motor control, the activity could have been arranged in a number of ways that would have been more rewarding and appropriate to her. She should have been working on a larger surface to accommodate her palmar grasp and whole-arm movement. Better activities to help her control and refine her arm movement would include filling and dumping play. Her fine and gross muscular control could be enhanced through activities such as moulding clay, painting or drawing. Most importantly, Nancy was robbed of an opportunity to engage in meaningful activity that was directed by her and supported her individual development.

Unfortunately, proactive legislation does not exist in Canada that supports the rights of children with special needs. "While all provinces and territories have made some provision for the inclusion of children with special needs, in no jurisdiction is it illegal to exclude a child from a child care on the basis of disability or other special needs. And while many provincial officials and child care consultants have worked diligently to make inclusion a reality in their jurisdiction, written policies, training requirements, and resource allocation seldom suggest systematic, stable support for inclusion" (Hope Irwin et al., 2000: xiii). It therefore falls upon individual child care centres to include children within their programs, often without the resources or support to do this.

Attitudes, Values and Beliefs About Inclusive Care

1. Bias

"**Bias** is a point of view or inclination that manifests itself through favoritism, dislike, or fear toward someone because of that person's particular looks, behaviour, or lifestyle. A bias can be conveyed to another through nonverbal, verbal, and physical interactions. In other words, one's point of view is clearly reflected by one's attitude and actions" (Saderman Hall & Rhomberg, 1995: 2).

Bias occurs regularly in everyday life. Individuals are influenced by what they see, hear, feel and smell. For example, Jasmine had been a refugee child. At the age of eight, she had been placed in a private institution until her parents could find a home for the whole family. One of the meals served once a week for lunch was horseradish soup. Jasmine found the taste "revolting." She refused to eat her soup. As a result, she did not get any lunch. To get any of the other lunch servings, she had to eat the soup first. Jasmine is now an adult. She still does not like horseradish. Even though she realizes that it could be good in other combinations, the experience left such a strong impression that she cannot force herself to try. "As soon as I smell horseradish, it brings back the memory of that awful soup. I remember the disapproving faces and how hungry I was every Monday."

Not all experiences lead to such a strong bias. Many instances of bias are much more subtle. For example, Marianna believed that Fisher-Price toys were the best toys to buy for her infant. When questioned why she believed this, she indicated that the magazines and television ads seemed to indicate that they were.

When one centre was faced with including a child with disabilities, some of the families did not want the child included and expressed their opposition. They did not inquire about the special need; nor were they interested in discussing the topic. The fears expressed were that:

- Less time would be available to spend with their child, as the child with special needs would demand more time from the two regular staff
- Less money would be available to spend as most of the resources would be needed to buy expensive equipment for only one child
- Children would pick up the negative behaviours modelled by this child
- Children would be hurt by the child's aggressive behaviours

The staff ultimately decided not to accept the child as too many families threatened to move their children to another centre should the child be accepted.

2. Sources of Bias

Any bias, including bias about children with special needs, can arise from a number of sources. The degree of bias an individual may hold is dependent on many factors:

- Knowledge about child development and special needs
- Experiences with individuals with special needs
- Physical indicators such as the appearance of an individual
- Belief systems such as ideas about how children learn or should be treated
- Socioeconomic status, which is an indicator of the social and economic values an individual holds
- Cultural influences that lead to certain ways of thinking and behaving
- Designation of roles such as male and female, parent or teacher
- Determinants such as skin colour or ethnicity
- Family dynamics
- Health status

A) KNOWLEDGE BASE Knowledge is one of the critical factors in anyone's ability to make informed decisions about how to interact with any child, how to select materials and resources, and how to develop a quality learning environment. Consider the following examples:

Two individuals were asked to identify what they thought of when they heard the phrase "children with special needs." Melanie, a first-year student in an Early Childhood Education program, responded: "You can usually tell if the kids are special needs by the way they look, like a Down's syndrome child or a child in a wheelchair. A lot of them are hyper, like disturbed kids, and they are hard to deal with. Most kids with special needs require a lot more work and attention. It would be hard to have them in a regular program with normal kids." Melanie clearly demonstrated her bias in several ways:

- She seemed to think that a child can be diagnosed based on the child's appearance. Although this might be true of some children, it is untrue of most (see Reflection).
- She also felt that most children with special needs share a behavioural characteristic: hyperactivity. All young children are active. Few children are actually diagnosed as hyperactive.

For the Student   **Reflection**

Look at the photographs presented at the beginning of the chapter. How many children could you identify as special needs simply by looking at them? Melanie obviously had limited experiences with children with special needs. Her experience and knowledge was based on physical characteristics and perceived behaviours of children with special needs. Reflect upon what you have seen or heard about children with special needs. What are some of the influences that might have caused Melanie to believe as she did?

For the Student

Read over some of the scenarios above and below (reflections about Nancy, Jasmine, Jeremy and Archibald). How many of these children showed similar behavioural characteristics? Reflect on some of the children you know. How many of these children show some of the characteristics of the children in the scenarios? Why is it dangerous to generalize about the behaviour of chil-

- Melanie also felt that working with children with special needs required more work. The amount of work required is not based on special needs alone. All children require more attention and work at some times than at other times. Not all children with special needs require a consistently large amount of attention.
- Melanie felt that it would be difficult to provide inclusive care. In fact, providing inclusive care should be very rewarding, not difficult. As with any child, the environment should be set up to accommodate the individual child's strengths and needs. When children are together in an inclusive setting, they learn to appreciate each other's strengths and weaknesses, and learn that everyone has some special needs.

The second person asked to identify what she thought of when she heard the phrase "children with special needs" was Arlene, a child psychologist. She answered: "All children have special needs. They are all individuals. I recognize that there is a code to identify the various types of disabilities, but children should be children. However, we should look at children as individuals who have different likes and dislikes, learning styles, and strengths and needs. The challenge is to try to gain insights into what the child understands so that we can interact in positive

For the Student

What are your experiences with young children? When do children tend to need more attention? At what times do children require more attention or work? Could the same answers be applied to children with special needs?

For the Student

Reflect upon the benefits of inclusive care to the individual with special needs and to his or her peers. What adaptations need to be made to the environment to meet the developmental levels of all the children in a child-care program?

ways to help his or her optimum growth and development." It is evident from Arlene's quote that she has a lot of knowledge and experience with children with special needs. She understands that:

- All children are unique individuals
- All children have special needs
- Adults need to interact with children based on their developmental levels
- Adults need to engage in positive interactions

B) EXPERIENCE WITH CHILDREN WITH SPECIAL NEEDS When Josh started in a nursery school program, the staff had no previous experience with children with special needs. As a result, Josh was treated as "special." One staff member was always near him to help him. All interactions with Josh were positive, but he had few opportunities to actively explore and interact with the materials in the environment independently. For example, when Josh tried to use the climber, one adult helped him up and another adult held him as he slid down the slide (Photo 1.13). This type of interaction can quickly lead to dependency. Josh's parents decided to take him to a different nursery school.

Photo 1.13

The staff in the new setting had experience in interacting with children with special needs. Josh was encouraged to participate independently. Josh thrived in this environment. He soon participated fully in all activities, independently (Photo 1.14).

The staff of the first centre that Josh attended were clearly biased about his abilities. They had decided that Josh needed careful supervision and help.

C) PHYSICAL INDICATORS Jeremy was born with cerebral palsy. He is able to walk by himself but lurches from side to side. Since Jeremy is very unsteady on his feet, people often try to help him walk. When Jeremy tries to tell them that he can walk by

Photo 1.14

Reflection

Reflection | *For the Student*

When you see someone in difficulty, what do you do? Do you jump right in and offer to help, or do you ask if the individual needs help first? Why might the latter strategy be more effective?

himself, he is most often not understood, as his speech is slurred and hard to understand.

This bias is clear. Jeremy looks unstable. He might fall and hurt himself. He needs to be helped.

D) BELIEF SYSTEMS It is a relatively new approach to include children with special needs in settings within their neighbourhoods or in settings of choice. This approach is based on the belief that inclusion is a system that removes barriers so children may participate in all aspects of their life (Voices 4 Children, 2003: 1). Belief systems of the past advocated partial to total segregation of children with special needs.

E) SOCIOECONOMIC STATUS Socioeconomic status dictates what a family can or cannot afford to do. Often families on lower incomes cannot give their children the same stimulation or experiences that families with higher incomes can. When children from low-income families are not as well dressed, or do not have the same experiences, as children from high-income families, sometimes negative assumptions are made about the care low-income families give their children. For example, Archibald, a three-year-old, often came to school with torn, dirty clothes. His hair was not combed, and his hands and face were dirty. He did not settle into routines easily. If crossed, he would scream, throw his toys, and sometimes bite or kick. The staff rarely saw his parents. He was usually dropped off by various extended family members. The staff tried to contact the family in writing and by phone, but these attempts were unsuccessful. The staff assumed that the family did not care and that the family did not use appropriate guidance techniques at home.

Reflection | *For the Student*

"The nature of developmentally appropriate practices allows for the inclusion of children with great variation in development within the same setting. Even in a group of young children without disabilities, of the same age, children can be as much as two years apart developmentally" (Udell, Peters & Piaza Templeman, 2001: 34). Reflect upon this statement. Have you noticed this age spread in abilities in a group of children?

F) CULTURAL INFLUENCES Throughout much of our country's past, children with special needs were often hidden away. Parents often placed children with special needs in institutions. More recently, a movement to keep the children living at home also saw them segregated into specialized schools or classes. Today the view is that it is better to integrate children into settings within their neighbourhoods.

Each of these three approaches was supported by the dominant Canadian cultures of the time. Huge institutions were built to house children with special needs for the rest of their lives. As society's values shifted toward keeping children at home, special schools were built and special classes were equipped and opened. It is only recently that most of the dominant cultures across Canada embrace inclusion as the appropriate methodology for caring for young children with special needs.

G) DESIGNATION OF ROLES Individuals have various roles they engage in every day. Each role carries its own bias. For example, Josh's mother was most concerned with developing his independence. This dictated her choice of program. The staff of the day care were more concerned with his safety. Subsequently, the interactions between Josh and the staff increased his dependency on adult intervention. Additionally, Josh's father served in the army and was often out of the country. As a result, Josh's mother's role was as primary caregiver of Josh and as the person responsible for most of the decisions concerning his care and education.

Reflection *For the Student*

Think about the neighbourhood you grew up in. What type of neighbourhood was it? Can you remember any bias that was held? Was this bias to your advantage or disadvantage? How was this bias expressed?

H) RACIAL AND SIMILAR DETERMINANTS, SUCH AS SKIN COLOUR OR ETHNICITY "The out-of-family perception of a family's need often misses the mark (Harry 1992). Instead, it is likely to represent the professionals' own bias and values" (Allen, Paasche, Langford & Nolan, 2002: 227). This observation is especially true if the child comes from a geographic area thought to be representative of higher numbers of children with special needs.

I) FAMILY DYNAMICS The types of interactions that occur within the home and family attitudes toward a child all have a profound impact on the child. Children who live in abusive or neglectful environments often do not receive the optimal attention and stimulation needed for healthy growth and development. As a result, these children live under constant stress and may exhibit many of the signs and symptoms of children with special needs. "A child who misses positive stimulation or is subject to chronic stress in the first years of life may have difficulty overcoming a bad early start" (McCain & Mustard, 1999; 52).

Often these children are labelled as children with special needs. The practitioner doing the labelling usually relies on someone else to provide the quality programs that these children need. However, if the child is enrolled in a program that is nurturing and of high quality, much of this early negative impact can be mitigated. "The evidence is clear that good early childhood development programs that involve parents or other primary caregivers of young children can influence how they relate to and care for children in the home and can vastly improve outcomes for children's behaviour, learning and health in later life. The earlier in a child's life these programs begin, the better. These programs can benefit children and families from all socioeconomic groups in society" (McCain et al., 1999: 52).

J) HEALTH STATUS Children who are medically fragile or often ill, or who live with family members who are ill, may also have a poorer head start. It is hard to stimulate someone to be involved in active play who is not feeling well. It is equally hard for someone who is not feeling well to have enough energy to stimulate a child.

Reflection *For the Student*

What do you perceive as symptoms of special needs? Might the symptoms you have identified be symptoms of something else? How can you ensure that you do not bring a personal bias to working with young children?

Reflection

For the Student   **Reflection**

Your personal health is critical to your ability to provide active and stimulating programs for young children. Reflect upon your energy level when you are not feeling well. How will this affect the children in your care? What strategies can you use to ensure your own well-being?

These children may also exhibit symptoms of special needs. As in the example above, a warm and nurturing child care program can provide the appropriate stimulation that is needed. Caregivers of young children need to take care of themselves in order to have the required energy to provide a healthy, stimulating program for the children in their care.

3. Anti-Bias Defined

Since the prefix "anti-" means against, taking an **anti-bias** approach "means taking a stand against unfair treatment associated with one of the areas of diversity where bias may exist" (Saderman Hall et al., 1995: 2). All individuals operate within the biases that are set by the time we live in, the environment we have been raised in or work in, and the social system we live in. It is therefore not feasible to be free from bias. "We will always have preferences, but to act on them in an exclusionary manner constitutes a bias" (Saderman Hall et al., 1995: 3). Adults working in inclusive settings must be aware of their personal biases and be prepared to overcome barriers that are imposed by a biased approach.

4. Strategies to Mitigate Personal Bias

Most of the types of biases referred to above can be mitigated by developing and using a number of strategies:

- Reflective practices and discussions, such as those featured in this chapter (see Table 1.1)
- Active listening strategies (see Figure 1.1)
- Appropriate self-care practices—Caregivers who feel tired or unwell may see things from a more negative perspective, resulting in negative interactions with children or other staff. Caregivers should ensure that they are healthy and well-rested by getting regular sleep, regular health-care checkups, and appropriate nutrition and exercise.
- Strategies to create an atmosphere of mutual respect for everyone—This includes children, families, other professionals and other staff. Applying reflective practices (Table 1.1) and active listening (Figure 1.1), developing lines of open communication with all partners and sharing information in a confidential, trustful manner will help set the stage for mutual trust and respect.

- Strategies to organize an inclusive learning environment (see section on elements of inclusive care)
- Identification of and elimination of subjective terminology that leads to bias in all observations, written documents and reports
- Organization of workshops with all team members—families, other professionals, community members and staff—to identify bias and to make recommendations toward elimination of biased perspectives

TABLE 1.1 **REFLECTIVE PRACTICES**

Stop and reflect	Think about what you have observed or heard. Do you have enough information? Can you make an unbiased interpretation based on what you have observed or heard?
Check your own feelings	How do you feel about what you have seen or heard? If you are feeling anxious or resentful, reflect upon why you feel this way. Do not respond until you have clarified how you feel. Try some of the other strategies below prior to responding.
Clarify	**Paraphrase**—Repeat what has been said to you in your own words. You might start with, "I understand that . . . " or "I believe you said . . . " **Pararead**—Repeat to yourself what you have read. You might write it down in your own words. Check what you have written against the original. If in doubt, clarify your perception in person.
Understand	Do you understand the information presented? Do you need to expand your knowledge with further research before you can interpret the information?
Mutual understanding	Are all individuals in agreement with the information? Are there differences? If there are differences, what steps must be taken to come to agreement?
Summarize	Summarize all of the information presented. Check to see that all the salient points have been covered.

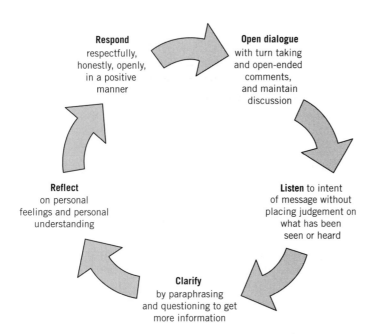

FIGURE 1.1
Active Listening Strategies

Elements of Inclusive Environments

1. Reasons for Individual Differences

The abilities of children in any age group vary greatly. This variance is the result of a number of factors. These include:

- Differential rates of development—Children generally pass through similar stages of development. However, not all children pass through the same stage at the same age or for the same amount of time. Some children may even skip a stage. For example, Jordan was a late talker. He used gestures and single words until he was three. He then started to talk in complete sentences.
- Accidents, problems during pregnancy or birth, identifiable genetic defects, chromosomal abnormalities, developmental delays, and exposure to abuse and neglect
- Genetic disposition—Heredity seems to influence intelligence, specific abilities, specific aspects of personality and some specific psychopathologies such as schizophrenia or depression. It is important to remember that the environment also plays a strong part in shaping the individual. "Children also mold their own environments by the choices they make—what they do and with whom—and their genetic makeup influences these choices....A child who has inherited artistic talent may spend a great deal of time creating 'masterpieces' in solitude, while a sibling who is athletically inclined spends more time playing ball with others. Thus not only will the children's abilities (in, say, painting or soccer) develop differently, but their social lives will be different as well" (Papalia, Wendkos Olds, Duskin & Feldman, 2001: 84).

- Background experiences—Children need appropriate stimulation and learning experiences, especially in the early years. These early experiences are critical to future success. "It is clear that the early years from conception to age six have the most important influence of any time in the life cycle on brain development and subsequent learning, behaviour and health. The effects of early experience, particularly during the first three years, on wiring and sculpting of the brain's billions of neurons, last a lifetime" (McCain et al., 1999: 52).
- Quality of the learning experiences—The High/Scope Perry Preschool Program has been long acknowledged as an excellent program. The outcomes for individuals who have attended the program have been tracked longitudinally. The results are illuminating: "More than 40 years of scientifically based research by the High/Scope Perry Preschool Program has found that adults born into poverty who participated in a high quality, active learning preschool program at ages three and four have a greater chance of experiencing more positive adulthood than individuals who do not" (High/Scope Research Foundation, 2004: 2). By age 27 the adults who had attended the Perry School Preschool, as compared with a control group, had:

  - 63% fewer habitual criminals
  - 68% fewer arrests for drug dealing
  - 21% fewer adults on social-service support systems
  - 31% more high school graduation
  - Almost twice the number of home owners
  - Three times as many individuals earning $2000 (US) or more per month
  - Significantly higher achievement and literacy scores (High/Scope Research Foundation, 2004: 1)

- Societal values and beliefs about raising and educating children—All children are unique. Children are shaped "by the many contexts in which the child lives—family, school, community, country, world" (Schickedanz, Schickedanz, Forsyth & Forsyth, 2001: xx).

Therefore, in any quality child care setting, a large number of elements must already be considered. These elements are similar in inclusive settings and are examined in the following section.

2. Organization of Learning Spaces to Encourage Active Participation

A) ACCESSIBILITY Active play involves making choices and decisions. In order for children to make these choices, the environment must be arranged in a way to encourage and enable children to navigate within the environment, so that they can find and use relevant materials and engage in appropriate learning experiences. To ensure accessibility, one must consider placement of materials and traffic flow.

TABLE 1.2 **ORGANIZATION OF MATERIALS**

Organization	Description
Install open shelves	• Heavy items should be on the bottom shelf, easy to access. • Lighter items can be stored on higher shelves. • Child can see and access materials readily.
Provide transportable containers	• Providing various containers (baskets, caddies, buckets, bags, cases) with handles helps children to transport items from on area to another. • If needed, provide containers that can slip onto handlebars of a walker, or sit on the tray of a wheelchair.
Organize by type	• Materials should be stored by type. This allows children to easily find and return the materials they wish to use. • Clear plastic containers are ideal, as the child can see what is in the container.
Label by picture and word	• Labelling helps children identify, find and return materials easily. • Labelling should include the picture and the word and/or, if appropriate, an outline of the object.
Use storage consistently	• Storage needs to be consistent. When materials are rotated, similar materials should appear on the same shelf.
Create a system that indicates ease of use	• The system could be as simple as easiest toys at the bottom and hardest ones on the top. • Storage could be colour-coded: red for easiest, green for hardest. Both shelves and toys should be colour-coded. This works well for items such as puzzles.
Ensure success	• If a child picks a toy that is too difficult to manage, he or she may become frustrated and leave all the pieces lying around. If trays, baskets or boxes are provided, the child is encouraged to put all the pieces in the storage container and put the container back on the shelf. In this way the child learns that it is OK to feel frustrated, but the materials still need to be put away. Additionally, often another child will come and complete the activity.
Store rotational materials accessibly	• There needs to be accessible well-organized storage for rotational materials. When a child wants an item, a staff member should be able to access it quickly and efficiently.

Photo 1.15

- Placement of materials—Since an environment that includes children with special needs may have especially broad age and developmental spans, it requires the corresponding equipment and materials to compensate. A system should be put in place that encourages children to find the appropriate materials they can use successfully. Table 1.2 outlines some ideas for the organization of materials.
- Traffic flow—The environment should be organized to encourage children to move from one area to another without difficulty, as shown in Figure 1.2. Some areas, such as the carpentry area, should be out of the traffic flow area (Area F). Other areas, such as drama (Area J) and blocks (Area B) should have large spill-out areas. These areas need lots of room for the play to extend into.

Outdoor play areas should also have clear pathways to encourage children to try different skills. In Figure 1.3, concrete pathways encourage riding. Access points to all of the climbing apparatus are via ramps starting from the concrete platforms. There are a variety of ways to get onto the apparatus: crawling, climbing or riding. All equipment is either totally or partially accessible to wheelchairs, and fully accessible if the child is mobile.

Some areas should be close to each other to encourage the use of materials in different areas. When areas are within visible range, children will start to use materials from one area in another area. This is especially important for children who are younger, either in age or by developmental delay. These children need to be able to scan the area to see what they might wish to use. For example, in Figure 1.2 the carpentry area is close to the creative art area. Children can easily take the structures created in carpentry to the creative art area to decorate (Photo 1.15).

The medium and large climbers are joined by ramps, platforms and gently rising stairs. Children can traverse from one area to the other above-ground. This often leads to more dramatic play. For example, a group of preschoolers were pretending that the large climber was a space station and the small climber was the space shuttle. The connecting platform was a tunnel they had to crawl through to get from one place to the other. One of the children in a wheelchair was also actively involved in this play. He was able to get to the platform but not to the higher parts of either climber. His job was to open and shut the "air gates" to make sure that individuals would not "choke and die 'cause they have no air."

Most areas outside are wheelchair-accessible. The terrain has been set up to maximize usability at various skills levels, with ramps, ladders, poles, concrete riding paths, gently rising stairs, grassy areas and sand areas. Children can safely ride, run, climb or jump irrespective of their individual abilities.

The flooring between areas in Figure 1.2 is flush. This prevents tripping and also provides an unobstructed access for a wheelchair to move from the carpeted to tiled areas.

All shelves that are not against walls are child-height. This increases ease of supervision and also makes it easier for children to see areas that they might wish to participate in.

Materials and shelves could be colour-coded to provide easier visibility for children with visual impairments. Labels should include symbolized forms, pictorial labels and Braille to make it easier for children to make their own choices.

Photo 1.16

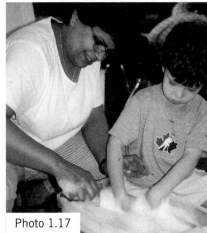

Photo 1.17

Ensure that the overall tone of the room does not distract from the activities or the children's work. High use of colour could distract children who have high activity levels or who are easily distracted. A display of children's creative efforts should provide the colour on the walls and other display areas. Reserve the use of colour for children's creations.

Supervision in the outdoor play area should be highly visible. However, staff members need to be stationed at different positions on the playground to interact in a timely manner in case of dangerous play. For example, Troy, an active four-year-old, wanted to climb over the railing. Melanie was close enough to him to remind him to stay on the platform.

Some parts of the indoor area, such as the sand area, are on the floor to encourage accessibility for all children (Photo 1.16). Other areas can be changed to accommodate the needs of children as the need arises. A platform can be used to raise or lower the level of play as needed. For example, Keegan was reluctant to use the water table. There were too many children around it. He was much more comfortable engaging in water play when the activity was more individual and located closer to the ground (Photo 1.17).

The outside play area is more difficult to adapt, as it is a permanent structure. However, care has been taken to add various levels of access to ensure maximum accessibility. Additionally, there is enough space to add mobile equipment as needed.

B) SAFETY CONSIDERATIONS Both indoor and outdoor areas shown in the figures have been set up to maximize the safety of all children. The following strategies were employed:

- Smooth flooring was used to prevent tripping and give easier access to children using walkers or wheelchairs.
- Some of the materials may be more dangerous for some children. For example, Dillon, a four-year-old, liked to put items in his mouth. The staff consequently placed the smaller items on higher shelves so they were not accessible to the children, reducing the chance of an injury caused by choking.

FIGURE 1.2

Indoor Learning Environment

Please refer to the key on the next page.

FIGURE 1.2

Continued

Area B: **Block Area** (see Photo 1.14)
Block shelf
1. Bottom shelf for wooden blocks
2. Second shelf for lighter cardboard blocks
3. Rotational materials—out of reach of children

Area C: **Manipulative Area**
4. Table and four chairs
5. Manipulative shelves
   a) Bottom shelf: lacing cards, large beads, easy puzzles, stacking toys, tracks, Duplo
   b) Middle shelf: small beads, small vehicles, sorting trays, sorting bears, puzzles
   c) Top shelf: sorting shapes, Lego, floor puzzles, small blocks

Area D: **Sand Area** (see Photo 1.16)
6. Floor-level large vehicle parking—The floor has lines drawn on it and pictures of the vehicles are mounted on the back of Shelf 5.
7. Shelf for sand toys: fences, digging toys, moulding toys, logs

Area E: **Water Play**
The water table changes from a regular water table to a low platform with several large water containers for individual use (see Photo 1.17).

8. Storage for pouring toys
9. Storage for bubble making materials

Area F: **Carpentry Area** (see Photo 1.15)
10. Top shelf for carpentry tools
11. Bottom shelf for wood
12. Carpentry table

Area G: **Creative Area**

13. Shelf with three-dimensional materials: dough, mixtures, clay, tools for dough and clay
14. Drying rack
15. Double-sided easel
16. Table with four chairs
17. Creative shelf—bottom shelves for use for children; top shelves for rotational materials

Area I: **Quiet Area**

FIGURE 1.2
Continued

18. Plant
19. Snake
20. Book shelf
21. Quiet games for concentration, such as puzzles, matching games
22. Small wall with plants on top

Area J: **Dramatic Area**
23. Cradles
24. Baby-bath area (see Photo 1.18)
25. Couch
26. Stove
27. Dress-up clothes
28. Child-sized kitchen cabinets

Area K: **Offices**

Area L: **Staff Lounge**

Area M: **Music Area** (see Photo 1.19)

Area N: **Cubbies**

Photo 1.18

Photo 1.19

When children requested to use these items, they were brought down and supervision was provided.

- The arrangement of the room maximizes the ability of staff members to supervise the room readily. In the outside spaces, staff members station themselves to be closer to the main activities.

- The riding spaces outside incorporate common safety rules. The riding path is wide enough to accommodate two vehicles. Children are encouraged to drive on the right side of the road. Stop signs and crosswalks have been placed on the pavement to prevent accidents and enforce road safety rules (Figure 1.3, A).

- Sand has been placed under all climbing equipment. The sand is raked daily to remove debris.

FIGURE 1.3
Inclusive Outdoor Space

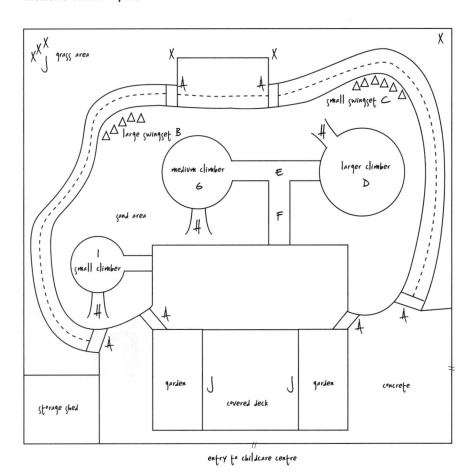

A: Crosswalks and stop signs
B and C: Swing sets
△:   Child height cedar hedge
D: Large climber—wheelchair-accessible to lower platform; upper platform has a
            playhouse; access by ramp, ladders, poles; also includes a slide
E: Platform connecting two climbers—wheelchair-accessible
F: Ramp to reach platform
G: Medium climber—wheelchair-accessible, access by ladders, gently sloping
            stairs chain ladder, pole and climbing rope
H: Slides
I: Small climber —totally accessible by wheelchair, access by ramps, gently
            sloping stairs
J: Benches
X: Mature trees

- The areas at the back of the swings are protected by a child-height cedar hedge, to prevent a child from accidentally running into the swing.
- The outdoor space is protected from the wind by a cedar fence and from the sun by a covered deck and a number of trees (Figure 1.3, X).

C) DISPLAY SPACES Display areas serve a dual purpose. They should be set up to attract children's attention. Areas may be set up to provide a point of interest, tweak the children's curiosity or focus on current activities. Children also need room to display their creative efforts, both two-dimensional and three-dimensional. For example, a group of preschool children had been interested in the insects that they had seen outside. They had created a mural through painting and printmaking. This mural was hung in the corner of the room. A platform was added in front of it. Children collected the plastic insects and some natural materials to place on the platform. They engaged in a number of activities—dramatic play using the insects, matching the insects to the insects in their mural and setting up an environment for the insects.

Through this activity the children learned in several ways:

- They learned to respect each other's efforts. Some of the children were able to make clear prints; others created more of a smudge. Some children were able to paint recognizable insects; others could not. Two children, Elsa and Michael, actively participated in this activity. At one point, Elsa watched Michael paint. Michael was covering an area in green paint. Elsa told him she thought green was a good choice as it looked like grass.
- They were able to use something they created to continue with the activity. The children matched the insects to the outlines that they had created.
- They saw that their creations were valued. Children gain pride in their achievements when it is appropriately displayed. When the families came to pick up

Photo 1.20

their children, they asked about what had been created. Elsa promptly described all the parts she had created. Keegan just looked over to the display and smiled.

- They helped in the set-up of the activity. When children have opportunities to help in organizing their learning environment, they tend to take a greater interest in the activity.

Displays can also be used to continue expanding children's learning. Jordan at three was communicating using gestures and some single words. He had been one of the children very interested in creating the mural. Anita, one of his teachers, noticed his interest in the mural. She started to talk to him about some of the things she saw. Jordan and Anita took turns in pointing out some of the insects in the mural and some of the plastic ones and naming them. Anita was thrilled when Jordan pointed to the snail and said "red snail."

D) SEPARATION OF LEARNING SPACES Spaces need to be separated according to their uses. Table 1.3 identifies some of the criteria needed.

E) SPECIALIZED AREAS Specialized areas are set up to meet the changing needs of children. Some examples of this type of area might include:

TABLE 1.3   CRITERIA FOR SEPARATION OF SPACES (FIGURES 1.2 AND 1.3)

Criteria	Description
Safety	• Areas such as carpentry should be situated away from the flow of traffic to avoid accidents while using tools (Figure 1.2, Area F). • Accidental collisions on playground equipment can be prevented by separating swings and the bottom of slides from major traffic areas (Figure 1.3, Areas B and C). • Kitchen and eating areas should be located away from washroom areas (Figure 1.2). • Sand needs to be confined to a corner to limit spilling (Figure 1.2, Area D).
The need to be alone	• Area should be protected from intrusion so that children can be alone by choice (Area I). • Use a sign to protect areas from intrusion, such as a "Do not disturb" or a stop sign.
Messy areas	• Messy areas such as sand, water and creative area should be on a tiled floor and near the water source to facilitate clean-up.

- Expanded sensory activities—These areas are often set up to provide soothing alternatives to children who at times may be experiencing stressful situations, may find it difficult to control their behaviour or may need to practise skills in other, less threatening ways. Some examples of extended sensory activities include:
  - Flour or coloured sand on different coloured surfaces to trace, draw or manipulate
  - Finger painting with different textures
  - Playdough or clay to pound or mould
  - Dry materials such as sand, beans, peas or rice to manipulate, fill and empty, or pour
  - Water to pour, fill and empty, or create bubbles
- Dramatic areas that encourage children to express their feelings in safe, non-threatening ways—The dramatic area often provides a safe outlet to express feelings that may otherwise not be expressed. Some examples of extended dramatic activities include:
  - Dress-up
  - Puppet play, with hand or finger puppets
  - Play with dolls and stuffed toys

- Areas following special interests of children—Any program for children should be based on the observations of children's interests, strengths and needs. The learning experiences emerge from these observations. This is referred to as an **emergent curriculum**. An example of an emergent curriculum is found in the insect example (see Photo 1.20 on page 26).

F) STORAGE OF CHILDREN'S LEARNING MATERIALS Children need to be able to make choices and solve their own problems. Appropriate storage is a key factor in children's ability to be involved in active play. Table 1.4 identifies aspects of storage that should be considered.

G) DEVELOPMENTALLY-APPROPRIATE AND AGE-APPROPRIATE PRACTICES "**Developmentally appropriate practice** refers to applying child development knowledge in making thoughtful and appropriate decisions about early childhood program practices—the understanding that 'programs designed for young children be based on what is known about young children.'" (Bredekamp & Copple, 1997: v; Gestwicki, 1999: 6)

Age-appropriate practices ensure that the decisions made about program practices are appropriate for the chronological age of the child, irrespective of his or her developmental level. For example, a four-year-old with a developmental delay of two years should be playing with toys that are appropriate for a four-year-old but with the appropriate developmental skill level. For example, this child should use a regular-rhythm instrument during music and movement times instead of a toddler or infant rattle.

All inclusive learning environments should be organized to reflect developmentally-appropriate and age-appropriate practices. Both developmentally- and age-appropriate practices are guided by the following principles:

TABLE 1.4   **ASPECTS OF STORAGE TO ENCOURAGE ACTIVE PLAY**

Storage Aspect	Importance
Organization by type	• When materials are organized by type, children learn to make connections about how things fit together. These connections are part of the real world. Language, math and science are categorized into groupings and sub-groupings (classification). • Materials organized by type also encourage children to find the specific items that they need to encourage their specific learning activity.
Predictability	• Children should be able to make the connection between what the materials are and where they are found. For example, generally, materials are stored in the area that makes it easy for children to find the required items. Plastic pails and shovels are stored in the sand area and blocks in the block area. • However, some materials can be used in more than one area. This means that the same materials should either be stored in two areas, or in close proximity to each other. For example, large trucks are suitable for sand or block play. If these are stored close to both areas, they can be used as needed in either area (Figure 1.2, Item 6). These vehicles are parked in a parking lot configuration. This further enhances the predictability of the storage of materials. Children have experiences to identify vehicle parking.
Clear labelling	• Materials should be labelled by word or sign, and picture or outline. This clearly identifies what is to be found in the storage container and where it needs to be returned to when finished. It also encourages the child to start to make the connections between symbols and written words.
Appropriate-sized, clear containers	• Too many items in a container will cause the child to dump out all materials to find what is wanted. This often leaves a mess. It also distracts the child from his or her play, as clean-up is usually required. • Containers that are predictable should be used . For example, if children are involved in sorting activities, one might store all the same-sized bears of different

TABLE 1.4 **CONTINUED**

	colours in one container. If children are interested in creating patterns, these bears should be stored in containers that contain bears of the same size and colour, such as a container of red bears or blue bears of the same size.
Consistency	• Children need to know where to find the materials and what system of organization is used. Frequent changes in where to find materials or how they are stored causes confusion and disrupts the long-term learning experiences of children. For example, Danny had been interested in playing with the large dinosaurs in both the block and sand area. They had been stored between the two areas in clear bins. The staff decided to change the bins and store vehicles there, instead. Danny looked for the dinosaurs in the regular spot. When he did not find them, he wandered aimlessly around the room. When asked what he wanted to do, he signed, "dinosaurs." He was told that the dinosaurs were put away, and it was time to play with the cars. Danny finally went to the book area and looked at some books about dinosaurs.
Accessibility	• Low, open shelves should be used to facilitate accessibility of materials. • Containers should be light enough to carry or move. • Small shelves on wheels can be easily moved from area to area. • Baskets or caddies allow collection of materials to be moved to other areas. • Materials should be stored logically within the specific learning area.

Storage separate from play area	• Toys should be stored separately from the play area. When toys are stored within the play area, such as the sand toys in the sandbox, the area becomes cluttered. The result could be any of the following:
	  • The toys take up so much space that there is no room to be creative.
	  • Toys get broken.

TABLE 1.4   **CONTINUED**

- The child does not have a clear concept of what can be achieved in the area. Children often get distracted by the activities or toys around them. When too many choices are available, the child may flit from one activity to another.
- Children do not play in the area at all because there is not enough space and there is no clear concept of what might be accomplished there.
- Children may get the clearly inappropriate message that it is all right to leave a mess.

- Knowledge of child development guides the application of all practices—This knowledge helps early childhood educators to be sensitive to typical variations in child behaviours.
- Interaction of all domains: physical, social, emotional, language, and cognitive—"Development in one domain influences and is influenced by development in other domains" (Gestwicki, 1999: 8). Caregivers must recognize the need to provide experiences to the whole child rather than trying to remediate only certain skills.
- Varied approaches to facilitate learning for all individuals—Strategies that work for one child may have to be adapted to the needs of a second child. For example, Jeremy identifies items verbally, in sentence structure with many descriptive words. In contrast, Dillon uses a combination of single words and sign language.
- Observation of children—"Observation is the cornerstone of effective teaching. Teachers and child care providers usually base intervention and curriculum planning decisions on careful observation of children's developmental needs." (Trawick-Smith, 2003:8) For example, had the staff observed Danny's interest in dinosaurs, they would have used his interest to continue to provide and enhance his skills through dinosaur play.
- An emergent curriculum—Structure is provided in the organization of the learning environment and planning of that environment based on the observed strengths and needs of the children. See the example of insect activity on page 26.
- Partnerships—Teachers and other professionals, families and children are active partners in providing learning experiences for children. When individuals collaborate toward a common goal, children benefit from a consistent approach at school, at home and (if needed) during therapy.
- Inclusiveness—All children actively participate in all learning activities.

In summary, inclusive, developmentally- and age-appropriate learning environments and practices focus on how each child learns, bearing in mind that each child is the best judge of what he or she needs to learn at a given time. "Effective early childhood instructional practices emphasize child-initiated, child-directed play activities, based on the assumption that young children are intrinsically motivated to learn by their desire to understand their environment" (Udell et al., 2001; Freiberg, 2001).

H) RESPECT FOR DIVERSITY All children have unique and diverse needs. "Diverse needs" refers to "variations in the needs or play and the learning styles of children of various cultural groups. For example, children of different cultures will have unique ways of learning or interacting with others, and in no group of students will all individuals be alike" (Trawick-Smith, 2003: 11). Respecting diversity includes:

- Creating an atmosphere that encourages children to feel good about themselves and about their identity
- Organizing the learning environment to respect the diversity of the children in the program and within the setting of the program by providing experiences, materials and displays that represent diversity
- Incorporating special social or cultural events within the learning environment
- Incorporating anti-bias materials in all learning activities within the playrooms, such as various markers or crayons to represent skin tones of different ethnic groups, and pictures and toys of individuals with handicaps
- Establishing an environment of mutual respect for all individuals: children, families, staff and other professionals
- Modelling behaviours that foster understanding and respect for diversity
- Providing a flexible program that meets the needs of all children and their families

I) APPROPRIATE ROUTINES Routines should centre on the basic needs and safety of children. Routines should be:

- Flexible about individual differences—For example, children should go to the bathroom as needed, and not as a time-tabled event.
- Consistent—Children need to learn that there are things that occur on a regular schedule. Consistent routines include examples such as washing hands after toilet visits, messy play or meal times; cleaning up toys when one is finished with an activity; and putting scraps in the garbage.
- Regular—Children also need to have certain activities occur on a regular basis. This helps the child learn to know what to expect. For example, creating a timetable that includes flexibility, consistency and regularity helps children predict and sequence their activities during the day.

J) APPROPRIATE SCHEDULING The schedule for children within an inclusive program should be flexible, consistent and regular. An example of a timetable is presented in Figure 1.4.

K) ADAPTATIONS AND ACCOMMODATIONS All learning environments for children will need to be adapted at times to accommodate the child with special needs.

Time	Activity	Description
7:00–8:00	Arrival	• Greeting of children and family members
		• Family members help children remove outdoor clothes and settle in for free play activities
		• Family members discuss pertinent information about the children's activities at home, how the children are feeling and any additional information
		• Family members sign children in and fill in information forms as needed
		• Family members tell children that they are leaving
	Snack	• Breakfast snacks are left out for children who have not had breakfast
	Free Play	• Active play within environment
9:00–11:30	Group Music	• Group music and movement activity
	Washroom	• Washroom routines and getting dressed to go outside
	Outdoor play	• Free play activities
11:30–12:30	Lunch time	• Washroom routines before and after lunch
		• Children set table for lunch
		• Lunch
		• Preparation for sleep time: story time, set-up
12:30–2:30	Sleep time	• Activities for non-sleepers
2:30–3:00	Washroom/Snack	• Quiet activities for non-sleepers and early
3:00–4:30	Indoor activities	risers
		• Transition to go outside
4:30–5:30	Outdoor play and free play activities	• Outdoor group physical activity, free play
5:00–5:30	Dismissal	• Family members pick up children
		• Staff member discusses child's day with family members
		• Family members sign out child, read over comments about child's day

FIGURE 1.4

Example of a Timetable in an Inclusive Setting

Accommodations may have to be made to include strategies for changes or adaptations to the environment and program in order to meet specific needs. These needs could be categorized as follows:

- Communication—Verbal, symbolic, body language such as gestures or signing, and formal devices such as the use of symbol boards
- Physical—Adapting physical space to accommodate children using wheelchairs or walkers; providing specialized equipment to aid activities such as drawing

and eating; adding adaptive devices to help individuals become more independent, such as door switches and light switches at child's level

- Cognitive—Developmentally- and age-appropriate materials and equipment to encourage active participation
- Social—Strategies for active play with opportunities to engage in solitary and group play
- Emotional—Establishing a climate that is respectful and encourages recognition of strengths and needs of all children

Collaborative Partnerships

One of the most critical factors in any inclusive setting is the need to collaborate with the many individuals who are involved with children, especially children with special needs. This team of individuals should always include children, parents, family members, early childhood educators, resource consultants and child support workers, to share expertise and knowledge about the child. Other professionals may join the team at other times depending on the needs of the child. These professionals could include medical professionals, specialists such as speech and language therapists or physical therapists, psychologists or child support workers.

The collaborative approach ensures that the unique needs of each individual are supported in the context of that child's family and community (see Figure 1.5).

FIGURE 1.5

Collaborative Approach

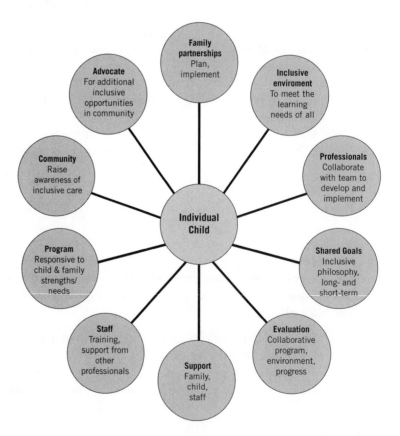

SUMMARY

Inclusive care is more than a philosophy. It is the right of every child. Research has clearly identified the benefits of inclusive care. (Schweinhart & Weikart, 1986) These benefits include:

- Educational benefits
- Social benefits for all individuals
- Cost savings
- Societal benefits (McCarthy, 2001)

Concern about the benefits of including children with special needs has been expressed regarding:

- Lack of resources to cope with children with high needs
- Lack of training of early childhood educators to cope with inclusive practices
- The fear that the disabling condition might be so severe as to negate the benefit of inclusion

Most jurisdictions within Canada offer support to children and families with special needs. However, in most instances this support is only provided if the child has been diagnosed with a special need. This means that children very early in life are identified and subsequently labelled. Some of the conditions with which children are commonly labelled today include attention deficit, autism and cerebral palsy.

Often the condition becomes more important than the child. For example, the child is treated as a child with cerebral palsy. Justin, a six-year-old with cerebral palsy, was enrolled in the Boy Scout Cub program. He was using a walker and a wheelchair to navigate. The Cubs planned a weekend winter camping trip at a regional educational outdoor facility. When the parents of Justin were approached, they were surprised to hear that Justin was to be included. The father volunteered to participate in the activities. Justin was very excited. He had attended the outdoor facility with his grade one class. He had heard about the outhouse that a porcupine had chewed a hole into. He had not seen the outhouse because he had been left behind with his teacher assistant in the outdoor class-room while the rest of the children explored the outdoor spaces.

Justin's father adapted his walker with skis. A group of children and one adult walked to the outhouse. A toboggan was taken in case Justin needed to rest. It took Justin and the children an hour to get to the outhouse. He walked the whole way by himself. He agreed to let the children take turns to pull him back on the tobog-gan on the way back. The whole Cub pack rejoiced and celebrated Justin's efforts.

This example clearly illustrates that:

- Some individuals limit children's efforts by their perception of what the child can do.
- Children can achieve their own goals if permitted.
- Adaptations in time and equipment may need to be made.
- All children benefit and enjoy the success of an individual's achievement.

KEY POINTS

Children's right to play

- Through active play children gain skills in commu-nication and all developmental domains, learn to solve problems, make decisions, build on what they already know and gain self-confidence
- Active play is supported by the UN Convention on the Rights of the Child

Bias

- Bias influences how we use all of our senses
- Bias results from lack of knowledge, experience, our perceptions of an individual, our belief sys-tems, cultural influences, roles, family dynamics, health status and socioeconomic status

Anti-bias

- Anti-bias means taking a stand against unjust treatment of individuals
- The anti-biased approach includes reflective practices, active listening, appropriate self-care practices, creating an environment of mutual respect and creating an inclusive environment

Inclusive environments

- Creating inclusive environments requires knowledge of individual differences
- Learning spaces must be organized according to many principles: accessibility, traffic flow, display spaces, safety aspects, separation of learning spaces, need for areas of specialization, children's storage, developmentally- and age-appropriate practices, respect for diversity, routines, scheduling, and adaptations and accommodations

Collaborative partnerships

- The team of individuals should include all children, families, staff, resource consultants, child support workers and, depending on the child's need, medical professionals, specialists, therapists and psychologists

EXERCISES

1. Reflect on the UN Convention on children's right to play as presented at the beginning of the chapter. How does reflection affect your philosophical viewpoint? Do you see this right to play equally applied to all children within day care settings? Explain why or why not.

2. Look over the list of possible causes of bias.
   a) Identify which ones could apply to you.
   b) What strategies could you employ to mitigate the bias identified?

3. Observe a group of children within a preschool environment engaging in fine motor tasks. What similarities and differences do you observe in the group of children? How might you account for these similarities and differences?

4. Visit a preschool setting. Draw floor plans of the indoor and outdoor environments. Using the criteria for organizing the environment on pages 18-34, identify what changes should be made to both floor plans to accept children with a variety of special needs—physical, social, cognitive and emotional.

5. Using Figure 1.5 on page 34, identify the individuals within your community that should become part of the partnership. For each individual, explain his or her role.

REFERENCES

Allen, K., Paasche, C., Langford, R., & Nolan, K. (2002). *Inclusion in Early Childhood Programs: Children with Exceptionalities.* Third Canadian Edition. Scarborough, ON: Thomson Nelson.

Bredekamp, S., & Copple, C. E. (1997). *Developmentally Appropriate Practice in Early Childhood Programs.* Revised Edition. Washington, DC: NAEYC.

Covell, K. H. B. (2001). *The Challenge of Children's Rights for Canada.* Waterloo, ON: Wilfrid Laurier University Press.

Crowther, I. (2003). *Creating Effective Learning Environments.* Scarborough, ON: Nelson Thomson Learning.

Freiberg, K. E. (2001). Educating Exceptional Children. *Annual Editions.* Thirteenth Edition.

Gestwicki, C. (1999). *Developmentally Appropriate Practices.* Second Edition. Scarborough, ON: Nelson Canada.

High/Scope Research Foundation (2004). High/Scope Perry Preschool Program. High/Scope Research Foundation [online]. Available at http://modelprograms.samhsa.gov/pdfs/FactSheets/HighScope.pdf.

Hope Irwin, S., Lero, D., & Brophy, K. (2000). *A Matter of Urgency: Including Children with Special Needs in Child Care in Canada.* Wreck Cove, NS: Breton Books.

IPA World (2004). The International Play Association [online]. Available at www.ipaworld.org.

McCain, M., & Mustard, F. (1999). *Early Years Study Final Report.* Toronto, ON: Publications Ontario.

McCarthy, M. (2001). Inclusion of Children with Disabilities: Seeking the Appropriate Balance. *Annual Editions Educating Children with Special Needs.* Thirteenth Edition, 8–11.

Papalia, D., Wendkos Olds, S., Duskin, & Feldman, R. (2001). *Human Development.* Toronto, ON: McGraw Hill.

Saderman Hall, N., & Rhomberg, V. (1995). *The Affective Curriculum: Teaching the Anti-bias Approach to Young Children.* Scarborough, ON: International Thomson Publishing.

Schickedanz, J., Schickedanz, D., Forsyth, P., & Forsyth, G. (2001). *Understanding Children and Adolescents.* Fourth Edition. Needham Heights, MA: Allyn & Bacon.

Schweinhart, L., & Weikart, J. (1986). Lasting Differences: The High Scope Preschool Curriculum Comparison Study Through Age 23. *Early Childhood Education Research Quarterly* 1, 15–45.

Trawick-Smith, J. (2003). *Early Childhood Development: A Multicultural Perspective.* Upper Saddle River, NJ: Pearson Education Inc.

Udell, T., Peters, J., & Piaza Templeman, T. (2001). From Philosophy to Practice in Inclusive Early Childhood Programs. *Annual Editions Educating Exceptional Children.* Thirteenth Edition, *2001/2002,* 32–36.

Voices 4 Children (2003). Fact Sheet #18: Children with Special Needs. Child and Family Canada [online]. Available at www.cfc-efc.ca/docs/vocfc/00018_en.htm.

2

CHAPTER

Inclusive Care in Canada

"Children with special needs are often excluded from child care in Canada. Despite the acknowledged role high quality early child care and education has in promoting children's development, most governments in Canada have failed to fully capitalize on the opportunities to use child care programs as a developmental resource for children with special needs. Moreover, exclusion of children with special needs from child care often means that their parents cannot participate in paid employment, or receive the kinds of support that could assist them as parents" (Hope Irwin, Lero & Brophy, 2000: xxi; Hope Irwin et al., 2000: xxi).

Learning Outcomes

After studying this chapter, you will be able to:

1. Describe various legislative requirements for children with special needs in Canada.
2. Identify reasons to explain why there is a lack of inclusive care in Canada.
3. Describe an inclusive setting. How is it similar to any quality setting? How is it different?
4. Describe the core elements of a quality inclusive setting.
5. Identify and describe the various program options for families and children with special needs in Canada.
6. Discuss the skills needed by an early childhood educator to provide inclusive care.

Introduction

Care for children with special needs in Canada is often haphazard and inconsistent (see Table 2.1). Many jurisdictions lack appropriate guidelines, policies or proactive legislation that addresses the inclusions for children with special needs. This often means that children may be prohibited from attending regular programs. Without appropriate guidelines, adequate resources are hard to obtain. When programs have been adequately resourced, the result has been a positive experience for all involved: children, families and staff (Hope Irwin et al., 2000: xiv). Adequate resources include staff training, additional support staff as needed, structural modifications of the physical environment and time to work in collaboration with all families and other professionals.

Additionally, one of the components of high quality care is the amount of education and training early childhood educators receive (Mayer, 1994; Doherty-Derkowski, 1994; Goleman, Doherty, Lero, LaGrange & Tougas, 2000). It is most disconcerting to note that in most jurisdictions in Canada, there are no additional training requirements for the staff in inclusive centres (Table 2.1). With adequate training, the child care professional is in a much better position to understand and apply that understanding to:

- Organizing inclusive environments that meet a variety of developmental levels and ages
- Providing learning activities that challenge a variety of developmental levels and ages
- Adapting and modifying the environment, materials and learning experiences to reflect the needs of all the children
- Developing skill in collaborating with families and other professionals
- Establishing partnerships to enhance the opportunities for children with special needs within their neighbourhood communities

It is difficult to get an accurate picture of what services for children with special needs are available on a national level. However, statistics are available for the percentage of children with special needs requiring services across Canada. These percentages are as follows:

- 1.6% of children under the age of four
- 3.7 % of children aged 5 to 9
- 4.2 % of children 10 to 14 years of age (Government of Canada, 2002)

"The rate of disability among younger children in Canada is lower than it is for adults. This is partly because some disabilities in children have not yet been detected and also because the majority of disabilities are acquired after childhood" (Government of Canada, 2002: 1).

Information about how many children are diagnosed with special needs and how many children are in inclusive care in a specific jurisdiction are not readily available. However, this information can be gleaned from some representational studies: You Bet I Care (Goleman et al., 2000) and a Matter of Urgency (Hope Irwin et al., 2000). These **representational studies** are conducted on a sampling of daycare centres in pre-selected regions as opposed to all daycare centres in all regions. The outcomes are then generalized as representative of Canada. These studies identify the following statistical information:

- Centres that did not have any children with special needs enrolled ranged from a low of 18.7% (Manitoba) to a high of 50% (Newfoundland and Labrador).
- The number of centres with at least three children with special needs enrolled was highest in Manitoba: 45.9% (Hope Irwin et al., 2000).

The statistical information presented by the representational study is significant. It means that less than half of the children in Canada have access to inclusive care. One of the problems with a representational study is that the results can reflect either over- or under-representation. If it is true that even more children with special needs are denied access to inclusive care, then the problem is even more dismal than reported. It is critical to obtain more specific provincial and territorial information about:

- The number of children diagnosed
- The number of children considered eligible to receive additional supports and funding for special needs
- The type of services provided
- The number of children receiving support and funding

With this type of data collected, a much clearer idea could emerge about how children with special needs are being served. Governments would have statistical information available to guide the process of policy and legislative development, to develop realistic budgets in support of resource and funding needs, and to evaluate the success of actions taken. Additionally, the data could be amalgamated with the national data to obtain a more accurate picture of the number of young children diagnosed with special needs in Canada as a whole.

There are a number of reasons for the seeming lack of inclusiveness in child care centres across Canada. Some of these reasons stem from two factors:

- Legislation and policy are lacking to make it illegal to exclude children with special needs.
- As a result, individual child care facilities have the choice to include or exclude children with special needs (Hope Irwin et al., 2000: xiii).

Additionally, some of the reasons for non-acceptance of children with special needs are expressed by individual child care centres. These reasons include:

- Insufficient and inconsistent funds to provide services to children with special needs
- Continual cutbacks in funding for child care in general
- Lack of appropriate resources
- Existing facility not accessible without modification to the physical structure
- Staff lack training to offer inclusive programs

TABLE 2.1   LEGISLATIVE REQUIREMENTS IN CANADA

Jurisdiction	Training of Staff	Description
Alberta	Not required	• Inclusive Child Care Program of Alberta provides for inclusive care • Funding depends on the needs of the child and the type of services needed • Funding may differ per region, and may or may not be available to child care facilities and for specialist consultation
British Columbia	Basic ECE training; special needs training	• Supported Child Care Initiatives provide recommendations to move toward more inclusive care • Special needs diagnosis required to access funds • Agencies or individuals contract for services
Manitoba	Consultation provided by Children's Special Services; no special training required for staff	• Integration of children into child care settings • Support paid to the child care facility and additional support provided if children are diagnosed with physical, cognitive or developmental delays • Children with behavioural disabilities and who are medically fragile supported by Child Day Care Organization • Grants available for renovations, equipment, materials, staff training and professional service • Children placed by Children's Special Services
New Brunswick	No special training required for staff	• Children identified as special needs if there has been a confirmed diagnosis at birth or developmental issues after birth, or if there are family risk factors • Children with special needs placed in Integrated Day Care Centres • Integrated Day Care Centres supported by funding for child with special needs and for support workers
Newfoundland	No special training required for staff	• No written policy established • Provision for children with special needs in one regulated centre exclusive to children with special needs • Centre funded by Health and Community Services • If eligible, welfare allowance paid to parents to hire support worker
Northwest Territories	No early childhood training requirements	• No segregated child care programs • Extra support to child care providers • Additional support available if eligible, based on financial needs assessment and medical referral
Nova Scotia	No special requirements	• Funding support for inclusive care • Funding eligibility based on evidence of special needs • Centres have designated number of spaces for children with special needs • Additional spaces dependent on grant availability

TABLE 2.1 CONTINUED

Jurisdiction	Training of Staff	Description
Nunavut	No early childhood training requirements	• No segregated child care programs • Support provided to child care centres through daily operating grants • Size of operating grant dependent on age of child and area centre is located in; preschool child with identified special need receives 50% increased funding • Health and Children's Initiatives provide funding for adaptive equipment or support worker • Parents eligible for fee subsidy after financial needs • Assessment and medical referral
Ontario	Resource consultants require ECE diploma and post-secondary program in working with children with special needs; no additional training requirements for child care staff	• No written policy established • Support provided for integration and inclusion • Responsibility for placement of children with special needs: Consolidated Municipal Service Managers (CMSMs) or District Social Services Administration Boards (DSSABs) • Support offered for staffing, equipment, supplies and services to child care centres • Resource consultants hired by CMSM or DSSAB to assist families and staff
Prince Edward Island	No additional training requirements for child care staff	• No segregated child care programs • Grants provided to centres based on training and experience of staff to be hired • Documentation such as social need required for additional grants • Funding covers additional staff to lower staff ratio
Quebec	No special requirements	• Policy in place to encourage inclusion • One-time grant available with a diagnosed need approved by ministry
Saskatchewan	No special requirements	• Funding granted by Child Care Inclusion Program to child care facilities • Individual funding available if child is referred, and enrolled for a minimum of 20 hours per month • Grant amount dependent on need • Additional funds available for inclusion of child with diagnosed high needs • Additional grants available for training, adaptive equipment and resources • Inclusion grant approved on a yearly basis • Enhanced accessibility grant lasts for six months, then requires reapplication

Adapted from Friendly, Beach & Turiano, 2002

- Lack of clear governmental directives
- Lack of availability of child care spaces in individual centres (Doherty, Lero, Goelman, LaGrange & Tougas, 2000)

Despite the somewhat gloomy picture presented nationally, there are many encouraging signs in all jurisdictions across Canada. "A large majority of front-line child care centre staff and centre directors in our sample believe that children with special needs should have the right to attend child care programs, and that legislation should be passed to prevent their exclusion. 89.5% feel that most child care centres would be willing to include children with special needs if adequate resources were in place to support their efforts." (Hope Irwin et al., 2000: xv) There are many centres across Canada that have, and continue to accept, children with special needs, despite the lack of adequate funding or resources. "In our opinion, it is a credit to this workforce that they have reached the level of commitment despite the lack of clear policy directives from the governments and in the face of insufficient funding, inadequate staffing and resources, and the general lack of support for inclusive care" (Hope Irwin et al., 2000: xv).

Reflection   *From the Author*

As I have travelled extensively across Canada from one coast to another, from the isolated communities of the north to the large urban centres of the south, I have seen many encouraging sights. I have visited many child care centres across Canada and talked to many individuals responsible for the provincial or territorial legislation of child care. I have observed and photographed a total of 52 centres, of which 40 had children with special needs enrolled. The support to centres that I observed ranged from exceptional to minimal. I observed the following elements of quality:

- Many jurisdictions had developed written policies, training requirements and resource allocations for the inclusion of children with special needs.
- Many child care centres across Canada included children with special needs, even when adequate funding was not available.
- Many centres had a long history of including children with special needs. I visited one centre that had been in operation for 30 years and had always had a policy to accept children with special needs.
- Twenty-one of the centres observed were adequately resourced to provide appropriate care for children with special needs.
- Strong leadership has emerged to move toward more inclusive care (Director Hope Irwin, 2004; Voices 4 Children, 2003; Friendly et al., 2002).

Challenges of Inclusive Practices

Including children with special needs may provide some additional challenges. These challenges may be grouped into two types: challenges that are relatively easy to overcome and challenges that require more in-depth consideration.

Some of the challenges of working in an inclusive setting may require extra time and effort but can be more readily overcome:

- Attitudes toward children with special needs—Some staff or families may be reluctant to include children with special needs because they do not understand the value of including these children. This requires a change of attitude. Changes of attitude do not occur overnight. A change of attitude does occur when individuals are given information (workshops, research findings, readings) that clearly identifies the value of inclusion. Additionally, when all individuals are given opportunities to observe the effectiveness of the process and see the value to all children involved, attitudes change. This can be done through including families as partners and documenting learning experiences of the children that show the value of inclusion.
- Time—There is a perception that children with special needs will require more one-on-one attention. However, if the environment is structured in ways that encourage active play for all children, this time can be significantly reduced. Some children with special needs will need more one-on-one intervention. This intervention is generally needed for children with more severe disabilities that lack the ability to fend for themselves and therefore need someone to help them. These children can usually receive additional help. In most jurisdictions the possibility of an additional support worker is possible.
- Specific needs—Often staff members feel that they do not know enough about a child with special needs. What needs to be remembered is that a child is a child first. All children have special needs. Knowledge of child development and observation will help to structure the learning activities to be inclusive of all children.
- Structural obstacles—Often structural changes may need to be made to the existing environment to make it more accessible. One-time funding opportunities are available to meet these needs.

Other challenges are more difficult to overcome:

- Lack of funding—This may lead to lack of ability to purchase the specialized equipment or materials needed. Available funding may not provide for hiring individuals with the additional training to support children with special needs. Since funding is provincial or territorial, stronger advocacy is needed to change funding requirements. Many centres are involved in fundraising and rely on volunteer workers to help overcome this challenge.
- Lack of specific education—One of the quality indicators of inclusive early childhood settings is adequate education. Individuals with education on inclusive care will be much more confident in their abilities and bring greater understanding to their work with the children and families. Although some information

Reflection   *From a Staff Member*

Reflection

I can still remember the first child with special needs who we had in our program. I remember how apprehensive I was. I did not recognize that I had any special abilities or knowledge of how to interact with this child. I also wondered how I was going to interact with the family.

At first, it did seem to be more time-consuming and a lot more work. However, I gradually began to realize that much of the time and effort that I was putting in was really due to my own fears. For example, I always wanted to protect him from falling when he was on the climber. I never worried about the other children in the same way. As I became more relaxed, I also realized that this child played along with the other children effectively as long as the materials and activities supported his skills and ability level.

I have learned so much and am so grateful for this first opportunity. I don't think that I could ever work in settings that do not include children with special needs. We all gain: children, staff, families and the society as a whole.

can be gained by independent research, there needs to be greater advocacy to encourage adequate education requirements for all early childhood educators.

Types of Programs for Children with Special Needs

1. Inclusive Programs

"Leigha, the five-year-old daughter of one of the authors, recently asked, 'Mom, will Kaelies always have possibilities?' Since she was just a year old, Leigha has attended a child-care program that actively includes children with disabilities, and she was trying to understand her friend Kaelies's disabilities. While she confused 'possibilities' and 'disabilities,' Leigha innocently identified the main reason for creating inclusive early education programs: to create normalized expectations for children with disabilities among the nondisabled" (Hanline & Daley, 2004: 42).

Teaching children in an inclusive setting is not as difficult as it seems. It requires that the early childhood educator look at best practices for teaching young children and the principles of setting up an inclusive environment (see pages 18–34). Best practices involve setting up a program for young children that:

- Emerges based on the observed interests, strengths and needs of the children
- Is supported by learning through active play
- Encourages children to become active partners in constructing their own learning

- Is supported by trained, sensitive and caring adults
- Is developed in collaborative partnerships among children, families, early childhood educators and other professionals

What does an inclusive setting look like? The basic premise of inclusive environments is that the majority of children progress through the same developmental stages irrespective of disability (Hanline et al., 2004). Early childhood education programs already provide a wide range of learning experiences for young children. Children in any grouping are unique individuals with a range of abilities and skills. For example, in a typical toddler setting in Ontario, one might expect to find children aged 18 to 30 months. The difference in skills and abilities between the 18-month-old and the 30-month-old toddler will be quite pronounced. The materials in the environment will reflect these differences. For example, in one toddler group the range of abilities for cutting skills ranged from toddlers who had never cut with scissors to toddlers who could cut a piece of paper in half. Consequently, two types of scissors were available to the toddlers: first scissors (spring-loaded scissors that are squeezed to cut) and safety scissors (child-sized scissors with blunt ends). Additionally, close supervision was provided when the toddlers were cutting to reinforce appropriate cutting habits such as keeping scissors on the table and redirecting a toddler to cutting when the scissors were put into the mouth.

The adaptations for most children with special needs are readily made. The child care provider must carefully identify the skills and abilities of the child to provide the expanded range of materials and activities needed. Children with special needs have the right to actively participate in the same core learning experiences found in all quality early childhood settings. In fact, to the casual observer, the children with special needs in an inclusive setting often cannot be distinguished. Children who are actively engaged in a variety of learning experiences are hard to distinguish from each other.

Harms, Clifford and Cryer have developed three inclusive rating scales—infants and toddlers, preschool children and school-aged children—that identify the core learning areas within quality early childhood settings. Children with special needs are included in all three scales. These scales identify core requirements for any quality early childhood setting. Core elements that are evaluated include space and furnishings; personal care and routines; language and reasoning; learning activities; interactions; program structure; and parents and staff.

A) SPACE AND FURNISHINGS In any environment, there are critical factors to ensure the children's comfort and safety. The elements that need to be considered include:

- Lighting—How much natural light is required? Although many of the jurisdictions in Canada recognize the need for natural lighting, many of them do not have formal guidelines. According to the Illuminating Engineering Society, windows should comprise at least 20 percent of wall space (Hawkins & Lilley, 1992).

What learning activities require natural light? Activities such as reading and writing should be placed near natural light. If possible, activities that involve the use of colour, such as drawing and painting, should also be conducted in natural light, where the colours are more natural.

There is mounting research that links hyperactivity, decreased productivity and poor health to the use of standard fluorescent lighting (Liberman, 1991; Hathaway, 1994; Crowther, 2003). Substituting **full-spectrum fluorescent lighting with ultraviolet enhancement** (the type of lighting closest to natural sunlight) has been shown to increase growth, development and student productivity, and to decrease absenteeism and depression due to seasonal affective disorder (SAD).

Children with visual impairments have a higher need for adequate lighting. For these children extra lighting may be needed for darker areas of the room. Colour coding could be used to attract attention to specific learning areas.

- Colour—Colour has also been shown to produce certain behavioural responses. Colour can be used to soothe and calm or to stimulate and excite. Colours like red, orange and yellow are used to stimulate and excite, whereas colours like blue or green can serve to relax, comfort and soothe individuals. "Light is required for our cells to function normally, and individual colours affect them by causing changes in growth and behavior. It therefore affects our system at a cellular level, and the vibrational patterns giving us life, holding us together" (Chiazzari, 1998: 16).

- Noise—Children engaged in active play make a lot of noise through their interactions with each other and the materials within the learning environment. The early childhood educator needs to find the balance between encouraging the natural enthusiasm of children and protecting the children from too much disruptive noise. For example, Jordan, a three-year-old, had been carrying the unit blocks over to the manipulative area. He dropped the blocks by accident as he was walking over the tiled floor. He immediately sat down on the tiled floor and started to stack his blocks to a certain height. He then knocked them down and clapped his hands in delight at the sound it made. Other children, who had been playing in other areas, quickly ran over to see what Jordan was doing. The noise level disrupted the children's attention, causing them to stop the activities they had been engaged in. This example clearly shows how children's attention can easily be refocused by a change in noise level. Continued exposure to high levels of noise can become disruptive to children's concentration and play activities.★★★Noise levels can be minimized by using some simple techniques:

  - Sound buffers—Materials such as carpets, upholstered furniture, padded dividers, acoustic tiles, grassy areas and hedges can absorb and minimize noise.
  - Protective surfaces in noisy areas—The block area should be carpeted to reduce the noise of falling blocks. Carpentry tables can be covered with a firm foam surface to decrease the noise of hammering.
  - Quiet areas—Separating the noisier aspects of a room, such as the block area, from the reading area helps children to monitor their own need to

find a quieter space. Placement of large pillow or cushions in the area can further reduce noise levels (see Figure 1.2 on page 22).

- Music—Music can be used to calm and soothe children. "[M]usic has proven to reliably alter young children's moods in the classroom. Helping them overcome anxiety and stress, calming them so that they can focus on a task, and enlivening their bodies sufficiently to maintain alertness, music works its magic whether or not the children consciously pay attention to it" (Campbell, 2000: 165)

Noise levels become particularly stressful for some children. Children who are sensitive to loud noises, children who are easily distracted (such as those with attention or hyperactivity disorders) and children who find it harder to concentrate will find noisy environments particularly difficult to deal with.

- Indoor and Outdoor Floor Space—All children need learning areas that can be negotiated freely. Children with special needs may have physical mobility problems such as lack of coordination in their movements, require assistive devices to move about such as walkers or wheelchairs, or may need the security of having stable learning spaces. The learning area should be organized to maximize all children's active exploration.
- Ventilation—Appropriate ventilation is important. It refreshes the air within the room. Stale air leads to lethargic behaviour. If possible, a good air filter attached to the furnace will also help to eliminate some contaminants in the air to reduce the effects of conditions such as asthma.
- Temperature—The room temperature needs to be comfortable for active exploration and play. The suggested temperature is around 20 degrees Celsius. This is especially important for young children who are less active. These children have less ability to regulate their body temperature through exercise. ★★★One of the leading causes of accidents is exposure to scalding water. The figure below identifies how quickly children can receive a burn from water that is too hot.
- Overall Repair—The environment should be well maintained to provide for the safety of all children. Floors and walls should be clean and free from debris, clutter and impediments such as raised tiles or carpet edges, as these can cause tripping. This is especially important for children who may have poor coordination or balance because of a special need.

FIGURE 2.1

Water Temperatures That Cause Scalding

Temperature of Water	Time to Cause a Bad Burn
66°C (150°F)	2 seconds
60°C (140°F)	6 seconds
52°C (125°F)	2 minutes
49°C (120°F)	10 minutes

Source: Pediatric Advisor, 2004

- Organization of Learning Areas—Inclusive program spaces need to be organized to include the core learning areas, as identified in Table 2.2, ensuring that they meet these standards:

  - All materials and equipment are accessible for active play for all children, with additional materials available for rotation.
  - Learning areas such as blocks or music are well defined, do not interfere with each other and are easily supervised.
  - Materials are organized to maximize the independence of all children through techniques such as labelling by picture and word and open, sturdy shelves.
  - Enough child-sized furniture is present that features appropriate adaptations for children with special needs.
  - Soft furniture or soft accessories such as pillows, rugs or stuffed toys appear in various parts of the room for relaxation.
  - A space for privacy is protected from intrusion by a sign or non-intrusion rule.
  - Spaces exist for the display of children's work.
  - Indoor and outdoor spaces are available for daily gross motor activity with a variety of gross motor equipment that is suitable for different skill development levels.

B) PERSONAL CARE AND ROUTINES Personal care routines include arrival and departure, meal time, sleep and rest, toilet visits or diapering, and health-related practices such as handwashing or toothbrushing. In an inclusive environment, these routines need to be flexible to meet the individual needs of each child. Some of these routines, such as handwashing, meal time and sleep time, should be predictable so that the child learns to associate each part of the routine with the next logical step. For example, when I arrive, I take off my coat and boots, and put them in my cubbies. After I have gone to the toilet, I wash my hands.

C) LANGUAGE AND REASONING Children need to have a variety of books and games for activities using both **receptive language** (understanding the message that has been communicated through speech, signing or symbols such as written words) and **expressive language** (expressing one's thoughts or ideas through verbal language, signing or symbols such pictures). These activities should be suitable for a variety of skill levels and interests.

D) LEARNING ACTIVITIES The types of learning activities that should be included in a quality centre are listed in Table 2.2. Children need to have the full range of activities to develop holistically. The learning activities provided should represent a balance of active or quiet play, activities for concentration or relaxation, and group or individual play.

E) INTERACTIONS The environment needs to be set up to encourage appropriate, safe interactions with all individuals and the materials within the learning spaces. Interactions between children and staff should be used to develop children's self-confidence, skills and abilities, foster their interest and enhance their self-esteem. Positive guidance techniques and appropriate social skills should be modelled to encourage children to learn appropriate patterns of behaviour and to interact positively with each other and adults.

F) PROGRAM STRUCTURE Much of the program structure is dependent on the daily scheduling. The following points should be considered:

- Does the daily schedule provide structure and predictability? Some events, such as meal or sleep time, should occur regularly every day. This gives all children a sense of personal control because they can predict what will occur during certain times of the day. Many children with special needs require these structured times to develop a sense of a regular, predictable sequence. This repetition and regularity helps children to anticipate and respond appropriately to regularly occurring events in their daily lives.
- Is the daily schedule flexible enough to meet all children's needs? If a child is hungry at nine o'clock, does he have to wait until ten o'clock, the scheduled snack time? If a child is actively engaged in a positive learning experience, does he or she have to stop to join a group activity? Does the child who is quick to dress himself or herself have to wait 20 minutes for all children to get ready to go outside?
- Does the schedule provide a balance between free play and structured group activities such as music and movement activities?
- Are there opportunities for children to participate in activities individually, in small groups or in large groups?

G) PARENTS AND STAFF Interactions with families and other professionals should be built on the principles of cooperation and partnership. All individuals should be recognized as equal partners in planning for children's growth and development.

It is also very important to recognize that a quality program must adequately meet the needs of the staff. Some of the following questions should be considered and addressed:

- Do staff members have a private space to withdraw to, relax in and store personal belongings?
- Do staff members have access to training, resources and professional development opportunities?
- Do staff have separate washroom facilities?

Table 2.2 identifies the core learning areas that should be included for various age groups.

2. Aboriginal Head Start Programs

"Aboriginal Head Start Program (AHS) is a Health Canada-funded, early intervention strategy for First Nations, Inuit and Métis children and their families liv-

TABLE 2.2   CORE LEARNING AREAS IN INCLUSIVE ENVIRONMENTS, BY AGE GROUPINGS

Infant/Toddler	Preschool	School-Age
• Books and pictures	• Books and pictures	• Arts and crafts
• Eye-hand coordination	• Fine motor activities	• Music and movement
• Active physical play	• Art	• Blocks and construction
• Art	• Music and movement	• Drama/theatre
• Music and movement	• Blocks	• Language/reading activities
• Blocks	• Sand and water	• Math/reasoning activities
• Pretend Play	• Dramatic Play	• Science/nature activities
• Sand and water play	• Nature/science	• Cultural awareness
• Cultural awareness	• Math/numbers	• Space for gross motor play
	• Use of TV, video or computers	• Space for privacy
	• Promoting acceptance of diversity	
	• Space for gross motor play	
	• Space for privacy	

Sources: Harms, Cryer & Clifford, 1990; Harms, Clifford & Cryer, 1998; Harms, Vineberg Jacobs & White, 1996

ing in urban centres and large northern communities. Aboriginal Head Start projects provide structured half-day preschool experiences by meeting their spiritual, emotional, intellectual, and physical needs" (Division of Childhood and Adolescence, 2003: 1).

Aboriginal children are often more disadvantaged than other children throughout Canada. Poverty is the single most disabling factor. According to the Canadian Council on Social Development:

- 52.1% of aboriginal children are poor.
- Aboriginal children are four times more likely to be hungry.
- Aboriginal children have more health problems (Canadian Council on Social Development, 2003).

It is therefore not surprising to find that AHS programs typically focus on a more global approach in six primary program areas, discussed on the following pages.

A) CULTURE AND LANGUAGE The environments of children in AHS programs reflect the cultural aspects of their community. Children's learning activities reflect the cultural events of their community. Typical activities may revolve around activities such as fishing, hunting or special festivals. Children also build upon their particular Aboriginal language. Through these activities, children develop a positive sense about themselves as aboriginal children. High self-esteem is a critical factor to an

Photo 2.1

individual's approach to learning. This is often the first step in any intervention strategies. Children who have a positive self-esteem will embrace new learning readily, with initiative and enjoyment.

B) EDUCATION AND SCHOOL READINESS Aboriginal Head Start Programs recognize the importance of play as a means to establish life-long learning skills. Emphasis is placed on:

- Initiation of learning by children
- Ensuring that learning experiences are enjoyable.
- Developmentally- and age-appropriate learning experiences, materials and equipment
- Respect for each individual child

C) HEALTH PROMOTION "The purpose of the Health Promotion Component is to empower parents, guardians, caregivers and those involved with AHS to increase control over and improve their health. More specifically, the projects will encourage practices for self care, working together to address health concerns, and the creation of formal and informal social support networks. The ultimate goal is for those involved with AHS to take actions that contribute to holistic health" (Division of Childhood and Adolescence, 2003: 3).

Healthy children come from healthy families. This approach recognizes the need to include family members if healthy practices are to be implemented. To be effective, good practices leading to good nutrition and effective self-care should be extended beyond the child's time in the program. They need to become an integral part of his whole life, in preschool and at home.

D) NUTRITION Nutrition is also covered to include all aspects of the child's life. Children are provided with healthy foods to meet their nutritional needs while in the program. Staff and families receive education to improve their understanding of the relationship between healthy nutrition, behaviour, learning and development. Meal times are used to provide opportunities to learn about nutritious foods, share and socialize.

E) SOCIAL SUPPORT Assistance is provided to families for these purposes:

- To increase awareness of community resources and services through such means as resource pamphlets, articles, books, referral information, workshops and community resource listings
- To facilitate access to community resources and services through direct referrals or provision of contact information
- To empower families to access services and resources within their communities by providing appropriate resource information, by guiding individuals through the help-access process and by encouraging families to seek help when needed

F) PARENTAL AND FAMILY INVOLVEMENT Involvement of families is the cornerstone of all quality programs. "Drawing families into full partnerships allows teachers to demonstrate their respect of the preeminent place of the family in children's lives. As the schools support family efforts, maximum communication between parents and teachers is essential to facilitate understanding and respect for the contribution of each party. Children benefit from greater consistency in their guidance, as teachers and parents work together to plan for major socialization and academic tasks" (Gestwicki, 1999: 311; Gestwicki, 1999: 311). There are several ways in which AHS programs involve the parents, including these:

- Direct involvement in the program—Family members volunteer time every month on a regular basis to help within the program.
- Special events—Family members help organize special events such as celebration feasts or prepare Aboriginal dishes.
- "Parents may bring forth special gifts" (Division of Childhood and Adolescence, 2003: 4)—This is an opportunity to share special talents and culturally important skills with children. For example, in one program an elder brought a variety of drums into the child care program and taught the children to drum. This was followed by another elder who taught the children simple dances to the beat of the drum.

In summary, AHS programs follow an inclusive philosophy that provides an early intervention strategy in support of the holistic development of Aboriginal children within their community.

3. Support Programs

Families with children with special needs can access support in a number of ways:

A) MEDICAL SUPPORT Often the family's first contact to obtain advice about their child is through their physician. Families may be worried about their child's progress. Physicians can diagnose certain physical conditions such as cerebral palsy or failure to thrive. Physicians may also be able to provide general guidelines of "normal development" of children. If children do not seem to meet these guidelines, the physician may refer the families to other professionals such as physiotherapists, speech and language pathologists or psychologists.

B) SUPPORT GROUPS When families and child care providers are suddenly faced with the need to provide appropriate care for children with special needs, they often feel lost and isolated. As a result, families of children with specific disabilities have formed support groups, both informal and formal, to share information and to support each other. An example of a support group that has expanded to provide support to families and other professionals is the Saskatchewan Cerebral Palsy Association. The services provided by this organization include:

- Supporting children with cerebral palsy and their families
- Developing and implementing programs such as swim programs or loaner programs

- Providing assistance to obtain grants for the purchase of equipment for educational purposes
- Providing a resource library of materials such as books, magazines or videos
- Sharing information on available resources, treatments and services
- Advocating for research on prevention and treatment of cerebral palsy
- Advocating for increased services and access to services
- Promoting education and public awareness through workshops and special events
- Exchanging information through publication of a regular newsletter
- Working with other groups and associations to provide referral and support services (Saskatchewan Cerebral Palsy Association, 2004)

4. The Role of Government

For children to be accepted into a program that is subsidized for children with special needs, there must be a diagnosis of special need and/or a referral to access these services. In most jurisdictions the eligibility for services or funding is set by the government. In most cases the ministry responsible for children and families sets these criteria.

British Columbia provides a good example of a jurisdiction in which services for children are provided through a centralized system. The Ministry of Children and Families is the provincial body responsible for providing funding for services for children with special needs. To be eligible for these services, the following criteria are used:

- IQ criteria—The child is diagnosed with an IQ of 70 or below.
- Diagnosis—The child has been diagnosed with autism spectrum disorder.
- Total Dependence—The child has been diagnosed with "severe disabilities that require long term medical supports and services and can be expected to cause extensive costs in maintaining the child at home. Severe disabilities is currently defined as total dependence for eating, toileting, washing, and dressing" (Wakeham, J., 2000: 3).

Staff members assist families to access funding through the Ministry of Children and Families and help families with the process:

- The social worker—This person is responsible for helping find the appropriate services and resources for the child with special needs.
- The intake worker—This is a social worker who will help families complete the initial intake process. The intake worker collects relevant information, makes referrals and sends this information to the social worker to ensure appropriate placement.

In the BC system a number of services are available to families, some of which may also be accessed in other jurisdictions in Canada:

- Home programs—These programs provide financial support to families to cover these expenses:
  - Approved medical equipment expenses
  - Repair and maintenance of equipment
  - Medical supplies and drug coverage
  - Medical transportation
  - Exceptional therapy costs
  - Dental and medical plans
  - Respite care

- Services of specialists, such as:
  - Behaviour consultants
  - Family support homemakers
  - Specialized helpers to assist in setting developmental goals for children

- Child Care Resource and Referral Services

5. Centralized Support Services

The Supported Child Care program in BC is a centralized access point for child care services for children with special needs. For families and the community, the advantage of a centralized organization is that all the service information and resources are accessible from one location. This saves both time and effort in locating the appropriate services for a child with special needs. Supported Child Care consultants (may be referred to as resource consultants in other jurisdictions) perform these functions:

- Helping the family access child care that meets the child's and family's needs
- Supporting child care providers by sharing information and suggestions to provide inclusive care to children
- Providing short-term staffing support
- Organizing workshops for families and child care providers
- Visiting child care settings (Wakeham, J., 2000: 15)

Children with special needs may be placed in any of a variety of licensed centres that may or may not be subsidized. These include family child care facilities, group child care centres, the child's own home, out-of-school programs and preschool programs.

6. Specialized Services

Some children, depending on their needs, may require specialized services from other professionals. Table 2.3 gives an overview of some of these services.

TABLE 2.3   **SPECIALIZED SERVICES**

Specialized Service	Description
Medical	Services provided by community health nurses, orthoptists, physicians or pediatricians to help diagnose possible health problems such as failure to thrive, or sight or hearing problems
Communication	Services provided by speech and language pathologists to children with language delays, or other speech or communication problems
Nutrition	Services provided by nutritionists to help plan and implement appropriate nutritional programs
Mental health	Services provided by psychologists, psychiatrists and mental health workers to support a child's emotional health and well-being
Physical needs	Services provided by physiotherapists to help plan and implement physical activities with children and to suggest specialized exercises and equipment

7. Additional Programs

A) PLAY THERAPY   Active play is the basis of play therapy. Children express themselves most readily through play. "Play is the child's symbolic language of self-expression and can reveal (a) what the child has experienced; (b) reactions to what was experienced; (c) feelings about what was experienced; (d) what the child wishes, wants or needs; and (e) the child's perceptions" (Landreth, 2002: 18).

In any play situation, the children express their past experiences and demonstrate their knowledge about the world around them. Careful organization of materials and learning experiences can present opportunities for observing the child's emotions, actions and experiences. This allows the therapist to respond to what has been expressed. "The selection of a variety of appropriate toys by the therapist can facilitate a wide range of feelings-oriented expression by children. Thus, children are not restricted to discussing what happened; rather, they live out at the moment of play the past experiences and associated feelings" (Landreth, 2002: 19). Through this process, the therapist then responds to and plans appropriate intervention strategies for the child.

In any child care setting, play therapy is used to some degree, and activities are set up that encourage both active play and quiet, relaxing activities. For example, Benjamin was able to relieve his feelings of frustration by engaging in sensory

Photo 2.2

Photo 2.3

finger-painting activitie (Photo 2.2). Danielle was able to relieve her feelings of stress by representing her "monsters" in more cheerful representations (Photo 2.3). Additionally, early childhood educators, through careful observation, may glimpse the first signs of problems. For example, Jonathan's father died in a car accident. He seemed to be handling the situation well. He seemed to be quite at ease in telling everyone that his father had died. A few weeks later, the staff noticed that his paintings started to change. He would paint intricate pictures, then cover the entire picture with black paint. When asked why he was doing this, he answered: "This is what my daddy sees. They put him into the ground. He can't see anything anymore." The staff told the boy's mother what was happening. She replied that she had noticed that Jonathan seemed quieter and more withdrawn at home. She decided to send Jonathan to a play therapist.

B) INFANT STIMULATION/DEVELOPMENT PROGRAMS   Infant stimulation programs, also known as infant development or early intervention programs, are provided for infants who have been diagnosed as developmentally delayed in one or more major skill areas or are diagnosed as being at risk for developmental delays. This type of program supports families by providing some or all of the following options:

- Home-based programs to help families expand their knowledge and skills about overall growth and development
- Home-based or centre-based programs to help families plan and implement learning activities to enhance the infant's social, emotional, physical and cognitive development
- Consulting services to provide information about:

- community resources such as medical, social or educational services
- family connections or support groups
- lending libraries of toys, adaptive equipment, books or other resources such as information about activities to stimulate an infant

C) WITHDRAWAL PROGRAMS   In some cases, a child may require specialized help that is in addition to inclusive care. This specialized care may be provided within the child care facility, or may require the family member to take the child to that service. In either case, the child is withdrawn from the regular program to attend the specialized session. Examples of this type of withdrawal program include speech and language therapy or physical therapy. Often the need for specialized equipment drives the need for a withdrawal type of program.

In most preschool settings, it is up to the parents to take the children to a withdrawal program. This may cause additional hardships to families, as time off work is needed and the children miss part of their day from the preschool. In some of the larger, more regularly funded centres, the specialists may spend a certain amount of time during the week within the centre itself. The centre is equipped with the needed resources for the specialized help. Of course, children still miss a part of their program. Often the specialists can offer guidance to the staff on how to provide some of the needed additional specialized help within the classrooms.

D) SEGREGATED PROGRAMS   Segregated programs are programs that are established based on specific needs of children, such as autism or giftedness. The idea of these programs, based on the belief that the child will benefit more from a specialized program, is to group children with like needs together. In most cases, segregated programs for children with special needs are within the school system, within separate education classes or schools. The rationale for segregated settings is based on these beliefs:

- A child with a severe disability will not gain any benefit from an inclusive setting.
- The child may be so disruptive that the education of other children is impaired.
- The costs are too high to include children with special needs in regular settings (McCarthy, 2002: 9).
- The child may need specialized resources that are not available within an inclusive setting.
- The staff does not have the appropriate training to manage children with severe disabilities.

On the opposing side, individuals argue that the benefits of inclusive care far outweigh the restrictive practices of segregated care. The rationale for integrated settings is based on these arguments:

- Every child, irrespective of ability, has the right to participate in the educational setting within their natural environments. This view is supported by the Canadian Charter of Rights.

- The National Association for the Education of Young Children has found that inclusion does work and identifies the following characteristics of children in inclusive settings:

  - Increased acceptance and appreciation of diversity
  - Better communication and social skills
  - Greater development in moral and ethical principles
  - Warm and caring friendships
  - Increased self-esteem (National Association for the Education of Young Children, 2002: 2–3)

- Studies such as "A Matter of Urgency" report positive findings. "The results of our study indicate that Canadian child care centres when appropriately resourced, can and do include children with special needs, and have substantial positive impacts on their development" (Hope Irwin et al., 2000: xv).

- All high-quality programs for young children are dependent on sufficient funding. In Canada, there has been a growing concern about the quality of child care, including inclusive care. Many of the studies conducted point out that a lack of support, funding, training and adequate policies undermines high-quality care. In high-quality programs, including inclusive programs that receive adequate funding and support, quality child care for all children is provided and the benefits are substantial and long-lasting. Refer to the Perry School Preschool study on page 18 (Schweinhart & Weikart, 1986; McCain & Mustard, 1999; Goleman et al., 2000).

Skills of Early Childhood Educators

Research clearly shows that training of the early childhood educator is the key to successful inclusive learning environments (Hope Irwin et al., 2000; Goelman, Doherty, Lero, LaGrange & Tougas, 2000). Training components should focus on:

- Specific techniques for working with children with severe disabilities
- Increased awareness about inclusive care to eliminate fears, misinformation and negative attitudes about children with special needs
- Provision of "best practices" in an inclusive setting
- Fostering self-confidence to adapt and modify the environment to meet all children's needs

Most skills that are needed are the same ones that any early childhood educator needs for working with young children, such as empathy, sensitivity, knowledge of child development and nurturing skills. In addition, the early childhood educator needs to develop skills in the following areas:

- Organizing the environment to provide materials and choices that are over a broad age range and range of developmental abilities
- Organizing the environment to provide security and safety to all children

- Developing learning experiences that are based on the individual strengths and needs of children
- Establishing routines that are flexible, predictable and consistent
- Varying approaches and techniques based on observation of children's individual learning styles, interests and abilities
- Working collaboratively with families and other professionals to facilitate observations, planning of learning experiences and evaluation of achievements, and to develop strategies to maximize children's chances of success

According to another study on inclusion in Canada (Hope Irwin, Lero & Brophy, 2004), additional characteristics should be considered. These characteristics relate to self-confidence, experience and education:

- Self-confidence—To be effective practitioners in an inclusive setting, adults need to build confidence and skills in:
  - Teamwork
  - Meeting individual children's strengths and needs
  - Research to identify sources of information and support
- Experience with children with special needs—Staff could request to observe inclusive centres or request staff exchanges to become more knowledgeable about specific children with special needs.
- Education—Staff should further their knowledge through attendance at conferences, specific courses, seminars or workshops related to inclusion.

SUMMARY

Anyone who wishes to work with young children should be aware that this includes working with children with special needs. In most cases, the child with special needs is included with children in his or her community. However, since services vary from jurisdiction to jurisdiction and also from centre to centre within each jurisdiction, child care providers must become knowledgeable of these topics:

- Regional legislative requirements or guidelines for children with special needs
- Local resources and support services
- Accessible funding
- Support networks
- How to advocate for the children and families within their care

KEY POINTS

Identification of numbers of children with special needs

- Lower percentages of children with special needs are identified in young children
- Specific statistics on type of services and number of children receiving services are not readily available
- Somewhere between 18.7% and 50% of centres in Canada do not accept children with special needs

Legislative requirements for working with children with special needs

- Training requirements range from no training to specialized training
- Funding for children with special needs is dependent on a diagnosis of needs in most jurisdictions
- Support to centres through grants and funding allocations is dependent on the assessed needs of the children

Reasons for non-inclusiveness

- Lack of funding and resources, training and child care spaces are the main reasons

Inclusive programs are developed on the principles of

- Best practices
- Active play
- Accessibility of all materials and learning activities
- Organization of learning environments to include age-appropriate access to all core curricular elements: books and pictures, fine and gross motor activities, dramatic play, nature and science activities, math and numbers, sand and water, cultural diversity, art, music and movement, blocks, TV and computers
- Observation of children's interests, skills and abilities
- Provision of materials and experiences based on a wide range of skills and abilities
- Recognition of individual safety needs

Aboriginal Head Start programs

- Holistic, inclusive approach
- Consist of six elements: culture and language, education and school readiness, health promotion, nutrition, social support and family involvement

Support programs

- Include medical support groups both informal and formal, centralized agencies, services of specialists, child-care resource and referral services, and supported child care

Role of government

- Sets legislation, policies and guidelines
- Sets criteria for funding, usually diagnosis of special need
- Hires qualified individuals to aid families through application and placement process
- Provides funding for home programs, specialist programs, referral services, supported child care services and specialized services for medical, communication, nutrition, mental-health and physical needs

Centralized services

- Provide all services in one location, such as collection of information, assessment of needs, placement of children, support to children within placement and support to day care facilities

Play therapy programs

- Use active play as central basis of therapy
- Therapist sets up materials and experiences to observe children's interactions in order to plan and implement intervention strategies
- Child care centres utilize play therapy techniques when setting up learning experiences to include sensory activities, soothing activities and opportunities to be alone

Infant stimulation programs

- Provide opportunities for families with infants diagnosed as at risk or developmentally delayed to learn about and participate in programs that serve to enhance infant development

Withdrawal programs

- Individual children are withdrawn from programs to receive specialized help such as speech and language or physical therapy

Segregated programs

- Children with special needs are placed based on a specific need, in rooms or buildings separated from other children

Skills of early childhood educators

- Training in specific techniques needed for children with severe disabilities; awareness about inclusive care and best practices; and self-confidence in ability to provide inclusive care
- Skill in organizing multi-level skill-based environment; providing a safe environment; establishing appropriate routines; and observing children's strengths, needs, learning styles, interests and abilities

EXERCISES

1. Describe how legislation influences the types of services provided to families and children with special needs.

2. Reflect upon the reasons given for not including children with special needs as outlined on page 59. Which of the reasons have some validity? What changes would need to be made to the present service delivery system to address these reasons?

3. Identify the benefits of inclusive settings.

4. Look over the section on Space and Furnishings on pages 47-50. Which of the elements discussed have particular relevance to children with special needs? Explain why you feel this way.

5. Identify what program options are available in your community for children with special needs. Discuss whether these services are adequate. What other services should be provided?

6. Reflect upon your own skills as an early childhood educator. What additional skills do you think you still need to be an effective early childhood educator in an inclusive setting? How might you gain these skills?

RESOURCES

Child care in the provinces and territories
www.childcarecanada.org/pt98/pre.html

Child care networks
www.cccf-fcsge.ca/links/links_en.html

Issue papers on child-care policy and programs in Canada
www.campaign2000.ca/ci/rep.html

The partners of Child & Family Canada
http://www.cfc-efc.ca/startup/orgs.htm

REFERENCES

Campbell, C. (2000). *The Mozart Effect for Children.* New York, NY: HarperCollins Publishers Inc.

Canadian Council on Social Development (2003). Aboriginal Children in Poverty. Candian Council on Social Development [online]. Available at www.ccsd.ca/pr/2003/aboriginal.htm (8-10-2004).

Chiazzari, S. (1998). *The Complete Book of Color.* Boston, MA: Element Books, Inc.

Crowther, I. (2003). *Creating Effective Learning Environments.* Scarborough, ON: Nelson Thomson Learning.

Director Hope Irwin, S. (2004). SpeciaLink: The National Centre for Child Care Inclusion. SpeciaLink [online]. Available at www.specialinkcanada.org (7-11-2004).

Division of Childhood and Adolescence (2003). Program Overview of Aboriginal Head Start. Health Canada [online]. Available at www.hc-sc.gc.ca/fnihb-dgspni/fnihb/cp/index.htm (18-7-2003).

Doherty, G., Lero, D., Goelman, H., LaGrange, A., & Tougas, J. (2000). *You Bet I Care! A Canada-wide Study on Wages, Working Conditions, and Practices in Childcare Centres.* Guelph, ON: University of Guelph.

Doherty-Derkowski, G. (1994). *Quality Matters: Excellence in Early Childhood Programs.* Toronto, ON: Addison-Wesley.

Friendly, M., Beach, J., & Turiano, M. (2002). *Early Childhood Education and Care in Canada.* Toronto: ON: Childcare Resources and Research Unit.

Gestwicki, C. (1999). *Developmentally Appropriate Practices.* Second Edition. Scarborough, ON: Nelson Canada.

Goelman, H., Doherty, G., Lero, D., LaGrange, A., & Tougas, J. (2000). *You Bet I Care! Caring and Learning Environments: Quality in Child Care Centres Across Canada* Guelph, ON: Centre for Families, Work and Well-Being, University of Guelph.

Government of Canada (2002). Chapter 6: Young Children with Disabilities in Canada. The Well Being of Canada's Young Children: Government of Canada [online]. Available at http://socialunion.gc.ca/ecd/2002/b-5.htm (16-8-2004).

Hanline, F., & Daley, S. (2004). "Mom, will Kaelie Always have Possibilities?" *Annual Editions Educational Psychology,* Nineteenth Edition, 42–45.

Harms, T., Clifford, R., & Cryer, D. (1998). *Early Childhood Environment Rating Scale.* Revised Edition. New York, NY: Teachers College Press.

Harms, T., Cryer, D., & Clifford, R. (1990). *Infant/Toddler Environment Rating Scale.* New York, NY: Teachers College Press.

Harms, T., Vineberg Jacobs, E., & White, D. (1996). *School-Age Care Environment Rating Scale.* New York, NY: Teachers College Press.

Hathaway, W. (1994). Non-visual Effects of Classroom Lighting on Children. *Educational Facility Planner, 23,* 12–16.

Hawkins, W., & Lilley, H. (1992). *CEFPI's Guide for School Facility Appraisal.* Columbus, OH: The Council of Educational Facility Planners International.

Hope Irwin, S., Lero, D., & Brophy, K. (2000). *A Matter of Urgency: Including Children with Special Needs in Child Care in Canada.* Wreck Cove, NS: Breton Books.

Hope Irwin, S., Lero, D., & Brophy, K. (2004). *Inclusion: The Next Generation in Child Care in Canada.* Wreck Cove. NS: Breton Books.

Landreth, G. (2002). *Play Therapy: The Art of the Relationship.* New York, NY: Brunner-Routledge.

Liberman, J. (1991). *Light Medicine of the Future.* Santa Fe, NM: Bear & Company Publishing.

Mayer, D. E. (1994). *National Statement on Quality Child Care.* Ottawa, ON: Child and Family Canada.

McCain, M., & Mustard, F. (1999). *Early Years Study Final Report.* Toronto, ON: Publications Ontario.

McCarthy, M. (2002). Inclusion of Children with Special Needs. *Annual Editions, Educating Exceptional Children,* Thirteenth Edition, 8–11.

National Association for the Education of Young Children (2002). The Benefits of an Inclusive Education: Making It Work. National Association fro the Education of Young Children [online]. Available at www.naeyc.org/resources/eyly/1996/07.asp (28-8-2004).

Pediatric Advisor (2004). Burn Safety: Hot Water Temperature. University of Michigan [online]. Available at www.med.umich.edu/1libr/pa/pa_hotwatr_hhg.htm (24-8-2004).

Saskatchewan Cerebral Palsy Association (2004). Saskatchewan Cerebral Palsy Association [online]. Available at www.members.shaw.ca/saskcpa (1-8-2004).

Schweinhart, L., & Weikart, J. (1986). Lasting Differences: The High Scope Preschool Curriculum Comparison Study Through Age 23. *Early Childhood Education Research Quarterly* 1, 15–45.

Voices 4 Children (2003). Fact Sheet #18: Children with Special Needs. Child and Family Canada [online]. Available at www.cfc-efc.ca/docs/vocfc/00018_en.htm (7-8-2004).

Wakeham, J. (2000). *Connections: A Resource Guide for Families with Children with Special Needs* (Rep. No. September, 2000). Vancouver, BC: Developmental Disabilities Association.

3

CHAPTER

Who Are the Children with Special Needs?

"Children who have differences that substantially change the way they learn, respond, or behave have been described in many ways. In fact, you will find these children referred to as children with exceptionalities, children with exceptional conditions, children who are handicapped, children with special needs, children with disabilities, or disabling conditions, and children who are challenged" (Winzer, 1999: 7).

Learning Outcomes

After studying this chapter, you will be able to:

1. Identify historical changes to the field of special education, and explain the significance of modern attitudes toward individuals with special needs.
2. Explain what behavioural and emotional disorders are and how they affect a child's growth and development.
3. Discuss how poor physical health may affect children's skills and abilities.
4. Identify the various types of physical disabilities, and discuss how each disability affects the child's ability to function within early childhood settings.

Introduction

Society has always influenced the way we view and treat individuals with special needs. Institutions such as churches and governments, as well as culture and economic circumstances, influence our belief and value systems. Over time, changing beliefs about how individuals with special needs should be treated and educated have reflected broader social trends.

In most cultures before the seventeenth century, children and adults with special needs were regarded as inferior beings. These children were mistreated and abused, and in some cultures their differences were seen as the sign of the devil. Families who had children with special needs tried to hide them away. Often these children were abandoned, put in an asylum for the insane or even put to death.

From the mid-seventeenth century on, there was a growing trend toward more humane treatment. But it was not until the nineteenth century that education for children with special needs was born. Children started to attend special schools for the deaf, the blind and the mentally retarded. In Canada, the first of these schools was opened in Montreal in 1831. This school for the deaf was forced to close five years later because of lack of funding. By 1848, permanent residential schools became firmly established. Families who had infants with a diagnosed special need such as Down's syndrome were often advised to place their child in an institution. Other children were placed in an institution when they got older and families found it more difficult to maintain them at home (Winzer, 1999).

Reflection   *From a Teacher*

I have been a junior and senior kindergarten teacher. I realized how important a good early start was and often wondered what kind of start children with special needs would have. I always felt that these children, in particular, often did not get the same chance as their more "normal" peers. The school board I was working for required that I had training in special needs before I could teach in a class for trainable retarded children. I decided to take the course during the winter semester. One of our assignments was to visit an institution in our area and write a report on our experiences.

We arrived on a Saturday morning. I was interested in the young children, so I was escorted to a locked ward for the preschool children. I cannot describe my shock in what I saw. The ward was arranged with several sleeping rooms along one side. Some of these held cribs, others had low beds. These small rooms opened to a large common room. There was a circular rug in the middle of the room. Under the adult-height windows were some adult-sized chairs and benches. At one end of the room, a TV set was showing Saturday morning cartoons. Some of the children were sitting in front of the TV. Many of the children were in their diapers or still in pajamas. Some were rocking back and forth, and others just sat staring blindly ahead. A few children were strapped into wheelchairs. Some of the children were still in their cribs. At one end of the room there was a toy box filled with toys, a bookshelf filled with an assortment of children's books, and two tables and chairs. Some attempts had been made to brighten the room. Pictures of nursery rhyme characters had been hung on the walls around the room. I was only there for 10 minutes, but I saw very few adult-child interactions during that time.

I was taken to the children's school room. This room had more materials, but predominantly materials geared to school readiness activities, such as alphabet and number cards. When I asked if the children could go outside to play, the answer was only in good weather.

I had not imagined that children could live in such an austere environment. What happened to the concepts of warmth, cuddling and stimulation? This was 1972, not 1872. How could anyone do this to a small child?

In 1906 special education classes were started in public schools in Canada. These classes were segregated classes within some schools for children with physical disabilities. By the 1940s, special education classes had expanded greatly to include a variety of other disabilities. Additionally, some school boards established segregated schools for children with special needs.

During World War II women were added to the workforce in large numbers. This resulted in the establishment of day care centres across Canada. Most of these facilities were closed after the war.

The 1960s brought increased change in social attitudes. "Social attitudes toward education, care, and training of individuals who are exceptional usually reflect more general cultural attitudes toward the obligation of society to its individual citizens" (Winzer, 1999: 32). This led to philosophies that placed value on the individual. Accordingly, the educational needs of individuals were also looked at and acknowledged. More special education classes evolved. Children were diagnosed for placement, usually based on an IQ test.

During the 1970s early childhood education started to flourish as more women entered the job market. Early identification became important. Programs such as Head Start and early intervention programs flourished. School systems and some day care centres started to move toward **mainstreaming** (placing children with special needs within segregated classrooms of elementary schools) and **integration** (placing children with special needs in classrooms for certain subjects, such as physical education, music and art). In some jurisdictions, children with special needs started to be integrated into regular day care programs, often with a support worker assigned to the child.

Reflection

Reflection | *From a Special Education Class Teacher*

In the mid-1970s, I was honoured to be able to teach in an experimental class of six children, in what was then called a class for trainable retarded children. The class was placed within an elementary school rather than in the school for the "Mentally Retarded." Children in my class ranged in age from four to eight. The special needs represented in the class included physical disabilities, what was then diagnosed as severe mental retardation, behavioural problems and significant language delays. The classroom had very few materials that I thought were developmentally appropriate or provided an adequate number of choices for active play. The children did not participate in the regular recess programs. In fact, some children outside the special needs class were afraid of the children in it.

Within two months, the classroom changed. Children could participate in active play. With the help and support of the rest of the school, all children also participated in the regular recess program. They could go out by themselves and come in by themselves. The children formed active friendships with their peers. Some of the children were even integrated into the music programs within the primary divisions. One of the children had been labelled as "untestable." I did not believe this diagnosis, and with great difficulty managed to convince the psychometrist to retest him. She was amazed to find that not only could he be tested, but now he tested in the mildly retarded range. Today I am very pleased to note that this experiment was so successful that more of the young children were moved into similar classes around the system, and some of the younger children were actually placed in some of the day care programs.

The 1980s brought a stronger legislative focus on education. Many jurisdictions passed legislation that paved the way for inclusive care. The right to inclusive education has become the norm within all Canadian jurisdictions. However, not all jurisdictions reinforce the concept of inclusion through policies, funding or other supports.

In all areas, children with special needs still face many hurdles that other children do not. In all jurisdictions in Canada, to obtain funding for support, children with special needs:

- Must be diagnosed with special needs by a recognized practitioner such as a doctor or a psychologist
- Must be diagnosed with the special need that is funded within the jurisdiction—For example, in Ontario, a child with special needs is defined as "a child who has physical or mental impairment that is likely to continue for a prolonged period of time and who as a result thereof is limited in activities pertaining to normal living as verified by objective psychological or medical findings..." (Government of Ontario, 1997: R1.1)
- May forfeit the right to attend the family's day care program of choice

As a result, children with special needs still do not receive equitable treatment. These children must have a confirmed diagnosis to receive support and funding for quality care. Funding arrangements are usually based on a categorical system. A categorical system labels the child with a specific disability in a broad category, such as communication disorders, physical disabilities or impaired health, developmental disabilities, behavioural disabilities, intellectual delays or disabilities, or sensory disabilities (Winzer, 1999; Baxter & Reid, 1999; Allen, Paasche, Langford & Nolan, 2002). The categorical approach presents several problems:

- Not all jurisdictions recognize all the categories. For example, the definition in Ontario does not cover behavioural or sensory disorders. Children with these disorders will find it difficult to receive the funding and support needed.
- Often the label may become a self-fulfilling prophecy. The child who was labelled as untestable was placed in a "trainable retarded class." It was assumed that because he could not be tested, he had a very low IQ, and as a result he was placed in a program with children of equally low IQs. As later testing showed, he was testable and did have a much higher IQ than expected. (See Table 3.1).
- Children may be refused service because the staff feel that the support is lacking or that they are not sufficiently trained to accept a particular special need.

Having special needs in one or more areas profoundly affects all aspects of a child's development. For example, a child with a physical disability will find it harder to explore the environment freely. This makes it more difficult for the child to gain first-hand knowledge about the particulars of that environment. Consequently, the child has fewer opportunities to form mental representations, with the result that both cognitive and language development could be delayed. It will also be much harder for the child to form a good concept about his or her own body, the functions of various body parts and the position of the body in relationship to other things within the environment. This may affect how the child perceives himself or herself.

The impact of a need in any one domain is like a domino effect: it affects all other areas because of the close interconnections of all developmental domains. To mitigate some of these effects, careful observation, early intervention and holistic care and treatment are required.

All children have special needs at one time or another. For example, at the age of three Michael had not started to talk. He was referred to a speech and language pathologist. A program was set up for him within the preschool environment. But when Michael did start to speak, he amazed everyone because he spoke in full sentences. Many children print letters backwards when they first start to write; however, as children mature, they learn to print letters appropriately. Within any quality program, the children continue to be involved in active play. The adults recognize the needs and adapt the materials, equipment and strategies to reflect the children's strengths and needs at that particular time.

Some children need more help than others. Depending on the severity of the need, some children may need more assistance, some adaptive equipment or greater

TABLE 3.1 **ADVANTAGES AND DISADVANTAGES OF LABELLING CHILDREN**

Advantages of Labelling	Disadvantages of Labelling
• Labels help children with special needs access services, funding and other supports. • Labels may help children access specialized equipment or instruction, such as Braille equipment or standing frames. • Labels may help families understand and deal with the problems of having a child with special needs. • Labels may help increase awareness and knowledge of individuals with special needs. Adults will often question or research information that they are not familiar with. • Labels may provide a common language for communications among professionals.	• Labels draw attention to one characteristic of the child. Often as a result of diagnosis, a program is then imposed that centres on the special need rather than looking at the whole child. The child's strengths may be completely overlooked. • Labelling ignores the fact that children are unique and do not fit neatly into fixed categories. • The label will not predict individual needs. For example, what does the label "Down's syndrome" mean? It is not helpful in setting up a program for that child. The child must first be observed for unique characteristics, such as interests, strengths and needs, before an appropriate plan can be created for him or her. • Labelling can lead others to infer that the diagnosis is accurate. An incorrect diagnosis could lead to inappropriate placement and programming. • Making an accurate assessment of a young child's special needs is difficult. Many of the standardized tests are not reliable or valid. • Labelling may lead to teasing by peers. • Labelling may lead to unrealistic expectations. Adults may concentrate on the remediation of needs and ignore the child's right to play. • Labelling may lead to needlessly lower expectations for the child. If the expectation is that the child cannot do a task, the opportunity may never be given to him or her. • For a child labelled "gifted," the label may burden the child with unrealistically high expectations.

adaptation to their program. To access funds to provide for all of the children's needs, caregivers must have children assessed and diagnosed with a special need. Classification for children with special needs is not precise. It tends to lump children together into arbitrary categories based on perceived needs. For example, Jordan was diagnosed with an overall developmental delay, but his teachers noticed that his gross motor skills were not delayed. He reached the same milestones as other children of his age.

Some of the major categorical systems used in different jurisdictions throughout Canada are identified below. These types of system are not geared to inclusivity.

They tend to label children and place them in categories, focusing on the need rather than the child. "In naming, a specific term is attached to something or someone. It is a powerful process that carries many messages about perceived value and human relationships" (American Association on Mental Retardation, 2002: 5). However, it is important for students learning about children with special needs to know about the major categories for children with special needs, in order to:

- Identify appropriate resources such as equipment, materials, toys and information about children with special needs
- Apply for relevant funding
- Become aware of varying strategies for effective interactions and appropriate program planning
- Interact effectively with families and other professionals

Children with Behavioural and Emotional Disorders

Children with behavioural or emotional disorders may exhibit feelings such as sadness, fear, anger, guilt or anxiety that change the way they behave and interact with others (Freiberg, 2004: 111). Behavioural and emotional disorders can include a wide range of disabilities, such as the ones described below.

1. Conduct Disorders

Children with a conduct disorder may have behaviours such as aggressiveness toward other children or materials, or disruptive behaviours such as constant interruptions or throwing temper tantrums when thwarted. For example, Ben had built an enclosure for his insects. Other children became interested in the enclosure he had built and they wanted to help. He immediately started to shout at them to leave his work alone. When this did not work, he physically tried to push the children away. Ben was often protective of his activities.

Conduct disorders include behaviours that can be classified as non-compliant oppositional defiant disorder. A **non-compliant oppositional defiant disorder** is defined by a pattern of behaviour that is consistently negative. Children may act with hostility—physically, verbally or both—and openly refuse to comply with expectations. These children frequently demonstrate behaviours such as these:

- Temper tantrums
- Arguments with adults or peers
- Expressions of anger
- Refusal to comply to expectations
- Blaming others for own behaviour
- Inappropriate behaviours such as deliberately trying to annoy others

2. Anxiety or Withdrawal

In reaction to stressful situations, some children may express anxiety or simply withdraw. For example, Melanie was one of the children involved when Ben had his outburst. As soon as Melanie heard Ben shout, she ran to the quiet area, sat on the couch and started to rock her body back and forth. Even when the episode was over, she still refused to leave the quiet area or become involved in any activities.

3. Attention Deficit Hyperactivity Disorder

The behaviour of children with an attention deficit hyperactivity disorder (ADHD) is characterized by a short attention span, distractibility, inattentiveness, impulsiveness and increased physical activity. For example, Donald was walking with his classmates to the bus. His caregiver was holding his hand. He was continually looking around him. When he spied a bird or a squirrel, he immediately tried to tug away his hand to try to run after it. When the bus arrived, the caregiver released his hand so that Donald could get on the bus. But Donald spied a stone on the road and immediately tried to crawl under the bus to get it. On the bus he continually tried to stand up in his seat to look at people either in front of him or behind him.

Research has shown that this category actually comprises two conditions: attention deficit hyperactivity disorder and attention deficit disorder (ADD). "Recent studies indicate that ADD without hyperactivity is uncommon, and today there is more use of the composite syndrome ADHD. There are some suggestions, however, that ADD occurs more often with students who are learning disabled, while ADHD may be more frequent among children with disruptive behavioral disorders" (Winzer, 1999: 289).

4. Pervasive Developmental Disorders

Pervasive developmental disorders (PDDs) are associated with stereotypical, repetitive behaviours and difficulties with social interactions and with communication skills. Autism and childhood schizophrenia are the most common PPD conditions.

Children with signs of **autism** seem to reject human contact. These children do not want to be cuddled and tend to avoid eye-contact. Autistic children often exhibit self-stimulation behaviours such as waving their fingers rapidly in front of their eyes, banging their heads or rocking. These children are easily upset by changes in routine or overreact to some sensory stimuli. They tend to lack appropriate communication skills. Unusual behaviours such as fixating on specific objects or lining up objects for long periods of time are indications of autism.

For example, when Peter arrived in the morning, he was greeted by his caregiver, Susan. She said, "Good morning, Peter. How are you today?" Without looking at Susan he responded in a high monotone voice, "Good morning, Peter. How are you today?" He walked over to the collection of small bears. He lined up all the bears in a long row, until he ran out of bears. Peter stopped his activity. He sat on the floor rocking back and forth, flicking his fingers in front of his eyes. Susan walked over to him. She gently put her hands on Peter's hands, and then held out her hand and said, "Let's clean up your bears." Peter echoed her words and refused to give her his hand but followed her to the bears. He stood beside her looking at the fish swimming in the aquarium. Susan gently prompted him to help her. He picked up a bear and spun it around on the floor. Other children had joined Peter and Susan and the bears were soon put away, back on the shelf. Peter immediately took the bears off the shelf and started to line them up again.

Since schizophrenia is extremely rare in children under the age of 12, **childhood schizophrenia** will not be covered in this text apart from the following definition: "Unlike children with autism, those with schizophrenia typically have a later age of onset of their problem, show less intellectual impairment, display less severe social and language deficits, develop hallucinations and delusions as they get older, and experience periods of remission and relapse" (Mash & Wolfe, 1999: 411).

Children with behavioural or emotional disorders may exhibit the following general characteristics:

- An inability to learn that cannot be explained by intellectual, sensory or health factors
- An inability to build or maintain satisfactory interpersonal relationships with peers and teachers
- Inappropriate types of behaviour or feelings under normal circumstances
- A general pervasive mood of unhappiness or depression
- A tendency to develop physical symptoms or fears associated with personal or school problems (Jolivette, Stichter & McCormick, 2002: 118)

Children with Cognitive Disabilities

Children with cognitive disabilities are characterized with limitations in a number of abilities, including intellectual functioning and the ability to adapt behaviours in social, conceptual and practical skills (American Association on Mental Retardation, 2002). A number of labels have been, and continue to be, applied to this disability: mental retardation, intellectual delays, cognitive delays and, sometimes, developmental delays.

Children may have any one of a number of symptoms. Some of these symptoms may also be part of normal development. The younger the child and the more restrictive the early experiences, the more likely it will be that the child will exhibit some of these symptoms.

Young children develop at different rates and in different ways. Each individual is unique. During the early years, young children learn the most they will learn in a lifetime. The young brain is remarkably active in forming numerous connections and "wiring" between these connections to help the individual master and transfer learning and skills in many situations. As a result, care should be taken to look at any symptoms in the context of the child's age, experience and present setting. These symptoms could include:

- Difficulty understanding directions—For example, Damian was participating in an obstacle course with the rest of the preschool children. The children were asked to proceed in one direction only. Damian consistently wanted to go back and do the obstacle course in the reverse direction when he had finished it.
- Difficulty learning new skills—For example, Bill, a four-year- old, had been in the same day care situation since he was two. The centre encouraged all children to recognize their own names. The staff had posted pictures and the children's names in many locations such as personal hooks and personal displays. Bill consistently needed help to find his picture and name.
- Difficulty remembering directions or skills previously learned—For example, Leona found it difficult to remember where material that she had used previously was kept. The environment had been structured carefully and consistently to maximize the children's ability to find and return materials. Leona would consistently ask where the materials were or return them to the incorrect spot. When a staff member gently reminded her where the toy that she was returning belonged, she would hit her head and say, "I forgot."
- A need for additional help to complete tasks such as self-help tasks or putting things back where they belong—For example, Timmy consistently needed help to put toothpaste on his toothbrush.
- An immature reaction or inappropriate response in social situations—For example, one group of preschool children had been reading stories and discussing how to be empathetic. One of the children, Jamie, was very sad when he arrived one morning. He shared that his dog had been hit by a car and died. Rodney heard the interaction and seemed to understand that something was wrong. He promptly came over to Jamie and gave him the "high-five" sign.
- Additional delays in other domains: physical, emotional, social and language— For example, Stevie was diagnosed as cognitively developmentally delayed. Additionally, this four-year-old used single words to communicate and found it difficult to master age-appropriate fine motor tasks such as putting on his own shoes or stacking blocks more than three blocks high.

The American Association on Mental Retardation (AAMR) has developed a classification system for children with cognitive disabilities that is widely used. The original AAMR system focused on the severity of the delays. According to this type of scale, children are tested, given an IQ score and then placed in an appropriate category. IQ scores are formal measures of intelligence that place children on a scale from non-competent to gifted. These are the categories of mental retardation identified from IQ testing:

- Mildly retarded—IQ score of 55–70
- Moderately retarded—IQ score of 40–55
- Severely retarded—IQ score of 25–40
- Profoundly retarded—IQ score below 25

Recently, the AAMR has begun to adapt its classification system for individuals with cognitive disabilities. "Rather than severity, the proposed system changes dependency to support needs, key terms to the level of services required, and describes them in ways that are prescriptive for programming needs. Specifically it replaces the levels of mild to profound with *intermittent, limited, extensive,* and *pervasive,* terms which refer to the supports needed" (Winzer, 1999: 195). This classification system looks at the adaptive behaviours needed to function appropriately within different settings. The new classification system is being created in collaboration with a wide range of participants, and in light of research and subsequent changing viewpoints about the best holistic way to treat individuals with this condition. "[W]e are in the midst of discussion about the nature of intelligence; the relationship between intelligence and adaptive behavior; the implementation of the supports paradigm; the best way to conceptualize disabling conditions; the impact of consumer and reform movements; and the effects of terminology upon individual lives" (American Association on Mental Retardation, 2002: xiii).

The reform of the classification system includes new terminology that focuses on:

- Support needs, availability of support and level of services required by an individual within his or her community
- Assessment of the individual that is sensitive to the individual's unique circumstances such as culture, language spoken at home and customs
- Sensitivity to both strengths and needs of the individual
- Development of a profile to identify necessary supports
- Personalized supports sustained over time (American Association on Mental Retardation, 2002)

Most jurisdictions in Canada utilize the old classification system developed by AAMR before 1992. However, most jurisdictions also advocate for inclusive care and support it to some degree. This represents a direct conflict between ideology and policy and provides support for the recommendations outlined in the study "A Matter of Urgency" (Hope Irwin, Lero & Brophy, 2000). Canada needs to develop policies and adopt guidelines that support inclusion.

1. Communication Difficulties

Just as children with special needs are categorized by their need, the domains of development are also categorized. In most systems, communication is regarded as part of the cognitive domain.

Communication is made up of three distinct components that are connected and dependent on each other (see Figure 3.1). **Receptive communication** refers to an individual's ability to understand what has been transmitted through verbal communication, body language and/or other means such as symbolized form or signing. **Physical communication** refers to an individual's ability to transmit signals by facial expressions and other body language such as shrugging the shoulders or using hand movements. Physical communications are culturally deter-

FIGURE 3.1
Communication Components

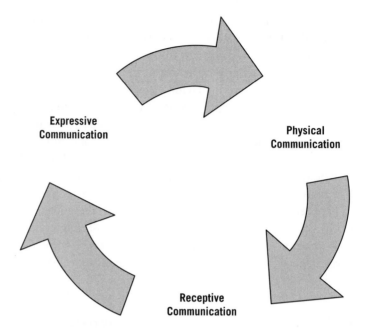

Expressive
Communication

Physical
Communication

Receptive
Communication

mined. For example, in some Asian cultures it is impolite to have direct eye contact with the speaker, which is in direct contrast to Western custom. **Expressive language** refers to an individual's ability to express himself or herself verbally or physically, including signing or using **augmentative devices** (devices that help an individual to communicate a message using devices such as symbol boards or talking computers) so that the message can be understood by others.

Children may experience difficulties in one or all of the communication areas. Difficulties in the receptive communication area are evident by a child's lack of understanding of:

- The meaning of words—For example, Jeremy was sitting beside one of his peers, Jonas. Jonas asked him to pass the shears. Jeremy looked around the table. He obviously understood that he was asked to find something and pass it to Jonas. He did not understand the word "shears." Jonas noticed his difficulty. He walked over, picked up the shears and said, "See, these are shears. They're kinda like scissors."

- Directions—For example, the children were lined up outside the gym. They received instructions to go into the gym, find a circle and jump inside the circle. When Dillon entered the gym, he stopped. He looked around and then started to jump around the room. Dillon had either not heard all of the instructions, or he had forgotten what he had been told, or he simply did not understand what was required of him. He watched the other children to see what was expected. He picked up that jumping was a requirement, so he jumped around the room.

- Conversations or dialogues—For example, Nancy was listening to the story of Goldilocks and the Three Bears with a group of her peers. Throughout the story, the child care provider asked questions about what was happening. Nancy was eager to answer but did not answer any questions correctly.

Difficulties in the expressive communication area are much more difficult to diagnose. Children's ability to express themselves is dependent on a number of factors. Children may have difficulty with one or all of the factors. These factors include:

- Understanding of the message—As in the example of Jeremy above, he could not respond to the message because he did not understand the meaning of the word "shears."
- Syntax—**Syntax** can be defined as the way words are put together to form phrases, clauses or sentences and the connection of the elements of language into an orderly system (grammar). Children develop sequence in an orderly system that progresses through orderly stages of development. Children with difficulty in syntactic development may exhibit the following behaviours:

  - Inability to ask questions correctly—For example, Jennifer, a five-year-old, wanted to have another drink of milk. Her way of asking for the milk was to say, "Me have milk." There was no inflection in her tone, nor any indication that this was a request for more milk.
  - Problems with use of various parts of speech—For example, Jetta consistently put verbs at the beginning of her dialogue, as in "Jump, me" or "Go fast, me."
  - Delayed use of the elements of language—For example, Jordan, a three-year-old, was communicating verbally in one-word or two-word utterances (though they did have the correct intonation patterns).

- Morphology—**Morphology** is the description of how words are built in the language. Some of the significant elements include **prefixes** (a part of speech placed in front of a word to change the word's meaning, such as "in-" or "re-") and **suffixes** (a part of speech placed at the end of a word, such as "-ly" or "-ness"). Children may avoid using any prefixes or suffixes. Sometimes this is not an inability to use the elements but the result of the language that the child has heard modelled. For example, many adults tend to omit the "-ly" suffix. It is quite common to hear, "Come quick" instead of "Come quickly."
- Phonology—**Phonology** is the system that builds sounds into words. The smallest unit of speech sound is called a **phoneme**. There are approximately 44 phonemes used in the English language. Children may have difficulties in expressing phonemes because of articulation disorders, voice disorders, fluency disorders or physical disorders of the speech mechanisms. Additionally, second-language learners may have difficulty with English phoneme production. There are a possible 300 phonemes that occur in the world's different languages. The phoneme structure of an individual's first language, therefore, could be quite different that of English.
- Phonetics—**Phonetics** represents the spoken language, as portrayed by the sounds of the 26 letters of the alphabet that are used in English to read and spell

words. Many children have difficulty with a phonetical approach. They may find it difficult to:

- Blend sounds into words—Some children cannot take individual letter sounds and put them together to make a word. For example, if one takes a word such as cat, it can be broken down into the individual letter sounds: c-a-t. When these sounds are verbalized separately, some children can quickly combine them into a word and some cannot.
- Utilizing beginning or end consonant sounds—This ability is similar to the ability to blend sounds together. Some children cannot hear the individual sound or distinguish it from the whole word.
- Distinguishing vowel sounds—This is much more difficult because there are two types of vowel sounds to distinguish—short and long—both of which come with a set of rules and exceptions. Inability to distinguish vowel sounds can become very confusing because the child who has difficulty following directions or sequences or with remembering will also find this difficult.

- Pragmatics—**Pragmatics** refers to how language is used. Language usage changes with the context of a situation. Children need to learn that it may be all right to use some words in certain conversations but not in others. For example, Lily, a four-year-old, told her caregiver to "shut up." Her caregiver responded that this was not a polite way to say this. Lily thought about it and replied, "Shut up, please?"

The use of physical communication is culturally and experientially dependent. Additionally, it can also be individualistic. Children's ability to express themselves physically is dependent on their ability to perceive messages through body language, their physical ability to imitate appropriate body language and their ability to understand and use body language. Here are some typical examples of children who use a different type of body language:

- Dillon nodded to mean no rather than yes.
- Melanie waved at people if she wanted them to go away, or if she wanted to be alone.
- Markus put his hands on top of his head when he was frustrated.

In addition to the possible disabilities described above, there are also a number of specific language disorders. Some of these include **aphasia**, an inability to communicate effectively using verbal language because of difficulty in comprehension or production difficulties, and **apraxia**, an inability to communicate verbally because the child cannot effectively use the muscles that control speech sounds.

Some children may simply not be able to learn through verbal communication. These children will need to be involved in nonverbal communication. These are some of the early warning signs of children in this category:

- The infant does not make early vocalizations or sounds, such as cooing or bab-bling.
- The infant started to coo and babble but stopped.
- The infant or toddler continues to coo using vowel sounds only.
- The child does not express any words.
- The child is not talking.
- The child does not follow simple directions.
- The child shows no evidence of recognizing familiar objects in the environment by pointing to them or following requests to get them.
- The child is difficult to understand.
- The child does not combine words into sentences or phrases.
- The child cannot relate experiences or tell stories in a relevant sequence.
- The child does not seem to understand verbal dialogue.

2. Advanced Cognitive Abilities

Children who fall into this category are often also referred to as intellectually superior, gifted or talented. These children have abilities that are advanced compared with other children of the same age. The identification of giftedness is difficult because:

- The identification is dependent on the particular values and beliefs about what abilities should be recognized as exceptional. Is the child only gifted if he or she is exceptional overall? Can a child be gifted in only one or two areas? What value is placed on giftedness in different areas such as art, music or academic achieve-ment?
- Various jurisdictions have different criteria for measuring giftedness. Is it meas-ured by an IQ score? Is it on the basis of a diagnostic assessment in a particu-lar area?
- Giftedness is somewhat of a subjective assessment in the early years. For exam-ple, Christopher started to talk in full sentences by the time he was 18 months old. He also used "big" words. He was continually identified as bright. He cer-tainly had an advanced skill in language, and since this was a very observable skill, assumptions were made about his general abilities.

Some of the behaviours that children who are gifted might exhibit include:

- Extensive vocabulary and advanced communication interactions—For exam-ple, Christopher at two was on a field trip in the department store. He was touching some of the clothes as he was walking by these on his way to the toy section. When asked to please not touch, he responded, "Will the sales clerk get annoyed with me if I touch the clothes?"
- Creativity in approaching tasks such as using materials symbolically when mate-rials are not readily available—For example, Olivia, a four-year-old, wanted to build a zoo for her toy animals. She started out by using rectangular blocks to

make fences. When she ran out of these blocks, she started to use wedges. But she thought that the animals might escape through the gaps, so she experimented and discovered that she could create rectangular shapes by putting two wedges together. Olivia also wanted to create a "terrain" that was more realistic. She created hills within her enclosure by placing boxes of various sizes in the enclosure and then placing a brown blanket on top of these. She also created a moat by using blue material to drape inside the fence she had created.

- Ability to solve problems independently—For example, Billy wanted to test which of the bottles held more water. He thought that the tall skinny bottle would hold the most. He collected a funnel, a measuring cup and some linking cubes. For every cup he poured into the bottle, he added one of the linking cubes. When he was finished, he could compare which bottle held more water visually. He was amazed to find that the shorter bottle held more. He repeated his experiment to make sure that it was "absolutely true."

- Perception of the world from another individual's perspective—For example, Emily, a toddler, saw another toddler fall and hurt herself. Before the adult could get to the injured child, Emily was already there. She said, "That hurt." She hugged the child and managed to calm her down.

- Transference of learning from one situation to another—For example, Jarred had discovered that he could create different colours of paint when he was finger-painting. He had discovered that yellow and red make orange. When he was at the paint station, he decided to experiment to create different colours. He was delighted to realize that he could create shades of colours and new colours.

- **Divergent thinking** ability (ability to think of a variety of ways to solve a problem)—For example, Braelyn and Yasmine wanted to test how fast the little cars could travel. They decided that they could test the speed of the cars in the following ways:

  - Pushing them quickly on a flat, clear surface
  - Testing them on the ramp they had built
  - Creating a new ramp that was higher
  - Creating a new ramp that was steeper
  - Using hollow cardboard tubes of varying lengths to roll the cars down

3. Learning Disabilities

"'Learning Disabilities' refer to a number of disorders which may affect the acquisition, organization, retention, understanding or use of verbal or nonverbal information. These disorders affect learning in individuals who otherwise demonstrate at least average abilities essential for thinking and/or reasoning. As such, learning disabilities are distinct from global intellectual deficiency" (The Learning Disabilities Association of Canada, 2004: 1).

Children who experience learning disabilities may have difficulty in the following areas:

- Oral language skills—For example, Charlie, a five-year-old, liked to tell stories. His stories would ramble on and on. He combined several stories into one oral narrative: "I got a dog. And mommy went to the dentist. And yesterday I hmmm. I like ice cream."
- Overall language skills—Jessica, a six-year-old, often confused words. She might ask for a shovel but in reality want a pail, or she might ask for something by saying, "I want hmmm, hmmm, thing, you know," and make a motion to describe the action of the object in the air.
- Visual spatial processing—Janie, a four- year-old, found it difficult to put a simple puzzle together. She would turn the piece around and around and try to force it into a specific spot.
- Visual sensory motor problems—Jeremy at age three had very poor coordinated movements. He ran with a jerky, awkward gait. He often lost his balance and fell. Jeremy also showed poor visual spatial processing. He was observed walking into walls or furniture.
- Visual perceptual tasks—At age four Olanda found it difficult to match two objects that were the same or different. She also found it hard to match a real object to a picture, such as a toy dog to a picture of a similar dog. Jeremy found it difficult to track a rolling object. He would chase a ball as it started to roll away, but stop chasing it because he lost the ball from his visual perspective.
- Visual-motor integration—Eight-year-old Jonathan found it difficult to try to grab the crib toy within his reach above him. He would swat at it, until he managed to grab it by chance.
- Memory—Alex often forgot simple sequential tasks. When he arrived in the morning he would need reminders to take his coat off, hang it on the hook, take his boots off and put his slippers on.
- Attention span—When Dillon arrived in the morning, he would visit four areas of interest within a 10-minute time span.
- Fine motor control—Jakob at four had great difficulties with fine motor activities such as stringing beads, holding scissors to cut and pasting items on a piece of paper. He generally avoided the painting and drawing areas of the preschool room.

Many additional learning disabilities do not surface until children start elementary school. At this time additional difficulties may surface in children's ability to solve mathematical problems, to read and to write.

Children with Impaired Health

Impaired health can be identified as a special need if the disease or condition—such as AIDS, diabetes, asthma, allergies or **cystic fibrosis** (a genetic condition that affects the respiratory and digestive systems)—affects daily functioning in that individual's life.

These conditions affect children, families and staff in the following ways:

- Children may need to take medication, and it may change their behaviour to make learning more difficult. The effects could include such behaviours as drowsiness, inattentiveness or lack of motivation.
- Children may be absent because of illness, which may increase family stress levels because there are few options for sick-child care.
- Children may need a variety of sophisticated interventions. Staff may need training to gain the knowledge to implement these procedures, such as knowing when and how to give an EpiPen to counteract an allergic reaction. This may create more stress on the staff because of the heightened responsibility for the safety of that child.
- There may be ethical problems and fears associated with some conditions such as AIDS.

High rates of absenteeism caused by impaired health may also affect other domains, such as social or cognitive development.

1. Cystic Fibrosis

Cystic fibrosis is a condition that is genetic and affects the respiratory and digestive systems. It is treated by medication and by diet. The physical manifestations of this condition include:

- Failure to gain weight
- Slow growth pattern
- Chronic episodes of pneumonia or bronchitis

2. Diabetes

There are two types of diabetes. Type 1, insulin-dependent diabetes, is the most common in young children, and Type 2, non-insulin-dependent diabetes, is most common after the age of 40. Type 1 diabetes can be treated by insulin intake, diet and exercise. Symptoms of children with diabetes are usually controlled by the medication. Sometimes a diabetic emergency is caused by a low or high sugar imbalance. Symptoms of a diabetic emergency include:

- Dizziness, drowsiness and confusion
- Rapid breathing
- Rapid pulse
- Feeling or looking ill

It is important to know what type of imbalance is evident—low or high sugar—because the treatment, such as giving a child more sugar, may cause a more severe reaction. If the condition is unknown, immediate consultation with a medical emergency authority is essential.

3. Allergies and Asthma

Allergies may also affect the child's performance. Allergies may be caused by genetic factors or by a large range of substances such as pollen, stings or dust. Allergies may be controlled by medication and by trying to minimize contact with the allergy-causing agent. Some common signs and symptoms of allergies include:

- Rashes, hives or itching
- Complaints of a tight feeling in chest or throat
- Swelling of specific areas of the body
- Wheezing
- Weakness, dizziness or confusion
- Feelings of nausea
- Vomiting

Asthma can be defined by a condition that obstructs the bronchial passages by narrowing or swelling of the tubes or by clogging of the tubes with mucus. Asthma may be controlled by a variety of drugs, usually administered by an inhaler. Common symptoms of an asthma attack include:

- Wheezing
- Violent coughing
- Shortness of breath

4. AIDS

Acquired immune deficiency syndrome (AIDS) is caused by a virus that attacks and disrupts the immune system. In most childhood cases, the HIV virus is transmitted to the fetus by an infected mother. It may also be transmitted through contaminated blood, such as a blood transfusion, or through abusive sexual contact. Children who suffer from AIDS have no defences to combat disease and are prone to eventual fatal infections and cancers.

Children with Physical Disabilities

Physical disabilities generally affect the child's ability to move effectively. Other domains such as cognitive, social, emotional or language may or may not be affected. Physical disabilities may be present at birth or caused by accidents, in particular, trauma to the head.

There are a number of physical disabilities that affect the child's ability to move around the environment effectively. Some children may need total support to help with any kind of movement. These children may have to be moved from one location to another with physical assistance. Other children may be able to navigate with minor assistance by using crutches or braces. Some children may not need assistive devices to walk, but may find it difficult to coordinate muscles smoothly, resulting in a lurching, disjointed gait. They may also find it difficult to keep their balance and will need clear, smooth passageways to navigate successfully.

Fine motor skills may also be ineffective, and children may need to use assistive devices such as Velcro straps on spoons, paint brushes or pencils. All fine motor utensils need to be checked to ensure effective use. The child's ability to hold and move the utensils should dictate the adaptations needed.

1. Cerebral Palsy

Cerebral palsy is an example of an **orthopedic condition** (a condition that involves the skeleton, joints and muscles). This is one of the most common conditions in young children with disabilities. Children with cerebral palsy find it difficult to coordinate muscle movements and therefore to maintain an appropriate posture or to balance effectively for movement. Cerebral palsy may be classified by the number of body parts that are impaired and by the type of brain damage that has occurred, as well as the subsequent motor patterns that are evident.

Spastic cerebral palsy refers to children who have suffered damage to the motor cortex of the brain. These children will have difficulty controlling voluntary movement. The condition is characterized by slow and difficult movement, poor coordination and weak, **hypertonic** (muscles tone is excessively tense) muscle tone.

The primitive reflexes that an individual exhibits at birth continue to be involved as the child grows. These reflexes are automatic and involuntary. Children may continue to exhibit primitive reflex movements, such as the rooting reflex, the startle reaction, the stretch reflex, the asymmetrical tonic neck reflex, protective extensive reactions and righting reactions.

Children with cerebral palsy will be affected in a number of ways:

- They will experience difficulty in reaching developmental milestones because they have little control over their muscles.
- They will need to learn to use braces or other assistive devices to walk.
- They may develop a multi-disabling condition affecting some or all other developmental domains.
- They may have difficulty communicating effectively because of impaired motor function of the speech organs.
- They may have visual or auditory problems.
- They may have deficits in the tactile senses causing decreased ability to feel pain, pressure or temperature.

2. Hearing Impairments

"Hearing loss is silent, painless, and invisible, one of the least recognized and most misunderstood disabilities. Severe and profound hearing loss (deafness) is a low-incidence condition; however, milder forms of hearing impairment (hard of hearing) are widely prevalent" (Winzer, 1999: 324).

Hearing loss is defined in terms of the individual's ability to distinguish the intensity of loudness over several frequencies. This is usually measured in **decibels**, the smallest measurable difference in loudness intensity between sounds. Hearing impairment is subsequently categorized into mild, moderate, severe or profound hearing loss. An individual with a mild hearing loss may have difficulty hearing faint sounds that are far away. An individual with a moderate hearing loss may find it difficult to follow conversations, especially in group situations. An individual with a severe hearing loss needs a hearing aid to understand language and will need speech and language training. With a profound hearing loss, individuals may hear loud sounds but cannot understand speech sounds.

Hearing is a critical component for the development of speech and language. Infants who are deaf will babble, but much later than other children—usually after they start to observe the movement of the lips and mouth, between six and ten months of age. The babbles produced by these infants are the labial sounds: sounds produced by the lips and mouth (Schickedanz, Schickedanz, Forsyth & Forsyth, 2001). Infants who are deaf will not respond to the normal soothing or interactive techniques used by family members, such as singing or sound games. As a result, families may attribute the infant's behaviour to other causes.

Children who suffer deafness or hearing loss will have some degree of difficulty. Predictable difficulties include:

- Inability to communicate using spoken language and consequent dependence on others around them to learn alternative means of communication
- Difficulty in interpreting the feelings and emotions of others, as many of these are portrayed through tone of voice
- Possible difficulty in acquiring early cognitive experiences through active exploration, unless care is taken to provide enriched opportunities through the other senses

Children who suffer from a loss of hearing or partial loss of hearing can still live active, normal lives. Their environment must be adapted to provide numerous opportunities to learn through alternative sensory experiences. Alternative communication strategies must also be provided, both to the child and to those individuals the child is in contact with.

3. Limb Deficiencies

Limb deficiencies may involve the loss of parts of limbs, such as toes and fingers, or the loss of a total limb, such as an arm or leg. Children may be born with this condition or suffer the loss due to an accident. A lost partial or total limb may be replaced by a prosthesis that allows the child to function relatively normally with some adaptations, such as ramps or gradually rising stairs on climbing equipment.

4. Muscular Dystrophy

Muscular dystrophy is an inherited condition, typically occurring in boys, that is associated with the degeneration of muscle fibre. Symptoms may not become evident until the child starts to walk. As the muscle tissue deteriorates, the child will find it difficult to climb stairs, and increasingly more difficult to walk effectively. Many children will be confined to a wheelchair by the time they are eight years old. This condition is associated with a shorter lifespan and is usually not associated with other disabilities.

5. Spinal Cord Damage

Damage or injury to the spinal cord will result in muscular damage below the point of injury, manifested by partial or total paralysis. As with other physical disabilities, children may need to use assisted devices for walking or may require a wheelchair. They may also have little control over bowel and urinary functions.

Spina bifida is a defect in the vertebrae that protect the spinal cord. The effects of spina bifida can range from minimal to severely disabling. Children may suffer neurological damage that results in delays in or impairment of growth and development. A resulting paralysis of the lower body may make it necessary for children to walk using assistive devices or in more severe cases to need a wheelchair. Children may have some perceptual and cognitive disabilities.

6. Tourette's Syndrome

Tourette's syndrome is characterized by involuntary muscle movement such as sporadic twitches or tics. Additional symptoms may include **hyperactivity** (higher motor activity levels than normal for children of this age), short attention span, increased impulsive behaviour, and restlessness.

7. Visual Impairments

Visual impairment is categorized by the severity of the loss: mild, moderate or severe. Vision is measured by two factors: the ability to see from a distance and visual acuity (clarity of vision). Normal vision is reported as 20/20 vision.

Infants whose visual acuity is impaired or completely lacking will find it more difficult to actively explore their environment. The motivation to move is not as strong when visual stimulation is missing. As a result, motor milestones may be delayed. Additionally, early symbolic and social play are limited. Both types of play are highly reliant on the visual senses. It is hard to use objects or actions symbolically when they cannot be seen.

Children may also experience difficulties with communication skills, as they will not be able to pick up visual cues such as body language or facial expressions. Interaction patterns may also be impaired. The body language of individuals who cannot see may differ from that of sighted people. For example, some of the cues that signal interest include smiling, eye contact or varied facial expressions. These may be missing totally, and this may interfere with peer social interactions.

Children with visual impairments need to learn about their world by relying on their other senses. These children can develop normally in all other areas if great care is taken to build their confidence in themselves and their environment so they can actively explore, and if children are provided other ways to learn than through visual stimulation.

Children at Risk

Risk factors that threaten early childhood development include biological and environmental conditions that may increase the likelihood of problems in physical, social, emotional, social or cognitive development. Risk factors include poverty, inadequate nutrition, child abuse, exposure to substance abuse and environmental factors.

1. Poverty

"In 1989, one in seven Canadian children lived below the poverty line. A unanimous, all party resolution, however, set out to change that. Child poverty would be eliminated by the year 2000. Twelve years on, the ratio stands at one in five, or a 43 percent increase. In human terms, the difference translates into approximately 500 000 more children living in poverty." (Martin, 2002). Children who live in poverty are vulnerable in all developmental areas. Poor families have few resources to spend on stimulative materials, appropriate nutritious foods and appropriate shelter, and often have less time to spend with children because of long working days. "Income seems to be strongly related to children's physical health, cognitive abilities, and school achievement in the early grades even after controlling for a number of other parental characteristics, and these effects of income are most pronounced for children who experience persistent and extreme poverty. Brooks–Gunn and Duncan also suggest that the timing of poverty is important. Low income during the preschool and early school years is more predictive of low rates of high school completion than low income during later childhood and adolescence" (Behrman, 1997: 9; Brooks-Gunn & Duncan, 1997).

2. Nutrition

The two most common problems in early childhood development that may not be identified as special needs are obesity and undernourishment. These conditions are often caused by unhealthy eating habits, but both obesity and undernourishment may also be caused by a diagnosable medical or psychological condition. Obesity may also result from a lack of appropriate physical exercise.

When children are so obese that it affects their physical activity, their social and physical development may lag. Children who are obese find it more difficult to keep up with their peers, may be teased and may be excluded. For example, Jonathan was a child who was obese as an infant. This made it very difficult for him to reach the normal physical developmental milestones. At 16 months of age, he had made no attempts to stand or pull himself to a standing position. The family finally sought medical help. With an appropriate diet, Jonathan not only lost weight but became physically more active. By the time he started in a toddler play-group program, he had almost reached all of his physical milestones.

Children who are undernourished consume too few calories for healthy growth and development. Reasons for undernourishment may include a specific disability such as fetal alcohol syndrome or severe cerebral palsy. Some children may have difficulty chewing or swallowing. A number of children in Canada may suffer from malnutrition because of poverty. Undernourishment may cause lack of appropriate growth and development. Children who do not meet the daily nutritional requirements may be listless, hard to motivate or seem tired all the time. For healthy growth and development in all domains, appropriate nutrition is paramount.

3. Exposure to Child Abuse

Child abuse in any form, whether physical, sexual or emotional abuse, or neglect, leaves a lasting effect on the developing individual, particularly in the early years. "It is clear that the early years from conception to age six have the most important influence of any time in the life cycle of brain development and subsequent learning, behaviour and health. The effects of early experience, particularly during the first three years, on wiring and sculpting of the brain's billions of neurons last a lifetime" (McCain & Mustard, 1999: 7). Unfortunately, "wiring and sculpting" are affected not only by appropriate experiences, but also inappropriate ones. A PET scan of the brain of a child who has been abused will show significantly less activity in the temporal lobes of the brain. Brain growth is stunted by any form of abuse. "As a result, regions in the cortex and in the limbic system (responsible for emotions, including attachment) are 20 to 30 percent smaller in abused children than in normal kids" (Begley, 1997: 32).

Brain development in the early years goes through periods when the brain is more sensitive to stimulation. "There are windows of opportunity for these sensitive periods. For attachment, the window closes at 18 months; for self-regulation at 24 months; and syntax at three to four years. Once a window closes, the potential for growth, differentiation and connection is much less. However, that does not mean that no further connections will be made—but to bring about change after windows of opportunity have lowered is fighting biology and like trying to swim upstream against a current" (Steinhauer, 1999: 15).

Children who have been abused in the early years will suffer permanent damage, for a variety of reasons:

- First, they will have difficulty regulating their feelings. They will be more negative, will smile less and may be more sullen or withdrawn.
- They may be more aggressive, show greater frustration and have fewer strategies to deal with their frustration.
- They may develop patterns of ADHD behaviours such as hyperactivity, short attention spans and distractibility.
- They are likely to be less empathetic toward peers.
- If abused as an infant, the child's ability to form strong attachments is also impaired. This will interfere with the ability to form positive relationships with peers in later years.
- All of these factors lead to eventual difficulty in the school years. These children tend to have difficulty learning and seek high levels of approval from their teachers (Steinhauer, 1999).

4. Exposure to Substance Abuse

Children who have been exposed to substance abuse in the fetal stages may exhibit a number of physical and behavioural differences. The most common studied areas of substance abuse include alcohol, tobacco and drugs such as cocaine and heroin.

Symptoms are generally associated with the type of abuse.

The most common syndrome associated with drug abuse is **fetal alcohol syndrome**. "Fetal alcohol syndrome refers to a physical and mental birth defect that may develop in individuals whose mothers consumed alcohol during pregnancy. It is an organic brain disorder which is characterized by central nervous system involvement, growth retardation, and characteristic facial features" (Graefe, 2003: 13). According to Graefe (2003), the symptoms are specific to different ages of the child:

- Infancy—Infants may have problems bonding, be irritable, have erratic sleep patterns or cry a lot. Many infants fail to thrive, which may be tied to feeding difficulties and a weak sucking reflex. Infants may have overall muscle weakness and tend to be highly susceptible to illness. Additional symptoms include sensitivity to touch, sound and sights, and slowness to reach developmental milestones.
- Preschool—Preschoolers tend to be highly sociable but indiscriminate with relationships. They tend to have poor motor control and a low attention span. They are easily distracted and may be hyperactive. Poor eating and sleeping habits are still evident. Delays may be noted in language development and in the ability to understand dangerous situations. They do not respond well to routines or verbal warnings, and may be prone to temper tantrums.

Smoking during pregnancy also causes a number of potential problems. "Over 2500 chemicals have been identified in cigarette smoke. Most likely, the majority of the adverse effects are attributed to two main ingredients: nicotine and carbon monoxide. During pregnancy, these chemicals decrease the oxygen available to the growing fetus, and increase fetal blood pressure" (Goldberg, 2002: 1). Potential problems include low birth weight, fetal and neonatal mortality, increased incidence of sudden infant death syndrome and spontaneous abortions. "The increase in carbon monoxide coupled with the decreased oxygen resulting from nicotine constricting the mother's capillaries affects brain development, which causes later deficits in learning and memory. Researchers have found that lung damage to the offspring can last into adulthood" (Schickedanz et al., 2001: 75).

Drug addiction during pregnancy results in addiction in the fetus and the newborn to the drug used. The newborn experiences drug withdrawal symptoms at birth that could include irritability, extreme sensitivity to touch, tremors, feeding problems, diarrhea and vomiting. Later effects may include impaired or excessive motor activity, impaired information-processing ability, difficulty in self-regulatory behaviours, impulsiveness and less responsiveness to stimulation.

KEY POINTS

Historical viewpoints
- Societal values and beliefs reflected in changing attitudes toward education of children with special needs
- Rise of institutional care from 1831 to 1970s
- Segregated settings from 1906 to present day
- Inclusive care in the 1990s

Behavioural and emotional disorders
- Feelings and emotions influence behaviour and interactions
- Conduct disorders—Aggressiveness, disruptive behaviours
- Anxiety/withdrawal—Withdrawing from stressful situations
- Attention deficit hyperactivity disorder—Impulsiveness, short attention span, inattentiveness, increased physical activity
- Pervasive development disorders—autism: avoidance of human contact, self-stimulation, fixation

Cognitive disabilities
- Difficulty following directions, learning new skills, remembering or responding appropriately to others or situations in other domains
- Classification system (AMMR)—Mild to profound retardation
- Reform of AMMR to reflect supports, individuality, sensitivity and personalized supports needed
- Communication difficulties—Receptive, expressive and body language difficulties; evident in difficulty with discerning meaning of words, following directions, engaging in communication; difficulty with syntax, morphology, phonology, phonics and pragmatics
- Advanced cognitive abilities—Giftedness dependent on value and belief system, subjective in early years, difficult to measure; signs include enhanced vocabulary, creativity in approach to tasks, independence in problem solving, perception of other perspectives, ability to transfer knowledge and skills, and ability to think divergently

- Learning disabilities—Difficulty with skills in oral language, overall language, visual spatial skills, visual motor memory, perceptual tasks, visual motor-integration, memory, attention span and fine motor control

Impaired health—Identified as a special need if the disease or condition affects the daily functioning of that individual

- May result in need to medicate or provide other specialized interventions
- May pose ethical problems
- May result in increased absenteeism
- May lead to developmental delays or social adjustment problems

Physical disabilities

- Cerebral palsy—Difficulty with coordination of muscle movement with continued primitive reflex behaviour; difficulty with reaching motor milestones, mobility without assistive devices, communication, visual and auditory channels, and tactile senses; may have multiple disabling conditions
- Hearing impairment—Classified from mild to severe; difficulty in communication, interpretations of feelings and emotions, and acquiring cognitive skills

- Limb deficiencies—Loss of single limb, part of a limb or multiple limbs
- Muscular dystrophy—Gradual deterioration of muscle fibre
- Spinal cord damage—Paralysis or partial paralysis below point of injury
- Tourette's syndrome—Hyperactivity with involuntary muscle movements such as twitching and tics
- Visual impairment—Classified from mild to severe; may be delayed in reaching motor milestones; difficulty with symbolic and social play, communication skills, self-confidence and peer interactions

Children at risk

- **Poverty**—Lack of appropriate stimulation, materials, shelter or nutrition leaves young children vulnerable in all domains
- **Nutrition**—Inappropriate nutrition can lead to obesity or undernourishment
- **Exposure to child abuse**—Child abuse affects brain development, resulting in lasting problems in ability to regulate behaviour or form appropriate social relationships
- **Exposure to substance abuse**—Includes alcohol, tobacco and drugs; children develop abnormal behaviour patterns and health problems

EXERCISES

1. Trace the historical steps in the evolution of the field of early childhood education. Explain how the current philosophical viewpoint has evolved.

2. Refer to Table 3.1 on page 72. There are far more disadvantages to labelling children than advantages. Reflect on your personal feelings. Where do you agree most strongly, least strongly? Explain why.

3. What positive guidance techniques would you draw upon to help a child who is having difficulties handling his or her behaviour?

4. Reflect on the following scenario: A new child has been registered in your toddler program. When you first meet Damian, he refuses to look at you or greet you. He cringes away from your touch, sits in the corner and rocks while flicking his fingers in front of his eyes. How do you feel? What are some strategies you might need to develop to help you interact with this child?

5. Identify what kinds of problems you might expect with children with (a) communication disabilities and (b) learning disabilities. What could you do to minimize the problems listed?

6. What strategies might you have to develop to include a gifted child within a preschool program?

7. A child with cerebral palsy who is using braces and crutches has enrolled in your program. Refer to the floor plan in Chapter 1 (page 22). What additional adaptations might be needed to accommodate this child?

8. How might you minimize the effects of poverty within a day care setting? How would you involve families? What resources might you need to gather?

RESOURCES

Historical overview of special needs in Canada
www.bced.gov.bc.ca/specialed/review/report/hist.htm

History of education: selected moments
http://fcis.oise.utoronto.ca/~daniel_schugurensky/assignment1

REFERENCES

Allen, K., Paasche, C., Langford, R., & Nolan, K. (2002). *Inclusion in Early Childhood Programs: Children with Exceptionalities.* Third Canadian Edition. Scarborough, ON: Thomson Nelson.

American Association on Mental Retardation (2002). *Mental Retardation Definitions, Classifications, and Systems of Supports.* Washington, DC: American Association on Mental Retardation.

Baxter, J., & Reid, M. (1999). *Children First: Working with Young Children in Inclusive Group Care Settings in Canada.* Scarborough: ON: Harcourt Brace & Company Canada, Ltd.

Begley, S. (1997). How to Build a Baby's Brain. *Newsweek, 28,* 28–32.

Behrman, R. E. (1997). Children and Poverty: Analysis and Recommendations. *The Future of Children in Poverty,* 7[2], 1–161.

Brooks-Gunn, J., & Duncan, G. (1997). The Effects of Poverty on Children. *The Future of Children and Poverty* 7[2], 55–72.

Freiberg, K. E. (2004). Emotional and Behavioral Disorders. *Annual Editions Educating Exceptional Children,* Sixteenth Edition.

Goldberg, B. (2002). Smoking in Pregnancy. Baby Corner [online]. Available at www.thebabycorner.com/pregnancy/info/preg0046.html (29-8-2004).

Government of Ontario. (1997). Day Nurseries Act. R.R.O. 1990, Reg. 262. Graefe, S. (2003). *Living with FASD: A Guide for Parents.* Vancouver, BC: Ben Simon Press.

Hope Irwin, S., Lero, D., & Brophy, K. (2000). *A Matter of Urgency: Including Children with Special Needs in Child Care in Canada.* Wreck Cove, NS: Breton Books.

Jolivette, K., Stichter, J., & McCormick, K. (2002). Making Choices—Improving Behavior—Engaging in Learning. *Teaching Exceptional Children, 34,* 24–29.

Martin, A. (2002). Child Poverty in Canada. PoliticsWatch News [online]. Available at www.politicswatch.com/child_poverty.htm (30-8-2004)

Mash, E., & Wolfe, D. (1999). *Abnormal Child Psychology.* Belmont, CA: Wadsworth Publishing Company.

McCain, M., & Mustard, F. (1999). *Early Years Study Final Report.* Toronto, ON: Publications Ontario.

Schickedanz, J., Schickedanz, D., Forsyth, P., & Forsyth, G. (2001). *Understanding Children and Adolescents,* Fourth Edition. Needham Heights, MA: Allyn & Bacon.

Steinhauer, P. (1999). How a Child's Early Experiences Affect Development. *Interaction* 13[1], 15–21.

The Learning Disabilities Association of Canada (2004). Learning Disability Defined. The Learning Disabilities

Association of Canada [online]. Available at www.ldac-taac.ca (18-8-2004).

Winzer, M. (1999). *Children with Exceptionalities in Canadian Classrooms*. Scarborough, ON: Prentice Hall Allyn and Bacon.

4 The Inclusive Learning Environment

CHAPTER

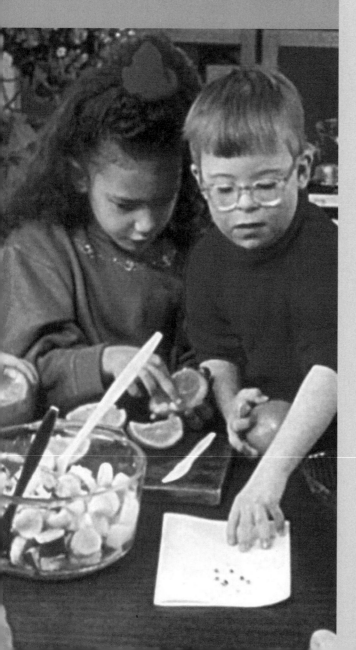

> "The Inclusive education movement focuses on the potential of learning environments for stimulating children's social and academic learning. Rather than focusing on the homogeneity of groups by asking children to conform to whole-group instruction, proponents of the inclusive approaches are asking teachers to create learning environments where children with diverse needs and abilities will be more likely to flourish" (Winter, 1999: 128).

Learning Outcomes

After studying this chapter, you will be able to:

1. Discuss the key components necessary to foster children's learning in an inclusive environment.
2. Explain how variables such as colour, the size and number of children in each learning area, light and maintenance of the learning areas affect children's activities and learning.
3. Analyze and discuss the various dimensions that are critical in the organization of inclusive settings.
4. Identify and discuss how the various core learning areas have been adapted to meet the needs of all children.
5. Define and explain what the relevant adaptations are and why they are critical to maximize learning.
6. Discuss what skills adults need to set up inclusive environments.
7. Define and discuss the role of an adult in an inclusive environment.

Introduction

The environment is a key component in fostering children's learning. In an inclusive environment, the range of abilities, the diversity of the group of children, the various learning styles and the varying needs of the children make the task of appropriate organization complex and challenging. Early childhood educators must consider all the aspects of the environment to meet the needs of the children. All dimensions of the learning environment must relate to the growth and development of all children as outlined in Table 4.1. In essence, the early childhood educators "set the stage" for learning.

The inclusive learning environment is not substantially different from other environments. The central focus is to encourage active play. The key differences are in the adaptations that have been made. These include:

- Spacing differences to allow access for individuals needing more room, such as individuals in wheelchairs
- Elimination of barriers by such means as providing ramps or adaptations to equipment to provide access and a sensory path (pavement, rugs, clear floor to guide individual to various learning areas) to the equipment or learning area
- Greater range of materials and equipment to meet all individuals' developmental levels
- Materials and equipment that are age-appropriate
- Labelling that uses pictures, symbols, Braille or colour schemes to help the child locate learning areas of choice
- Materials, equipment and organization of learning spaces that foster interactions with peers and materials
- Flexibility in routines, time and activities that acknowledges and respects the child's ability to complete activities
- Stable, structured environment that encourages predictability and comfort in knowing where things are
- Collaborative planning (including families, professionals and staff members) to develop individual program plans that identify the individual child's strengths and needs, set goals and objectives for an individual program, list strategies and evaluate the progress of the child regularly (this type of planning is referred by different names across Canada: individual education plans, family services plans or functional program plans)

Setting the Stage

"The physical elements of a learning environment help to create a psychological climate of ambiance. Whether the message is overt or symbolic the physical environment communicates information about the kinds of behaviors and performances expected of children" (Winter, 1999: 135). It is critical that adults think about the messages that the organization of the learning environment is sending. A number of variables can either impede or facilitate learning.

TABLE 4.1 **ASPECTS OF OPTIMAL CHILDREN'S LEARNING ENVIRONMENTS**

Environments	Optimal Aspects
Learning spaces that foster emotional development	• Secure, safe environment to encourage active exploration • Spaces for individual and group play to encourage child to recognize and respect personal feelings and the feelings of others • Organization that encourages independence • Materials and toys that represent diversity to foster understanding of self and others
Learning spaces that foster social development	• Organization of learning spaces to encourage individual, small-group or large-group interactions • Organization to provide opportunities to practise a variety of role play situations • Materials and equipment that encourage individual or group play • Organization to support the growth of respect and cooperation with each other
Learning spaces that foster cognitive development	• Encouragement of a variety of skills such as problem solving, decision making, divergent thinking, transferring knowledge and skills from one situation to another, and experimenting with materials and equipment
Learning spaces that foster physical development	• Open spaces to practice gross motor skills such as running, crawling, riding or balancing • Equipment that encourages development of motor skills such as strength, endurance, agility, balance and coordination • Materials to encourage fine motor development to refine grasps, eye-hand coordination and skill development such as constructing, painting, drawing, cutting and pouring
Learning spaces that foster language development	• Materials and equipment that encourage children to talk about their play, as in dramatic role play situations • Materials that foster language development, such as books, word games, picture games, videos, computers, photographs, pictures and puzzles
Learning spaces that foster individual development	• Adaptations to meet individual needs, such as a large variety of learning materials to meet a wider age range of abilities, or adaptations to the physical environment to facilitate active choices • Materials, organization and equipment to encourage individual and group learning activities

1. Use of Colour

Colour, as discussed in Chapter 2, page 48, can be used to soothe or excite children's activities. Careful consideration must be given to the colours used in the environment.

The use of bright, primary colours in rugs or furniture will place emphasis on the rugs and the furniture, as these items will stand out in the environment. Children's learning activities will be de-emphasized. In fact, these colours might also serve as a real detractor to the children's activities. Many of the materials and toys are colourful. For example, materials such as Lego or Duplo blocks are usually in

Photo 4.1

bright primary colours. When these are used on a bright surface, or a colourful rug, the materials tend to blend in and are hard to pick out. This makes the activity much harder to accomplish. In addition, children who have difficulty with **visual figure ground** (ability to pick out individual items from a background such as that shown in Photo 4.1), or with any visual problems, will find this task almost impossible. When children work on bright table surfaces, with materials such as coloured paper and various colours of crayons and markers, these are also difficult to pick out. The bright surfaces also reflect light and may lead to eye strain. This affects the ability of the child to be creative and to sustain activity.

When the walls are brightly coloured, it is hard to display children's work appropriately. Their creative efforts become lost in a sea of colour. When too much colour exists within the learning environment, children may become distracted more easily, find it harder to settle into a routine or may tend to avoid certain areas altogether.

For example, in an integrated preschool room, the following colour scheme was used: One wall was painted a bright red, with colourful depictions of the alphabet and associated pictures marching across the middle of the wall. Two bookshelves in dark blue were placed at right angles to this wall to create a book corner. The cushions in the area were bright yellow and red. The rug in the block area was an alphabet rug in yellow with brightly coloured letters, numbers and pictures in various squares. The other three walls were painted in a darker blue. The overall effect gave the impression of a dark, dull day. The room seemed very small. The furniture was in variations of primary colours: yellow, red and blue. Within this environment, the following behaviours were observed within one hour:

- Children were wandering around. Some children were running and had to be reminded to walk (eight times).
- No children were observed in the book area.
- Children only used blocks that were of a natural colour.
- There was a high noise level in the room. Children became progressively noisier during the hour of observation. The lights were flicked on and off four times to remind the children to settle down.
- The papers that children chose to draw on tended to be large and white or off-white.

From the Author   **Reflection**

Reflection

One of the integrated settings I observed left a memorable impression on me of what *not* to do. When I entered the preschool room, I became overwhelmed with the bright profusion of colours. The effect of the colours was worsened by the bright sunlight streaming in. It hurt the eyes! I was also overwhelmed with a sense of disorganized bedlam. Children were in continual motion. The noise level was overpowering. The learning areas were in disarray. Toys had been left scattered on brightly coloured rugs. These toys were hard to pick out because they blended in so well with the background. There was no area that had been created to provide a relief from the over-stimulation of senses.

I eventually noticed that one child had created an area of calm for himself. He was sitting under a table and hidden from view by a bright tablecloth. When I peeked under the tablecloth, he placed his finger on his lips to say "Shhh!" He also whispered, "You can come and draw with me if you like." I crawled under the table to sit with him. The atmosphere was much cozier and the noise was somewhat diminished. When I emerged from under the table, one of the staff members explained that this child worked there most of the time. I asked why she thought he did that. The answer was that he was very bright, but that he did not like interacting with other children very much. The staff did not seem to realize the effect that the environment had on the children.

- One child, who was visually impaired, brought the beads over to the rug area. She accidentally dropped the beads. She sat down to try to find them, spreading out her hands to try to feel the beads. She eventually gave up and found another activity.

The observer questioned the staff to find out if these were normal behaviours during free-play activities. The staff indicated that these behaviours were fairly typical. When asked why this particular colour scheme had been chosen, the staff responded that children liked primary colours. When asked if they liked the colour scheme themselves, some staff members indicated that they did not find it restful.

In contrast, another inclusive setting had decided to de-emphasize the background colours and emphasize the children's activities. In this centre, all the walls were a very pale green. The furniture was natural wood, and the floors and rugs were neutral colours. The children's creative efforts dominated the walls and display areas. When you entered this room, your eye was immediately drawn to what the children had accomplished. None of the behaviours observed in the first example were evident in the second setting.

Colour schemes should be carefully selected to ensure that:

- The focus is on children's creative efforts through displays of their art work, photographs or documentation of their activities.

- The colour does not interfere with the children's ability to accomplish their activities.
- Colour is selected to promote an appropriate atmosphere of learning and relaxation.
- The choice of colour promotes the development of aesthetic appreciation.

2. Size of the Learning Area

The nature of the activity should dictate the size of the learning area. A simple system can be used to define the size of any learning area (Shipley, 2002; Crowther, 2003).

- **Simple units**—A simple unit is one play space. Children involved in individual play such as working on a puzzle, reading a book or painting use simple units.
- **Complex units**—A complex unit is made up of four spaces. Children involved in complex units are usually involved in some sort of group play such as **parallel play** (play beside another child, using similar materials but not sharing ideas or materials) or **associative play** (children share materials and ideas, but may continue to be engage in individual play activity). Children use complex units when they are involved in learning areas such as sand, water or carpentry.
- **Super units**—Super units are made up of eight play spaces. Dramatic play and block play usually involve super units. Larger spaces are needed because block play can spread over a larger area, and dramatic play often utilizes a number of larger pieces of equipment and furniture or may involve larger groups of children.

In a flexible environment, depending on the children's interactions or needs, the size of the play area may change. For example, a single unit may change to a more complex unit because children have decided to work on a larger puzzle together or a child with a wheelchair in a simple unit needs more room to navigate in. In contrast, a complex unit can become a single unit if, for instance, sand play is provided in individual containers on a platform or on a tabletop.

3. Number of Children per Learning Area

The number of children in a play area should be flexible. Children who are actively involved in play should continue to play together without interruption. Consider the following examples:

In the first example, a symbolized form of four stick figures on a piece of paper was mounted on the sandbox. Five children were playing in the sandbox. The children were emptying and filling containers of sand. Each child had a container and a scoop. The children were talking to each other about how full their container was: "Mine is almost full." "Mine is overflowing." One child, Josh, signed, "Full." Amie, another child, promptly signed back and verbalized that his was fuller than hers.

Rachel, a staff member, walked over to the area. She indicated that there were too many children in the sand centre. She asked one of the children to count the stick people. She then said, "See, you counted four. How many individuals are there here?" Josh signed, "Four." She responded that that was not correct; there were five people. Rachel stated that there were too many people and that one child had to leave. She asked who had joined the activity last. The children continued with their filling and dumping activity. She finally arbitrarily selected one child to leave, assuring that child that she could come back when there was room.

In this situation, the adult has not realized the value of the children's play. All children were actively involved. All children were communicating effectively with each other. Each child had found enough space and materials to engage in the sand activity without causing a problem for another child. This type of arbitrary assignment and reinforcement of rules is developmentally inappropriate and cheats children of valuable learning experiences. It is developmentally inappropriate for two reasons:

- Most young children do not make the connection between symbols (stick figures) and the number of children engaged in an activity. There were enough materials for five children to use, and therefore there was room enough to play. The young child sees the world from his or her own perspective.
- Since the play was peaceful and appropriate, asking one child to leave was inappropriate. What was the message given? The children may have concluded that the activity they were involved in or the way they were interacting was inappropriate. It would be difficult for a child to find any other reason for disrupting their play.

In the second, more positive example, at a water centre great excitement was being expressed. A group of six children had discovered that they could cover the water table with bubbles and then hide items in the water under the layer of bubbles. They had also discovered that by using straws, they could blow away the bubbles to create a clear space to see and find the objects hidden. Their enthusiasm attracted other children. Harmon rolled over in his wheelchair. He consistently asked to see, but the children were too excited to hear him. Joyce, the early childhood educator, walked over and said, "Harmon would like to join you." The children promptly moved over and made room for Harmon to participate. The table might have been too crowded for that many children, but since this was a valuable learning experience for the children and since the children were interacting appropriately, there was no reason to disrupt their play.

In summary, the number of children that can participate in a learning activity should depend on three factors:

- The interest of the children—If children are actively engaged, then obviously they have made a decision on how to utilize the space effectively.

- The type and number of materials available (although the number of materials can quickly be increased if needed)—Sometimes a small group of children can be very innovative in using materials perceived to be suitable for just one individual. For example, three children were using a small six-piece transport puzzle. They created a road out of small blocks to pretend to drive the vehicles along. The puzzle frame was utilized as a parking lot.
- The type of interaction—If children are interacting appropriately, they should not be disturbed. If there is a problem, this situation can be used as a problem-solving situation. Note how Joyce prompted the children to solve the problem to include Harmon. In the following situation, Melanie, an early childhood educator, used the situation to encourage the children to solve a problem: Jordan joined a group of four children who were creating strings beads. He found a long pipe cleaner to use, but could not find an individual container of beads. He grabbed a container from another child. She promptly shouted that it was hers and grabbed it back. Melanie heard the child and asked all of the children what the problem was. Joseé said that Jordan was grabbing beads. Melanie looked at Jordan and asked him what he would like to do. He pointed to his pipe cleaner. "I see," said Melanie. addressing all of the children. "Jordan would like to put some beads on his pipe cleaner." Jordan nodded. Andrew replied, "There's none more." Melanie said, "We seem to have a problem. Jordan would like some beads but can't find any. How could we solve this problem?" The children thought about it and then decided that each could give a few beads to Jordan.

4. Type of Lighting

Appropriate lighting is important in many activities where children need to use their visual skills more effectively than usual (see the discussion on pages 47-48 in Chapter 2). The need for adequate lighting for children who have visual impairments is even more critical. Any visual work will be greatly enhanced if it takes place near natural light, or if additional light is provided such as floor lamps or table lamps to improve the quality of the light in all areas of the room. Additional lights also give some ability to the children to learn to select the amount of light they need by turning lights on or off.

5. Maintenance of Learning Environment

An environment should be aesthetically pleasing. This means that walls, furniture and floors should be clean and free of scratches, dents or holes. Tables should be tidied and cleaned after use. If the environment is left in a messy state, the wrong messages are imparted to children (Photo 4.2). Children learn that:

- leaving a mess is appropriate
- someone else is responsible to tidy up

Photo 4.2

- areas that are unattractive or have no room to engage in meaningful activity should be avoided
- some learning activities are not valued
- independent action or problem solving is not a requirement

All children need to be engaged in a regular routine. This is an excellent way to expand their sequential skills in a natural way. When I engage in an activity I need to pick up after myself, clean the table and put the materials back where they belong. Consistent expectations not only help children to become more independent, but also encourage growth and development in all skill areas.

6. Additional Dimensions

In summary, the environment in an inclusive setting plays a critical role. The environment can act as a "teacher." Adults need to carefully consider all aspects of the environment to create learning spaces that are appropriate for all children. There needs to be collaboration among families, teachers, other professionals and children to design, change and evaluate the physical learning environment.

Additional dimensions should also be considered in the effective organization of learning environments (Winter, 1999). These dimensions include:

- Softness and hardness—The softness in the environment is provided by soft furniture and items such as large pillows, carpets or grassy surfaces. Softness provides children with opportunities to relax. Hardness in the environment is provided by some of the materials such as blocks and ground surfaces such as tiled floors or pavement. Hardness encourages a different type of play such as stacking, riding or running.
- Open-ended versus closed learning materials—**Open-ended materials** provide children with a variety of ways to accomplish tasks. Examples of open-ended activities include blocks, painting or beading. **Closed materials** are materials that usually can only be used in one way. Examples of these types of activities are puzzles, dominoes or nesting cups.

- Simplicity and complexity—It is critical that the materials and experiences encourage children to move from the simple to the complex. Providing a range of materials encourages children to progress at their own rate and speed. An example of a type of material that can range from simple to complex is puzzles, which range from single knob puzzles to interlocking puzzles with a background picture, to interlocking puzzles with no background picture, to interlocking puzzles with ever-increasing numbers of pieces. Providing ever-more-challenging puzzles is a form of scaffolding, an approach described by the learning theorist Vygotsky (Vygotsky, 1962). **Scaffolding** involves a "process of providing and gradually removing, external support for learning. During scaffolding, the task itself is not changed, but what the learner initially does is made easier with assistance. As the learner takes more responsibility for performance of the task, less assistance is provided. The child receives a decreasing amount of guidance to accomplish a task" (Bodrova & Leong, 1996: 162).

- Intrusion/seclusion and large group or individual activity—Intrusive settings are those that encourage children to join others in ongoing play. For example, when Harmon heard the children's excitement at the water centre, he immediately wanted to join in. The environment should be organized in such a way as to encourage children to interact with each other in small and large groups. There should be enough flexibility in the organization to accommodate a change from simple to complex or super units of space. Secluded areas should be set up to encourage privacy. It is important that children have an opportunity to get away from the pressures that result from continual interaction with peers. "Privacy space can be created by physical barriers such as bookshelves, by reinforcing the rule that children may not interrupt one another; by limiting the number of children working at a table placed in an out-of-traffic area. Examples of space for privacy are a small loft area; activity centres where use is limited to one or two children; a large cardboard box with cut-out windows, door, and a cushion inside; a small outdoor play house" (Harms, Clifford, & Cryer, 1998: 13).

- High mobility/low mobility—The scheduling and the environment should provide areas that are conducive to high-mobility activities such as running or riding and low-mobility activities such as looking at books or drawing. Both indoor and outdoor environment should be organized to have spaces appropriate for both types of activities. For an example of both, see the floor plans in Chapter 1 on pages 22 and 25.

- Risk/safety—Children need to be able to explore safely. For example, when infants start to crawl they need the assurance that they can navigate around the environment without fear of injury from sharp objects on the floor or falls down stairs. Crawling infants also need to take risks. They need to learn to crawl not only on flat surfaces but also up and down stairs. Never letting an infant crawl up or down stairs would be a disservice to the infant. By providing appropriate supervision, helping the infant to learn how to climb down safely and providing safety gates when supervision is not possible, the adults are providing safe risks for the infant to grow and develop through active exploration.

- Accessibility/inaccessibility—All items that children can use safely should always be accessible through a system of child-sized open shelves and clearly labelled containers. Some materials such as cleaning products or medication should be kept in locked areas away from the children. Additionally, there are some materials that might be dangerous to some children, such as small beads that might be swallowed by a child who puts things in his or her mouth. These items should be placed out of reach of the children but accessible visibly. In this way, children may ask for the items and staff can supervise the activity.

- High stimulation/low stimulation—In addition to colour, discussed previously, the number of activities and materials provided to children should differ according to age range of the children. The younger the child, the fewer materials are needed.

    Young children, when offered too much choice, will get distracted from their play by other materials and activities. Preschool-age children can handle a great many choices. They have learned to concentrate on the task of choice and are not as likely to become distracted. Some children with special needs may find a full preschool setting overwhelming. Care must be taken to offer an organization that provides secluded corners in many areas of the room. In this way, the child is encouraged to take his or her materials to a location that provides opportunities for non-distracted activity.

    Timmy, a toddler, visited the preschool room. He was immediately attracted to the block area and started to play with the blocks. He saw the cars in the area and dropped the blocks and started to play with the cars. He saw another child playing with Duplo. He immediately dropped his cars and picked up some Duplo. Timmy was overwhelmed with all the choices. In contrast, the preschoolers continued to play with the activity that they had chosen.

- Predictability/unpredictability—Some parts of the day should occur in a predictable pattern. For example, children generally arrive and leave at the same time. Lunch and sleep or rest time should occur at similar times. Similarly, some routines should be predictable. For example, children should always take their shoes off before lying down for a nap and wash their hands after going to the washroom. However, life is not always predictable, and predictability can become boring. Children need to learn to cope with uncertainty. Unpredictability can be introduced by using a variety of different materials in a variety of different settings. For example, the children had been interested in rolling different types of balls. This play was extended outside to rolling the balls down a hill. This provided varying results: a light, large ball may be influenced by the bumps in the hill or the wind and roll to a different area, whereas a small ball may not roll very far at all if it gets stuck in the grass.

- Familiarity/novelty—Children need to have some sense of familiarity in their environment from day to day. This is easily established by maintaining the core learning areas in relatively static positions. If changes are made, they should be made with the involvement of the children. Children will gain a sense of security in knowing where things are and also a sense of ownership as they feel themselves able to help in creating change. The introduction of new materials and experiences maintains interest, expands learning and provides motivation to learn. For example, "Understanding of other cultures can be promoted when novel items from various cultural heritages are provided. On the other hand, more familiar items enable the children to link new information to their prior knowledge" (Winter, 1999: 141).

Josh enjoyed the baby bath area every day. He had a new baby brother at home and this was a familiar routine. He could follow a regular routine of bathing the baby, drying the baby, adding powder and diapers, dressing the baby and putting the baby to sleep. When he came in one morning the area had changed and he could not find the materials he needed. He got frustrated and stomped out of the area.

Putting the Pieces Together

The creation of inclusive learning areas must be undertaken in light of all the topics covered in the previous chapters, such as children's right to play, the elements of core learning areas, the strengths and needs of all children and the various dimensions of individual learning areas.

The following information draws upon actual observed learning areas in a variety of inclusive environments across Canada. Areas have been included based on the core learning areas as described in Table 2.2 on page 52. Representation is included from all age groups. Individual centres have not been identified, to ensure confidentiality of the children with special needs who participated in these inclusive settings.

1. Books

In a preschool setting shown in Figure 4.1, the book corner has been set up in the corner of the room on the opposite side from the noisier areas such as blocks, sand and water. This corner has been designated as a quiet area for concentration and manipulation.

One of the children, Jamie, uses a wheelchair with a basket attached to the side. Jamie wheeled himself directly to the bookshelf (Figure 4.1, 3). He got a book from the second shelf, put it in his basket and went over to the table. He navigated his wheelchair under the table, took out his book and started to look at it. When he had finished looking at the book he returned it to the bookshelf.

Children also read books outdoors. A quiet sheltered area is set up for reading in the corner of the playground. The area has soft plastic cushions on the ground covered by a blanket. It is protected from the wind. In winter, the area is in full sunlight. Children may collect books in baskets to take outside to read (Photo 4.3).

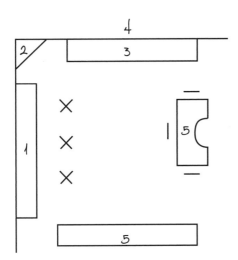

FIGURE 4.1
Books and Pictures

Key

1. Bookshelf
   - picture books and board books on bottom shelf
   - easy-to-read books on middle shelf
   - books suitable to read to children on top shelf
2. Stuffed toys

3. Manipulative shelf
   - puzzles, matching games, board games
   - easiest materials on bottom shelf
   - hardest materials on top shelf
4. Window above bookshelf
5. Table with three chairs, wheelchair-accessible
6. Adult-sized couch
X Large cushions

2. Fine Motor Activities

In the preschool setting above, the environment is adapted and organized based on the emergent interests of children and the observations made by the staff. The staff made the following observations about the children:

- They were interested in animals and in small vehicles.
- They were sorting and patterning the materials. For example, one child lined up all the red cars.
- They used the beads infrequently.

As a result of these observations, the manipulative area was organized as indicated in Figure 4.2. Since two of the four-year-old children put most of the materials in their mouth, the small animal and vehicle beads were only placed on the table when a staff member could supervise the area directly. When there was no direct supervision of the children in this area, these beads were moved to a shelf out of the reach of the children. Children could request to use these beads but could use them only when supervised.

The staff continued to observe the children in the manipulative area. Examples of these observations on manipulative materials are listed in Figure 4.3A. These observations identified the type of manipulative activity the child was engaged in and the type of learning strategy used. Based on these observations, the staff was

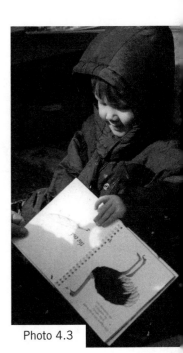

Photo 4.3

FIGURE 4.2
Fine Motor Activities

Spill Out Area
from Block Play

Key
1. Manipulative table with six chairs
2. Manipulative shelf
   a) bottom shelf
      • blocks, unit blocks, small cubes
   b) second shelf
      • accessories, tracks, vehicles, people
   c) third shelf
      • large beads, 3 puzzle racks, one piece knobbed puzzles, interlocking with background picture, 12 or more interlocking pieces
      • sorting bears, one container of each: blue, red, yellow, green
      • two large bowls and 4 dishes: blue, red, yellow, green
3. Display area

Photo 4.4

satisfied with the revisions made to the manipulative materials. They also added a display area (Figure 4.2, 3) to document the children's progress and to use the documentation to encourage continued activity. The staff also decided to add milestone documentation to the display area in the hall outside. Dillon's first beading effort was posted in this area.

Additional opportunities to increase fine motor development were available in other parts of the room. Staff observed the children's continued interest in using crayons, markers and pencil crayons. A table was set up with a variety of paper and writing tools in organized containers. Children could decide what to use and how to use these materials.

3. Art

The creative art area in another preschool room has a variety of creative activities available. These activities include painting, sculpting, cutting and pasting, and drawing (see Figure 4.4). The art area is in a corner of the room, on a tiled floor with access to water for both children and adults. Adults actively participate in creative art efforts.

The art area is a popular learning area. Children experiment with the materials in a variety of ways and for a variety of purposes. Art provides all children

FIGURE 4.3A

Examples of Observations of Manipulative Activities

Dates: Oct. 7, 9, 10, 11
Key: R = random, **S** = sorting, **P** = patterning
Setting: beading activities

Child's Name	Type of Activity	Comments
Timmy	R, R, R, R	Stringed using gimp Used only vehicle beads
Marcia	P: ABAB pattern P: AABBAABB pattern S: Elephants of different colours S: Zoo animals of different colours	Uses animal beads Fills length of gimp
Dillon	R: Used pipe cleaners R: Poured beads onto plate, then started to bead on pipe cleaner R: Put one train bead on gimp	Filled more than one pipe cleaner When Dillon put bead on gimp immediately ran to teacher to show what he had done

FIGURE 4.3B

Frequency Count of Interests of Group of Children

Dates: Oct. 6, 7, 8, 9, 10
Key: t = tally, #### = bundle of five tallies

Activity	Number of Children Observed	Coments
Tracks and small vehicles	#### #### #### #### ####	Dillon dumps bears into bowls, gets a scoop from the sand area and scoops them onto the plates, then dumps back into bowls. Usually repeats activity at least three times.
Puzzles	#### #### #### III	Jeremy has tried the vehicle puzzle five times. He puts the pieces on the tray, waits for someone to finish it, looks at it, dumps it out and tries to fit the pieces in. He refuses help from peers or adults.
Matching games	III	
Matching bears	#### #### #### #### ####	
Small blocks	#### #### III	

FIGURE 4.4

Art Activities

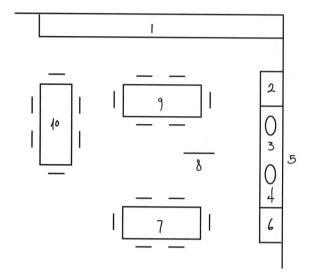

Key

1. Storage shelf
   - Bottom 3 shelves hold materials of choice for children to access
     - paper of various types
     - decoratives materials: buttons, cotton balls, glitter, scraps of material and cloth
     - natural materials: pine cones, seeds, sand, stones
     - play dough and play dough tools
     - scissors, glue
     - drawing materials: pencils, crayons, markers
     - brushes: different sizes and shapes
   - Top shelves
     - rotational materials or materials that can only be used with supervision; children request

2. Drying rack
3. Child-sized sink
4. Adult-sized sink
5. Adult-height lockable shelves
6. Three-dimensional display shelf
7., 9., 10. Tables for creatve art work: finger painting, painting, cut and paste, dough or clay, drawing and writing
8. Double-sided easel

with opportunities to actively participate at their own level, irrespective of ability. Some children simply engage in art for the sheer pleasure of watching colours explode under their fingertips. Other children experiment and try different techniques to increase their understanding of the world around them. Others create with a specific purpose in mind. The following examples capture only some of the many possibilities.

Photo 4.4

- Josh and Ted collected all the materials they needed to make their own playdough (Photo 4.4). Both boys had learned to make playdough in the past. They got out the large bowls. They went to the storage bins and got a cup of flour and a quarter cup of salt each. To facilitate this process, staff had placed the correct size of cup in each bin. Next each boy got a small container of water. The boys mixed their playdough (Photo 4.4). When they had added too much water, they added more flour to "make it less wet." Eventually they asked for the fruit-flavoured drink crystals to add colour and a fruity smell to their playdough. Josh and Ted not only gained a skill; they also became more independent and developed greater confidence in their abilities.
- Benjamin had been playing in the block area. He had created an elaborate structure for his animals. When he left to get some more animals, some of the other children changed the structure. Benjamin reacted instantly. He shouted at the children and told them to leave. When they did not leave he tried to pull them away from the structure. Michael, the early childhood educator, immediately went over to the children. He gently reminded Benjamin to tell the other children what he had wanted to do. Benjamin shouted, "I did. They didn't listen." He then promptly burst into tears. Michael suggested that perhaps Benjamin should find a soothing activity until he calmed down. He also told Benjamin that he would post a "Do Not Disturb" sign until they could all solve this problem.

  Benjamin immediately went to the creative area and started to fingerpaint (Photo 4.5).

  He created a variety of designs, covered them up and recreated them. He eventually stopped crying. When he was satisfied with his efforts, he put his work on the drying rack, washed his hands and said he was ready to "talk calmly." Benjamin was able to engage in sensory experiences to find relief from a personally frustrating experience.
- Many children visit the creative area for the pure enjoyment of creating. It is an area that encourages children to create free of restrictions and expectations. Braelyn had started to glue buttons to her paper. She decided to change the colour both of her buttons and the paper to "enhance the brightness of my efforts." She was pleased to note that she could paint the buttons to change the colours (Photo 4.6). Braelyn was disappointed when some of the colour dropped off her buttons. But she also noticed that some of the colour stuck to the buttons, and that this colour seemed to be mixed with the glue. She promptly mixed some glue and paint. She was very pleased when this time the colour stuck to her buttons.

Photo 4.5

Photo 4.6

Photo 4.7

- Dillon had watched Benjamin fingerpainting, but when asked if he wanted to join in, he quickly indicated no. Anne noticed his interest. She knew that Dillon regularly used the flour to create playdough. Ann quickly set up a table with flour on it and sat down and drew some lines. She described what she was doing. Dillon came and watched. He soon started to draw lines and shapes in the flour. He continued with this activity over several days. Dillon could use an alternative material for a result similar to the fingerpainting (Photo 4.7). Anne had recognized Dillon's interest and reluctance to fingerpaint and provided him with an acceptable alternative.
- Danielle often talked about monsters. She refused to look at books about them. Much of her art work represented monsters (Photo 4.8). She often represented

Photo 4.8

the monsters in bright, cheerful colours, and almost always identified them by female names. When asked why she painted the monsters in this way, she replied, "Happy." The staff knew that Danielle was experiencing a stressful time at home. They surmised that this was her way of coping with her stressful situation.

4. Music and Movement

Music activities provide excellent opportunities to explore and discover skills associated with such musical concepts as sound, rhythm, beat and volume, individually and in groups. Young children from very early ages enjoy creating sounds. One need only observe any infant with a rattle, a toddler with pots and pans, or a preschooler with sticks on the ground or on a pail enjoying the sounds they create.

The music area in this preschool setting (see Photo 4.10) was organized on a shelf adjacent to the block area. This organization allowed children to spill out into the block area if necessary for group or movement activities.

The staff noticed varying degrees of musical skill in the children. The children aged 3 to 5 ranged in ability from being able to beat out the rhythm of a known tune to enjoying creating sounds with various instruments (Photo 4.9).

The staff provided the appropriate number and types of rhythm instruments. Not only did abilities range in music, but also in physical competence. The area was organized to fully encourage participation by all children (Photo 4.10).

Photo 4.9

Photo 4.10

Photo 4.11

5. Blocks

Another preschool centre found that they were forced into a more inclusive approach when one of their children, Keith, arrived with a broken leg and crutches one morning. Keith usually started in the block play area. But on that morning Keith quickly became frustrated because the blocks on the bottom shelf were too heavy for him to move, and the lighter blocks were too high for him to retrieve. The staff decided to make some quick changes to the block area, but they also decided to look at this area more closely to see what overall changes could be made. During their discussions, the staff also realized that the children really did not use the area effectively.

To make the block area more accessible, they decided to leave the heavy unit blocks on one shelf at the bottom, but to add some of the lighter blocks to the bottom shelf on the other side. They created labelled bags for the unit blocks and hung these on hooks on the wall beside the building block shelf (see Figure 4.5). The staff thought that this arrangement would be more accessible for all children, as two toddlers were enrolled within the preschool setting.

The next morning the staff eagerly awaited the arrival of the children. They were happy to note that not only was Keith able to effectively build again, but the toddlers were also starting to stack the cardboard blocks (Photo 4.11).

Photo 4.12

6. Sand

Sand play is a naturally sensory activity. Children of all ages and adults enjoy the sensation of sand running through their fingers (Photo 4.12). Sand activities can be provided in a variety of ways to meet the needs of all children:

- Sandbox on the floor (see Figure 1.2 on page 22) or ground outside—Venice is ladling sand into her bucket using a full palmar grasp (Photo 4.13). The success of this activity has been enhanced by providing a ledge to place her pail on, so that she can concentrate on the action of filling. She would find it difficult at her stage of development to hold the pail and fill it at the same time. The success of her digging and filling activity has been further enhanced by providing her with a ladle that has a shorter handle. This increases her ability to get the sand into the pail.
- Sand on a platform—The placement of the sand on a platform provides greater accessibility to the activity (Photo 4.14). Children find it easier to access the sand as there is no lip to obstruct access. Additionally, children can kneel or sit on the ground to access the sand activity.
- Sand in individual containers on the table. —Putting sand on the table makes almost all types of play possible: **solitary play** (playing alone without interacting

Photo 4.13

FIGURE 4.5

Block Area

1. Block Shelf
   - First Shelf: ✱ large hollow wooden blocks
                     ● cardboard and foam blocks
   - Second Shelf: accessories, small cars, tracks, fences, natural materials such as pine
                     cones, wooden rounds
2. Hooks for bugs with unit blocks
3. Vehicle Shelf: large vehicles on bottom shelf, construction books on top shelf
4. Pictures of children engaged in block play

Photo 4.14

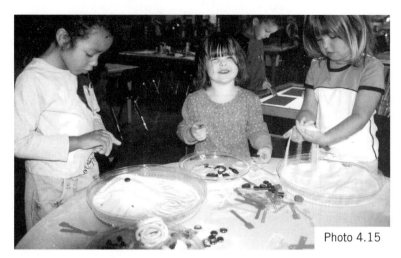

Photo 4.15

with others), **parallel play** (playing beside others, and with similar materials, but without interaction), **associative play** (playing with others, sharing materials and ideas, but continuing with own activity; Photo 4.15) and **cooperative play** (play toward a common goal that involves planning, role designation and sharing of ideas and materials). Therefore, this activity becomes very inclusive. Children at different social levels can interact effectively. For example, children who have not yet developmentally learned to share do not need to. All materials are duplicated.

- Alternatives—Using alternative materials for sand gives children opportunities to transfer knowledge and skills from one setting to another. Examples of sand alternatives include dried seeds such as peas or rice, shredded paper (see Photo 1.1 on page 4) and snow (Photo 4.16).

Photo 4.16

7. Water

Like sand activities, water activities are also naturally soothing. Children are fascinated by the various aspects of water, such as movement and bubbles, and will spend much time exploring both sensory and conceptual aspects (Photo 4.17). Water is also like sand in that it can be provided in various ways to encourage different types of play.

- Water table—Dillon and Autumn are taking turns at the water table pouring water into the water wheel to make it turn (Photo 4.18). As one child pours, the other child watches the wheel turn. The water table has been adapted to ensure the success of the children's activity by providing a clear Plexiglass centre to rest containers on. The clear surface provides opportunities to continue to observe what is happening to the water. The Plexiglass surface leaves hands free to pour and observe. This type of activity encourages associative play.
- Water containers on a platform—This type of set-up (see Photo 1.17 on page 21) encourages a variety of types of play: solitary, parallel, associative and cooperative. Children can engage in the type of social activity most comfortable to them using the supportive materials around them.
- Water in individual containers on the table—The children had been on a field trip to the ocean. They had collected many items. The children and their families continued to collect relevant items and bring them to the preschool. Individual clear tubs were set up to encourage children to recreate their "ocean experience." Michael chose his items to place into his tub from a variety of items kept on a shelf beside him (Photo 4.19). He explored various aspects of the activity by putting things into floating shells, dropping things into the water to watch them splash and stirring the water with his hands to watch the objects move. The activity was adapted to make it more successful for him. The tub was the size of the small table and therefore accessible from all sides. A towel cov-

Photo 4.17

Photo 4.18

Photo 4.19

Photo 4.20

Photo 4.21

Photo 4.22

ered the table to soak up any spilled water. A drying rack was placed on the shelf to encourage children to facilitate additional learning about water, but also to facilitate clean-up.

- Alternative water experiences—Some of these experiences could include blowing bubbles of various sizes (Photo 4.20), walking in the rain (Photo 4.21) or observing flowing water outside (Photo 4.22).

8. Dramatic Play

In one inclusive toddler setting, the toddlers had been interested in picnics. They had had picnics outside on the playground. The toddlers were also interested in housekeeping activities. The organization of the dramatic play area represented their interests.

Photo 4.23

Photo 4.24

The organization ensured maximum successful participation of the toddler group. The area was made more attractive by adding familiar items to the toddler environment. The canopy that had previously covered the outside picnic area was brought inside. To attract the children's attention, icicle lights were hung from the edges of the canopy (Photo 4.23). Some of the children were crawling, some were cruising (walking while holding on to furniture) and the rest were walking independently. The furniture that was added was accessible to all groups. In addition, the tables and chairs were sturdy enough to allow children to pull themselves up to a standing position.

The staff also created a dramatic play area outside. A large mirror was positioned securely on the fence and dress-up clothes, large material pieces and scarves were set up beside the mirror.

9. Nature and Science

Nature and science activities tie into most of the learning areas in the children's environments. Children learn about the natural world around them in various ways such as these:

- Mixing materials to create playdough—They learn about consistency and how to change it (see Photo 4.4 on page 113).
- Mixing colours when painting to create new colours (see Photo 4.6 on page 114)
- Experiencing natural events such as rain and snow (see Photos 4.21 and 4.16)
- Creating bubbles by adding soap to water and stirring (see Photo 4.17) or by blowing (see Photo 4.20)
- Learning about how materials perform differently if wet or dry (see Photos 4.14 and 4.15)

Often children discover things that fascinate them. Although the magnets had been in the science area previously, they had not attracted much attention. Mario found one of the magnets under the carpentry bench. He was delighted when he found that a nail had stuck to it (Photo 4.24). The children immediately became interested in how magnets work and what is attracted to magnets, and began actively exploring the environment to find things that the magnet would attract.

The staff set up a special magnet area in the room, with the active involvement of the children. The children thought they needed to have baskets to "collect things to test." They also decided they needed some way of showing what things were attracted to the magnets and what things were not. They finally decided that they would put the things that were attracted to a magnet on the green paper, as green means go, and things not attracted on a red paper, as red means stop (see Figure 4.6). The staff helped create documentation panels in the area that children could refer to. These panels included photographs and comments about the children's activity.

When one of the children mixed up all the items on the table, Mario told him he would help him get them back in the right place. Dillon and Mario picked up all the pieces and put them in a basket. They next took turns testing each piece. Mario would remind Dillon where the piece belonged: "That's not attracted. It stops the magnet, so put it on red."

FIGURE 4.6

Magnet Area

Key

(1) Documentation panel

(2) Red paper on table - taped down

(3) Green paper on table-taped down

(4) Shelf - magnets - bar and horseshoe
       - baskets for collections

(5) Books about magnets

10. Math and Numbers

In one preschool program, math and number activities were used across the curriculum in all areas. Table 4.2 identifies the types and distributions of these materials.

TABLE 4.2 SUPPORTIVE MATERIALS FOR MATH AND NUMBERS

Area	Materials	Activities
Books	• Base, G. (2001). *The Watering Hole*. Toronto, ON: Random House. • Bateman, R. (1998). *Safari*. Toronto, ON: Madison Press Ltd. • Dale, P. (2000). *Big Brother Little Brother*. Cambridge, MA: Candlewick Press. • Davis, A., and Petrièiæ, A. *The Enormous Potato*. Toronto, ON: Kids Can Press. • Krebs, L., and Cairns, J. (2003). *We All Went on Safari: A Counting Journey Through Tanzania*. Cambridge, MA: Barefoot Books. • Selman, M., and Donnelly, M. (1995).- *Big Tracks Little Tracks*. New York, NY: HarperCollins Publishers.	Children used these books to: • Count objects, animals etc. • Compare sizes • Compare items the child was using to items in a book Books were found in the book corner, but also in the manipulative beading section and the science corner to support current interests.
Manipulatives	• Counting bears • Sorting trays of various colours • Colour tiles • Shape tiles • Peg boards (small knobs and large knobs) • Beads: animal and vehicles available on request, large beads of various sizes, colours and shapes of various sizes and colours, gimp and long pipe cleaners for ease of stringing • Puzzles: single pieces, large and small knobbed pieces, interlocking pieces • Lacing cards • Small cubed blocks • Light table with clear glass shapes of various sizes and colours	Children engaged in: • **Patterning** activities—Child creates a pattern that is repetitive, such as red bear, blue bear, red bear, blue bear, an ABAB pattern. • **Seriation** activities—Child lines up materials according to size, such as small bears to large bears. • **Matching** activities—Child places exact duplicate of objects side-by-side, for instance matching two large bears, or two dominoes with six dots each, end to end. • **Sorting** activities—Child places a number of materials with similar characteristics together, such as lining up all the red bears on a red tray. • **Counting** —For instance, how many beads on a string, how many cars in a row, how many pegs on a peg board.

TABLE 4.2   CONTINUED

Area	Materials	Activities
	• Dominoes: with pictures and numbers • Interlocking tracks for small cars and trains • Small vehicles and trains • Duplo blocks	• **One-to-one-correspondence** —Child places one object onto another object, for instance, one bear on one circle or one shape per hole.
Sand/water	• Digging and pouring tools, such as scoops, spoons, measuring cups and containers to pour or scoop into • Measuring tools, such as measuring cups or spoons • Scales	• Measuring activities—Which is heavier or lighter: placing water containers or sand containers on the scale to see which has more or less, or is heavier or lighter • Associated vocabulary: equal to, more than, fewer, most • Counting activities—Such as how many scoops in a pail • Comparison activities—Such as more full of water, more sand or heaviest
Music	• Bells, drums, tone blocks • Bells of different pitches • Shakers of different volumes	• Beat four times • Walk and follow same beat • Listen and follow a beat • Compare sounds according to volume or pitch
Blocks	• Unit blocks • Hollow blocks • Cardboard blocks • Foam blocks	• Count how many • Compare size—build a tower taller than individual • Compare which is longer, shorter • Associated vocabulary: long, short, heavy, light
Dramatic play	• Setting the table • Making playdough	• One-to-one correspondence—One spoon per plate • Measuring amounts to make playdough
Carpentry	• Nails of various sizes • Wood of various sizes • Hammer	• Measure correct size of nail to hammer into wood • One-to-one correspondence—One nail per hole • Count—Number of times needed to hit a nail into the wood

11. TV, Video and Computers

Television watching and the use of computers is a disputed field. Much of the research talks about the hazards of technology in early childhood settings. However, there are also benefits. Thus the issue becomes one of appropriate use and adult monitoring.

"Computers should be used in developmentally appropriate ways beneficial to children, and like any other tool they can also be misused. There is considerable research pointing to the positive effects of technology on children's learning and development. That research also indicates that computers supplement and do not replace highly valued early childhood activities, and materials, such as art, blocks, water, books, exploration with writing materials, and dramatic play" (National Association for the Education of Young Children, 2005: 1).

Similar comments may be made about the benefits of watching television. There are a number of appropriate television programs that can become part of the healthy development of young children. "Children need a variety of activities for healthy development and television can be a fun and educational part of a child's daily routine, if managed properly" (Media Awareness Network, 2005:1).

12. Space for Gross Motor Play

Outdoor play is one of the important indicators of the quality of a program. Among the programs surveyed for this book, there seemed to be a general recognition that gross motor play was an important activity. Additionally, most centres scheduled regular activities outdoors. All centres had appropriate outdoor play areas. A few centres had additional indoor gym areas. For a more detailed description, refer to Chapter 8, pages 274–277.

13. Summary of Adaptations

Overall, the inclusive environment is organized in the same way that any quality environment for young children is organized. The same core learning areas are represented. Adaptations are made immediately to accommodate the need of any child. Adaptations may be needed to:

- Ensure the safety of the children
- Ensure accessibility of materials and activity
- Maximize success
- Accommodate various learning styles
- Provide for opportunities for active play

To maximize all children's learning, all of the inclusive settings make relevant adaptations based on the observed strengths and needs of the children. The adaptations made within each core learning area are summarized in Table 4.3 below.

TABLE 4.3   SUMMARY OF RELEVANT ADAPTATIONS

Adaptations to Enhance	Use of Assistive devices
Independence	• A basket was added to a wheelchair to facilitate carrying items to other areas. Organization: • The organization of materials encouraged children to find the appropriate level of difficulty such as finding a book or puzzle that was at their level.
Adaptations to the environment	Adaptations to furniture: • Tables were adapted so that wheelchairs could fit under them Traffic flow: • All learning areas were accessible by wheelchair or other assistive devices. Accessibility: • Furniture such as chairs or couches was low on the floor to encourage access by all individuals. • Furniture such as a table could provide access to child in a wheelchair.
Adaptations for safety	Potentially dangerous objects: • Objects that were potentially dangerous were stored out of reach. • Children could receive the objects, such as beads, by request, as long as the staff provided close supervision. • Furniture was sturdy enough for children to safely balance against or pull themselves up to a standing position.
Adaptations to enhance varying levels of abilities	Adaptation of materials: • Pipe cleaners, gimp and shorter tools were provided to enhance success of manipulation activities. • Ledges in the water area were provided to facilitate filling and pouring activities. • Large bowls and plates were provided to encourage filling and dumping activities. • Dress-up clothes used Velcro to make putting them on more manageable for little fingers. • Various levels of materials such as rhythm instruments and books were provided to accommodate individual differences. Limitations: • Some materials were put out in limited amounts to maximize the success of the activity, such as the flour and water for making play dough. Safety: • Sturdy materials were provided to encourage active participation without fear of breakage.
Adaptations to encourage relaxation	Relaxation: • Soothing activities such as fingerpainting were provided to help children relax. • Soft areas were set up in various parts of the room such as couches, large pillows and carpets.

TABLE 4.3 CONTINUED

Adaptations to Enhance	Use of Assistive Devices:
	Expression of feelings: • Art activities were used as a means for children to express their feelings (as with Danielle's monsters) to help them cope with these feelings. Alternative activities: • Activities more acceptable to some children, such as using flour to draw on rather than fingerpainting, were set up.
Adaptations to recognize individual differences	Maximizing learning: • Materials were changed to maximize children's success, such as providing lighter blocks for ease of building. Individualizing activities: • Greater access was provided by placing some activities on the floor, such as the sand. • Activities were provided in a variety of ways to encourage different types of play activities, such as individual sand and water containers.
Adaptations to maintain/enhance interest	• Materials were added, such as beads, to encourage sorting or patterning activities. • Points of interest were provided to attract attention, such as the canopy and hanging lights (see Photo 4.23 on page 120).

Planning an Inclusive Environment

The adults who planned the inclusive learning environments described above used consistent planning strategies. These included the following steps:

1. Observe the children—To make the learning activities meaningful to the children, the early childhood educator must first be aware of the children's strengths and needs. Observations and relevant adaptations are critical in this process (see Figure 4.3 on page 111). All domains should be observed: physical, social, emotional, cognitive and language. Observations also provide valuable information about the need for early intervention strategies. The earlier a need can be identified, the earlier intervention strategies may be implemented. Early intervention often plays a significant role in mitigating some of the negative impact of a disability (see author's Reflection).

2. Plan the learning activities and learning environment—Organize the learning spaces based on the observations and interpretations (see the section on planning of the manipulative area on pages 109-110).

3. Implement the learning activities and spaces.

4. Evaluate and observe—Evaluate if the environment has been effectively set up. If the answer to the following questions is yes, then few changes and adaptations need to be made at this time:

   a) Are the children using the materials appropriately?

   b) Is the traffic in the learning area appropriate?

Reflection   *From the Author*

Joey, the first son of friends of mine, was a child with Down's syndrome. The family became actively involved in learning how they could nurture his growth and development. One of the strategies used was to offer him enhanced stimulation. They participated in an infant stimulation program. Friends and relatives became involved to offer support and relief for the parents. When Joey was two, he was enrolled in an inclusive preschool program. Joey adjusted extremely well to the preschool setting. The family and early childhood educators worked together to provide an appropriate active learning program for Joey.

Joey moved from the preschool program into a regular kindergarten program. He handled the transition well and had a successful year. He progressed to a regular grade one program. Joey handled some aspects of the structured program well. However, he did start to fall behind his age peers with respect to many of the more academic requirements, such as reading and writing. At a case conference it was decided that Joey's gains in social skills and the social benefits to the other children warranted keeping Joey in a regular program with adaptations.

Today Joey is in grade six. He is still in a special program within a regular classroom but is coping well. He has friends his age and is participating in team sports such as baseball. He is also learning to play the piano. Without the early intervention, I doubt that Joey would have had the same opportunities.

c) Can you identify relevant learning taking place in various learning areas?
d) Do the children seem to enjoy the activities?
e) Can children use the materials and equipment independently?
f) Are a variety of skill levels provided for?
g) Are the activities accessible to all children?

5. Adapt, revise, change—Adapt and revise where needed. Change if interest is dropping or no interest has been expressed.

In summary, planning children's learning spaces requires a continual cycle of observing, planning, implementing, evaluating and observing, adapting and changing (see Figure 4.7).

Individual Program Plans

Many different names exist in Canada for individual program plans, such as individual education plans, functional program plans and family-centred program plans. The development of individual programs provides opportunities to:

- Summarize individual strengths and needs
- Provide short- and long-term developmental goals

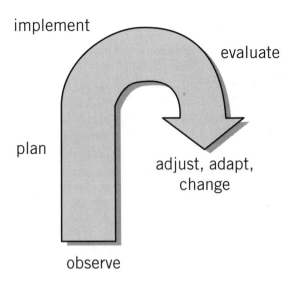

FIGURE 4.7
Planning Cycle

- Provide a summary of information about an individual
- Provide recommendations and strategies for successful intervention strategies

An individual program plan is developed collaboratively among family members, children, staff and other professionals. Each individual program plan has a number of phases:

- Collection phase—This includes collecting information from all partners, such as observations and reports from specialists.
- Planning phase—This phase should involve all individuals involved in the process. The following information is developed and agreed upon in a series of meetings:

  - Identification of strengths and needs
  - Setting long- and short-term goals
  - Identification of resources, materials and appropriate strategies
  - Support strategies needed to assist all individuals to meet the goals

- Implementation Phase—All individuals will implement the agreed-upon strategies.
- Evaluation Phase—It is important to set up a system of information sharing that gives all partners opportunities to reflect upon the progress of the child. This facilitates any necessary adjustments or modifications. A regular meeting should be set up to evaluate the progress made in all settings.

The Role of Adults

The adults' role in the inclusive environment is multifold. Some of the topics have already been covered and are summarized in Figure 4.8. One of the key concepts is to establish a collaborative process. Since many individuals are involved in the lives of all children, proceeding collaboratively is critical both to maximizing learning and to organizing successful learning experiences and environments. These individuals include parents, children, family members, staff, other professionals, community agencies and the community. A collaborative system provides opportunities for all of its members to be actively involved at all levels, organizing the environment, evaluating, setting policies and procedures, and sharing information. Each member has a key role to play in the life of the child:

- Parents and families—Families are key to the collaboration because they have vital information about their children. They have first-hand knowledge of their children's physical, social, emotional and cognitive traits (Duckworth & Kostell, 2002). Family members also have the most at stake in their children's lives. They are the individuals with the primary responsibility to their child's health and well-being.
- Staff—All staff members need to have continued support and training to help create inclusive environments for all children.
- Other professionals—All children at some times in their lives will be involved with other professionals, such as medical personnel or specialists. Children with special needs will be involved with a much greater variety of specialists. The early childhood educator must collaborate with all professionals to ensure that a team approach is taken to the health, well-being and education of the child. Other professionals can support the staff in developing strategies to help facilitate growth and development in all areas.
- Children—Children need to be recognized as individuals who are active participants in their learning. Adults need to encourage full participation of the children to plan, organize and implement learning activities. Adults should follow the lead of the child.

Staff's efforts need to be supported. The key individual to support the staff is the supervisor or executive director. The research clearly shows that a supportive director can make a very positive contribution to inclusive care and to staff morale and motivation (Hope Irwin, Lero, & Brophy, 2000; Hope Irwin, Lero, & Brophy, 2004). Support can be provided through:

- Applying for assistance in dealing with particular problems, such as applying for funding to gain support for another adult on the floor or requesting the services of a specialist to help build effective strategies
- Active listening strategies supported by the director and all staff
- Engaging in brainstorming sessions with other staff to develop solutions and strategies for common problems
- Providing training opportunities through workshops, courses and conferences

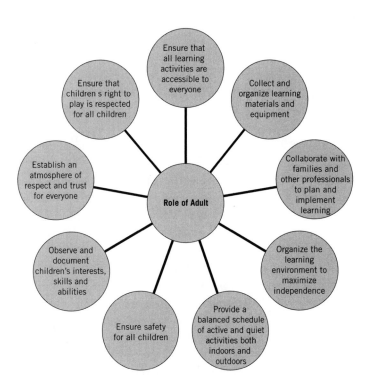

FIGURE 4.8

Role of the Adult in the Learning Environment

- Engaging in a collaborative process that encourages and values all members of the team
- Providing staff with a private space to withdraw to, as needed
- Providing resources to staff to increase their opportunities to engage in personal professional development

SUMMARY

To nurture all children and their families, the inclusive environment must be organized effectively. Effective organization should achieve several ends:

- Respect for the right to learn through play
- Nurture of all children's individual learning styles
- Establishment of a collaborative process between all individuals involved

- Maximization of learning by review of all quality dimensions of learning environments, such as the use of colour, space, developmental appropriateness and stimulation
- Adaptation of the environment based on the needs of individuals and groups of children
- Establishment of core learning experiences and learning areas within indoor and outdoor learning environments

KEY POINTS

- **Aspects of inclusive learning environments—** All aspects must foster emotional, social, cognitive, physical and language development.
- **Setting the stage for inclusive environments—**Elements to consider include use of colour, size of the learning area, number of children in a learning area, type of lighting and maintenance of learning spaces.
- **Dimensions of the learning areas—** Softness/hardness, open-ended materials versus closed ones, simplicity/complexity, intrusiveness/seclusion, high mobility/low mobility, risk taking/safety, accessibility/inaccessibility, high stimulation/low stimulation, predictability/unpredictability, familiarity/novelty
- **Inclusive core learning areas—**Books; fine motor; art; music and movement; blocks; sand; water; dramatic play; nature and science; math and numbers; TV, video and computers; gross motor

- **Relevant adaptations—**To enhance independence, to adapt the environment for safety, to provide for varying levels of abilities, to encourage relaxation, to recognize individual differences, to maintain interest
- **Planning for an inclusive environment—**A cycle of activities starting with observation, then continuing with collaborative planning, implementation, evaluation, and adaptations and/or changes, and then returning to observation to start the cycle again
- **Role of the adult—**Multi-fold: collaborative planning, implementation, evaluation and organization; organization of safe learning materials and environment; development of team effort with all partners; provision of balanced schedule; observation and documenting of children's interests, skills and abilities; establishment of an atmosphere of respect and trust; provision of developmentally appropriate learning activities and materials

EXERCISES

1. Define the key components of a learning environment. Explain the impact each component has on children's learning.

2. Using the chart provided, explain the critical nature of each of the components listed in relationship to children's learning.

Components	Relationship to Children's Learning
Use of colour	
Size of the learning area	
Number of children per learning area	
Type of lighting	
Maintenance of learning spaces	

3. Describe and explain the importance of additional dimensions of effective learning environments as listed on pages 105–108.

4. Compare an inclusive setting to a non-inclusive setting. What similarities do you notice? What differences are evident? Use the attached chart to help you with this process.

COMPARISON OF INCLUSIVE AND NON-INCLUSIVE SETTINGS

	Inclusive Setting	Non-inclusive Setting
Type of learning experiences		
Organization of the environment		
Type of learning materials		
Accessibility		
Free choice		

5. Focus on three of the inclusive organized learning activities as outlined on pages 108–125. Identify what strategies have been used to:
   • Provide for the safety of all children
   • Provide for accessibility
   • Maximize success

6. Reflect on the planning cycle on page 129. Develop a plan of action for a new inclusive toddler program based on the cycle. How will you gather observations on the children you do not know? What strategies could you use to ensure maximum accessibility? How will you decide on the type of materials to include and the type of effective organization?

7. Describe the role of the adult in any learning environment.

REFERENCES

Bodrova, E., & Leong, D. (1996). *Tools of the Mind: The Vygotskian Approach to Early Childhood Education*. Upper Saddle River, NJ: Prentice Hall.

Crowther, I. (2003). *Creating Effective Learning Environments*. Scarborough, ON: Nelson Thomson Learning.

Duckworth, P., & Kostell, P. (2002). The Parent Panel. *Annual Editions Educating Exceptional Children*, Thirteenth Edition, 12–15.

Harms, T., Clifford, R., & Cryer, D. (1998). *Early Childhood Environment Rating Scale*. Revised edition. New York, NY: Teachers College Press.

Hope Irwin, S., Lero, D., & Brophy, K. (2004). *Inclusion: The Next Generation in Child Care in Canada*. Wreck Cove. NS: Breton Books.

Hope Irwin, S., Lero, D., & Brophy, K. (2000). *A Matter of Urgency: Including Children with Special Needs in Child Care in Canada*. Wreck Cove, NS: Breton Books.

Media Awareness Network (2005). Special Issues for Young Children. Media Awareness Network [online]. Available at www.media-awareness.ca/english/parents/television/issues_children_tv.cfm?RenderForPrint=1 (30-6-2005)

National Association for the Education of Young Children (2005). Computers and Young Children. National Association for the Education of Young Children [online]. Available at www.naeyc.org/resources/eyly/2001/01.htm (30-6-2005)

Shipley, D. (2002). *Empowering Children*. Scarborough, ON: Nelson Thomson Learning.

Vygotsky, L. (1962). *Thought and language*. Cambridge, MA: MIT Press.

Winter, S. (1999). *The Early Childhood Inclusion Model: A Program for All Children*. Olney, MD: Association for Childhood Education International.

5

CHAPTER

Communication Strategies in Inclusive Settings

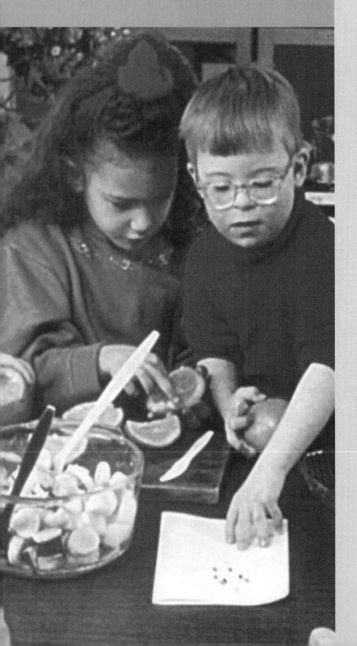

Chapter Outline

"Children develop language at different rates, and in different ways. While you can be confident that a child who is fast to talk and understand is intellectually bright, the opposite is not necessarily true—many children who are slow to talk are also bright. For other children, slowness to speak and understand is a sign of a language disorder or more general problem of development, or perhaps a hearing deficit. Language delays need to be taken seriously, because sometimes—but not always-they point to problems that need early diagnosis and treatment" (Needlman, 2000: 1).

Learning Outcomes

After studying this chapter, you will be able to:

1. Identify the components of communication.
2. Describe the importance of language milestones.
3. Identify the range of communicative abilities within an inclusive setting.
4. Discuss the various factors that affect language development.
5. Identify and discuss essential communication strategies and adaptations within inclusive settings.
6. Identify and discuss collaborative relationships to enhance communication.

Introduction

The ability to communicate is one of the most important areas of human development. All living organisms communicate in one way or another. Communications form the cornerstone of receiving, understanding and responding to a multitude of stimuli. "Speech and language are the typical human activities in communication. Language is a system of symbols organized into conventional patterns of meaning. Speech is essentially a mechanical production of language. Other methods than speech may be appropriately employed to express language—sign language and writing for example. However, while it is possible to possess language and lack the ability to speak, it is not possible to have speech without language" (Winzer, 1999:117).

Communication can be broken down into various components. These components include:

- Receptive language—This refers to understanding the intent of a message or communication (see Figure 5.1). Understanding of communication precedes expression.
- Expressive language—We're using expressive language when we respond to a message or communication, or initiate communication through verbalizations

FIGURE 5.1

Receptive Language

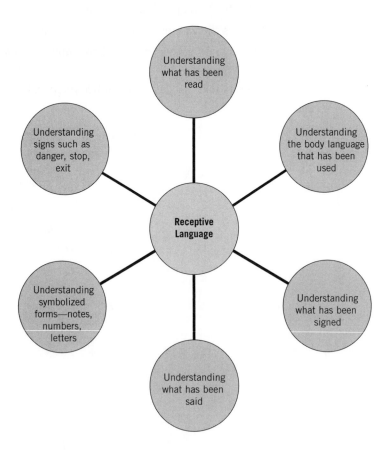

or body language (see Table 5.1). Expressive language is based on the understanding of receptive language development.

- Body language—This means understanding and responding through such physical mechanisms as facial expressions or movement of particular body parts (see Table 5.1).

TABLE 5.1   EXPRESSIVE AND BODY LANGUAGE

Type of Communication	Description
Verbal expression	- Using verbalizations such as grunts, squeals or babbling to communicate meaning - Talking in single words or sentences ranging from simple to complex - Using intonation patterns such as raising voice at the end of a question - Telling stories or relating events
Facial expression	- Smiles, frowns, raising eyebrows - Expressions to indicate feelings such as puzzlement, tiredness, anger or surprise
Eye contact	- Eye contact or avoidance of eye contact - Eye movement to look at specific items - Staring at items
Body language	- Flaying of arms and legs to express excitement - Gestures such as waving goodbye - Pointing - Turning head toward source of stimulation - Using ritualistic forms such as shaking head to mean "no" or raising shoulders to express "I don't know." - Physiological signs such as flushing or increased breathing - Blinking - Mouth movements
Alternative modes of communication	- Sign language - Assistive devices such as computers to write, or pictures or symbols to identify what is desired - Writing - Drawing

Development of Language

Language development is universal. All children pass through similar stages, but the rate of acquisition is individual. Most children acquire communication skills in their first three years; however, differences in language development can be related to the supportive environments that children are exposed to. "Differences in language development can be detected in the first years of life and by 24 months, differences in vocabulary words can be detected among children from different classes. This development is strongly related to communicative words spoken to the child during the early period of life. This period of development has a significant effect on later language development and literacy and for males, is related to anti-social behaviour as teenagers. It also appears to be related to IQ, which is influenced by the effects of the care giving environment on experience-based brain development in the early years, particularly the first year" (McCain & Mustard, 2002: 12).

Language development is also dependent on brain development. Research points to **critical periods** of brain development. "This means that the developing brain is best able to absorb language, any language, during this period. This ability to learn a language will be more difficult, and perhaps less efficient or effective, if these critical periods are allowed to pass without exposure to language" (National Institute on Deafness and Other Communication Disorders, 2001: 2). Additionally, during the periods of language acquisition, coinciding periods of brain growth spurts become evident. The first of these periods occur between the ages of one and a half and two years, the age of emergent language abilities, and the second between three and six years, when children start to use their language skills to guide individual behaviours.

Communication and language skills are learned in an interactive environment. As children observe and hear language used appropriately, they will learn to make the connections between what they hear, what they see and how to use this information. To facilitate language development, it is critical to understand how language develops and what to expect at different ages. This knowledge provides opportunities to plan and implement developmentally- and age-appropriate programs for children. Developmental milestones are outlined in Figures 5.2A–E. These charts will:

- Help identify children's developmental levels
- Serve as a basis to develop specific observational tools
- Serve as the basis for identifying communication problems or delays
- Provide a quick reference for the selection of appropriate learning experiences for young children

It takes special skills to recognize and respond to the communication signals that very young infants send (see Figure 5.2A). This is difficult because the infant's mode of communication is crying and body language. These signals can easily be ignored or misinterpreted. To respond with sensitivity and understanding, adults need to be familiar with the infant's language milestones.

At the age of four to twelve months, children quickly gain skill in communicating (see Figure 5.2B). Differential crying changes to more deliberate sound

FIGURE 5.2A

Developmental Language Milestones: Birth to Four Months

Communication Method Used	Description
Differential cry	- Crying changes in intensity to indicate needs such as hunger, pain, discomfort, need for comforting, thirst, frustration, boredom, illness
Making sounds	- Gurgling and a variety of throat sounds
Listening	- Turns head toward auditory stimulation - Looks at face of individual speaking to him or her - Waves arms, hands or legs when spoken to - Stops crying to listen to see if there is a response - Listens to vocalizations
Body language	- Uses eye contact to continue communication - Expresses excitement by waving arms or kicking - Avoids eye contact, turns head away, stops moving or yawns to signal a desire to stop to interact - Uses facial expressions to indicate likes and dislikes
Cooing	- Various vowel sounds such as "eeee" and "oooo" with addition of pitch, volume and into-nation patterns
Maintaining communication	- Turns toward sounds or voices and responds appropriately before speaker is in visual range - Imitates cooing, facial expressions and gestures such as waving or shaking the head - Takes turns: listens, then responds, listens again

patterns that mimic adult speech. **Proto-words**—verbalizations that sound like words and are accepted as words such as "da-da-da" for daddy—are the start of intentional vocalizations. Real words soon follow.

Communication skills in the twelve-month to two-year age group (see Figure 5.2C) are marked by increasing vocalizations and intentional communications. Children start to use:

- **Deictic gestures**—Gestures used to communicate infant's intent, such as pointing to or reaching for a desired object
- **Representational gestures**—Gestures used to symbolize an object, a request or an event, such as supporting side of head with two hands to indicate tiredness

FIGURE 5.2B

Developmental Language Milestones: Four Months to Twelve Months

Language Skill Used	Description
Babbling	- Combinations of vowel and consonant sounds such as "ma-ma-ma-ma" take on the characteristics of adult intonation patterns
Intentional communication	- Speech patterns and sounds resemble native language - Recognizes and responds to own name - Responds to simple requests such as wave goodbye - Imitates and initiates intonation patterns and non-speech sounds such as lip smacking or coughing - Reacts differentially to variations in voice tone expressing anger or happiness and to unknown sounds or sudden, loud noises Uses differential vocalizations to express feelings: frustration, happiness or fright - Uses babbling, intonation pattern, physical actions to express requests and to get a response - Uses proto-words - Follows simple directions such as pointing to a picture in a book upon request
Listening	- Listens to simple rhymes, songs or music and reacts through movements, gestures or facial expressions
Understanding of Words	- Understands meaning of everyday words such as items of clothing, food or body parts (an average of 36 words by eight months)
Vocabulary	- Uses up to 2–6 words by 12 months

- **Joint attention**—Child looks at an object, points to it and then looks back at the adult to focus the adult's attention on the desired object; by 16 months 65 percent of pointing is accompanied by joint attention
- **Underextensions**—One word used to represent many meanings, such as "hat" as a general term to mean all types of hats
- **Overextensions**—Single words used to represent broad categories, such as using "dog" for all animals that have a tail and four legs
- **Holophrastic speech**—One-word utterances representational of questions or statements, depending on the inflection pattern used
- **Telegraphic speech**—Utterances resembling sentences but expressed only in two or three essential words, such as "Want milk!"

FIGURE 5.2C

Developmental Language Milestones: Twelve Months to Two Years

Language Skill Used	Description
Words	- Starts to use babbling to mimic real words - Uses words related to games, routines, food and drink, people, body parts, animal names, clothing, household items, toys and vehicles, as well as prepositions such as "up" and "down" - Confuses words that sound similar, such as "dish" and "fish," until about 20 months - Imitates animal sounds and sound effects such as "yum-yum"
Intentional Communication	- Uses gestures to support intentional communication - Uses deictic gestures - Uses representational gestures - Uses joint attention—By 16 months 65 percent of pointing is accompanied by joint attention - Uses underextensions - Uses overextensions - Uses holophrastic speech - Uses telegraphic speech
Listening	- Listens to stories, looking at books as book is read and pointing to pictures when asked
Understanding	- Identifies body parts, familiar objects, toys or animals by pointing - Locates objects when asked to - Uses "yes" or "no" to answer questions - Understands increasing number of words
Vocabulary	- Uses up to 26 words at 13 months - Uses up to 210 words at 16 months - Understands 0–52 words by 12 months - Understands 0–347 words by 16 months - Understands 3–544 words by 20 months -Uses identification—"My ball" or "Look, plane!"
Expression of meaning	- Location—"Daddy here" or "Me on chair" - Nonexistence—"No more" or "All gone" - Negation—"No go" or "No hat" - Ownership—"My cookie" or "Mommy's hat" - Recurrence—"More cheese" or "Again" - Simple sentences—"Daddy drive car" or "Drink milk" - Attribution—"Red car" or "Big ball" - Questioning—"Where ball?" or "What that?"

Adapted from Schickedanz, Schickedanz, Forsyth, & Forsyth, 2001: 213.

During the preschool years (see Figure 5.2D) there is an explosion of language acquisition. Children gain rapid competence in becoming adept language users. Language is starting to be used to describe, to tell stories and for enjoyment. Also, as children approach the school years, other forms of communication are added to the child's repertoire. Children learn to read, write and use other symbolized forms such as math and music symbols.

FIGURE 5.2D

Developmental Language Milestones: Preschool Years

Language Skill Used	Description
Words	**Three-year-old:** - Expands sentence structure to three or more words - Asks why and what questions repeatedly - Uses comparative words—more, longer, faster - Repeats simple rhymes, finger plays, simple songs - Talks about things not evident—"Mom's car is black." - Describes actions, events, and feelings—"I went to the circus. I liked the clowns." - Maintains conversations by adding comments ("It's a *blue* car."), asking questions ("Why did she jump in the water?"), making suggestions ("Let's read another book.") or answering questions appropriately **Four-year-old:** - Creates more complex sentences—"I went shopping with mom and we bought a new doll for me and some clothes for my brother." - Asks and answers questions using who, what, why - Identifies words that sound alike—ball and fall - Tells stories or pretends to read to peers - Changes manner of dialogue depending on who is spoken to—for example, simplifying language to speak to younger children
Grammar	**Three-year-old:** - Uses plurals—dolls, cats - Uses "-ing" endings on verbs - Uses negatives—"not mine" or "no more water" - May overextend grammatical rules—"feets" or "hurted" **Four-year-old:** - Uses spatial terms—"on," "in" and "under" - Uses prepositions—by the tree, with Mommy - Uses possessive pronouns—hers, his, theirs; and nouns—Mom's - Uses past tense - May continue to overextend grammatical rules – "feets" or "hurted" **Five-year-old:** - Uses past tense correctly, both regular and irregular forms - Uses "would" and "could"

Communication development in the early school years (see Figure 5.2E) is focussed on refinement of skills such as increased competence with grammatical structures, reading and writing, and the continued expansion of vocabulary.

FIGURE 5.2E

Developmental Language Milestones: School Years

Language Skill Used	Description
Grammar	**Six-year-old:** - Uses verb tenses, word order and sentence structure appropriately **Seven-year-old:** - Understands and follows grammatical rules in conversations and in written form **Eight-year-old and older:** - Uses increasingly complex grammatical structures correctly
Vocabulary	**Six-year-old:** - Understands 10 000 to 14 000 words - Learns five to ten new words a day **Seven-year-old:** - Enjoys learning new words, especially long words - Looks up words in dictionary for meaning **Eight-year-old and older:** - Continues to increase vocabulary and understand more complex words
Conversations	**Six-year-old:** - Talks with peers and adults; may interrupt if excited; makes up stories to tell - Uses language to express a variety of feelings: dissatisfaction, frustration, enjoyment or anger - Uses slang and profanities - Uses humour to attract attention—jokes, riddles—and makes up funny stories **Seven-year-old:** - Speech patterns start to reflect culture and geographical areas - Exaggerates verbalizations; e.g., "My Dad's stronger than a bear." - Language becomes more descriptive with more use of adjectives and adverbs - Conversations become more coherent **Eight-year-old and older:** - Uses and enjoys word plays - Becomes fluent conversationalist - Talks to friends on the telephone - Imitates colloquial language – slang words, swear words, and curses - Compliments and criticizes others

Sources: Crowther, 2005; Schickedanz et al., 2001; Berk, 2002.

Ranges of Communicative Abilities

In any setting, children will reach developmental milestones at different rates and at different times. They will use language in different ways, understand verbal and or physical communication differently and respond depending on their ability, age and level of development. The ranges of abilities within inclusive settings can be identified as:

1. Normal range—Children who fall into this range tend to meet developmental milestones (as identified in Figure 5.2) in all aspects of communication.
2. Gifted range—Children who fall into this category may demonstrate:

    a) Early and extensive language skills
    b) An extensive vocabulary
    c) Use of complex sentence structures
    d) Discussion of elaborate ideas
    e) Creativity in making up stories and telling them
    f) Interest in reading

3. Exceptional range—Children who fall into this range may demonstrate difficulties in a number of areas. These include:

    a) Receptive language abilities—Children may demonstrate difficulties in receptive language abilities. These difficulties may include:
    *   Lack of understanding of what is expressed
    *   Inability to follow directions
    *   Inappropriate or irrelevant responses to auditory signals
    *   Lack of attentiveness to auditory expressions, shown, for instance, in lack of eye contact, absence of reaction to auditory stimulation or inattention to auditory signals
    b) Expressive language abilities—Children may demonstrate difficulties in expressive language skills. These may include difficulties in:
    *   Vocalizing wants and needs
    *   Using words and word meanings appropriately
    *   Expressing themselves coherently
    *   Learning new vocabulary
    *   Recalling information
    c) Articulation abilities—Children may mispronounce sounds and words or may stutter.
    d) Attentiveness—Children may have difficulties attending to language activities and interactions. These difficulties may include:
    *   Inattentiveness while listening to stories
    *   Lack of turn-taking skills while interacting verbally with others
    *   Difficulty in attending to conversations
    *   Continual interruptions while others are talking
    *   Self-stimulating behaviour, such as rocking or flicking of the fingers

- Easy distractibility in communicative settings
- Ignoring of requests or questions

e) Reading and writing abilities—Children may have difficulties with print materials. Difficulties may be evident in the child's ability to:

- Read
- Comprehend what has been read
- Identify differences and similarities between letters and numbers
- Learn the alphabet
- Identify letter sounds
- Spell words
- Perceive the correct order of letters in words

Factors Affecting Language Development

In addition to the potential communication difficulties listed above, children may also experience a number of problems that will reflect on their ability to communicate effectively. These include:

- Structural problems—Some children may have physical problems that interfere with their communication, such as a hearing loss, lack of visual acuity, cerebral palsy, cleft lip or a cleft palate.
- Frustrated behaviours—Children may become frustrated with themselves and others due to an inability to communicate effectively. This may lead to inappropriate behaviours such as withdrawal from interactive situations, physical aggression or temper tantrums.
- Language disabilities—Some children may have a language disorder, such as a language delay or aphasia that has a subsequent adverse affect on academic achievement.
- Learning disabilities—These affect many of the language domains. Children may experience difficulty in:

  - Listening—This not only impairs children's ability to perceive language appropriately, but also impairs their ability to respond appropriately.
  - Expressive language—Some children tend to have difficulty in using language to express themselves.
  - Articulation problems—Speech may be immature, often unintelligible, with substitutions of inappropriate words, or with some speech irregularities.
  - **Semantics** (word meaning)—Vocabulary repertoire is poor and children fail to understand many underlying concepts or multiple meanings, such as the various meanings of "fork."
  - Syntax —The children's utterances have many grammatical errors. Children often string together a series of unrelated thoughts that ramble on and on repetitively.
  - Pragmatics — Children are unable to utilize skills such as recognizing cues or turn-taking, and have difficulty communicating their intent.

- Lack of stimulation—Children who are not stimulated to talk or to listen will often suffer language delays or have a limited vocabulary.
- Restricting conditions—Some conditions such as autism, attention deficit disorder or neurological conditions will result in difficulty in conversing with others.
- Cognitive impairment or delay—The ability to produce and understand language is closely tied to cognitive development. Language learning requires that children form **mental representations** (mental pictures) of the world around them and learn to associate the words that correspond to these mental images. Any delay in cognition will cause a delay in language acquisition.
- Auditory processing disorders—Some children may have difficulty in decoding auditory speech sounds. These children will have difficulty understanding verbal messages.

Essential Strategies within Inclusive Settings

A number of essential strategies must be considered when setting up an inclusive environment. These include collaboration with partners, observing communication behaviours of children, developing individual program plans or portfolios, and planning for an inclusive environment.

1. Collaborative Processes

Collaboration can be defined as several individuals cooperating with each other to work together toward a common goal. The collaborative team consists of the child, family members, staff members and other professionals. The common goal is to improve the communication competence of the child.

A) PARTNERSHIPS WITH FAMILIES Families are the key individuals in the communicative process. Family members are the child's first teachers. Developing fetuses start to react to sounds by 25 weeks through motor activity. "And in the last week of pregnancy, they learn to prefer the tone and rhythm of their mother's voice. In one clever study, mothers read aloud Dr. Seuss's lively book *The Cat in the Hat* to their unborn babies over the last six weeks of pregnancy. After birth, their infants were given a chance to suck on nipples that turned on the recording of the mother reading this book or different rhyming stories. The infants sucked harder to hear *The Cat in the Hat,* the sound they had come to know while still in the womb" (Berk, 2003: 91). After birth, continued interactions between the infant and family members lead to increased growth and development of communication skills. Thus, children arrive in child care with a communication competency that is best known to the family members. It is vital that this information is shared and that continued collaboration is encouraged.

Involvement of the family members in all aspects of planned communication and language activity within the child care centre leads to increased:

- Consistency of learning activities for the child
- Ability to transfer language learning from one setting to another
- Increased knowledge about the child's communicative abilities
- Extended expertise—Family members, child, staff and other professionals each bring a different piece of knowledge to the table, all relevant and important
- Inclusive treatment of the child
- Respect for the child and family

B) PARTNERSHIPS WITH OTHER PROFESSIONALS   Children with perceived communication difficulties should be referred to other professionals such as speech and language pathologists. Often this has happened prior to the child's entry into a program. All professionals involved with an individual child need to become part of the working team. Collaboration with other professionals as part of the team leads to:

- Improved diagnosis of strengths and weaknesses
- Improved planning for communicative success
- Inclusive communicative activities that focus on all children's strengths and needs
- Identification of appropriate resources
- Increased use of developmentally-appropriate and age-appropriate techniques
- A coordinated effort between all individuals: staff, family members, professionals and the child.

2. Observing Communicative Behaviours

To ensure the success of planned activities, observation of the child's progress is critical. Accurate and complete information about a child's communicative abilities leads to:

- Improved diagnosis of strengths and needs
- Individual and pertinent planning
- Identification of appropriate strategies and resources
- Collaboration among partners: family members, other professionals and the child
- The ability to plot progress
- Maximizing the success of experiences through use of the child's observed strengths, interests and abilities in the planning and implementation of activities

When a language difficulty is suspected, a screening tool should be used. Screening tools are usually age-specific, geared to infants (see Figure 5.3), toddlers (Figure 5.4) and preschoolers (Figure 5.5). Each tool is further divided into smaller age groups. This makes it easier for the observer to identify a specific age group in

FIGURE 5.3

Screening Checklist for Infants

Age	Skill	Comments
By 3 months	Coos Establishes eye contact Looks at and listens to caregiver Turns toward source of sound Startles at loud or unexpected sounds Reacts by smiling	
By 6 months	Adds babbling to cooing sounds Imitates and initiates sounds Takes turns—listens, responds, listens Reacts differentially to different voices Responds to facial expression	
By 9 months	Uses body language to express intent, such as pointing to a desired object Responds to own name Mimics adult intonation patterns Takes turns during vocal play Responds appropriately to "no" Uses vocalizations during play	
By 12 months	Points to items in environment or books Imitates gestures Demonstrates understanding of simple sentences —For example: "Go out?" Child runs to door Uses proto-words Listens to simple rhymes, music, songs, books Plays games such as peekaboo	
By 15 months	Repeats words, phrases Uses words Uses holophrastic speech Follows simple directions, such as "Get the car"	
By 18 months	Names familiar objects Talks while playing with toys Answers questions by pointing or using words Uses "no"	

order to observe a specific skill set associated with it. When competency in one or more items is identified as lacking, referral to a speech and language specialist should be made. Screening tools help in many ways. They can:

- Confirm or deny the suspicion of language difficulties
- Isolate the type of problem
- Provide a means of sharing information with families, staff and other professionals
- Compare the language of the child to developmental norms to assist with decisions about the next steps

- Form the basis of a referral to a specialist
- Facilitate the development of a specific communication program to meet the strengths and needs of individual children

FIGURE 5.4
Screening Checklist for Toddlers

Age	Skill	Comments
By 2 years	Uses telegraphic speech Locates objects upon request Identifies body parts, familiar objects, animals, people, by naming or pointing Asks questions, such as "Why?" or "What?" Uses descriptive words Repeats simple rhymes, finger plays or songs Initiates and maintains verbal interactions Uses words to indicate non-existence Uses "no" appropriately Uses possessives, such as "my," "Mommy's" Requests more of something	

FIGURE 5.5
Screening Checklist for Older Toddlers and Preschoolers

Age	Skill	Comments
By 3 years	Uses sentences of three or more words Asks questions repeatedly Follows two-step directions, such as "Get your ball in the hall, please" Uses plurals Talks about things not present May overextend grammatical rules	
By 4 years	Uses complex sentences Asks and answers questions Tells stories Uses pronouns: I, me, you, he, she Uses possessives: hers, his, theirs, Mom's Uses spatial terms: on, in, under May overextend grammatical rules	
By 5 years	Explains concepts Talks about past, future, present Uses word endings for irregular verbs	

Sources: Crowther, 2005; Hanen, 2002

3. Individual Program Plan

The individual program plan (IPP) is a written plan that describes the communication program and services required by an individual child. A typical communications IPP will include observations and assessments, identification of strengths and needs, goals and objectives, strategies, implementation activities and evaluation and review. Figure 5.7 is an example of a communications IPP that was set up and implemented in collaboration with the speech and language pathologist, the staff and the family members within the Loyalist College Preschool Curriculum Lab.

The IPP usually starts with a section that identifies a specific communication problem. The identification of this problem has been diagnosed through observations (by family members and staff) and most often is accompanied by a formal assessment by a speech and language therapist. The assessment information is then used to develop a profile of the child that includes strengths, needs, goals and objectives. This profile forms the basis of a plan of action: strategies and implementation activities. The child's progress is tracked through the implementation, and the IPP is reviewed regularly to identify adaptations, additional strategies or new strategies as needed. Simplified, the process can be represented in the flow chart shown in Figure 5.6.

FIGURE 5.6

IPP Process

problem identification → observation & assessment → identification of strengths & needs → setting goals & objectives → identifying strategies → implementation → review → adaptations & changes

FIGURE 5.7

Communications IPP

Name: Jordan   **Age:** 2.8
Date: October 5, 2004
Summary of Diagnosis

1. **Diagnosis by Speech Pathologist**
    a) **Expressive language**—Severe speech delay caused by a choroid plexus cyst located near the speech centre of the brain
    b) **Receptive language**—Within high normal range

2. **Observations of Family Members**
    a) **Expressive**—Uses only grunts, pointing and pulling individuals to what he wants
    b) **Receptive**—Family feels that Jordan understands well
    c) **Behaviour**—Jordan and family members are frustrated at his lack of ability to speak

FIGURE 5.7

Continued

---

3. **Observations of Day Care Staff**
   a) **Expressive**—Uses cooing and babbling sounds; grunts; points or pulls staff toward what he wants
   b) **Receptive**—Normal
   c) **Behaviour**—Usually engages in solitary play. He is self-sufficient in choosing his activities and finding his own materials. He is easily frustrated when he is not understood; he cries and withdraws from the situation.

Observations and Assessment
Language Screening Checklist for Jordan (Home)
Date: September 30, 2004   **Observers:** Family members

Skill	Comments
Telegraphic speech	No verbalizations used
Location of objects upon request	Willingly and accurately brings requested item
Identification of body parts, objects, people, animals	Uses pointing to identify—all major body parts, common objects around house, family members and friends, farm animals around our farm; especially likes pet cat
Asking questions	Points to items and grunts to indicate he wants them, or pulls one of us to the object and points
Use of descriptive words	Indicates size by hand motion
Repeating of rhymes, finger plays, songs	- Listens to rhymes, finger plays and songs - Smiles, laughs and uses appropriate hand gestures - Favourites: Twinkle, Twinkle Little Star; Pat-a-Cake; Baa, Baa Black Sheep; Head and Shoulders - Brings over nursery rhyme book to have it read to him
Use of words to indicate non-existence	Uses head shake or moves hands back and forth
Possessives	Pats his chest to indicate something is his
Requests for more	Points or pulls person to what he wants; shows empty container to indicate he wants more

FIGURE 5.7
Continued

Language Screening Checklist for Jordan (Preschool)
Date: September 25-30, 2004   **Observers:** Jane, Jonathan

Skill	Comments
Telegraphic speech	Uses series of grunts, some babbling and cooing sounds
Location of objects upon request	Brings items requested immediately; also brings items requested of another child
Identification of body parts, objects, people, animals	Uses pointing to identify; seems to understand plays with animals as well as other children in his group and makes some animals sounds: moo, baa
Asking questions	- Tends to play by himself - Does not indicate what he wants but rather gets it himself - Stops to listen when questions are asked by other children
Use of descriptive words	Shows big, small, tall, long, short, heavy using hand motions
Repeating rhymes, finger plays, songs	First to arrive at story time; uses appropriate body language to support what he has heard
Use of words to indicate non-existence	Empty—looks at container and places hands palms up More—uses sweeping finger motion to indicate more
Possessives	Pulls object toward him, clutching it tightly to his chest
Requests for more	- Points or pulls person to what he wants - Holds container upside down to indicate he wants more to drink - Points to food then plate to indicate he wants more to eat
Behaviour	- Tends to stay away from other children - Cries and withdraws if not understood

Identification of Strengths and Needs

Strengths	Needs
Receptive language skills in normal range	Expand sound production of vowels and consonants
Communicates with gestures	Combine sounds into words
Uses babbling and cooing sounds	Interact with other children to communicate

FIGURE 5.7

Continued

Interests
Interested in books, songs, finger plays
Plays with animals

Goals
Jordan will
1. Increase his vocalizations
2. Develop an expressive vocabulary
3. Interact with other children

Objectives
Jordan will:
1. Use initial sounds every time he requests something or answers questions, such as "mm" for milk
2. Interact with a small group of children with similar interests during free play activities

Strategies
1. Objectives will be implemented at home, within speech therapy sessions and at pre-school.
   • Within preschool daily: at meal times, at reading or music and movement times, and during animal play
   • At home daily with similar animals and books, and at meal times
   • At weekly sessions with the speech therapist
2. Jordan's interests will be used to encourage interactions with other children. Strategies:
   • Set up the manipulative area to encourage parallel play with animals
   • Set up a similar play area at home to encourage play with siblings
3. Positive feedback will be given every time Jordan uses vocalizations.
4. Progress will be monitored at home, during therapy and within preschool.
   • Observation evaluations filled in at home and at day care, with the master form kept at day care
   • Observations sent to speech pathologist weekly
   • Team meetings held as directed by speech and language pathologist or as requested by other team members
   • Monthly review of communication plan

Evaluation of Jordan's Progress
Evaluator(s): Jane, Mother

Date	Type of Vocalization	Setting
Oct. 6	Requested milk—"M?"	Snack table
Oct. 6	Listened to Alicia say "Grr." smiled. picked up another dog and grunted	At home with sister during animal play

4. Individual Portfolio

Another strategy that is receiving increasing acceptance and use is the creation of an individual portfolio. The portfolio is written as a collaborative process with all individuals involved. Jordan's portfolio was developed collaboratively with Jordan, his family members, the speech and language pathologist and the preschool staff. A communication portfolio particularly lends itself to reporting the progress in speech and language. The portfolio grows with the changing abilities of the child. This serves to give a complete picture over time about a child's abilities. The same information is provided about Jordan, but in a way that tells the story of his progress (see Figure 5.8).

In summary, the portfolio provides an alternative way of capturing a child's abilities over time. The biggest advantage of the portfolio is that the child becomes an active partner in the creation of the portfolio, in the ongoing evaluation of his or her skills, and in the tracking of his or her successes and adaptations.

5. Planning for an Inclusive Environment

The IPP or portfolio processes are similar to what should be used when planning activities within an inclusive setting. Planned activities should focus on the strengths, needs and interests of all the children. The activities should be a collaborative effort between all partners: children, staff, families and professionals such as a speech creationists, resource consultants and speech and language pathologists.

The steps in the planning process for an inclusive communication environment need to include the following elements: identification of the communication needs, skills, abilities and interests of the children within the program, and possible strategies for implementation. The steps used will reflect the process used in the Loyalist College Preschool Curriculum Lab.

A) IDENTIFICATION OF SPECIFIC COMMUNICATION NEEDS The following conditions were identified within this preschool setting:

- Speech delay (see Jordan's IPP)
- Overall language delay; uses signing to communicate—one child
- Expressive language delay—three children
- Superior communication skills—three children
- Attention deficit disorder—one child

B) COMMUNICATION SKILLS OF CHILDREN WITHIN THE PROGRAM The staff created a milestone graph to indicate the overall communication skills and abilities of the group of children (Figure 5.9). This information was gathered from individual observations of staff, family and assessments from the resource consultant and speech and language therapist.

FIGURE 5.8
Jordan's Individual Communication Portfolio

Purpose of Jordan's Portfolio

"My name is Jordan. This is my portfolio. It will tell you about me and my communication skills. It will tell you who I am, what I can do and about my interests. This portfolio will help all of us to improve my ability to talk and interact with others."

This portfolio has been developed for Jordan by his grandmother, his teachers and his speech and language pathologist. The portfolio was developed on October 5, 2004. At this time, Jordan was 2.8 years old. He attended a half-day preschool program five mornings a week. He visited a speech and language pathologist once every week.

This portfolio will provide a record of Jordan's communication activities. The portfolio will contain the following sections: Likes and Dislikes, Things That Jordan Does Well, Individual Goals and Objectives, Strategies to Help Calm Jordan, Activities and Evaluation.

The information in this portfolio was gathered with Jordan's help. He initiated many activities such as pointing to or bringing things to indicate what he liked. Any information that was put into the portfolio was always read to him. Jordan often took his portfolio to his speech therapy sessions and home, so he could add information.

What I Like

I like to listen to stories. I like the book Classic Nursery Rhymes.

I like books about animals.

I like to paint on the divider.

I like to build houses for my animals.

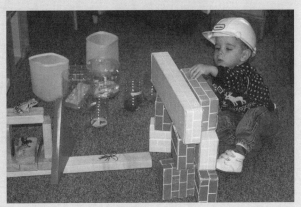

FIGURE 5.8
Continued

I like to make necklaces with animal beads.
I like to make necklaces with Shanleigh.

I like to play with Colin.
We like to make tornadoes.

FIGURE 5.8
Continued

I like to play the triangle.
I like playing to "Twinkle, Twinkle, Little Star."

What I Don't Like

I get angry when people don't understand me.
I want people to understand me.
I don't like it when someone takes my things away.
I don't like it when someone breaks my buildings.
I don't like it when some kids don't leave me alone.
I don't like it when my grandmother leaves. I cry.

What I Can Do Well

I understand everything.
I can do the actions to songs and finger plays.
I can make the sounds of animals: "Sssss" for
a snake and "Moo" for a cow.
I can make things work. I can do it by myself.
This is an "um." I can say some sounds.

FIGURE 5.8
Continued

I can sort. I can sort all the fish and all the farm animals. I can sort all the coloured vehicles: blue cars, red fire trucks and orange planes.

I can clean up by myself. I don't need someone to remind me. I clean up my toys at home.

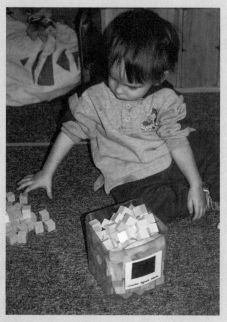

My Goals

I am going to increase what I can say. I will make more sounds.

I will learn to say words.

I will play with other children.

My Objectives

I will make a sound every time I want something.

I will say short words like "not," and "my."

I will join other children who are doing things I like.

FIGURE 5.8
Continued

What to Do When I Get Upset

When I get upset and cry when my grandmother leaves, I want to wave goodbye from the window.

When I get upset when you don't understand, hug me and try again.

Activities

I want to do things I like.

I like you to tell me when I have done good work.

I want to put shapes on my chart.

I want to mark on paper when I can do something.

I like going to see Ann (speech and language pathologist).

I like to play with Colin and Shanleigh.

Evaluation

1. Tracking Progress

When Jordan used letters or words to interact, the sound or word was added to the chart. Jordan would then place a sticky shape on his chart.

2. Collections

When Jordan presented any work that he then chose to talk about, it was collected and put into his portfolio.

Jordan's Art Work
October 11
Jordan used orange, red, green and blue markers.
He brought his art work to Jane and pointed to and said "o" for orange, "boo" for blue and "gr" for green.

Jordan's Progress
Oct. 10, Oct. 11

Letters I use

m
s
k
b
o
gr

Letters I can say

moo
no
my

FIGURE 5.9
General Range of Communication Skills of the Children in the Program

Area	Range of Skills
Expressive language skills	babbling, proto-words, holophrastic speech, telegraphic speech, complex sentences, story-telling, explaining concepts
Receptive language	turns toward voice or sound, listens and uses body language to respond, points to identify, follows simple directions, follows complex directions
Body language	No eye contact, eye contact, uses facial expressions, uses gestures, points or pulls individuals to indicate desire
Signing	Uses sign language to communicate

C) INTERESTS OF THE CHILDREN Additionally, the staff created a frequency count to identify the most common interests of the children (see Figure 5.10). The staff also created a bulletin board to encourage input from families. The bulletin board (shown in Figure 5.11) served to identify interests and encouraged families to add information.

FIGURE 5.10
Common Interests of Children

Dates: October 2–4
Observers: Jane, Jonathan

Interest Areas	Frequency	Interest Activities	Frequency
Sand	||||/ ||||/ ||||/ ||||/ ||||/ ||||/ ||||/ ||||/ ||||/ ||||/ ||||/ III	Beading:	
		- Animal beads	||||/ ||||/ II
Water	||||/ ||||/ III	- Vehicle beads	||||/ IIII
Carpentry	||||/ ||||/ ||||/ ||||/ ||||/ ||||/ ||||/ ||||/ III	**Baby bathing**	||||/ ||||/ ||||/ II
Art	||||/ ||||/ ||||/ ||||/ III	Dinosaur structures	||||/ ||||/ ||||/ ||||/
Sculpting	||||/ III	Animals in sand play	||||/ ||||/ III
Sewing	||||/ ||||/ ||||/ ||||/ III	Vehicles and tracks	||||/ ||||/ ||||/ III
Books	||||/ IIII	Rhythm instruments	||||/ ||||/ III
Quiet	||||/ ||||/ ||||/ ||||/ ||||/ ||||/ III	Lego construction	||||/ IIII
Drama	||||/ ||||/ II		
Music	||||/ ||||/ ||||/ ||||/ ||||/ ||||/ I		
Blocks	||||/ ||||/ ||||/		
Gross motor manipulatives	||||/ ||||/ ||||/ ||||/ IIII		

FIGURE 5.11

How to Display a Bulletin Board

We like Animals and Cars
Children's Dictation

- We like to use animals in the sand box.
- We like to make animal environments.
- We construct vehicles from Lego.
- We like to play the rhythm instruments. Shanleigh likes to keep time to "Listen to the Horses Clipping Clopping."

- We like to make long strings of animals or vehicles.
- We like the magnetic animal puzzles.
- Jordan likes the animal books. He just pointed to them.
- We like to make animals swim in the water.

What I like

What I like

FIGURE 5.11
Continued

What I like

"Our horses are galloping. They like to gallop quickly. The Arabian stallion is the quickest. The colts are the slowest."

What We Created

"We collected log rounds, small logs and rocks to create a pond. We used pond animals like snakes, lizards, frogs, turtles and insects. The blue bulletin board is our water."

Please Add Photographs or Other Interests to Our Board

Ted likes to use plastercine to make dinosaurs.

Jessica particularly likes the book *Where the Wild Things Are*.

D) STRATEGIES FOR IMPLEMENTATION The information collected was used to plan the organization of the environment and the specific related language activities. The information gathered about the children's abilities served to help staff to understand the range of language activity that needed to be represented within the environment. This understanding made it possible for staff to:

- Utilize the information on individual IPPs; for example, in Jordan's case, to engage Jordan in daily language activities while he was enjoying his active play of choice and while he was with other children
- Engage in spontaneous language activities as children were engaged in the regular activities of the day
- Plan for language activities in the variety of interest centres—The staff in collaboration with the speech pathologist brainstormed activities that could occur while children were actively engaged in activities around the room
- Use the children's interests to motivate language development as needed
- Provide the resources and materials needed to encourage continued development and interest

i. Strategies to Encourage Expressive Language Activities Activities should be set up in ways to encourage active interactions between children and adults. This can be done by:
- Providing sufficient materials of interest

   An example would be duplicate sets of animal beads and vehicle beads, with enough beads to engage more than one child in active play (see Figure 5.12 and Photo 5.1).
- Providing space to play in close proximity with each other

   For instance, using a long, narrow table so that all children can see each other and retrieve materials readily.
- Observing children's play and spontaneously facilitating appropriate expressive language activities

   For example, Jane, the early childhood educator, noticed that Jordan and Shanleigh were beading. She sat down near the two children and started to identify the animals that Jordan was putting on his string. She then also verbalized the animal sound. Shanleigh quickly imitated Jane. Jordan became involved as he too started to imitate the animal sounds made. The two children laughed at each other as they put the beads on the string and made the sounds. In this way, two of Jordan's needs were met: his need to interact with other children and his need to vocalize during play.
- Encouraging dialogue with children in a variety of interest centres

   Michael was using sea animals and other related materials at an individual water play area (Figure 5.12, Photo 5.3). Jonathan noticed his activity. He verbally reinforced Michael's activities by labelling the animals he was using: "The crab is sitting at the bottom." He also described the activities that Michael was engaged in: "Oh, look! You put the crab into the shell. The crab and the shell are floating on top of the water." Michael responded by looking at the shell and crab and smiling.

FIGURE 5.12

Documentation of Children's Skills and Interests

We are interested in animals.

Photo 5.1

Photo 5.2

- We like to make necklaces out of animal beads.
- We know the names of the animals and the colours.

- I like to paint the animals, especially the green ones.

Photo 5.3

Photo 5.4

- I like to make the water animals float.

- We like to learn more about the various types of horses.

FIGURE 5.12

Continued

Photo 5.5

- I like to play along to "Listen to the Horses Clipping Clopping."

Photo 5.6

- I like to look at the animals closer.
- They look larger.
- I can see things like how many legs. I can see the feelers and wings.

Photo 5.7

- We like to create habitats for our animals and dramatize their activities within the habitats.

I like Building Vehicles

I like:
- big trucks
- long trucks

Photo 5.8

Photo 5.9

- Becoming aware of the type of language that the adults could reinforce at each area

For example, the staff recognized that some of the children had superior language abilities. The staff also recognized that they did not always have the language expertise in some content areas. Liesl and Hannah had been very interested in the different type of horses (Figure 5.12, Photo 5.4). The staff created a list of all the toy horses available within the centre. They also created a display of the various horses on a bulletin board, along with various books on horses. Pictures of the toy horses were mounted on cards that were labelled so that children could match the picture to the real horse. This gave staff the opportunity to label the horses and activities appropriately.

- Providing additional materials to continue children's interests or expand the learning activity

The children's interest was expanded by providing additional animal puzzles. These puzzles also expanded the learning activity by providing opportunities to complete puzzles in an alternative way, by using a magnetized pole. Children gained the opportunity to talk about magnetism. Interest was also expanded to encourage looking at the details of the pictures of the animals on the puzzle with a magnifying glass. Miranda was able to identify the number of legs the insect had, that a moth had long feelers and that some insects had two wings (Figure 5.12, Photo 5.6). Her excitement sparked the interest of other children. Soon there were a number of children communicating with each other to look for and identify different items.

- Following a set program as developed in collaboration with the speech and language pathologist and the family members

The target sounds for Jordan for the week might be "k" and "s." The pond activity (Figure 5.12, Photo 5.7) presented a wonderful activity to practice the "s" sound, as a variety of snakes were available for this type of play.

- Reading related stories about animals to children

Reading provides children with opportunities to:
  - Hear spoken language
  - Make associations between the printed word and the verbalization, or sign language
  - Answer questions verbally or through pointing
  - Gain understanding of words in context and through picture clues
  - Enjoy listening activities

- Providing language materials and activities at various levels that are both age appropriate (appropriate for the chronological age) and developmentally appropriate:
  - Books, including picture books, **easy reading books** (with large pictures and few words, with words explaining the meaning of pictures), picture dictionaries, **research books** (books that encourage children to find infor-

mation for themselves), **read–aloud books** (books that adults read to children) (see page 176, resources for reading)
A variety of literature should be provided: nursery rhymes, finger plays, fairy tales, fables, poetry, fiction and non-fiction.
- Music to listen to, to use musical instruments with, to move to or to sing along with. Songs can include:
  - Simple and repetitive songs such as "Mary Had a Little Lamb"
  - Action songs such as "Head and Shoulders" or "I'm a Little Teapot"
  - Action games such as "Ring Around the Rosie"
  - Music or songs to play rhythm instruments to, such as "Listen to the Horses Clipping Clopping"
  - Songs supported by books, where the child can look at the book while listening to the song (Siomades.L., 1999; Adams, 1973)
- Language games such as picture dominoes, matching card games, match a sound, rhyming words or what goes together
- Puppets: finger puppets, hand puppets, puppet theatre
- Feely boxes—The feely box is used to hide things in. The child puts his or her hand into the sleeve to find the object in the box and guesses what it is. Children can be encouraged to describe what they feel.

ii. Strategies to Encourage Receptive Language Activities   Children need to hear or see (in writing or signing) language used. The child needs to learn to associate the words with items, ideas, events, people or animals. This allows the child to form the mental representations needed to remember and use the words. Strategies to use for children who need to develop receptive language skills include the following:
- When the child is engaged in activity such as looking at something, pointing at something or playing with something, the facilitator should use this opportunity to talk about what the child is looking at.

FIGURE 5.13
Feely Box

Photo 5.10

Photo 5.11

Photo 5.12

For example, Ann said to Robert, "Those are red sparkles, red sparkles." This was both verbalized and signed.

Dillon turned the container of sparkles around repeatedly. Ann: "I see the sparkles are moving!" Dillon stopped and looked at Ann and smiled.

Dillon spread glue on his creation and shook sparkles on the area. Ann: "The sparkles are sticking to the glue."

Dillon looked at the area with the sparkles in it. Ann: " Look, this red area is shiny. This one is not." Dillon pointed to the shiny area. Ann: "It is shiny." (Photo 5.10)

- Encourage children to look at books or read books to them.

Ann had read a book about insects to the children. Levi had been playing in the sand area. He continually stopped his activity and looked over at Ann and the book she was reading to the other children. When Ann had finished reading the book, Levi went over, picked up the book and looked at it (Photo 5.11).

Ann noticed his activity. She followed Levi's lead and verbalized what he was doing. He was counting the ladybugs. Ann counted them aloud to him.

- Use an approach that is multi-sensory.

Pritti had set up individual bubble play areas to involve some of the children who normally avoided larger group activities. Keegan was fascinated by the texture of the bubbles. He listened to Pritti describe the activity. He eventually started to feel the bubbles that Pritti held. Eventually, Keegan placed his hands into the bubble mixture and started to explore the bubbles himself (Photo 5.12). When Pritti said she was going to blow some bubbles, Keegan stopped, watched and smiled. He imitated the action immediately.

- Utilize materials that encourage listening—Activities that lend themselves to listening include those shown in Table 5.2.

- Model appropriate language. Avoid using slang. Enunciate words clearly. Look at the child while speaking. Speak at the appropriate volume and slowly. Use a variety of expressive intonation patterns to speak.

iii. Strategies to Encourage Communication Through Body Language Communication involves a number of different supportive body language signals. These include hand movements and gestures, facial expressions, eye contact, body posture and body movement. "Gestures and body language communicate as effectively as words—maybe even more effectively. We use gestures daily, almost instinctively, from beckoning to a waiter, or punctuating a business presentation with visual signals to airport ground attendants guiding an airline pilot into the jetway or a parent using a whole dictionary of gestures to teach (or preach) to a child" (Imai, 1966: 1).

Body language varies from culture to culture and from individual to individual. "As the global village continues to shrink and cultures collide, it is essential for all of us to become more sensitive, more aware, and more observant to the myriad motions, gestures, and body language that surround us each day. And as many of us cross over cultural borders, it would be fitting for us to respect, learn, and understand more about the effective yet powerful 'silent language' of gestures" (Imai, 1966: 1).

TABLE 5.2 **MATERIALS TO ENCOURAGE RECEPTIVE LANGUAGE DEVELOPMENT**

Materials	Description
Puppets	Puppet shows tell a story or illustrate a poem, encouraging children to watch and listen. This activity reinforces understanding as children can make the connections between what they hear and the puppets' actions.
Props such as pictures, photographs, flannel board pieces or real objects	Props may be used to encourage children to make the connections between what is said and the words used. For example, telling a story about bears is enhanced by using stuffed-toy bears to illustrate the story.
Language audio card reader	An audio card (picture and word) is fed through the reader. "First children slide an audio card through our reader and listen to a recorded voice. Then they record their own response and listen to the recorded voice" (Wintergreen, 2003: 154).
Listening centres	Children can listen to stories or music through earphones while following along in a book.
Rhythm instruments	Children listen and move in accordance to the type of beat that is heard, such as slow, fast, quiet or noisy. Children can take turns creating the beats themselves.
Action songs	Action songs such as "Head and Shoulders" reinforce the words with the corresponding action.

It is most important that caregivers understand and know how to use body language effectively to help communicate with young children. Supportive body language becomes extremely important with very young children or with children with communication difficulties. Table 5.3 provides some ideas of various types of North American body language and how they might be used and interpreted. Body signs may be used to:

- Help interpret the behaviour of children
- Express feelings
- Enhance understanding of messages
- Help to model a different communication technique

Table 5.3 provides some general guidelines into various types of body language. However, it is important to be aware that knowledge of the individual will help to interpret how body language is used and what it might mean.

TABLE 5.3   **USE OF BODY LANGUAGE**

Message	Types of Body Signs
Approval	• Smile • Getting down to the child's level • Leaning toward the child • Relaxed body posture • Hand gestures such as thumbs up
Respect	• Eye contact (not respectful in Asian cultures) • Allowing personal space as required by the individual child
Puzzlement or lack of knowledge	• Raising eyebrows • Shrugging shoulders • Raising forearms and hands, palms up
Interest	• Smile • Getting down to child's level • Eyes level with child's activity and child
Unhappiness	• Walking or standing with shoulders hunched • Mouth turned down, sad facial expression
Boredom	• Ritualistic behaviour such as swinging legs, spinning around on the floor, gazing into the distance
Defensiveness	• Ridged body posture • Arms crossed on chest
Aggressiveness	• Raised open hand (ready to hit) • Shaking a fist at someone • Angry expression on face
Tiredness	• Rubbing eyes or ears • Hands folded and head rested on folded hands
Warning	• Waving forefinger at someone
Stop	• Hands held up, palm faced outward
Impatience	• Drumming fingers on desk • Tapping foot on floor
Uncertainty	• Pulling hair • Biting nails
Avoidance	• Lack of eye contact
Self-stimulation	• Rocking back and forth • Flicking fingers in front of face
Stop interaction	• Looking away

iv. Strategies to Maintain Attention   Some children find it difficult to maintain attention. To improve a child's attention span, the caregiver must first have some idea of what a normal attention span for that individual might be and what circumstances lead to increased or decreased attention span. For example, Peter would engage in self-stimulating behaviour, such as rocking and flicking his fingers in front of his face, during all group times. He would listen to an individual story if sitting on someone's lap while they looked at the book together. He also left interest areas when more than three children started to play in that area. It seemed that Peter adjusted better to individual and small group activities. The program needed to be adjusted to accommodate his needs.

Strategies used to increase and maintain interest include the following:

- Observing the child to identify his or her interests and skills
- Using the interests of the child to motivate the child to engage in language activities
- Providing appropriate challenges and materials to maintain the activity, such as expanding the language activity of Liesl and Hannah (see Photo 5.4)
- Following the child's lead—Dillon's interest in the sparkle activity (Photo 5.10) was enhanced by the adult's interactions. The adult observed Dillon and followed his lead to maintain attention.
- Providing enough time—John had been painting. He was asked to come and listen to a story. He responded that he was not finished and did not want to listen to a story. When the routine was enforced, John threw a temper tantrum. The result was that he did not listen to the story, the other children's time was interrupted and he could not finish his painting. Routines should be set up to meet the needs of the child, not to enforce a strict timeline. The whole negative episode could have been avoided had one of the following strategies been used:

  - Giving John a choice to finish his painting after the story
  - Allowing John to finish his painting and listen to the story from where he was
  - Giving John a choice as to what he wished to do

- Providing appropriate resources to encourage continued interest, such as those provided for Michael during his water play activity (Photo 5.3).

Communicative Adaptations in Inclusive Settings

Communication takes many forms. Not all children learn the same way, nor will all children be able to learn in the same way. Table 5.4 identifies some adaptive methodologies that might be used.

TABLE 5.4 **ADAPTIVE COMMUNICATION**

Type	Description
Braille	• Braille is a writing system based on raised dots that will help a child with a visual impairment to read and write.
Signing	• **American Sign Language** is a visual-spatial language that uses gestures, facial expression such as eyebrow or lip movements and the surrounding space to help in describing individuals or places. • **Signed English**—Every word in the English language has a corresponding sign. Signed English is similar to spoken English. • **Finger Spelling**—Each letter of the alphabet has a corresponding sign. Words are spelled out letter by letter.
Pictorial representations	• Pictures familiar to the child give the child the opportunity to communicate desire or choice. This child is indicating that he wants more rice.
Labelling	• Labelling in the environment should include pictures, words and signs such as ASL or Braille. This maximizes the child's ability to independently find and return materials. • Colour coding labels helps to speed up AAC. For example, all verb signs might be colour-coded pink (Musselwhite, 1999).
Augmentative/alternative communication (AAC)	• "ACC is any device or method that improves the ability of a child with communication impairment to communicate effectively" (Ballinger, 1999: 1; Ballinger, 1999). 1. Developmental approach—Provision of intervention strategies based on normal language development; works well with preschool children. 2. Ecological inventory—Identification and adaptation of relevant activities within the common environments children spend time in.
Multimodal communication	• Using more than one method of communication, such as verbal and signing—Advantage of greater diversity in approaching language learning.
Adaptive devises	• Adaptive devices help children to communicate with greater ease and flexibility—This includes reading, writing and interactions with others. Examples: computers—speech activated or hands-free—and flashing lights to "grab" attention. • Adaptive writing devices to hold writing/drawing tools.

Role of the Early Childhood Educator

Early childhood educators have a profound affect on young children's communication development. They are in a key position to coordinate activities between all partners—children, specialists, families and staff—to maximize the child's success. These are the key roles of the early childhood educator:

- Careful observation of children's communicative skills and interests—Jane had observed Hannah and Liesl's interest (Photo 5.4). Based on this interest, additional language activities were created.
- Setting up language activities to encourage active play situations within each interest area in the room—For example, the beading area was set up to encourage interactions among the children (Photo 5.1).
- Using spontaneous play to create "teachable moments"—Pritti had observed Keegan's reluctance to get involved in larger group activities. Setting up a small water play area encouraged Keegan to participate. She then used this situation to involve Keegan in a spontaneous language activity.
- Setting up displays to document children's learning and activities (Figure 5.11)
- Evaluating children's progress
- Creating an IPP (Figure 5.7) or a portfolio (Figure 5.8)
- Adapting communication strategies as needed (Table 5.4)
- Providing materials to maintain attention and interest over time—The pond area (Photo 5.7) continued to be active over many weeks. Many spontaneous language activities and "teachable moments" were continued over time.

SUMMARY

Children learn to communicate effectively when:

- Language is modelled appropriately from adults and peers
- Children interact with each other in active play
- There is a consistent approach to learning at home, in therapy and in care
- Alternative strategies are used to facilitate communication as needed
- Learning is fun, based on children's interests
- Individual strengths and needs are acknowledged and planned for

KEY POINTS

Components of communication
- Receptive language
- Expressive language
- Body language

Development of language
- Universal, with individual rate of acquisition
- Critical periods
- Dependent on environment
- Developmental milestones in predictable progression through the ages

Range of communicative abilities in inclusive settings
- Normal
- Gifted
- Exceptional: receptive, expressive, articulation, attentiveness, reading and writing

Factors affecting language development
- Structural problems
- Frustrated behaviours
- Language disabilities
- Learning disabilities
- Lack of stimulation
- Restricting conditions
- Cognitive impairments
- Auditory processing

Essential strategies within inclusive settings
- Collaborative approach
- Partnerships with other professionals
- Observation
  - Screening tools
  - Language behaviours
  - Importance of observing—For diagnosing problems or skills; planning activities; identification of skills, interests and abilities; plotting progress; preparing referrals; developing plan of action

Individual Program Plan
- Written plan of action for an individual
- Contains observations and assessment, identification of strengths and needs, goals and objectives, implementation activities and evaluation

Individual portfolio
- Ongoing, collaboratively created summary about an individual
- Contains purpose, likes and dislikes, abilities, goals and objectives, strategies, activities and evaluation

Planning inclusive learning environments
- Collaborative effort
- Process oriented—Identification of communication needs; children's skills, abilities and interests; implementation strategies

Strategies for implementation
- Expressive language—Encourage active play; observe children's play; interact in planned and spontaneous ways; encourage dialogue between children; reinforce language in all areas; expand materials based on interests; follow guidelines provided by professionals; read to children; provide language materials, music and experiences across different levels of abilities
- Receptive language—Follow child's lead, utilize teachable moments, encourage looking at books, use a multi-sensory approach, utilize a variety of materials that encourage listening, model appropriate language
- Body language—Identify and interpret different types of body language indicating approval, respect, puzzlement, feelings, interest, defensiveness, aggressiveness, tiredness, warning, action, avoidance
- Maintaining attention—Observe, use interests, provide individual challenges, provide enough time, provide the appropriate resources

- Communicative adaptations—Braille, signing, pictorial representations, labelling, augmentative/alternative communication, multimodal communication adaptive devices

- Role of the early childhood educator—Observing children's interests, strengths and needs; setting up language activities; responding to teachable moments; displaying children's efforts; creating IPP or individual portfolios; adapting communication strategies; maintaining interest over time

EXERCISES

1. Divide the class into three groups. Each group picks a children's story that can be easily dramatized. Each group then dramatizes in one of these ways:
   - Using body language only
   - Telling the story without props
   - Telling the story using a variety of props

   Identify which technique you enjoyed the most and why.

2. Using the developmental milestone charts on pages 139–143, observe a group of children within a preschool setting. How many children seemed to fit into the normal range? How many were exceptional? What types of exceptionalities could you identify?

3. Discuss what range of communicative abilities might be found in a preschool setting.

4. Reflect upon your personal language abilities. Which areas do you excel in? Which areas do you need to work on? How does this compare with children in inclusive settings?

5. Identify the importance of the essential communicative strategies for inclusive settings, utilizing the chart provided below.

6. Compare the IPP and the individual portfolio. What are the advantages and disadvantages of each? Reflect on which one you might wish to use and why.

7. Utilize the adaptive communication table (Table 5.4). Develop an observation tool using this chart. Implement the tool in an inclusive setting. Discuss which strategies seemed most effective and why?

COMPARISON OF INCLUSIVE AND NON-INCLUSIVE SETTINGS

Essential Area	Importance
Collaboration	
Observation	
Individualized programming	
Planning strategies	
Implementation strategies	

RESOURCES

Evaluation of children's books

Circle of Inclusion, Nine Ways to Evaluate Children's Books That Address Disability as Part of Diversity
www.circleofinclusion.org/english/books/section1/a.html

Council for Exceptional Children, Evaluation of children's books about disabilities
http://ericec.org/fact/kidbooks.html

Stewart Resources Centre, Saskatchewan Teachers' Federation, evaluation of picture books
www.stf.sk.ca/teaching_res/library/teach_mat_centre/TMC/E11287/picture_book_unit.pdf

Specific types of children's books

Internet School Library and Media Center, discussion and listing of various types of books suitable in inclusive settings
http://falcon.jmu.edu/~ramseyil/picture.htm

Articles on Practices

Beginning Literacy: Research-Based Principles and Practices
www.sadlier-oxford.com

Tips for sharing picture books with young children
www.libsci.sc.edu/BEST/readaloud/ReadAloudInfo/Tips%20for%20Sharing%20Picture%20Books%20with%20Young%20Children.ppt

Resources for Specific Needs

Braille alphabet
www.nbp.org/ic/nbp/braille

Braille alphabet and numbers
www.afb.org/braillebug/braille_print.asp

Signing With Your Baby
www.signingbaby.com

A Basic Guide to ASL, a resource dictionary for Internet users
www.masterstech-home.com/ASLDict.html

American Sign Language Alphabet
http://where.com/scott.net/asl/abc.html

Learn to finger spell
www.iwaynet.net/~ggwiz/asl

Augmentative and Alternative Communication (AAC)
http://aac.unl.edu/yaack

Auditory Processing Therapy Program
www.rmlearning.com/auditoryprocessing.htm

Technology

Assistive Technology and Augmentative Communication
www.lburkhart.com/main.htm

Assistive Technology
http://pediatrics.med.miami.edu/mailman/assist_tech.htm

Associations

Speechville Express, useful associations for families
www.speech-express.com/associations-disability.html

The Canadian Association of Speech-Language Pathologists
www.caslpa.ca/english/careers/careers.asp

Hanen Centre Canada
http://library.hcs.ucl.ac.uk/Links/SLT.htm

Speech and Language Development

Disorders associated with speech and language disabilities
www.kinderstart.com/childdevelopment/speechverbaldevelopment/disabilities.html

Language ages and stages
http://members.tripod.com/Caroline_Bowen/devel2.htm

Receptive language disorder
www.betterhealth.vic.gov.au/bhcv2/bhcarticles.nsf/pages/Receptive_language_disorder?Open

Children with Communication Disorders
http://ericec.org/digests/e617.html

REFERENCES

Adams, P. (1973). *There Was an Old Lady Who Swallowed a Fly*. Singapore: Child's Play International Ltd.

Ballinger, R. (1999). How to Get Started. What Is Augmentative and Alternative Communication (ACC)? Available at http://aac.unl.edu/yaack/ 21/09/2004.

Berk, L. (2002). *Infants and Children*. Fourth Edition. Boston, MA: Allyn & Bacon.

Berk, L. (2003). *Child Development*. Canadian Edition. Toronto, ON: Pearson Education Canada Inc.

Crowther, I. (2005). *Child Development Primer*. Scarborough, ON: Thomson Nelson.

Hanen (2002). Understanding Language Delay and Disorders. The Hanen Centre [online]. Available at www.hanen.org/Hanen2002/pages/Parents/Understandi ngLanguageDelay/UnderstandingLanguageDelay.htm (10-11-2004).

Imai, G. (1966). Gestures: Body Language and Nonverbal Communication. California State Polytechnic University, Pomona [online]. Available at www.intranet.csupomona. edu/~tassi/gestures.htm (29-12-2004).

McCain, M., & Mustard, F. (2002). *The Early Years Study*. Toronto, ON: The Founders' Network.

National Institute on Deafness and Other Communication Disorders (2001). Language Developmental Milestones. National Institute on Deafness and Other Communication Disorders [online]. Available at www.comeunity.com/disability/speech (8-11-2004).

Needlman, R. M. (2000). The Importance of Language. drSpock [online]. Available at www.drspock.com/article/0,1510,4829,00.html (25-9-2004).

Schickedanz, J., Schickedanz, D., Forsyth, P., & Forsyth, G. (2001). *Understanding Children and Adolescents*. Fourth Edition. Needham Heights, MA: Allyn & Bacon.

Siomades, L. (1999). *The Itsy Bitsy Spider*. Honesdale, PA: Bell Books.

Wintergreen, (2003). Wintergreen Learning Materials. Concord, ON: Wintergreen.

Winzer, M. (1999). *Children with Exceptionalities in Canadian Classrooms*. Scarborough, ON: Prentice Hall Allyn and Bacon.

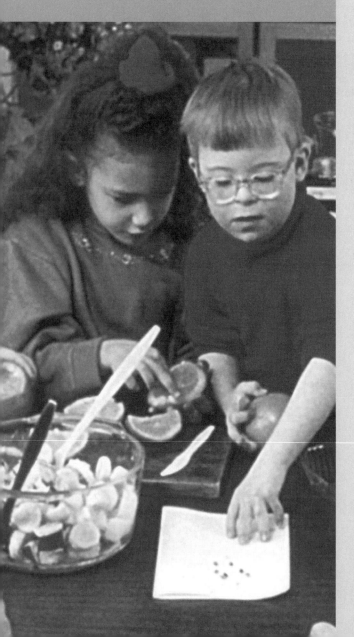

6 Play in Inclusive Settings

CHAPTER

"The universal importance of play to the natural development of the wholeness of children has been underscored by the United Nations proclamation of play as a universal and inalienable right of childhood. Play is the singular central activity to childhood, occurring at all times and in all places. Children do not need to be taught to play, nor must they be made to play. Play is spontaneous, enjoyable, voluntary, and non goal-directed" (Landreth, 2002: 9–10).

Learning Outcomes

After studying this chapter, you will be able to:

1. Identify how play affects a child's development.
2. Define the various types and stages of play.
3. Discuss the various stages of play found in inclusive settings and the reasons for a range of developmental play stages.
4. Discuss the importance of establishing a collaborative process with families and other professionals.
5. Discuss the various factors that should be considered when organizing an environment in which children's play is valued.
6. Discuss the importance of observing and documenting children's play.
7. Define and discuss the importance of the following adaptations in inclusive settings: environmental support, material adaptation, simplified activities, children's preferences, special equipment, adult support, peer support, invisible support.
8. Describe the role of the early childhood educator in encouraging active play within children's learning spaces.

Photo 6.1

Introduction to Play

Play is a natural way of learning for all children. Through active play, children lay the foundations of all future learning. According to Bodrova and Leong (Koralek, 2004: 7), there are four principles through which play influences development. It affects the child's motivation, facilitates cognitive decentring, develops mental representations and fosters deliberate actions.

1. Play Affects the Child's Motivation

When children can make choices, receive gratification through their efforts and interact in positive situations, a cycle of learning develops. This is particularly important for young children with special needs. These children are often placed into situations in which they are required to engage in activities where they do not have a choice and that may not be developmentally appropriate for them. These situations arise to meet adult expectations for children with special needs to "catch up" to normal development. Children make greater gains when they are left to work in an environment that provides developmentally appropriate choices and engages their interests. For example, one of the goals for Dillon's IPP was to improve his fine motor skills. Dillon was encouraged to choose his own activities for reaching this goal. He discovered that he could use the large chalk to create marks on the board (Photo 6.1). He experimented endlessly to create straight lines and circles in various colours. When he had covered the area he had used, he erased the shapes and started again. Through this activity Dillon gained:

- Self-confidence in his ability to interact with the materials in his environment
- Practice to refine his fine motor skills
- Insight into cause and effect relationships—Dillon could see the different marks he made, and he could erase them and start again.
- Gratification in his ability to produce different shapes

2. Play Facilitates Cognitive Decentring

All young children's thinking is centred on their individual perspective. It is difficult for a young child to take on a different perspective. The child is focused on one aspect of his or her perspective and is unable to think about other aspects. For example, Jamie, a three-year-old, had finished a painting. When her grandmother telephoned a little while later, Jamie enthusiastically ran to get her painting. She held it up to the phone and said, "Look at the painting I just finished." Jamie's focus was on her painting. She was talking to her grandmother, and Jamie could see her painting, so she assumed her grandmother could see it too.

Through play, children gradually learn to take on different perspectives. When children learn to take on another perspective, they are developing the skill of decentred thinking. As children experiment with materials during block or water play or sand play, they gain experience in seeing and manipulating objects from different perspectives. Benjamin decided to try to use the water wheel with sand, instead of water, to see if he could make the wheel turn (Photo 6.2). He was able to transfer learning from one situation to another. Through this activity he gained experience in:

- Observing how different materials cause a similar effect
- Using equipment and materials in different settings effectively
- Seeing the result of individual actions from different perspectives

Through dramatic play children further develop decentred thinking skills. Children gradually take on different roles during pretend play. As children practise the various roles they take on, they are learning about how to act differently depending on the role they assume. They gradually learn to coordinate various roles and negotiate the different play scenarios. For example, Jenna, a four-year-old, had been playing the role of a child in the daily living centre. She explained, "I am crying because I want the toy my brother is playing with. I am only pretending to cry. He is only my pretend brother." Later she decided to switch roles. She became the mother. When her two "children" were arguing about a toy she said, "There are enough toys for both of you. Timmy, you could find a new bucket." Jenna clearly was able to take on and understand the different roles she assumed.

Photo 6.2

3. Play Develops Mental Representations

"This development occurs as the result of a child separating the meaning of objects from their physical form. First children use replicas to substitute for real objects; then they use new objects that are different in appearance but can perform the same function as the prototype. Finally, most of the substitution takes place in the child's speech with no object present. Thus the ability to operate with symbolic substitutions for real objects contributes to the development of abstract thinking and imagination" (Bodrova & Leong, 2004: 7).

For example, Ben had been very interested in animals. Initially he played with the animals in different settings, such as sand play or water or block play or the light table. Occasionally he would hold up an animal and look at Yenka, his teacher. Yenka would supply the name. As he looked at books, he was able to point to the animal upon request. Eventually Ben was able to make the word "lizard," copied from a dictionary card. Gradually Ben was forming mental representations of the animals he was playing with. He started by becoming familiar with what the animals looked like: their shapes, textures, colours or sizes. He gradually understood the labels associated with each animal and was finally able to reproduce the label in symbolized form—an outline of the lizard and the printed word (Photo 6.3).

Photo 6.3

4. Play Fosters Deliberate Actions

As children gain experience in play situations, their actions become more deliberate. For example, Melanie, a nine-month infant, kicked the mobile at the foot of her bed to make it move and squeak. Melanie would watch and listen. When the sound and movement stopped, she would kick it again. Jake, a five-year-old, knew the rules for snakes and ladders. He would patiently explain them to anyone who wanted to play with him. If other children made mistakes, he would correct them. Because Jake had memorized rules, he was able to monitor the game to ensure that everyone played by the same rules.

In summary, play provides opportunities for children to accomplish many things:

- Learn through making personal choices
- Learn in a natural setting with real materials
- Learn through interactions with others and materials
- Establish positive attitudes toward learning
- Engage in meaningful activity
- Develop autonomy
- Acquire skills associated with cognition, socialization, self-awareness, motor control, language and emotional control

Development of Play

Play develops in an orderly, predictable pattern. Figure 6.1 provides an overview of play stages as they develop from one age to the next. Many of the stages overlap because children may enter a different stage of play depending on their development, interactions and the stimulation received. For example, solitary play evolves through the infant years and into the toddler years. As the toddler is given opportunities to play with other children, parallel play evolves. Play stages are cumulative and play stages may continue to exist over time for different purposes.

Not only is it important to know what the various stages are, it is also critical to understand what skills are prevalent at each stage. Figure 6.1 provides an overview of the various stages of play.

The type of play changes with age and with the experiences that children have had. Solitary play may be a sensory exploration of a toy by touching, mouthing or throwing. It will continue throughout all ages with a different purpose, such as wanting to be by oneself to read a book. As children develop more and more skills, the purpose of their play will change in accordance with those skills. The toddler may be content to listen to a story, or look through a book, whereas the preschool child may start to read words and may pretend to read a story to others.

It is important to understand the development of play in order to facilitate optimal active play situations that meet the needs, interests, abilities and skills of all children. Knowledge of the stages of development enables the child care provider to:

- Provide appropriate materials and resources
- Continue to adapt and change learning environments as needed
- Be sensitive to the needs of all the children
- Maintain an environment of positive social interaction
- Understand how and when interactions are needed

FIGURE 6.1
Play Defined

Type of Play	Definition	Example
Onlooker play	Child watches others play without interacting.	Josh watched the children fingerpaint without interaction or joining in.
Solitary play	Child plays alone.	Photo 6.4
Parallel play	Children play side by side, using similar materials, but without interacting with each other.	Photo 6.5
Associative play	Children play with similar materials, sharing ideas and materials, but engage in personal activities.	Photo 6.6

FIGURE 6.1

Continued

Type of Play	Definition	Example
Cooperative play	Children play together toward a common goal, planning their play and designating roles to achieve the goal.	
Functional play	Children repeatedly practise skills through interacting with objects, other individuals and language.	
Symbolic play	Children use one action or object to represent another idea.	Lauren represents sleepy.

FIGURE 6.1

Continued

Type of Play	Definition	Example
Constructive play	Children use materials or objects to create something.	
Dramatic play	Children create imaginary roles and situations with or without props. **Sociodramatic play** occurs when two or more children are involved in dramatic play situations.	
Games with rules	School-aged children have the understanding of preset rules. They agree to play by these rules.	Competitive sports such as tennis or hockey

Range of Stages of Play

Children in inclusive settings will exhibit all types of play behaviour as identified in Figure 6.1. Children may be engaged in specific play behaviours for a number of reasons, including these:

- Developmental ability—Children's participation may be limited depending on their abilities. For example, a child with a developmental delay may find it difficult to share toys and materials. A child who is in a wheelchair may find it difficult to access all activities independently. Adaptations to the materials and the environment will need to be made to maximize these children's opportunities to engage in active play.

- Background experiences—Children who have received limited stimulation prior to enrolling in the child care program may find the environment overwhelming, with too many things to choose from. Additionally, these children may not have the skills or knowledge to use the materials in appropriate ways. These children will need time, positive interactions and guidance to adjust to an environment rich in resources.

- Family values—Some families do not put a value on play, believing that children must be taught what they need to know. Play may be seen as a frivolous activity. It is important to interact with these families to demonstrate that during active play, the child will learn all of the necessary skills in a more enjoyable and long-lasting way.

- Family expectations—All families have expectations of what their child should be able to do. Sometimes families make the child's disability the focus of that child's educational need. In these cases, the child is often expected to perform tasks such as learning to print the letters of the alphabet or complete a puzzle, rather than engaging in active play. Collaboration among therapists, child care staff and family members will facilitate the process to set up a play-based program for that child.

- Type of disability—Many disabilities may interfere with the child's ability to become involved in active play. Irrespective of the disability, care should be taken to provide each child with the opportunity to become involved in active play. This may mean providing the centre with additional resources, such as Braille materials, or adaptive equipment, such as wheelchair swings.

- Societal pressures—There are increasing pressures to prepare children academically. This often means formal instruction at early ages. "Academic training is increasingly replacing imaginative play and experiential hands-on learning in the early years of our children's lives. Education is now seen as a race, and the earlier you start, the sooner and the better you finish. Yet there is no evidence that this push for early academics, such as the effort to have children start reading by age five, produces any lasting advantage for children. If anything, research and experience point in the opposite direction" (Alliance for Childhood, 2004: 1). Early childhood educators need to develop skills of advocacy. They need to familiarize themselves with information about the value of play and share it with families, community members and policy-makers. This information sharing should always be backed up by research and experience.

Strategies to Develop a Play-Based Curriculum

A number of strategies should be considered when an active play-based curriculum is being set up. These may be categorized into collaborative processes and setting the stage for play to occur. As previously discussed, collaboration forms the cornerstone of a quality program. Collaboration among children, staff, families and other professionals not only enriches the knowledge about learning through play, but also ensures congruence among practices in the child's various settings: home, centre-based and therapy-based.

1. Collaboration with Families

When families and child care staff work together toward a common goal, everyone benefits. This may involve initial information sessions with families to promote a play-based approach. An information session can be conducted in different settings:

- Individual sessions—These sessions can be part of the intake procedure. The session could include a tour of the facility and an open discussion about the value of play to the child's development. If needed, support documentation would be available to show how a play-based approach works and how the child's strengths and needs are met.
- Group sessions such as discussion groups, or seminars on the topic of play—This gives families opportunities to further explore the topic of play and to ask staff about concerns that might need to be addressed.

Families play an important part in helping to create a positive learning environment for their children, both at home and at the centre. Families share information about:

- Children's interest—a mechanism needs to be provided to encourage information sharing. This could be done by posting documentation about children's interests on bulletin boards, creating a portfolio of evolving interests (either individual or group) or providing space on daily recording charts that encourage families to record children's interests upon arrival or departure at the centre.
- Progress in different settings—There needs to be a regular flow of information between families and staff. Families should be encouraged to participate to keep similar observation tools to those the centre uses (see Tables 6.2 and 6.3 on pages 201 and 202). Families should have access to the information about

their child. A system needs to be developed that ensures confidentiality of individual children and families but also keeps families informed about their child's progress.

- Concerns—When concerns arise it is best to set up a time to meet, either in a face-to-face meeting or through a telephone call. This should be done immediately, as the longer a concern remains unaddressed, the harder it becomes to deal with it. The tone of the meeting should be respectful and involve active listening. The outcome should involve mutual problem solving to reach a consensus about the action to be taken.

- Celebrations of success—Often celebrations of successes are forgotten. A celebration for success gives all individuals opportunities to feel good about progress made, validate the child's efforts, acknowledge the efforts of families, staff and other professionals, and create a positive atmosphere.

2. Collaboration with Other Professionals

Various types of professionals can play an important role in helping child care practitioners set up an appropriate play-based program for children. These could include specialists such as play therapists, occupational therapists, sandplay therapists or music therapists. The therapist is a highly trained individual with specialized skills.

Following is a brief description of the type of services each of these professionals might offer with respect to play and the child with special needs.

A) PLAY THERAPY   Play therapy has long been established as a mode to encourage children to express their feelings and explore relationships. Play therapy is defined as "a dynamic interpersonal relationship between a child (or person of any age) and a therapist trained in play therapy procedures who provides selected play materials and facilitates the development of a safe relationship for the child (or person of any age) to fully express and explore self (feelings, thoughts, experiences, and behaviours) through play, the child's natural medium of communication, for optimal growth and development" (Landreth, 2002: 16).

There are a number of play therapy associations around the world. According to the Canadian Association for Child and Play Therapy:

> It is a therapeutic approach for human service professionals and as stated by Virginia Axline, "provides an opportunity for the child to 'play out' his or her feelings and problems just as, in certain adult therapy, an individual 'talks out' his or her difficulties." A child's self-understanding is one of the goals in this approach. Play Therapy can be used either as a primary or adjunct therapy in settings such as Children's Services, Community Agencies, Psychiatric Centers, Children's Hospitals, Schools, and Women's Shelters (Canadian Association for Child and Play Therapy, 2004: 1).

B) THE LUDIC MODEL: OCCUPATIONAL THERAPY In an interview with Francine Ferland, professor in Occupational Therapy at the University of Montreal, the connections between play and the Ludic Model were discussed. Based on research and her experiences in working with children and families of children with special needs (neurological disorders, physical disabilities, developmental delays and cognitive disabilities), Professor Ferland has developed the Ludic Model ("Ludic" meaning related to play) to use with children in occupational therapy settings. This model was created as a reflection of the importance of play in the life of any child. It is based on research conducted with parents of children with physical disabilities and interviews with the occupational therapists who worked with these children and with adults who had lived with someone with permanent physical disabilities since birth. The subjects of the research study were individuals with physical disabilities, developmental delays and intellectual deficiencies. The research was conducted after the first publication of the *Ludic Model* and reported in a second edition of the publication (Ferland, 2005).

The Ludic Model embraces the philosophical underpinnings of the child's right to learn through play. Play has three components that relate to all aspects of treatment of the child: assessment, planning a treatment program and implementation. The Ludic Model embraces play in the following ways:

- Nurturing a playful attitude (Ludic attitude)—Play is seen as more than engaging the child in "play-like" tasks, for instance asking the child to do a task such as drawing shapes with colourful pens on a piece of paper. Playful attitude is what leads to active play—the desire to play, the enjoyment that arises with play and the positive interactions that arise from play. The Ludic attitude is characterized by pleasure, curiosity, a sense of humour and spontaneity.
- Involving the interests of the child—Careful consideration is given to identification of the child's interests. This information is gathered from family members and the observations of the therapist, and could include information from the child care centre. Using the child's interest to develop a program is a strong motivator for the child to want to participate, which is necessary to awaken the desire to act and to maintain pleasure in action.
- Involving the child in active play (Ludic action)—Active play involves decision making, problem solving and interacting with materials and other individuals in meaningful ways. When children are actively involved, learning occurs that is relevant to their abilities, is **intrinsic** or self-motivated (motivation that is internal and is expressed by the individual) and leads to greater autonomy. Ludic actions are instrumental components that permit the actions of play.

C) SANDPLAY THERAPY Sand therapy was first used by Margaret Lowenfeld in 1930. It was further developed by Dora Dalff, who developed the use of sand as a tool for therapy and named it sandplay. Sandplay is similar to play therapy because it also engages the child in active play through the medium of sand and expresses the child's thoughts and feelings. Sandplay has been used extensively in Germany, England and the United States and has had recent acceptance and use in certain jurisdictions in Canada.

During sand play the therapist observes the child carefully and follows the child's lead as appropriate. According to the Sandplay Therapists of America:

> The essentials of sandplay therapy are a specially proportioned sandtray, a source of water, shelves of miniatures of multitude variety: people, animals, buildings, bridges, vehicles, furniture, food, plants, rocks, shells—the list goes on—and an empathetic therapist who provides the freedom and the protection that encourages children (or adults) to experience their inner, often unrealized, selves in a safe and non-judgmental space. The therapist as a witness is an essential part of the method, but this therapist is in the mode of 'appreciating,' not 'judging,' what the sandplayer does (Bradway, 2004: 2–3).

D) MUSIC THERAPY Music therapy has strong historical roots. Many of the ancient philosophers, historians and scientists have alluded to the power of music as a therapeutic agent. Music can evoke different types of moods and can be used to change moods. The effects of music are measurable. Research has identified the following effects:

- Music can influence physiological processes, such as speeding up or slowing down the heart rate.
- Music may be used for medical purposes. For instance, classical music is sometimes provided in infant intensive-care units. Studies have found that these infants tend to gain more weight, leave the hospital earlier and have better survival rates.
- Regular, continued experiences with music in early childhood relate to improved competence in many domains: physical, social, language, emotional and cognitive.
- Music can be used to evoke various moods. It can be used to change moods; for example, calming a child (Campbell, 2000; Canadian Association for Music Therapy, 2003)

The Canadian Association for Music Therapy defines the term this way: "Music therapy is the skillful use of music and musical elements by an accredited music therapist to promote, maintain, and restore mental, physical, emotional, and spiritual health. Music has nonverbal, creative, structural, and emotional qualities. These are used in the therapeutic relationship to facilitate contact, interaction, self-awareness, learning, self-expression, communication, and personal development" (Canadian Association for Music Therapy, 2003: 1).

E) BENEFITS OF COLLABORATION WITH PLAY SPECIALISTS Each of these kinds of specialist is an expert in play with children with special needs. Interactions with these specialists will help the child care staff to:

- Create an atmosphere of calmness and therapeutic value in the classroom—Sand and music are excellent ways to offer relief in times of stress or frustration.
- Organize play areas with appropriate toys and resources—Children will become more independent in making appropriate choices and solving their own problems.

- Gain insight into how to use play opportunities to foster children's well-being and development—Provide opportunities to children that are relaxing, soothing and enjoyable.
- Gain expert advice on how to handle certain behaviours—Examples include fear, withdrawal from situations or lack of interest in play.
- Become more knowledgeable about alternative ways of helping families and children—Early childhood educators will be able to offer a greater variety of choices to families if a referral is needed.

3. Setting the Stage for Play

"When children are playing they are thinking, innovating, negotiating, and taking risks" (Jones, 2004: 24). Learning environments should be organized to encourage active play activities by supplying children with appropriate learning spaces, enough time and materials. Child care providers should encourage children to solve problems and provide challenges by presenting children with new problems to solve. These problems should emerge from careful observation of the children's evolving interests, in a spirit of acceptance and appreciation of the children's curiosity about the world around them.

Key considerations for organizing the environment for active play—setting the stage for play—have been described by Carr (2005). These include observation, material and resources, program format, "teachable moments," documentation of children's successes, a variety of self-expressive materials, organization of learning spaces and mediation between children (Carr, 2005: 4).

A) OBSERVATIONS OF CHILDREN For effective play planning for a group of children, knowledge of the children's usual play behaviour, interests, abilities and frustration levels is critical. Gathered by all team members—other professionals, family members and staff—this information will help early childhood educators plan and organize developmentally-appropriate and age-appropriate play experiences for all the children (see section on observations, pages 200-202.)

B) MATERIALS AND RESOURCES To optimize children's success and decrease possible frustration, a number of points should be considered when choosing toys, materials and resources in inclusive settings (Carr, 2005; Lekotek, 2005):

- Durability—Toys and equipment should be tough enough to withstand active play.
- Safety—Care should be taken to choose materials that are unlikely to chip, splinter or break with repeated use and do not contain any harmful substances such as lead paint. Larger equipment should be sturdy enough to prevent tipping or falling when used.
- Potential for various levels of play—Learning materials should be available to support all levels of play within the centre. They should be chosen to meet a variety of developmental needs. For example, choose materials that could be used by more than one developmental age, such as buckets with a broad base to

prevent tipping and a larger diameter across the top to facilitate filling and emptying individually or in small groups. Choose play buildings such as barns or houses that are large enough to facilitate a number of types of play: solitary, associative or cooperative.

- Involvement of more than one sense:
  - Visual—Different, perhaps contrasting colours; clear detail; realistic appearance; movement
  - Auditory—Interesting sounds
  - Tactile—Varied textures, contours or surfaces
  - Smell—Scented dolls (powder scent), scented play dough

- Opportunity for success
  - Open-endedness—The learning materials can be used in more than one way, without a right or wrong way.
  - Avoiding frustration—Children of different abilities can effectively manipulate or experiment with the learning materials.
  - Accessibility—The learning materials can be used in various places or positions, such as on the floor, on a table or on a tray while sitting in a wheelchair.
  - Adaptability—Adjustments can be made to equipment to accommodate different heights, volumes or speeds, such as adjustable paint easels, listening centres with appropriate volume control or a variety of ground surfaces to encourage running or riding at different speeds.

- Appropriate interests—The learning materials are appropriate for a variety of current interests and abilities.
- Developmental- and age-appropriateness—The learning materials are age-appropriate for all children. For example, the materials should relate to the culture of the setting by providing items such as storybooks on disabilities, dolls in wheelchairs or pictures of individuals working in communities with disabilities.
- Self-expression—The materials encourage creativity, uniqueness and the opportunity to make choices. Children should gain experiences with a wide variety of media (Lekotek, 2005: 1).
- Interactivity—The learning materials provide opportunities for a variety of interactions: verbal, body language, individual or group.
- Simplicity—The materials look realistic, are devoid of distracting backgrounds, are easy to understand and are attractive.
- Scaffolding—Learning materials that encourage increased skill levels are available. For example, provide a variety of puzzles to encourage skill development from simple to complex.
- Cause and effect—Provide learning materials that encourage children to see the result of their actions. For example, when the child turns a knob, a light will flash; when the child pushes a car, it will roll; or when a child opens a book, he or she will see a picture.

- Familiarity—Provide learning materials that are familiar to the children's experiences and backgrounds.

C) PROGRAM FORMAT Often the format of the program may deter children from engaging in active play. Programs that are too rigid or too open in scheduling tend to inhibit active play. Key components that encourage active play are flexibility and predictability. Adults should carefully consider appropriate strategies for transitions, allot an appropriate amount of time for active play, provide overall stability in day-to-day experiences, observe and interact with children spontaneously, document children's efforts, provide a variety of self-expressive materials, organize the learning spaces to encourage active play and mediate between children as needed.

- Transitions—Transitions should be kept simple and to a minimum. Major transitions, such as from indoor to outdoor play, meal times, sleep times or dismissal, should be carefully considered. Ample warning should be provided and children should be included through such techniques as actions, songs or visual cues.
- Time to complete tasks—Ensure that there is enough time for all children to complete activities. At least one hour of free play in the morning and in the afternoon should be considered. Provide opportunities to complete activities over time by creating storage for projects in progress.
- Predictability—Children should get a good sense of what is happening next. There needs to be a schedule that establishes continuity from day to day. In this way, they can gradually learn to anticipate and get ready for the next routine.
- Stability—Continual, massive changes, such as total room changes to the environment to accommodate new themes, should be avoided. Children need the security of knowing where things are and how to find them. Changes and adaptations should be made based on the children's abilities and interests. These changes should involve the children and should not affect the overall organization of the room.

D) "TEACHABLE MOMENTS" "Teachable moments" occur when an early childhood educator observes children's play and identifies a situation that can be used to increase interactions between children or foster growth and development. For example, Jamie had been watching Dillon draw on the chalkboard (see Photo 6.1 on page 180). Both boys tended to be involved in solitary play. Kaya asked Jamie if he wanted to draw on the chalkboard. Kaya created a set of chalk similar to Dillon's and brought it over to the chalkboard, telling Dillon that Jamie also wanted to draw on the board. Both boys continued to draw. Kaya had created an opportunity for the two boys to be involved in parallel play.

E) DOCUMENTATION OF CHILDREN'S SUCCESSES Documentation of children's successes is important in several ways. It serves to inform visitors, other professionals and families of the children's accomplishments and it also serves to reinforce the value of play as a primary mode of learning. Additionally, children's efforts are acknowledged and documented. This leads to increased pride in achievement and may motivate children to continue with current activities or move on to new challenges.

Documentation of children's achievements also helps the adult to recognize the significance of even small achievements and the importance of sharing these achievements with family members. For example, Jeremy, a teacher in a class of children diagnosed with learning disabilities, reported: "One of my profound moments in teaching occurred when I called one of the parents of Scott, an eight-year-old child with dyslexia, to inform the parents that Scott had created a poem on the new voice-activated computer. Scott and I had decided to submit this poem to a children's magazine and needed his parents' agreement. I had not met Scott's parents before. Neither parent had attended the parent night in the fall. When I called the mother during lunch hour, I politely introduced myself. Her response was very abrupt. I explained what Scott had achieved and what he wanted to do with this achievement. There was a long silence. Eventually she responded: 'You mean you called me to tell me something good about my son? In all the years that Scott has been in school, first preschool, then kindergarten and now elementary school, we have never been called about something he has done well.' I was stunned. I thought back over the number of times that I contacted family members and had to admit that it was usually because of a problem that had occurred. This was a teachable moment for me. I have since then strived to share as many of the successes as I can in as many ways as I can. I have found that the results have been most rewarding. I now teach happier children, have more supportive families and enjoy my job so much more."

Several types of documentation could be used. Two of the most common are documentation panels and portfolios. Both techniques involve all partners: children, families, staff and other professionals. The purpose of both documentation panels and portfolios is to clearly identify the activities the children have been engaged in and the learning that resulted, and to be open to adding additional information as the learning activity continues to evolve. Examples of the two techniques are provided in Figures 6.2 and 6.3.

These sample pages from a portfolio followed a field trip to look for signs of spring. They include the children's expression through art and dictations about the signs of spring. The children decided what to include. One of the advantages of a portfolio over a documentation panel is that children can take home the portfolio to show to families. Individual copies can also be provided at the families' request.

F) VARIETY OF SELF-EXPRESSIVE MATERIALS Communication is central to all interaction. There are many forms of expression. The Reggio Emilia approach to education talks about the "Hundred Languages of Children" (Malaguzzi, 1997). Communication can take many forms, such as verbal, written, symbol, signing, art, body language or music. It is essential to provide materials that engage children in a variety of ways to express themselves (see Table 6.1). It is also a fundamental right of children to have their personal way of expression acknowledged, understood and valued.

FIGURE 6.2

Example of One Part of a Documentation Panel

Ideas About Signs of Spring

The information was gathered from the children. Ideas were communicated through verbalizations, pointing to pictures and signing. The list was expanded over several days. Sometimes the child and a family member or other professional would add items to it.

growing things	ice disappears	ride our bikes
snow melts	put winter things away	spring cleaning
gets warmer	play outside longer	collect things
rain	see things on the ground	work in the yard
sing spring songs	birds come back	insects come out
animals come out		

The children decided that they would like to go on a field trip to gather signs of spring.

We found many signs of spring.

Katie found pussy willows. "They are fuzzy."

"I discovered that the ground is soggy. When you step on it water seeps over your boots."

Anastasia found a flower: "Yellow." Braelyn said, "It's a dandelion, Anastasia, and it's actually a weed."

Yasmine was excited that the ice had disappeared from the river. She said, "I see shells, stones and tiny little fish."

FIGURE 6.3

Sample Pages of a Project-Based Portfolio

What We Learned About Spring

Children learned to represent their ideas in different ways. They used different media: crayons, oil pastels, glue, different coloured foil scraps and play dough. They were able to articulate various concepts about spring verbally, in writing, through signing and by providing visual cues:

- changing weather patterns—rain and snow, what to wear, observing rain on the window
- effects of temperature—melting
- new growth—flowers
- activities related to spring—splashing in puddles

Danielle drew a picture of rain. She signed that her picture was about "rain falling."
When Jordan heard Danielle's message, he ran to get a pair of boots, an umbrella and a raincoat.
Damian saw the boots and said, "In the spring there are puddles. I like to splash in puddles.

Jenna had been fascinated with watching raindrops run down the window pane. She traced their path with her fingers. She said, "Shiny." Later she created her own raindrops. She used a paste brush to create a circle of glue on her paper. Then she added scraps of shiny foil to the circles of glue.

FIGURE 6.3

Continued

What We Learned About Spring

Christopher created a flower using oil pastels. He also created a frame for his picture made of rolled paper. He explained, "The flower is growing because the sun is warmer. It is a violet. It is one of the first flowers to appear in the spring."

Olivia created a snowman. She indicated that sometimes it snowed in the spring and that sometimes she could still make a snowman. "My snowman will soon melt. He will slowly disappear."

TABLE 6.1   **SELF-EXPRESSIVE ACTIVITIES**

Type of Activity	Range of Self-Expressive Activities
Art	• Painting—With tools such as brushes or rollers; fingerpainting or foot-painting; painting on different surfaces such as paper, clear surfaces, boxes • Drawing—With tools such as oil pastels, chalk, pencil or wax crayons, markers, sticks, or fingers or hands; on a variety of surfaces: boxes, paper, booklets, lined paper, unlined paper, trays filled with sand or flour, the ground or sand in the sandbox • Sculpting—Clay, play dough, wet sand, papier mâché, boxes; with tools such as knives, spatulas, rollers, hammers or fingers and hands • Decorating—Glue, scissors and materials to decorate with: paper products such as shiny paper, regular or tissue paper in various colours and sizes; collections from nature such as shells, colourful stones, pine cones, grasses or seeds; material such as scraps of fabric, yarn or felt; glitter; wood products such as popsicle sticks or wooden shapes; wire, such as plastic-covered wire or pipe cleaners
Carpentry	Carpentry tools—For attaching, cutting and decorating activities, plus appropriate materials such as soft wood and appropriate-sized nails. Coordinate with art area to encourage decoration.
Music	• Rhythm instruments—Drums, sticks, bells, cymbals, tambourines, maracas, triangles • Musical instruments—Xylophone, keyboards, bells • Music—Appropriate to play along with or move to • Props—Scarves, capes, ribbons
Blocks	Wooden-unit, soft-unit, cardboard, foam and hollow blocks
Manipulative toys	Lego, Duplo, Interlinks, tinker toys
Dramatic play	• Props—Dress-up clothes, scarves, blankets • Role play materials • Combining dramatic area with other areas—Riding toys, sand and water areas, block areas
Writing	• Writing area—Dictionaries, dictionary cards, papers (lined and unlined) and writing tools of various sizes, booklets, books, photographs, alphabet letters • Scribe centre—Area that children can come to in order to dictate a story
Sewing	• Tools—Plastic large-eyed needles, hole punch, scissors, pinking shears • Material—Cardboard, plastic, fabric, yarn, gimp

G) APPROPRIATE SPACE AND ORGANIZATION "When indoor and outdoor learning centres are designed to do the bulk of the direct teaching, children's pretend play in those centres can support and foster the bulk of their learning. When children play without relying on the accomplished skills of an adult, they tackle complex challenges of language skills, perspective taking, representational thinking, problem solving, and turn taking as they work hard to keep their games going" (Perry, 2004: 17).

The organization of the learning environment has a great impact on children's ability to participate in active play. The following factors should be considered:

- Visibility—All interest areas should be clearly visible from all areas of the room. This facilitates the ease with which a child can find an area of interest and also better supervision.

- Accessibility—All areas (indoors and outdoors) are accessible by wheelchair and unobstructed floors and passageways to prevent tripping, falling or blocking a route of travel. Materials are accessible on low, sturdy shelves and organized by type.

- Labelling system—Materials are labelled by pictures, words, symbols and/or outlines to facilitate retrieval and return of the materials.

- Aesthetics—Materials should be arranged in such a way as to invite the child to touch, explore or handle. For example, in one inclusive setting children spent a lot of time painting. There were several alternative paint centres set up. One centre was set up with new colours: bright pink, dark indigo, lime green, eggshell white, tangerine and cardinal red. The paint was set up in clear plastic containers set on circular mirrored surfaces. Brushes were placed in a brush container with bristles up. The centre was set up on a rectangular table near a water source to encourage children to clean their brushes after use.

  In the hour of free play, this centre was used consistently by most of the children. The children talked about the paint being "mirrored in the glass." Some children put paint on their paper and gently touched the paint with their fingers. One child looked at the paint from many different perspectives. In contrast, areas left messy or dirty tend to be ignored.

- Choices that represent a holistic approach—A full range of choices—including creative, manipulative, dramatic, construction (sand, blocks, carpentry), experiment (water, sand, science, math), language, music, gross motor, fine motor, books and space to be alone—should be available in both indoor and outdoor environments (Harms, Clifford & Cryer, 1998; Crowther, 2003).

H) MEDIATION BETWEEN CHILDREN Young children are at the egocentric stage of life. They see the world from their own perspective. They are also eager to learn and embrace new learning vivaciously. Children may not always understand the signals that are communicated. It is up to the adult to interpret and help children make sense of what they have seen or heard.

For example, Liu, a second-language learner, was playing in the block area. She had built several structures. Mario joined her and started to add to her structure. Liu said, "我想要一個人靜一靜" Mario looked at her with a blank look on his face. Min, the early childhood educator, had heard Liu's comment. She walked over to the two children. She looked at both and said, "Mario, Liu said that she wants to be alone." Mario smiled and left.

I) FOCUS ON PROCESS The process that the child is involved with during play should be the emphasis rather than the end product. Children should be encouraged to extend their play through:

- Asking exploratory questions—Such as asking a child what he or she will do next, or asking the child to explain or demonstrate how a task has been accom-

FIGURE 6.4

Examples of Labelling Systems

1. Photograph and label

scissors

2. Outline and label

scissors

3. Picture and label

scissors

plished. "You have worked hard to build the block structure. What are you going to do now?"

• Commenting on what the child is doing—For example, describing the colours, shapes or lines made in an art creation. "I can see that you have made large red circles, and fat blue lines."

• Labelling feelings—Identifying how the child feels and why they are feeling this way. "I understand it is frustrating when someone takes away your toy."

4. Observing Children's Play

There are a number of factors that should be considered when observing play, such as types of play, the child's interests, who the child plays with and attention span. Each is related to play but provides its own pertinent information.

A) OBSERVING TYPES OF PLAY It is important to know what type of play children are involved in, in order to provide the appropriate settings, materials and resources to maintain or expand the play opportunities. Table 6.2 provides an overview of some types of tools that could be used to observe the type of play children are involved in.

TABLE 6.2 **OBSERVING TYPES OF PLAY**

Name: Josh (3.6)　　　　　　　　**Observer:** Jane
Date(s): November 2, 3, 4, 2004

Type of Play	Setting	Circumstances	Comments
Solitary	Puzzles		Completed a six-part single-piece puzzle by trial and error; put it back on shelf
Solitary, functional	Water	Chose individual water tub	Filled pail with scoop, emptied it; repeated filling and emptying five times; needed reminder to replace toys on shelf
Parallel, constructive	Blocks	Beside Damian	Created a horizontal structure, watched it fall, rebuilt it; Damian built enclosures; stopped building when Damian did; both boys were reminded to clean up
Parallel, functional	Duplo	Beside Damian	Followed Damian to Duplo; attached pieces and took them apart
Parallel, functional	Sand	Beside Hannah	Both used dump trucks and shovels to fill and dump; made appropriate truck noises
Associative	Puppets	With Shanleigh and Damian	Children shared puppets, laughed at funny actions, but continued to use own puppets individually

How might the observations in Table 6.2 be used? Josh is engaged in age-appropriate types of play. He seems comfortable with other children, especially with Damian. This observation could be used to encourage interactions between the two boys.

Josh's interests include filling and dumping activities. This activity could be encouraged by providing additional materials in both water and sand. Adding a shelf to the water centre (placed in the water centre to provide the child with opportunity to place a container on it and pour water into the container) might facilitate more parallel and or associative play in water.

B) OBSERVING INTEREST Observations of interest help the care provider to organize settings that encourage children to participate with each other. Based on the interest shown by Josh (Table 6.2), the tool shown in Table 6.3 was used.

How might the observations in Table 6.3 be used?

- To confirm previous observations—It would seem that the strategy to use a shelf in the water centre worked. Josh finds it hard to hold a container and fill it at the same time. This strategy eliminated his difficulty. He also seems to play more often with Damian.

TABLE 6.3 **OBSERVATIONS OF INTEREST**

Name: Josh   **Observer:** Jane
Dates: November 5, 6, 9   **Key:** S = Solitary; P = Parallel; A = Associative

Interest	Frequency	Comments
Play with Damian	PPP AA	Using construction toys—Blocks and Duplo Puppet area, fingerpainting
Filling and dumping	SSS PPP	Water, puzzles, book Noticed shelf in water centre; started to fill and dump

- To plan for interactions—Since the two boys are often seen together, this situation can be used by an adult to generate spontaneous interactions with both boys.

C) OBSERVING ATTENTION SPAN Observing a child's attention span gives information about his or her ability to sustain interest over time. The easiest method is to use a graph like that shown in Figure 6.5. This technique can be combined with types of play and interests. This saves the observer some time and gives the added benefit of recording all the information on one sheet.

How might the observations in Figure 6.5 be used? Inferences can be made about the child's skills and abilities:

- Josh has a normal attention span for activities that he is interested in.
- The type of play Josh engages in is also age-appropriate.
- He has a variety of interests.
- He is interested in filling and dumping activities and taking things apart and putting them together again—mostly functional play activities.

This information could be used to adapt materials in the environment:
- Add the small cubed blocks to the block area. This may encourage more fine motor control to build towers.
- Add construction vehicles to the block area. This may encourage a different type of building.
- Add building wheels and round peg stackers to the manipulative area to encourage further skill in attachment.

5. Adaptations for Play in Inclusive Settings

Children with special needs may find it difficult to participate in play activities. Special adaptations may need to be made to encourage participation in play. Sandall (2004) identifies eight categories for curriculum adaptation: environmental support, materials adaptation, simplifying the activity, using child preferences, special equipment, adult support, peer support and invisible support (Koralek, 2004:44–45).

Key S - Solitary Play
P - Parallel Play
A - Associated Play

Obsrvation of Attention Span, Interest, Type of Play

Name: Josh

Observer: Jane

Chart: Time in minutes (y-axis) vs interest centres (x-axis)

Nov. 12 — P Damian; P Hannah Ben ②; S ①; P Damian

Nov. 13 — P Jordan; P Damian; A Shanheigh

x-axis labels: Block Play - towers; Water ① tab ② centre; Duplo - attach/take apart; Sand - fill dump construction toys; Beading - animal beads random strings

---

A) ENVIRONMENTAL SUPPORT To maximize free choice and facilitate positive inter-actions, a number of adaptations could be made. These adaptations might include:

- Photograph display to help children find the interest centre that they would like to participate in (see Figure 6.6)
- Posted picture symbols to help children communicate what they wish to have or do
- Organization of the environment to facilitate various types of play, such as individual or small group play (see Photos 6.4 and 6.6 on page 183)

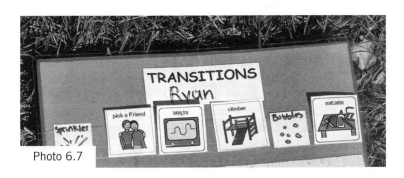

Photo 6.7

FIGURE 6.6

Example of a Photograph Display of Interest Areas

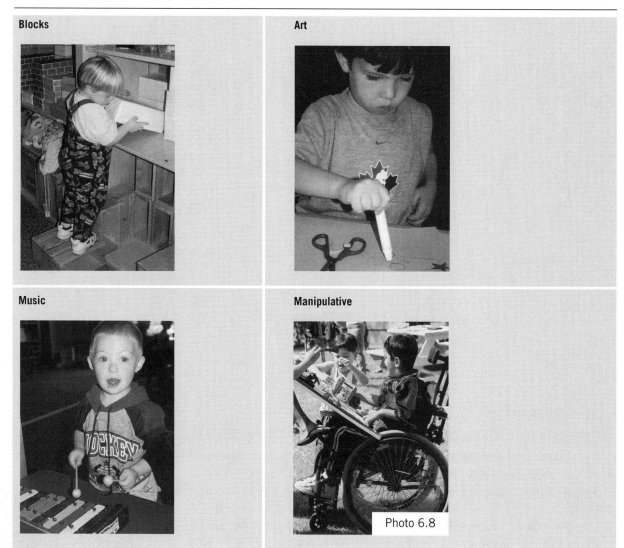

Blocks

Art

Music

Manipulative

Photo 6.8

B) MATERIALS ADAPTATION Materials may be adapted to maximize children's ability to manipulate the objects effectively. Several levels of adaptability could occur: accessibility, comfort and ease of manipulation.

- Accessibility—Children need to be able to freely reach all materials and activities.
- Comfort—Not all children can access materials or activities successfully. For example, putting a wheelchair into a group setting is uncomfortable for the children and for the individual in the wheelchair. Providing a special chair for a child in a wheelchair will enable all children to interact at the same level (Photo 6.9).

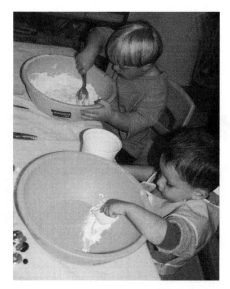

Photo 6.9

- Ease of manipulation—For example, Melanie had only one arm with just two digits on the hand. She liked to play with small vehicles. To pick up small vehicles, she needed to use a tray to trap the vehicles and to have vehicles with open undersurfaces or windows to help her grasp them more easily.

C) SIMPLIFIED ACTIVITIES Activities that involve more than one step may be difficult for some children to accomplish. Children may need to have these types of activities simplified. Simplification could be accomplished in a number of ways:

- Reduction of number of pieces or number of steps—Provide puzzles with fewer pieces. Games such as musical chairs could be changed to listening to the music and sitting down when the music stops without removing chairs.
- Changing the timing of activities—Some children may need more time than others to complete an activity such as painting. Songs such as "Head and Shoulders" may need to be sung much more slowly so that children have time to point to the correct body part.
- Scaffolding—For example, Josh and Ted had learned to make their own play dough. This task was broken down into a number of small steps. These steps were represented pictorially. The boys were able to complete the task with minimal supervision (see Figure 6.7).

D) CHILDREN'S PREFERENCES Children who are interested in what they are doing will continue to work on an activity over long time periods. Benjamin enjoyed painting. He was often observed covering paper with paint using tools such as brushes, but also often using his hands. He rarely participated in writing activities or printing. Christopher, his teacher, noticed his interest. He set up a fingerpainting activity at one table. Christopher then sat down, covered his page with paint and started to draw designs on the page with his fingers. Benjamin watched for a while, clearly intrigued. He finally covered his paper in red paint. He then proceeded to draw

Photo 6.10

FIGURE 6.7

An Example of Scaffolding: Making Play dough

What you need:

Flour

Measuring cup

Spoon

Water

Salt

Mixing bowl

Recipe Cup sizes: Use full cup for flour and water and quarter-cup measure for salt. You could also add steps to add food colour and/or drink crystals to add colour and or pleasant smell.

Step 1: Add 1 cup flour.

Step 2: Add 1 cup salt.

Step 3: Add 1 cup water.

Step 4: Mix.

shapes on his paper. He beamed when Jeremy identified the shapes by size, shape or letter name. This activity lasted over several weeks (Photo 6.10). Benjamin's efforts were displayed (see Figure 6.8).

E) SPECIAL EQUIPMENT Some children may need special equipment to help them interact appropriately with other children. For example, John is using a weighted bag over his legs to help him concentrate on the music activity he is involved with (Photo 6.11).

F) ADULT SUPPORT Adult support is a critical factor in any children's environment. Adult support includes:

* Encouragement of the activity the child is engaged in—Benjamin was encouraged to continue to fingerpaint by the posting of his results, and by the adult's interest in his activity.

Photo 6.11

FIGURE 6.8
Sample Display of Benjamin's Efforts

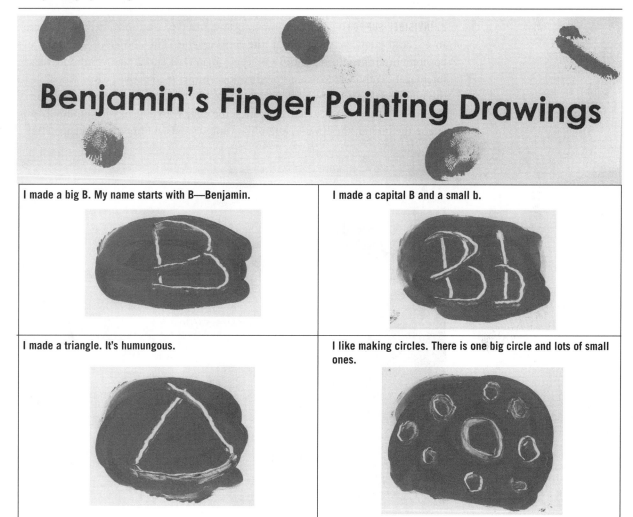

- Joining in—An example would be playing along with the children during musical activities. Harmon was encouraged to join in by providing him with a chair that helped him to be at the children's level (see Photo 6.9).
- Modelling—Jeremy modelled fingerpainting strategies to Benjamin.
- Commenting—Jeremy made relevant comments on Benjamin's fingerpainting.

G) PEER SUPPORT The early childhood educator uses opportunities to encourage children's peers to join in the play. Jonathan was finding it difficult to find something to do. He had been wandering around the room asking if he could join in. Several times he had been rejected. Susan noticed that Jonathan was walking over to Gracie, who was reading to herself. She walked over to Gracie with Jonathan and said, "Gracie is reading. Would you like to listen?" Jonathan nodded. Gracie looked up and smiled and asked Jonathan if Jonathan's baby liked the story. Jonathan smiled and smacked her hand enthusiastically to indicate his pleasure. The two children continued to play together (Photo 6.12).

H) INVISIBLE SUPPORT The environment is organized to maximize children's success. In effect, the environment acts as the third teacher. The choice of materials and equipment and the organization of these materials encourage children to learn interdependently. Materials are stored on low, sturdy, open shelves, easily accessible to the children. The shelves and containers are labelled for easy retrieval and return (Figure 6.4). Labelling is used to encourage the child with difficulty in communicating to use the pictures or photographs to communicate (see Photo 6.7 on page 203).

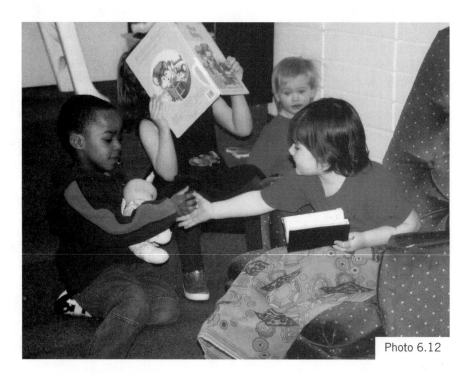

Photo 6.12

Role of the Early Childhood Educator

The early childhood educator's role of encouraging active play in the learning environment requires many skills. These include:

- Collaboration with all partners—To set up a learning environment that maximizes children's learning through play, a collaborative process should be established with children, families and other professionals to identify and utilize children's skills, interests and abilities.
- Creation of an atmosphere of warmth, respect and acceptance—Children need to feel comfortable that their interactions, self-expressions and learning are accepted and valued (see Figures 6.6 and 6.8).
- Arrangement of materials and equipment to encourage active play situations within each interest area in the room—Children need to be continually observed to utilize spontaneous "teachable moments."
- Careful consideration of outdoor play spaces—Play spaces outside should reflect a smooth transition from indoor to outdoor play (see Photos 6.5 and 6.8).
- Adaptation—Identification of necessary adaptations to the learning spaces, the materials and equipment in these spaces, and the interactions occurring there is critical (see pages 202-208).
- Use of displays to document children's learning and activities—Displays help to maintain interest and keep all individuals informed about the learning and activities of the children (Figures 6.6 and 6.8).
- Observing children—Adults observe and document children's activities to enable them to adapt the environment as needed (see pages 200–202).
- Documentation of learning—Adults facilitate in the creation of portfolios (Figure 6.3) or documentation panels (Figure 6.2) that describe children's interests and learning.
- Modification—Play strategies are modified as needed (see pages 202–208).
- Maintaining interest—Materials are added, rotated or adapted to maintain attention and interest over time (Photo 6.3).

SUMMARY

Best practices for all children require that children have the right to learn through play. Through play children establish positive attitudes toward learning that last a lifetime. Research has identified that withdrawal from play situations has implications for academic success and provides a "strong predictor of peer rejection, social anxiety, loneliness, depression, and negative self-esteem in later childhood and adolescence" (Bergen, 2004: 4). Play builds the foundations for all future skills, abilities and learning. It is therefore critical to foster children's play to develop skills in:

- Social competence
- Communication competence

- ...forming objects and actions symbolically
- ...egotiating with peers and adults
- ...olving problems

- Learning to take different perspectives
- Learning how to learn

KEY POINTS

Principles that influence play
- Play affects the child's motivation.
- Play affects cognitive decentring.
- Play develops mental representation.
- Play develops deliberate actions.

Types of play in developmental order
- Solitary, parallel, associative, cooperative
- Functional, symbolic, constructive, dramatic, games with rules

Reasons for diverse play abilities in inclusive settings
- Developmental ability, background experiences, family values, family expectations, type of disability, social pressures

Collaborative process
- Families identify interests, monitor progress, mitigate areas of concern, celebrate successes
- Other professionals: play therapists, occupational therapists, sand therapists, music therapists—Create appropriate play atmosphere, organize play areas, gain insight into behaviour, gain expert advice, become more knowledgeable about the services specialists provide

Setting the stage for play
- Observation of children's abilities and interests
- Materials and resources—Durable, safe, multi-functional, multi-sensory, avoid frustration, accessible, adaptable, based on children's interests
- Developmental- and age-appropriateness
- Maximization of self-expression, interactivity, mediation
- Maximization of success—Scaffolding, familiarity, spontaneity

- Program format—Flexible transitions, time to complete tasks, predictability, stability
- Documentation of success
- Organization of learning areas—High visibility, accessibility, labelling, holistic approach

Observations of children
- Types of play, interests, attention span

Adaptations of play in inclusive settings
- Environmental support
- Material adaptations—Accessibility, comfort, ease of manipulation
- Simplified activities—Number of pieces, changed timing, scaffolding
- Use of children's preferences
- Special equipment
- Adult and peer support

Role of early childhood educator
- Collaboration—Children, families, staff and other professionals
- Creating an atmosphere of warmth, respect and acceptance
- Organizing materials and equipment to maintain interest over time
- Smooth transitions from indoor to outdoor play
- Identification of adaptations
- Documenting with documentation panels, portfolios
- Observing and documenting children's interests, skills, progress, successes

EXERCISES

1. Reflect on the following situation: A mother complains that her child is not meeting the goals as set out by her physiotherapist. She feels that the staff is allowing her daughter to play too much. She indicates that she wants to see an IPP set up that addresses her child's needs specifically. She would like to see less involvement in play and more time spent on structured activities such as tracing letters and other manipulative tasks. How would you respond to this mother?

2. Observe a group of preschoolers in an integrated setting. Identify how often you see the children involved in various types of play. Explain why the children might be involved in each type of play.

3. Identify the key individuals in your area whom you might wish to collaborate with to set up an appropriate inclusive play-based program. What type of collaboration would you seek from each individual identified? What are the benefits of this collaboration to the child, the family, the specialist and the staff?

4. Utilize the criteria developed for materials and resources on pages 191–193. Develop an observation chart. Take the tool to a local toy store and identify which toys would be suitable in inclusive settings. Justify each answer.

5. Utilize the chart below to identify various documentation methods in child care centres in your area. Compare your results with your classmates. Discuss which methods are most effective and why.

6. For each of the adaptive criteria listed, develop specific strategies that will provide for best inclusive play practices:
   • Providing environmental support
   • Adaptations of materials
   • Providing support from adults and peers
   • Simplifying materials and activities

7. Describe the role of an early childhood educator in an inclusive setting. How is that role the same as in other settings? How is it different?

DOCUMENTATION TYPES

Type	Description	Effectiveness
Displays		
Documentation panels		
Portfolios		
Other		

RESOURCES

National Lekotek Centre
www.lekotek.org

Playground Safety for Your Child with Special Needs
www.cshcn.org/resources/Playground-Safety.htm

Caring for Children with Special Needs: Physical Differences
www.ces.ncsu.edu/depts/fcs/human/pubs/nc15.html

Resource listing on various topics
www.letshomeschool.com/specialneeds.htm

Institute for Play
www.instituteforplay.com/5importance_of_play.htm

National Network for Child Care
www.nncc.org/Curriculum/better.play.html

HaLife
http://halife.com/family/play.html

Invest in Kids
www.investinkids.ca/DisplayContent.aspx?name=playing_with_baby

Alliance for Childhood
www.allianceforchildhood.net/projects/play

Canadian Association for Child and Play Therapy
www.cacpt.com

Child and Family Canada—Special Needs
www.cfc-efc.ca/menu/specneed_en.htm

Occupational Therapy
www.otworks.com/otworks_page.asp?pageid=761

The Canadian Play Therapy Institute
www.playtherapy.org

The British Columbia Association for Play Therapy
www.vcn.bc.ca/bcapt

Sand Therapy Canada
www.primal.bc.ca/ptsandpl.htm

Sandplay: Christina Becker, Jungian analyst and psychotherapist
www3.sympatico.ca/cjbecker/sandplay.htm

Canadian Association for Music Therapy
www.musictherapy.ca

REFERENCES

Alliance for Childhood (2004). The Importance of Play Children from Birth to Five: A Statement of First Principles on Early Education for Educators and Policymakers. Alliance for Childhood [online]. Available at www.allianceforchildhood.net/projects/play/index.htm (5-12-2004).

Bergen, D. (2004). Pretend Play and Young Children's Development. ERIC Digest [online]. Available at www.ericdigests.org/2002-2/play.htm (25-9-2004).

Bodrova, E. & Leong, D. (2004). Chopsticks and Counting Chips Do Play and Foundational Skills Need to Compete for the Teacher's Attention in an Early Childhood Classroom? In D. Koralek (Ed.), *Spotlight on Young Children and Play* (pp. 4–11). Washington, DC: National Association for the Education of Young Children.

Bradway, K. (2004). Sandplay with Children. Sandplay Therapists of America [online]. Available at www.sandplayusa.org (12-1-2005).

Campbell, C. (2000). *The Mozart Effect for Children*. New York, NY: HarperCollins Publishers Inc.

Canadian Association for Child and Play Therapy (2004). Play Therapy. Canadian Association for Child and Play Therapy [online]. Available at www.cacpt.com (1-3-2005).

Canadian Association for Music Therapy (2003). What Is Music Therapy? Canadian Association for Music Therapy [online]. Available at www.musictherapy.ca (8-2-2004).

Carr, A. (2005). Play and Relationships: Programming for Inclusion. Child & Family Canada [online]. Available at www.cfc-efc.ca/docs/cccf/00021_en.htm (10-1-2005).

Crowther, I. (2003). *Creating Effective Learning Environments*. Scarborough, ON: Nelson Thomson Learning.

Ferland, F. (2005). *The Ludic Model: Play, Children with Physical Disabilities and Occupational Therapy*. Second Edition. Ottawa, ON: CAOT Publications ACE.

Harms, T., Clifford, R., & Cryer, D. (1998). *Early Childhood Environment Rating Scale*. Revised Edition. New York, NY: Teachers College Press.

Jones, E. (2004). Playing to Get Smart. In D. Koralek (Ed.), *Spotlight on Young Children and Play* (pp. 24–27). Washington, DC: The National Association for the Education of Young Children.

Koralek, D. E. (2004). *Spotlight on Young Children and Play*. Washington, DC: National Association for the Education of Young Children.

Landreth, G. (2002). *Play Therapy: The Art of the Relationship*. New York, NY: Brunner-Routledge

Malaguzzi, L. (1997). *The Hundred Languages of Children*. Second Edition. Reggio Emilia, Italy: Reggio Children.

National Lekotek Centre (2005). Resources... Top 10 Tips for Choosing Toys. National Lekotek Centre [online]. Available at www.lekotek.org/resources/informationontoys/tentips.html.

Perry, J. (2004). Making Sense of Outdoor Pretend Play. In D. Koralek (Ed.), *Spotlight on Young Children and Play* (pp. 17–21). Washington, DC: The National Association for the Education of Young Children.

7 Managing Behaviours in Inclusive Settings

CHAPTER

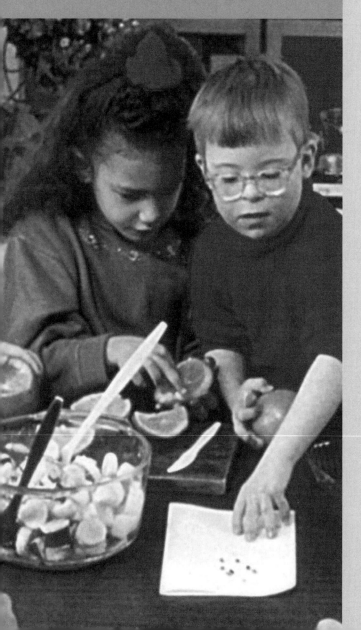

"Children with challenging behaviours desperately need to learn social skills to protect them in the future. Their socially competent peers, who can act as role models and reinforce their attempts at positive behaviour every day, are the best possible teachers (if there are enough properly trained adults around to support them of course).

"The other children are learning, too. They learn how to help a friend, how to stand up for themselves, how not to become victims. Above all, they learn that people are different and that everyone is a valuable individual" (Kaiser & Sklar Rasminsky, 1999: 14).

Learning Outcomes

After studying this chapter, you will be able to:

1. Describe why it is difficult to diagnose challenging behaviours.
2. Identify and describe the types of challenging behaviours of children.
3. Explain why it is important to understand the causes of challenging behaviours.
4. Identify the partners in a collaborative process, and explain why this collaboration is critical with each partner.
5. Identify how and why to observe challenging behaviours of children.
6. Describe the similarities and differences between a standard IPP and a behavioural IPP.
7. Describe the types of environmental adaptations that should discourage the occurrence of challenging behaviours, considering the social context, the overall program, the use of interaction approaches and the child's perspective.
8. Describe the roles of the early childhood educator in organizing a positive learning environment.

Photo 7.1

Introduction

It is often difficult to formally diagnose children with behaviour problems because a challenging behaviour in one setting may not be challenging in another setting. This is a result of the expectations placed on individuals, cultural values and the type of environment a child is in. Rashawne at age two was an active, curious child. He actively explored the environment, and he especially loved filling and dumping activities (Photo 7.1). But the resulting disarray caused several reactions, depending on where he was playing or whom he was interacting with:

- At home, this activity was acceptable, as long as Rashawne helped clean it up afterwards.
- When he played at a friend's house, he was told it was not appropriate to create a mess—"These beads are meant for stringing, not dumping."
- Within the day care situation, this type of activity was discouraged because it was too noisy, too messy and might cause another child to trip and fall. Additionally, the pieces were deemed too small for toddler use because the toddler might choke on them.

This type of play behaviour would also have been inappropriate in more formal settings such as a church.

When Rashawne was asked to clean up his beads, his immediate action was to continue to play. When asked again, he said, "No." Again the reactions to Rashawne were varied:

- His parents calmly ignored his behaviour and made a game of cleaning up the beads. The clatter that the beads made when tossed into a container made a pleasing sound. Rashawne was soon absorbed in the clean-up activity.
- His friend's mother, Janelle, told him not to be naughty, and to help clean up the beads. Rashawne ignored her. When she insisted, Rahawne ran away, kicking the beads in front of him. Janelle's impression was that he was a hard-to-manage child.
- Rashawne visited the preschool room. He found the beads and proceeded to dump them. One of the adults noticed his behaviour and quickly redirected his dumping behaviour by providing alternative containers to dump into.

Each of these settings produced different perceptions about Rashawne's behaviour. At home, he was encouraged to explore freely with some limitation: he had to clean up. His parents realized the value of the activity Rashawne was involved in and encouraged his behaviour. The toddler room did not provide these types of toys because they were considered dangerous. His friend's mother had expectations that were not appropriate for toddlers. It is a natural developmental activity for toddlers to fill and dump. It is natural for toddlers to assert their independence by refusing to help. The preschool teachers understood the toddler's developmental stage and redirected his behaviour positively so he could continue to actively explore.

Behaviour should always be looked upon as positive when children are:

- Actively involved in play
- Using materials and toys appropriately
- Interacting positively with each other
- Learning from their interactions with materials and toys
- Enjoying their activities

In contrast, challenging behaviours are behaviours that:

- Interfere with children's learning, development and success at play
- Are harmful to the child or other children
- Put the child at risk for later social problems or school failure (Kaiser et al., 1999: 7)

Types of Challenging Behaviour

It is estimated that from three to fifteen percent of preschool children in Canada are considered challenging (Vitaro, De Civita & Pagani, 1996). Challenging behaviours are varied; they depend on the child's temperament, the circumstances and the setting in which these behaviours occur. Some of these behaviours are frustrating to adults and peers; others may be dangerous to peers or to the child; and some may escape notice as a challenging behaviour. Children who are quiet, shy or withdrawn may not be identified as having challenging behaviours because the behaviours are less obvious and are more socially acceptable. Challenging behaviours may be grouped into several categories: emotional, conduct, hyperkinetic, developmental or diagnosed.

1. Emotional-Related Behaviours

It is often difficult for adults to separate what they think is the imagination of young children from what the young child thinks is real. A shadow on a wall may become a monster; a hot breath of wind may be a lion chasing the child: these in the child's mind are real. However, many of these instances are based on a combination of correctly observing what has been seen and heard and using the imagination to fill in the blanks.

Adults are not always able to judge what the incident was that started a train of thought. They tend to judge the child based on the outcome of the imaginary episode. For example, as a young child, my family emigrated from Germany. I overheard my family discussing Hurricane Hazel. I heard them talking about the hurricane's ability to tear the roofs off buildings and to throw cars into the air. I heard them say that the hurricane would arrive tomorrow. I had never heard of a hurricane before. I could not make sense of what they were saying. Nothing in my life had ever exposed me to something that could rip the roofs off buildings and throw cars into the air. The only thing that made sense was that a monster would come and create this havoc. Not wanting to be eaten by this monster, I refused to go to school the next morning.

How do adults separate what is real from what is imaginary to a child? The adult needs to understand the development of children, listen closely to what the child is saying and put what the child has said into the context of what the child is experiencing. Early childhood educators need to gain understanding of the child's world.

Some of the emotional behaviours that children exhibit may stem from:

- Phobias and anxiety states—It is estimated that between five and twelve percent of children are affected by phobias or anxiety states. A **phobia** is a persistent and irrational fear expressed about an object, event, animal or person. Common examples include the young child's fear of the dark. An **anxiety state** is a fear of something that might happen in the future. Jenna, a four-year-old, was reluctant to go outside. She became very agitated and clung to her caregiver's legs. It turned out that Jenna was afraid of being shot. She had seen a news program about children who had been shot in a school. This had not happened in her community, but she was convinced it would happen to her.
- Depression—There is mounting evidence that some preschoolers suffer from depression. An ongoing five-year longitudinal study found that preschoolers who are depressed may be irritable, grouchy, sad or withdrawn. The child may cease to enjoy activities that had previously been enjoyed and may act out negative feelings during play (Weingarden Dubin, 2001; Winzer, 1999).

2. Conduct-Related Behaviours

Children who seem to be hard to manage because they exhibit a number of extreme behaviours are often diagnosed with conduct disorders. Up to 10 percent of children fall into this category (Weingarden Dubin, 2001). Some of these behaviours are developmentally appropriate for young children who have not yet developed the understanding of their behaviours One longitudinal survey of children in Canada concluded that physical aggression starts at about nine months and peaks between 27 and 29 months. During these ages, 53.3 percent of boys and 41.1 percent of girls exhibit aggressive behaviours (Kaiser et al., 1999: 7). Typical behaviours one might expect of children include those listed in Table 7.1.

3. Hyperkinetic-Related Behaviours

Kinetic behaviour is behaviour associated with the energy of movement. **Hyperkinetic** behaviour involves increased energy and movement. Hyperkinetic behaviour is part of a diagnosed disability such as attention deficit hyperactivity disorder. Depending on the diagnosis used, it is estimated that from three to five percent of children suffer from this disorder (National Institute of Mental Health, 2003; Winzer, 1999). Typical behaviours exhibited may include all or some of the following behaviours, depending on the severity of the condition:

TABLE 7.1 **CONDUCT-RELATED BEHAVIOURS**

Behaviour	Description
Physical aggression	Biting, hitting, punching, pushing, pinching, kicking
Verbal aggression	Name-calling, swearing, using derogatory terms, shouting
Destructive behaviour	Breaking materials or toys, destroying other children's creations
Lying	Blaming others, refusing to accept responsibility for actions
Refusal to follow directions	Defying attitude when asked to do something, ignoring requests, refusing to follow routines
Running away	Trying to leave if he or she does not want to do something

- Overactiveness—Children who exhibit this behaviour are continually on the move, continually talking or interrupting, and flitting from activity to activity. They also tend to have short attention spans.

- Impulsiveness—The child acts without thinking about the consequences. Joseph picked up a stone, looked at it and threw it. The stone hit another child. It had not been Joseph's intent to hit another child. He simply had a stone in his hand and to him the logical thing to do was to throw it.

- Inattention—The child ignores verbal interactions; for instance, he or she is unable to follow directions or answer questions about a story. The child's attention easily wanders from the task at hand.

4. Development-Related Behaviours

Some challenging behaviours would be considered appropriate at a younger developmental age. "Human beings are not born with social skills. Very small children

From a Mother   Reflection

Christy was always an active child. She was continually on the move. I did not associate this with any problems until one day Christy brought me one of her favourite stories to read. During the time I read her the story, she squirmed, fiddled with toys on the floor and ran away. I finally started to watch her more closely and realized that she was not just active but unable to sustain her activity for any length of time.

Reflection *From an Early Childhood Educator*

Dillon was always eager to learn. I found that he was easily distractible. If he heard something that attracted his interest, he was gone. We finally set up areas in the room that decreased the degree of visual distraction. When Dillon was in these areas, he seemed to be much less distracted.

don't have words to express their feelings and needs. They don't yet connect actions to consequences, they are impulsive and self-centred, and even though they may notice others' feelings they don't begin to develop the ability to empathize until they are about two years old. They use any means at their disposal to get what they want and to make themselves understood" (Kaiser et al., 1999: 7). Children need to learn which behaviours are appropriate and which ones are not.

When children continue to use behaviours that were appropriate for younger ages, this may be indicative of other underlying conditions such as delays in acquiring skills, or more pervasive conditions such as autism or learning disabilities.

5. Diagnosed Conditions

Some conditions, such as attention deficit disorder (ADD), attention deficit hyperactivity disorder (ADHD), fetal alcohol syndrome (FAS) or fetal alcohol effect (FAE) may be the cause of differences in behaviours. Some typical behaviours include:

- Lack of eye contact
- Lack of response to others
- Self-injury, such as head banging or biting
- Self-stimulating behaviours such as flicking fingers in front of eyes while rocking back and forth
- Continuous repetitive movements such as spinning around or running in circles
- Switching from passive to nervous or active behaviours and back to quiet activity again; for instance, sitting quietly rocking, then spinning on the spot, then sitting quietly and then rocking again
- Showing extreme dislikes for some stimuli such as certain sounds
- Finding changes in the environment or routines difficult to cope with

Causes of Various Types of Behaviour

The causes of children's behaviour must be understood in order to provide successful intervention strategies. Not all strategies are successful for all situations. Causes of behaviour may be classified using the following categories: developmental, environmental, functional and psychological.

1. Developmental Causes of Behaviour

To identify possible problems, as well as advanced abilities, it is important to recognize and understand the typical behaviours of children. Behaviour like all other domains is dependent on interactions with the environment and other individuals, and on normal growth and development. Children learn to control their behaviour along a developmental continuum. Table 7.2 identifies some of the milestones needed to develop self-control. These milestones are helpful in:

- Developing tools to observe behaviour
- Gaining understanding about normal, delayed and gifted behaviours
- Identifying potential problems

2. Environmental Causes of Behaviour

Often behaviour problems arise from an external source: the learning environment. The organization of the learning environment can lead to either the development of pro-social skills or inappropriate behaviours. Factors to consider are the functionality of the learning spaces, noise levels, choices, use of space, type of organization and type of toys. The factors and resulting possible behaviours are described in Table 7.3. The information can be used to develop a checklist to evaluate the environment to identify if the organization of the environment might lead to challenging behaviours.

In addition to the arrangement of the environment, the interaction between adults and children may also lead to some challenging behaviours:

- When adults pay more attention to negative behaviour than positive behaviour, the negative behaviour itself may become rewarding. The focus of staff interactions with children should be a predominance of positive-behaviour reinforcement.
- When expectations are inconsistent from time to time or between individuals, the children quickly learn to ignore these expectations. This leads to frustration for all individuals, children and adults alike. Expectations should be realistic and consistent for all children.
- Often frustration occurs because the child was not able to understand what was expected of him or her. Care must be taken to ensure that all interactions are clear and tailored to fit the comprehension level of each individual child.

3. Functional Causes of Behaviour

When an early childhood educator has identified that a challenging behaviour exists, has eliminated the possibility of a developmental cause, has assessed the environment, has analyzed the child–staff interactions and has still not been able to solve the problem, a functional behaviour assessment should be completed.

TABLE 7.2   **DEVELOPMENT OF SELF-CONTROL**

Milestone	Age	Importance
Mutual regulation	Infancy	When caregivers recognize and respond immediately to the signals that infants give, the infant gains trust in his ability to communicate and have his communications understood and responded to.
Exploration and observation of body parts	Birth to 3 months	As infants move and touch body parts they start to gain awareness about their own bodies and how they move. This is the first step toward establishing self-confidence.
Recognition of other people	Birth–3 months	Recognition of others also leads to increased awareness of self as a separate individual.
Expression of emotions	3 months and up	Recognition of and reaction to various emotions expressed is needed in order to gain self-control.
Recognition of own name and response to own name	4–12 months	Recognizing and responding to one's name is a major milestone in the development of self-awareness.
Imitation	1 year	Imitation leads to greater ability to communicate, to act upon the environment and, as a result, to establish greater autonomy.
Self-regulation	1 year	Once infants start to eat by themselves, they are becoming more independent and are starting to do things for themselves—"I eat when I am hungry."
Establishment of cause and effect relationships	1–2 years	As infants and toddlers actively explore the environment, they begin to realize that they have the power to make things happen by their actions.
Acquisition of language	Preschool age	Increased skill in language parallels increased skills in the ability to think and reason, which in turn lead to greater self-control.
Direct independent actions	1–2 years	Toddlers understand simple concepts. They listen to a simple request and comply or do not comply. Toddlers are learning to express their autonomy.
Finding alternative solutions	2 years and up	When children realize that they can control the situation by using a different approach, such as finding a different book to read rather than grabbing a book from someone else, another milestone in self-control is established.
Reaction to personal feelings	About 3 years and up	When children recognize that they are tired and find a quiet activity to engage in, they are learning to respond to and respect personal needs.

TABLE 7.3   **ENVIRONMENTAL FACTORS THAT MAY CAUSE CHALLENGING BEHAVIOURS**

Description of Factor	Description of Possible Behaviours
Overcrowding—Either too many people in a space or not enough room for active play	Children may become frustrated because they cannot get involved in active play. Aggressive behaviours such as throwing materials, grabbing toys or hitting a child who took a toy may occur.
Too many open spaces	Young children like to run. Large open areas encourage running activities such as chasing each other.
Disorganized storage of material	When children cannot find a toy they are looking for, or materials are placed in large containers, dumping will occur. Often this leaves a mess. If children do not have clear guidelines that indicate where materials are found, they tend to leave the area without cleaning up. This may also lead to frustration and non-compliance. The task becomes too difficult.
Noisy environment or overpowering background noises such as continuous loud music	When environments become too noisy, the noise level tends to continue to increase. This becomes frustrating and disruptive to some children. Some children will not be able to concentrate. It is particularly hard for children who are hard of hearing and children with ADD/ADHD or FAS. These children may withdraw from the situation or become even noisier in their attempt to be heard.
Too many choices	When too many choices are provided, children can easily become confused. Children typically will get distracted by the variety of choices and flit from one choice to the next. This is particularly true of younger children and many children with special needs.
Too few choices	Too few choices lead to conflict. Children may become aggressive to enable them to play with an activity of choice.
Choices that are developmentally- or age-inappropriate	Children may become frustrated because the activity is too easy or too hard. Materials may be destroyed.
Competitive activities	The very nature of competition causes frustration for some children because there is always a loser and a winner.
Provision of violent toys	This often results in aggression against the toy or peers.
Learning experiences not based on the interests or background experiences of the children	Children may not actively engage in play because of a lack of interest, because the activity is inappropriate or because they do not know what is expected.
Too much waiting during transitions	When children are waiting, they are bored and will resort to other activities to entertain themselves. These activities may include aggressive behaviours, withdrawal, non-compliance and noisiness.

"A functional assessment assumes that the behaviour in question serves a purpose or 'function' for the child. Simply put, it 'functions' to get the child something she or he wants, such as attention of staff, access to a favourite toy/activity or escape from a disliked activity. In most cases we find that the behaviour compensates for a skill deficit which is related to the child's special needs" (Orr & Cavallaro, 1997: 1-2). For example, when Jade wanted something that another child had, she would simply take it. If an adult noticed, she would sweetly smile at the child and say, "Sorry." The strategy worked; she rarely got a lecture, and she usually got to keep the toy. Jade used the strategy because it had worked in the past, not because she had been able to reason that this was a good strategy to use.

To prevent the challenging behaviour from recurring, it is necessary to find out why the child is engaging in this behaviour. Once that is known, the solutions are usually natural consequences of that behaviour. For example, Jade, a three-year-old, consistently grabbed toys from other playmates. When Jade was observed, it was discovered that she was at the parallel play stage and that there were not enough similar toys to play with. Similar toys were placed in the area. When Jade started to grab, she was told: "Jamie is playing with that toy. Here is another one for you."

4. Psychological Causes of Behaviour

"Although psychological abuse leaves no physical scars, it shakes children's feeling of security and disrupts their development. If Alex, Esther or Ryan is reported to child welfare authorities for suspected physical abuse or neglect, caseworkers will be aware that the child may also be a victim of psychological abuse. Prevention involves working to help these children grow up feeling good about themselves" (Chamberland, Laporte, Lavergne & Baraldi, 2003: 1).

Psychological abuse is often an invisible cause of challenging behaviours. Some forms of psychological abuse might include:

- Ridiculing the child
- Ignoring the child or the child's efforts
- Verbal aggressiveness
- Discrediting the child's achievements and efforts
- Comparing the child unfavourably to others
- Making negative judgments about the child's behaviours

"Children who are victims of psychological abuse experience more emotional problems than children who are not victims of this type of maltreatment." Victims of direct psychological abuse are:

- More socially withdrawn
- More depressed
- More insecure
- Much likelier to engage in behaviours that put them at risk (Chamberland et al., 2003: 3)

Range of Behaviours in Inclusive Settings

Within any setting, many of the behaviours previously described may be found. The range of behaviours evident depends on the type of special needs, the age of the children, how the environment is organized and the interaction patterns between the adults and the children within the learning environment. Typical behaviours include difficulties in:

- Interacting with peers, resulting in a range of behaviours such as aggression, withdrawal and tantrums
- Attending or interacting in group settings, resulting in behaviours such as interrupting, self-stimulation or fidgeting
- Coping with making choices, resulting in behaviours such as flitting from activity to activity, withdrawal or aimless wandering
- Concentrating, resulting in distractible behaviours such as continually being attracted to a new toy or activity, or taking all toys off the shelf but not playing with any one
- Controlling emotions, resulting in behaviours such as temper tantrums, verbal or physical aggressiveness or defiance
- Accepting praise, which results in low self-esteem and often underachievement: "I can't do this. It's too hard."

Positive Guidance Strategies in Inclusive Settings

1. Establishing a Collaborative Process

Collaboration among all partners is critical. Approaches to guiding children's behaviours must be agreed upon and be consistent to effect any lasting changes in behaviour. Children need to know that expectations are constant. They quickly learn to adjust their behaviour depending on the situation they are in. This is learned behaviour.

For example, Jillian, a three-year-old, had learned to use the phrase "Shut up!" When she used it with her older peers, they thought it was cute and they would burst out laughing. When her teacher asked her to do something, she responded, "Shut up!" and smiled. Her teacher smiled back and said that this was an inappropriate word to use. Jillian thought about it and said, "Shut up, please?" Jillian had obviously had a pleasant experience in the past when she had used this phrase. She was reluctant to give it up. She also knew that "please" was an appropriate word in her preschool. So she tried to create a winning situation.

Children can learn to conform to different expectations in various environments. However, when the expectations are consistent, the child can make better sense of the world and this leads to growth in self-control.

A) COLLABORATION WITH FAMILIES Families share many of the concerns that relate to challenging behaviours. They face the same difficulties at home as are evident in the child care centre. A collaborative process helps deal with the behaviour in the most positive and expedient way for all individuals involved. The collaborative process should include:

- Observations of the child's behaviour
- Development of an IPP
- Evaluation of progress

B) COLLABORATION WITH OTHER PROFESSIONALS Depending on the severity of the problem, other professionals who might become involved with the child include psychologists, psychiatrists, resource consultants, behaviour management experts, mental health workers or play, music or sand therapists. These professionals offer valuable insight into problems. Their collaborative role has many aspects:

- Assisting in setting up an appropriate IPP
- Offering suggestions for positive guidance techniques
- Offering suggestions for how to organize the environment effectively
- Advising on the types of materials and resources that are most effective for dealing with challenging behaviours

C) COLLABORATION WITH OTHER STAFF MEMBERS Dealing with challenging behaviours should be approached consistently by all staff members who may interact with the child. Staff need to be informed of the appropriate strategies to use and should be involved in the evaluation and adaptation process. This gives all staff members opportunities to become more involved and to model appropriate behaviours so that the children can gain from a consistent approach.

2. Observing Children's Behaviours

It is critical to observe the behaviour of the child to try to diagnose the cause of the problem. Does the problem lie in the way the environment is organized? Is it due to the interaction pattern between the children and the staff? Is it a functional behaviour? If the cause cannot be determined and the behaviour continues to exist, it is usually wise to refer the child to a specialist. Observation of children should be conducted in consideration of the following:

A) HOW OFTEN DOES THE BEHAVIOUR OCCUR? The best method for collecting this type of information is through a frequency count. This is best done by making a note of the behaviour each time it occurs (see Figure 7.1).

This type of observation is useful in determining whether a behaviour pattern exists or not. For example, Melanie identified Jordan as being aggressive. She had caught him biting a child once and hitting another child. When she started to count his aggressive behaviours on a regular basis, she found that these had been isolated incidences. If Melanie had discovered instead that Jordan was hitting and biting more often, she should have continued her observations to find out more about his behaviour.

B) WHEN AND WHERE DOES THE BEHAVIOUR OCCUR? Knowing the times of day and how often the behaviour occurs at those times can yield important insights. Is

FIGURE 7.1

Counting Behaviours

Name: Jordan   **Dates:** February 1-10
Observer: Melanie

Behaviour	Frequency
Hitting	I
Biting	I

there a certain routine or activity that might lead to disruptive behaviour? Figure 7.2 provides an example of how this might be accomplished.

This type of observation not only confirms that the child is hitting, it also gives the circumstances under which the child is behaving aggressively. It would seem that Jason is engaging in functional behaviour. He is using the aggression to get what he wants: a toy. During circle time, he is also getting what he wants. When he bites, he is removed from the activity. Since biting only occurs during circle time, it is safe to assume that Jason does not want to participate in circle time.

C) HOW LONG DOES THE BEHAVIOUR LAST? For some behaviours it is not only impor-tant to know how often the behaviour occurs but also how long it lasts (**duration count**). Observation of this type of behaviour works well for behaviours such as separation anxiety or temper tantrums. Knowing know how long a child may engage in this type of behaviour answers the question of whether intervention is needed or the child is likely to settle down by himself. The easiest method is to use a graph to document the information. The circumstances and setting can be added to give the detail needed for planning effective intervention strategies.

The information gleaned from the observation shown in Figure 7.3 indicates that Amanda will continue to be upset for a long time. This may cause disruptions to the program and to the other children. This is also a functional behaviour. She wanted a certain book and continued her behaviour until she got it. She did not

FIGURE 7.2

Behaviour Occurrence

Name: Jason   **Dates:** February 11–15
Observer: Pritti

Behaviour	Frequency	Setting
Hitting	++++ ++++ III	During free play—hits a child who has a toy he wants, then grabs toy: or if toy taken from him, he hits
Biting	++++ ++++	Circle time—bites children sitting near him

FIGURE 7.3
Duration Count

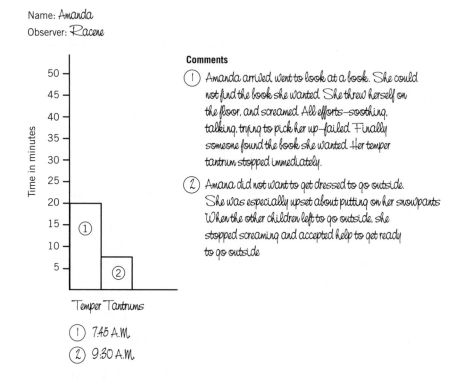

Name: Amanda
Observer: Racene

Comments

① Amanda arrived, went to look at a book. She could not find the book she wanted. She threw herself on the floor, and screamed. All efforts—soothing, talking, trying to pick her up—failed. Finally someone found the book she wanted. Her temper tantrum stopped immediately.

② Amana did not want to get dressed to go outside. She was especially upset about putting on her snowpants. When the other children left to go outside, she stopped screaming and accepted help to get ready to go outside.

Temper Tantrums

① 7:45 A.M.
② 9:30 A.M.

want to get dressed and continued her behaviour until all the children had gone outside. This seems to indicate that she is willing to cooperate to be with the other children.

Additional information needs to be gathered to learn what strategies have been tried in the past, and which were successful or not successful (see Figure 7.4). This information will give a better idea about how to plan appropriate intervention strategies for the individual child.

As always, it is better to develop a learning environment and experiences for children by using their interests. Tools for observing interest have been covered in previous chapters (see Figure 5.12 on page 164 and Table 6.3 on page 202).

FIGURE 7.4

Recording Intervention Strategies

Name: Damian
Observer: Rachelle

Behaviour	Strategy	Result
Temper tantrum	He wanted to eat macaroni and cheese.	It was not available that day. Provided explanation. Showed him that none was there. Unsuccessful; cried harder. Stopped; asked for it the next day.

3. The Behavioural IPP

Once the observation process has been completed, and the staff has some awareness of the types of strategies that may be used to calm individual children, an IPP can be developed.

The development of an IPP for behaviours follows a slightly different pattern from other types of IPPs. The primary purpose of a behavioural IPP is to either increase incidence of a behaviour, such as using words instead of hitting, or decrease a behaviour, such as pushing or pinching. In order for the IPP to be effective, there needs to be some measure against which progress can be measured. This is called a base line. A **base line** is a method used to determine how often behaviour has occurred prior to formal intervention strategies. It is usually established prior to implementing an intervention process. An observation process such as the one shown in Figure 7.1 could be used. However, recording only the number of times that a behaviour has occurred would limit the IPP's potential for success. Gathering of other information, as illustrated in Figures 7.2 to 7.4, needs to be undertaken through observations from all partners: family members, staff and other professionals.

The goal of the IPP is generally to increase or decrease behaviours. Objectives are not always stated, but if they are, they usually identify how the incidence of the behaviours should increase or decrease within a particular time span.

In an IPP for behaviours, children's strengths and needs are usually not stated. Instead, there is a statement about what causes the behaviour (if known) and the strategies that are effective and ineffective. It is critical to avoid using a strategy that the child has already learned to ignore or that may cause the behaviour to worsen. When the best strategies have been identified, similar strategies can be used in the implementation process.

Evaluating the process should occur daily. A simple method is to use a line graph (see evaluation section of the IPP on pages 231-234). Through this process:

- Success is monitored.
- The need for adaptations and/or revisions can be identified.
- All partners have a record of achievement. This provides opportunities to celebrate success.

The behavioural IPP is usually implemented over longer periods of time than other IPPs and is reviewed weekly to gauge the success of the strategies used. Figure 7.5 is an example of a behavioural IPP.

Implementation of the behaviour strategies usually causes behaviours to spike. The reason for this is that the child reacts to the new strategies imposed, and the only strategy that the child has is the old behaviour. This behaviour worked in the past and therefore will be tried again. With consistent efforts of all partners and with appropriate strategies, there should be a gradual drop or more modest rise of appropriate behaviours after one week.

Bringing about behavioural change is a long process; it may take weeks or even months. The five-part Figure 7.5 presents an example of an IPP developed for the challenging behaviours of a toddler named Gabriella.

FIGURE 7.5A

Behavioural IPP

Name: Gabriella   **DOB:** February 12, 2000
Date: October 5, 2003

i.   **Summary of Diagnosis**
     a. **Summary of Observations by Resource Consultant**
        i. **Attachment**—Separation anxiety caused by traumatic events in the child's life: death of a grandmother, separation of parents and illness of mother.
        ii. **Aggressive Behaviours**—The physically aggressive behaviours seem to be mostly functional, as they occur when she wants something or does not want to follow directions.
     b. **Summary of Observations of Mother**
        i. **Separation**—Gabriella has had a hard time because she has been faced with so many difficulties. I was ill for about a month and was separated from my daughter. She finds it difficult to be separated from me, especially when she visits her dad, and sometimes at day care, and especially if she knows her dad will come to pick her up. She cries and clings to me.
        ii. **Behaviour**—I first noticed her aggressive behaviour when she was one-and-a-half. She would bite, pinch, kick or punch if she didn't get her way or if she was upset. She is an emotional child, which is understandable given what she has gone through.
     c. **Summary of Observations of Day Care Staff**
        i. **Separation**—The staff noted that Gabriella suffered from tremendous separation anxiety. She would cry for at least half an hour when dropped off in the morning, and start to cry right after lunch when she knew sleep time was close. She would wake up, crying for her mother, father or grandmother. When either parent came to pick her up, she did not want to go home.
        ii. **Behaviour**—Her behaviours included kicking, punching, throwing herself on the ground and screaming wildly. Her crying and/or temper tantrums could last up to 45 minutes. She is very sensitive and empathetic toward other children and will try to comfort them.

2.   **Observations of Behaviours**
     Observations were conducted at home by the mother and at the day care by one of the child care staff. The process was guided by the resource consultant.
     a. **Challenging Behaviours at Home**—See Figure 7.5B.
     b. **Challenging Behaviours at the Centre**—See Figure 7.5C.
     c. **Interests**—See Figure 7.5D.

3.   **Base Line**
     a) Maximum number of aggressive behaviours observed: 12
     b) Separation-anxiety behaviours
        • Four times daily—Arrival, before sleep time, after sleep time and at dismissal
        • Maximum duration—45 minutes

4.   **Successful Behaviour Management Strategies**
     • Provide her with a picture of her family that she can access and hold when she is upset.
     • Provide her with comfort toys.
     • Hold her and cuddle her.
     • Sing to her.

5.   **Goals**
     a) Reduce the number of aggressive acts.
     b) Reduce the time spent in separation-anxiety behaviours.

FIGURE 7.5A

Continued

6. **Strategies**
   a) Reduce the number of aggressive acts:
      i.   Observe her to try to intervene before the aggressive behaviour occurs and redirect her to a positive behaviour.
      ii. Focus on her positive interactions and reinforce these.
      iii. Model asking for something that is wanted.
      iv. Clearly state the expectations that Gabriella needs to use words.
      v.   Prompt her as needed.
      vi. Provide pillows and blankets to scream into and to kick when angry.
      vii. Graph personal success.
   b) Reduce the time spent in separation-anxiety behaviours:
      i.   Assign one consistent teacher to Gabriella.
      ii. Provide activities of interest to Gabriella immediately when she arrives.
      iii. Encourage her to use her comfort items as needed.
      iv. Prepare Gabriella for transition times. Focus on positive possibilities with comments such as, "When your mom arrives, you can show her the play dough model you made."
      v.   Provide soothing activities such as play dough or books that Gabriella likes to look at.
      vi. Provide a quiet place, safe from interruptions.
      vii. Extend the transition between drop-off and pick up times—mother stayed 20 minutes during each time slot.

FIGURE 7.5B

Challenging Behaviours at Home

Date: September 30–October 4, 2002
Observer: Mother
Child: Gabriella

Behaviour	Situation
Clingy, crying: IIII	When I tell her she is going with her dad
Hitting: III	When she is upset

FIGURE 7.5C

Challenging Behaviours at the Centre

Child: Gabriella
Observer: Kaya

Dates: Sep. 29, 30

Aggressive Behaviours—Kicking, punching

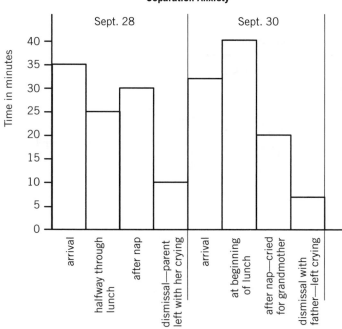

Separation Anxiety

Comments
The only thing that seemed to work was to let her hold her dog and be cuddled. If put down she screams. If teachers switched off, G's behaviour changed dramatically.

FIGURE 7.5D

Interests

A collaborative effort between home and centre

Interests	Description
Dough	Kneading, poking, moulding
Drama	Role-playing, especially grandmother
Books	Likes to be alone to look at books or have an adult read to her
Finger plays	Participated within group or individually

FIGURE 7.5E

Evaluation of Gabriella's Progress

Gabriella's progress was charted daily. The progress was reviewed and adaptations were made to the IPP. Adaptations to the IPP were primarily in the area of removing more adult control and reinforcing Gabriella for her positive interactions. The number of adults in the classroom was reduced to one for as much of the day as possible. Children within the grouping had high problem-solving skills and were good peer role models. Gabriella also attended an art therapy program one morning a week for two months.

✱ Transition Days: first and last day of the week (going to a different home)

FIGURE 7.5E
Continued

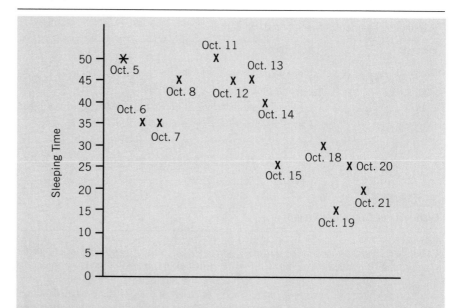

Evaluation Chart of Gabriella's Progress Within two weeks, some positive results were noted, especially with Gabriella's separation-anxiety behaviours. Over the next six months, her behaviour slowly improved. The number and duration of incidences of separation-anxiety behaviours started to gradually decrease. To include Gabriella more in the process, an individual portfolio was begun within seven months of the initiation of the IPP. This offered Gabriella opportunities to discuss how she felt and to start to develop personal strategies to cope with her feelings and her interactions with others.

4. The Individual Portfolio for Behaviours

The individual portfolio for Gabriella was created to reinforce and maintain her positive behaviour gains. Gabriella was able to share information that was to be put into the portfolio. She was proud of her accomplishments. Some sample pages of her portfolio have been included in Figure 7.6. At the time of starting the portfolio, Gabriella was four years old. The sample pages are taken from her portfolio when she was five years old. It is interesting to note that she has become more aware of her own feelings, that she is confident in expressing herself openly and that her interests have expanded tremendously.

5. Adaptations in Inclusive Settings

There are a number of ways to intervene to maximize children's opportunities to be successful: the physical environment can be reorganized, the social context of

FIGURE 7.6

Sample Pages of Gabriella's Portfolio

Things I like to do:

I like to draw using markers.

I am practising making my name.

I also like to paint, especially flowers.

Flowers need the sun to grow.

Things I am good at:

I am a good cutter.

I folded my paper, and now I am cutting out pieces to make a snowflake.

FIGURE 7.6
Continued

Doing big puzzles!

I can finish them by myself.

I like it when others help me do the puzzles.
Big puzzles are hard.

I counted the pieces. There are 32 pieces.

I am really good at tracing.

I get angry when . . .

I get angry when my friends tease me.

I get angry when my friends don't let me play with them.

When I get angry I don't hit anymore.

When I get angry sometimes I shout at my friends,
sometimes I shout in my pillow, sometimes I just cry.

interactions can be changed, the program can be adapted and interactions with early childhood educators can be reviewed and adapted. The situation should always be viewed from the child's perspective. (Kaiser et al., 1999)

A) ORGANIZATION OF THE ENVIRONMENT Effective organization of the indoor and outdoor environments can decrease the incidence of challenging behaviours. Interest areas should be clearly defined in both indoor and outdoor learning areas. This not only serves to provide a defined space for an activity such as water play or block play; in indoor spaces it will also serve to eliminate large open areas that encourage running (Photo 7.7).

Outdoor spaces should have large open areas to encourage running activities. Areas should be set up outside that encourage activities that are similar to indoor activities (Photo 7.8), along with a number of gross motor activities that encourage gross motor development at a number of ability and skill levels (Photo 7.9).

Careful consideration should be given to the appropriate size of each area. Some areas, such as the block area, require larger areas to provide ample room for appropriate play. Other areas such as the book area should be in a smaller, comfortable area to encourage quiet reading activities (Photo 7.10). Areas should be set up to encourage individual, small and large group activity (Photo 7.11).

Limits to the number of children in an area should be imposed by the number of pieces of furniture in the area (Photo 7.12), the number of materials available or the sides of equipment such as the water table. If more children are in the area than expected, the area should be monitored closely. If the children continue to play appropriately, there is no need for intervention.

Photo 7.11

Photo 7.7

Photo 7.8

Photo 7.9

Photo 7.10

Photo 7.12

Photo 7.13

Photo 7.14

Photo 7.15

A quiet area should be available that children can withdraw to (Photo 7.13). This area should be protected from intrusion. This can be done by creating a doorway or posting a stop sign when children wish to be left alone.

The room should offer a number of activities that are sensory in nature to provide a calming effect. Examples include sand and water, music, play dough or fingerpainting. These activities encourage children to develop self-control. The child is able to choose to engage in an activity that meets his or her needs at the moment. When upset, the child can find an alternative activity to soothe his or her feelings (Photo 7.14).

Materials and resources should be clearly organized and labelled to encourage children to find the materials they need and to return them independently (Photo 7.15).

Photo 7.16

Materials more suitable for children with higher-level skills could be placed on higher shelves. Extra materials should be available for rotation or brought out as needed to maintain interest and create new challenges. This is especially important for children who are gifted.

Areas should be separated into quiet areas and noisy areas. The quiet areas should be removed as far as possible from the noisy areas. Children need to have choices to withdraw from noisier play. Some noise reduction can be achieved by placing shelves or padded dividers around the noisy area. Noisy areas such as blocks should be on a rug to absorb some of the noise. Carpentry areas could have a sound-absorbing surface placed on the carpentry table.

Since the interests and abilities of children in an inclusive setting vary greatly, a large variety of materials should be available for use. Avoid including toys or materials that are related to violent themes, as these may incite aggressive interactions. To help those children who have difficulty focusing, a planning board could be provided to help them make choices prior to participating (see Photo 6.7 on page 203). There should be a clear table or surface in the area that children can utilize after they have chosen their activity. Areas that require greater concentration should have some visual barriers around them. This can be achieved with low shelves or dividers (Photo 7.16).

B) CHANGING THE SOCIAL CONTEXT The most important social environment that can be created is one in which all participants will feel welcome and accepted. The centre staff must set a climate that respects all learners, set appropriate policies and times, and be flexible to change as needed.

Reflection	*From the Author*
	I have visited many inclusive environments and make it a point to walk through toy stores and book shops. Within child-care settings, I usually see genuine attempts made to try to represent the diversity of the community with very limited resources. Usually there are some books and some photographs or posters representing diversity of cultures and needs, and some gender-related topics. What I see very little of are toys that represent people with special needs, books about individuals with special needs working in communities or stories including children with special needs. It is also difficult to find the resources of this type that are available. In fact, in most cases you have to order this type of material and equipment from specialized sources, at increased prices. As result, some centres have created their own resources. Figure 7.7 lists a few of these.

FIGURE 7.7

Ideas for Inclusive Environments

1. Centre-based resource materials were created for display purposes. Photographs were taken of the children engaged in various activities. The photographs were enlarged, mounted and laminated. Not only did these photographs represent the various cultures and special needs, but the children were also engaged in the process.
2. In some centres, the children and staff created their own books. These books were simply made. They involved feelings such as likes or dislikes, and could involve a great many more topics. For example, Dillon created his own book about what he likes to do. A sample page is included.

"I like to draw."

Dillon chose the activities, and the words that are bolded are the words he used or signed. The book was laminated and then coil-bound. An excellent source of ideas for creating books is *Making Books* by Diehn (1998). Additionally, similar techniques could be used to create books about adults with special needs. For books on community helpers, families could incorporate family members and other adults in the community.

3. Broken dolls were used to represent individuals with special needs. These dolls had slings for broken arms, a cane, a crutch or an attached prosthesis for a missing limb.
4. Simple instructions for the creation of toy wheelchairs to use with dolls are found in Figure 7.8.
5. In many cases, the staff approached seniors to help them create special toys (carpentry) or special clothing for dolls or for the dress-up areas, or to help them within the classroom in offering one-on-one activities to children, such as reading to a child or helping a child complete a project.
6. Several centres had borrowed child-sized wheelchairs for children to use from a local hospital. Neither centre had children in wheelchairs.
7. In one centre the dress-up area included child-sized crutches and canes.
8. Several centres had activities children engaged in that involved exploration through only tactile exploration, or visual cues without sound, or sound without visual cues.
9. One centre had developed labelling that included Braille, pictorial symbols and words.

FIGURE 7.8
How to Build a Toy Wheelchair

You need:
- Four pieces of 1/4 plywood large enough to seal one of the dolls
  - Two pieces of the same size for the sides
  - One piece for the bottom
  - One piece for the back
- Four wheels and four nails to fit through the hole in the wheel

Directions:
1. Sand all pieces and all sides of wood until smooth.
2. Nail sides, bottom and back together.
3. Attach nails by sliding through hole of wheel, then hammering the nail into the wood. Make sure that the wheel is not tight. It should move freely.
4. Put some wood glue into wood to cover the nail that has been hammered in.
5. Paint wheel chair.

In collaboration with the staff and families, policies need to be set that describe appropriate child guidance techniques. Policies need to be reviewed at least on a yearly basis and revised as needed. Behaviour policies should stress positive guidance techniques, consistency in managing all behaviours and safety—physical and emotional.

Limits with children should be simple and logical. They should be based primarily on the safety of the child. Any rules that are set should be based on respecting the rights of others, avoiding dangerous situations and taking care of the environment (Kaiser et al., 1999: 19). Rules should be posted pictorially and in writing, too, as a reminder to everyone of what is expected. For example, the photograph of Dillon's signal for quiet had been enlarged, laminated with the word "quiet" under it to post in the quiet area (Photo 7.18).

C) ADAPTING THE PROGRAM Program adaptations usually are concerned with routines, transitions, stability, scheduling and flexibility. The routines should be kept consistent and predictable—such as washing hands after using the washroom. Setting predictable, stable routines encourages children to start to accept responsibility for their actions; they can learn to "do the next thing." Behaviours practised over time in different settings, at home and at the centre, will be easier to learn and use, leading to greater child autonomy.

Transitions are often the cause of behaviour problems. Children who wait too long with nothing to do will find alternative ways to amuse themselves. This often

Photo 7.18

leads to inappropriate behaviours. Transitions should be kept to a minimum. When approaching a transition, children should be given a warning so that they can finish what they are doing or save it to finish at another time. Some strategies for more effective transitions follow:

- Minimize the waiting time—The transition could be staggered so that children who take longer can start to get ready (go outside or get ready for lunch) and the ones who are faster could join them later so that everyone is ready at the same time.
- Make transitions fun—Provide activities to do during transitions. Good activities are singing songs, or doing finger plays.
- Minimize the number of transitions—Group transitions should only need to occur before major scheduled events such as going outside or getting ready for lunch or sleep time.
- Post a pictorial routine of the day—Children will learn to look to see what is coming next.
- Ensure the children know what will happen when they get to the next activity—For example, ask children what they intend to do once they are outside.
- Avoid waiting after the transition—When children get to the lunch table, they may have to wait for everyone to arrive before lunch is served. This might be a good time to read a story or continue with the songs or activities that had been ongoing during the transition.

D) CHANGING INTERACTION APPROACHES The first and most important thing that the staff must learn to do is to carefully observe the children. If a potential challenging behaviour can be anticipated, it can often be turned into a positive situation. For example, Jennie noticed that Yasmine had a frown on her face as she was playing beside Jenna. Jenna was starting to use the blocks in front of Yasmine. Realizing that Yasmine was not happy, she quickly brought over some more blocks and said, "I noticed that you do not have enough blocks, so I got some more." Jennie prevented a potential negative behaviour episode. She also modelled to both children what they could do if they did not have enough of something. Signals that indicate a potential problem differ from child to child. The adult needs to be observant and to be able to identify these signals. Some common signals include:

flushed look	frowns	angry look
increased breathing	sweating	clenched teeth
fidgeting	tears	sucking thumb
twirling hair	rocking	whining
loss of eye-contact	screaming	loud voices or laughter
withdrawal		

Early childhood educators should be responsive to the intent of the child's message. They should acknowledge what has happened, as Jennie did by indicating to the children that there were not enough materials, and by offering a positive solution to the problem. To give another example, Jodi was upset because she had not had a chance to use the new tricycle. Melanie knew that Jodi also liked to play with balls. She offered to get a new ball for Jodi to play with. Jodi was pleased with the suggestion.

Supportive body language is another critical component. The early childhood educator should get down to the child's level, with a smile on his or her face, and respond with gestures such as nodding. However, not all children respond to touching or hugging. Any techniques used should correspond to what the child is most likely to respond positively to. For example, Aiden would shrink away if someone came too near to him. He enjoyed group story time but would sit far away from the rest of the children.

Open communication should be used. This involves active listening, responding appropriately to the message received, clarifying the intent of the message, paraphrasing if needed and taking the appropriate action. Dillon had been playing in the dramatic area. The noise level had risen because a group of children were creating a marching band that was marching to music. Most of the children had become involved in the activity. Dillon finally sat down and put his finger up to his mouth (Photo 7.18). Kaya walked over to Dillon and said, "Is it too noisy for you?" Dillon nodded. Kaya asked Dillon to watch the children marching, but he shook his head and again raised his finger to his mouth. His lower lip started to tremble. Kaya said, "You are finding it very hard to play with all the noise around you. It's hard to concentrate, isn't it?" Dillon nodded. Kaya asked Dillon what they should do. Dillon signed that he would like the music quieter. Kaya stopped the children and said, "Dillon has something to tell you." Kaya translated Dillon's signing. One of the children immediately ran over to the CD player and turned the music down. He ran back to Dillon and said, "Is that better?" Dillon beamed. Kaya had correctly interpreted Dillon's message. She encouraged him to find a solution. She helped him to communicate his message to the other children. In this way, the children managed to solve their own problem with Kaya's help.

If the the child's signals have been missed and a challenging behaviour is the result, or if the child does not follow expectations, some different strategies may have to be used. The strategies used are again dependent on the child and his or her reaction to different behaviour techniques. Here are some techniques that might work in this situation:

- Keep the statement brief and to the point—Jodi was throwing sand at Jenna. Kaya observed what was happening and called out, "Stop, Jodi!" As she quickly walked over to Jodi and Jenna, she quietly but firmly said, "The sand belongs in the sandbox or in your bucket."
- Make the statement only once. Repeatedly asking children to do something teaches them that they do not have to listen the first time.

- The message should be delivered in a calm but firm manner that sets the expectation that the child will follow through on what has been asked.
- Wait for a response from the child. What happens next dictates the next move. Kaya stayed close to Jodi to see if her message had been understood. Jodi picked up some sand in her hand and lifted her hand. Kaya quickly lifted up a bucket and showed it to Jodi. Jodi put the sand in the bucket, sat down and continued to fill her bucket.
- Ask the child how he or she might solve the problem, or provide alternative suggestions to the child to help him or her cope and if a choice is made reinforce that choice—If Jodi had continued to throw sand, Kaya might have given her an alternative choice: "It's time to calm down. Let's read a good book." This choice would have been a good one for Jodi because she enjoyed reading books. Alternative choices should not be used as a punishment for a previous behaviour and should be based on the interest of the child. If the child is directed to another choice that he or she does not like, the previous challenging behaviour will likely continue in another form or even escalate.
- If these strategies do not work, direct the child to an alternative activity—These could include going to another similar activity, or finding an activity that will allow the child to work through his or her frustrations.
- Recognize the child's feelings and respect them—"I know you are angry. We'll talk about this when you have calmed down."
- The child should not be forced to do something or be forcefully restrained—Restraint should only be used when a child is in danger of hurting himself or hurting someone else, and only as a last resort. Jeremy was very angry. He picked up one of the chairs and threw it. When Josie, his teacher, came near him he picked up another chair and threw it at her. Josie dodged the chair. She knew that this behaviour was getting dangerous and she had to stop Jeremy from hurting someone. Before she could get to Jeremy, he had picked up a unit block and was ready to throw it. When Josie took it away from him, he attacked her, hitting and kicking her. Josie held Jeremy firmly from behind, sat down with him on the floor, still holding him from behind to protect herself. She gently rocked Jeremy and sang to him. When Jeremy started to relax, she asked him if he was ready to do something else with her. Jeremy nodded. Josie realized that talking to Jeremy in his state of anger would not work. The first priority was to protect others from injury and the second priority was to soothe and calm Jeremy down. Once these goals were accomplished, the behaviour could be talked about.
- Ignore other behaviours that the child may be exhibiting if he or she is following through on the stated expectation—Li was asked to clean up the beads she had left on the floor. She started to shout: "No, I don't want to. I don't have to. It's not my responsibility." As she was shouting, she was cleaning up her beads. When she had finished putting the beads away, she had also stopped shouting. Her positive behaviour was reinforced. "Good job of putting away your beads."
- If the child is out of control and nothing else seems to work, the following strategy might be used:

- Stand between her and the rest of the world—but at a safe distance. Don't try to move her.
- Don't confront her. To keep her from feeling trapped, stand sideways, compose your face, and don't look in her eye.
- Don't talk. She isn't ready to listen yet.
- When she's calm, talk to her quietly. Help her to name her feelings ("You were pretty angry") and to distinguish between feelings and actions ("It's OK to feel angry, but it's not OK to lie on the floor screaming"). Let her know that you love her, and help her to think about how she can solve the problem the next time (Canadian Child Care Federation, 2000: 2).

E) USING THE CHILD'S PERSPECTIVE At all times the adult should try to understand the situation from the child's point of view. Behind most behaviours there is a reason. If the reason is understood, the solution can be found. Not all children are able to voice or communicate their reasons. It is essential to learn to understand the child's signals and to react to them appropriately and immediately. When warning signals are ignored, behaviours can quickly escalate.

Changing behaviour is difficult. An empathetic, calm and consistent approach should always be taken. Collaboration with family members and other professionals will help produce a greater understanding of a child's behaviour and will help find solutions that can be implemented by all individuals.

F) KNOWLEDGE OF CHILD DEVELOPMENT AND CHILD GUIDANCE TECHNIQUES Early childhood educators need to have a firm understanding of children, their development and their typical responses to various situations. Challenging behaviours usually do not simply appear in a vacuum. There are usually triggers that cause a behaviour to start. Often that trigger may be something that is caused by anxiety or frustration. This is the easiest stage in which to deal with the problem. Positive reassurance or active listening will usually solve the problem.

However, if the anxiety is not recognized or the frustration is not noticed, the child often becomes agitated and will seek an outlet for the agitation. Again, if the behaviour is noticed, the adult can use it as a teachable moment. The behaviour should be acknowledged: "I know you find this difficult." Then a solution should be offered: "Do you need some help?" Failure to notice the child's agitation may result in aggressive behaviours or withdrawals. "When children have reached the aggressive state, they are no longer responding from a logical, reasoned state of mind" ("Irwin Hope, 1999: 81). Children in withdrawal are in a similar state of mind. At this stage, the behaviour is much harder to deal with and the child finds it much harder to revert to his or her normal state. (See page 243 for appropriate guidance techniques.)

If aggressive behaviours are not halted, they can quickly lead to an assaultive state. "In an assaultive state, they begin to take out their anger, hurt, fear, and rage and direct it towards you. There are two primary tasks that you want to accomplish when a child is in this state. You want to protect yourself and those in your care, and you want to move the child out of the assaultive state" (Irwin Hope, 1999: 82).

In summary, the consequences of lacking the appropriate knowledge of how to deal with children's behaviours can quickly lead to situations that become difficult to manage for the staff, are extremely detrimental to the emotional health and well-being of the child and lead to frustration for all individuals involved.

Role of the Early Childhood Educator

The role of the early childhood educator actually consists of several roles: observer, collaborator, planner, manager, supporter, evaluator and researcher. Each role is equally critical in helping the child gain greater self-control.

1. The Role of Observer

Observation is a critical role of the early childhood educator. Observation is an ongoing process that helps the early childhood educator understand behaviours and develop strategies for intervention based on what has been learned through the observation process. The observation process is an ongoing cycle of observing and interpreting behaviours, implementing strategies, more observing and evaluation in order to adapt strategies as needed (see Figure 7.9).

Early childhood educators need to observe children to learn to understand their behaviours and possible causes of behaviours, as Jennie did by observing Yasmine's frown (page 242). Jennie knew that when Yasmine started to frown it indicated that she was upset about something. Once there is an understanding of the type of behaviour a child uses and the signals that the child exhibits prior to the occurrence of a challenging behaviour, intervention strategies can be developed.

FIGURE 7.9

Observation Process

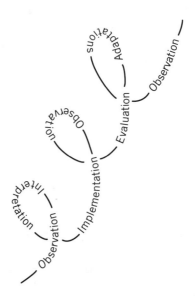

Additionally, the learning environment needs to be observed and assessed to identify any adaptations that might need to be made to the environment. Interactions between children and between children and adults should also be observed and assessed to identify possible adaptations. For example, is the staff dealing with the behaviour consistently with all children in all settings? Do more problems occur when certain peers play together?

Once an IPP has been established, daily observations and team meetings need to be held to discuss the outcomes of the IPP strategies and to develop new strategies or revise existing ones.

2. The Role of Collaborator

As previously stated, collaboration with partners—families and other professionals—is extremely important. Similar behaviours occur in all settings, and it is very confusing to a child for different behaviour strategies to be acceptable in different settings. Children will adapt to varying expectations, but learning is increased when the expectations are consistent in all settings. This way, children learn to transfer what is expected of them from one situation to another. Gabriella's IPP and portfolio are a good example of what can be achieved if a collaborative process is used.

3. The Role of Planner

The early childhood educator may take the lead in the development of an IPP or portfolio. Planning is an ongoing process. As a plan is implemented, it needs to be evaluated in order to adapt or revise strategies as needed.

An appropriate learning environment needs to be established and organized to effectively meet the behavioural needs of all children. Ongoing assessment of the environment will lead to new adjustments as needed.

Routines and policies should be established and revised as needed to create predictability and stability. This will lead to a more secure environment for all children. Children can anticipate what will happen during their day at the centre.

4. The Role of Manager

The early childhood educator acts as a manager. Team meetings need to be organized to collaborate with partners. Information needs to be shared with all centre staff in order to ensure consistency of programming and implementation of specific strategies. After Gabriella's IPP was completed, Kaya arranged regular meetings with staff to ensure that everyone knew of the expectations and could collaboratively implement them. Realistic limits should be collaboratively set and consistently reinforced by all partners. Interactions between children need to be mediated and encouraged.

5. The Role of Supporter

Behaviour is learned. Early childhood educators need to model appropriate behaviours and reinforce appropriate behaviours when they occur. This sets the tone for creating a positive learning environment.

Children and families need encouragement. Inappropriate behaviours take a long time to change. It is easy to give up. Celebrating success, sharing this information and continued acceptance of the child will lead to more positive long-term successes.

Early childhood educators must learn to anticipate challenging behaviours in order to prevent them, or to ignore challenging behaviours whenever possible. For example, Gabriella was asked to find her pillow to scream into. She shouted, "I am not going to use my silly old pillow!" as she was walking over to the pillow. This behaviour can be ignored, since the child is already complying with the expectation. The early childhood educator should focus on positive behaviours and reinforce them to set the tone for more positive behaviours.

6. The Role of Evaluator

The early childhood educator needs to continually monitor and assess the learning environment, interaction patterns and strategies used to cope with all behaviours in order to identify necessary changes or adaptations. When it was noticed that Gabriella needed more positive peer modelling, the staff decided to provide opportunities for Gabriella to interact with a group of children who had strong appropriate social skills (see Figure 7.5E on page 233).

7. The Role of Researcher

There is always one child who will challenge the abilities of everyone to find acceptable behaviour-management strategies. Rather than give up on that particular child, acceptable alternatives should be looked for. There are a number of resources listed at the end of the chapter to help the practitioner find alternative solutions.

SUMMARY

Challenging behaviours are difficult to manage for everyone and can be extremely frustrating and emotionally draining for all individuals working with that child. The early childhood educator needs to become part of a collaborative team to help the child, the family and the centre staff cope most effectively with these behaviours.

Some strategies that are currently used in Canada include:

- Support and development of an IPP in collaboration with mental health care workers, families, resource consultants and staff members
- Referral to a mental health service
- Referral to a medical team for possible drug treatment—"This practice is controversial and the consensus among investigators seems to be that drug therapy for children should be used with extreme caution, and only with those children for whom other alternatives simply do not work" (Hawkins-Clarke, 1998: 3).

- Removal of the child from the program— "Centres are highly reluctant to take this step knowing there are often few other resources for families. However, the all too likely result of including children with disruptive behaviour disorders is all too likely to increase staff stress and affect morale. It appears that challenging behaviours are the most problematic inclusion issue in Canadian child care after specialized health related issues. A significant number of early childhood educators across the country feel that children who are uncontrollably aggressive should be excluded" (Hawkins-Clarke, 1998: 3–4).

KEY POINTS

Types of challenging behaviours

- Emotional, conduct, hyperkinetic, developmental, diagnosed conditions

Causes of challenging behaviours

- Developmental, environmental, functional, psychological

Range of behaviours in inclusive settings

- Aggressive, interrupting, low attention span, difficulty concentrating, difficulty with self-control, low self-esteem

Collaboration

- With families, other professionals, staff

Observations

- Frequency counts, duration counts, graphs

Individual program plan

- Summary of diagnosis, observations of behaviour, base line, successful behaviour management strategies, goals, strategies, evaluation

Individual portfolio

- Reinforce and maintain behaviour, involvement of child

Adaptation to inclusive settings

- Organizing environment, changing social context, adapting program, changing interactive approaches, using the child's perspective

Role of the Early Childhood Educator

- Observer, collaborator, planner, manager, supporter, evaluator, researcher

EXERCISES

1. Reflect upon the challenging behaviours you have seen children engage in within a centre-based program. What were the behaviours? How did they affect the child and the staff? Why do you think these behaviours occurred? Why do you think behavioural disabilities are hard to diagnose?

2. Using the chart provided at the top of page 250, identify some of the behaviours that might fit into each category.

Category of Behaviour	Types of Behaviour
Emotional	
Conduct	
Hyperkinetic	
Diagnosed conditions	

3. Identify the causes of behaviour and discuss how behaviours are similar or different in each case.

4. Discuss why it is important to know the normal development of children to guide behaviour.

5. Using the following table, observe a group of preschool children in a centre-based program to identify the types of challenging behaviours that might occur because of the factors listed on the left side. What adaptations might you suggest to decrease the number of challenging behaviours? If no challenging behaviours were observed, reflect on the information to identify why you did not observe any.

Description of Factor	Types of Behaviour Observed
Overcrowding	
Too many open spaces	
Disorganized storage of material	
Too noisy	
Too many choices	
Too few choices	
Developmentally- or age-inappropriate choices	
Competitive activities	
Provision of violent toys	
Organization not based on the interests or background experiences of the children	
Too much waiting during transitions	

6. Define functional causes of behaviour. What strategies might be used to mitigate the occurrence of functional behaviours?

7. Reflect on an experience that you have had that caused you to feel badly about yourself. What was the cause? How did you feel? What strategies did you develop to overcome this situation? How can you help children in similar situations?

8. For each of the following, develop specific strategies that lead to a collaborative process: families, other professionals, other staff members.

9. Identify the purposes of each of the following observational techniques: frequency count, duration count and use of a graph. When might each of the techniques be of the most use?

10. Compare the similarities and differences between a standard IPP and a behavioural IPP and justify the differences.

11. How is an individual portfolio useful in helping a child learn to control his or her behaviour?

12. Describe each of the possible adaptations to inclusive settings and list at least three strategies for each one.

13. Identify and explain each of the roles of the early childhood educator in an inclusive environment.

RESOURCES

Intervention Strategies
www.cfc-efc.ca/docs/cccf/00020_en.htm

http://dmoz.org/Health/Child_Health/
Special_Needs/

www.library.utoronto.ca/equity/familycare/
parenting/features_arch_challenging_
behaviours.html

Aggressive Behaviours
www.community.nsw.gov.au/documents/
aggression_discussionpaper.pdf

www.excellence-earlychildhood.ca/
documents/Webster-StrattonANGxp.pdf

www.ces.ncsu.edu/depts/fcs/human/pubs/
nc10.html

www.statcan.ca/cgi-bin/IPS/display?cat_
num=89-599-M2004001

Disruptive Behaviours
www.cfc-efc.ca/docs/cccns/00001248.htm

Causes of emotional and behavioural disabilities
www.parliament.uk/post/pn092.pdf

Parenting—various topics
www.cfc-efc.ca/menu/parenting_en.htm

Assessment
www.rnld.co.uk/cb.html

Canadian Child Care Federation—Resources
www.cccf-fcsge.ca/subsites/familytp/english/
resources_en.htm

SpeciaLink: The National Centre for Child Care
Inclusion
www.specialinkcanada.org/books/challenge.
html

Preschoolers with depression
http://news-info.wustl.edu/clip/page/normal/
2678.html

http://health.yahoo.com/health/centers/
depression/2179

www.wrongdiagnosis.com/news/very_young_
children_can_and_do_suffer_from_depression.
htm

Study of children with attention deficit hyperactivity
disorder
www.nimh.nih.gov/publicat/adhd.cfm

Fetal alcohol syndrome
www.acbr.com/fas

REFERENCES

Canadian Child Care Federation (2000). Tips for Parenting Children with Challenging Behaviour. Child & Family Canada [online]. Available at www.cfc-efc.ca/docs/cccns/00001248.htm (23-1-2005).

Chamberland, C., Laporte, L., Lavergne, C., & Baraldi, R. (2003). Psychological Abuse: Children's Invisible Suffering. Child & Family Canada [online]. Available at www.cfc-efc.ca/docs/cwlc/00001_en.htm (23-12-2004).

Diehn, G. (1998). *Making Books That Fly, Fold, Wrap, Hide, Pop Up, Twist and Turn*. Hong Kong: Oceanic Graphic Printing Productions Ltd.

Hawkins-Clarke, D. (1998). Disruptive Behaviour Disorders: Implications for the Child Care Community. Child & Family Canada [online]. Available at www.cfc-efc.ca/docs/cccns/00001248.htm (19-1-2005).

Irwin Hope, S. E. (1999). *Challenging the Challenging Behaviours*. Wreck Cove, NV: Breton Books.

Kaiser, B., & Sklar Rasminsky., J. (1999). *Meeting the Challenge: Effective Strategies for Challenging Behaviours in Early Childhood Environments*. Ottawa, ON: Canadian Child Care Federation.

National Institute of Mental Health (2003). Attention Deficit Hyperactivity Disorder. National Institute of Mental Health [online]. Available at www.nimh.nih.gov/publi-cat/adhd.cfm (20-1-2005).

Orr, L., & Cavallaro, G. (1997). Intervention for Children with Challenging Behaviour and Special Needs. Child and Family Canada [online]. Available at www.cfc-efc.ca/docs/cccf/00020_en.htm (19-1-2005).

Vitaro, F., De Civita, M., & Pagani, L. (1996). The Impact of Research-Based Prevention Programs on Children's Disruptive Behaviour. *Exceptionality Education Canada* 5[105].

Weingarden Dubin, J. (2001). More Than a Mood. *Psychology Today* 34, 21. Winzer, M. (1999). *Children Exceptionalities in Canadian Classrooms*. Scarborough, ON: Prentice Hall Allyn and Bacon.

8

CHAPTER

Strategies for Facilitating Motor Growth in Inclusive Settings

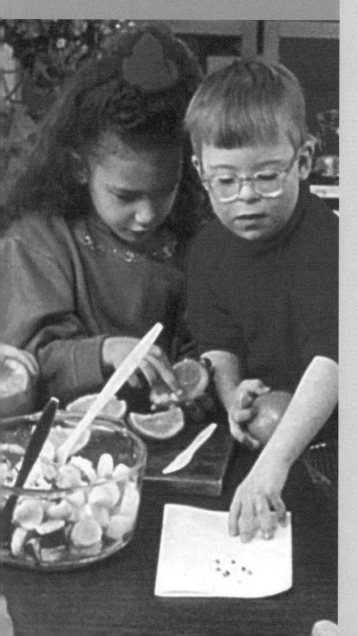

Chapter Outline

"Movement is a part of everyone's everyday life and has many manifestations. The urge to achieve physical skill mastery and capitalize on the body's capacity for movement is common to all children. They delight in physical accomplishment and enjoy movement for its own sake. Children use movement to express feelings, manipulate objects, and learn about their world" (Sanders, 2002: xiv).

Learning Outcomes

After studying this chapter, you will be able to:

1. Identify the importance of movement to early learning.
2. Describe the connection between perceptual skills and fine and gross motor skills, and identify the importance of knowledge of normal perceptual and motor development.
3. Explain the relationship of perceptual and motor development to other developmental areas.
4. Explain the importance of collaborating with families and other professionals.
5. Identify and describe how observations are used to develop an appropriate motor program.
6. Discuss why it is important to have an expert involved in helping to set the direction of a motor IPP.
7. Identify relevant adaptations that should be made to the indoor and outdoor environments to optimize motor development.
8. Describe the various roles of the early childhood educator in helping to develop an appropriate motor program for all children.

Introduction

Movement is innate to all human beings. Movement is evident at birth with the first breath and first cry. Newborns use movements to express themselves. This repertoire of body language continues to grow and become refined as children gain control over their muscles and start to understand the world around them.

Expression through movement is demonstrated in many ways, some more obvious than others. Infants express excitement through a flailing of the arms and legs, or more placidly through increased sucking while feeding or using a soother. Toddlers express their curiosity of the world around them by active exploration of the environment or by observing others and reacting with facial expressions. Preschoolers express their enthusiasm in an increasing number of ways. Their feelings and knowledge about the world can be observed in their actions, language and creations. As children's control over both fine and gross muscles increases, their creative expressions may begin to be expressed in an increasing number of ways, such as through dance, art, writing or music.

Studies of children who have been institutionalized at an early age demonstrate that movement is critical to learning. When infants were placed into an institution and lacked the opportunity to actively explore the environment, their motor development was delayed. Infants in these institutions spent the majority of time in their cribs with no toys to stimulate development. By age three to four, the majority of these infants could not yet walk. However, infants transferred to a more developmentally appropriate environment were all able to walk by age three (Schickedanz, Schickedanz, Forsyth & Forsyth, 2001).

Movement is also critical to all other domains. As children gain increased motor abilities such as walking and the ability to manipulate objects, they also:

- Are increasingly able to act independently
- Make choices about what, when and how they wish to engage in learning activities
- Actively explore the environment to learn about the world around them
- Discover relationships between their actions and the results of their actions
- Develop understanding about themselves, their actions and the materials and experiences in their environments

Motor development is often categorized into perceptual motor development, gross motor development and fine motor development. However, it is important to remember that it is the interplay of all motor domains that leads to healthy growth and development. Children with a challenge in any of these areas often need to learn to compensate by developing skills in another domain. For example, the child with a visual disability will need to rely more on auditory perception in order to freely explore his or her environment.

Development of Motor Skills

Normal development of perceptual skills and gross and fine motor skills occurs in a predictable, universal pattern. Individual differences in reaching milestones may arise from culture or family expectations, early stimulation in milestone development or disability. For example, infants who are born blind will attempt to reach for and try to grasp objects that they can hear. These infants are usually not successful in grasping the objects because they do not know how far away the object is. If this listening and grasping behaviour is not reinforced and guided, these infants will cease to try to grab objects they hear (Schickedanz et al., 2001).

Knowledge of normal motor development will facilitate the adult caregiver's ability to:

- Identify relevant motor skills and milestones to foster further growth and development
- Identify potential motor problems
- Plan appropriate learning experiences for children
- Create appropriate indoor and outdoor environments to encourage optimum growth and development.

1. Perceptual Development

Perceptual development is characterized by visual and auditory perception and by sensory awareness: tactile, body, spatial, directional and time awareness. Knowledge of developmental milestones in these areas will help adults make informed decisions about children's perceptual and motor behaviours and will guide the formation of realistic expectations.

A) VISUAL PERCEPTION Visual perceptual ability involves the physical ability to see and a process of making sense of the information that has been seen. The ability to see is usually referred to as visual acuity. This term "refers to how well the elements of a pattern can be seen by someone at a specific distance" (Schickedanz et al., 2001: 95). Development of visual acuity starts at birth and is fully developed by the time a child is three years old. Development of motor abilities hinges on the young infant's ability to see and understand what he or she has seen. The simple act of reaching for a toy involves the ability to see the toy, to centre attention on that toy, to reach toward that toy and finally to grasp it. Visual perception is an integral part of the process. As previously stated, if the infant is unable to see the object, other strategies must be used to reinforce the motor behaviours and to help the child continue to develop normal motor behaviours.

Developmental milestones in visual acuity normally follow a predictable pattern:

- Birth—Cannot fixate on an object; poor eye coordination; poor ability to discriminate colour; shows poor visual acuity
- One month—Tracks slowly moving objects; has developed visual preferences for strong contrast, complex designs and human faces; still shows poor visual acuity

- Three months—Can fixate on objects for longer periods of time; can see smaller objects and differentiate colours; pays attention visually by maintaining eye contact; searches for objects visually
- Four months—Shows improved visual acuity; begins to show interest in own body parts; tracks objects moving in all directions
- Five months—Starts to examine things visually; achieves **eye-hand coordination** (can reach and grasp intended object)
- Six months—Coordinates eye movements smoothly; shows increased ability to differentiate near and far objects
- Two years—Completes **myelination** of optic nerve: formation of protective sheath that forms around nerve cells to improve transmission of impulses (see Figure 8.1). A myelin sheath can be compared to the coating on an electrical cord. If the wires are left bare, the electricity can still reach the end point, but the signal will be weakened as the electricity will also be diverted to other points along the bare wire. A weak signal to a light bulb would result in a weak light. The cord protects the wires and provides an efficient means of transmission of signals. Similarly, the impulses travelling along myelinated nerve branches will be faster and stronger.
- Three years—With full maturity of retinal tissue, has ability to see virtually as well as adults

The ability to see is also linked to the child's understanding of what he or she sees, and understanding of what is seen is closely related to the child's experiences. Understanding is linked both to the growth and development of both motor and cognitive skills. When children actively explore the environment, they learn through touching, manipulating and hearing others describe and talk about their experiences. Infants with motor delays or physical challenges need to experience similar explorations. Adults should be creative in organizing learning expe-

FIGURE 8.1

Myelination

Photo 8.1

Photo 8.2

riences that provide opportunity to learn about the world through active physical participation. As children grow and mature, they gradually gain skills and abilities in all domains that reinforce and transform learning:

- Children acquire the ability to use language to identify and describe what they are experiencing—Language ability progresses from differential crying to cooing, to babbling, to first words, and then jumps rapidly to forming sentences and complete ideas.
- Children gain understanding about their personal actions—Infants and toddlers are centred on the self and the needs of the self. Understanding is based on the individual behaviours and the sensory motor experiences of that child. Hannah has decided to use her hands to paint (Photo 8.1). Notice the intense concentration on her face. She is involved in a sensory motor experience. She is gaining experience with:
  - How the paint feels (texture, temperature, consistency)
  - What happens when you put paint on paper
  - How to make things change (hands, paper)
  - How to use her fine and gross muscles to retrieve and spread the paint

- Understanding moves from the sensory-motor activity to active exploration of how things work and how things function—Preschool children actively explore the environment to experiment with various techniques of making things happen.

Yasmine is experimenting with different ways of painting (Photo 8.2). She had found a dried flower and was upset because it had "lost its colour." She started out by trying to paint colour onto it. Eventually she switched to using the dried flower to paint with. She was very excited to make various discoveries: the patterns that the flower made on the paper; other things in the environment that she could use; that different materials made different marks; that some materials broke very easily; and another way of representing her experiences—through art. Through this process, Yasmine gained greater understanding of the world around her. She used her perceptual abilities to find the materials needed, and her fine and gross motor abilities to represent her experiences on paper.

B) AUDITORY PERCEPTION "Auditory perception is the ability to hear different sounds and to distinguish one from another. Listening, the ability to remember sounds, and sound patterns form a part of auditory perception" (Nyisztor & Rudick, 1995: 17). Hearing matures during the fetal stage. The fetus begins to hear during the last two months of pregnancy and is well equipped to hear at birth. Newborns already recognize the voices of their primary caregivers and are soothed by the familiar mother's voice. Over the next two years, the infant gradually develops the understanding of language.

Auditory perception plays a role in movement activities, especially in helping the child to:

- Understand the relationship between movement and language
- Participate in music and movement activities
- Rely to a greater extent on the auditory channel when there are challenges in other domains such as visual

C) SENSORY AWARENESS Sensory awareness develops at the fetal stage and matures over a lifetime of experience in a variety of settings and with a variety of materials. As children actively explore the environment, they gain understanding of many of the sensory concepts such as spatial and body awareness.

Tactile awareness develops at the fetal stage. The skin is very sensitive to touch because of that area's many receptors. The fetus floats in the embryonic fluid, stretching, bouncing and moving in other ways, and with each movement feels the fluid embrace and flow around the body. Through this sense, individuals learn to detect differences in many variables such as temperature, texture and consistency. Children with special needs need more sensory motor experiences than other children to gain understanding about their world. Tactile behaviours such as continually putting things in one's mouth may persist for longer periods of time. The caregiver must take note of the development of the child and carefully provide tactile experiences that promote safe and healthy development. Knowledge of developmental guidelines helps practitioners plan appropriate learning experiences. Some developmental guidelines follow:

- Neonates are extremely sensitive to touch. Touch calms a newborn. A premature infant who has been held and soothed by touching gains weight more quickly than one who has not had this experience (Photo 8.3) (Schickedanz et al., 2001).
- All newborns respond to pain, felt in response to such things as a pinprick or circumcision.
- All infants respond to different tactile stimulation differently and selectively.
- As children start to actively explore their environments, they learn to differentiate between tactile sensations and start to establish distinct preferences for a larger

Photo 8.3

variety of tactile experiences, such as swimming, rolling down a hill or simply running to feel the breeze around their bodies.

Another type of sensory awareness is body awareness. As children develop an awareness of their bodies and how the different body parts function and move, they also gain a sense of self. There is a developmental sequence to gaining body awareness. Children who do not engage in the following behaviours should be carefully observed to identify if they are at risk:

- As infants kick and move their extremities, they start to gain an awareness of how to move their limbs and the location of these limbs (Photo 8.4).

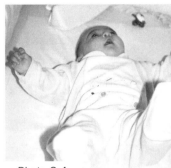

Photo 8.4

- Increased mobility brings increased independence and increased ability to practise skills. Toddlers attempt to achieve and maintain balance as they engage in a variety of activities, such as climbing, squatting, running or manipulating objects in various positions (Photo 8.5).

- Preschoolers continue to refine and practise a variety of motor skills, for instance, riding (Photo 8.6), jumping and the manipulation of small parts to put together and take apart (Photo 8.7).

A third type of sensory awareness, spatial awareness, includes the understanding of one's own body, the relationship of one's body to things that are near or far away and the awareness of space between objects. It makes it possible for the child to move freely around a designated space and to identify where his or her body is in relationship to that space and how to appropriately move through that space. Children who lack a good sense of spatial awareness may have difficulty in handling large open areas and may find certain perceptual tasks, such as discriminating similarities and differences, difficult. This may lead to later disabilities in such tasks as reading and writing. Spatial awareness:

Photo 8.5

- Develops in infancy—As infants are touched, cuddled, played with and hear the language associated with the actions ("I am tickling your tummy") (Photo 8.8), they start to gain awareness about their bodies and the location of body parts.

Photo 8.6

Photo 8.7

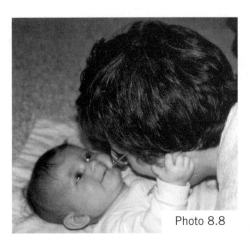

Photo 8.8

- Increases through such activities as dressing, undressing or bathing—Language activities (verbal or signing) should accompany all activities: "Oh, you have bubbles on your nose!" or "Where is that arm? Is it in the sleeve?"
- Increases with maturation as the infant can start to put body parts into his or her mouth such as fingers, hands or feet.
- Changes dramatically when children start to actively explore the environment— The kind of mobility associated with each stage—crawling, sitting or walking— enables children to see their world from different perspectives. Children are able to place themselves in different positions such as on, inside, outside or under, as they hear or see the appropriate labels that are associated with these actions.
- Changes dramatically with active manipulation—Children can place items in different locations and learn the associated vocabulary that corresponds to the position.

The development of directional awareness, another form of sensory awareness, entails increased understanding of one's own body, such as the knowledge that:

- Each individual body has a front and a back
- The body can move in different directions as a unit
- The different body parts can move separately

Understanding of directionality develops with active movement over the early years. By the time that children are about six years old, they develop an understanding of right and left. A healthy development of directional awareness will help children with special needs obtain a better understanding of their bodies. Children who are unable to move efficiently may require help and guidance to gain a normal awareness of how their body moves.

Time awareness is yet another form of sensory awareness. Consciousness of time starts to develop in infancy and continues to grow and expand in the early years. Here are some developmental milestones:

- Reciprocal actions—During infancy, the interactions between caregiver and infant are punctuated by the infant's growing ability to listen, respond, listen and respond again. When an infant engages in an interaction, such as smiling at another individual, and that individual responds by smiling back, the infant gains some awareness of the concept of after.
- Independence in routines—As toddlers and preschoolers gain increasing independence they gain further experience in the concepts of before and after: Before I go to bed, I brush my teeth. After breakfast we get dressed and go to day care.
- A general understanding of various times and the sequence of the day—This understanding arrives at the preschool stage. Lunch time, for instance, is followed by a nap. After the outdoor time, Daddy will come to pick me up. A preschooler does not yet have a specific concept of time. Jenny woke up on Sunday morning to get ready to go to day care. Her mother informed her that it was Sunday, and that Sunday was a holiday. Jenny understood the concept of a holiday but, clearly worried anyway, she responded. "Could you phone my day care to see if it is Sunday there too?"

- School-aged children start to develop a more sophisticated understanding of time—For example, they learn the hours of the day and the days of the week.

Children who have not developed an appropriate sense of time will find it difficult to predict what will occur next in their day. These children will need reminders and stable routines to help them make sense of their world.

2. Gross Motor Development

Dependent on perceptual development, fine motor development and maturation, gross motor development is also directly related to the experiences and stimulation in a young child's life. Although motor milestones develop in a predictable and universal sequence, there is variation in when individual children reach milestones based on individual characteristics, as well as family and cultural expectations. Table 8.1 identifies the major developmental milestones of gross motor development.

TABLE 8.1   **MILESTONES OF GROSS MOTOR DEVELOPMENT**

Age Range	Gross Motor Milestones
Birth–4 months	• Lifts and clears head from surface when lying on stomach • Rolls over from front to back • Can be pulled into sitting position
4–8 months	• Sits without support • May pull self to crawling position and rock • Rolls over front-to-back and back-to-front • May push with feet to move backwards • Can be pulled to standing position
8–12 months	• Crawls • Pulls self up to standing position • Climbs stairs • Walks holding onto furniture • Walks independently
12–18 months	• Walks independently • Runs
18–36 months	• Jumps on the spot and jumps down from higher positions • Uses riding toys, first pushing with feet and using pedals by end of period

Sources: Crowther, 2005; Schickedanz et al., 2001

3. Fine Motor Development

Control over fine motor skills develops in a process that is smoothly interactive between perceptual and all motor activities. The simple act of picking something up requires an individual to coordinate seeing the object, reaching the object and grasping it, and using gross muscles to bend and reach for the object. Fine muscle control develops in a predictable pattern. Children with physical disabilities may continue to use specific grasping skills, such as the palmar grasp, for longer periods of time. Major milestones are included in Table 8.2. One of the important milestone developments in the early years is the ability to grasp and manipulate objects. Figure 8.2 identifies major grasping milestones.

TABLE 8.2   **MILESTONES OF FINE MOTOR DEVELOPMENT**

Age	Milestone	Description
Birth—4 months	Hands and feet	Uses hands and feet to wave or kick to express excitement or interest
	Grasp	Reaches for and swats at items with hands or feet, often missing
		Reflexively grasps object when near hand (see Figure 8.2)
4 months – 8 months	Grasp	Palmar grasp (see Figure 8.2)
	Transfers objects	Transfers objects from one hand to other
	Release	Starts to release objects voluntarily by end of period
	Exploration of objects	Puts things into mouth
12 months – 2 years	Grasp	Releases objects voluntarily—skill well established
	Drawing	Scribbles with whole arm movement
	Feeding	Uses spoon, fork to feed self
8 – 12 Months	Release	Uses voluntary release to drop, to transfer or throw, and to place
	Manipulation	Pokes, transfers items from hand to hand, looks intently, starts to stack items
	Grasp	Pincer grasp evolves (see Figure 8.2)
2 – 3 years	Self-help	Undoes buttons and zippers; holds glass in one hand; opens doors; turns pages of book
	Filling and dumping	Fills and dumps repetitively—sand, water or other solid objects such as beads
3 years and older	Increased abilities	Is more independent, feeding and serving self and catching and throwing by self
	Grasp	Performs tripod grasp (see Figure 8.2), leading to increased ability to complete fine motor tasks such as colouring in lines, drawing, painting, building and printing

Sources: Schickedanz et al., 2001; Crowther, 2005

FIGURE 8.2

Grasping Milestones

Description	Example

Reflex grasp

When something is placed near the infant's hand, the hand reflexively closes

Primitive grasp

When something is placed in an infant's hand, the object is reflexively grasped, but it is dropped when hand becomes tired.

Palmar grasp

The young child uses his or her whole hand to grasp, hold or manipulate objects.

Pincer grasp

The child uses forefinger and thumb to pick up smaller objects.

Tripod grasp

This grasp is used to draw print or write more effectively.

4. Relationship of Motor Development and Other Domains

Often when children have a special need, there is an emphasis on just that area of development to the exclusion of other areas. Such methods are ineffective because they do not recognize the underlying interactions of behaviour (see Figure 8.3).

Lara at two months looked at the rattle that was shaken in front of her face. Her attention focused on the rattle because of the rattle's bright colours, movement and sound. When the rattle was placed near her hand, her fingers closed around it in a reflexive grasp. Soon her hand tired and the rattle dropped to the floor. She did not look for the rattle or seem upset that the stimulation was gone. When Lara was six months old, she was able to initiate her own action. She grabbed the rattle, shook it and then brought it to her mouth. When she was placed near the same toys again at another time, she immediately shook the same fish rattle. She had gained greater control over her physical actions, learned to make choices and remembered past actions.

Photo 8.14

FIGURE 8.3

Interaction of Movement and Other Developmental Domains

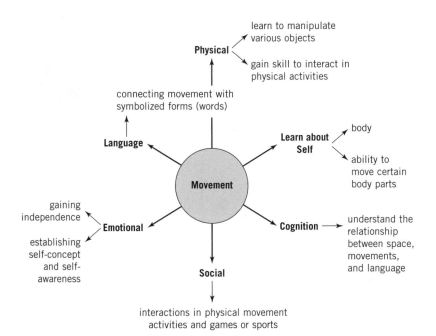

Lara at 12 months actively explored the environment. She engaged in filling and emptying activities. She enjoyed taking toys apart, then giving them to someone to put them together again (Photo 8.15). Lara had learned to expand her choices of play to include others in her play. She remembered what she could do with toys and used her knowledge to interact with other individuals effectively. Lara at 19 months actively explored her environment. She was able to find her own materials to engage in play. She found the animal beads and the metal bowls, and used these materials to fill and dump. Lara usually retrieved the metal bowls for this activity as she liked the sound the beads made when they dropped into the bowl. Lara was by this time also attracted to the various colours of beads and often started to find like colours to drop into the bowl (Photo 8.16).

Over time, Lara has gained a number of skills. As she interacted with similar materials over time, she strengthened her knowledge and understanding of the world around her. Initially, her interactions were dependent on adults and limited to listening and watching. Lara at six months used her cognitive skills to remember past actions, involved gross and fine motor skills to reach, pull, shake and manipulate the rattle. Lara at 12 months was actively mobile to make her own choices, solve some of her own problems and involve others in social play. Lara at 19 months had combined many skills: memory of past actions, increased dexterity to manipulate materials, the ability to take the initiative and observation of objects to identify detail.

The Ludic Model of occupational therapy exemplifies the effective use of the concept of interacting modalities with children with disabilities. The model is used to "stimulate, develop, and maintain play skills of children, involving the sensory, motor, cognitive, and social sphere" (Ferland, 2005: 106). Children are assessed on the criteria listed in Table 8.3. The assessment includes emotional, sensory, motor, cognitive and social components. It is only when all characteristics are considered that a therapy program is developed.

Photo 8.15

Range of Motor Behaviours in Inclusive Settings

The range of motor behaviours in inclusive settings varies greatly from centre to centre in Canada. In most centres behaviours range from slightly delayed motor abilities to normal and gifted behaviours. However, at times it is necessary to accommodate children who require assistance to be mobile such as children in a wheelchair.

Photo 8.16

The types of motor behaviours that might be expected include the following:

- Delayed motor abilities—These children will exhibit behaviours that are at a lower developmental level than their chronological age. Since these preschool or school-aged children might still walk with the toddler's unsteady gait or be involved in sensory motor exploration, safety becomes an issue. Organization of the environment must consider the safety needs of all the children, such as putting small parts out of reach and encouraging children to use these with supervision.

TABLE 8.3   **DEVELOPMENT OF LUDIC BEHAVIOUR: ATTITUDE AND ACTION**

1. Sensory stimulation and response
2. Exploration of objects and space, and manipulation of materials
3. Ludic activity: functional and unconventional use of play materials leading to the acquisition of a personal play repertoire.

Stage 1	Stage 2	Stage 3
LUDIC ATTITUDE		
Characteristics		
• awakening of attention • awakening of curiosity • awakening of interest • desire to know	• interest sustained • sensation of pleasure • desire for initiative • desire to explore • desire to act	• interest in action • pleasure in action • initiative • humour • spontaneity
Emotional Components		
• feelings of confidence	• feelings of control of objects • expression of needs • beginning of autonomy	• feeling of mastery • expression of needs and feelings • autonomy • decision-making • self-esteem
LUDIC ACTION		
Sensory Components		
• looks • touches • smells • hears • puts in mouth • moves		
Motor Components		
• grasps • manipulates • maintains a position • moves	• grasps/releases • opens/closes • throws/catches • empties/fills • piles • carries • changes position • moves around	• uses tools (crayon, scissors...) • uses several objects • combines various actions

TABLE 8.3   CONTINUED

Stage 1	Stage 2	Stage 3
Cognitive Components		
• experiments with relationships of cause and effect (beginning) • experiments with permanence of the object (beginning) • recognizes basic characteristics of objects	• understands the relationship of cause • understands the concept of permanence of the object • understands how objects work • helps solving problems • understands how activities proceed	• imitates • pretends • creates a play situation • uses symbols (make-believe play, drawing, language) • solves problems • understands symbols
Social Components		
• plays with the adult • plays alone	• plays in parallel • grasps the notion of property	• shares the play materials • plays with other children • cooperates in shared play • knows how to ask for and accept help • can help others • expresses ideas

Source: The Ludic Model

- Challenges with balance—Some children will find it difficult to maintain their balance while walking or trying to manipulate materials because of spastic movements or rigidity of muscles. Special adaptations need to be made for these children to ensure that they can participate safely and without becoming frustrated.
- Mobility with assistive devices such as a wheelchair—The environment must be made accessible both indoors and outdoors to provide maximum opportunities for independent participation.
- Normal range of abilities—These children need to become aware of their peers and develop understanding of their peers' strengths and needs.
- Giftedness—These children usually have exceptional motor abilities in fine and/or gross motor skills. Children in this category need to be provided with challenges to avoid potential boredom and inactivity.

Intervention Strategies

Intervention strategies for children with special physical challenges are usually developed by a specialist such as an occupational therapist or a physiotherapist. It is generally not left to the child care providers to offer physical training programs. Their responsibilities are usually more centred on collaboration with specialists and families to ensure that children are included in programs to their maximum abilities.

1. Collaboration with Specialists

Children who have physical challenges usually attend therapy sessions with a specialist. The specialist develops a program based on his or her assessment and will provide the therapeutic program for the individual child. For example, Simon is a five-year-old with cerebral palsy who uses a wheelchair for mobility. Simon's occupational therapist conducted an assessment of his abilities and used the results, shown here in Table 8.4, to recommend a therapy program based on Simon's strengths and needs.

The results were shared with Simon's day care staff. Regularly scheduled meetings were set up among the occupational therapist, the family members and da care staff. In collaboration with the occupational therapist, the staff were able to:

TABLE 8.4   RESULTS OF SIMON'S ASSESSMENT

1. Sensory stimulation and response
2. Exploration of objects and space, and manipulation of materials
3. Ludic activity: functional and unconventional use of play materials leading to the acquisition of a personal play repertoire.

Stage 1	Stage 2	Stage 3
LUDIC ATTITUDE		
Characteristics		
• **awakening of attention** • **awakening of curiosity** • **awakening of interest** • desire to know	• interest sustained • **sensation of pleasure** • desire for initiative • desire to explore • desire to act	• interest in action • pleasure in action • initiative • **humour** • spontaneity
Emotional Components		
• **feelings of confidence**	• feelings of control of objects • **expression of needs** • beginning of autonomy	• feeling of mastery • expression of needs and feelings • autonomy • decision making • self-esteem
LUDIC ACTION		
Sensory Components		
• **looks** • **touches +** • **smells** • **hears** • **puts in mouth** • **moves**		

TABLE 8.4 CONTINUED

Stage 1	Stage 2	Stage 3
	Motor Components	
• **grasps** • manipulates • **maintains a position** • **moves**	• *grasps/releases* + • *opens/closes* • *throws/catches* • empties/fills • piles • carries • **changes position** • **moves around**	• *uses tools (crayon, scissors...)* • uses several objects • combines various actions
	Cognitive Components	
• **experiments with relationships of cause and effect (beginning)** • **experiments with permanence of the object (beginning)** • **recognized basic characteristics of objects**	• *understands the relationship of cause* • *understands the concept of permanence of the object* • *understands how objects work* + • helps solving problems • understands how activities proceed	• imitates • pretends + • creates a play situation • uses symbols (make-believe play, drawing, language) • solves problems • understands symbols
	Social Components	
• **plays with the adult** + • **plays alone**	• plays in parallel • grasps the notion of property	• shares the play materials • plays with other children • cooperates in shared play • knows how to ask for and accept help • can help others • expresses ideas
Legend: • bold: present • italics: in development	• normal type: absent • + : strong interest	

Source: The Ludic Model

- Develop an individual program plan for Simon
- Share observations on a variety of skills
- Gain expert advice on equipment/material needs to include in the program
- Foster experiences that supported Simon's growth and development in a variety of settings

2. Collaboration with Families

Collaboration with family members helps to identify, evaluate and reinforce learning activities that are implemented in the home, at the centre and at the therapy program. This collaboration is critical to ensuring that:

- The child's program is consistent in all settings
- Information about the child's progress is shared with all partners
- Appropriate revisions and adaptations are implemented as needed
- Evaluations are developed and implemented as a team

Observing Children's Motor Development

Observing children's motor development is important in planning an inclusive environment that provides for active motor participation of all children. To plan the motor experiences and the organization of the materials within the learning environment, child care staff should conduct an observation of children's motor milestones (for examples, see Figures 8.4 and 8.5). This type of observation helps to identify gross and fine motor skills and abilities.

How can an observation such as that shown in Figure 8.4 be used? It is evident that Sam seems to participate in gross motor activity regularly. He seems to like challenges such as walking across tree stumps. But he is also aware of his capabilities—he holds onto the fence, and crawls down the stairs backwards. He engages in balancing activities: walking up stairs, on the line and over the stumps. This seems to indicate that more activities—for instance, balance beams, inside and outside—should be set up to enable him to practise various types of balancing activities.

FIGURE 8.4

Observation of Gross Motor Skills

Child: Sam
Observer: Nadia

Date	Skill	Comments
Oct. 2	Climbing	• Climbed stairs one foot at a time, holding onto rail • Crawled down stairs backwards • Repeated behaviour four times • Refused when encouraged to try to walk down holding someone's hand
Oct. 3	Walking	• Followed line on the floor by moving with one foot on either side of the line; lost his balance and fell twice, but continued to try
Oct. 4	Rolling	• Rolled sideways down hill outside (six times)
Oct. 5	Balancing	• Watched children walk across tree stumps; joined in by holding on to the railing; continued with activity after other children had left

FIGURE 8.5

Observation of Grasping Skills

Child: Sam   **Dates:** Oct. 3–5; 7–11
Observer: Nadia

Type of Grasp	Setting	Description	Intervention
Palmar	Sand	Used shovel frontwards, then flipped it over backwards into the bucket, but most of the sand landed outside the bucket	Provided larger bucket: Sam filled it without spilling
Pincer	Beads	Picked up gimp to thread beads; could not get beads onto gimp; started to frown	Provided some long pipe cleaners: Sam could place beads onto gimp

Observation of fine motor skills (as shown in Figure 8.5) provides information about the type of grasp that is being used, what type of activity the child is engaged in and intervention strategies that can be used to enhance success of the activity.

A summary of the observations shown in Figure 8.5 could be used to create a tool to observe other characteristics of Simon, such as sensory components, as shown in Figure 8.6. This kind of observation provides valuable information to the therapist about activities and behaviours that are prevalent in other situations and provides insights into what sensory activities might be organized to encourage Simon's interactions.

FIGURE 8.6

Observation of Sensory Components

Child: Simon
Observers: Combination of family and centre staff

Sensory Component	Setting	Description
Observing	Watched finger play	• Five children and Tracey engaged in Itsy Bitsy Spider finger play as Simon watched from a distance; when asked if he wanted to join, moved wheelchair away • Watched me bake cookies; refused to help but stayed and watched
Tactile activities	Tactile tiles	• Picked up tile and placed it in front of him; rubbed his finger over it several times; repeated process for set of tiles; smiled and continued to rub the ones he liked; placed the ones he liked in one pile—Melanie asked him if she could play; he let her use all tiles, even his favourite ones; she told him that they were her favourite ones too
Listening	Requested to listen to the song and look at the book about Itsy Bitsy Spider	• Listened and looked at book four times

How can an observation like that shown in Figure 8.6 be used? This type of tool is useful in establishing the child's interests and interactions with both materials and other children. It provides a basis to collaboratively plan experiences in various settings.

The IPP for Motor Skills

Individual program plans are usually not developed by practitioners for motor skills development. Dealing with challenges in motor behaviour is a skill that needs specialized training. Physiotherapists and occupational therapists can provide guidance on the types of motor activities that the child should engage in and the types of specialized equipment that he or she might need.

The individual program set up for Susan was initiated by the physiotherapist. The IPP shown in Figure 8.7 started with a goal set by the physiotherapist. Strategies and materials to reach the goal were collaboratively developed by the family members, the staff, the support staff and the physiotherapist. Progress was tracked by everyone.

Adapting the Environment

General adaptations should be made to accommodate motor abilities of all the children. These general adaptations are usually concerned with accessibility. Adaptations should reflect the ability of any child to access all activities irrespective of the mode of movement used, such as a walker or wheelchair. The principles behind the adaptations include these:

- Movement around the indoor or outdoor environment—Clear passageways should accommodate free movement between various learning spaces.
- Areas free from clutter—Clutter is dangerous as children may trip and fall. Some mobility may be inhibited by trapping the wheels of such devices as wheelchairs and walkers.
- Clear visibility of learning areas—Children should be able to be able to identify the various learning areas from different positions and from various points in the room.
- Access to all learning activities and routine care areas—All areas should be accessible to wheelchairs and other devices.
- Access to the facility—Ramps and automatic door openers should be provided to all entrances to the facility that children use.

In addition to the general adaptations, a number of specific adaptations must be made to both indoor and outdoor environments to reflect individual motor needs. In all instances, these adaptations should encourage maximum autonomy and optimal interactions among children and with learning experiences.

FIGURE 8.7

Individual Program Plan

Name: Susan   **DOB:** Jan. 1, 2001

Overview of Susan's Skills:

Susan has cerebral palsy. She is confined to a wheelchair. She can use her wheelchair independently. She uses a full palmar grasp to manipulate objects. She is persistent in her attempts to pick items up and examine them, but finds it difficult to manipulate objects that are on a slippery surface. She needs to be allowed the time to complete manipulative tasks.

Summary of interests observed in various settings (home, therapy centre and day care):

1. Tactile experiences—tactile tiles, feely bag, tactile books, creative activities with tactile materials
2. Sand—filling and dumping activities; needs help to dump sand out
3. Listening—finger plays and stories told or read

Goal:

To improve manipulation skills

Strategies:

1. Utilize regular play experiences with other children to support goal.
2. Adapt environment to make manipulation easier.
   - Add low, firm pile carpeting to manipulative table to make picking up easier
   - Provide trays in areas with lips and carpeting to prevent toys from falling off surface
   - Provide individual sand containers on tables to encourage filling and emptying activities, with a variety of smaller containers to make it easier to fill and dump the sand
   - Provide large crayons and markers to facilitate palmar grasp creative activities
   - Add basket to wheelchair to facilitate independence in gathering materials of choice

Evaluation:

The following observation form (only a portion of which is shown here) was used to fill in behaviours as they occurred in the centre and at home. The information was reviewed once every two weeks to plan for any needed adaptations or revisions.

Date	Setting	Activity
Oct. 25	Individual sand tray	Solitary play, filled small buckets with a shovel; much of the sand spilled, persisted until pail was full; called teacher over to look at full pail; dumped out sand and repeated activity

1. Indoor Learning Spaces

Indoor learning spaces should provide opportunities for children to actively participate in all learning activities organized with peers using the materials and equipment available. These adaptations can be classed in six categories:

- Environmental control devices—These devices are usually special switches that allow an individual to move around or to access equipment independently. Examples include automatic devices such as door openers, water taps, toilet flushers, light switches or remote controls to such equipment as computers.

Photo 8.17

- Daily living aids—There are a number of assistive devices that encourage independence. Examples include specially designed toilet seats, hand rails beside toilets, tilted mirrors in washrooms and specialized cutlery and dishes to assist independence at meal times.
- Visual aids—These aids are designed to assist maximum participation. Signs should be posted in sign language, Braille and symbolized formats to encourage all children to understand and find the learning activities and materials they wish to engage in (Photo 8.17).
- Alternative communication devices—These devices help children communicate with each other and with adults.
- Mobility devices—These include equipment such as wheelchairs, walkers and adaptive bicycles.
- Positioning equipment—This equipment may be used to maximize children's ability to interact with others and the materials and equipment in their learning environment. Examples include wedges to provide support for various body positions; adjustable chairs, tables and easels; standing frames; and specialized chairs and cots.

2. Outdoor Environments

A number of specific adaptations need to be made to outdoor environments to facilitate active participation of all children. These include:

- Clearly defined paths that are paved to allow access to all learning areas with wheelchairs or other mobile equipment (Photo 8.18)

Photo 8.18

Photo 8.19

Photo 8.20

Photo 8.21

Photo 8.22

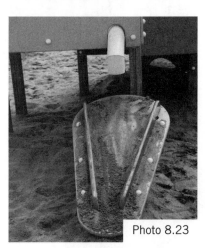

Photo 8.23

- Ramps to access play equipment (Photo 8.19 and 8.20)
- Adaptive playground equipment (Photo 8.21 and 8.22)
- Play at various levels to encourage a variety of interactions (Photo 8.23)

Role of the Early Childhood Educator

The role of the early childhood educator in the physical environment actually comprises five roles: observer, planner, collaborator, organizer and advocate.

1. Observer Role

The observer role is critical to helping children with motor challenges to participate fully in the learning environment. Children's motor skills and abilities must be observed to enable organization of an appropriate learning environment. Ongoing observations need to occur to identify:

- Safety issues that affect children of varying abilities—For example, it might be wise to create a one-way system on paths to ensure that children in mobility devices or on riding toys do not bump into each other. Additionally, marked crosswalks and stop signs can be placed at intersection points to avoid collisions and to reinforce safety rules.
- Modifications or adaptations that need to be made to allow for active participation by all individuals.
- Modification of activities to maintain interest and to continue to build capabilities through providing appropriate challenges such as setting up an obstacle course.

2. Planner Role

Motor activities need to be planned to take place in different ways: spontaneously, individually and/or in small or large groups.

- Planning for spontaneous activity—If the environment is organized appropriately, there should be opportunities for children to become actively involved in perceptual, gross and fine motor activities. The environment acts as the third teacher. Kyler had watched the children walking across the stumps. He seemed reluctant to try. Claudia noticed his reluctance and asked if he wanted some help. Kyler nodded. He used the stumps several times during outdoor play activities (Photo 8.24).
- Planning for individual skill development—Some skills can be planned for by providing the appropriate equipment and materials. All young children need opportunities to coordinate visual perception skills and motor skills. Jordan was able to manipulate the digger to scoop up snow so he could load up his dump truck (Photo 8.25).
- Planning for group activity—Children need opportunities to explore activities together. Outdoor water activities often lend themselves to a variety of motor skills through experiences such as these (Photo 8.26):

Photo 8.24

Photo 8.25

Photo 8.26

- the feeling of water on various parts of one's skin (and the opportunity to share one's impressions)
- awareness of directionality and spatial awareness
- running through water
- splashing other children
- directing the flow of water at others
- blowing bubbles and catching them

3. Collaborator Role

Early childhood educators need to collaborate with others to ensure that programs offered are of the highest possible quality. Through a collaborative process, the early childhood educator can enhance quality by:

- Discussing progress in motor skills and identifying new goals or target behaviours
- Ensuring that a consistent approach to the child's motor needs is used
- Providing opportunities to try motor skills in different settings, which will lead to transfer of skills
- Sharing successes—Nathan was two years old. He had been diagnosed with an overall delay. He had learned to pull himself into a standing position and cruise along with the support of furniture. While at day care he took his first independent step. The staff member quickly took a photograph. In this way this important developmental milestone could be shared.
- Sharing resources—The centre decided that they wanted to replace the indoor playhouse and provide a new setting that was more accessible to all children. A planning meeting with all the families and staff was arranged. One of the fathers was a carpenter. He helped the staff devise plans for a new structure, organized the parent group to procure materials and finally organized all participants to help build the structure.

4. Organizer Role

Early childhood educators are involved in several organizing roles. These include organizing of physical and human resources.

The physical environment needs to be set up to maximize motor activity for all children. Organization of the physical environment comprises various functions:

- Identifying appropriate resources, materials and equipment to ensure that all children's strengths and needs are met
- Organizing the resources, materials and equipment appropriately to ensure that children have opportunities to practise motor skills on a daily basis
- Providing opportunities to rotate resources, materials and equipment to maintain interest and pose challenges

- Providing toys and play materials that encourage social interactions
- Organizing safe indoor and outdoor environments that encourage children's independence
- Ensuring that an emergency plan is in place that includes children with physical disabilities
- Developing an appropriate schedule that includes regular motor activities
- Organizing displays and materials that showcase diversity, such as pictures, books or photographs

The organization of human resources includes these functions:

- Providing opportunities to children to express their concerns about their physical differences
- Collaborating with families and other professionals to develop IPPs, plan activities and evaluate the program, the environment and the progress of individual children
- Collaborating with staff to identify and develop consistent interaction strategies
- Demonstrating appropriate interaction patterns through modelling behaviours

5. Advocate Role

Materials and equipment to enhance motor development are often expensive to purchase and to install. Early childhood educators need to learn to advocate for appropriate funding to procure resources, adaptive technology, equipment and accessibility to all children and their families.

SUMMARY

Gross motor activities should be looked upon as a vital component of healthy growth and development. Active movement ensures that children develop:

- Independence skills
- A positive self-image
- Healthy living habits
- Healthy attitudes toward physical activity
- The ability to use their fine and gross muscles in a variety of active play

- The ability to coordinate a number of skills in various domains—sensory, physical, cognitive, social and emotional

Movement and learning is central to the child's healthy development. The interplay between movement and all other domains forms a cornerstone of healthy growth and development. Figure 8.3 demonstrates the interaction between active motor activity and all other domains. With careful planning and organization of the learning environment, every child can maximize his or her potential. "Our society has an underlying value structure that makes us think of disability in terms of 'tragedy,' having an 'impaired body' or being 'abnormal.' We must change this negative definition. Many things that make a person 'disabled' have to do with not having access to his or her environment. A flight of stairs makes a person who uses a wheelchair disabled. Put in a ramp and the disability disappears—until that person gets to a narrow doorway" (Greenstein, 1998: 1).

KEY POINTS

Perceptual development
- Visual perceptual ability—Acuity and understanding of visual stimuli
- Auditory perception—Distinguishing individual sounds and making sense of what has been heard

Sensory awareness
- Tactile awareness—Touch, temperature, texture, consistency
- Body awareness—Function of different parts of the body, self-awareness
- Spatial awareness—Awareness of self in relation to other objects and within a physical space
- Directional awareness—Understanding of own body and how to move body parts in different directions
- Time awareness—Develops through reciprocal actions, independence in routines, daily routines and formal understanding of time such as hours and days of the week

Motor development
- Interaction of gross, fine and perceptual motor development
- Interaction of all domains—Physical, social, cognitive, language and emotional

Fine motor development
- Grasping skills—Reflex, palmar, pincer, tripod grasps

Range of motor behaviours in inclusive settings
- Normal, delayed, gifted, requiring wheelchair accommodation

Intervention strategies
- Collaboration with specialists
- Collaboration with families

Observing children's motor development
- Observation of gross motor milestones
- Observation of grasping skills
- Observations of sensory components

Individual program plan
- Overview of motor skills, summary of interests, goals, strategies, evaluation

Adapting the learning environment
- General adaptations
- Adaptations to indoor learning spaces: environmental control; daily living aids; visual aids; alternative communication devices; mobilization devices; positioning devices
- Adaptations to outdoor learning spaces: defined paths; adaptive equipment; various levels of play

Role of the early childhood educator
- Observer—Safety, modifications, adaptations
- Planner—Spontaneous/planned, individual/group activities
- Collaborator—Progress, consistency, sharing successes and resources
- Organizer—Identify resources, organize physical resources and environment
- Advocate—Funding, procure resources and equipment

EXERCISES

1. Reflect on your personal ability to participate in fine and gross motor activity. How does this affect your self-awareness? How does it affect your self-concept?

2. Define each of these terms: perceptual development, gross motor development and fine motor development. Why are these developmental areas related?

3. Blindfold yourself in your kitchen. Find a glass and take it to the sink. Fill it with water and have a drink. Describe your experience? How did you feel about this experience? How did your movement change?

4. Explain how the following affect motor development:
   a) Visual perception
   b) Auditory perception
   c) Sensory awareness

5. Describe the changes that occur as grasping behaviour develops. What are the limitations of each type of grasp? What type of material might you provide to encourage children to gain better control over their manipulative abilities?

6. Describe the relationship of motor development to other developmental domains.

7. Describe the importance of each intervention strategy identified on pages 269–272.

8. Observe children in an inclusive setting. Identify the range of gross and fine motor behaviours.

9. Compare the IPP developed for motor behaviour to a behavioural IPP. How are they similar or different?

10. Using the chart provided, identify the adaptations that could be found in inclusive settings to encourage motor development.

11. Identify the key role an early childhood educator should demonstrate to provide a learning environment that provides children with opportunities to optimize their motor development.

Adaptation	Description
General adaptations	
Adaptations in indoor environments	
Adaptations in outdoor environments	

RESOURCES

Child's spatial awareness
**www.partnershipforlearning.org/article.asp?
ArticleID=2539**

Spatial relations development
www.tsbvi.edu/Education/early-years.htm

Visual perceptual development, Microsoft PowerPoint
**www.le.ac.uk/pc/tmw3/Perceptual%20develop
ment%20(6%20per%20page).pdf**

Perceptual-development problems, frequently asked
questions
**http://home.att.net/~rperhardtdp/
faq_VPM.html**

Auditory development
**www.hon.ch/Dossier/MotherChild/postnatal/
hearing_dev.html**

Assistive technology
www.nymc.edu/wihd/at/at_loanprogram.html

Programming ideas, conductive education
www.boostcamp.org/Conductive_Ed.html

Physical Challenges in Childcare: Let the Children
Lead
www.cfc-efc.ca/docs/cccf/00022_en.htm

Service initiatives—links
**http://sph.umdnj.edu/HSAP/service/fc_links2
.html**

Cerebral palsy
http://cnet.shs.arizona.edu/infonet/cp.html

REFERENCES

Crowther, I. (2005). *Child Development Primer.* Scarborough,
ON: Thomson Nelson.

Ferland, F. (2005). *The Ludic Model: Play, Children with Physical
Disabilities and Occupational Therapy,* Second Edition.
Ottawa: CAOT Publications ACE.

Greenstein, D. (1998). Physical Difference and Impairments.
Cornell University [online]. Available at
www.ces.ncsu.edu/depts/fcs/human/pubs/nc15.html
(10-1-2005).

Nyisztor, D., & Rudick, E. (1995). *Moving and Learning.*
Toronto, ON: Harcourt Brace & Company Canada, Ltd.

Sanders, S. (2002). *Active for Life: Developmentally Appropriate
Movement Programs for Young Children.* Washington, DC:
National Association for the Education of Young
Children.

Schickedanz, J., Schickedanz, D., Forsyth, P., & Forsyth, G.
(2001). *Understanding Children and Adolescents,* Fourth
Edition. Needham Heights, MA: Allyn & Bacon.

9

CHAPTER

Social and Emotional Growth in Inclusive Settings

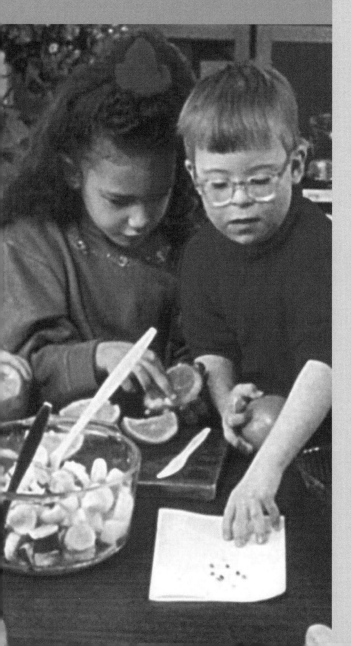

"Children in group care live in a kind of 'forced growth' situation that involves a great variety of relationships with adults and peers. They may be expected to acquire behaviours and learn the social meanings that go with many feeling and actions, in ways that can easily contradict the demands and limitations of individual temperaments and developmental stages. Infants may be asked to practice cooperative and sharing behaviours, toddlers to follow abstract rules, preschoolers to thread their way through various kinds and degrees of friendship and rivalry" (Kilbride, 1997: 120).

Learning Outcomes

After studying this chapter, you will be able to:

1. Define and describe social and emotional development.
2. Explain the relationship of Erikson's Stages of Development and how these stages relate to organizing a social-emotional environment that is both inclusive and effective.
3. Discuss how the following factors affect social-emotional behaviours: type of attachment pattern; child-rearing practices; background experiences; and temperament.
4. Define and describe social attributes.
5. Describe the types of social-emotional behaviours that might be found in inclusive settings.
6. Explain why it is important to understand the six principles of guiding behaviour in inclusive settings.
7. Identify how to observe children's social-emotional behaviour.
8. Identify and describe the key components of a social-emotional IPP.
9. Identify and describe strategies for guiding social-emotional behaviours in inclusive settings.
10. Identify how to effectively organize the social-emotional environment.
11. Describe the role of the early childhood educator in inclusive social settings.

Introduction

Social development and emotional development are closely linked. As children become more socially competent, they become more adept at social interactions with peers and adults in their lives and are able to react appropriately to a variety of different social and cultural situations. These interactions build friendships and relationships with others. Positive early social interactions lead to increased self-confidence and increased self-esteem. In contrast, the research clearly shows that negative early interactions leave lasting and sometimes permanent disabilities in emotional and social development that may affect much of the child's success in later academic years (McCain & Mustard, 1999; McCain & Mustard, 2002).

Social skills are also linked to the types of play interactions that children demonstrate at various ages and to the behaviour patterns that evolve. However, it is the interplay of all domains that leads to healthy development (see Figure 9.1).

Healthy social interactions depend on a child's ability to communicate; understand how to interact with others in different situations; form relationships; and express emotions in acceptable ways. The social setting that children interact in has tremendous influence on how children feel about themselves. When an environment is set up to encourage children to work together and with adults to try new challenges, make appropriate choices and solve problems, children gain confidence in their abilities and skills. When the efforts of children are valued, children receive modelling to learn to respect others. Emotional well-being flourishes in an atmosphere of respect. Children learn to accept each other's varying abilities and learn to function more effectively in a diverse social setting. "Child psychologists, early childhood educators, and others working with young children will readily agree that there is no one factor that can be accredited for determining the quality of children's self-esteem. Rather, many factors interact in shaping the way in which chil-

FIGURE 9.1

Interplay of Developmental Domains

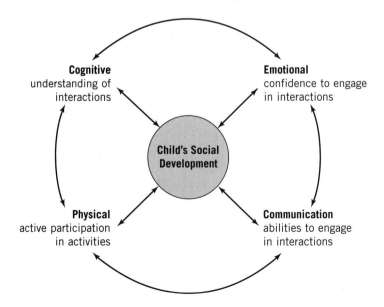

dren feel about themselves. It is also well known that the nature of this feeling further affects children's motivation, learning, and achievements" (King, Chipman & Cruz-Janzen, 1994). "Primary among the factors frequently identified as being at the core of the children's self esteem are a sense of belonging, feeling of worth, and a sense of competence" (Kilbride, 1997: 84).

When children have difficulties in any one of the developmental domains, they may find it a struggle to engage in appropriate social interactions. To sup-

TABLE 9.1   **ERIKSON S STAGES OF DEVELOPMENT**

Stage	Description	Positive Outcomes	Negative Outcomes
Stage 1: **Infancy** **(birth–18 months)**	Infants depend on primary caregivers for food, warmth, affection and stimulation.	**Development of Trust** When the infant's needs are met consistently and immediately, secure attachment with primary caregivers is established. The infant learns to trust that his or her signals are responded to and learns to trust the environment.	**Development of Mistrust** If the infant's needs are not met or met inconsistently, the infant will develop mistrust of the individuals and things in the environment.
Stage 2: **Toddlers** **(2–3.5 years)**	Toddlers learn to do things by themselves, such as walking, talking or feeding themselves. Toddlers start to develop self-control and confidence in their own abilities.	**Development of Autonomy** If toddlers are encouraged to become independent and are reinforced for their efforts, they develop confidence in their ability to make choices and act upon their environment effectively. As a result they develop greater independence.	**Development of Shame or Doubt** If toddlers' independence is discouraged or their efforts are disapproved of or ridiculed, they may develop feelings of shame about their behaviours or may start to doubt their abilities.
Stage 3: **Preschool** **(3.5–6 years)**	Preschoolers have developed a number of skills (motor, cognitive, language, social, emotional) and are able to interact more effectively with others. They are very curious and more independent but are still learning to assume responsibility and self-control.	**Development of Initiative** Preschoolers need to be encouraged to solve their own problems and make their own choices. They need positive and consistent guidance. If preschoolers' choices and actions are valued, they will develop the initiative to try new challenges.	**Development of Guilt** If preschoolers' choices or actions are not valued, or if their activities are mostly directed, they may cease to try and become dependent on the adults in their environment. If their efforts are ridiculed or rejected, they may develop a sense of guilt.
Stage 4: **School-Age Years** **(6–12 years)**	Children at this stage learn academic skills such as reading and writing. Independence increases and friendships proliferate.	**Development of Industry** Children need to be encouraged to become independently productive, to strive for success and to enjoy intellectual activities in order to develop a sense of being a competent individual.	**Development of Inferiority** Children who have become dependent, need continual assistance to accomplish tasks and do not enjoy intellectual activities may develop a sense of inferiority.

port all children's healthy social and emotional development, a number of areas need to be considered. Adults working in an inclusive setting must have a firm knowledge of social and emotional development, the types and ranges of social and emotional behaviours that young children engage in, how to observe these behaviours and how to develop an emotionally secure and socially responsive inclusive environment.

Social and Emotional Development

Social and emotional development starts at birth. The early interactions between primary caregivers and the infant have a profound influence on all future development. "The evidence from neuroscience and child development studies is clear: The first years of life are crucial in setting a good foundation for each child's future" (McCain et al., 1999: 51). As the infants grow and develop, they pass through predictable stages of development. For optimal growth and development to occur, children need to be exposed to a nurturing, stimulating environment at each stage.

According to Erik Erikson's theory of psychosocial development, individuals pass through eight psychosocial stages in their lifetimes. Four of these stages occur between birth and the age of 12 years. At each stage of development, the child achieves either positive or negative outcomes depending on the type of stimulation and interactions that the child is exposed to (Schickedanz, Schickedanz, Forsyth & Forsyth, 2001). Table 9.1 outlines these stages and the outcomes associated with each. Understanding the psychosocial development of children is important because caregiver interaction patterns directly affect the optimal development of each child.

Children's social and emotional behaviour progresses along a developmental continuum. Normative data are sensitive to cultural and individual family values. For example, studies have shown that children raised with different parenting styles behaved differently socially. The least competent children were those raised with very permissive or neglectful parenting styles. The children raised with parents with a more authoritative parenting style tended to be the most competent (Schickedanz et al., 2001).

Practitioners need to know and understand social-emotional milestones in order to:

- Plan appropriate social environments for children
- Provide a safe and nurturing environment for all children's skills and abilities
- Identify potential problems
- Provide appropriate social experience to meet all children's strengths and needs
- Nurture appropriate social and emotional development

An outline of social-emotional growth in infancy is given in Table 9.2. These social-emotional milestones and those shown in subsequent tables can be used to help early childhood educators and families create observational tools to identify children's behaviour and evaluate their abilities, skills and progress.

Social-emotional growth starts at birth with interactions between infant and caregivers and rapidly develops into interactions with others. It is easy to miss the

TABLE 9.2   **SOCIAL-EMOTIONAL MILESTONES: INFANCY**

Age	Milestone	Importance
Birth–6 months	Differential crying	Signals different needs
	Cooing and babbling	Establishes communication patterns between infant and adult
	Attachment patterns formed	Develops sense of trust and security
	Social smiling	Provides opportunity for social interactions
	Differential reaction to different voice tones	Learns to recognize the mood expressed by tone of voice
	Initiating, imitating and maintaining interactions through use of body language and vocalizations	Learns to listen and develops skills of turn-taking
6–12 months	Selective smiling	Controls interactions with individuals of choice
	Social referencing	Opportunities for social interactions between infant and caregivers
	Beginning of stranger anxiety	Leads to selective social interactions
	Responding to stress of others	First indication of awareness of other individuals' feelings
	Using repertoire of gestures to indicate meaning	Initiates and maintains social interactions
	Enjoying attention	Initiates social interactions and expresses feelings through physical acts such as kissing and hugging
	Demonstrating assertiveness by refusing to do something	Development of autonomy
12–18 months	Peak of separation anxiety	Demonstrates increased awareness of own emotional needs and preferences
	Symbolic actions	May be used to initiate and maintain social interactions
18–24 months	Demonstrating empathetic responses to distress	Demonstrating greater awareness of others in the environment
	Using words to interact	Showing greater ability to interact socially with others
	Showing inability to share	May cause some anti-social behaviours

importance of some of these early interactions because of the infant's seeming helplessness. Caregivers must learn to recognize the interactions for what they are to identify possible problems and to nurture optimal social and emotional growth.

The toddler years are marked with growth in autonomy. Social-emotional development at this stage is outlined in Table 9.3. Many toddler behaviours may be looked upon as inappropriate, such as the tendency toward non-compliance and their use of aggressive acts to gain what they want. However, these behaviours are developmentally appropriate and arise from the toddlers' inability to adequately express themselves or gain control over their own actions (see author's Reflection). Knowledge of developmental milestones is critical in planning and implementing appropriate social-emotional activities for toddlers.

Reflection

Reflection	*From the Author*
	I observed a group of toddlers at play within a physical play group setting. Two of them actively explored their environment. The toddlers were closely observed by the early childhood educator. She seemed to know when she needed to step in. For example, both active explorers continually tried to climb a piece of equipment at the same time. Another two toddlers were lying on a blanket with a number of toys between them. One of these toddlers continually tried to take a toy away from his peer. Another adult quickly intervened to put an identical toy within reach of the "grabbing toddler." Each of these early childhood educators realized that the toddlers' behaviour was not a negative behaviour but a simply a result of their developmental competency.

TABLE 9.3   SOCIAL-EMOTIONAL MILESTONES: TODDLERS

Age	Milestone	Importance
2 years	Responding verbally to other individuals' stress signals	Increased understanding of the feelings of others
	Starting to include other children in play activities	Start of social play interactions with peers
	Enjoying helping	Creates awareness of some social functions such as chores
	Decrease in physical aggression as communication skills improve	Demonstrates greater awareness of the use of symbolized forms (language) to interact
	Sharing and turn-taking still difficult	Causes anti-social behaviours
	Making demands and expecting compliance	Development of greater autonomy

The preschool years are, as indicated in Table 9.4, the start of much pro-social behaviour, such as starting to form friendships and increased independence. Knowledge of social-emotional milestones will help identify possible problems and form the basis of an appropriate social-emotional learning environment.

Effects on Social-Emotional Behaviours in Inclusive Settings

Children's social and emotional behaviours are dependent on a variety of factors. These include attachment patterns, child-rearing practices, background experi-

TABLE 9.4   **SOCIAL-EMOTIONAL MILESTONES: PRESCHOOLERS**

Age	Milestone	Importance
3 years	Starting to share and take turns	Start of pro-social behaviour
	Participating in group activities	Ability to interest in a group situation
	Defending possessions	Still finds sharing difficult
	Engaging in make-belief play	Start of ability to take on another individual's perspective
	Showing affection to peers	Greater awareness of own feelings in more socially acceptable ways
4 years	Using voice tone to express feelings	Increased ability to express feelings in more socially acceptable ways
	Showing pride in accomplishments	Greater self-awareness
	Ability to label feelings	Greater awareness of personal feelings
	Engaging in role play	Practice of familiar roles
	Rapid mood changes	Reaction to personal challenges such as frustration
	Starting to tell jokes and funny stories	Initiation of alternative reasons for communication with peers
	Striving for independence but easily frustrated	Leads to greater autonomy
	Start of friendships	Leads to ability to maintain relationships
	Possible taunting of peers	Has learned and imitates inappropriate behaviours
5 years	Sudden mood swings	Reacts to personal challenges but also to peer perceptions
	Need of approval from peers and adults	May lead to positive or negative self-image depending on reaction of peers or adults
	Start of moral development	Shows feelings of disappointment and self criticism

ences, temperament, special needs, social attributes and opportunities in the learning environment.

1. Attachment and Social-Emotional Development

Researchers have measured the attachment behaviours demonstrated in infants' responses to personal needs, potential danger or expectations. "The parent's overall pattern of behaviour toward the baby influences strongly the kind of attachment the baby will develop. Each attachment pattern seems to reflect different histories of parental response. When the parents respond sensitively to the baby's signals, the baby tends to become securely attached. When the parents respond inappropriately, or not at all, the baby tends to form an insecure attachment of some kind" (Schickedanz et al., 2001: 236). Four different types of attachment behaviours have been identified: secure, ambivalent, avoidant and disorganized. The latter three categories describe the behaviours of infants who are not securely attached. The impact of attachment patterns in infancy continues to be demonstrated in later years. Expected behaviours of children who are not securely attached might include these:

- Crying more
- Playing less
- Engaging in fewer symbolic activities
- Showing more aggression and destructiveness in interactions with peers
- Showing more dependence on adults for attention and support
- Exhibiting a greater variety of challenging behaviours

2. Child-Rearing Practices and Social-Emotional Development

Child-rearing practices also influence the social behaviours of children. Children who are raised too permissively, without warmth or nurturance, or with high levels of control over their behaviours also exhibit social-emotional behaviours that affect their overall abilities over time. Children raised under these conditions are:

- Less self-reliant
- Less self-controlled
- Lacking in social skills to interact with peers
- More apprehensive of engaging in learning activities
- Likely to experience stress
- Less compliant

3. Background Experiences and Social-Emotional Development

Children are raised in many different environments. The type of social-emotional behaviours children might engage in can depend on the amount and types of stimulation they have previously received. Children who have never been exposed to certain situations, who have never been empowered to use certain tools or utensils, or who are not securely attached to their primary caregivers might find it difficult to adapt to a setting with choices that are foreign to them.

In Western cultures, the ability to read and write is highly valued. Not all children come from backgrounds that nurture this approach. There are a number of cultures, such as many Aboriginal and some Asian cultures, that favour verbal communication instead. Children from these cultures will not have the background experiences to utilize the many print-based resources within an early childhood setting. Child care providers will need to adjust expectations and strategies to create an enjoyable and positive environment for these children.

Children who have not had the relevant background experiences to engage in some learning activities may exhibit some of the following behaviours:

- Lack of interest in certain things such as reading books
- Avoidance of certain learning areas such as the writing, painting or book area
- Developmental lag in certain activities such as knowledge of the alphabet
- Seemingly inappropriate social behaviours such as lack of eye contact (considered rude in some cultures)
- Shyness or withdrawal
- Continual talking or interrupting
- Reluctance to initiate social contact
- Reluctance to show emotions

Caregivers need to learn to understand the behaviour expectations of the various backgrounds that the children are from. With this understanding, developmentally-appropriate learning experiences can be developed and implemented.

Some children have grown up in backgrounds that are very enriching. These children often seem to be advanced for their age (gifted). The behaviours of these children may vary greatly. Typical behaviours may include:

- Desire to play with older children
- Boredom with activities
- Compassion and empathy for those around them
- Non-compliance
- Challenging of roles or expectations
- Preference for solitary play
- High energy levels
- Intense curiosity about everything
- Impatience with others
- Dislike of routines
- Interactions based on making rules and trying to get others to play by these rules
- Excessive self-criticism (The Council for Exceptional Children, 2005)

4. Individual Temperament and Social-Emotional Development

"Temperament refers to the patterns and style of a person's behaviour such as energy, quality, and intensity of expression of emotions, persistence, attention, tendencies to approach or withdraw from the unfamiliar, and self-regulation which appears later and develops with maturation" (National Association of School Psychologists, 1998: 1). Temperament is thought to be an inherited trait. However, expressions of temperament can be modified by maturation, experiences and the environment.

One aspect of temperament that may influence children's behaviours is initiation. When young children are able to initiate their own learning activity, they develop **intrinsic motivation** (motivation that is originating from the individual). Tasks that are intrinsically motivating are more likely to spur children on to learn with enthusiasm. When young children's learning is controlled by adults, children may:

- Become dependent on adults and require attention and encouragement to try different learning activities
- Be unable to regulate their own behaviour and as a result wait for others to initiate activities
- Lack the necessary self-confidence to try some learning activities

Another aspect of temperament that may influence behaviour is fear. Fear inhibits children from actively exploring the environment or activities within the environment. All children have fears, and they are considered a normal part of childhood development. Children's fears could be caused by a variety of factors, real or imagined. Some fears are triggered by remembered events, such as falling off a tricycle; others may not have an obvious cause. Toddlers' fears tend to focus on separation from primary caregivers, sudden or unexplained noises, some animals and insects, being in the dark or taking a bath. Preschoolers' fears expand through their imagination to include fears of such things as monsters or ghosts, and potentially more justifiable fears of real-life events such as losing a parent, terrorist activity or war. Children express their reactions to fear through physiological and behavioural signals. Fear reactions could include:

- Physiological signals such as sweating, increased breathing, increased heartbeat or tense muscles
- Avoidance or withdrawal from situations
- Refusal to participate
- Anxious behaviours such as continually looking toward the source of the perceived fear or taking a detour around the object of the fear to get to another activity

Frustration is another aspect of temperament that may influence behaviour. Frustration can be caused by a number of social situations that are a normal part of growth and development. Children are exploring different roles and practising various social skills, such as maintaining relationships or showing affection appropriately. During normal social interactions frustration may arise if the child is not understood, or if the child is rejected from a social situation. Children's frustrated behaviours may range from withdrawal to physical or verbal aggression against other individuals or things in the environment. Jamie had been told that she could not play with a group of her friends. As she stormed away, she shouted, "I hate you. I don't want to play with you anyway." She picked up one of the dolls the group was playing with, threw it and shouted, "Dolls are sissy stuff."

A fourth aspect of temperament that may influence children's behaviours is attention span. A significant factor in any childhood social situation is the length of attention span the children have. Children with long attention spans can maintain play with others over time. Children with short attention spans will find social activity and interactions difficult. These children may continually drift from activity to activity, interrupt interactions, avoid group activities or engage in challenging behaviours at times of stress.

5. Diagnosed Special Needs and Social-Emotional Development

Certain conditions such as ADD, ADHD, FAS or FAE make it much harder for children to engage in social interactions. Children with high needs usually demonstrate all of the socially challenging behaviours already listed.

Social Attributes in Inclusive Settings

There are a number of attributes of social behaviour that need to be considered when interacting with children and when organizing learning environments and activities. These include individual attributes, social skill attributes, and peer relationship attributes (McClellan & Katz, 2001).

1. Individual Attributes

Individual attributes are those behaviours that children exhibit based on personal temperament, personal learned behaviours or developmental abilities (McClellan et al., 2001). Since all children have different characteristics, it is important to know the individual attributes of the children. This will give the early childhood educator guidelines to:

- Plan for various social interactions to meet all children's needs
- Identify adjustments or adaptations needed to improve social interactions
- Help develop strategies for children with challenges in emotional or social interactions
- Develop sensitivity to creating a social environment suitable for all individuals

  Individual attributes include the following:

- Moods of children
- Dependency on adults
- Separation from adults
- Willingness to come to the centre
- Coping strategies
- Capacity to empathize
- Types of relationships with peers
- Types of interactions with peers
- Capacity for humour

2. Social Skill Attributes

Social skill attributes determine the types of interactions and skills the children bring to social situations. Through use of these skills, children learn to interact positively, maintain relationships with other children and assert themselves as needed. Child care providers need to understand what types of skills are used by children in order to facilitate and maintain positive interactions between individual children and groups of children. Children may use the following social skill attributes:

- Ability to engage in positive or negative interactions with peers
- Ability to assert self
  - To express preferences
  - To explain reasons for actions
  - To explain feelings (anger, frustration) effectively and appropriately
  - To be unintimidated by peers

- Ability to initiate contact with peers:
  - To approach peers
  - To negotiate and compromise
  - To seek to join groups successfully
  - To show interest in what others are doing
  - To accept all individuals
  - To engage in appropriate nonverbal interactions as needed

- Ability to maintain interactions:
  - To takes turns
  - To add to interactions by offering comments or suggestions, or asking for information

3. Peer Relationship Attributes

Peer relationship attributes refer to other children's interactions with a child. Children are either accepted or rejected by other children. They may be invited to engage in play activities with other children or ignored. Caregivers need to be able to determine which children have social-emotional strengths and which children are often excluded to help develop strategies for social inclusion.

Range of Behaviours in Inclusive Settings

Social and emotional behaviours within inclusive settings will include the full range of specific behaviours discussed already. In terms of their behaviours, children will fall into one of these categories:

- Children with a normal range of social-emotional skills
- Children with advanced social-emotional skills—These children will often act as models for other children in the program. Identification and assessment of the

skills of these children will help caregivers in several ways. Social settings may be organized to encourage peer modelling. They may also be organized to provide opportunities and encouragement for children to initiate contact with peers who may need help or encouragement to participate.

- Children who lack some social-emotional skills—Knowledge of the specific skills that the children do have will help to plan social settings based on these children's strengths. Caregivers will also be able to respond to spontaneous interactions in accordance with the specific needs of the children.

Interaction Patterns in Inclusive Settings

Guiding children's social and emotional interactions requires that caregivers have a firm understanding of expected social and emotional behaviours and set the stage for positive interactions to occur within the environment. There are six principles to setting the stage – recognition of the complexity of social skills, reduction of mistaken behaviours, practices of positive adult-child relations, solution-oriented intervention methods, partnerships with families, and a teamwork approach (Gartrell, 2004).

1. Recognition of Complexity of Social Skills

Gaining social-emotional skills is a lifetime achievement. With every new social setting, a new set of expectations and skills is acquired. Adults in children's lives need to recognize that the child is still learning. Adults set the stage on which social learning takes place. "The teacher takes a comprehensive approach. He seeks to understand the problem, modifies the child's program to reduce crisis, intervenes consistently but nonpunitively, builds the relationship with the child, involves the parents, teams with staff and other professionals, and develops, implements, and monitors a long-term plan" (Gartrell, 2004: 30).

2. Reduction of Mistaken Behaviours

Many behaviours that children exhibit may be classified as mistaken behaviours because they arise from the child's limited perspective of how to interact in social settings. Very young children resort to aggressive behaviours such as grabbing or hitting. They have not yet gained the maturity in skills such as language or negotiation to enable them to interact more acceptably. Some children have had models of behaviours such as using inappropriate words in their background experiences. Children will try the social behaviours that they have within their repertoire. Adults need to understand that the child is not "misbehaving" but using behaviours that are based on his or her background experiences and understanding. Guidance needs to focus on modification of the behaviours through positive interactions and modelling. "When children's development, learning style, and family background become the main priority of the program, children become positively involved and feel less need to show mistaken behavior" (Gartrell, 2004: 31).

Photo 9.1

Put toys away.

3. Fostering Positive Adult–Child Relations

As Erikson (see page 287) has identified in his stages of psychosocial development, adults play a key role in setting a positive learning environment. Positive adult–child relations occur when adults:

- Establish limits—Often limits are expressed as rules, which are often stated in the negative, the emphasis being on something that cannot be done. Limits should be stated in positive terms to guide behaviour. Instead of telling children what not to do, they should be told what to do. This is easily reinforced by placing picture and word messages in various centres as needed (Photo 9.1).
- Ensure that children understand the guidelines—Children need to be given explanations of why they should do something. Guidelines should make sense to them. "We wear a smock so that our clothes don't get dirty."
- Concentrate on reinforcing positive behaviours—Adults should be observing children carefully to anticipate a negative behaviour in order to prevent it. Jamie was watching the children play in the block area. He kept walking around them, getting closer and closer. Jamie usually engaged in solitary play. Other children often told him that he couldn't join their play. Corinne, an adult, had noticed Jamie's interest. She asked Jamie if he would like to play. Corrine told the children, "Jamie and I would like to play, too. What can we do?" The children quickly assigned roles to Jamie and Corinne. Corinne had accurately assessed the situation. She knew that Jamie wanted to join the play. She knew that the children would most likely reject his request. She made it more acceptable to the children because she also joined in their play. She also worded her request in a way that assumed that the children would be happy to include them. In this way, she was able to set up a positive experience for Jamie and the other children.
- Model appropriate behaviours and reinforce them when they occur—Charmaine greeted each of the children as they arrived in the morning. She had a smile on her face, remarked on something personal about each child and inquired pleasantly what he or she was going to do once in the preschool room.

4. Solution-Oriented Intervention Methods

Organization of the learning environment and learning experiences fosters individual and group problem solving. One aspect of organization involves making materials and equipment accessible and available. Storage should be arranged so that children can find the items that they want and use them appropriately. For example, children's dress-up clothes should be stored logically and visibly. Children are already familiar with how clothes are organized at home. Clothes can be put on hooks, hats on shelves and shoes on shoe racks. This offers a consistent scheme. Children are able to transfer information from one setting to another and in the process reinforce expectations in both. This, according to Erikson (see page 287), will lead to the development of greater autonomy.

Another aspect is helping children find their own solutions to problems. Two children were starting to argue about who could use the cement truck. Corral told the children that she could see that they had a problem. She asked the children to tell her what the problem was. Jordan answered, "We both want the cement truck." Jill nodded. Corral said: "Hmm, that is a problem. You only have one cement truck and two people want to use it. What could we do about this problem?" Jordan thought and said, "We could play together. I'll use the dump truck and Jill can dump the cement into my truck." Jill smiled and nodded again. Corral said, "That sounds like a good solution. You both seem to agree." She continued to watch to see what would evolve.

Corral identified the problem to the children, asked them to help find a solution and then monitored them to make sure that they continued to interact positively.

5. Partnerships with Families

Collaboration with families is critical. Through this process information can be shared about social behaviours in different settings, emotional adjustments to new experiences and joint strategies to guide behaviour. "Through positive notes home, phone calls, visits, meetings, and conferences, [the child-care provider] builds partnerships. It is her job to build partnerships even with hard-to-reach parents" (Gartrell, 2004: 32).

6. Teamwork Approach

All individuals who are interacting with the child need to be part of a team effort to reinforce positive social behaviours and ensure that the child's emotional needs are met. Some of the partners in this process might include a social worker, a psychologist, a music therapist or a resource consultant. Strategies should be planned as a team, involve all partners—including staff and family members—and be reviewed regularly.

Observing Children's Behaviours

Observations should be undertaken to identify the existing attributes of social behaviours within a group of children. Anecdotal records are well suited to this work, since most of the behaviours to be observed are related to the affective domain, and effective terminology—such as moods, dependency or separation—is open to interpretation. The terms are non-specific but the behaviour needs to be clearly described, and therefore anecdotal records are appropriate tools (see Figure 9.2 for examples). This type of record requires the observer to write down specific information about the child related to the criteria set. Individuals might ask a question such as, "What are the child's moods?" Records of just the moods would give an incomplete picture of what is happening. The particular mood might make more sense if analyzed in the setting and circumstances it occurred in.

FIGURE 9.2

Observing Individual Attributes

Name: Joanie   **Dates:** October 15, 16
Observers: Collaborative process between home and centre
Centre: Corral = C   **Home:** Mother = M

Attribute	Description of Behaviour	Setting	Circumstances
Mood	Ran up to Corral and gave her a hug, smiled	Upon arrival	M dropped her off
	Sat in quiet area, quietly reading book, laughed at pictures	15 minutes after arrival	C asked her what was the matter; she shook her head and turned away
Mood	At home—temper tantrum lasted 20 minutes	After we got back from day care	Was upset because I told her she was visiting her dad this weekend
Mood	Cried, clung to M, threw self on floor in cloakroom and screamed for 15 minutes	After arrival at day care	Temper tantrum started when mother left
	Clung to C when M came, refused to look at M, refused to get dressed to leave	At time of dismissal	Temper tantrum ended when Olivia came and brought her favourite doll. M indicated that this was the weekend when she was dropping her off at her father's house

This type of tool is useful in gathering information about individual children's ways of handling themselves in various situations. As new attributes are observed, they can be added to the chart as necessary. The chart should yield information about when certain behaviours might be expected and what might be a trigger. Joanie's parents are divorced. Her father has remarried. One of the triggers seems to be when she is expected to stay at her father's house. The staff and Joanie's mom continued to observe Joanie's behaviour to confirm this pattern of behaviour or to reject it as an isolated incidence.

Additional information that could be observed includes play behaviours as covered in Chapter 6, page 200. Play is a form of social interaction. Noting how children play with each other provides caregivers with information on:

- What types of social interaction to plan for
- What types of materials to provide to encourage social interactions
- How to utilize spontaneous activities to encourage children's interactions

Observations of interest should centre on children's social activities (see Figure 9.3). Examples of such activities could include:

FIGURE 9.3

Observing Interests

Name: Liam, age 3.2   **Dates:** April 5, 6

Observer: Shane

Interest Area	Activity	Peers
Block area	Stacked blocks end to end on floor to create a race track; used small cars to push across track; pretended to be race-car drivers	Jonathan and Jake
Sand area	Construction vehicles; pretended to build a road	Jake and Matthew
Tricycles	Raced tricycles around track; pretended to be race-car drivers	Jake and Jonathan

- Pretend play
- Working together to complete a task
- Playing games
- Completing a project

This type of observation reveals some valuable information about Liam's interests and the types of social activities he is engaged in. It would appear that he has formed a closer relationship with two of his peers. The three boys share an interest in racing. This interest could be used to expand their play activity to other areas such as water, or other concepts could be added to their play such as different speeds on different surfaces.

Observation tools based on the developmental social-emotional milestones given on page 291 could be developed to identify milestones reached and also to use as a guide to determine if a referral is needed.

Individual Program Plans

The development of an IPP for education would resemble that of the behavioural program plan outlined in Chapter 5 on pages 229–234. Desired outcomes are usually used to specify social behaviours that need to be increased or decreased. An IPP (Figure 9.4) was developed for Dillon to increase his interactions with peers.

The results of the first week were discussed with the family and resource consultant. It was felt that good progress was being made and that no adaptations needed to be made at this time. Dillon's mother noted that she had set up a creative area on a table at home, and Dillon and his siblings (two boys) had painted a mural together this week. It was decided to bring the mural to the centre and display it to give Dillon a chance to talk about his artwork to other children.

FIGURE 9.4

IPP to Increase Interactions with Peers

Name: Dillon   **DOB**: January 8, 2000
Date: April 5, 2004

i. **Summary of Diagnosis**
   a) **Resource Consultant's Observations**
      i. **Type of Play**—Dillon tends to shy away from other children. He is observed mostly as an onlooker or in solitary play.
      ii. **Peer interactions**—If a peer enters Dillon's space, he usually gets up and leaves. He will participate in small group activity at story time and during music and movement activities. He avoids other group activities and will cry if staff tries to encourage him to join in.
   b) **Mother's Observations**
      i. **Peer interactions**—Dillon was always shy. He has had two heart surgeries already and may have to have another one. He spends a lot of time in the hospital recovering. The first operation did not succeed, so they had to do another one. He really doesn't play with any of the kids in the neighbourhood. I have invited the boys over to play with him, but that didn't work. I think the boys were too active. It scared him.
   c) **Day Care Staff's Observations**
      i. **Play Behaviours**—Dillon engages in solitary play in the book area, creative art area, small blocks and puzzles. He often watches the children build with the larger blocks from a distance but resists joining their play.
      ii. **Peer Interactions**—He does not seem to have formed any close relationships with the other children. They tend to leave him alone. He avoids children who are too noisy or too active. He will move to an opposite side of the room to play.

2. **Observations of Behaviours**
   Observations were conducted at home by the mother and at the day care centre by one of the child care staff. The process was also guided by the resource consultant.
   a) **Play Behaviours at Home**

Date: March 27–April 4, 2001   **Observer:** Mother

Play Activity	Description
Reading	Likes Dr. Seuss books; asked to have them read to him; father read book to him
Track and vehicles	Built a track for his small cars; his brother came and asked him if he could play; Dillon agreed, but when Danny started to change the track and move his cars quickly along the track, Dillon left to draw some pictures
Outdoor playground	Dillon's cousins came over and we went to the playground; Dillon sat in the sand and played by himself; he watched the boys play tag on the climbers

   b) **Play Behaviours at the Centre**

Dates: March 27–April 14   **Observers:** Mandy and Kaya

Solitary play	With books, puzzles, small blocks; listened to music; used rhythm instruments (drum, sticks) to play along to the songs on a Raffi CD
Group activity	Participates in music and movement activities: singing (knows all the words of the songs) and rhythm instruments (especially likes the drum); always joins group of children if a story is read or told
Observer activities	If play is too loud or too active will move to quieter spot and may watch the activity; watches large block play

FIGURE 9.4

Continued

3. Interests

Observers: Collaborative effort between home and centre
Dates: March 27–April 14

Interests	Description
Painting	Uses bright colours and covers whole page; creates a shape, then paints it in, very careful not to go over lines; then uses another colour and repeats the process; then fills in the gaps left with a new colour
Music and movement	Always participates in marching-band types of activities, if given a choice always uses the drum; will join a singing group; quickly learns the tunes and words of songs
Books	Likes to be alone to look at books or have an adult read to him; can read several of the simple books
Puzzles	Usually completes at least three puzzles a day
Small blocks	Builds towers and enclosures; sometimes uses his structures with farm animals; will dramatize farm scenarios

4. Number of peer interactions
March 27: 0—participated in rhythm activity but ignored other children
March 28: 1—parallel play with Cynthia with small blocks
March 29: 1—read a book to Cynthia
March 30: 2—sang songs with group of children; continued to sing with Jeremy after the rest of the children left; followed Jeremy to creative area and engaged in parallel painting activity

5. Base Line
Maximum number of interactions: 2

6. Goals
To increase the number of social interactions

7. Objectives
- **Weeks One and Two:** Increase the number of social interactions to two per day.
- **Weeks Three and Four:** Increase the number of social interactions to three per day.

8. Strategies
a) Set up the areas of interest to encourage parallel play (small blocks, puzzles); switch painting from easel to tabletop; provide more drums during rhythm play.
b) Observe Dillon and use spontaneous opportunities to engage him with peers.
c) Use Dillon's ability to read to encourage him to read to peers.
d) Move the small blocks closer to the large blocks to encourage Dillon to participate in large-block structures.

9. Evaluation of Dillon's Progress
Dillon's progress was charted daily.

FIGURE 9.4
Continued

Peer interaction: number of times Dillon was involved

	Solitary play	Parallel play	Onlooker	Other
Week 1	IIII	I	II—blocks	
	IIII	II	II—tag outside	
	++++	III	II—water play	
	III	II		Associative with Cynthia
	II	III		Associative fingerpainting

Guiding Social-Emotional Behaviours in Inclusive Settings

Adults need to observe the learning environment together with interaction patterns in order to encourage the active participation of all children. Often children may find it difficult to engage in social interactions because they may be:

- Too timid to join in
- Reluctant to share
- Exhibiting challenging behaviours that make it difficult for other children to join in
- Unwilling to take turns
- Avoiding communication
- Unable to give or read nonverbal messages (Macintyre, 2002: 25)

Most children sometimes have difficulties in dealing with social situations. Adults need to be sensitive to these needs to foster social-emotional growth and development and to set up appropriate learning environments.

The first principle of organization of any social-emotional learning environment is to ensure that the environment is a safe and nurturing place in which children can interact in meaningful ways, express themselves freely and be supported in their actions and behaviours. Several steps should be considered when creating an emotionally secure social environment. These include providing opportunities for children to understand and accept individual differences, creating an atmosphere of mutual trust and cooperation, and observing the children to encourage social interactions.

1. Encouraging Acceptance of Individual Differences

It is human nature to perceive each situation and each individual from a personal perspective. Adults have the ability to analyze their perspectives and adjust them as needed. Janine had never taught toddlers before. She was very nervous about her first morning in the toddler room. She planned an interesting welcome circle. She was dismayed when the toddlers were not interested in her activity and engaged instead in what she thought were inappropriate activities. After circle time, she asked her co-worker why her circle had not interested the children. Her co-worker explained that it was really not an age-appropriate strategy for toddlers. Janine researched developmentally-appropriate activities for toddlers and changed her group time into an active participation experience. She was pleased to see how much the toddlers enjoyed the activity.

Children lack the ability to analyze and adjust their perceptions. A young child sees the world from his or her perspective. Often adults chuckle at the humorous notions that this creates: "Milk comes from trucks." "Grandmothers borrow other people's children 'cause they don't have any of their own."

Children's attitudes reflect their experiences: what they have heard, what they have seen and how they make sense of these experiences. Jeremy had never seen an individual in a wheelchair before. When Jodi arrived with her wheelchair, he was fascinated. He finally asked Jodi when she would get out of her chair so that she could play with him. Jeremy had not made the connection between the wheelchair and the inability to walk.

Early childhood educators need to create opportunities to involve the children in activities that will increase their understanding of the special needs within their environments. General activities might include:

- Providing books and display materials about children with various special needs
- Providing opportunities to ask questions
- Involving children with special needs in answering questions about their needs whenever possible
- Encouraging children to help find solutions to overcome barriers to active participation
- Involving families and other professionals in planning and reinforcing suitable activities

To help children fully understand the problems that children with disabilities might have, role-playing opportunities should be provided to simulate some disabilities. When children are actively involved, they are much more likely to understand the nature of the problem and more likely to gain a more positive attitude toward the problem. Table 9.5 offers some suggestions for activities that are relevant for some specific needs. These activities should be followed with discussions about how the children felt. Children's efforts should be documented through documentation panels that reflect children's learning. Documentation panels could include photographs, written descriptions and the creative efforts of the children.

TABLE 9.5   ACTIVE ROLE PLAY TO GUIDE UNDERSTANDING OF SPECIAL NEEDS

Need	Description of Activities
Physical disability	Borrow child-sized equipment as needed such as a cane, crutches, braces or a wheelchair. For example, borrow wheelchair to give children an opportunity to explore what it feels like to use one.
Visual impairment	Create opportunities to participate in activities without sight. Simple activities include guessing what an object might be by using a feely box. Children may try to guess what sound they hear or where it came from without seeing the object that made the sound. Asking children to navigate using a blindfold should only be used as a choice activity. This activity may frighten some children. Provide books and signs in Braille.
Hearing impairment	Games could be set up to ask children to distinguish what they can hear when the sounds become very quiet. Involve children in short activities without sound such as watching a short video without sound. Provide some activities that include children in sign language such as singing and using sign language simultaneously.
Challenging behaviours	Provide acceptable alternatives to relieve feelings of frustration or anger, such as a pillow to scream into or punch in a corner of the room. Provide alternative activities that help release stress, such as pounding play dough or a work bench, or soothing activities such as water, finger-painting or sand. Discussions with children could focus on feelings and how to express feelings appropriately, noting that all feelings are appropriate but sometimes how they are expressed is not appropriate.
Low self-esteem	Foster self-esteem through: • Displays of children's creative efforts • Documentation of children's learning • Reinforcement of efforts • Encouraging children to help each other whenever possible • Encouraging discussion of individual abilities—Children need to gain an understanding that all people have things they do well, other things they do not do so well and some things they may need help with.

2. Creating an Atmosphere of Trust and Understanding

Children need to feel that they can express their feelings in a variety of ways, that their expressions of their feelings are respected, that their interactions are valued and that appropriate consistent guidance is provided.

Adults can use a variety of strategies to help them create an environment that encourages trust and respect for everyone. Strategies are outlined in Table 9.6.

TABLE 9.6   **CAREGIVER STRATEGIES TO ESTABLISH TRUST AND UNDERSTANDING**

Strategy	Example
Learn to recognize and understand the various signals that children communicate	When Venice is unsure of a situation or of new individuals in her environment, she becomes quiet and observant, and puts her hands in her mouth. When her signals are missed, she starts to cry and withdraw from the situation.
Know when to step in and when to let children solve their own problems	Lauren and Kamaya had been playing together. Kamaya saw Elsa and ran to talk to her. The two girls decided to go and pick daisies. Lauren became upset and ran away. She sat in the playhouse, visibly upset. Kamaya noticed that Lauren had gone. She looked for her and saw that she was in the playhouse and ran to join her. Kamaya asked Elsa if she would like to pick some more daisies with them. At first Lauren refused, but eventually she decided to join the girls. Pritti had observed her charges. She gave the girls an opportunity to try to solve the problem themselves.
Acknowledge feelings and provide comfort	Michael had been hit by a ball while playing in the sandbox. This was not a serious injury, but Maureen understood that Michael's pain needed to be acknowledged. She put an ice pack on his head and reassured him that he would soon feel better. She also acknowledged his feelings by telling him that she knew that the episode had frightened him and that it hurt.
Provide the level of comfort a child needs	Jesse and Kaghu had been arguing about who had a toy first. They were trying to pull the toy away from each other. Kaya's attempts to help the boys solve their own problem were not successful. She said, "I think we should find something else to do. We could read a book or perhaps paint a picture." Both boys decided that they wanted to read a book. Jesse was still upset. He ran to get a book and then sat on Kaya's lap.
Share a child's accomplishments	Shannon had completed a drawing. She ran excitedly to show the children and Hardeep. Hardeep quickly took a photograph of her drawing. The drawing was framed and mounted on the bulletin board.
Help children as needed	The noise level around the creative table had escalated. Hardeep realized that the children needed some help to calm down. She sat down with them and started interacting. She referred to what they were doing and what colours they were using. The children became more relaxed and the activity continued.

TABLE 9.6 **CONTINUED**

Strategy	Example
Refer children to each other	Jonathan had built a structure with blocks. He was using some of the toy people and animals to place strategically on and in his structure. Emily watched him from a distance. She moved closer and closer to his activity. Monique noticed what Emily was doing. She said to Jonathan, "Emily is admiring your structure. Can you tell her what you are doing?' Jonathan replied, "I built a city. Now I am strategically placing things like vehicles, people and eventually trees in my city." Emily pointed. Monique said, "Emily would like to know what one of your buildings represents." Jonathan looked at Emily, smiled and said, "An office building. Do you want to get some trees and stuff to plant?" Emily wheeled away in her wheelchair and went to get the required things. Jonathan continued to involve her by asking her to retrieve items and asking her where they should be placed.
Interpret communications	Jocelyn tried to join a group of girls pretending to have a picnic. The girls said no because there wasn't enough room. Jocelyn picked up some toys and said, "There!" as she pointed to another area of the room. Kaya had noticed the interchange and quickly said, "Jocelyn is trying to tell you that there is room over there." The girls looked and said, "OK, let's move."

3. Observing to Encourage Social Interaction

In an environment that provides children with opportunities to engage in active play, make their own choices and interact with peers and adults, many opportunities arise to expand children's learning. If the caregivers have a good understanding of the children, these opportunities may be used as teachable moments. For example, on one occasion the children had built an obstacle course out of the hollow blocks. They were walking along the blocks and then jumping off at the end. Esta noticed that Rachel was watching the children. Rachel had difficulty with balance when walking or running, and so it would have been difficult for her to participate. Esta said to the children, "I wonder how else you could move across the blocks. Do you have any ideas, Rachel?" Rachel said, "Crawl?" The idea quickly caught on. Soon all the children were crawling, including Rachel.

Organizing the Social-Emotional Environment

The second organizing principle of any social-emotional learning environment is to ensure that the environment maximizes opportunities to engage in social-emotional activities. Inclusive settings need to be organized to consider the familiarity of the children with various social activities, the stability and predictability of the environment and the promotion of independence.

1. Familiarity of Social Activities

Young children's activities should be based on their background experiences. Children need to be able to explore various roles of individuals or activities that they have observed, imitating and refining as the skills involved are practised and gain acceptance by others. Much of children's social play is based on symbolized actions and imitated behaviour. The ability of children to engage in imitative and symbolized play is largely dependent on the materials and learning experiences in their environment.

Very young children's play is dictated by the props around them. A child will use a bucket for filling or a spoon for stirring. Play is more likely to occur when the child is familiar with the objects that he or she is using. Familiar objects for young children include items that are used for everyday activities. To encourage imitative social play, the play environment should include realistic items associated with activities such as eating, sleeping, dressing, cooking, cleaning, driving, gardening, driving and communicating.

Children naturally move from a dependence on props to using other materials symbolically. Children may use a curved block as a telephone or a stick to stir with. Symbolic activity depends very much on the experiences children have had with real materials. As children manipulate the real materials, they learn about the materials' shapes, sizes and uses. They can then transfer this knowledge to new settings with new materials. The caregiver should take careful note of what materials are in the environment and place alternatives in other areas to increase children's ability to use situations symbolically. Some suggestions are included in Table 9.7.

2. Stability and Predictability

It is essential to establish stability in the environment to provide children with continuity and comfort, so they can learn where to find things and what experiences are possible in various settings. Continual changes to the configuration of learning spaces leads to fragmentation and sporadic activity. The emphasis needs to be on children's continued social activity. Changes and adaptations should reflect learning needs and changing interests.

TABLE 9.7   EXAMPLES OF MATERIALS FOR SYMBOLIC USE

Material	Purpose	Example	
Sticks of different sizes	Drawing, stirring	Benjamin used the popsicle sticks as road graders, the dowelling as the start of telephone poles along a road and logs as the ditch at the side of the road	
Various materials, including plastic sheets and materials from nature	Creating various scenes for dramatic play	Colin and Jordan decided to build a fishing camp in the sandbox. They created a river with blue plastic strips, leaves for an island, logs to sit on, toy boats, fishing poles and plastic shrubs.	
Boxes of various sizes	Encouraging group activity, dramatic play	Petra and Madison used boxes as part of their dramatic house play. They pretended the boxes were cars they used to do their shopping.	

Figure 9.5 shows how, at the centre, the block area was originally organized. It had been observed that children used some of the manipulative materials in the block area. However, although the area received high use, all of the children had tended to use the blocks and the manipulative materials in the block area. The area became overcrowded and some challenging behaviours started to be observed.

The staff discussed some strategies. They realized that the children were actively using the area. The children were finding the materials they needed and were returning materials appropriately. The following changes (illustrated in Figure 9.6) were decided on:

- Increase the size of the area, but leave the configuration the same.
- Replace the open-sided shelf with two shelves to limit access to manipulative materials from each side.
- Rearrange the manipulative materials.

The changes were effective. Children continued to actively use the block area. There was increased use of the manipulative area, and the challenging behaviours dropped.

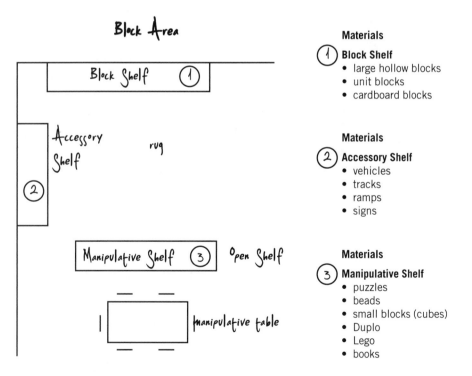

Materials

① **Block Shelf**
- large hollow blocks
- unit blocks
- cardboard blocks

Materials

② **Accessory Shelf**
- vehicles
- tracks
- ramps
- signs

Materials

③ **Manipulative Shelf**
- puzzles
- beads
- small blocks (cubes)
- Duplo
- Lego
- books

FIGURE 9.5

Initial Organization of the Block Area

Problems Observed
- block area became congested with items from manipulative shelf
- overcrowding in block area

FIGURE 9.6
Revised Floor Plan

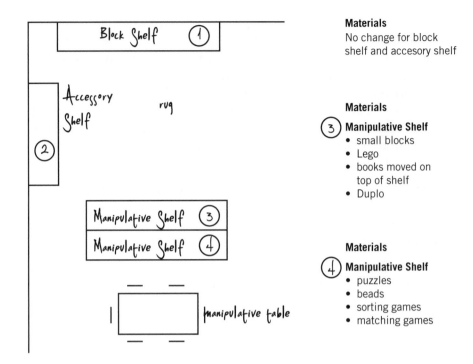

Materials
No change for block shelf and accesory shelf

Materials

③ **Manipulative Shelf**
• small blocks
• Lego
• books moved on top of shelf
• Duplo

Materials

④ **Manipulative Shelf**
• puzzles
• beads
• sorting games
• matching games

3. Promotion of Independence

Children's activities and materials should maximize their ability to do things for themselves. General principles of setting up an environment to nurture independence include using appropriate labelling systems (see page 200), installing low, open shelves accessible to all children, organizing materials by type and ensuring that all areas remain free of clutter. Some specific factors relating to social skills directly influence the growth of independence:

• Self-help skills—Children love to help with adult tasks. Provide children with child-sized cleaning materials so that they can help in routine clean-up activities. Thee materials could include:
  • Child-sized brooms, dustpans and mops
  • Spray bottles of water and sponges to clean tabletops
  • A place to put dirty dishes after eating
  • A posted sequence for doing things, such as the sequence of washing hands
  • A container to put dirty supplies in, such as toys that have been sneezed on or dirty brushes

• Dressing skills—Children often find it difficult to put on dress-up clothes. To make it easier to use dress-up materials, try these strategies:
  • Put Velcro tabs on dress-up clothing to make it easier to fasten.
  • Cut down clothes to child's size so there is less danger of tripping.
  • Avoid providing adult-sized shoes. These can cause tripping.

- Add elastics to waists of pants or skirts. This will make it easier to slip them on and keep them on.
- Provide similar clothes for dolls to encourage children to use an actual sequence of dressing.

The third principle of organization for any social-emotional learning environment is to make any needed adjustment to the individual interest centres to maximize social-emotional activities.

4. Dramatic Play

Dramatic play activities lend themselves to social-emotional development. All levels of dramatic play provide for opportunities to plan for social-emotional growth (Crowther, 2003: 176–177). Table 9.8 identifies the levels of dramatic play, the types of interactions to expect and specific examples of learning activities.

5. Music and Movement

Music is also particularly suited to social-emotional growth and development. Music can be used in a variety of ways, at individual levels of comfort and skill development, and in individual or group settings. Musical activities involve active interaction with materials, can involve interactions with others and can be used for different purposes, including relaxation, mood changing, skill development, active listening, active participation, concept learning (language, beat, rhythm, volume, tone and pitch), creativity development and, of course, simple enjoyment. "Music builds and strengthens bonds of trust and communication between adults and children. Music gives children a reference point, a way to respond appropriately. Simple songs, incorporated into daily activities, communicate without nagging or endlessly repeating directions. Since the children are already 'tuned in' musically, singing will capture their imagination. Transitions will be smoother and children will be more likely to remember the daily routines. Better yet, the children will begin to help each other by singing the songs together, as they anticipate the planned activity" (Ensign Baney, 2002: 7).

- Music for relaxation—In the Loyalist College Curriculum Lab, music was used to calm children down when the activity level was too noisy. When soft background music was played from a variety of CDs (Gibbon & Gibbon, 1991; Gibbons & Gibbons, 1992; Milner, 1993), the children immediately calmed down, play became less noisy and harmony within the room was restored.
- Music to change the mood—It is an acceptable practice to play soothing music during sleep time. This technique can also be used to help children calm down or cheer up. Jeremy, a toddler, was very upset. Someone had taken his toy away. He was sobbing and clinging to the caregiver, Jennifer. Jennifer picked him up and sat on a rocking chair with him. She knew that he was too upset to listen

TABLE 9.8   STAGES OF DRAMATIC PLAY

Stage/Age	Interactions	Examples of Learning Activities
Stage 1: prop-dependent, imitative (1–2 years)	Imitation of facial expressions and actions	Play imitation games with objects or actions: "Put the cup on your head, on your head." Children can initiate the activity or follow the lead.
	Mirror play, parallel play	Set up dress-up activities (scarves, blankets) in front of mirrors to encourage imitation, interactions and self-awareness.
Stage 2: familiar roles (2–3 years)	Play involving roles that children have observed, such as those associated with household activities (cleaning, food preparation, meal times, personal care routines) trips or visits to doctor's office	Coordinate adjacent learning areas such as blocks and dramatic play to encourage use of materials in both settings. Josh had built a simple school bus with the blocks. He is the bus driver to pick up children to go to school. Other ways to coordinate learning areas include putting books in every area to encourage looking up information or to use as sources of ideas for extending play. Water and sand could be combined to encourage exploration of mixtures. Or provide mobile creative units that encourage social activity by encouraging drawing and painting in various areas of the room, such as making signs or documenting activities.
Stage 3: diverse roles (4–5 years)	Play that involves less familiar roles that children might have read about, heard about or seen on TV or in a movie. These include adventure roles, less frequently observed roles of familiar adults or roles from favourite stories.	Provide materials that can be easily converted to assume a variety of purposes, such as blankets, scarves and other dress-up clothes, fabric flowers, pieces of hose, pillows or boxes. Children will be creative in their interpretations. Emily, for instance, is a bride.
Stage 4: communicative-cooperative (5 years and up)	Various forms of dramatic play in which children create their own characters, scripts and props	After a visit from a police officer, the children re-created their own version of what to do if "some bad people" wanted to come into their house. They used a cage from the veterinarian's office dramatic-play area to act out their story.

to her words. She quietly sang his favourite songs to him. He gradually calmed down as he listened. Eventually he sang along with her.

- Music for skill development—"Each component of music affects a different part of the brain, e.g. a familiar song activates the left frontal lobe, timbre the right frontal lobe, a pitch the left posterior. One side of the brain processes the word while the other processes the music—activating the whole brain to ensure retention. Short-term memory has the ability to hold onto seven bits of information. If bits of information are bonded together as in a song, it can be processed as one piece. By condensing the information, the brain is able to receive and process more" (Harman, 2002: 1). Thus, when we sing with children to encourage them to engage in activities, skill development is enhanced. Examples of songs are listed in Figure 9.7.
- Music for active listening—Listening is the first stage of music development. Involve children in various types of listening activities, such as singing a book (Siomades, 1999); listening to music or a song and playing along on a rhythm instrument; or listening to the words of a song such as "If You're Happy and You Know It, Clap Your Hands" and doing the actions.
- Music for active participation—Music is a natural combination with movement. It gives the child specific signals for how to move, such as fast or slow, or the type of movement, such as heavy or light. Children may move to an instrument played (drum, piano, guitar), to music played on a CD or to songs that are sung ("This Is the Way We Walk Indoors"). Providing props such as scarves, banners or flags encourages children to also become creative in how they move.
- Music for concept learning—Examples of concepts that could be learned include language concepts, speed and volume, self-awareness, responses to feelings or relaxation.

FIGURE 9.7

Examples of Songs to Sing During Activities

Pick an easy song that the children are familiar with. Adjust the words of their activity to the melody.

"Clean-up"
(sung to the tune of "Mary Had a Little Lamb")
[Child's name] picking up the blocks, up the blocks, up the blocks. [Child's name] picking up the blocks, and stacking them up high.

"Counting"
(sung to tune of "One Little, Two Little, Three Little Indians," during activities such as climbing stairs or setting the table)
One fork, two forks, three forks, four forks. Five forks, six forks, seven forks, eight fork. Nine forks, ten forks, put them on the table. Now we have ten forks.

- Music for enjoyment—Children naturally enjoy music. In one preschool setting, the teachers used music in many ways to help children through transitions and to learn new concepts. One child, a four-year-old named Ted, was curious about everything around him. One day he was heard humming to himself, "I just love insects, I just love grass and I just love my friends." The children heard him and soon imitated him. Soon this became a regular part of the program.

6. Activities to Encourage Group Play

Alternative arrangements of standard activities such as sand and water may encourage more interaction between children. For example, when the sand was placed in shallow containers on a table, children interacted with each other to describe what they were doing. Raven said, "The sand is flowing through my fingers. I love the feel of it." Kamaya, who was busily decorating her sand with glass beads, responded, "I know. I like doing it at the beach. It's cool 'cause the sand is nice and hot." Lauren said excitedly, "Look! I made a weird face." The other girls stopped and looked at Lauren's creation and told her that it was "cool" and "weird" (Photo 9.2).

Creative activities can be set out on a table or the floor to encourage more children to participate and interact with each other.

Some strategies are listed here:

- Place a long piece of paper on a wall or the floor to encourage children to create a mural together.
- Provide large boxes and encourage children to decorate them and use them as playhouses.

Photo 9.2

- Take large papers along on field trips and ask children to record their impressions.

Learning areas in the room should be carefully monitored to identify when changes or adaptations need to be made. Areas may need to be increased or decreased in size depending on the interests or activites of the children. Caregivers may have to provide additional materials to maintain interest. The adaptation of the learning area should be based on the activities and interactions that children engage in.

Role of the Early Childhood Educator

The role of the early childhood educator in organizing a social-emotional environment is primarily to create an atmosphere that provides children with safe and secure learning spaces and experiences so they can express their feelings and interact positively with each other and other adults. The early childhood educator's role comprises these functions:

- Being an active listener and encouraging active listening skills—Kaya listened to the children's interactions and interpreted what Jocelyn wanted to do. She was able to communicate Jocelyn's intent to the other children in order to involve Jocelyn in their interactions.
- Observing children's body language in order to respond appropriately—Children may not always express themselves with words. They may communicate using body language, as was evident with Emily's behaviour, when she observed Jonathan's play but needed Monique's help to join in the play.
- Providing opportunities for children to initiate and maintain activities—A table was set up outside for creative art activities. This provided opportunities for

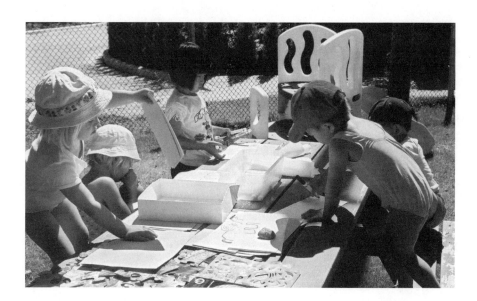

children to engage in creative activities, to share ideas and to set their own
pace to complete what they wished to do.

- Observing children to identify behavioural causes such as fear or frustration. Kim
  was afraid to go outside because she was afraid of flying insects. She uses
  crutches to walk and finds if difficult to get away. But Kim agreed to go outside with her teacher, Melina, when Melina promised to make sure that none
  of these insects would land on Kim.
- Observing children to identify teachable moments—Esta utilized a teachable
  moment when she challenged the children to use alternative methods for cross-
  ing their obstacle course. This involved Rachel in a physical activity with the
  other children.
- Coordinating team efforts—The activities of the IPP were coordinated by
  Dillon's teacher. She set up regular meetings with staff, family and the resource
  consultant.

SUMMARY

Social and emotional behaviours are closely linked.
When a child participates successfully within social settings, his or her emotional well-being is also improved.
Caregivers must be aware of all the factors that influence
social-emotional behaviours of children in order to:

- Understand each individual child's behaviour
- Plan an effective social-emotional environment for children
- Implement effective social interactions
- Be sensitive to children's emotional needs
- Collaborate effectively with families and other professionals

KEY POINTS

Healthy social interactions—Communicate, understand
interactions, form relationships and express emotions

Social-emotional development
- Starts at birth
- Predictable stages

Erikson's psychosocial stages
- Trust versus mistrust
- Autonomy versus shame or doubt
- Initiative versus guilt
- Industry versus inferiority

Effects on social-emotional behaviours
- Attachment
- Child-rearing practices
- Background experiences
- Temperament

Social attributes
- Individual attributes
- Social skill attributes
- Peer relationship attributes

Range of behaviours in inclusive settings

- Normal range
- Advanced social-emotional skills
- Delayed social-emotional skills, or lack of them

Guidance principles

- Recognition of complexities of social skills
- Reduction of mistaken behaviours
- Positive adult–child interactions
- Solution-oriented intervention methods
- Partnerships with families
- Team approach

Observing behaviour

- Anecdotal records
- Interests
- Checklist to observe milestones

Individual program plan—Background information, summary of diagnosis, observations, base line, goals, objectives, strategies, evaluation

Guiding Behaviour

- Accepting individual differences
- Creating an atmosphere of trust and understanding
- Observing children

Organize the social-emotional environment—Familiarity, child developmental levels, stability and predictability, promoting independence

Learning activities

- Dramatic play—Prop-dependent, imitative, familiar roles, diverse roles, communicative-cooperative
- Music and movement—Relaxation, change mood, skill development, active listening, active participation, learning concepts, enjoyment

EXERCISES

1. Using the information developed in Tables 9.1, 9.2, 9.3 or 9.4, develop a screening tool for one age group that would help identify potential problems in social-emotional development.

2. In a small group, discuss and record major points about factors that affect social–emotional behaviours. Utilize the chart provided to facilitate your discussions.

Factor	How the Factor Affects Social-Emotional Behaviour
Attachment	
Child-rearing practices	
Background experiences	
Temperament	
Attention span	
Diagnosed special need	

3. Utilize the individual, social and peer relationship attributes on pages 295–296 to develop a screening tool for observing children. Implement the tool with two different age groups. How are the results different? What social behaviour differences did you observe in the two groups? Explain the differences.

4. Define mistaken behaviour. What type of mistaken behaviours might you find in a group of infants, toddlers or preschoolers?

5. Amy is a four-year-old. She has been diagnosed with ADD. She rarely interacts with other children. Describe a solution-oriented model that you might use to increase her peer interactions.

6. You are a staff member in a toddler program. You suspect that one of the children has a social delay. How would you confirm or deny your supposition?

7. You have been informed that a new child is to be admitted to your program. This child has cerebral palsy and is confined to a wheelchair. What steps might you take to prepare the children and the environment for the new child?

8. What strategies might you use to help a child who has been identified as gifted become more socially active?

9. Reflect on the roles of an early childhood educator in an inclusive setting. How are the roles similar to or different from settings that have not included children with special needs? Explain your answer.

RESOURCES

Music
www.earlychildhood.com/Articles/index.cfm

Promoting Positive Attitudes
**www.findarticles.com/p/articles/mi_m0HDG/
    is_2_21/ai_102909983**

**www.ncrel.org/sdrs/areas/issues/students/
    earlycld/ea400.htm**

**www.specialednews.com/early/earlynews/
    preschoolfriends121299.html**

www.projectappleseed.org/aaceptance.html

Supporting Social and Emotional Growth
**www.education.gov.ab.ca/EducationGuide/
    spec-ed/partners/chapter4.pdf**

**www.kidsource.com/kidsource/content2/
    social_development_gifted.html**

**www.enableonline.com/theory/stages_in_
    emotional_development.htm**

**http://chiron.valdosta.edu/whuitt/files/
    socialdev.html**

Social-Emotional Development of Gifted Children
http://ericec.org/digests/e527.html

**www.mcgt.net/Articles/nurturing_social_
    emotional_devel.htm**

Self-Regulation
www.ldonline.org/njcld/preschool.html

Erikson
**http://psychology.about.com/library/weekly/
    aa091500a.htm**

www.ship.edu/~cgboeree/erikson.html

Assessing Children's Social Competence
**www.athealth.com/Consumer/disorders/
    ChildSocialSkills.html**

**www.vtaide.com/png/ERIC/
    Social-Competence-Checklist.htm**

Temperament: Educational Testing Service,
    Princeton, New Jersey.
www.temperament.com/ordercoping.html

Children's Fears
**www.keepkidshealthy.com/parenting_tips/
    fears.html**

REFERENCES

Council for Exceptional Children (2005). Nurturing Social-Emotional Development of Gifted Children. The ERIC Clearinghouse on Disabilities and Gifted Education [online]. Available at http://ericec.org/digests/e527.html (27-1-2005).

Crowther, I. (2003). *Creating Effective Learning Environments.* Scarborough, ON: Nelson Thomson Learning.

Crowther, N., & Sommer, M. (1997). Building Social Relationships. In K. E. Kilbride (Ed.). *Include Me Too: Human Diversity in Early Childhood.* Toronto, ON: Harcourt Brace & Company Canada Ltd.

Ensign Baney, C. (2002). Wired for Sound: The Essential Connection Between Music and Development. Earlychildhood.com [online]. Available at www.early-childhood.com/Articles/index.cfm?FuseAction=Article&A=141 (15-1-2005).

Gartrell, D. (2004). *The Power of Guidance: Teaching Social-Emotional Skills in Early Childhood Classrooms.* Clifton Park, NY: Thomson Delmar Learning.

Gibbon, D., & Gibbon, G. (1991). *Solitudes: The Classics.* Toronto, ON: Solitudes Ltd.

Gibbon, D., & Gibbon, G. (1992). *Solitudes: Peaceful Classics.* Toronto, ON: Solitudes Ltd.

Harman, M. (2002). Music and Movement: Instrumental in Language Development. Earlychildhood.com [online]. Available at www.earlychildhood.com/Articles/index.cfm?FuseAction=Article&A=361 (11-1-2005).

Kilbride, K. E. (1997). *Include Me Too: Human Diversity in Early Childhood.* Toronto, ON: Harcourt Brace & Company Canada Ltd.

King, E., Chipman, M., & Cruz-Janzen, M. (1994). *Educating Young Children in a Diverse Society.* Boston: MA: Allyn and Bacon.

Macintyre, C. (2002). *Play for Children with Special Needs.* London, UK: David Fulton Publishers.

McCain, M., & Mustard, F. (2002). *The Early Years Study.* Toronto, ON: The Founders' Network.

McCain, M., & Mustard, F. (1999). *Early Years Study Final Report.* Toronto, ON: Publications Ontario.

McClellan, D., & Katz, L. (2001). Assessing Young Children's Social Competence. ERIC Clearing House on Elementary & Early Childhood Education [online]. Available at www.vtaide.com/png/ERIC/Social-Competence-Checklist.htm (12-8-2004).

Milner, D. (193). *Mystical Call of the Loon.* Plymouth, MN: Metacom.

National Association of School Psychologists (1998). Implications of Temperament for the Practice of School Psychology. National Association of School Psychologists [online]. Available at www.nasponline.org/publications/sprsum274.html (15-1-2005).

Schickedanz, J., Schickedanz, D., Forsyth, P., & Forsyth, G. (2001). *Understanding Children and Adolescents.* Fourth Edition. Needham Heights, MA: Allyn & Bacon.

Siomades, L. (1999). *The Itsy Bitsy Spider.* Honesdale, PA: Bell Books.

10

CHAPTER

Cognitive Growth in Inclusive Settings

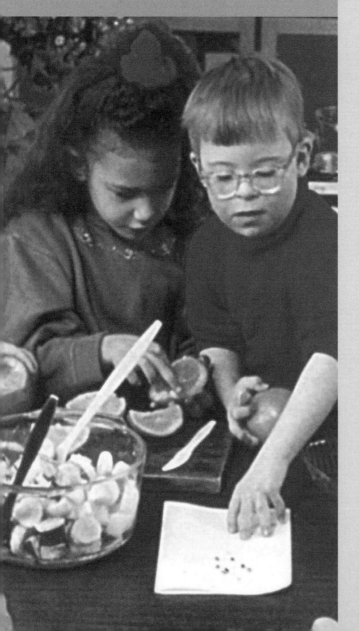

"Effective early childhood instructional practices emphasize child-initiated child-directed play activities, based on the assumption that young children are intrinsically motivated to learn by their desire to understand their environment" (Udell, Peters & Piaza Templeman, 2001).

Learning Outcomes

After studying this chapter, you will be able to:

1. Identify and discuss the importance of Howard Gardner's theory of multiple intelligences.
2. Identify stages of cognitive development of the various age groups.
3. Identify the variations of children's cognitive behaviours in an inclusive setting.
4. Explain how variations of children's cognitive behaviours may affect children's abilities.
5. Discuss the importance of forming partnerships.
6. Identify and discuss various methods of observing cognitive behaviours.
7. Explain why a portfolio is an appropriate tool to document cognitive behaviour.
8. Identify and discuss how to set up an environment to enhance cognitive growth.
9. Describe the role of the adult in fostering children's cognitive development.

Introduction

How intelligence develops has been disputed for a long time. For many years, it was thought that intelligence was inherited and could not be altered. John Locke (1632–1704) believed that a child was born with an "empty mind." He compared the mind of a newborn to an empty slate (tabula rasa) that experience writes on (Landry, 2004). In the 1960s it was believed that most behaviours were learned through a system of rewards and punishments (behaviourist theory; Naik 2001). This theory was followed by social learning theory, built on the behaviourist theory but including the use of imitation and modelling. Jean Piaget (1896–1980) developed the constructivist theory, which was based on the notion of learning through stages of cognitive development (Piaget, 1962). Piaget's theory clearly recognized the interplay between nature and nature. Modern theorists believe that intelligence is shaped by both heredity and the environment.

One of the modern theorists, Howard Gardner, proposed that there is no single entity of intelligence but that there are seven different types of intelligences: linguistic, logical-mathematical, musical, bodily kinesthetic, spatial, interpersonal and intrapersonal (see Table 10.1). Although Gardner's theory has been disputed by many academic psychologists, it has received wide acceptance by educational theorists, teachers and policy-makers within the educational system. This acceptance reflects the fact that "the theory validates educators' everyday experiences: students think and learn in many different ways. It also provides educators with a conceptual framework for organizing and reflecting on curriculum assessment and pedagogical practices. In turn, this reflection has led many educators to develop new approaches that might better meet the needs of the range of learners in their classrooms" (Smith, 2002: 20).

Gardner's theory of intelligence clearly focuses on the change in thinking today. Children need to learn within inclusive environments that foster opportunities to grow in all domains: social, emotional, physical, communicative and cognitive. Cognition is the underlying glue that binds all development together. "We know that learning and memory are strongly connected to emotions, and thus, the learning environment needs to be both stimulating and safe. Classroom experiences can be designed to allow children to investigate, reflect, and express ideas in a variety of ways that are increasingly complex and connected. Gardner proposed that each individual draws on multiple intelligences and generally relies on some more than others (Gardner, 1993). Thus, learners need ample opportunity to use and expand upon their preferred intelligences as well as to adapt and develop other intelligences which are all interdependent within one brain" (Rushton & Larkin, 2005: 21).

Cognitive Development

Cognitive development is evident through the interactions of children with others and the materials and equipment within their learning environments. Stages of

TABLE 10.1   GARDNER'S THEORY OF MULTIPLE INTELLIGENCES

Intelligence Type	Description
Linguistic	• Learns and uses language effectively • Understands and uses verbal and symbolized language such as body, signed and written language • Uses language creatively Example: Yasmine story—see Figure 10.1.
Logical-mathematical	• Performs mathematical operations such as addition and subtraction • Explores materials and the environment to find out why or how things work • Solves problems • Uses reasoning in an orderly, sensible fashion Example: Billy decided to see which pail of sand was heavier. The scale that was in the room was too small. He decided to bring his bathroom scale from home to see which pail was heavier. He could not read the numbers on the scale but was able to explain, "It's heavier if the little line goes more this way" (pointing to the right).
Musical	• Follows musical patterns such as beat and rhythm • Recognizes differences and similarities in musical elements such as pitch, tone, mood, tempo and rhythm • Creates simple rhythms, songs or tunes • Learns to play a musical instrument Example: Wolfgang Amadeus Mozart played the harpsichord by age three, composed solos for the harpsichord by age four and produced his first symphony by age eight.
Bodily/kinesthetic	• Uses body or parts of body to solve problems in gross motor activity such as climbing, moving or moving around obstacles • Coordinates mental abilities and bodily movements Example: Madison started formal gymnastic classes at age three. By age four, she could walk across the balance beam, somersault and swing on the bars, jump from the trampoline to land on various parts of her body and hang upside-down from the rings.
Spatial	• Uses different sizes of spaces appropriately for movement • Recognizes and uses spatial terminology correctly Example: As Josh was putting the animals in different containers, he signed "in," "out," "on top of" and "beside" correctly.
Interpersonal	• Uses effective social skills that include understanding of the desires, motivations and intentions of others Example: Melanie, age four, saw that Jamie, one of her peers, was crying. She correctly interpreted the situation to mean that Jamie was sad because she wanted the same toy as another child's. Melanie got her a pail that was the same colour and size and said, "See, now you have a pail 'xactly the same."
Intrapersonal	• Understands self: fears, feelings and personal motivations Example: Joanie, a five-year-old, created a book of drawings inspired by her personal feelings. She used the book to "get rid of my sad and angry feelings."

FIGURE 10.1
Yasmine's Story

Yasmine decided to create a storybook by dictating a story on most days. The following is an example of one of her stories.

I feel like being creative today.
I am going to illustrate my story with lots of pictures.

My mommy and I are in this picture. The small one is me and the large one is my mommy. We look alike because we have red dresses on.

cognitive development may be inferred through these interactions. Although children tend to go through similar stages in cognitive development, the timing and rate of progress through these stages is varied and depends on background experiences. It is important to know what some of the typical behaviours of the various age groups are in order to learn:

- What types of behaviours might be demonstrated by each age group
- How these behaviours might be interpreted
- What types of observation tools might be developed
- How to encourage cognitive growth and development

1. Infant Cognitive Development

Infants are at the **sensory motor stage** of development. Learning during the sensory motor stage involves exploring the learning environment through the use of all the senses. In the first few months, much of the infant's behaviour is reflexive. As the reflexes disappear, the infant's behaviours become more deliberate and purposeful. Infants learn about their world through manipulation, listening, observing and interacting with individuals in their environment (see Table 10.2). Learning

TABLE 10.2   **INFANT COGNITIVE DEVELOPMENT**

Age Range	Skill	Description of Behaviour
Birth–1 month	Random manipulation	Swats at items; grasps reflexively at items near hand
	Observation	Follows objects slowly if held close to face
	Preferences	Prefers familiar voices, sweet tastes; turns away from strong, unpleasant odours
	Memory	Turns toward familiar voices
1–6 months	Visual perception	Looks at various parts of face—eyes, mouth
	Preferences	Prefers high contrasts such as black and white patterns; familiar faces or voices; soothing music such as Mozart, Vivaldi and Brahms; familiar odours
	Memory	Remembers familiar objects, individuals, voices; demonstrates understanding of how to keep toys in motion, such as hitting mobile to make it move
	Imitation	Imitates familiar gestures such as waving bye-bye, sticking out the tongue, making sounds
6–12 months	Imitation	Imitates new behaviour if familiar, e.g., pat-a-cake
	Interactions	Repeatedly drops item, looks for it, then waits to have item returned
	Object permanence	Searches for completely hidden object
	Preferences	Prefers to look at things with more details such as scrambled faces
	Trial-and-error learning	Tries a variety of ways to make something work, such as trying to place a circular shape into each hole of a shape sorter until it fits
12–18 months	Reciprocal play	Includes others in play activity, such as an adult building a block tower and the child knocking it down
	Pointing	Points to objects or pictures to request information or answer question, e.g., "Bring the ball, please."
	Following simple directions	Child brings ball when requested to get ball
	Pretend play	Pretends with familiar objects such as stirring with a spoon
	Understanding causality	Starts to understand cause and effect, such as banging on a lid will make a noise

is cumulative. Skills and knowledge gained at one level will continue to be used and refined at subsequent levels of development.

2. Toddler Cognitive Development

Toddlers actively explore their environment to learn about people and things and to learn how to make things work. They demonstrate their new understanding of their world through unique mental representations. These representations start to be expressed in various ways:

- Actions, such as shrugging their shoulders if they don't know something
- Language, such as labels for items or language to express thoughts
- Symbolized play, such as the use of a hand and appropriate noises to represent a digger in the sand
- Body language, such as jumping for joy or dancing to music

Toddlers continue to build on the skills and knowledge gained throughout infancy to practise new tasks and or refine existing ones (see Table 10.3). Toddlers view their world from their own perspective, and consequently, many of their skills reflect the absence of a skill in another area, such as an inability to share.

3. Late Toddler/Early Preschool Cognitive Development

As toddlers gain more control over their bodies and more communication skills, their cognitive development also becomes more evident. They start to remember and use background experiences to solve problems. They begin using the names of other individuals and labelling objects in their environment. They also learn to recognize other means of communication, such as books and music.

TABLE 10.3   TODDLER COGNITIVE DEVELOPMENT

Age Range	Skill	Description of Behaviour
18–24 months	Object permanence	• Will continue to look for an object even if the location is unknown, for instance looking for a favourite toy in common places such as a drawer or toy box
	Deferred imitation	• Copies behaviours previously seen, such as scratching head to indicate puzzlement or smacking the lips to indicate that something is delicious
	Pretend play with familiar objects	• Pretending to do such things as use a phone or drive a car
	Functional relationships	• Demonstrates understanding of common relationships between things, for instance placing a spoon with a bowl or standing up a doll beside a chair
	Functional play	• Takes thing apart and puts them together
	Matching	• Finds things that are the same, such as two red cars
	Sorting	• Starts to put like things, such as red cars, together, but easily confused and may switch—For example, Jamie was lining up cars. But as he lined up a red car, he noticed a red plastic bear and switched to lining up bears.
	Inabilities	• Unable to share ideas and or materials, or to take another person's perspective—For example, Jordan held up a painting he had done to show his teacher, but he held the painting facing him.

Toddlers' play is rich in symbolic and imitative actions. As toddlers mature, they increasingly substitute objects for other things in pretend play. Actions are used to represent ideas and or communicate intent. As toddlers grow into the preschool years, they move from sensory motor activity into **preoperational thinking**—they begin to demonstrate their knowledge of the world around them through symbols such as words. Thinking during this stage is inflexible and tied to the situation the child is involved in. For example, Christopher saw a harvest moon in the evening sky. He said excitedly, "Look my mommy. There is the sun." His mother replied, "It's the moon, Christopher." Christopher thought about it and said, "No my mommy, it is the sun. It is big, round and orange. It is the sun. OK, my mommy?"

Cognitive development is dependent on the experiences and interactions that children are exposed to. As children grow and develop, differences in their cognitive abilities become more individualistic and varied. Typical abilities are listed and described in Table 10.4.

4. Preschool Cognitive Development

Preschoolers continue to practise preoperational thinking. Children at this stage see the world mostly from their own perspective, but by the end of the preschool

TABLE 10.4   LATE TODDLER/EARLY PRESCHOOL COGNITIVE DEVELOPMENT

Age Range	Skill	Description of Behaviour
14–36 months	Symbolic activity	• Increased use of objects to represent other, unrelated objects, such as a block to represent a telephone
	Theme play	• Pretend play is related to known activities such as washing babies, cooking or cleaning
	Prop-dependent play	• The props available give direction to the type of play engaged in—For example, Jenna was in dramatic play area. She saw a whisk and some bowls. She immediately pretended to make scrambled eggs.
	Sorting	• Objects are grouped together by function, such as things we eat or things we wear
	Inabilities	• Unable to understand different perspectives from their own; to think in abstract thoughts; or to distinguish what is real and what is not—For example, Jonathan noticed a stone tumbling down a stream and was upset because he thought it was getting hurt.

TABLE 10.5 **PRESCHOOL COGNITIVE DEVELOPMENT**

Age Range	Skill	Description of Behaviour
3 years	Counting	• Uses conventional words • Counts to five by rote
	Comparison/Seriation	• Solves nesting cup problems by comparing each size and placing it in or on top of the next size; may miss some cups in the process
	Labelling	• Starts to recognize and name geometric shapes: circle, triangle, square
	Dramatic play	• Pretends with realistic scenarios such as dressing a doll and taking it for a walk in a stroller
3½ years	Counting	• Counts five objects without error
	Drawing	• Draws shapes (triangle, square, circle) and letters
	Sorting	• Sorts by single dimensions: colour, size or shape
	Comparison	• Identifies size differences: larger or smaller
	Inabilities	• Has difficulty distinguishing false beliefs; understanding different perspectives; classifying by more than one attribute; and patterning such as forming a consistent pattern (e.g., red bear, blue bear, red bear, blue bear). Also has difficulty with seriation, such as consistently ordering items by size; observation, such as recognizing that quantities remain the same even when the container changes; and abstract thinking (thinking is restricted to situation)
4 years	One-by-one correspondence	• Uses one-to-one correspondence to form rows of objects of equal length
	Reading	• Recognizes name in print
	Writing	• Prints name; recognizes some printed words; may read simple books
	Seriation	• Stacks up to five objects in increasing order of size
4½ years	Counting	• Counts up to 15 by rote
	Patterning	• May start to create simple patterns but is inconsistent
	Different perspectives	• Starts to understand false beliefs—may say, "This is just pretend"; identifies feelings in others
	Classification	• Classifies using more than one attribute
	Inabilities	• Unable to understand conservation of mass, volume or weight, or to think abstractly
5 years	Classification	• Classifies using one defining attribute, e.g., food, animals, vehicles
	Concepts	• Combines shapes to create new shapes, such as putting two triangles together to form a square
	Number and letter recognition	• Identifies similarities and differences in items, for instance, matching letters that are the same • Orders objects, for instance by size or identification of first or last • Recognizes written numbers to 10

TABLE 10.5 **CONTINUED**

Age Range	Skill	Description of Behaviour
5½ years	Conservation	• Recognizes that sets of numbers are the same even when arranged differently
	Counting	• Counts 20 objects without error
	Concepts	• Understands mathematical concepts such as half, more, less
	Patterning	• Forms consistent simple patterns
	Inabilities	• Unable to understand conservation of mass, volume or weight, or to classify using more than one attribute; incapable of abstract thinking

period they gradually become aware of different viewpoints. Preschoolers continue to build on previous skills. Play activities become more social, and children expand upon their abilities to engage in symbolic activities. As children continue to actively explore their learning environments, emergent skills are practised and refined. Table 10.5 outlines some of the additional cognitive skills children gain during the preschool years.

5. School-Age Cognitive Development

Children in their school years, aged six to twelve, demonstrate concrete operational thinking. "Children begin more and more to use logic and mental operations to understand situations and to think about how things work" (Schickedanz, Schickedanz, Forsyth & Forsyth, 2001: 439). For example, Janine, a seven-year-old, counted 10 birds sitting on a telephone wire outside. She also counted three birds that flew away. She then identified that there were only seven birds left.

During the school-age years, children make dramatic gains in cognitive development. They learn to:

• Think more logically—For instance, they may decide not to do something because the consequences of the action are not desirable.
• Use abstract reasoning—This is most evident in their ability to add, subtract, divide and multiply, and to take on and understand different viewpoints and perspectives.
• Gain increased ability to use symbolized forms—Examples include increased reading and writing skills, and greater facility with mathematical symbols.
• Begin to recognize and use time appropriately—John found the quickest way to get to school by timing himself to see how long it took him to get there.
• Use rehearsal strategies to increase ability to remember, such as repetitive practice of skills
• Play strategy games—Examples include Monopoly and Scrabble.

FIGURE 10.2
Christine's Book Report (age 9)

The book I read was The Three Little PUA'A written by Sherry Forkum.

This story is really the story of the Three Little Pigs. It takes place in Hawaii. Instead of a wolf, there was a scary creature Mo'o. A Mo'o is like a giant lizard. The rest of the story is the same except that the Mo'o was tricked into falling into a trap filled with hot lava rocks. He disappeared after eight hours.

I read this book because I like different versions of fairy tales.

- Summarize information without including irrelevant information (for an example, see Figure 10.2)
- Understand conservation
  - Six-year-olds: conservation of number
  - Eight-year-olds: conservation of area
  - Nine-year-olds: conservation of weight
  - Eleven-year-olds: conservation of volume

In summary, cognitive development is demonstrated through children's actions and behaviours. Although predictable stages can be identified, children pass through these stages at varying rates and at different ages. Cognitive development is dependent on the experiences children have in various tasks, such as problem solving, interacting with others to identify solutions or to explain a process used in collaborating with other children and adults. It is also affected by various experiences and conditions, such as individual life experiences, degree and type of disability, individual attitudes toward learning. cultural expectations and exposure to learning opportunities.

Range of Cognitive Behaviours in Inclusive Settings

Within any inclusive setting, a wide range of cognitive behaviours will be evident. Ranges in cognitive behaviours include children's ability to understand the world around them; to act on the learning environment; and to interact with others.

1. A Child's Understanding of the World

Children's ability to understand the world around them is based on their knowledge, skills, interests, background experiences and abilities. Specific behaviours that might be observed include:

- Inability to find appropriate learning activities—Jamie wandered around from area to area. He had roamed around the room twice before he decided to stay in the water area. There, Jamie grabbed one of the bubble wands from one of the girls. Instantly an argument erupted. The girl tried to grab back the wand, shouting, "I had it first." Jamie had a tight grip on the wand, and as the two children struggled, the wand broke. Jamie fell down and started to cry. Sue, the early childhood educator, came over. She checked to see if Jamie was hurt and consoled him. She brought out two new wands for the children to use. When Jamie tried to create bubbles with his wand, he was not successful. He tried to grab another wand from another child. Sue quickly came over and indicated that he already had a wand, but in frustration he threw his wand on the floor. He was redirected to another activity. Jamie obviously had difficulty trying to find something to do. He was attracted to the bubble play but lacked the skill to use the materials successfully.

Photo 10.2

Photo 10.3

- Inappropriate use of materials—Jordan was trying to fit a puzzle piece into the appropriate slot. He was unsuccessful. He ran over to the carpentry area and grabbed a hammer. He proceeded to try to hammer the puzzle piece into place. The vibration of the hammer hitting the puzzle caused the puzzle piece to shift and land in the correct slot. Jordan immediately tried another piece. When he hit this one it broke.

- Inappropriate use of equipment—Samantha was five. She had been in this particular day care since she was two. The playground was used by all age groups. Samantha climbed up the slide instead of climbing up the stairs. She was redirected. She went over to the climber and climbed on top of the tube tunnel connecting two areas. She was again redirected. Samantha obviously had excellent motor abilities. The existing climbing structures no longer challenged her abilities, so she created her own challenges.

Photo 10.4

- Lack of understanding of how to use materials—Michael picked up a pair of scissors and looked at them. He watched the other children cutting. He picked up a piece of paper and tried to cut it without opening his scissors. Eventually he gave up and put the scissors down.

- Frustrated behaviours—Michael came back to pick up the scissors again. Once more he tried to cut without opening his scissors. Finally he threw the scissors on the floor and ripped up his paper. Alice, another child, was at the puzzle area. She took out all the puzzles and put them on the table. She gave a big sigh. Her caregiver asked her why she didn't pick one puzzle. She replied, "I can't find one I like. They are all too easy."

- Self-expression through various forms at various levels of ability:
  - Art (Photos 10.2 and 10.3)
  - Movement (Photos 10.4 and 10.5)

- Creation of intricate structures or scenarios—Ben, a four-year-old, created a structure of three towers in the block area. He placed toy insects according to types on the various towers (see Figure 10.3).

Photo 10.5

FIGURE 10.3

Observation of Ben's Insect Towers

Ben organized the insects according to the following criteria:

(1) Large flying insects—dragonfly, butterfly, moth, bumble bee

(2) Small flying insects—bees, ladybags, flies, flying grasshopper

(3) Crawling insects—ants, aphids, walking sticks

2. Acting on the Learning Environment

Children demonstrate their cognitive abilities through their interactions with the environment. Their acts represent their knowledge about the world:

- Various ability levels—Mikayla (see Photo 10.2) and Michael (see Photo 10.3) demonstrate their ability to draw at different skill levels.
- Various degrees of problem solving—Dillon wanted a toy, so he tried to take the toy from someone else. In contrast, Nick wanted to expand his flower garden, so he asked to go to the storage room to find materials for his garden.
- Varying ways of utilizing the space—When the children went to the large gym, they behaved in various ways. Some children immediately started to run around the room. Others picked up a piece of equipment, such as a hoop or a ball, and started to play with it in a more confined area.
- Varying ways of using materials—Kim played in the sand by creating various structures with moulding containers, whereas Jodi used similar containers to fill and dump the sand.
- Varying approaches to learning—Timmy completed a six-piece puzzle through **trial-and-error learning** (learning by trying different techniques until one that works is found). Tammy completed the same puzzle by looking at each piece, finding the shape of the piece on the puzzle board and placing the piece into that slot.

- Background experiences—Braelyn could name all the shells in the collection in the room. Michael had difficulty finding two shells that looked the same. Braelyn had just returned from a holiday at the beach. She had not only added additional shells to the collection but also brought a book to identify them. Michael had not had any past experience with shells, nor had he expressed an interest in them or manipulated them.

3. Interactions with Others

Children's understanding may also be expressed in the way they interact with others. Children range in their ability to interact through:

- Type of play engaged in—Solitary to cooperative
- Ability to follow directions—Ranging from inability to follow simple directions to ability to follow complex directions
- Ability to initiate and maintain interactions—Ranging from inability to exceptional ability
  Children may also experience difficulty in these areas:
- Knowing what to do
- Being able to make suggestions to take the game forward
- Short-term memory—not remembering what happened before, poor verbal skills (e.g., limited vocabulary), remembering what was said
- Ability to follow the rules of the game (Macintyre, 2002: 25)

Effects of Various Cognitive Behaviours in Inclusive Settings

The presence of varying ranges of cognitive abilities affects all learning areas in the room. It may affect children's ability to do certain things:

- Understand directions—Therefore children may have difficulty remembering routines
- Play effectively with peers or the materials within the learning environment
- Negotiate for themselves
- Solve problems
- Find appropriate challenges
- Sustain activity over time

The learning environment needs to be structured and organized to address the range of abilities of all the children. This requires that there are enough materials to interest and challenge all abilities. The materials must be organized to maximize children's ability to find and succeed in self-directed tasks.

Caregivers must model and scaffold appropriate interaction patterns. Scaffolding refers to "verbal interaction between teacher and child that helps the child to solve a problem, carry out a task or achieve a goal beyond efforts that are unassisted" (Genisio & Drecktrah, 2002: 43). "Modelling" means "physical demonstration, showing the child what needs to occur, while demonstrating the activity to the child" (Genisio et al., 2002: 43-44). When scaffolding and modelling are combined in any circumstances, learning is nurtured and enhanced. For example, Jonathan noticed that Michael was having difficulty trying to use the scissors. He showed and explained to Michael how to open and shut the scissors. Michael was delighted to try. Next Jonathan cut a piece of paper. He then held up a piece of paper to Michael. Michael made a few snips on the paper. Jonathan scaffolded the task. He broke it down into manageable parts to help Michael gain success with the cutting activity.

Early childhood educators must therefore carefully observe children to identify when they need help or become frustrated, or when adult intervention is needed.

Forming Partnerships

Caregivers should form partnerships with family members and other professionals to coordinate learning activities effectively. Partners play a critical role in helping to:

- Observe children
- Provide expert advice
- Provide help and resources
- Ensure that consistency for the child is maintained in all settings

Observing Children's Behaviours

Careful observation and documentation is the cornerstone to building a quality program. Observations have many uses:

- Developing an IPP or portfolio for individual children
- Understanding and interpreting children's behaviours
- Providing appropriate adult intervention strategies
- Providing appropriate materials and interactions to encourage cognitive development
- Assisting with preparation of progress reports and referrals
- Enabling the appropriate organization of learning environments

Since cognitive behaviour cannot be observed directly, techniques need to be developed to identify and collect information about various demonstrated behaviours that can be interpreted. Some of these techniques include collections of children's work, photographs or diagrams of their products, checklists of specific skills and anecdotal records of specific behaviours.

1. Collections of Children's Work

Collections of children's efforts could include artwork, writings, photographs of structures made or video recordings of specific episodes. Examples of pieces of children's efforts could be collected periodically in individual portfolios (see page 154). Each specific item collected should be accompanied with an interpretation (see Figure 10.4 for an example). Information gathered from this type of process provides opportunities to:

* Interpret aspects of children's cognitive development
* Document changes over time
* Determine appropriate challenges to encourage further development
* Select materials, experiences or equipment to foster sustained interest and development over time
* Explain and illustrate changes in cognitive behaviour

2. Photographs

Photographs provide wonderful opportunities to record the achievement of milestones in children's cognitive activities (see Figure 10.5). Photographs can also be

FIGURE 10.4

Observations of Kikayla's Work

Date: May 2004 DOB: **January 22, 1999**

Circumstances: Drawing reflects follow-up of a field trip to look for signs of spring

Description	Comments	Interpretation
"My flowers are in front, so they are bigger. My house is in the background, so it's smaller."	Uses symbols to represent recognizable objects.	Able to take on a different perspective: size. Schematic stage of art development. Creative in recreating past experiences.

FIGURE 10.5

Explore to Discover Meaning

Date: April 02, 2004 DOB: **June 5, 2001**

Circumstances: Jordan had discovered the "Tornado in a Bottle." He had difficulty creating the tornado. Colin noticed and came to help him. Colin showed Jordan how to "make the tornado spin." Jordan eventually was successful.

Description	Comments	Interpretation
	J: "I can't." C: "Sure, you can. See, it's easy. Just turn the bottle." J: "The water's going around." C: "It's not really a tornado. It's a water spout." J: "Water spout." C: "Now you try!" J: "I did it, I did it. I made a water spout."	Jordan is at the math and science stage of exploration to discover meaning. He was able to interpret his discovery with Colin's help.

placed in a child's individual portfolio. The caregiver should include descriptions and interpretations of the event.

3. Diagrams of Children's Products

Sometimes it is not possible to take a photograph or adequately describe a child's actions or accomplishments. A quick diagram may best capture the child's efforts. These can then be interpreted. Diagrams can also be placed into a portfolio.

FIGURE 10.6

Interpretation of Ben's Insect Tower

Date: September 21, 2004   **DOB: April 22, 2000**

Circumstances: Ben was fascinated with the various kinds of insect. He often looked up information in books. He could name most of the collection of plastic insects that were available in the room. He built a special tower for his insects.

Description	Comments	Interpretation
[See Figure 10.3 for diagram.] He named the categories he had created—large and small, flying insects and crawling insects. He named all the insects he used.	Ben is able to classify using more than one attribute. Structures show his grasp of balance and order.	He placed blocks in order of size to effectively build his structure.

4. Checklists of Specific Skills

A number of checklists can be created to interpret cognitive behaviours. Checklists lend themselves to the identification of skills such as matching, sorting, seriation or patterning. Skills need to be observed more than once and in various settings to be sure that the skill has been acquired. These checklists give valuable information to ensure that children's developmental levels are being addressed and that appropriate challenges are provided for children. Figure 10.7 provides a few examples of appropriate checklists.

FIGURE 10.7

Samples of Checklists

Sample 1: Matching

Name: Josh   **DOB:** 12/03/1999

Skills	Date	Evidence
Colour	02/02/04	Matched vehicles by colour into egg carton container—yellow, red, blue, orange
Shape	03/04/04	Paired animals that were the same in the sandbox

Sample 2: Seriation

Name: Josh   **DOB:** 12/03/1999

Skills	Date	Evidence
Ordering items	05/02/04	Placed three nesting cups in order from smallest to largest
	05/04/04	Placed three rings in order from smallest to largest on sorter; used three of the six rings

Sample 3: Patterning

Name: Marlene   **DOB:** 10/05/2001

Skills	Date	Evidence
Colour	05/02/04	Created red-and-blue pattern with round beads
Size	05/04/04	Created large-fish, small-fish pattern with pattern cards

Sample 4: Sorting

Name: Marlene   **DOB:** 10/05/2001

Skills	Date	Evidence
Colour	05/04/04	Created necklace of all red beads from round beads of various colours

5. Anecdotal Records

Anecdotal records may be used to identify behaviours that need more explanation or do not occur very often. One example would be the child's use of language that demonstrates understanding. These types of records are useful as they preserve the total incident, making the information easy to interpret.

Individual Portfolios

Since cognitive behaviour is very difficult to observe, building a portfolio with the help of the child is an excellent way to document cognitive abilities. This works particularly well with children who are very verbal or who have been identified as gifted. Portfolios should be built in partnership with children, families and other professionals. Sample sections—reports, collections and personal reflections—are included in a sample portfolio (Figure 10.9). Portfolios are excellent ways to:

- Keep track of individual interests and skill development
- Maintain a record of progress over time
- Provide ongoing documentation that the child and family can keep as a record
- Provide a record of demonstrated cognitive skills and abilities
- Provide documentation that is easy to interpret and share

FIGURE 10.8

Sample Anecdotal Record

Name: Jill   **DOB:** 09/30/2000

Jill's Dialogue	Interpretation
"I hurted my finger. I cried. Mommy didn't cry. She is brave."	Has recognized that verb endings change when talking about the past. Sees the world from her perspective.

FIGURE 10.9A

Christopher's Portfolio: Introductory Page and Reports

Date: July 2, 2004

My name is Christopher.

I am almost four years old.

My birthday is on September 30. I will be four then.

The picture I drew is of me and my mommy.

Psychologist's Report

Christopher took part in a research study at Braceton University.

The purpose of the study was to test young children from three to five years of age who had an extensive vocabulary to see if this was an indicator of overall proficiency. Christopher's test results put him in the high superior range, overall.

Preschool Report

1. **Social adjustment:** Christopher gets along with all the children and adults in the program. He is very popular with all the children.
2. **Creativity:** Christopher is very creative in everything he does. His abilities in art far surpass the normal expectations of his age group.
3. **Overall Abilities:** Christopher excels at everything he does. He continually keeps the staff on their toes with his unique questions. He always seems to want to know everything. He can read most of the books on the shelf, and sometimes reads to other children.
4. **Summary of Observations:** Christopher is at an advanced level in all skill levels observed.

FIGURE 10.9B
Christopher's Portfolio: Collections

Christopher's Report
What I Can Do

I am good at painting, drawing and music.
I am good at sports like skiing, swimming and gymnastics.
I like preschool. I like pretend playing with my friends.

1. Art

I really like to draw.

I really like trucks. They can go anywhere. I wish my mommy
would drive a truck.

I like to use paint. I experiment to create interesting designs.
I mixed the colours blue and green to get turquoise. I used
really thick paint to create dots and thin paint to create
lines.

2. Projects

I especially like to use clay.

I decided to make a dinosaur. I formed it out of clay. Then I
decided to make it be two different things, like my trans-
formers. So, I made a dinosaur rabbit. Then we took it down
to the kiln to be fired. We then painted it and glazed it and
next it was fired again.

This is my dinosaur.

This is the dinosaur transformed into a rabbit

3. Stories

I love to write stories. I still need help to write them.

Dictated Story: "My Pets"

We have a pet cat and some fish. I love them. I think that I am
lucky. I have four fish. They like to swim in an aquarium. I feed
the fish.

I like to play with our pet cat. I love her. Her name is Simsim.

FIGURE 10.9C

Christopher's Portfolio: Personal Reflections

---

1. What I Like to Do

I like to play the piano. We had a concert and I got to play a solo.

I like all kinds of sports.

I love the art lessons. I take them at the Art Gallery. We got to see a show about South American art. It was cool. I liked the colours the artists used.

I like to play with my friends.

I like the rooftop playground at our nursery school, and I like to roll down the big hill with Darren when we go to the nursery school.

2. What I Don't Like

I don't like to sit and wait to go outside. Some kids are so slow.

I don't like spinach. I don't care if it's good for you.

I don't like to be always interrupted when I'm busy.

3. What Makes Me Sad

I was really sad when my grandfather died. I still miss him.

4. What Makes Me Happy

I'm really happy when people give me presents, like on my birthday and at Christmas.

I like to make my mommy happy. I draw her pictures.

My mommy tickles me.

5. What Makes Me Angry

I get really mad when people hurt animals.

I get annoyed when people won't leave me alone when I tell them to.

6. What Scares Me

Sometimes I get scared that a plane will drop bombs on us.

FIGURE 10.9D

Christopher's Portfolio: Samples of Observations of Christopher's Skills

All information was gathered by the staff and family members.

Name: Christopher   **DOB:** 09/30/00

Skills	Date	Evidence
Matching		
missing pieces	02/05/04	Matched set of cards
Interior detail	03/04/04	Matched identical pieces hidden in a background of many pieces
Seriation	02/29/04	Ordered 10 shells from smallest to largest
	03/02/04	Built set of 15 towers, each getting larger
	03/04/04	Helped Josh to order stacking cups from smallest to largest several times
	03/04/04	Used clay to create series of dinosaur eggs from largest to smallest

Patterning Skills

Name: Christopher   **DOB:** 09/30/00

Skills	Date	Evidence
Colour	03/02/04	Created turquoise-and-blue pattern of sponge print
Shape	03/04/04	Used toy animals to create a pattern of mother, baby animals
Size	04/06/04	Used beads to create two-small, two-large pattern

Sorting Skills

Name: Christopher   **DOB:** 09/30/00

Skills	Date	Evidence
Colour	05/04/04	Sorted all the beads (which had been dumped) by colour
Classification	06/07/04	Placed the toy animals into two groups, then asked teacher to guess the groups; teacher was unable to do so; had correctly separated animals with and without hooves.

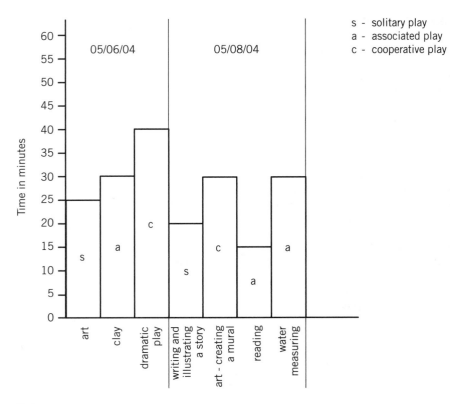

FIGURE 10.9E

Observation of Interests and Attention Span

Comments

Dramatic play involved planning and creating a zoo in the block area. Christopher was the "engineer" and later the "veterinarian." All five children assumed different roles.

Organizing the Cognitive Environment

The indoor and outdoor environments should be organized to maximize children's opportunities to solve problems, make decisions, experiment, transfer knowledge and skills from one situation to another and engage in self-reflective activities. There should be a smooth flow of activities from indoors to outdoors.

1. Opportunities to Solve Problems

Opportunities for children to solve their own problems should be available in every centre. Caregivers should ensure that materials at the appropriate level are available and accessible (see Table 10.6).

2. Opportunities to Make Decisions

Organization of the materials in the environment should ensure that materials are accessible, categorized with an appropriate labelling system (Chapter 4, pages 105-108)

TABLE 10.6 **SUGGESTIONS FOR CREATING OPPORTUNITIES TO SOLVE PROBLEMS**

Learning Area	Description of Opportunities
Dramatic play areas • **Housekeeping** • **Role play** • **Pretend play**	• One-to-one correspondence when setting the table: one spoon for every plate • How to mix ingredients to make a meal • How to dress for certain roles • How to interact when role-playing • How to set a table
Music area	• Counting the beat • How to play an instrument • Learning words of songs, or names of instruments • Matching sounds to different instruments • Keeping time to music
Manipulative area	• How things fit together • Matching shapes to put them into a puzzle or shape sorter • How to create patterns • One-to-one correspondence: one bear in one container • How to fit nesting cups together
Creative arts	• How to mix colours • How to create different designs • How to create different shapes • How to use different tools such as brushes or scissors • How to make things stick
Sand area	• How to create moulds • When to use wet or dry sand • How to build structures in sand • Which tools are most effective for digging or filling • How to measure: heavy, light, full, empty
Water area	• Which tools are most effective to pour or fill with • How to create flow • How to make bubbles • Identifying what sinks or floats
Math and science area	• How to make things sink • How to notice detail • Counting to find out what has more or less • One-to-one correspondence • Sorting objects by size or colour or shape • Identifying which items are attracted to a magnet
Carpentry area	• How to attach things together • Identifying appropriate tools to use for different tasks • Identifying which size of nails to use • How to shorten pieces of wood • How to use tools safely

TABLE 10.6 **CONTINUED**

Learning Area	Description of Opportunities
Book area	• How to use books for different purposes • How to read • Answer questions • How to retell a story using props such as felt pieces • Finding an appropriate book
Block area	• How to build stable structures • How to fit blocks together to form different structures • How to build to different heights • How to transport blocks effectively • How to represent different ideas such as tunnels, platforms or towers
Gross motor play	• How to get to the top of a climber • How to stop • How to balance on a balance beam • How to ride a riding toy • How to move around obstacles

and are easily visible from various areas of the room. Materials should reflect the following criteria:

• Open-ended—Children should be able to make decisions about how to use the materials (see Photo 10.14).
• Multi-purpose—Materials should be usable in a variety of settings for a variety of purposes. Children can make the decisions about where or when the materials might be used (see Photo 10.15).

Photo 10.14

Photo 10.15

Photo 10.17

Photo 10.16

Photo 10.18

- Providing choices—Children should be able to choose materials from a variety of alternatives. This provides opportunities to make decisions about when or which materials will be used.

3. Opportunities to Experiment

Children learn about their world through active participation. They need to explore their learning environments in order to discover many important things:

- How things work (Photo 10.17)
- What will happen as a result of certain actions (Photo 10.18)
- How things change or can be changed for different purposes (Photos 10.19 and 10.20)
- How to work together or independently (Photo 10.21)

Photo 10.19

Photo 10.20

Photo 10.21

4. Opportunities to Transfer Knowledge and Skills

Learning occurs as children explore and learn about their environment. However, learning is reinforced and strengthened when learning can be transferred from one situation to another. Children learn that similar actions can be used in similar ways in different circumstances. Table 10.7 offers some suggestions of how different materials may be used in similar ways in different settings.

5. Opportunities to Engage in Self-Reflective Activities

Children need to learn to reflect on what they have learned, what they still wish to learn and the value of their activities. Self-reflection activities might include discussion, writing, or drawing.

TABLE 10.7   SUGGESTIONS FOR CREATING OPPORTUNITIES TO TRANSFER SKILLS

Skill	Transfer Opportunities
Pouring	• Sandbox—Dry sand • Water—Filling and emptying • Snack—Pouring own drink • Manipulatives—Pouring gems or beads into containers
Pouring	• Blocks - Transporting blocks in construction vehicle toys and dumping them where needed • Cooking—Preparing food
Stacking	• Blocks • Manipulatives—Duplo, Lego or small blocks • Dramatic play—Dishes, bowls • Outdoor play—Rocks
Mixing	• Sand—Making wet sand • Water—Creating mixtures with various things such as soap or food colour • Painting—Creating new colours • Dramatic play—Creating meals • Sand—Adding alternatives such as scraps of materials or paper
Reading	• Blueprints for creating carpentry projects • Recipes for making own play dough or snack • Books to read for pleasure • Books placed in all learning areas to look through for ideas, expand knowledge
Drawing/painting	• Block area—Create maps, signs, roads, scenery • Creative area—Free exploration of materials • Outdoors—Natural extension from indoor to outdoor activity • Field trips—Recording what has been observed • Carpentry—Decorating projects • Sand—Mixing sand and paint to create sand pictures

A) DISCUSSION Discussion opportunities should be provided that help the children reflect. Children might be asked the following questions:

- How do you feel about what you have done/created?
- What did you like about what you have done/created?
- How might you do things differently next time?
- What other materials might you need to continue working on what you are doing?
- How did this experience make you feel?

B) WRITING AND DRAWING Children could be encouraged to create personal booklets to record their reflections. A **scribe** (someone who listens and writes down exactly what the child says) should be provided to aid younger children with this process. The advantage of a booklet is that children can refer back to their reflections over time and also share them with others. Reflection booklets should be personal and should only be shared if the child wishes to share them.

Role of the Early Childhood Educator

The role of the early childhood educator is to observe, monitor and organize developmentally- and age-appropriate learning activities to meet the learning needs of all children within the group (see the author's Reflection). Some specific strategies have been adapted from Gensio and Drecktrah (2002):

Reflection	*From the Author*

One of my most memorable incidents concerning facilitator interactions occurred during a practice teaching occasion. The children had been very interested in dinosaurs. Much of this dinosaur play had occurred in a large sandbox on the floor. One of the student teachers, Tammy, decided that since it was spring, she should change the activity to reflect the season. She collected a number of plastic flowers and created a flower garden in a corner of the sandbox.

When Benjamin and Damian arrived, they immediately went to the sandbox. "Where are our dinosaurs?" Tammy explained that it was springtime and wouldn't they rather plant a garden? "No!" was the instant reply. "Let's go and get the dinosaurs!" Tammy responded that she did not know where the dinosaurs were kept. "Come, we will show you!" The two boys took her to the storage room to retrieve the dinosaurs. They also showed her where to find the other things they needed for their dinosaur play.

When they got back to the sand area, Benjamin asked Tammy to tell them the names of the dinosaurs. Tammy responded with phrases like "That is a ferocious looking dinosaur," or "That one is a green one." Benjamin finally looked at her, put his hands on his hips and said, "Don't you know any of their names?

| | Reflection |

continued   *From the Author*   **Reflection**

Even I know some of them." He pointed to the dinosaurs and said, "This is a tyrannosaurus rex, this is a triceratops and this is a pteranodom."

The next day Tammy was ready. She had brought appropriate books, expanded the dinosaur collection and brought in some tall grasses that the children could use in creating the dinosaur play. Benjamin and Damian were enthralled with the new activity. This time when they asked her the names of the dinosaurs she knew some of the names. If she did not, she offered to find the dinosaur in the book and read about it.

When Tammy reflected on the experience she said: "I never realized how smart the kids could be or how important it was to follow their lead. I know you always told us how important it was to know more about the child's play and know the names of the materials they are playing with. I now realize just how important that is. This has been a great learning activity for the children, but a much more powerful one for me!"

1. Focus on Important Activities

Children with special needs in the cognitive domain may not always have the ability to focus on what is important. The early childhood educator should guide the children's focus. This could be done through:

- Focusing on the interest of the child—Jamie had been looking at the dinosaur play but had not interacted.
- Guided dialogue—Tammy: "I see you are interested in the dinosaur. I wonder what he feels like."
- Modelling—Tammy picks up the dinosaur and runs her fingers over the back. "It feels bumpy." She hands over the dinosaur to Jamie. Jamie touches the dinosaur's back but does not hold it. Tammy describes Jamie's actions and the sensation he feels.
- Guided action—Tammy: "Let's put the dinosaur in the sand," still holding the dinosaur in her hand. Jamie takes the dinosaur and places it in the sand. Tammy continues to observe his actions and guide his behaviour. Jamie eventually plays with the dinosaur in the sand by himself.

2. Use Concrete Examples

Young children have difficulty dealing with abstract concepts. For example, when my father died my son was two and a half. We followed my father's wishes and had his body cremated. My son was very upset when he realized that his grandfather was not to be buried. He said, sobbing, "But he has to be buried, so I can water him and he can grow again." It was spring and my son had associated flower bulb planting with the process of burying the dead. We have to be continually aware of the impact of what we do and say on young children. Children make connections that are rooted in their daily experiences. Explanations and interactions also need to be rooted in concrete experiences that the children can relate to.

3. Provide Lots of Practice

To learn any new task, practice is required. Young children often engage in repetitive activity, which provides them with the necessary practice needed to develop and gain confidence in new skills and to refine existing skills. Facilitators need to ensure that:

- Enough time is available to practise skills
- Appropriate materials and equipment are available
- Skills can be practised in a variety of settings
- Appropriate encouragement is given to maintain activities
- Appropriate indoor and outdoor spaces are available

4. Observe and Document Children's Progress

All skill and ability development progresses at individual rates. Caregivers need to carefully observe children so they can gauge individual abilities and interests—knowledge of which is essential to providing the appropriate materials, time and space to encourage cognitive growth and development.

5. Modify Learning Activities

Learning activities need to be continually evaluated and monitored to ensure that children's learning needs are met. Changes and adaptations should reflect individual needs and abilities. Josh had been very interested in the children's beading activities. He tried to bead but found it difficult to manage the gimp. Given some long pipe cleaners, he was able to complete the activity.

6. Scaffold Learning Activities and Learning Experiences

Children's understanding of learning is also individual. Learning situations need to be structured so that the children can understand and complete the activities. Materials should be arranged to give choices of simple to more difficult to meet all children's needs. For example, in the centre's book area the books that were displayed were related to the children's prevailing interest: farm animals. There were:

- Simple dictionaries that displayed the picture of the animal with the word
- Picture books that showed animals involved in a variety of movements
- Storybooks about different animals
- Illustrated poetry books

7. Provide Supportive Feedback

Children need feedback to encourage them to continue to be actively involved in learning activities. "Throughout childhood, children practice a skill and the feedback they get from the result encourages them to continue. But when they become repeatedly successful in their own judgment, the skill holds no more challenge and they abandon it to try something else. Similarly, if they are consistently unsuccessful they give up trying. It seems that intermittent feedback is the result that keeps children longer on the task—an important point for those planning teaching" (Macintyre, 2002: 3).

Feedback to children should always be honest and realistic. The child's process should be referred to as opposed to the product. Consider the following observations. Jenna was intent at the easel. She was covering the paper with blue paint. When she had finished she started to paint over the blue paint with green paint. She discovered that the paint mixed and new colours appeared. Jenna put her brushes down and started to use her fingers to create different swirls and loops. One of the adults in the room noticed her efforts and said, "Jenna, that is a beautiful painting. I love the colours you used." Jenna ignored her and continued to create shapes. Jenna did not gain anything from this interaction. She was not painting a "picture." She was exploring mixing colours and creating designs.

In contrast, Benjamin was fingerpainting. He covered his papers with various sizes of circles. Charmaine noticed his efforts and said, "Wow, you made a lot of circles. I see five little ones and six large ones." Benjamin nodded and said, "Watch, I can squeeze another little circle in this corner. Now I have one, two, three, four, five, six small circles. That's the same as the big ones." Ben gained gratification for his efforts. The adult added another dimension: counting.

8. Model a Variety of Skills

Caregivers should model a variety of skills to encourage and maintain interactions:

- Patience—This gives children a clear message that it is all right to do things differently and at the same time creates understanding that each individual is able to finish activities in accordance with his or her own needs.
- Persistence—Children need to learn that sometimes things do not go as expected the first time, but that it is important to try again. Dillon was trying to fit a puzzle piece into a slot. He was not experiencing any success. He put the piece down and tried a different piece. Thomas noticed his efforts and quietly said, "What a good idea to try another piece. I wonder if it will fit." Dillon smiled

and tried the piece, but it did not fit. He looked up at Thomas and frowned. Thomas smiled and said, "What are you going to do now?" Dillon smiled and picked up another piece. This time it did fit. "Good job!" Thomas said.

9. Encourage Independence

Children should be encouraged to be as independent as possible. Caregivers need to carefully observe in order to encourage individual independence as much as possible. For example, a child may not be able to start a zipper but may be able to pull it up once started. A careful balance needs to be struck between insisting that a child does a task and helping him or her do it. For example, a behaviour that is commonly observed is hand-over-hand helping. The child gains nothing from this activity. The adult is directing all the actions. If a child is having difficulty, the following questions should be asked:

- Is this is an important task for the child to master at this time?
- Does the child have the skills to do this task?
- Can the task be broken down to make it easier to accomplish?
- Are there alternative activities that can be used to reinforce that skill?

10. Provide Challenges

Children who are actively and meaningfully engaged in developmentally-appropriate learning activities are satisfied with themselves and the tasks they are engaged in. However, children also need to be challenged to continue to learn. Children who are not challenged often find other things to do, some of which may not be appropriate.

For example, I was asked to observe a group of children early in the morning to advise the centre staff about what might be done about the inappropriate behaviours the children were engaged in. The centre opened at 7:00 a.m. Two staff members were present to admit the children. Only six children arrived before the next staff member was scheduled to arrive. The mix of the children included one infant, two toddlers (one with special needs) and three four-year-olds. The children were in one room for the first half-hour of the morning. The room of choice was the toddler room. The inappropriate behaviours observed were all with the three four-year-olds: James, Rachel and Jeb. These behaviours included racing vehicles down the toddler slide; using the mats to tumble on; and throwing soft toys back and forth to each other. Once the next staff member arrived, the preschoolers went to their own room. It took the staff some time to settle the children into the routine of the morning.

I decided to ask the children themselves about their behaviour and report what they had said back to the staff. I asked the children why they behaved the way they did. Their responses were as follows:

James: "I don't know. There's nothing else to do. I hate being in the dumb toddler room. I'm four years old."

Rachel: "I don't like going in that room. It's too boring."

Jeb: "I like to race toys. I can't reach our slide to race cars."

The room the children were in clearly did not provide enough challenge for them, so they created their own challenge. When the staff heard the responses of the children, alternative arrangements were made. The inappropriate behaviours stopped.

SUMMARY

To interpret cognitive behaviour, children's activities must be carefully observed. The actions of the children provide clues about their understanding of the world. Children demonstrate their understanding of the world around them by the way they interact with the materials in their learning environment, the way they interact with others and what they communicate about these interactions. Children need opportunities to engage in active play that includes solving problems, making decisions and becoming increasingly independent.

KEY POINTS

Cognitive development
- Nurture versus nature
- Multiple intelligences—Linguistic, logical–mathematical, musical, bodily/kinesthetic, spatial, interpersonal, intrapersonal
- Infant—Sensory motor, reflexive, manipulative, imitative
- Toddler—Sensory motor, start preoperational stage, symbolic play, deferred imitation
- Preschool—Preoperational, inflexible thinking, increased refinement of cognitive skills
- School age—Concrete operational, appearance of abstract thought, increased ability to use abstract concepts

Range of Cognitive Behaviours—Related to ability to understand the world, act upon the environment and interact with others.

Effects of Range of Cognitive Behaviours—Affects children's understandings, abilities, skills and organization of the environment

Observations—Collections, photographs, diagrams, checklists, anecdotal records

Individual portfolio—Introduction, reports, collections, personal reflections, observations

Organization of the environment—Opportunities to solve problems, make decisions, experiment, transfer skills and knowledge, reflect

Role of early childhood educator—Focus on important activities, use concrete examples, provide practice, observe and document, modify, scaffold learning, provide supportive feedback, model a variety of skills, encourage independence, provide challenges

EXERCISES

1. In a small group discussion, discuss Gardner's theory of multiple intelligences. Reflect upon which of the listed intelligences best represents you.

2. Utilize one of the developmental charts listed in Tables 10.2–10.5 (pages 327–330). Develop an observation tool to identify cognitive milestones. Implement the tool. Discuss what behaviours you have observed that demonstrate cognitive behaviour.

3. Discuss why there is a great deal of variation of cognitive behaviours in any setting. What adaptations need to be made to accommodate these differences?

4. Discuss the importance of forming partnerships.

5. Utilize two of the observation tools listed on pages 336–340. Implement the tools with an individual with special needs and an individual without special needs. Compare the results.

6. Reflect on the individual portfolio on pages 341–345. What makes the portfolio a useful tool to the child, the teacher and the family member?

7. Observe an inclusive environment. Identify what adaptations have been made to:

a) Accommodate individual cognitive needs
b) Caregiver interaction patterns
c) The materials and equipment within the centre

RESOURCES

Howard Gardner's Multiple Intelligences and Education
www.infed.org/thinkers/gardner.htm

John Locke's philosophy of the tabula rasa
www.answers.com/topic/tabula-rasa

Behaviorist theory
www.personalityresearch.org/papers/naik.html

Assistive Technology
http://spot.colorado.edu/~dubin/bookmarks/ b/445.html

Intellectual developmental delays
www.cyh.com/HealthTopics/ HealthTopicDetails.aspx?p=114&np=306&id =1876

Gifted children Association of British Columbia
www.worldgifted.org/xwebix.htm

Gifted children in Canada
www3.telus.net/giftedcanada

REFERENCES

Gardner, H. (1993). *Multiple Intelligences: The Theory in Practice.* New York, NY: Basic Books.

Genisio, M., & Drecktrah, M. (2002). Emergent Literacy in an Early Childhood Classroom: Center Learning to Support the Child with Special Needs. In K. Freiberg (Ed.), *Annual Editions Educating Exceptional Children* (pp. 40-47). Guilford, CT: McGraw-Hill/Dushkin.

Landry, P. (2004). John Locke (1632–1704) The Philosopher of Freedom. Blupete [online]. Available at www.answers.com/topic/tabula-rasa (4-10-2005).

Macintyre, C. (2002). *Play for Children with Special Needs.* London, UK: David Fulton Publishers.

Naik, P. (2001). Behaviorism as a Theory of Personality: A Critical Look. Northwestern University [online]. Available at www.personalityresearch.org/papers/naik.html (5-1-2005).

Piaget, J. (1962). *Play, Dreams, and Imitation in Childhood.* New York, NY: Norton.

Rushton, S., & Larkin, E. (2005). Shaping the Learning Environment: Connecting Developmentally Appropriate Practices to the Brain Research. In K. Cauley, F. Linder & J. McMillan (Eds.), *Educational Psychology* (Dubuque, IA: McGraw-Hill/Dushkin).

Schickedanz, J., Schickedanz, D., Forsyth, P., & Forsyth, G. (2001). *Understanding Children and Adolescents.* Fourth Edition. Needham Heights, MA: Allyn & Bacon.

Smith, K. (2002). Howard Gardner's Multiple Intelligences and Education. Infed [online]. Available at www.infed.org/thinkers/gardner.htm (9-4-2005).

Udell, T., Peters, J., & Piaza Templeman, T. (2001). From Philosophy to Practice in Inclusive Early Childhood Programs. *Annual Editions Educating Exceptional Children,* Thirteenth Edition, 2001/2002, 32–36.

11

CHAPTER

Issues Concerning Inclusive Care in Canada

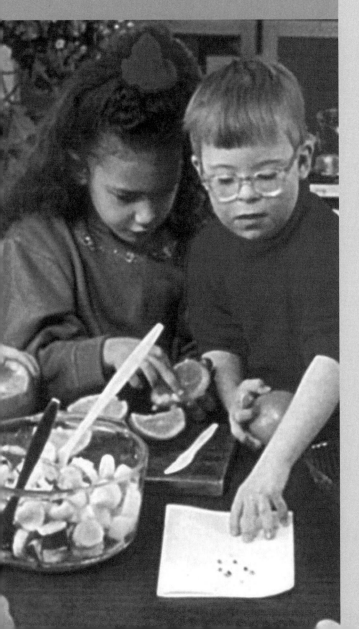

"In 1982, under Canada's Charter of Rights and Freedoms, children with special needs finally gained the right to attend school in all provinces and territories.

"In signing the UN Convention on the Rights of the Child in 1991, Canada made additional commitments to children with special needs. Today it is a matter of urgency that children with special needs finally gain the right to attend child care programs in all provinces and territories with their non-disabled peers, and that these programs be adequately resourced to meet their needs. These children must no longer be excluded and segregated" (Hope Irwin, Lero & Brophy, 2000: xiv).

Learning Outcomes

After studying this chapter, you will be able to:

1. Discuss the issues associated with equitable access; lack of space; need for proportionate care; and need for appropriate policies.
2. Define the eleven components of quality care.
3. For each of the eleven components of quality care, identify associated problems.
4. Describe issues associated with diagnosis and assessment of children with special needs.
5. Describe how culture may influence the treatment of children with special needs.
6. Identify the barriers that exist to funding programs for children with special needs.
7. Describe the issues related to the education of individuals working with children with special needs.
8. Describe the effects of poverty on children with special needs.

Introduction

All provinces and territories have some legislation that provides for care and education of children with special needs. However, the definitions of inclusive care and education vary. On the one hand are simple statements such as this one: "Inclusion as a value, supports the right of all children, regardless of their diverse abilities, to participate actively in natural settings within their communities" (The Council for Exceptional Children, 1997: 1). Other definitions are multidimensional: "SpeciaLink for example proposes that, in full inclusion no children are excluded because of level or type of special need. Building on a base of high quality core child care, this definition includes five elements: 1) zero rejection; 2) naturally occurring proportions of typically developing children and children with special needs; 3) full participation of all children in all activities; 4) same range of options for attendance of all children (e.g., part-day, full-day, casual); 5) advocacy, pro-action, and parent participation to the maximum extent desired by parents" (Hope Irwin et al., 2000: 5). A definition of inclusiveness provides a starting point to the dialogue that is necessary to the establishment of appropriate philosophies and the creation of proactive policies for inclusive care. Without a common definition, it is not surprising that a number of approaches and a variety of policies or lack of policy have been implemented across the country.

The absence of a universally acceptable definition of inclusive care is but one of the issues that can be identified in Canada. Issues concerning inclusive care in Canada have been clearly articulated in the research (Hope Irwin et al., 2000; Hope Irwin, Lero & Brophy, 2004; Hope Irwin et al., 2004; Goleman, Doherty, Lero, LaGrange & Tougas, 2000; Valentine, 2001) and by many individuals who work with children with special needs.

In this chapter, a summary of the prevailing issues will be presented through the eyes of individuals who are involved with the education of children with special needs. A series of interviews was conducted with individuals involved in ongoing research: family members, staff, supervisors, directors, consultants, board members, licensing officials and faculty involved in training programs for special needs certification.

Those interviewed were asked to identify what they perceived to be the outstanding issues concerning the care of children with special needs. The issues identified can be grouped into several categories, including these: access; diagnosis and assessment of special needs; funding; family concerns; staff concerns; effects of poverty; and legislative policies. A final category of issues, quality care, comprises many aspects: the learning environment; equipment and materials; the role of the director; support for staff; training of staff; provision of therapy; individual program planning; inclusion of families as partners; facilitation of social interaction among children; support from board members; and establishing a smooth transition from centre to elementary school.

From the Author   **Reflection**

Reflection

I have always spent a lot of time reading the research about the care of children with special needs in Canada. Reading about the issues and problems is always a very abstract experience. You might reflect upon what you have read, but after you have put the readings aside, the information gleaned quickly recedes. It is only when you actually become involved with the children, families and professionals caring for children with special needs that the issues become more personal, real and understandable.

I wanted to bring this more personal perspective to the readers of this text. That is why I decided to conclude by interviewing individuals working with children with special needs. I thought it would be valuable to catch a personal glimpse into the issues and problems associated with working with children with special needs.

Equitable Access

Equitable access involves the inclusion of children with special needs within community care settings of the family's choice. All individuals interviewed identified equitable access as a concern. Research clearly supports this viewpoint: "The Canadian Council on Social Development's original survey of 112 Canadian agencies demonstrated that ... there are many barriers to services for these children and families. This results in a number of unmet needs. In their report, The Canadian Policy Research Network has concluded that 'full citizenship demands the easy access to inclusive supports, services and community settings. They argue that the provision of a package of portable and flexible supports targeting the particular needs of children with disabilities and their families must be readily accessible in local communities' (Valentine, 2001: 68). This is clearly not the case." (Canadian Council on Social Development, 2000: 53). The issues of equitable access identified included the lack of child care spaces, the need for proportionate care and the need for appropriate policies.

1. Lack of Child Care Spaces

A common problem identified was an overall lack of child care spaces. It was estimated that approximately one out of every eight child care centres in Canada do not include children with disabilities.

Many individuals reported that they could not meet requests to accommodate more children either with or without special needs. One centre reported a huge waiting list that included 250 space requests for children not identified as special needs and 40 requests for supported spaces. All centres reported that they had waiting lists for children with special needs.

The number of available spaces has also decreased because many of the part-day and nursery school programs have closed in many jurisdictions. For example, with the opening of junior kindergarten in Ontario, many preschool programs were closed. Children with special needs often attend programs part-time to accommodate the many other services that they are involved with. Without available half-day or part-time programs, these children now compete for spaces within full-day settings. Many centres cannot afford to offer part-time services to their clients, even if spaces did exist.

One director of a full-day child care centre, Susan, reported that children with special needs could not be accepted into the program. The reasons for refusal included these:

- The staff was already overburdened with a number of challenging behaviours of children enrolled in the program. These children had not been diagnosed with a behavioural problem, but Susan felt that in reality the program should be receiving funding to help with these problems. She did not feel that the centre could accept more children with special needs.
- The staff, Susan felt, did not have adequate training to provide quality programming for children with special needs.
- Additionally, Susan felt it was difficult if not impossible to access appropriate expertise to help with programming for children with special needs.

What can you do to address the lack of child care spaces? Here are some suggestions:

a) Become informed about equitable care issues. Talk to individuals involved with the care of young children with special needs to find out what the issues are.
b) Learn to advocate for better care for children with special needs. Attend workshops on how to become a better advocate.
c) Join community groups that meet regularly to discuss issues concerning children with special needs, such as the Canadian Council for Children with Exceptionalities.
d) Read appropriate resources (see references and additional resources at end of chapter).

2. Need for Proportionate Care

One of the principles of inclusion is that the care of children with special needs should be in naturally occurring proportions: "in proportion to their occurrence in the general population" (Hope Irwin, 2002: 2). This is generally about 10 percent of the group size. When the number of children with special needs within a program is higher than 10 percent, the resources of the program often become stretched. It becomes more difficult to meet the needs of individual children and their families, and to access appropriate resources. Care for children with special needs varies across Canada. Individuals interviewed indicated that special needs care ranged from proportionate to disproportionate.

June, a staff member in an inclusive setting with a higher number of children with special needs, summed up the situation in the following way:

- Nine of our sixteen children have special needs. This is too high a proportion for us to provide a high-quality program.
- Sometimes I feel that our typical children lose out because they do not get the same individual attention. We seem to spend more time with the children with special needs because they often need the one-on-one approach to cope.
- We have a support worker in the room, so we do have an extra pair of hands, but it never seems enough.
- I realize the importance of the social interactions that take place. All our children benefit from these interactions. However, sometimes children pick up inappropriately modelled behaviours, and it is hard to explain to a young child why the behaviour is not appropriate.
- I believe in inclusion, but I do think that all the children and the staff would benefit more from a more balanced approach.

What can you do to address the need for proportionate care?

a) Become informed about the benefits of proportionate care.
b) If more help is needed on the floor, encourage volunteer support in the room: family members, senior citizens or community members.

3. Need for Appropriate Policies

All individuals interviewed identified that there was a need for proactive policies. All were concerned that there were no proactive policies consistently in place in Canada. The lack of proactive policies makes it essential that practitioners working with children with special needs engage in proactive activities. This activity is defined in another principle of inclusive practices: the inclusive program "actively promotes legislative and policy change, encourages enrolment of children with disabilities and involves parents at the level they choose" (Hope Irwin, 2002: 2).

Interviewees agreed that appropriate proactive policies provide the framework for quality inclusive care. One director indicated that these policies should not be linked to the need to label children but should be tied to providing adequate resources to inclusive child care centres such as funding for higher staff–child ratios, resources (human, physical and material) and training.

Concerns were also expressed by several individuals that often there are provincial or territorial pressures to reduce standards. One supervisor indicated: "There have been pressures to reduce standards in BC. During a review of legislation in BC, care has been made more affordable by reduction of standards. We should strive toward national policies that will drive local applications."

What can you do to advocate proactive policies that support inclusive child care?

a) Become informed about the policies concerning children with special needs in your jurisdiction.
b) Identify what proactive policies may be needed in your area.
c) Participate in public forums or internet-based forums.
d) Write letters to your MPP to indicate your concerns.

Quality of Inclusive Care

All those interviewed expressed concern about the generally low overall quality of care for children with special needs in Canada. This concern is clearly supported by the research. The results of a national research study, "Inclusion: The Next Generation in Childcare in Canada" (Hope Irwin et al., 2004), clearly support this concern. Based on the Early Childhood Environmental Rating Scale—Revised (ECERS-R) (Harms, Clifford & Cryer, 1998) and reports from the 32 participating centres, the study reached these conclusions:

- Three centres (9.4%) had quality scores that indicated inferior program quality.
- Fourteen centres (43.8%) had scores in the minimal-to-mediocre range.
- A similar proportion (46.9%) had scores in the good-to-excellent range (Hope Irwin et al., 2004: 158).

Aspects of quality inclusive environments include the physical environment, equipment and materials, the role of the director, support for staff, training of staff, provision of therapy, individual program planning, inclusion of families as partners, facilitation of social interaction between children, supportive board members and a smooth transition from centre to elementary school (Hope Irwin et al., 2004: 151). Some individuals raised concerns about the quality of at least one of these aspects.

1. Physical Environment

All individuals expressed concern about the impact of the physical space on the quality of the learning experiences for the children. Specific concerns included these:

- Lack of space to make necessary adaptations—One staff member reported that she felt the quality of the program for the children had decreased because of the modifications that had to be made to the physical environment. The environment had been changed to include wheelchair access. To accommodate access, a number of learning areas had to be removed. These learning experiences were now offered on a rotational basis. "I do not think that this is ideal. We had to make the adjustments because we all wanted to accept the child in the wheelchair. The consequences are that children now have fewer choices and the adults are working harder to rotate a variety of experiences that have similar outcomes. It has been both challenging and frustrating. We simply need a larger space."

- Lack of funding to make the relevant modifications—A number of directors and board members indicated that they would like to make modifications that would make the centre more inclusive but that they lacked the necessary funds. Sandy, an executive director, reported: "We found it quite easy to make some of the physical adjustments, such as adding an elevator to the building, ramps and accessible washroom spaces because we received a one-time grant to make modifications to the physical space. What has been most difficult is to receive funding for ongoing equipment needs such as standing frames, communication boards, adaptable devices and switches, or adaptive playground equipment. The grants given provide only access. There is no consideration given toward ongoing funding to provide for quality experiences for the children once they are in program."

2. Equipment and Materials

Most individuals interviewed indicated that it was difficult to obtain specialized materials and/or equipment to encourage independent choices and abilities. These specific difficulties were mentioned:

- Finding specialized equipment and materials can be difficult. Material may have to be purchased at a distance from specialized suppliers, such as adaptive eating utensils or adaptive switches.
- Much of the highly specialized equipment, such as standing frames, is needed by only a few children.
- Equipment may require a lot of storage room. Many centres may not have adequate storage space.
- These materials and equipment may be too expensive to purchase.

3. Role of the Director

Directors interviewed were very conscious of their role in supporting inclusive care. There was a general concern that related to attracting suitable staff. One director commented: "I realize that training is one way to enhance the quality of the program. Trained individuals have presumably learned the relevant skills and knowledge necessary to interact with children with special needs. However, there are also other dynamics at work. I have noticed that standards of practice may change with the dynamics of the group. Often when a new staff member is hired, there is a change in practice. If we have selected the individual carefully, we may find that quality actually improves. Unfortunately, some of the factors I look for in individuals are generally not things we can teach: good people skills, passion, respect for children, nurturing attitudes and knack for creative programming."

Kim, another director, found that much of her time was involved in supporting and challenging the staff to continually find new ways of doing things, to help find various ways to resolve conflicts and to actively provide real choices to all children.

Directors who were in centres with a high degree of support for inclusive care had very low staff turnover. The opposite was true of centres with low support. In one instance, the director reported that within a single year there had been a continual need to hire new staff and sixteen new individuals had been hired. She also indicated that the behaviour of the children changed drastically with the constant staff turnover.

All staff members interviewed readily identified that the director was a key individual in advocating and maintaining quality inclusive care.

4. Support for Staff

Staff concerns centred on these issues:

- Child–adult ratios—Often enhanced support is provided for individual children with a diagnosed need. One staff member, Vivian, stated: "Since funding is usually tied to diagnosed need, only children with high needs tend to get support. There are many children within our inclusive setting who have not been diagnosed and have similar high needs but do not get any support. In these cases we rely on a resource consultant who comes in once in a while to offer suggestions. This is really helpful, but what we need most is an extra pair of hands on the floor to help us cope. What do you do when you have three children who are throwing temper tantrums and another child who needs your help, and you have only four hands to cope? It can become very frustrating."
- Time relief—All staff members interviewed indicated that it was difficult to address the needs of all the children, confer with consultants or other specialists to help provide better programming for the children, meet the families' needs and meet the needs of regular programming during the daily schedule. One staff member, Charmaine, noted: "There are not enough hours in the day to do all the things we need to do. Also, we never have time to meet as a team. We need to find some way to function without continually spending our own time to meet. This can very quickly lead to resentment and to burnout."

5. Training of Staff

All interviewees were aware that training to work with children with special needs was not something that was universally mandated across Canada. All individuals expressed the belief that specialized training should be mandatory for all individuals working with children with special needs. They identified these areas of concern:

- Education—Vivian stated: "I feel that I do not know enough about how to deal with a child with special needs. I had only one course about special needs in my college diploma program. That was not enough to prepare me for this job.

Don't get me wrong—I love what I do, but I wish I could get more training to help the kids more."

- Additional training—Another staff member summed up the lack of supplementary training as follows: "I know that education is important. I have participated in training. I have obtained a certificate to work with children with special needs. I financed the additional training by myself. It does help me to do my job better, but do I get more money? Of course not! Quite frankly, I am getting tired of the lack of acknowledgment for my additional skills. I keep saying that I won't take any more training, but you know what? I always do."

- Ongoing training—As new children with special needs are accepted within programs, ongoing training may become necessary. Staff members indicated that they needed ongoing training to help them plan an appropriate environment, gain expertise to know what types of materials or equipment are needed and manage the group dynamics of a wide range of abilities and skills.

- Consultative support—Most staff members identified that the support received from a resource consultant or other specialists was very valuable. However, they identified a need for a more gradual transition to move from consultative support to independent handling of children within the program.

6. Provision of Therapy

Parents interviewed clearly identified the high need for resources to help the family cope with a variety of therapy needs. Parents identified the following issues:

- Difficulty of obtaining assessments—Janine and Rob suspected that there was a problem with their daughter. She seemed delayed in all her milestones. When they attempted to have their child assessed they were told that they should be patient and that the child was too young to be accurately assessed and would probably outgrow the problem.

- Long waiting lists—Janine and Rob believed that their child needed to be assessed immediately. They felt that the longer they waited, the more behind their daughter would be. They insisted on a referral to a child psychologist. They were referred but were told that the next available appointment was in nine months.

- High cost and lack of choice—Janine and Rob did not want to wait nine months. They decided to see if they could get a private referral. They found someone who could see their daughter within one week. When they inquired if they could get funding to pay for the private consultation, they were refused. They could not afford the cost themselves.

Often children in regular care need additional therapy such as physical or speech therapy. In most cases it is up to the family members to bring children to the various required therapy sessions. Several problems were identified:

- Disruption of family schedules—Many families were often unable to take time off work to take their children to the required doctors, specialists or therapists.

As a result, some of the children were not receiving all the help they needed. Other families found that the schedule added continual stress to family life.

- Disruption of program schedules—In some instances, staff reported that the children found it difficult to settle into the program because of the periodic absences of children who required additional therapy.
- Isolation—Some staff members indicated that they felt that the child's program seemed fragmented. Information sharing between agencies was often incomplete or non-existent. The staff felt that this made quality programming difficult.

7. Individual Program Planning

There was consensus that individual programming was needed for children with special needs. Several individuals pointed out that this should be a standard policy for all children. Some of the problem areas identified included these:

- Time—Many staff members indicated that while the development of an individual program plan was important, there was little time to develop an individual plan and to implement it.
- Nomenclature—Several individuals felt that a common professional vocabulary seemed to be lacking. Rachel summed up this point well: "We get very concerned about what to call a special plan for children with special needs. I have worked in the system for a long time. I have heard a number of terms used: functional program plan, developmental service plan, individual training plan, family service plan and so on. I think it is time that we get more concerned about the quality of what is in the plan and how it is implemented than what it is called. Additionally, it gets very confusing for non-professionals to sort through all the acronyms: IPP, IFP, FSP,..."
- Access to resource consultants—Interviewees noted that collaborative access to a resource consultant was not consistently available. Children who had been identified with special needs were most likely to receive help.

8. Families as Partners

All interviewees agreed that families needed to be involved in developing appropriate programs for children with special needs. However, disagreements were expressed about the ideal degree of involvement:

- Treating families as partners—Some felt that the family members did not have the experience or the knowledge to know what was best for their child. Nancy, a parent of a child with special needs, vehemently disagreed: "I do not understand the patronizing attitude of some professionals toward me and, I am sure, other parents. Who better than I to know what my child needs? I have been traipsing to every specialist conceivable since my son was an infant. I have read their reports, have disagreed with some, have sought second opinions, have read a lot about my child's disability and I live with my child for most of his day. I am truly the greatest expert on my son."

- Regular information sharing—All individuals agreed that information sharing was critical. In all cases information sharing was done in writing and through meetings. However, some professionals did not include family members in professional team meetings in the belief that family members would not understand the information presented. Some of the family members interviewed wanted to be included in professional meetings, while others did not.
- Program planning—The individuals interviewed, both family members and professionals, varied in their responses to the issue of involving parents in program planning. Some felt that family members should be full partners in all aspects of the child's program, while others felt that the professionals should handle programming, sharing only progress reports.

9. Social Interactions

All individuals interviewed agreed that social interactions among all children were critical. Problems identified were more concerned with how to handle three particular issues:

- Diversity—Concern was expressed about how to meet mandated diversity requirements within the child care setting. For example, some staff and directors identified the difficulty in providing appropriate role models for children with special needs. One commented: "Children with special needs often grow up in 'normal' families and attend care with children of 'normal' abilities. These children continually live in situations that identify them as different. It is sometimes difficult to foster a nurturing attitude among peers and adults that fosters the uniqueness of the child without the continual focus on the special need."
- Abilities—Some difficulty was identified among staff members in meeting the increased range of needs. This difficulty translates into the need to provide a greater range and variety of learning materials, take more care in organizing materials to challenge the developmental needs of all children, provide safety to actively explore the learning opportunities and gain additional skill in providing opportunities for active social interaction for all children.
- Communication—Staff noted that it was often difficult to receive appropriate training, resources and materials to meet the needs of various children. They expressed the belief that training outcomes should include increased competency in signing and augmentative communication techniques and devices.

10. Supportive Board Members

Board members are critical individuals to involve in efforts to achieve quality practices for inclusive care. Supportive board members are able to initiate the development and implementation of an appropriate philosophy and proactive policies that value and support quality inclusive care. Several issues were identified by staff, directors and board members interviewed:

A) STAFF MEMBERS' PERSPECTIVE Staff members identified that often the philosophy developed and the policies set had little connection with the realities of working with children and families on a daily basis. Jeremy, one staff member, summarized this viewpoint: "It is one thing to set a philosophy and policies, and it is another to try to work in this situation. So, sure, we advocate inclusive care and will not turn away any children. The reality is that we have turned away children because we do not have the training or resources to help the child and family. For example, we had a child that needed to be tube-fed. None of us knew how to do this, nor was any training opportunity available to learn the process. Additionally, our centre is very small. There is no room to set up an area in which we can do this. The child was turned away. I think it is too easy to state wonderful things in writing, but not so easy to follow up and actually implement them. Part of setting philosophies and polices should include strategies and resources to make sure that it is feasible to actually implement the expectations implied."

B) DIRECTORS' PERSPECTIVE Some of the directors indicated that it was difficult to get "good" board members and keep them. Often it was particularly difficult to encourage family members with children with special needs to participate on the board because they were already overwhelmed with the burden of coping with the demands made on their time. A failure to include family members could leave the board structure lacking in adequate representation of the perspectives of children with special needs.

C) BOARD MEMBERS' PERSPECTIVE The common problems identified by the board members interviewed were concerned with time, expertise and expectations:

- Time—All board members interviewed noted that they did not regret the commitment made to sit on the board. Most, however, stated that they found it difficult to balance their family, work and volunteer commitments.
- Expertise—Several board members indicated that they wished that more parents and professionals dealing with children with special needs could be part of the board representations. One board member stated: "Although I have a child with special needs, I am continually astounded at the variety of special needs that are evident in my daughter's program. My child has a physical disability. My husband and I have learned how to make adaptations to her learning environment and are very happy to interact with the staff and board to offer our help. However, most of the needs in this program seem to be social and emotional. I wish I had more experience to help. As a board, we have tried to recruit individuals with that expertise but have been unsuccessful. As a result I sometimes think that we set philosophies and policies that may not be in the best interests of the children or the families."

- Expectations—Often board members seem to feel that too many expectations are placed on their time. Jonathan, another board member, commented: "I agreed to sit on the board to develop policies, help evaluate the program to ensure congruency between the program and our mission statement, and possibly volunteer for committee work as needed. I now find that it seems expected that I am at the bingo hall to raise funds every month and that I am on a program review committee to identify needed program adaptations identified in the last evaluation of the centre. I have also been asked to assume an executive position because one of our board members resigned. My one evening a month for three hours is now four evenings a month and sometimes more. Most meetings last for more than three hours. I do not have time for this in my schedule. I will not be able to return to the board for another term."

11. Transition from Centre to Elementary School

Most individuals interviewed indicated that there was a complete break in the child's life from the early childhood setting to the elementary school. In most cases the information about the child's diagnosis, progress and treatment strategies was lost. Most school boards re-evaluated the child upon entry into the elementary school system. Family members were concerned about the time this took. Mary, a mother of a child diagnosed with ADD, indicated that it took six months before any action was taken. Mary tried to share previous assessments with the teacher but was told that the school board would initiate its own diagnosis. Mary said: "By the time they got around to it, Jimmy was worse than he had ever been. He had adjusted so well at the day care. He was actually making progress. Now it seems nothing helps. I think that by the time he got help, it was too late. They moved him into a special class for kids with behaviour problems by the middle of grade one. It was so frustrating and we felt so helpless. He is now in grade three and has been identified as a problem child."

What can you do to play a greater role in obtaining high-quality inclusive care?

a) Utilize opportunities to get information from different perspectives. Attend board meetings, staff meetings or parent groups.
b) Become skilled in active listening skills. Learn to listen to the intent of the message rather than from a personal perspective.
c) Become knowledgeable about quality issues through personal reading, courses or workshops.
d) Utilize the resources in your community to become more knowledgeable about the issues of quality care. Resources could include libraries, faculty at colleges or universities, family members with children with special needs, local support groups or resource consultants and other professionals.

Diagnosis and Assessment

The survey identified several problems related to labelling, type and number of disabilities; misdiagnosis; and cultural expectations:

1. Labelling

The process of **labelling** a child involves two aspects:

- Assessment or diagnosis—The child is assessed to identify level of functioning in all developmental domains, or to identify specific medical or psychological problems.
- Application of a label—The label is applied as a result of the assessment or diagnosis. Examples of labels include learning disability, ADD, mental retardation and autism.

In most jurisdictions in Canada, the process of assessment and labelling may result in funding or programming for the child. Funding depends on the label applied. Additional purposes of labelling include:

- Providing a direction to programming
- Identifying appropriate resources or ideas
- Identifying potential approaches to implement

In addition to the problems of labelling identified on page 72, the following disadvantages were identified by interviewees:

- From a teacher: "The label provides you with a general idea about what difficulties the child may have, such as reading disability. You may suspect that the child will find it difficult to learn to read. [The label] does not tell you where the difficulties lie or what strategies to use to teach the child to read. You still need to observe the child in order to utilize appropriate strategies. That will work for that individual child."
- From an early childhood educator: "I have found that the label can be used to excuse our inability to cope with the child's behaviours. For example, I remember one child who had a number of behaviour problems. He was referred for assessment and diagnosed as ADHD. Once it was identified that he had a disorder that could be diagnosed, the attitude seemed to change from trying to cope with the behaviour to using the label as an excuse for not being able to cope. I have actually heard a staff member say, 'How do they expect us to cope with this child? He is impossible to deal with. He needs specialized help.' The child's behaviour had not changed but the staff attitude toward him had."
- From a psychologist: "I think there is too much attention paid to labels. Often the label sticks and follows the child through life. We should emphasize that a child is a child and that every child has some special needs. We need to deal with the child, not the label."

From the Author

I had returned to work after a maternity leave, having obtained a new position as a learning resource teacher. I remember my first case conference. Everyone used a number of acronyms such as DAP, IEP and IFP. I didn't have a clue what they were talking about. I felt so stupid. After the conference, I did some research on the new terminology so I wouldn't be in a similar position again.

- From a resource teacher: "Early childhood educators and family members already know the child's needs best. Sufficient documentation on a child's needs already exists for a diagnosis (IPP/IFSP). This should be adequate to provide needed resources to help the child, the family and the centre without trying to label the child."

2. Misdiagnosis

Several individuals expressed concern about the increased number of children diagnosed with behavioural types of disabilities. One director of a program identified that there had been an increased number of children diagnosed with autism. She said that half of the children within their program had been diagnosed with autism. Other individuals—both staff members and directors of programs—noted that more children were being diagnosed with ADD or ADHD. They expressed concern about the correctness of these diagnoses and wondered if a mere diagnosis of mistaken behaviours might be have been more accurate in some cases.

Cindy, one director, observed: "I have had several children diagnosed with autism in my program. Two children certainly demonstrated behaviours consistent with autism. However, two of the boys did not. Initially both boys demonstrated very high activity levels. Once they had settled into the program, the activity levels dropped, and I really saw very little evidence of any behaviour that even remotely resembles autism. Both boys maintained consistent eye contact, used language appropriate to their age group, sat on an adult's lap to read a story, interacted socially in a similar manner to their peers and maintained activities of choice for age-appropriate periods of time. These are not normal behaviours of children with autism. I think this diagnosis was definitely based on mistaken behaviours."

Some of the individuals interviewed also addressed the controversial issue of medicating children to control their behaviour. Generally there was agreement that medication at times was necessary, such as for childhood depression. However, individuals expressed concern that medication was an external control and did not help the child achieve self-control.

3. Assessment Strategies

Formal assessment is usually provided by professionals who are trained to assess young children, such as psychologists, psychiatrists, speech and language pathologists, occupational therapists or pediatricians. These services are often hard to access for families with children with special needs. Penelope, a mother with twins with special needs, stated: "I knew something was wrong with my twins. They were just not developing as they should. At first I thought that I was not doing something right. But when I saw my doctor he agreed [with my parenting approach]. Then began the long search for answers—we went from specialist to specialist. I was lucky because my doctor referred us, so the services were free. Nothing conclusive was discovered, however. We were told that perhaps it was a developmental delay and that time and stimulation might mitigate the problems. On the advice of our physician we started an infant stimulation program. I am so thankful that we had such a good doctor."

Appropriate assessment tools for staff members to use are based on observation. These tools, such as the Brigance inventory, the Portage guide or the DISC assessment, are expensive to purchase and require some training to successfully implement and interpret. Additionally, the tools compare the subjects with children of normal development. The comparison does not indicate the type of treatment that is required. Often, as a result, the child's program becomes based on meeting special needs rather than active play. Janice, a mother, noted: "It really bothers me when the teachers tell me all about my son's needs and how they will ensure that the program is built to strengthen his needs. He is just a little boy. He needs to actively play. I feel learning through play is much more appropriate for him. He will learn to make choices, solve problems, play with his peers and build on his strengths."

The most appropriate assessment strategies to use in early childhood settings are observations. Interviewees identified the problems that prevent adequate observation:

- Insufficient time—Many of the staff members felt that they did not have time to observe and record children's behaviours because they were too busy interacting with children.
- Insufficient experience—Staff members identified that they needed training to help them select appropriate tools and interpret what they had observed.
- Insufficient staffing—Staff felt that ideally all children should be observed, not just children with special needs, but given present resources this was felt to be an unrealistic expectation.

What can you do to improve the assessment process?

a) Become more knowledgeable about the various assessments that are implemented—Ask questions of the individuals doing the testing. Ask them to explain why they are using a particular tool and what the advantages and disadvantages might be.

b) Increase your skill in personal observations—You can do this by utilizing the variety of tools presented in the various chapters of this text.

Cultural Expectations

As it does in all experiences, culture plays a large part in how children are diagnosed and treated. On executive director indicated that Italian cultures are much more tolerant of active children, and as a result fewer children are labelled as ADHD or ADD than in the US and Canada. In fact, there has been an increase of 200 to 300 percent in the number of prescriptions, such as Ritalin and Prozac, used by preschoolers in the US (Bergquist, 2000). Individuals interviewed indicated that they felt that similar increases have taken place in Canada.

In some areas in Canada, there is a refusal to label young children. It is felt that as children grow and mature, their behaviour may change. However, often in these jurisdictions, funding is not available without the labelling.

What can you do to determine the extent to which culture influences diagnosis and treatment in your community?

a) Become informed about the incidence of various types of disabilities diagnosed in your community. Are the numbers comparable to national averages? If different, ask questions to identify why there are differences.
b) Become informed about the advantages and disadvantages of labelling children.
c) Interview the family of an older child with special needs. What challenges have they faced? What recommendations would they make?

Funding of Programs

In Canada diversity is celebrated, but this attitude is not evident in early childhood settings. Early childhood programs are not funded for optimal growth and development. As discussed previously, there are a number of barriers to obtaining funding to ensure equal access for children with special needs. Because of insufficient funding for programs, necessary adaptations of equipment and modifications of the environment are often not undertaken. But worse yet, the time children with special needs spend in centre-based programs is often reduced. Many programs offer half-day services only. One director stated: "We have a large waiting list for children with special needs. To accommodate that need, we offer half-day programs for these children. It is not ideal, but at least we can provide services to more children with special needs."

What can you do to advocate better funding for programs?

a) Become informed about how children with special needs are funded in your area and in other areas.
b) Develop advocacy skills to advocate for increased funding.
c) Participate in fundraising events in your community.

Education of Staff

Training standards across Canada vary greatly. Interviewees identified an overall lack of training concerning accommodation, adaptation, social-emotional disabilities and how to include family members as partners. Lack of training for staff was seen to lead to a variety of problems:

- Higher burnout rates
- Decreased capacity for coping with diverse abilities of children
- Inability to identify relevant resources and materials
- Decreased ability to manage the variety of behaviours demonstrated in child care settings
- Higher frustration levels
- Inability to interact appropriately with families
- Diminished overall self-confidence in personal child guidance techniques

What can you do to attain adequate training and avoid these problems?

a) Search out opportunities to gain additional education, such as courses at universities or colleges, conferences and workshops.
b) Develop a resource library containing articles, newspaper clippings, journals and internet references.

Poverty

Poverty has a long-lasting detrimental effect on children's growth and development. In recent years, child poverty has increased in Canada. "Since 1989, when the House of Commons passed a unanimous resolution to 'seek to eliminate child poverty by the year 2000,' poverty among children has increased by 21 percent. One in six children, or 1 139 000 children, still lives in poverty in Canada" (Campaign 2000, 2000: 1). Children with special needs living in poverty are doubly affected. According to the Urban Poverty Consortium of Waterloo Region:

> "Poverty brings with it many costs that have a long-term influence on children:
>
> - Poor nutrition, hunger
> - Family stress, parental depression, reduced supports and family conflict
> - Fewer resources for learning, lower quality child care, financial barriers for activities
> - Crowded and dilapidated housing problems, homelessness, problem neighbourhoods, frequent moves, lack of safe places to play" (The Urban Poverty Consortium of Waterloo Region, 2000: 3).

The result of poverty on children is evident in children's abilities to learn. Most often this is a long-term effect, unless the conditions of poverty can be reversed. Poverty itself may be a contributing factor in diagnoses such as special needs.

"Poverty has a negative influence on learning. In comparison with other children, children living in poverty have:

- Lower IQ levels
- Lower math and reading abilities
- Shorter attention spans
- Greater speech delays
- Vocabulary limitations

Poverty during childhood is related to poor intellectual outcomes and general learning or overall educational attainment. This means:

- Lower average grades
- Fewer years of education
- Lower rates of going to college or university
- Lower adult productivity (as measured by annual earnings, wages and work hours)" (The Urban Poverty Consortium of Waterloo Region, 2000: 7)

In addition, children who live in poverty experience fewer recreational activities. Children rarely have opportunities to participate in organized activities such as swimming, physical activity programs for family members and children, organized sports or clubs or community groups such as Beavers or Guides. As a result poverty often acts as an exclusionary factor in the child's life.

What can you do about the effects of poverty on childhood development?

a) Learn about the effects of poverty on children.
b) Research ways in which the effects of poverty can be mitigated, such as providing nutritious meals throughout the day.
c) Join community groups to advocate against poverty.
d) Become aware of and support programs to mitigate the effects of poverty, such as Better Beginnings and Healthy Babies Initiatives.

From the Author   **Reflection**

I wanted to end the text on a positive note. I wanted to share many of the positive feelings and attitudes that individuals talked about across Canada. I believe that with increased awareness, we will also forge change. I have seen many families, professionals and community members striving to make Canada a better place for children with special needs. In my lifetime we have seen the demise of the horrific institutions that children with special needs were once placed in. I believe that the future will bring additional positive changes.

Attitude

In this section, I will provide quotes of various individuals who have cared for, or lived with, children with special needs.

Parents of child born with Down's syndrome:

"We were so excited about our son's birth. I couldn't wait to hold my new son in my arms. It was a profound shock when the doctor told us that there was something wrong with our baby. After the first shock wore off, I just wanted to hold him. I remember that first time I held him. I remember the strong feelings of joy to look on my son's face. So what if he wasn't perfect? As the years passed, we have never regretted having Darren. He has taught us many lessons, such as patience, tolerance for others and acceptance of individual differences. Darren has been a blessing in our lives."

Staff member:

"I find it highly rewarding to work with children with special needs. It gives me a sense of accomplishment and a sense that I am making a difference."

Director:

"I have worked in many different settings, but I must admit that I most enjoy working in inclusive settings. The rewards are so rich. I love to see the acceptance and tolerance of individual differences that grow between the children and the families who attend the centre. It is such a win, win and win for everyone."

School-aged child:

"I knew that there were children around who didn't act or look the same as the rest of us, but I had never really met one. We had a new classmate, Sheilagh, who had cerebral palsy. At first, I tended to avoid her. She looked so different. Our teacher was really great. She noticed that some of us were rather hesitant. She helped Sheilagh explain to us about her condition. I never had really thought of her as a person like me. After she had told us about herself, I began to realize how funny and brave she was. We became good friends. I began to realize that she wasn't so different from me after all."

Licensing professional:

"I have been so pleased to see a gradual change in our community. Twenty years ago, when I first started my position as a licensing officer, children with special needs went to one preschool for children with special needs. When the centre first closed, there was a lot of resistance to including these children. Today I am proud to say that all of our centres accept children with special needs. I am not aware of one instance in which a child has been refused access to centre-based care in our community."

Learning Resource Consultant:

"I just love my job. It is so great to go into a centre and support the staff, family and child with special needs. I have found most staff members very open to suggestions and very willing to try to new things. It is refreshing to see all children play together. After all, we are a society that embraces diversity."

SUMMARY

Although there are still many issues involved in caring for children with special needs, great strides have been made over the last century. For the most part, segregated preschool settings have disappeared. Most jurisdictions in Canada embrace the concept of inclusive care. This means that children can attend the centre of their choice, with the peers from their community, in a community setting. Additionally, there is abundant research available that increases awareness about the benefits of inclusive care. As a result, more proactive policies are being developed in some centres and jurisdictions across Canada.

KEY POINTS

Equitable access
- Lack of space—One out of eight child care centres does not accept children with special needs; long waiting lists
- Proportionate care—Children with special needs in proportion to their occurrence in general population
- Appropriate policies—Lack of proactive policies

Quality care
- Physical environment—Lack of space for adaptations; lack of funding to make relevant modifications
- Equipment and materials—Difficult to obtain; specialized equipment for few children; problem to store bulky equipment; expensive to purchase
- Role of director—Attracting and maintaining suitable staff; supporting role to staff; leadership role
- Support for staff—Concerns about child–adult ratios; need for time relief from meetings and planning
- Training of staff—Lack of training opportunities; no support for additional training
- Provision of therapy—Difficult to initiate assessment; long waiting lists; few choices; disruption of schedules; lack of coordination between therapy and child care program
- Individual program plan—Need time to develop; standard nomenclature; access to resource consultants

- Families as partners—Attitudinal differences with respect to degree of involvement, type and manner of information sharing and family involvement in program planning
- Social interactions between children—Difficult to implement because of lack of role models, large diversity of skills and abilities and various communication methods
- Supportive board members—Lack of connection between setting policies and philosophies and daily program implementation; difficulty in attracting and maintaining board members; time involved in volunteer role of a board member; lack of expertise on board; too many expectations of board members
- Transition from centre to elementary school—Re-evaluation of child upon entry to school

Diagnosis and assessment
- Labelling—Tied to funding; labels fail to provide programming strategies and provide excuses for lack of programming; child stuck with label; focus on disability not programming needs
- Misdiagnosis—Increased number of ADD/ADHD children diagnosed; controversy of medicating children
- Assessment strategies—Formal assessment by trained professionals; training needs of staff to use informal tools and observation; lack of time and experience to implement and interpret

Cultural expectations

- Role of culture to determine how children are diagnosed and treated
- Variation among cultures in diagnosis of behavioural disorders

Funding of programs

- Need to provide equality of access to children with special needs

Education of staff

- Lack of training leads to burnout, decreased coping ability, decreased ability to procure relevant resources, decreased ability to manage a variety of

behaviours effectively, higher frustration levels, decreased ability to interact with families and overall lack of confidence

Poverty

- Compounded influence on children with special needs
- Influences development—Through poor nutrition, increased stress, access to fewer resources and poor living conditions
- Negative effect on learning—Lower IQ, lower math and reading abilities, shorter attention span, greater speech delays, limited vocabulary
- Fewer recreational opportunities

EXERCISES

1. Review the definitions of inclusive care on page 360. Identify how each definition might place limits on or enhance inclusive care.

2. Conduct a survey of your community. Consider the following questions:
   a) How many centres accept children with special needs?
   b) How many spaces are available to children with special needs?
   c) What is the ratio of children with special needs to other children in the program?
   d) What policies are in place to ensure equal access to programs for children with special needs?

3. You are a staff member of a program that has previously not had children with physical abilities enrolled. Therefore, no physical adaptations have been made to the play spaces. You are on a ground floor and ramps are provided for all entries into the building. You are going to accept a child who is in a wheelchair. What types of adaptations need to be made to the playrooms, washrooms and play yard to accommodate this child?

4. Look over some of the resources listed for children for special needs, such as the website at www.irsc.org.

Identify some additional resources you might need for:
   a) Physical disabilities
   b) Social-emotional disabilities
   c) Cognitive disabilities
   d) Communication disorders

5. What types of support are needed to increase the effectiveness of child care centre directors? Staff? Board members?

6. Identify strategies that might be used to overcome barriers to accepting families as partners within all aspects of the program.

7. What are some strategies that could be developed to provide appropriate social interactions in settings of diverse abilities and skills?

8. What strategies might be developed to decrease the lack of transition from centre-based care to the elementary school system?

9. Describe some of the problems associated with diagnosis and assessment of young children.

10. Explain why the effects of poverty are compounded for a child with special needs.

11. Reflect on the attitudinal statements made by the various individuals on page 378.
    a) Which reflections strike a core within you? Identify why.
    b) Are there any reflections that you do not understand? Explain why not?

RESOURCES

Advocacy
**snow.utoronto.ca/resources/disability/
disorg.html**

Assessment
**www.childpsychologist.com/testing/
preschool.htm**

www.ericdigests.org/1996-3/preschool.htm

www.oafccd.com/factshee/fact15.htm

Inclusive care and education in Canada
www.childcarecanada.org/pt98/fur.html

**www.campaign2000.ca/ci/issue/
SocialInclusion_ISSUE.pdf**

Medicating young children
**www.sciencefriday.com/pages/2000/Mar/
hour1_030300.html**

Poverty
**www.campaign2000.ca/rc/rc02/
NOV02reportcard.pdf**

www.waterlooregion.org/poverty/talk/6.html

Canadian Policy Research Network
www.cprn.com/en

REFERENCES

Bergquist, C. (2000). Hour One: Medicating Preschoolers/ADHD. Science Friday [online]. Available at www.sciencefriday.com/pages/2000/Mar/hour1_030300.html (3-4-2005).

Campaign 2000 (2000). Poverty Amidst Prosperity: Building a Canada for All Children. Campaign 2000 [online]. Available at www.campaign2000.ca/rc/rc02/NOV02reportcard.pdf (4-3-2005).

Canadian Council on Social Development (2000). *Children and Youth with Special Needs*. Ottawa, ON: Canadian Council on Social Development.

Goleman, H., Doherty, G., Lero, D., LaGrange, A., & Tougas, J. (2000). *You Bet I Care Caring and Learning Environments Quality in Child Carte Centres Across Canada* Guelph University, ON: Centre for Families, Work and Well-Being.

Harms, T., Clifford, R., & Cryer, D. (1998). *Early Childhood Environment Rating Scale*. Revised Edition. New York, NY: Teachers College Press.

Hope Irwin, S. (2002). Including All Children. Child & Family Canada [online]. Available at www.cfc-efc.ca/docs/cccf/00017_en.htm (18-12-2004).

Hope Irwin, S., Lero, D., & Brophy, K. (2000). *A Matter of Urgency: Including Children with Special Needs in Child Care in Canada*. Wreck Cove, NS: Breton Books.

Hope Irwin, S., Lero, D., & Brophy, K. (2004). *Inclusion: The Next Generation in Child Care in Canada*. Wreck Cove. NS: Breton Books.

The Council for Exceptional Children (1997). Inclusion Defined. Council for Exceptional Children [online]. Available at www.projectexceptional.org/pdf/inclusion_defined.pdf (5-1-2005).

The Urban Poverty Consortium of Waterloo Region (2000). Let's Talk About Poverty: Fact Sheet 6. waterlooregion.org [online]. Available at www.waterlooregion.org/poverty/talk/6.html (4-3-2005).

Valentine, F. (2001). *Enabling Citizenship: Full Inclusion of Children with Disabilities and Their Parents* (Rep. No. F/13). Ottawa, ON: Canadian Policy and Research Network.

Glossary

Active listening Listening to the content of a message without personal bias and clarifying the intent of the message when the meaning is unclear or to ensure that the meaning is clear.

Addictive behaviours Habits that are out of control, with a resulting impact on a person's health (Insel, & Roth, 1999: 312).

Age-appropriate Appropriate for the chronological age.

Age-appropriate practices Practices that are appropriate for the chronological age of the child, irrespective of his or her developmental level. For example, a four-year-old with a developmental delay of two years should be playing with toys that are appropriate for a four-year-old but one with the appropriate developmental skill level.

American Sign Language A visual-spatial language that uses gestures, facial expressions such as eyebrow and lip movements and the surrounding space to communicate.

Anti-bias "An anti-biased approach means taking a stand against unfair treatment associated with one of the areas of diversity where bias may exist" (Saderman Hall et al., 1995: 2).

Anxiety state A fear of something that might happen in the future.

Aphasia An inability to communicate effectively using verbal language because of difficulty in comprehension or production difficulties.

Apraxia An inability to communicate verbally because the individual cannot effectively use the muscles that control speech sounds.

Associative play Children share materials and ideas but may continue to be engaged in individual play activity.

Asthma A condition that obstructs the bronchial passages by narrowing or swelling of the tubes or by clogging of the tubes with mucus.

Attention deficit hyperactivity disorder (ADHD) Behaviour is characterized by a short attention span, distractibility, inattentiveness, impulsiveness and increased physical activity.

Augmentative devices Devices that help an individual to communicate a message, such as symbol boards and talking computers.

Augmentative/alternative communication (AAC) Any device or method that improves the ability of a child with communication impairment to communicate effectively" (Ballinger, 1999: 1).

Autism Pervasive developmental disorder leading to social and communicative problems.

Base line A method used to determine how often behaviour has occurred, prior to formal intervention strategies.

Bias "Bias is a point of view or inclination that manifests itself through favoritism, dislike, or fear toward someone because of that person's particular looks, behaviour, or lifestyle. A bias can be conveyed to another through nonverbal, verbal, and physical interactions. In other words, one's point of view is clearly reflected by one's attitude and actions" (Saderman Hall et al., 1995: 2).

Childhood schizophrenia "Unlike children with autism, those with schizophrenia typically have a later age of onset of their problem, show less intellectual impairment, display less severe social and language deficits, develop hallucinations and delusions as they get older, and experience periods of remission and relapse" (Mash & Wolfe, 1999: 411).

Closed materials Materials that usually provide only one effective solution to completing a task, such as puzzles, dominoes and nesting cups

Complex units Activity units containing four play spaces to encourage group play such as sand, water or carpentry activities

Concrete operational thinking "Children begin more and more to use logic and mental operations to understand situations and to think about how things work" (Schickedanz et al., 2001: 439)

Conduct disorders Patterns of behaviour characterized, for instance, by aggressiveness toward other children or materials; disruptive behaviours such as constant interruptions; throwing temper tantrums when thwarted; or withdrawal from the situation

Constructive play Children use materials or objects to create something

Cooperative Play Play toward a common goal that involves planning, role designation and sharing of ideas and materials

Critical periods of brain development Times when "the developing brain is best able to absorb language, any language... This ability to learn a language will be more difficult, and perhaps less efficient or effective, if these critical periods are allowed to pass without exposure to language" (National Institute on Deafness and Other Communication Disorders, 2001: 2)

Cystic fibrosis A genetic condition that affects the respiratory and digestive systems

Decibels The smallest measurable difference in loudness intensity between sounds

Deictic gestures Gestures used by infants to communicate intent, such as pointing to or reaching for a desired object

Developmentally-appropriate practice "Refers to applying child development knowledge in making thoughtful and appropriate decisions about early childhood program practices—the understanding that "programs designed for young children be based on what is known about young children" (Bredekamp et al., 1997: v) (Gestwicki, 1999: 6)

Divergent thinking Ability to think of a variety of ways to solve a problem

Dramatic play Children create imaginary roles and situations with or without props

Duration count A record of how long a behaviour lasts

Easy reading books Books with large pictures and few words; pictures illustrate the meaning of words

Emergent curriculum A program for children based on the observations of children's interests, strengths and needs. The learning experiences emerge from these observations.

Emotional and behavioural disorders Children with these disorders may exhibit feelings such as sadness, fear, anger, guilt or anxiety that may alter the way they behave and interact with others.

Expressive language Expressing thoughts, desires or ideas through verbal language, signing, body language, or by using symbols such as pictures

Eye-hand coordination Ability to reach and grasp intended object

Fetal alcohol syndrome Brain disorder involving physical and mental birth defects developing during pregnancy, caused by mother's consumption of alcohol during pregnancy; central nervous system involvement, growth retardation and characteristic facial features

Finger spelling A spelling method in which each letter of the alphabet has a corresponding sign, and words are spelled out letter by letter

Full-spectrum fluorescent lighting with ultraviolet enhancement Type of artificial lighting closest to natural sunlight

Functional play Children practise skills through repeatedly interacting with objects, other individuals and language

Holophrastic speech One-word utterances representing questions or statements; dependent on the inflection pattern used

Hyperactivity Condition characterized by higher motor activity levels than normal for individuals of a given age

Hyperkinetic Denoting behaviours that involve increased energy and movement

Hypertonic Muscle tone is excessively tense

Impaired health A disease or condition—such as diabetes, asthma, allergies, cystic fibrosis or muscular dystrophy—that affects the daily functioning of the individual's life

Intrinsic motivation Motivation that originates from the individual

Joint attention Child looks at an object, points to it, then looks back at the adult to focus the adult's attention on the desired object

Kinetic Behaviours associated with the energy of movement

Labelling Involves two aspects: assessment or diagnosis (the child is assessed to identify level of functioning in all developmental domains, or to identify specific medical or psychological problems) and application of the label (the label—for example, "learning disability," "ADD," "mental retardation" or "autism"—is applied as a result of the assessment or diagnosis)

Matching activities Exact duplicates of objects are placed side by side, such as two large bears or two dominoes

Mental representations Mental pictures

Morphology Description of how words are built in language

Multimodal communication Using more than one method of communication, such as verbal and signing

Muscular dystrophy An inherited condition, typically occurring in boys, that is associated with the degeneration of muscle fibre

Myelination Formation of a protective sheath around nerve cells to improve transmission of impulses

Non-compliant oppositional defiant disorder A consistently negative pattern of behaviour in which children may act with hostility—physical, verbal or both—and openly refuse to comply with expectations

One-to-one correspondence The process of assigning one object to another, such as one spoon to one cup.

Onlooker play Child watches others play without interacting

Open-ended materials Materials that provide children with a variety of ways to use them, such as blocks, paint and beads

Orthopedic condition A condition that involves the skeleton, joints and muscles

Overextension Using single words to represent broad categories such as "dog" for all animals that have a tail and four legs

Parallel play Children play side by side, using similar materials, but without interacting with each other

Paraphrase Repeat what has been said in one's own words. Start with statements similar to "I understand that…" or "I believe you said…"

Pararead Repeat to yourself what you have read. You might write it down in your own words. Check what you have written against the original. If in doubt, clarify your perception in person.

Patterning Creation of a pattern that is repetitive, such as ABAB or red bear, blue bear, red bear, blue bear

Phobia A persistent and irrational fear expressed against an object, event, animal or person

Phoneme The smallest unit of speech sound

Phonetics A language system that breaks spoken language down into vocal sounds; used to read and spell

Phonology The system that builds sounds into words

Physical communication An individual's ability to transmit signals by facial expressions and other body language, such as shrugging the shoulders or using hand movements. Physical communications are culturally determined.

Pragmatics Refers to how language is used. Language usage changes with the context of a situation.

Prefixes Part of speech placed in front of a word to change the word's meaning, such as in- or re-

Preoperational thinking Children begin to demonstrate knowledge of the world through symbols such as words. Thinking is inflexible and tied to situations.

Proto-words Verbalizations that sound like words and are accepted as words, such as "da-da-da" for "daddy."

Read-aloud books Books that adults read to children

Receptive communication An individual's ability to understand what has been transmitted through verbal communication, body language and/or other means such as symbolized messages or signing

Receptive language Understanding the message that has been communicated through speech, signing or symbols such as written words

Representational gestures Gestures used to symbolize an object, a request or an event, such as supporting the side of the head with two hands to indicate tiredness

Representational study Study conducted on a sampling of day care centres in pre-selected regions as opposed to all day care centres in all regions. The outcomes of the study are then generalized as representative of all of Canada.

Research books Books that encourage children to find information for themselves

Risk factors Include biological and environmental conditions that may increase the likelihood of problems in development—physical, social, emotional and cognitive.

Scaffolding The process of providing and gradually removing external support for learning

Scribe Someone who listens and writes down exactly what the child says

Scribe centre Area to which children can go to dictate a story

Semantics Word meaning

Sensory motor stage Learning involves exploring the learning environment through the use of all the senses

Seriation Activity in which materials are lined up in order according to size (such as small bears to large bears)

Signed English Every word in the English language has a corresponding sign. Signed English is similar to spoken English.

Simple units Single play spaces to encourage individual play, such as working on a puzzle, reading a book or painting activities

Sociodramatic play Occurs when two or more children are engaged in dramatic play

Solitary play Play alone without interacting with others

Sorting Activities in which a number of materials with similar characteristics are placed together, such as collecting all the red bears on a red tray

Spastic cerebral palsy Refers to children who have suffered damage to the motor cortex of the brain. These children will have difficulty controlling voluntary movement. The condition is characterized by slow and difficult movement, poor coordination and weak, hypertonic (excessively tense) muscle tone.

Spina bifida A defect in the vertebrae that protect the spinal cord. Effects include neurological damage that results in delays in or impairment of growth and development, paralysis of the lower body, impeding the ability to walk without assistive devices, and some perceptual and cognitive disabilities.

Suffixes Parts of speech placed at the end of a word, such as -ly or -ness

Super units Activity units containing eight play spaces to encourage individual or group play such as dramatic or block play

Symbolic play Children use an action or object to represent something else

Syntax The way words are put together to form phrases, clauses or sentences and the connection of the elements of language into an orderly system (grammar)

Telegraphic speech Utterances that resemble sentences but are expressed only in essential two-to-three-word phrases such as "Want milk!"

Tourette's syndrome A condition characterized by involuntary muscle movement such as sporadic twitches or tics

Trial-and-error learning Trying different techniques until one that works is found

Underextension One word is used to represent many meanings, such as "hat" as a general term to mean all types of hats

Visual acuity "Refers to how well the elements of a pattern can be seen by someone at a specific distance" (Schickedanz et al., 2001: 95)

Visual figure ground Ability to pick out individual items from a background.

APPENDIX A

SECTION 1

The SpeciaLink Child Care Inclusion Practices Profile

"The *SpeciaLink Inclusion Child Care Practices Profile* and the *SpeciaLink Child Care Inclusion Principles Scale* are tools for assessing inclusion quality in child care centres. Used together, they provide a picture of sustainable and evolving inclusion quality—an emerging issue as more children with special needs attend community-based centres and as inclusion pioneers leave their centres and a new generation of directors and early childhood educators take on the challenge."

The SpeciaLink Child Care Inclusion Practices Profile and the SpeciaLink Child Care Inclusion Principles Scale (Final Workshop Version, May 2005) by Sharon Hope Irwin (SpeciaLink: The National Centre for Child Care Inclusion). Reprinted with permission.

Recommendations for Inclusive Care, from Sharon Hope Irwin, Donna S. Lero and Kathleen Brophy: Highlights From Inclusion: The Next Generation in Child Care in Canada *(SpeciaLink: The National Centre for Child Care Inclusion), pp. 23-25. Reprinted with permission.*

Practice 1: Physical Environment and Special Needs.

Inadequate 1	Minimal 3	Score: 1 2 3	Good 5	Excellent 7 4 5 6 7
1.1 ☐ Y ☐ N No modifications for children with special needs.	3.1 ☐ Y ☐ N Minor modifications (e.g., placement of furniture).		5.1 ☐ Y ☐ N Major permanent modifications (e.g., ramps; step-up changing table).	7.1 ☐ Y ☐ N Universal design principles are evident throughout*
1.2 ☐ Y ☐ N Building entrance and/or classroom entrance not accessible.	3.2 ☐ Y ☐ N Some classroom areas are accessible.		5.2 ☐ Y ☐ N Many classroom areas are accessible.	7.2 ☐ Y ☐ N All classroom areas are accessible, as are washroom, coatroom and hallways.
1.3 ☐ Y ☐ N Classroom is too noisy and/or too bright or too dim.	3.3 ☐ Y ☐ N Some efforts made to soften noise and light.		5.3 ☐ Y ☐ N Many efforts made to ensure that noise and light are appropriate.	7.3 ☐ Y ☐ N Sound and light are at appropriate levels.
1.4 ☐ Y ☐ N Playground entrance not accessible.	3.4 ☐ Y ☐ N Some playground areas are accessible.		5.4 ☐ Y ☐ N Many playground areas are accessible.	7.4 ☐ Y ☐ N All playground areas are accessible.

* Universal design principles are part of a concept of design, right from the beginning, that embodies characteristics that make a physical environment accessible to all people. Hallways are wide enough for wheelchairs, bathrooms are accessible, kitchen counters are reachable. At its best, universal design is so well done that adaptations are invisible. There is no ramp, because the threshold of the building is at ground level. The field of universal design is opening up rapidly, as a large proportion of our adult population ages— and wants to remain active and independent. We should expect no less for our youngest children.

"Some" means at least 3 interest areas are accessible; "Some efforts" means at least 3 examples are evident. "Many" means at least 5 interest areas are accessible; "Many efforts" means at least 5 examples are evident.

Comments:

Practice 2: Equipment and Materials.

Inadequate 1	Minimal 3	Score: 1 2 3 Good 5	4 5 6 7 Excellent 7
1.1 ☐ Y ☐ N No adaptations or special equipment for children with special needs.	**3.1** ☐ Y ☐ N Some* adapted typical toys and specialized equipment for children with special needs.	**5.1** ☐ Y ☐ N Many* adapted typical toys and specialized equipment for children with special needs.	**7.1** ☐ Y ☐ N Equipment and materials are individualized to meet unique needs. Universal design principles are evident throughout.
1.2 ☐ Y ☐ N No adapted gross motor equipment available for children with mobility, coordination and sensory issues.	**3.2** ☐ Y ☐ N Some gross motor equipment adapted for children with limited mobility, coordination, and sensory issues.	**5.2** ☐ Y ☐ N Many items of gross motor equipment adapted for children with mobility, coordination and sensory issues.	**7.2** ☐ Y ☐ N Substantial gross motor equipment adapted for children with mobility, coordination and sensory issues.
	3.3 ☐ Y ☐ N At least 1 example of assistive technology is evident.**	**5.3** ☐ Y ☐ N At least 3 examples of assistive technology are evident.	**7.3** ☐ Y ☐ N At least 5 examples of assistive technology are evident.
	3.4 ☐ Y ☐ N Adapted and assistive equipment occasionally*** used in regular routines and activities.	**5.4** ☐ Y ☐ N Adapted, specialized and assistive equipment frequently*** used during regular activities.	**7.4** ☐ Y ☐ N Adapted, specialized and assistive equipment integrated into all regular activities.

As universal design principles are applied to equipment and materials, items such as door handles, kitchen utensils (such as "Good Grips"), pens and pencils, forks and spoons, and hair brushes are designed so people with motoric problems can use everyday items. In a child care centre you would look for specialized equipment, adapted equipment and well-designed regular equipment that allow children with motoric issue and other issues to participate fully in routines and activities. Look for visual cue systems (such as PECS), knobbed puzzles, crayons with good grips, two-person scissors, sensory materials fur children with high needs, touch screens and head switches for computers, and touch switches for mechanical toys. Note whether height and design of tables, housekeeping area. and easels allow access by children who use walkers, standing braces or wheelchairs, is respectful of children and convenient for staff

* "Some" means 3 or 4; "Many" means 5 or more.

** "Assistive technology" refers to equipment such as specialized computer software, input devices (such as head switches, touch screens, voice recognition software), output devices (such as speech simulation software), cause-effect switches, and FM switches;

***"Occasionally" means 25% of the time; "Frequently" means over 50 % of the time—as appropriate.

Comments:

Practice 3: Director and Inclusion.

Score: 1 2 3 4 5 6 7

Inadequate 1	Minimal 3	Good 5	Excellent 7
1.1 □Y □N Director expresses no interest in inclusion.	3.1 □Y □N Director expresses willingness to include children with special needs.	5.1 □Y □N Director takes an active role in inclusion program.	7.1 □Y □N Director is an inclusion leader** within the centre.
1.2 □Y □N Director plays no advocacy role regarding inclusion.	3.2 □Y □N Director is an advocate in at least one area—the community, the ECE field, education system or with government.	5.2 □Y □N Director is an advocate in at least 2 areas—the community, the ECE field, education system with government.	7.2 □Y □N Director is an inclusion leader*** within the community, in the ECE field, with the education system, and with government.
1.3 □Y □N Director does not encourage staff to become knowledgeable about inclusion.	3.3 □Y □N Director allows staff to attend yearly workshops or conferences on inclusion with either lieu time or some funding.	5.3 □Y □N Director promotes staff participation in courses/workshops/conferences related to inclusion, with lieu time and funding.	7.3 □Y □N Policies are developed that reward staff development, skills and credentials related to inclusion.
1.4 □Y □N Director does not encourage board to be supportive of inclusion.	3.4 □Y □N Director passes along information on inclusion to board members.*	5.4 □Y □N Director promotes board* knowledge of inclusion through speakers at meetings, information sessions.	7.4 □Y □N Director actively recruits board members* who are supportive of inclusion and educates them on issues, policy, trends in inclusion.
1.5 □Y □N Director does not work with related early childhood intervention agencies.	3.4 □Y □N Director attends occasional meetings with agencies related to inclusion.	5.5 □Y □N Director is a partner in at least one agency or community group related to inclusion.	7.5 □Y □N Director collaborates with many community agencies related to inclusion.

* Or to other similar unit, such as parent committee;

** Proving in-services on inclusion and modeling participation in advocacy activities to staff;

*** Provides workshops in community, ECE field and to government; participates us task forces, committees, working groups; promotes broad participation in advocacy for inclusion.

Comments:

Practice 4: Staff Support.

Inadequate 1	Minimal 3	Score: 1 2 3 Good 5	4 5 6 7 Excellent 7
1.1 ☐Y ☐N There is little or no consultative assistance available to staff on inclusion.	3.1 ☐Y ☐N Scheduled consultative assistance is available during period when children with special needs enrolled.	5.1 ☐Y ☐N Consultative assistance plans are developed collaboratively.	7.1 ☐Y ☐N Level of consultative assistance flexible to centre's needs.
1.2 ☐Y ☐N There is no in-centre staff, in addition to ratio, to support the children with special needs.	3.2 ☐Y ☐N There is at least a part-time support staff, in addition to ratio, to support the children with special needs.	5.2 ☐Y ☐N Reduced child-to-staff ratio to include children with special needs OR one-to-one staffing, as needed.	7.2 ☐Y ☐N Reduced child-to-staff ratio to include children with extra needs, and one-to-one staffing, as needed.
	3.3 ☐Y ☐N Resource support staff have some training in ECE, special needs, or the individual child's issues.	5.3 ☐Y ☐N One permanent staff (in-house RT) in addition to ratio, facilitates inclusion (at least part time).	7.3 ☐Y ☐N In-centre RT, in addition to ratio, facilitates inclusion (full-time position).
		5.4 ☐Y ☐N In-centre Resource Teacher has ECE diploma and post-diploma special needs certificate, or BCE diploma and at least 10 years experience with children with special needs and 10 workshops in special needs/inclusion.	7.4 ☐Y ☐N In-centre RT has degree in ECE or related field and post-diploma certificate in special needs/inclusion.

Comments:

Practice 5: Staff Training.

Inadequate 1	Minimal 3	Score: 1 2 3 4	Good 5	Excellent 7
1.1 ☐ Y ☐ N No regular staff With special needs/inclusion training.	**3.1** ☐ Y ☐ N One staff partially trained in special needs/inclusion[5].		**5.1** ☐ Y ☐ N One staff has certificate in special needs/inclusion.	**7.1** ☐ Y ☐ N More than one staff has certificate in special needs/inclusion.
1.2 ☐ Y ☐ N Staff not encouraged to attend workshops, conferences, in-services on special needs issues.	**3.2** ☐ Y ☐ N Some** staff attend periodic*** workshops, conferences, in-services on special needs issues.		**5.2** ☐ Y ☐ N Many*** staff attend periodic workshops, conferences, in-services on special needs issues.	**7.2** ☐ Y ☐ N Most staff attend periodic workshops, conferences, in-services on special needs issues.
1.3 ☐ Y ☐ N Director does not participate in inclusion training.	**3.3** ☐ Y ☐ N Director either participates in inclusion training OR encourages staff to do so.		**5.3** ☐ Y ☐ N Director participates in inclusion training.	**7.3** ☐ Y ☐ N Director provides inclusion training at in-services, workshops, conferences or at community college.
				7.4 ☐ Y ☐ N Some inclusion training provided as in-services, with topics developed collaboratively.
				7.5 ☐ Y ☐ N Director/board promote inclusion training through funding of workshops, lieu days, career laddering, etc.

* "Training" means a diploma or certificate in special needs/inclusion beyond basic ECE training;

** "Some" means less than 25% of staff;

*** "Periodic" means at least once a year; "Many" means over 50%. "Many" means over 50%.

Comments:

Practice 6: Therapies: Physiotherapy (PT); Occupational Therapy (OT); Speech & Language (S&L); Behavioural Consultation.*

Score: 1 2 3 4 5 6 7

Inadequate 1	Minimal 3	Good 5	Excellent 7
1.1 ☐ Y ☐ N Director has little or no knowledge of therapeutic interventions and goals for children with special needs.	3.1 ☐ Y ☐ N Director has information about therapeutic interventions and goals for some of the children with special needs.	5.1 ☐ Y ☐ N Director is knowledgeable about children's therapies and encourages liaison between therapists and staff.	7.1 ☐ Y ☐ N Director successfully promotes collaborative goal setting among therapists, parents and staff.
1.2 ☐ Y ☐ N Staff has little or no knowledge of therapeutic interventions and goals for children with special needs.	3.2 ☐ Y ☐ N Staff has information about therapeutic interventions and goals for some of the children with special needs.	5.2 ☐ Y ☐ N Staff is knowledgeable about children's therapies and meet occasionally with therapists for most of the children.	7.2 ☐ Y ☐ N Staff is knowledgeable about children's therapies and participate collaboratively with therapists and parents in developing and assessing therapeutic interventions for all of the children.
	3.3 ☐ Y ☐ N Therapies may be provided at clinics, or at the centre.	5.3 ☐ Y ☐ N Some therapies are provided at centre, in group settings; when therapies are provided at clinics, staff periodically attend therapy sessions.	7.3 ☐ Y ☐ N Most therapies are provided in group settings.
	3.4 ☐ Y ☐ N Staff sometimes carry out follow-up activities suggested by therapists.	5.4 ☐ Y ☐ N Staff are consistent in carrying out follow-up activities.	7.4 ☐ Y ☐ N Staff are creative, as well as consistent, in implementing follow-up activities.
	3.5 ☐ Y ☐ N Follow-up activities may be carried out outside of classroom or within activities and routines.	5.5 ☐ Y ☐ N Follow-up activities are often carried out within group activities.	7.5 ☐ Y ☐ N Goals are embedded into regular routines and activities.

* Since the availability of therapeutic interventions, their adequacy, frequency and duration are issues beyond the control of child care centres, we do not address this issue in #6. Obliquely, however, we do address the issue under "advocacy" in the SpecialLink Child Care Inclusion Principles Scale.

Comments:

Practice 7: Individual Program Plans (IPPs).

Inadequate 1	Minimal 3	Good 5	Excellent 7
1.1 ☐ Y ☐ N Children with special needs are present, but none have Individual Program Plans (IPPs).	**3.1** ☐ Y ☐ N Children with special needs are present, and some* have IPPs.	**5.1** ☐ Y ☐ N Most* children with special needs have IPPs.	**7.1** ☐ Y ☐ N All children with special needs have IPPs.
	3.2 ☐ Y ☐ N IPPs may be carried out in one-to-one pull-out sessions and/or within regular routines and activities	**5.2** ☐ Y ☐ N IPPs are generally used in either small group pull-out sessions or in regular group.	**7.2** ☐ Y ☐ N IPP goals are embedded in regular group activities.
	3.3 ☐ Y ☐ N IPP goals of the children with special needs are known by at least the one-to-one workers and/or the RT.	**5.3** ☐ Y ☐ N IPP goals are shared with all staff at staff meetings and/or planning sessions.	**7.3** ☐ Y ☐ N IPP goals are posted at interest centres so that all staff with work on them.
	3.4 ☐ Y ☐ N IPPs are developed by therapist or consultant/RT.	**5.4** ☐ Y ☐ N IPP goals are developed by consultant/RT, with staff and/or parent input.	**7.4** ☐ Y ☐ N IPPs are developed collaboratively by consultant/RT, staff, parents.
		5.5 ☐ Y ☐ N IPPs goals and objectives are reviewed periodically.	**7.5** ☐ Y ☐ N Child progress is monitored to document acquisition toward IPP goals, and ineffective practices are modified.

Score: 1 2 3 4 5 6 7

* "Some means at least 25%; "Most" means at least 75%.

Comments:

Practice 8: Parents of Children with Special Needs.

Inadequate 1		Minimal 3		Good 5		Excellent 7
Score: 1	2	3	4	5	6	7
1.1 ☐Y ☐N Director makes no additional effort to involve parents of children with special needs, in the regular activities of the centre, beyond attendance at mandatory IPP meetings.		3.1 ☐Y ☐N Director makes minimal effort to involve parents of children with special needs in the regular activities of the centre.*		5.1 ☐Y ☐N Director encourages involvement of parents of children with special needs in the regular activities of the centre.*		7.1 ☐Y ☐N Director actively promotes involvement of parents of children with special needs in IPP meetings, regular activities of the centre, collaborative meetings with therapists for goal setting, committees, board membership[5].
1.2 ☐Y ☐N Parents are not treated as sources of information about their children with special needs.		3.2 ☐Y ☐N Parents are treated as sources of information about their children with special needs.		5.2 ☐Y ☐N Parents are also seen as contributors to program planning and goal setting.		7.2 ☐Y ☐N Parents are encouraged in their role as advocates for their children.
1.3 ☐Y ☐N Parents of children with special needs are not given information concerning progress of their child on IPP goals, unless they ask for it.		3.3 ☐Y ☐N Parents of children with special needs are given information concerning progress of their child on IPP goals, at least twice a year.		5.3 ☐Y ☐N Parents of children with special needs are encouraged to participate in regular planning sessions and reviews of their child's progress, at least twice a year.		7.3 ☐Y ☐N Parents of children with special needs are encouraged to develop greater knowledge about IPP processes, transition to public school procedures, therapies, and/or disability organizations.
1.4 ☐Y ☐N Parents of children with special needs are not encouraged to join committees, the Board or other governance/specialty groups.		3.4 ☐Y ☐N Parents of children with special needs are told about opportunities to join committees, the board, or other governance/specialty group.		5.4 ☐Y ☐N Parents of children with special needs are encouraged to join committees, the board or other governance/specialty group.		7.4 ☐Y ☐N Parents are encouraged to participate in panels, workshops, staff training and advocacy.

* To achieve a "3" rating, the centre must provide at least 2 supports, such as transportation, babysitting, translation, meeting at site convenient to parents, encouragement to bring relative or trusted friend/advocate. To achieve a "5" rating, the centre must provide at least 4 supports. To achieve a "7", all must be available.

Comments:

Practice 9: Involvement of Typical Children.

Note frequency and intensity of play that involves children with special needs and typically developing children—especially in housekeeping area, block area, and out of doors, during free play times.

	Inadequate 1	Minimal 3	Score:	1	2	3	4	Good 5	5	6	7	Excellent 7

Inadequate 1

1.1 ☐ Y ☐ N
Typically developing children rarely interact with children with special needs.

1.2 ☐ Y ☐ N
Staff take no active role in encouraging social inclusion.

1.3 ☐ Y ☐ N

Minimal 3

3.1 ☐ Y ☐ N
Typically developing children sometimes* interact with children with special needs in group social play situations. (That means that during at least 25% of the time when children with special needs are in group play situations such as the Dramatic Play area and the Block area, they are not ignored and left out of the play.

3.2 ☐ Y ☐ N
Staff make comments or gestures to promote social inclusion.

3.3 ☐ Y ☐ N
Cooperation is motivated occasionally, by adult requests.

Good 5

5.1 ☐ Y ☐ N
Children with special needs are often* included in group social play.

5.2 ☐ Y ☐ N
Staff suggest appropriate roles or dramatic situations that are inclusionary.

5.3 ☐ Y ☐ N
Cooperation is stressed, through planned activities that require more than one child to accomplish.

Excellent 7

7.1 ☐ Y ☐ N
Children with special needs are included in group social play most of the time.*

7.2 ☐ Y ☐ N
Staff systematically use techniques of scripting, cooperative learning, valued object sharing, etc., to promote social inclusion.

7.3 ☐ Y ☐ N
Staff receive specific training in promotion of inclusive social play.

7.4 ☐ Y ☐ N
Cooperation is motivated frequently by adult verbal statements and by activities that need more than one child to accomplish.

* "Sometimes" means 25% of the time; "Often" means 50% of the time; "Most OF the time" means over 75% of the time.

Comments:

Practice 10: Board of Directors and Other Similar Units.

In privately owned centres, inquire about parent committees. Replace the word "board" with "committee."

Inadequate 1	Minimal 3	Score: 1 2 3 Good 5 4 5 6 7 Excellent 7
1.1 ☐ Y ☐ N Board of Directors (or Parent Committee) has not addressed the issue of inclusion.	**3.1** ☐ Y ☐ N Director occasionally provides information about inclusion issues to Board of Directors (or Parent Committee).	**5.1** ☐ Y ☐ N Board of Directors (or Parent Committee) has adopted a written policy on inclusion.	**7.1** ☐ Y ☐ N Board of Directors (or Parent Committee) actively promotes inclusion in the community.
1.2 ☐ Y ☐ N Board of Directors (or Parent Committee) includes no parents of children with special needs.	**3.2** ☐ Y ☐ N Board of Directors (or Parent Committee) occasionally* includes a parent of a child with special needs.	**5.2** ☐ Y ☐ N Board of Directors (or Parent Committee) always includes at least 1 parent of a child with special needs.	**7.2** ☐ Y ☐ N Board of Directors (or Parent Committee) actively recruits parents of children with special needs for board positions.
1.3 ☐ Y ☐ N Board of Directors (or Parent Committee) given no orientation/information about inclusion of children with special needs.	**3.3** ☐ Y ☐ N Board of Directors (or Parent Committee) given orientation/ information about inclusion of children with special needs.	**5.3** ☐ Y ☐ N Board of Directors (or Parent Committee) receives regular report about inclusion/special needs.	**7.3** ☐ Y ☐ N Board of Directors (or Parent Committee) continuously updated about inclusion issues at meetings, written information, speakers.

* "Occasionally" means 25% of the time.

Comments:

Practice 11: Preparing for Transition to School.

Inadequate 1	Minimal 3	Score: 1 2 3 Good 5	4 5 6 7 Excellent 7
1.1 ☐ Y ☐ N Centre has not addressed this issue.	3.1 ☐ Y ☐ N Director and/or staff actively seek information about school system practices related to children with special needs. 3.2 ☐ Y ☐ N School system staff may telephone or visit centre in regards to individual children with special needs in preschool year.	5.1 ☐ Y ☐ N Staff implement suggestions from school system—from kindergarten teachers or special educators. 5.2 ☐ Y ☐ N Centre staff meet with some school staff (e.g., special education staff, resource teachers, principals, teachers, classroom assistants) regarding many* children with special needs in Spring of preschool year.	7.1 ☐ Y ☐ N Staff actively collaborate with teachers and parents to design and implement transition strategies during preschool year. 7.2 ☐ Y ☐ N Centre holds regular case conferences with school staff, in Spring of preschool year, about all children with special needs. 7.3 ☐ Y ☐ N Centre shares information with school system, only as requested by parents, and only after discussion with parents about potential pros and cons of such disclosure.

* "Many" means at least 50%.

Comments: _____

_____

_____

_____

_____

_____

The SpeciaLink Child Care Inclusion Principles Scale

Principle 1: Zero Reject.

In fully inclusive child care centres, *all children are welcome, regardless of type or level of disability.* Many child care centres that are referred to as "inclusive" actually integrate only children with mild to moderate disabilities, or children with a single disability. Children who are not toilet-trained, who are not ambulatory, who have behavioural disorders, or who have special health care needs, are most likely to be excluded. (Read this statement to Director as you begin to discuss Principle #1 in a non-judgmental tone. Then use probe questions, as necessary, and record comments.

Some probe questions: (1) Have you, or would you be, unable to accept children with any particular level or type of disability? If "yes," what type of disability(ies) or level(s) are these? (2) Children with what disabilities and levels of disability (mild/moderate/severe/profound) have you been able to accommodate in your centre? Record as "comment."

Inadequate 1	Minimal 3	Good 5	Excellent 7
1.1 ☐ Y ☐ N — Director describes previous and present inclusion of children with disabilities in terms of very subjective criteria, such as "very nice parent," "seemed easy to include," "we were forced to."	3.1 ☐ Y ☐ N — Director specifies some* types and levels of disability that the centre can accommodate.	5.1 ☐ Y ☐ N — Director specifies many* types and levels of disability that the centre can accommodate.	7.1 ☐ Y ☐ N — Director specifies that the centre will enroll children with all levels and types of disability—actively following the principle of zero reject.
1.2 ☐ Y ☐ N — Lead BCE is not aware of previous or present enrollment of children with disabilities in her classroom.	3.2 ☐ Y ☐ N — Lead ECE is aware of previous or present enrollment of some* children with disabilities in her classroom.	5.2 ☐ Y ☐ N — Lead ECE is aware of many* children with disabilities, previously and presently enrolled, including some specifics about accommodations and modifications made to include them.	7.2 ☐ Y ☐ N — Lead ECE, another ECE, a support staff (such as secretary or cook), and a parent*** all articulate zero reject principle as their own and as the centre's.
1.3 ☐ Y ☐ N — The centre has no written or verbal policy on inclusion.	3.3 ☐ Y ☐ N — The centre has an informal policy on inclusion (evidenced by Director's comments and supported by such evidence as accessible materials on diversity including pictures, books, dolls with disabilities, or by the presence of information and training opportunities on inclusion being available to staff.	5.3 ☐ Y ☐ N — The centre has a written policy statement that supports inclusion.	7.3 ☐ Y ☐ N — The centre has a written inclusion policy statement that affirms the zero reject principle, with a phrase such as "all children."

Score: 1   2   3   4   5   6   7

* "Some" means three or fewer; "Many" means four or more.
** "Types of disability" refers to diagnosis, such as autistic, intellectual, physical, visual, auditory. "Levels" refers to intensity, such as mild, moderate or severe.
*** "A parent" means the first parent (or close family member) of a child with special needs whom you see—in locker room, at arrival or departure, or identified through probe question.

Comments:

Principle 2: Natural Proportions.

In fully inclusive child care centres (those with a "7" rating), **the proportion of children with disabilities is roughly that of their natural proportion in the general population (10-15%).** Many child care centres that are refereed to as "inclusive" enroll only one or two children with special needs at any one time. Other child care centres that are refereed to as "inclusive" are actually programs with a very high proportion of children with special needs. Sometimes called reverse mainstreaming, these programs typically enroll a few typically developing children as role models, or include 50% typically developing children and 50% children with disabilities. (Read this statement to Director as you begin to discuss Principle #2 in a non-judgmental tone, Then use probe questions, as necessary, and record comments.)

Probe questions: (1) What percent of children with disabilities do you think you could enroll (or, do you enroll) in your centre? If they answer with a number, convert this to a percentage by using the licensed capacity figure. (2) Do you think that there is a percentage that would be too high? What is it? (3) If she says, "It depends on the child/ren," ask what she means. Record as "comment."

	Inadequate 1	Minimal 3		Good 5			Excellent 7
Score:	1	2	3	1	2	3	4 5 6 7
	1.1 ☐ Y ☐ N Centre never enrolls a child/ren with disabilities.	**3.1** ☐ Y ☐ N Centre occasionally* enrolls at least a few (less than natural proportions which is roughly 10-15%) children with disabilities,		**5.1** ☐ Y ☐ N Centre usually* enrolls nearly a natural proportion of children with disabilities (roughly 10-15%).			**7.1** ☐ Y ☐ N Director actively follows "natural proportions" as a working principle in the centre, enrolling a natural proportion of children with disabilities nearly all of the time.*
	1.2 ☐ Y ☐ N Centre mainly enrolls children with disabilities, with a few typically developing children as role models.						
	1.3 ☐ Y ☐ N Centre enrolls 50% children with disabilities and 50% typical children.	**3.2** ☐ Y ☐ N Lead BCE is aware of the number of children with disabilities currently in her classroom because she is involved in arranging and/or carrying out accommodations and adaptations to support these children.		**5.2** ☐ Y ☐ N Lead BCE is aware of the number of children with disabilities currently in the centre because she is involved in developing and carrying out IPP goals and because inclusion strategies are discussed at staff meetings.			**7.2** ☐ Y ☐ N Lead ECE, another ECE, a support staff (such as secretary or cook) and a parent articulate the principle of natural proportions as their own and as the centre's.
	1.4 ☐ Y ☐ N Lead ECE is not aware of number of children with disabilities currently in her classroom.	**3.3** ☐ Y ☐ N The centre has an informal policy on inclusion (evidenced by Director's comments and supported by such evidence as accessible materials on diversity including pictures, books, dolls with disabilities, or by the presence of information and training opportunities on inclusion being available to staff).		**5.3** ☐ Y ☐ N The centre has a written policy statement supporting inclusion.			**7.3** ☐ Y ☐ N The centre has a written inclusion policy affirming the principle of natural proportions.
	1.5 ☐ Y ☐ N Centre has no written or verbal policy on inclusion.						**7.4** ☐ Y ☐ N The centre's policy statement is visible to visitors and available to staff, parents, community.

* "Occasionally" means at least 25% of the time; "Usually" means at least 75% of the time; "Nearly all of the time" means around 90% of the time.

Principle 3: Same Hours/Days of Attendance Available to All Children.

In fully inclusive child care centres, all attendance options (such as full day, mornings, two days per week, etc.) that are available to typically developing children are also available to children with special needs. Many child care centres that are referred to as inclusive only include children with special needs for part of the day. The center may be open until 5:30 but the child with special needs is required to leave early. Funding is often cited as the limitation, because too often what is being funded is not "child care" but is, rather, "development." (Read this statement to Director as you begin to discuss Principle #3 in a non-judgmental tone. Then use probe questions, as necessary and record comments.)
<u>Probe question:</u> (1) Are there any limitations on the hours or number of days that children with disabilities can attend your centre? For example, if the parent is not employed, can the child with a disability attend five days per week, until closing time? Record as "comment."

	Inadequate 1		Minimal 3		Good 5		Excellent 7
Score:	1	2	3	4	5	6	7
	1.1 ☐ Y ☐ N Director states that many* children with disabilities attend limited hours per day, or limited number of days per week, despite parent preference—not the same options that other children have.		**3.1** ☐ Y ☐ N Director states that at least some* children with disabilities attend the same hours and days that other children attend—with the same options that other children have.		**5.1** ☐ Y ☐ N Director states that at least most* children with disabilities attend the same hours and days that other children attend—with the same options that other children have,		**7.1** ☐ Y ☐ N Director actively follows the principle of "same hours of attendance available for all children." No children with disabilities are limited to schedules that do not apply to typically developing children.
	1.2 ☐ Y ☐ N Children with disabilities are often** required to stay at home when particular staff members are absent.		**3.2** ☐ Y ☐ N Occasionally a child with a disability <u>may be asked to stay at home</u> because a particular staff member is absent.**		**5.2** ☐ Y ☐ N Children with disabilities are never asked to stay home because a particular staff member is absent.		**7.2** ☐ Y ☐ N The absence of a particular staff does not have a major impact on the child with disabilities, because s/he is accustomed to interacting with several members of the staff.
	1.3 ☐ Y ☐ N Lead ECE is unaware of centre policy on "not same hours/days of attendance" for children with disabilities.		**3.3** ☐ Y ☐ N Lead BCE is aware of centre's policy on attendance options for children with disabilities,		**5.3** ☐ Y ☐ N Lead ECE recognizes inequity in a hypothetical policy that does not provide same hours/days of attendance option.		**7.3** ☐ Y ☐ N Lead BCE, another BCE, a support staff (such as secretary or cook) and a parent articulate their support and the centre's support of the principle of "same hours/days of attendance available for all children,"
	1.4 ☐ Y ☐ N Parents are required to be present to perform related health procedures—such as tube-feeding or catheterization—as a condition of enrollment.		**3.3** ☐ Y ☐ N ☐ N/A Parents are requested to be present to help with training of staff in related health procedures, such as tube-feeding or catheterization. (N/A is possible.)		**5.4** ☐ Y ☐ N Parents are invited to participate in the development of a Special Health Care Plan for their child with special health care needs, and to collaborate in related staff training.		**7.4** ☐ Y ☐ N Parents are acknowledged as experts in their child's health care needs, and are fully accommodated so that they can participate in training and information sessions.
	1.5 ☐ Y ☐ N Centre has no written or verbal policy on inclusion,		**3.5** ☐ Y ☐ N The centre has an informal policy on inclusion (evidenced by Director's comments and supported by such evidence as accessible materials on diversity including pictures, books, dolls with disabilities, or by the presence of information and training opportunities on inclusion being available to staff).		**5.5** ☐ Y ☐ N The centre's written policy statement affirms the centre's support of inclusion.		**7.5** ☐ Y ☐ N The centre's written inclusion policy statement affirms the principle of "same hours/days of attendance available to all children."

* "Some" means at least 25%; "Many" means more than 50%; "Most" means at least 75%; **5 "Occasionally" means 3-4 times a year; "Often" means more than monthly.

Principle 4: Full Participation.

In fully inclusive child care centres, children with special needs have their needs met within the regular group activities and routines, through accommodations, modifications, and extra support where necessary. They are celebrated, not simply tolerated or accepted. Many child care programs that are referred to as inclusive are actually programs that merely *physically* include children with special needs, but which make insufficient provision for their full participation. These children often are "observers" rather than "participants" for a large part of the day, or are engaged in pull-out activities rather than those of the group. (Read this statement to Director as you begin to discuss Principle #4 in a non-judgmental tone, Then use probe questions, as necessary and record comments.)

Probe questions: (1) Does the ability of a child ever cause exclusion from certain activities? (2) If "no," What sorts of accommodations and modifications have you made to include children with disabilities in all activities? (3) if "yes," What exclusions have been necessary for which children? Record as "comment."

	Inadequate 1		Minimal 3		Good 5		Excellent 7
Score:	1	2	3	4	5	6	7
	1.1 ☐ Y ☐ N Children with disabilities are never included in *all* activities and routines.		**3.1** ☐ Y ☐ N Children with disabilities participate in some* regular activities and routines, at least a substantial part of the day.*		**5.1** ☐ Y ☐ N Children with disabilities participate in most* regular activities and routines, at least most of the day.*		**7.1** ☐ Y ☐ N Director actively follows and promotes the principle of full participation, assuring that children with disabilities can participate in *all* activities and routines *all* of the time.
	1.2 ☐ Y ☐ N Children with disabilities and resource support staff are an obvious "pair," not part of the group, almost all of the time.		**3.2** ☐ Y ☐ N ☐ N/A** Resource support staff enhance ratios or ratios are reduced by enrolling fewer children, so that all staff have additional opportunity to interact with and support children with special needs.		**5.2** ☐ Y ☐ N ☐ N/A** While enhancing ratio, resource support staff also bring specialized knowledge (or reduced ratios provide time for regular staff to become familiar with additional resources) about individual children and inclusion strategies to staff and community.		**7.2** ☐ Y ☐ N Resource support staff are "invisible—all staff work as a team and demonstrate a positive, *celebratory* attitude in their modifications and adaptations for children with special needs. Expertise is shared, not hoarded.
	1.3 ☐ Y ☐ N Lead ECE verbalizes no strategies for including children with disabilities in regular activities and routines of classroom.		**3.3** ☐ Y ☐ N Lead ECE verbalizes some* strategies for including children with disabilities in activities and routines.		**5.3** ☐ Y ☐ N Lead ECE verbalizes a wealth of experience and knowledge about disabilities and about inclusion strategies.		**7.3** ☐ Y ☐ N Lead ECE, another ECE, a support staff (such as secretary or cook) and a parent articulate their support and the centre's support of the principle of "full participation."
	1.4 ☐ Y ☐ N Centre has no written or verbal policy on inclusion,		**3.4** ☐ Y ☐ N The centre has an informal policy on inclusion (evidenced by Director's comments and supported by such evidence as accessible materials on diversity including pictures, books, dolls with disabilities, or by the presence of information and training opportunities on inclusion being available to staff).		**5.4** ☐ Y ☐ N The centre's written policy supports inclusive child care.		**7.4** ☐ Y ☐ N The centre's written inclusion policy statement affirms the principle of "full participation."

* "Few" means 2 or 3; "Some" means more than 3; "Most" means more than 5; "A substantial part of the day" means at least 1/3 of the time that all children are there (generally 9-3), "Most of the day" means 75% or more. **If there are fewer than 4 children with disabilities in the centre, if the disabilities are mild , if the staff are experienced at including children with disabilities, and if high quality consultation and therapeutic support is available, there may be no need for either additional staffing or ratio reduction, Use N/A for this situation.

Principle 5: Maximum Feasible Parent Participation at Parent's Comfort Level.

In fully inclusive child care centres, adjustments are made by the centre to encourage attendance at IPP planning meetings, committee meetings, and training sessions, arranging times convenient to parents; transportation and babysitting when necessary; translators at no cost to parents; encouraging parents to bring relatives and/or trusted advisors to meetings and/or observations, etc. With these adjustments in place, parents participate in IPP planning meetings, committees, training sessions, etc., to the maximum extent of their comfort level. Many child care programs that are referred to as inclusive report that parents of children with special needs are just too busy to participate. (Read this statement to Director as you begin to discuss Principle #5 in a non-judgmental tone. Then use probe questions, as necessary, and record comments.)

Probe questions: (1) Do you have difficulty in getting parents of children with special needs to participate in meetings and training sessions? (2) If "yes," "What have you done to try to increase such participation? (3) If "no," To what do you attribute your success? Record as "comment."

	Inadequate 1		Minimal 3		Good 5		Excellent 7
Score:	1	2	3	4	5	6	7
	1.1 ☐ Y ☐ N Parents of children with disabilities almost never participate in meetings or trainings at the child care centre.		**3.1** ☐ Y ☐ N Parents of children with disabilities sometimes** participate in meetings or trainings.		**5.1** ☐ Y ☐ N Parents of children with disabilities often" participate in meetings and trainings at the child care centre.		**7.1** ☐ Y ☐ N Director actively follows the principle of maximum feasible parent participation. Parents of children with disabilities are active on board or committees, and very frequently participate*** in IPP meetings and trainings. Parents are not "guilted" into being involved.
	1.2 ☐ Y ☐ N Centre has made no adjustments to encourage greater parent participation.*		**3.2** ☐ Y ☐ N Centre has made at least one adjustment to encourage greater parent participation.**		**5.2** ☐ Y ☐ N Centre makes some adjustments to encourage greater participation such as transportation, babysitting, translators, parent-sensitive scheduling.***		**7.2** ☐ Y ☐ N Centre encourages participation through many adjustments such as transportation, babysitting, location, translators, parent-sensitive scheduling.****
	1.3 ☐ Y ☐ N Lead BCE is unaware of any adjustments made to encourage maximum feasible participation.		**3.3** ☐ Y ☐ N Lead ECE is aware of an adjustment made to encourage maximum feasible participation or spontaneously articulates at least one reason why this is important.		**5.3** ☐ Y ☐ N Lead ECE is aware of some adjustments made to encourage maximum participation and spontaneously articulates at least one reason why this is important.		**7.3** ☐ Y ☐ N Lead BCE, another ECE, a support staff, and a parent list several adjustments made to encourage maximum parental participation and articulate at least two reasons why this is important.
	1.4 ☐ Y ☐ N Centre has no verbal or written policy on inclusion.		**3.4** ☐ Y ☐ N The centre has an informal policy on inclusion (evidenced by Director's comments and supported by such evidence as accessible materials on diversity including pictures, books, dolls with disabilities, or by the presence of information and training opportunities on inclusion being available to staff).		**5.4** ☐ Y ☐ N Centre has written policy on inclusion		**7.4** ☐ Y ☐ N Centre has written policy on inclusion that affirms the parent participation principle.

* Must list at least I adjustment (such as transportation, babysitting, location, translators, parent-sensitive scheduling) to achieve a "3" rating. **"Sometimes" means roughly 25% of the time; "Often" means roughly 50% of the time; "Very Frequently" means 75% of the time. Two factors are combined in this item—percentage of parents of children with disabilities who participate and frequency that each participates. If 25% participate 25% of the time, 3.1 applies. (Add the two percentages and divide by 2.) If 10% participate 40% of the time, 3.1 still applies. ***Must list at least 3 adjustments to achieve a "5" rating; ***Must list at least 5 adjustments to achieve a "7" rating.

Principle 6: Leadership, Pro-active Strategies and Advocacy for High Quality, Inclusive Child Care.

Even when the regular child care program is available and adequate, many families of children with special needs are excluded by reasons such as staff training, support staffing, transportation, funding and therapeutic support. In fully inclusive child care centres, these limitations are not passively accepted by the director, board, parents or staff. Advocacy activities on behalf of high quality inclusive child care include appeals to civic organizations, work with government officials to change rules that limit the inclusion of children with special needs, and presentations on inclusion to staff, associations and community—these types of actions exemplify fully inclusive child care centres. (Read this statement to Director as you begin to discuss Principle #6 in a non-judgmental tone.) Then use probe questions, as necessary and record comments.)

Probe questions: (1) Does your centre try to change policies and funding arrangements that impede full inclusion? (2) If "yes," What sorts of actions have you taken? (3) If "yes," who is involved (such as the director, staff, board, and/or parents)? Record as "comment."

Score: 1 2 3 4 5 6 7

Inadequate 1	Minimal 3	Good 5	Excellent 7
1.1 ☐Y ☐N Neither director, board, staff nor parents participate in advocacy activities or in providing workshops on inclusion.	3.1 ☐Y ☐N Director participates in advocacy activities or in providing training for inclusion.	5.1 ☐Y ☐N Director and lead BCE staff participate in advocacy activities or in providing training for inclusion. (Either/or for each person.)	7.1 ☐Y ☐N Director takes a leadership role in *both* advocacy *and* in providing training for inclusion.
1.2 ☐Y ☐N Centre passively uses funded supports, and doesn't seek additional supports such as summer grants, service clubs, or volunteers.	3.2 ☐Y ☐N Centre uses funded supports, and once in a while* seeks additional supports, such as summer grants, service clubs and volunteers.**	5.2 ☐Y ☐N Centre uses funded supports and often[5] seeks additional supports such as summer grants, service clubs, volunteers, students, in-kind donations, fund-raising, other government programs.**	7.2 ☐Y ☐N Lead BCE staff, and board or some parents participate in advocacy activities and in providing training for inclusion. (staff-both; others-1)
1.3 ☐Y ☐N Centre does not have a verbal or written policy on inclusion.	3.3 ☐Y ☐N The centre has an informal policy on inclusion (evidenced by Director's comments and supported by such evidence as accessible materials on diversity including pictures, books, dolls with disabilities, or by the presence of information and training opportunities on inclusion being available to staff).	5.3 ☐Y ☐N Centre has written policy supporting inclusive child care.	7.3 ☐Y ☐N Centre uses funded supports; constantly seeks additional supports; and is creative in obtaining additional resources—both human and financial.**
			7.4 ☐Y ☐N Centre has written inclusion policy that affirms leadership/advocacy principle.

* "Once in a while" means less than yearly; "Often" means at least yearly; "Constantly" means as integral part of administration, at least several limes a year.

** For "Additional Supports" (such as summer grants, service clubs, volunteers, students, in-kind donations, fund-raising, other government programs), the centre must score at least 2 for "3"; 5 for "5"; and 7 for "7".

*** In 5.1, 2 out of 3 must participate for a "yes" answer.

Comments:

Notes On Rating and Scoring

1. Read the entire scale carefully, including the Items, Notes for Clarification and Questions. In order to be accurate, all ratings have to be based exactly as possible on the indicators provided in the scale items.

2. Examples that differ from those given in the indicators but seem comparable may be used as a basis for giving credit for an indicator.

3. Scores should be based on the current situation that is observed or reported by staff, not on future plans. In the absence of observable information on which to base your rating, you may use answers given by staff during the question period to assign scores.

4. When scoring an item, always start reading from 1 (inadequate) and progress upward till the correct score is reached.

5. Ratings are to be assigned in the following way:

    *   A rating of 1 must be given if any indicator under 1 is scored Yes.
    *   A rating of 2 is given when all indicators under 1 are scored No and at least half of the indicators under 3 are scored Yes.
    *   A rating of 3 is given when all indicators under 1 are scored No and all indicators under 3 are scored Yes.
    *   A rating of 4 is given when all indicators under 3 are met and at least half of the indicators under 5 are scored Yes.
    *   A rating of 5 is given when all indicators under 5 are scored Yes.
    *   A rating of 6 is given when all indicators under 5 are met and at least half of the indicators under 7 are scored Yes.
    *   A rating of 7 is given when all indicators under 7 are scored Yes.

6. The total mean scale score is the sum of all the item scores for the entire scale divided by the number of items scored."

7. Transfer your ratings to the score sheets on the following pages.

Score Sheet

SpeciaLink Child Care Inclusion Practices Profile

Observer: _____
Centre/School: _____
Room: _____
Teacher(s): _____
Number of Staff Present: _____
Number of Children Enrolled in Class: _____
Number of Children Present: _____

Observer Code: _____
Centre Code: _____
Room Code: _____
Teacher Code: _____

Date of Observation: _____
Number of Children with Identified Disabilities: _____
Check Type(s) of Disability: □ Physical/Sensory □ Cognitive/Language □ Social/Emotional □ Other

Birthdates of Children Enrolled: Youngest _____ Oldest _____

Time Observation Began: ____ : ____   □ AM □ PM
Time Observation Ended: ____ : ____   □ AM □ PM

Any Unusual Occurrence During Observation: _____

1. Physical Environment and Special Needs

1 2 3 4 5 6 7   Notes:

Y N	Y N	Y N	Y N
1.1	3.1	5.1	7.1
1.2	3.2	5.2	7.2
1.3	3.3	5.3	7.3
1.4	3.4	5.4	7.4

2. Equipment and Materials

1 2 3 4 5 6 7   Notes:

Y N	Y N	Y N	Y N
1.1	3.1	5.1	7.1
1.2	3.2	5.2	7.2
	3.3	5.3	7.3
	3.4	5.4	7.4

3. Director and Inclusion

1 2 3 4 5 6 7   Notes:

Y N	Y N	Y N	Y N
1.1	3.1	5.1	7.1
1.2	3.2	5.2	7.2
	3.3	5.3	7.3
	3.4	5.4	7.4
	3.5	5.5	7.5

4. Staff Support

1 2 3 4 5 6 7   Notes:

Y N	Y N	Y N	Y N
1.1	3.1	5.1	7.1
1.2	3.2	5.2	7.2
	3.3	5.3	7.3
			7.4

5. Staff Training

1 2 3 4 5 6 7   Notes:

Y N	Y N	Y N	Y N
1.1	3.1	5.1	7.1
1.2	3.2	5.2	7.2
1.3	3.3	5.3	7.3
			7.4
			7.5

6. Therapies: PT; OT; S&L; Behavioural

1 2 3 4 5 6 7   Notes:

Y N	Y N	Y N	Y N
1.1	3.1	5.1	7.1
1.2	3.2	5.2	7.2
	3.3	5.3	7.3
	3.4	5.4	7.4
	3.5	5.5	7.5

7. Individual Program Plans (IPPs)   1 2 3 4 5 6 7

Y N	Y N	Y N	Y N	Notes:
1.1	3.1	5.1	7.1	
	3.2	5.2	7.2	
	3.3	5.3	7.3	
	3.4	5.4	7.4	
		5.5	7.5	

8. Parents of Children with Special Needs   1 2 3 4 5 6 7

Y N	Y N	Y N	Y N	Notes:
1.1	3.1	5.1	7.1	
1.2	3.2	5.2	7.2	
1.3	3.3	5.3	7.3	
1.4	3.4	5.4	7.4	

9. Involvement of Typical Children   1 2 3 4 5 6 7

Y N	Y N	Y N	Y N	Notes:
1.1	3.1	5.1	7.1	
1.2	3.2	5.2	7.2	
1.3	3.3	5.3	7.3	
			7.4	

10. Board of Directors and Similar Units   1 2 3 4 5 6 7

Y N	Y N	Y N	Y N	Notes:
1.1	3.1	5.1	7.1	
1.2	3.2	5.2	7.2	
1.3	3.3	5.3	7.3	

11. Preparing for Transition to School   1 2 3 4 5 6 7

Y N	Y N	Y N	Y N	Notes:
1.1	3.1	5.1	7.1	
	3.2	5.2	7.2	
			7.3	

Total and Average Scores

	Total Score	# of Items Scored	Average Score
Physical Environment and Special Needs			
Equipment and Materials			
Director and Inclusion			
Staff Support			
Staff Training			
Therapies			
Individual Program Plans			
Parents of Children with Special Needs			
Involvement of Typical Children			
Board of Directors and Similar Units			
Preparing for Transition to School			
TOTAL			

Score Sheet
SpeciaLink Child Care Inclusion Practices Scale

Observer: _____
Centre/School: _____
Room: _____
Teacher(s): _____
Number of Staff Present: _____
Number of Children Enrolled in Class: _____
Number of Children Present: _____

Date of Observation: _____
Number of Children with Identified Disabilities: _____
Check Type(s) of Disability: ☐ Physical/Sensory ☐ Cognitive/Language ☐ Social/Emotional ☐ Other
Birthdates of Children Enrolled: Youngest _____ Oldest _____
Time Observation Began: ____ : ____   ☐ AM ☐ PM
Time Observation Ended: ____ : ____   ☐ AM ☐ PM

Any Unusual Occurrence During Observation: _____

1. Zero Reject   1 2 3 4 5 6 7   Notes:

Y N		Y N		Y N		Y N	
1.1		3.1		5.1		7.1	
1.2		3.2		5.2		7.2	
1.3		3.3		5.3		7.3	

2. Natural Proportions   1 2 3 4 5 6 7   Notes:

Y N		Y N		Y N		Y N	
1.1		3.1		5.1		7.1	
1.2		3.2		5.2		7.2	
1.3		3.3		5.3		7.3	
1.4				5.4		7.4	
1.5							

3. Same Hours of Attendance Available to All Children   1 2 3 4 5 6 7   Notes:

Y N		Y N		Y N		Y N	
1.1		3.1		5.1		7.1	
1.2		3.2		5.2		7.2	
1.3		3.3		5.3		7.3	
1.4		3.4		5.4		7.4	
1.5		3.5		5.5		7.5	

4. Full Participation   1 2 3 4 5 6 7   Notes:

Y N		Y N		Y N		Y N	
1.1		3.1		5.1		7.1	
1.2		3.2		5.2		7.2	
1.3		3.3		5.3		7.3	
1.4		3.4		5.4		7.4	

5. Maximum Feasible Parent Participation   1 2 3 4 5 6 7   Notes:

Y N		Y N		Y N		Y N	
1.1		3.1		5.1		7.1	
1.2		3.2		5.2		7.2	
1.3		3.3		5.3		7.3	
1.4		3.4		5.4		7.4	

6. Pro-Active Strategies and Advocacy for High Quality, Inclusive Child Care   1 2 3 4 5 6 7   Notes:

Y N		Y N		Y N		Y N	
1.1		3.1		5.1		7.1	
1.2		3.2		5.2		7.2	
		3.3		5.3		7.3	
		3.4		5.4		7.4	

continued

continued

Total and Average Scores

	Total Score
Zero Reject	_____
Natural Proportions	_____
Same Hours of Attendance to All Children	_____
Full Participation	_____
Maximum Feasible Parent Participation	_____
Pro-Active Strategies and Advocacy for High Quality, <u>Inclusive</u> Child Care	_____
TOTAL	

# of Items Scored	Average Score
_____	_____

A

Recommendations for Inclusive Care

From *Highlights from Inclusion: The Next Generation in Child Care in Canada*

A Focus on Leadership

Inclusion: The Next Generation confirms the critical role of the child care centre director as inclusion leader. Some of the programs in this study lacked resource teachers; some lacked regularized funding for the extra costs of resource supports; some lacked strong boards — but none of the successful programs lacked strong, committed directors. Activities and programs that enhance that role are critical. Fully inclusive child care centres are still rare, and their sustainability is in question as founding directors retire or move on. We strongly recommend that:

1. **Governments must target inclusive directors as key change agents, and fund projects that enhance their impact on the broader child care community.**

   This can be achieved through projects that:

   - Bring key people from successful inclusive child care sites together to share learnings and best practices, and to strategize about practical initiatives;
   - Sponsor inclusion leadership training institutes for directors, and for potential directors, with demonstrated commitment to inclusion;
   - Support networking opportunities for directors/supervisors of inclusive centres;
   - Create a national mentorship program for inclusion, with successful directors/supervisors of inclusive centres as mentors, nominating in-province leaders who are "ready to include";
   - Support field-based speakers' bureaus on inclusion, with directors/supervisors—credible practitioners—as key figures;
   - Promote a career ladder and encourage existing successful inclusion practitioners to become trainers.

   There is a tremendous reserve of "practice wisdom" that should be widely shared and utilized to enhance inclusive practice and to encourage the next generation of directors and child care professionals.

2. **Governments must fund a variety of opportunities (using in-person presentations, print materials, videos, and web-based resources) to share with others knowledge acquired by leaders in inclusive child care programs.**

A Focus on Training

3. **Provincial and territorial governments must ensure that there is a variety of courses, conferences and workshops on inclusion that are accessible, affordable, and available to staff and directors on an ongoing basis, addressing the range of topics and issues that are important for successful inclusion.**

4. **College and university programs in ECE must incorporate more materials about inclusive practice in their curricula and in post-diploma and graduate courses.**

5. **Practical and placement courses in ECE and related programs must be strategically developed to ensure that students have the opportunity to learn about inclusion by participating in successful centres.**

6. **Colleges and universities must reconceptualize (in consultation with the field) post-diploma/ graduate programs for resource teachers and special needs workers in early childhood education.** These should reflect the multiple roles of direct service, collaborative practice, consulting, and adult education. They should also address the needs of short-term contract workers who work in inclusive child care settings, oftenwithout training.

7. **Intensive inclusion quality enhancement programs, such as *Keeping the Door Open* in New Brunswick; *Measuring and Improving Kids' Environments (MIKE)* in Prince Edward Island; and *Partnerships for Inclusion* in Nova Scotia, must be offered to centres in all provinces.**

A Focus on Policy

Provincial/territorial/municipal policy must support effective inclusion practice. Funding must be provided to ensure that centres and their staff have access to the resources (both financial and human resources) they need to continue to be effective and to expand their capabilities, and are compensated for the valuable work they do. Among policy concerns to be addressed are:

8. **Child care centres that enroll children with special needs must have timely access to child assessments, both to determine eligibility and to help child care staff in their planning efforts.**

9. **Child care centres must have additional funds to enhance ratios (or employ an in-house resource teacher) when four or more children with special needs are enrolled, or when any children have extremely high special needs. Funding should be stable and adequate to recruit and retain trained and experienced ECEs for this work.**

10. **Itinerant resource teachers must be available to child care programs to support the effective inclusion of children with special needs.**

11. **Child care centres must have appropriate levels of support from therapists and other related specialists in the community when they enroll children with special needs.**

12. **Child care centres must have additional assistants when they enroll children with more challenging needs.**

13. **Since accessibility and physical structure are so closely related to both inclusion quality and global quality, all new centres must be purpose-built to meet current standards, and older centres must be eligible for capital grants to increase accessibility.**

A Focus on Planning for Transitions

Provincial/territorial policy must support a collaborative, interdisciplinary approach among early years professionals, including school personnel.

14. **Early years personnel must develop protocols and strategies for effective planning and coordination of efforts to assist with child care transitions (from home or early intervention/infant development to child care, and from child care to school).**

A Focus on Research

15. **Governments must fund thorough evaluations of the effectiveness of different models of inclusion support.**
16. **Governments must fund the monitoring of progress toward *"inclusiveness"* in child care programs.** Instruments for monitoring inclusion quality, such as the *SpeciaLink Inclusion Profile* and the *SpeciaLink Inclusion Practices Scale*, are available and are familiar to the field.

A Focus on the Profession

Wide variance exists in the roles, training, caseload size, duration and frequency of visits, focus of service, etc., of resource teachers in child care.

17. **As an emerging profession, leaders in the field of resource teachers/specialists in Early Childhood must define their own code of ethics, mandates, appropriate caseloads, and standards of training and practice.** Funding must be allocated for research and development projects oriented toward this goal.

Toward a System of High Quality, Affordable, Accessible, Inclusive Child Care Programs Across Canada

The continued under-funding and undervaluing of child care professionals is a serious concern that will affect the recruitment and retention of skilled individuals in this field.

A renewed commitment to a national child care program must consider the quality of early learning and child care, along with issues of affordability and expansion of spaces.

18. **Federal/provincial/territorial governments must strengthen the funding component of the *Multilateral Framework on Early Learning and Child Care* to build a national Canadian child care system that includes career ladders with graduated salaries, and assures a continuing infrastructure to support high quality, inclusive programs.**

B Provincial and Territorial Profiles

Excerpts from *Early Childhood Education and Care in Canada 2004* by the Childcare Resource and Research Unit (University of Toronto). Reprinted with permission.

Newfoundland and Labrador

Kindergarten

Legislation

Newfoundland and Labrador House of Assembly. *School Act*. 1997. (Amended 1999, 2000, 2001). *S.N.L. 1997 c. S-12.2*.

The legislation applies to both public and private schools.

Children With Special Needs

There is no written policy. However there is an expectation that all children will be included in the regular kindergarten classroom. A variety of support is available, primarily from special education teachers if need is demonstrated. There is also the provision of student assistants who, under the direction of a teacher, assist children with personal care and behaviour management.

The number of kindergarten children with special needs in 2003/04: 325

Regulated Child Care Services

Children With Special Needs

Newfoundland and Labrador does not have a written policy regarding children with special needs.

One regulated centre works exclusively with children at-risk and their families, serving approximately 50 full- and part-time children. The centre receives core funding from Health and Community Services. Parents, who pay no fees, are not income tested.

Parents whose children require additional support to attend typical child care programs may receive a child welfare allowance if they meet eligibility requirements under a means test. The allowance is paid directly to the parent who hires an individual to provide support to the child in a child care setting. The setting may include a child care centre, family child care home or unregulated home. Parents who do not meet eligibility requirements for the special welfare allowance must pay for additional supports themselves.

There are no special training requirements for staff working with children with special needs.

Aboriginal Child Care

In January 1998, the first on-reserve child care centre was licensed for the Miawpukek First Nation at Conne River, the only reserve in Newfoundland and Labrador. It was the choice of Conne River Health and Social Services to apply for a provincial license and comply with provincial regulations. A second centre (not licensed) was opened at Conne River in 2001. There is also a centre in Hopedale under First Nations/Inuit funding and centres serving largely Innu and Inuit communities in coastal Labrador at Sheshatshui, Nain, Rigolet, Postville and Natuashish. First Nations and Inuit child care centres that are licensed receive the same funding as other centres in the province and parents are eligible for subsidy.

Aboriginal Head Start funds projects in Hopedale, Sheshatshiu, and Happy Valley–Goose Bay.

Space Statistics (2003/04) (March 2004)

Number of regulated child care spaces	
Centre-based	
Infant	48
Full-time (excluding infant)	3,499
Part-time	556
School-age	578
Family child care (agency approved)	210
Family child care (individually licensed)	30
Total number of licensed spaces	4,921

Children with special needs in regulated child care
Statistics are not kept on total number of children with special needs attending typical child care facilities bur approximately 273 children with special needs received a fee subsidy. There are also 50 children with special needs at Daybreak Parent/Child Centre which receives core funding.

Children receiving subsidies	**1,350**

Number of centres and homes	
Number of child care centres	**151**
– Full day	104
– Part-day nursery schools/preschools	27
– Stand-alone after-school programs	20
Number of family child care agencies	2
Number of family child care providers	35

Sponsorship of full-time regulated centre spaces	
Non-profit	1,242
For-profit	3,439

Openings and closings (2003/04)	
New child care centre licenses issued	12
Number of child care centre closures	2
Number of new licenses issued to family child care agencies	0
Number of new licenses issued to individual family child care providers	3
Number of family child care agencies/individual providers who ceased providing care	0

Standards And Regulations

Regulated Centres

Staff qualification requirements

CERTIFICATION LEVELS: *Entry Level* certification requires completion of an orientation course of 30 60 hours depending on the age group with which the staff will be working.

Level One certification requires a minimum of a one year certificate in Early Childhood Education. Staff are certified to work with particular age group. (See note below)

Level Two certification requires a minimum of a two year diploma in Early Childhood Education. Staff are certified to work with particular age groups. (See note below)

Level Three certification requires Level Two certification plus an ECE-specific or an ECE-related post diploma specialization.

Level Four certification requires an ECE-specific university degree or a university degree plus an ECE diploma.

Note: Prior to 1997, the focus of early childhood training was on children aged 2-12. After that time, training included an infant care component. Since certification was introduced, individuals with ECE qualifications received before 1997 are certified to work with children 2-12. Those wishing to be certified to work with infants must complete a 50-hour self study program. Graduates of the community college and some private ECE training programs after 1997 are certified to work with children 0-12. ECE graduates from private colleges that choose not to include infant care in their course content are required to complete the 50-hour self-study program if they wish to be certified to work with infants.

Centre operators must have Level Two certification in the age groups for which the centre is licensed and two or more years experience working with children in those age groups, or its equivalent from another jurisdiction.

One staff person with each group of children requires Level One certification for the age group in which the staff is assigned and a minimum of one year's experience in that classification.

All other staff who are included in the staff:child ratio must have Entry Level certification (30-60 hour orientation course). Note: there is no entry level certification for infant care; the minimum qualification is Level One infant care.

A minimum of 30 hours of professional development every three years is required to keep any certification level valid.

The Department of Health and Community Services contracts with the Association of Early Childhood Educators of Newfoundland and Labrador to certify staff and to deliver the orientation courses at no cost to the individual.

PARENT INVOLVEMENT Parent involvement is not specified.

LICENSING, MONITORING AND ENFORCEMENT Regional staff employed by the Department of Health and Community Services carry out monitoring and enforcement of standards. Each of the six regions has a director of child care services, one or more child care consultants and social workers. The child care consultants must have Level Four child care certification and three years experience.

Centres are inspected at least once per year. Child Care Services staff visit centres regularly (monthly where possible) and are available upon request to provide support, advice and direction.

Fire/life safety and health inspections are done annually by officials of the provincial Government Service Centre, Department of Government Services, Labour and Lands.

Minor infractions of the regulations result in a verbal warning. More serious infractions result in a violation order to the centre requesting immediate compliance. If the infractions are not remedied within the designated time, a conditional license, a license suspension or centre closure follows.

Regulated Family Child Care

REGULATION The province licenses non-profit family child care agencies that enter into contractual arrangements with providers to provide child care in compliance with the regulations. The province also licenses individual providers.

MAXIMUM CAPACITY Care for up to six children including the provider's own children not attending school on a full-time basis. Not more than three children may be under 36 months; of these, no more than two may be under 24 months. Under exceptional circumstances (and with director's approval). the provider may add two school-age children if she has two children of her own who are younger than school age. With director's approval, a seventh child may be added for a maximum of 1.5 hours per day, or for a maximum of 12 continuous hours once a week.

A provider may care for three children under 24 months providing that there are no other children being cared for at the same time.

PROVIDER QUALIFICATION REQUIREMENTS Providers who work under the supervision of an agency or who are individually licensed are required to have Entry Level certification (30-60 hour course). A minimum of 30 hours of professional development every three years is required to keep the certification valid.

LICENSING, MONITORING AND ENFORCEMENT In agency-based family child care, home visitors make both announced and unannounced visits at least once a month to monitor the home and provide support to the provider. Home visitors also conduct annual inspection visits at least once a year at which time a written evaluation of the child care service and related requirements is completed. In addition, annual fire/life safety and health inspections are conducted by Government Services Centre inspectors.

Home visitors are responsible for a maximum of 20 homes and are required to have at least Level Two certification in family child care and two years experience in a family child care setting.

Agencies are inspected annually by staff of regional Health and Community Services Boards.

Individually licensed homes are monitored and supported through monthly visits (where possible), and receive annual inspections from staff of regional Health and Community Services boards. In addition, annual fire/life safety and health inspections are conducted by Government Services Centre inspectors.

Municipal or Other Local Government Role

There is no municipal or other local government role in regulated child care.

Child Care Planning and Development

There is no formal plan for the development of child care.

Related Programs

Family Resource Programs

Since 1999, nine family resource programs serving 144 communities have been funded through the National Child Benefit (NCB).

Since 2002/03, federal Early Childhood Development (ECD) funding has resulted in the establishment of six additional family resource programs serving 102 communities. ECD funding also allowed for enhancements to five existing family resource programs to assist in expansion to new communities.

Health Canada through the Community Action Programs for Children (CAPC) and Canadian Prenatal Nutrition Program (CPNP) supports an additional nine family resource programs.

There are also three Military Family Resource Programs in the province.

Key Provincial ECEC Organizations

Association of Early Childhood Educators of Newfoundland and Labrador
P.O. Box 8657
St. John's, NL A1B 3T1
Telephone: 709-579-3004 or 1-866-579-3004
Facsimile: 709-579-0217
Email: aecenl@nfld.net
Website: www.cfc-efc.ca/aecenfld/

Teachers' Organizations and Associations

Newfoundland and Labrador Teachers' Association
3 Kenmount Road
St. John's, NL A1B 1W1
Telephone: 709-726-3223 or 1-800-563-3599
Facsimile: 709-726-4302 or 1-877-711-6582
Website: www.nlta.nf.ca

Prince Edward Island

Kindergarten

Prince Edward Island introduced publicly funded kindergarten in September 2000.

Legislation

Kindergarten in PEI is part of the early childhood system. The act governing kindergarten is the Child Care Facilities Act, Regulations, and Guidelines R.S.P.E.I. 1988.

Children With Special Needs

There is a philosophy of inclusion. Child-specific special needs grants are available to centres for additional staffing from the Department of Health and Social Services. A school-aged child with special needs may attend a second year of kindergarten.

The number of kindergarten children with identified special needs 2003/04: 64. Fifty-five had services of a Special Needs Assistant.

There are no segregated child care programs for children with disabilities.

Centres may apply for a special needs grant on behalf of a child. A grant of up to $11.50/hour based on the training and experience of the staff hired is available. Some documentation is required in order to receive the additional support but it is flexible and social need of the child maybe considered. Special needs funding usually provides for additional staff to lower the ratio of the group. The funding is capped, and in 2001, there was a waiting list for the first time. Parents of children with special needs are not required to be employed or in training to receive a subsidy

No specific training is required for staff to work with children with special needs.

A pilot project is underway with the Early Childhood Development Association of Prince Edward Island using the ECERS-R for centres enrolling children with special needs.

Aboriginal Child Care

Prince Edward Island does not fund or license child care programs on-reserve. There are no First Nations/Inuit Child Care Initiative programs in PEI. There is one unlicensed kindergarten centre on-reserve.

The Abegweit First Nation on the Scotchfort reserve operates an Aboriginal Head Start program, It serves 2-6 year olds, operates from 8 a.m. to 3 p.m. and is unregulated.

Space Statistics (2003/04) (March 2004)

Number of regulated child care spaces

Centre-based	Full-day	Part-day*
Infants	40	0
Preschool	1,918	571
School-age	—	695
Kindergarten	836	671
Total	2,794	*1,937

Note: there are a total of 1,507 children attending kindergarten, 671 who attend part-time kindergarten only and 836 who attend both kindergarten and child care for the balance of the day.

*For purposes of comparison with other provinces where kindergarten is in the public education system, the figure 1,266 part-day spaces (preschool-571 and school-age-695, but excluding part-day kindergarten-671 = 1,266) is used to calculate figures in Tables 9, 12 and 26.

Family child care	40
Total regulated spaces	4,771

Children with special needs in regulated child care	215

Children receiving subsidies	**1,077**

Number of centres and homes

Number of child care centres:	142
— Full day	66
— Part-day nursery schools/preschools	2
— Stand-alone after-school programs	19
— Kindergarten centres	49
Number of individual family child care providers	6

Sponsorship of regulated spaces (2003/04)

Non-profit	1,902
For-profit	2,869

Note: For the purpose of comparison with other jurisdictions where kindergarten is in the public education system, the part-day kindergarten spaces are excluded from the figures in Table 10.

Openings and closings (2002/03)*

New child care centre licenses issued	8
Number of child care centre closures	9
Number of new licenses issued to individual family child care providers	0
Number of family child care agencies/individual providers who ceased providing care	0

*Information for 2003/04 not available

Standards and Regulations

Regulated Centres

STAFF QUALIFICATION REQUIREMENTS Centre supervisors and one full-time staff member in each program must have at least one year Early Childhood Development diploma or university Child Study degree.

Thirty hours of in-service training every three years is required for all staff.

PARENT INVOLVEMENT Not specified

LICENSING, MONITORING AND ENFORCEMENT Each year centres are visited for licensing purposes by Early Childhood Services staff, who observe programming, and by the Child Care Facilities Board, which concentrates primarily on administration. Annual inspections are required by the Fire Marshall's office and the Environmental Health Division of the Department of Health and Social Services.

If a centre is not in compliance with the legislation it may operate under a regular license but is given a specific time frame in which to comply. A centre may have a provisional license for a period of six months, or it may have its license revoked or not renewed. A centre receiving a provisional license or having its license revoked or not renewed may appeal directly to the Minister who then must establish an Appeal Board. This Board must conduct an inquiry and render a decision within 30 days.

The Department of Health and Social Services and the Early Childhood Development Association provides training to the staff of early childhood centres to use the (ECERS-R) and the Canadian Supplementary Scale (CSS) developed for *You Bet I Care!* In addition, they also provide training to supervisors to use the SpeciaLink Child Care Inclusion Profile (SCCIP) to maintain and/or improve inclusive environments.

The Department of Education has appointed a staff resource to the Child Care Facilities Board to be responsible only for inspections in Kindergarten centres.

Regulated Family Child Care

REGULATION Providers are individually licensed.

MAXIMUM CAPACITY Up to seven children including the provider's own children under 12 years, with a maximum of three children under two years.

PROVIDER QUALIFICATION REQUIREMENTS A 30 hour training program, two letters of reference and current first-aid certificate

LICENSING, MONITORING AND ENFORCEMENT Early Childhood Services conducts a program review using the Family Day Care Rating Scale (FDCRS). Annual inspections are made by a Child Care Facilities Board inspector, an inspector for the Fire Marshall's office and an Environmental Health officer.

Municipal Role

There is no legislated municipal role for the development or delivery of child care.

Child Care Planning and Development

Five principles guide the planning of child care: quality, affordability, accessibility, providing for children with special needs, and parent involvement.

Application to the Child Care Facilities Board for a license must include a needs assessment that documents the need for child care in a particular area.

Related Programs

Employment Initiatives

Employment Enhancement and Job Creation are programs for social assistance recipients. Parents enrolled in either program access regular child care subsidies to use the regulated system. The only exception is for those with infants who cannot find a space, or those who work odd, irregular hours. Those parents may access the same fund in the welfare system that provides for occasional babysitting. The provincial social assistance budget has $50,000 for unregulated care.

Key Provincial ECEC Organizations

Early Childhood Development Association of Prince Edward Island
40 Enman Crescent, Room #228
P.O. Box 23055
Charlottetown, PE C1E 1Z6
Telephone: 902-368-1866 or 1-866-368-1866
Facsimile: 902-569-7900
Website: www.ecda.pe.ca

Teachers' Organizations aqnd Associations

Prince Edward Island Teachers' Federation
24 Glen Stewart Drive
P.O. Box 6000
Charlottetown, PE C1A 8B4
Telephone: 902-569-4157 or 1-800-903-4157
Facsimile: 902-569-3682
Website: www.peitf.com

Nova Scotia

Kindergarten

Legislation

Nova Scotia. Legislative Assembly. *Education Act and Regulation*. 1995-96. Amended 1998, 2000, 2002.

Children With Special Needs

There is a policy of including children with special needs in the least restrictive setting. Extra support is available and children have Individual Program Plans (IPPs). Resources such as assistants and technology are provided. A per pupil special education grant is available to school boards.

In 2003/04 287 students (approximately 3% of all Grade Primary students) had IPPs.

Regulated Child Care

Children With Special Needs

Licensed child care centres may receive Supported Child Care funding of between $19 to $82 per full-day and $20 per part-day to support the inclusion of children with special needs who have either a developmental delay or behavioural issue that requires intervention. The funding is intended to cover the additional costs of including children with special needs in child care programs. Funds may be used towards the salary of an early childhood special educator or to purchase materials, equipment or resources that will assist with inclusion.

Eligibility is based on evidence of the child's disability. Parents of children with special needs are not income tested for additional supports. The funding depends on availability and is not an entitlement.

Supported Child Care funding is not available in family child care but may be available in part-day child care centres.

Aboriginal Child Care

Development of on-reserve child care as part of the First Nations/Inuit Child Care Initiative is the responsibility of the Nova Scotia Tri-Partite Social Working Committee: Child Care Facilities and Licensing Agreement Sub-Committee. There are 13 on-reserve child care centres with 233 spaces. Centres follow provincial regulations but are not provincially licensed or funded.

Space Statistics (2003/04) (March 2004)

Number of regulated child care spaces

Centre-based

Full-day	9,318
Part-day	3,282
Family child care	159
Total regulated spaces	12,759
Number of children receiving subsidies	*3,700

Note:This figures includes children that share subsidized spaces. Further breakdowns are not available.

Subsidized child care spaces

Total subsidies: 2,706. Of these 2,426 spaces are allocated to specific non-profit centres and 280 "portable spaces" may be used in either for-profit and non-profit centres and follow the child.

Children with special needs in regulated child care	376

Number of centres and homes

Number of child care centres	382
— Full day	278
— Part-day nursery schools/preschools	43
— Stand-alone after school programs	11
Number of family child care agencies March 2004:	3
Number of family child care providers	34

Sponsorship of regulated centre spaces (2004)

	Full time	Part -time	Total
Non-profit	5,060	1,927	6,987
For-profit	4,258	1,355	5,613
Total	9,318	3,282	12,600

Openings and closings (2003/04)

New child care centre licenses issued	28
Number orchid care centre closures	24
Number of new licenses issued to family child care agencies	0
Number of family child care agencies that ceased providing care	0

Standards and Regulations

Regulated Centres

STAFF QUALIFICATION REQUIREMENTS The centre director and 2/3 of the staff must have completed a training program in early childhood education or its equivalent. To be considered equivalent staff must have completed grade 12, have a minimum of two years experience in a day care centre and have successful completion of a full credit course of two semesters of post-secondary education in at least one of the following areas:

- human growth and development with an emphasis on the young child;
- curriculum development and implementation of programs for young children in child care centres;
- and successful completion of 25 hours in training programs, seminars or workshops in the other area not completed by way of post-secondary education.

Note: Workshops that are directly related to planning the child care curriculum are also offered at conferences. These workshops may be considered as meeting the requirements of equivalency (as stated above).

PARENT INVOLVEMENT Parent meetings must be held at least four times in a year for full-day programs and twice a year for part-day programs.

LICENSING, MONITORING AND ENFORCEMENT Initial and ongoing inspections are conducted by provincial Early Childhood Development Officers (ECDOs). ECDOs require education, experience and expertise in early childhood education, child development or special needs.

Licenses can be issued for up to 24 months for part-day programs and up to 12 months for full-day programs. If a centre is not in compliance with the Day Care Act and Regulations, clear direction and written communication of the enforcement requirements and the compliance dates are sent to the program (centre) director and/or to the operator. The non-compliance will be documented and conditions may be attached to a license requiring that the violations be corrected. To assist with compliance with the Day Care Act and Regulations, ECDOs are guided by the Department of Community Services' Compliance/Enforcement Policy.

If the centre fails to meet the legislative requirements in this period, the Day Care Act and Regulation authorizes the Minister to cancel or not renew the license. A license may not be renewed if there is evidence of a threat to the health or safety of children, or if there is a pattern of noncompliance to regulations that impacts on the physical, social, emotional, or intellectual development of children. Health inspections are conducted by inspectors from the Department of Agriculture and Fisheries. Fire inspections are conducted by the Department of Environment and Labour.

Regulated Family Child Care

REGULATION Family child care providers are supervised by licensed agencies.

MAXIMUM CAPACITY Up to six children of mixed ages including the provider's own preschool children, or up to eight school-age children including the provider's own school-age children.

PROVIDER QUALIFICATION REQUIREMENTS Providers must be at least 18 years old, be screened through the Child Abuse Register and have undergone a criminal record check by the RCMP or local police. No early child-hood training or experience is required by the province.

LICENSING, MONITORING AND ENFORCEMENT A licensed family child care agency staff must have ECE qualifications as per the provincial regulations. The agency is responsible for recruiting, screening and selecting providers, and for approving and monitoring homes. Provincial Early Childhood Development Officers (ECDOs) conduct annual visits and evaluations of agencies to confirm adherence to provincial guidelines for child care homes.

Funding

Supported Child Care funding

Between $19 and $82/day/child with special needs intended to cover additional costs associated with including children with special needs. Special needs are described as either a developmental delay or behavioural issue presented by the child that requires intervention. Eligibility is based on evidence of the child's disability. This grant depends on availability of funding.

Municipal or Other Local Government Role

There is no legislated municipal or other local government role.

Child Care Planning and Development

Nova Scotia developed *Our Children: Today's Investment, Tomorrow's Promise* (2001), which serves as the foundation for the province's Early Childhood Development/ Early Learning and Child Care investments.

The Early Childhood Development Initiative (ECDI) was created as part of Nova Scotia's commitment to "support families and improve opportunities for children to have a healthy start in life" and is reported in Nova Scotia's Early Childhood Development Initiative Annual Report April 2003.

Key Provincial Early Childhood Education and Care Organizations

Child Care Connection-NS
Suite 100, 1200 Tower Road
Halifax, NS, B3H 4K6
Telephone: 902-423-8199 1-800-565-8199
Fax: 902-492-8106

Certification Council of Early Childhood Educators of Nova Scotia
c/o 100 1200 Tower Road
Halifax, NS, B3H 4K6

Coalition of Non Profit Directors of Nova Scotia
c/o 17 Earnscliff Avenue,
Wolfville, NS, B4P 1X4

Private Licensed Administrators Association
2695 Dutch Village Road
Halifax, NS, B3L 4G5

Société Provincial des Intervenant(e)s du Prescolaire (SPIP)
CP 117
Pointe de L'Eglise, NS, B0W 1M0

Teachers' Organizations and Associations

Nova Scotia Teachers' Union
3106 Dutch Village Road
Halifax, NS, B3L 4L7
Telephone: 902-477-5621
Fax: 902-477-3517
Website: www.nstu.ca

New Brunswick

Kindergarten

Legislation

New Brunswick. *Legislative Assembly Education Act, 1997. c.E-1.12*

Sections of the Education Act specific to kindergarten are: Section 8 (school privileges), Section 15 (compulsory attendance), and Section 16 (exceptions).

Children With Special Needs

The *Education Act* mandates the inclusion of exceptional pupils. A policy on Special Education is under development. Extra supports include physical accommodations such as ramps or elevators, assistive technology, development of special education plans, and teacher assistants and school intervention workers. If the child's needs warrant it, a Teacher Assistant may be provided (see Classroom Assistants below for details).

Regulated Child Care

Children With Special Needs

Children with identified special needs may be referred for integrated day care services through the Early Childhood Initiatives (ECI) Program. To be identified as special needs, the child must fall into one of three categories: a confirmed diagnosis at birth, developmental issues after birth or family risk factors.

Facilities providing integrated day care services to children referred under ECI may receive an average of $3, 150/ year/child for children age 2-5. The maximum payment for a child with high needs is $5,150/year, primarily to provide a support worker. However, the funding may also be used for transportation, materials and equipment and/or additional nutritional needs of the child.

There are no additional training requirements required for support personnel who may be hired under the Early Childhood Initiatives.

Aboriginal Child Care

New Brunswick approves child care centres on-reserve upon request from a First Nations community. There are four centres on-reserve currently approved by the Department and in 2004 applications were pending from two others. Ongoing monitoring and renewal functions are managed locally. Licensed centres on-reserve are not eligible for provincial funding and parents are not eligible for fee subsidy.

Some Head Start programs receive funding through an agreement between the First Nations of New Brunswick and the Department of Indian and Northern Affairs (New Brunswick Head Start) and by Health Canada (Aboriginal Head Start). These programs are not licensed by the provincial government.

Space Statistics (2003/04)

Number of regulated child care spaces

Centre-based		11,747
Family child care	150	
Total regulated spaces	11,897	

New Brunswick approves day care centres for a total enrolment based on usable space and does not allocate spaces according to specific age groups.

Enrolled spaces by age group

	Full-time	Part-time
Child care centres		
Infants	451	162
Preschool	3,432	2,688
School-age	3,669	1,178
Family child care		
Infants	12	5
preschool	46	37
School-age	24	15

Note: The number of enrolled spaces by age group is reported through the Quality Improvement Funding Support which includes 338 of the 357 licensed centres in the province.

Children with special needs in regulated child care   589

Note: This figure represents the number of children receiving Integrated Day Care Services.

Children receiving subsidies   2,652

Number of centres and homes

Number of child care centres:		357
— Full day	216	
— Part-day nursery schools/preschools	33	
— Stand-alone after-school programs	76	
— Combined nursery school/school-age programs	13	
— Other*	19	
— Number of family child care providers	25	

* There are 79 centres that did not apply to receive the Quality Improvement Funding Support and information on the part-day/full-day nature of their operations is not available.

Sponsorship of full-time regulated centre spaces

Data are not available but according to provincial officials, approximately 70% are for-profit and 30% non-profit.

Openings and closings

New child care centre licenses issue in 2003/04	0
Number of child care centre closures in 2303/04	0

Number of new licenses issued to individual family child care providers in 2003/04: Information not available

Number of family child care providers who ceased providing care: Information not available

Standards and Regulations

Regulated Centres

STAFF QUALIFICATION REQUIREMENTS Effective April 1, 2003 the Director OR his/her designate OR one in four staff were to have been required to have a one-year community college ECE certificate or equivalent- New applicants for child care centres must meet this training requirement prior to approval. Existing centres that do not need the requirement have been provided with funding and access to training, and are expected to meet the requirement by April 1, 2006.

The one-year certificate program is offered through distance education over a three-year period. Eligible students receive 80% of the tuition costs to complete the training.

Staff must be at least 16 years old. Staff 16-19 years old are required to be supervised by a primary staff member who must be at least 19 years old. All staff must have first-aid training.

PARENT INVOLVEMENT Non-profit centres are required to be managed by a board of directors whose members include at least two parents of enrolled children. There is no requirement for parent involvement.

LICENSING, MONITORING AND ENFORCEMENT Nine regional Early Childhood Services coordinators are responsible for monitoring compliance with the regulations. Regional coordinators must have an ECE credential or equivalent. Child care centres receive one annual inspection and may receive up to three unannounced monitoring visits per year. Centres determined to be in noncompliance with standards are given a time frame in which to comply. Where the child care service is considered necessary and where the Minister is satisfied that the requirements will be met within the designated period of time, the regulation permits the issuance of a temporary approval for a period not to exceed six months.

The *Family Services Act* provides the Minister with the authority to investigate, recommend changes, suspend the operation or terminate the approval of a child care facility. While the functions of approval and monitoring are delegated to regional offices of the department, the authority for openings and closings has not been delegated. Regions recommend and approvals are granted or terminated by the Minister.

Regulated Family Child Care (Community Day Care Homes)

REGULATION Individually licensed

MAXIMUM CAPACITY

Infants: Three
2-5 years: Five
Six years and over: Nine
Combination of ages: Six
The capacity maximums include the provider's own children under 12 years.

PROVIDER QUALIFICATION REQUIREMENTS No early childhood education training or experience is required. Providers must be at least 19 years old and have first aid training. Training requirements implemented in April 1, 2003 do not apply to operators of community day care homes.

LICENSING, MONITORING AND ENFORCEMENT The regional Early Childhood Services Coordinators are responsible for licensing and monitoring community day care homes. Community day care home providers are issued an initial license and must make an annual request for renewal. The regional coordinators spot-check homes to ensure compliance with the regulations.

Municipal or Other Local Government Role

There is no legislated municipal or other local government role.

Child Care Planning and Development

The Department of Family and Community Services has lead responsibility for the initiatives of the Early Childhood Development Agenda and the Early Learning and Child Care Agreement.

The Department is currently working on a child care plan.

Key Provincial ECEC Organizations

Early Childhood Care and Education New Brunswick
Soins et Education à la Petite Enfance du Nouveau-Brunswick
30 Gordon Street, Suite 103
Moncton, NB E1C 1L8
Email: edcc@nb.aibn.com
Telephone (506) 382-8143 or 1-888-834-7070
Facsimile (506) 854-8533

Teachers' Organizations and Associations

Association des Enseignantes et des Enseignants
Francophones du Nouveau-Brunswick
650, rue Montgomery
C.P. 712

Fredericton, NB E3B 5B4
Telephone: 506-452-8921
Facsimile: 506-453-9795
Email: aefnb@nbnet.nb.ca
Website: www.aefnb.nh.ca

New Brunswick Teachers' Association
650 Montgomery St.
P.O. Box 752
Fredericton, NB E3B 5R6
Telephone: 506-452-8921
Facsimile: 506-453-9795
Email: nbtainfo@nbnet.nb.ca
Website: www.nbta.ca

New Brunswick Teachers' Federation
Federation des Enseignants du Nouveau-Brunswick
650 Montgomery St.
P.O. Box 1535
Fredericton, NB E3B 5G2
Telephone: 506-452-1736
Facsimile: 506-453-9795
Website: www.nbtf-fenb.nh.ca

Quebec

Kindergarten

Legislation

Quebec. National Assembly. Education Act. R.S.Q, c.1-13.3

Quebec. National Assembly. An Act to amend the Education Act concerning the Conseil scolaire de l'ile de Montréal, Bill 41(2001, c. 30).

Quebec. National Assembly. An Act to amend the Education Act, Bill 35. (2001, c. 46).

Quebec. National Assembly. Education Act for Cree, Inuit and Naskapi Native Persons. R.S.Q., c.I-14.

Children With Special Needs

There is a Quebec policy—Politique d'adaptation scolaire—that addresses inclusion, specialized services and corresponding budgets. School boards can adopt additional policies that expand on it but cannot restrict it.

About 50% of children with special needs are included in regular classes. Others either attend special classes in schools or attend specialized schools (for instance, schools for the deaf).

For four year olds with special needs (handicaps as defined in Quebec), the school board has the obligation to deliver a kindergarten program if the parents so request.

In 2003/04, 778 children out of 1,552 identified with special needs were included in regular kindergarten classes.

There are additional budgets tied to inclusion of children with special needs.

Regulated Child Care

Children With Special Needs

Quebec has a policy encouraging inclusion of children with special needs in regular programs. For a child who has a diagnosed disability or who meets the ministry definition of a "disabled" child, a one-time grant of $2,200 and an additional $25/day/child on top of the regular operating grants is available. Admission is at the discretion of the CPE.

Aboriginal Child Care

Quebec regulates child care on-reserve. In 2004, there were 41 child care centres, three family child care services and no garderies on-reserve. Other centres were under construction. On-reserve child care is funded through agreements between First Nations communities and federal and provincial governments. The Quebec Native Women's Association, Band Councils, the Cree and the Kativik regional administrations play key roles in First Nations child care in Quebec.

Space Statistics (2003/04)

Number of regulated child care spaces

Centre-based

Infant/toddler	17,755 (CPE and garderie)
Preschooler (18 mos-4 yrs)	76,240 (CPE and garderie)

Note: Breakdowns by type by age are no longer available

	Child care centres (CPE)	Day care centres (garderie)
Total centre-based spaces	68,274	29,437
Family child care	82,044	
Total spaces regulated by the Ministère de l'Emploi, de la Solidarité sociale et de la Famille (MESSF)		179,755
Total school-age child care spaces		141,977

Note: School-age child care for children aged 5-12 is the responsibility of the Ministry of Education (MEQ).

Total spaces regulated by MESSF and under the aegis of MEQ	321,732

Children with special needs in regulated child care:	2,274

Number of child care programs

Number of child care centres	996

Note: Breakdown by CPE and garderie is no longer available

Stand-alone after school programs	Information not available
Number of family child care agencies (part of CPEs)	852
Number of family child care providers	13,000 (estimate)

Openings and closings

New child care centre licenses issued	16
Number of child care centre closures	Information not available

Note: Breakdown by CPE and garderie not available

Number of new licenses issued to family child care agencies:	44

Number of family child care agencies who ceased providing care: Information not available

Sponsorship of centre-based spaces	
Non-profit (CPE)	68.274
School-board operated school-age spaces	141,977
Total non-profit spaces	210,251
For-profit and other non-CPE centres (garderies)	29,437
Note: The majority of garderies are for-profit.	

Standards and Regulations

Regulated Centres (Centres Under CPES and Gardèries)

STAFF QUALIFICATION REQUIREMENTS Two-thirds of staff in centre-based CPEs must have a college diploma or university degree in ECE. Centres operated by CPEs that have been modified to expand capacity have until the third anniversary of the expansion to comply with these training requirements (introduced in 2001). Until that time, staff qualifications in these centres must conform to the previous regulations requiring 1/3 of staff to have the training outlined above.

In garderies (for-profit centres and non-profit centres not operated by a CPE), 1/3 of staff must have a college diploma or university degree in ECE.

PARENT INVOLVEMENT CPE board structure requires 2/3 of board membership to be parents.

LICENSING, MONITORING AND ENFORCEMENT The Ministère de l'Emploi, de la Solidarité sociale et de la Famille (MESSF) issues permits (licenses) for up to a three-year period. MESSP inspectors may visit any licensed operation to monitor its compliance with regulations.

There is no regulatory requirement for the frequency of visits by inspectors. Inspectors are not required to have a degree, diploma, or training in early childhood education.

Quebec does not issue conditional or provisional licenses. If a centre is found to be in noncompliance with legislative requirements but there is no immediate danger to the health or well-being of the children, MESSE informs the centre's board (in writing) that the program is in noncompliance with a specific regulation(s) and requests rectification. A follow-up check is done by an inspector when sufficient time is deemed to have passed. Repeated instances of noncompliance which do not pose an immediate threat may result in a court hearing.

The operator may appeal the loss of license (or the refusal by MESSF to renew a license) or may contest a decision to the Tribunal administratif du Québec. Its decision is binding.

REGULATED FAMILY CHILD CARE Family child care providers are supervised by a CPE.

MAXIMUM CAPACITY Up to six children including the provider's children under nine years; no more than two children may be under 18 months. If the provider is assisted by another adult, they may care for nine children, including both providers' own children, with not more than four children being under 18 months.

PROVIDER QUALIFICATION REQUIREMENTS Family child care worker

Staff duties include approving/recognizing people responsible for family child care, providing technical and professional support to such persons, and exercising control and supervision for such persons. Staff responsible for supervision must have at least three years of full-time experience working with children or supervising or directing people.

Family child care provider

Family child care providers must hold a first-aid certificate and complete a training program, lasting at least 45 hours, pertaining to child development, health, safety and diet issues, and organization and leadership in a "life environment". Many CPEs provide training for providers.

LICENSING, MONITORING AND ENFORCEMENT Family child care workers are required to do on-site home visits. The CPE is responsible for ensuring that providers meet the regulations. MESSF monitors records of home visits and activity reports.

Special needs school-age grants

From the Ministry of Education, school-age child care services receive a flat rate per child with special needs of $1,000 for each child attending the service on a regular basis, and $500 for each child that attends on an irregular basis

The basic allowance for child care centres and family child care equals the allowable expenses less the parental reduced contribution (PRC)

Municipal and Other Local Government Role

Municipalities may no longer hold licenses to operate child care facilities. School boards provide school-age child care for children attending kindergarten and elementary school.

Child Care Planning and Development

Quebec uses a province-wide planning process. Les conseils régionaux de développement, with representation from municipalities, social services, and child care organizations, set priorities by region. They develop five-year plans based on population and labour force statistics, funding and relative regional equity.

The Quebec government historically had a policy that strongly favours the development of child care services that are controlled by user-parents. MESSF licenses (permits) new child care services as the requirements of the Act and Regulations are met.

Key Provincial ECEC Organizations

Association québécoise des CPEs
6611 rue Jarry est, bur.2
Saint-Leonard
Montréal, PQ H1P 1W5
Téléphone: 514-326-8008
Télécopieur: 514-326-3322
www.aqcpe.com

Association des services de garde en milieu scolaire du Québec
13, rue Saint-Laurent est
Longeuil, PQ J4H 4B7
Téléphone: 450-646-2753
Télécopieur: 450-646-1807
www.familis.org

Syndicats des travailleuses et travailleurs en garderie.
FSSS-CSN
1601 avenue de Lorimier, #105
Montreal, PQ H2K 3W5
Téléphone: 514-598-2210
Télécopieur: 514-598-2223
www.fsss.qc.ca

Teachers' Organizations And Associations

Association québecoise des éducateurs et des éducatrices du primaire
85, rue Saint-Charles Quest
Bureau 2201, 2e étage
Longueuil, PQ J7H 1C5
Téléphone: 450-463-4300
Télécopieur: 450-928-0387
www.aqep.org

Federation nationale des enseignantes et des enseignants du Québec
1601, rue de Lorimier
Montreal. PQ H2K 4M5
Téléphone: 514-598-2241
Télécopieur: 514.598-2190
www.fneeq.qc.ca

Ontario

Kindergarten

Legislation

Ontario. Legislative Assembly. *Education Act,* R.S.O. 1990, c. E.2

Section 16 of the *Education Act* is specific to private schools.

Ontario funds and delivers denominational education. Both "public" and Catholic school boards are publicly funded.

Children With Special Needs

The *Education Act* requires that all publicly funded school boards provide special education programs and services to students who have been identified as exceptional. This requirement extends to all enrolled pupils. Inclusion is not specified.

Number of kindergarten children with special needs: Information not available

Regulated Child Care

Children With Special Needs

Ontario does not have a written policy regarding children with special needs but encourages integration and inclusion of children with special needs into community child care services. Special needs resourcing provides assistance for staffing, equipment, supplies or services to support the inclusion of children with special needs in child care.

Resource teachers generally work for agencies that provide a variety of services for children with special needs, and may serve children in several child care settings. The level of service per child can vary depending on the child's needs, the local service model, and available resources. Consequently the previous ratio of one resource teacher to four children with special needs is no longer applicable in all areas. A resource teacher must hold a diploma in early childhood education or academic equivalent and have completed a post-secondary school program related to children with special needs. If working with children with multiple disabilities, the resource teacher must also have a current standard certificate in first aid.

There are no training or experience requirements for staff other than resource teachers who are working with children with special needs.

Aboriginal Child Care

Ontario funds and regulates on-reserve child care.

As of March 2004, there were 64[3] licensed child care centres on-reserve with a licensed capacity of 2,513. There were also two licensed private-home day care agencies with 36 homes on-reserve.

Ontario cost-shares fee subsidies for licensed on-reserve child care programs on an 80/20 basis with First Nations, and the province pays 100% of other child care financing (wage subsidies, special needs resourcing and family resource centres). First Nations manage the fee subsidy system in their communities. Ontario recovers the majority of expenditures on fee subsidies through the federal government under the 1965 Memorandum of Agreement Respecting Welfare Programs for Indians.

Space Statistics (2003/04)

Number of regulated child care spaces	
Infants (0-18 mos)	5,981
Toddlers (18-30 mos)	18,877
Preschool (2.5-5 yrs)	86,163
JK (3 yrs 8 mos)	6,355
SK (4 yrs 8 mos)	6,916
School-age (6-12 yrs)	62,613
Private home day care	19,838
Total (estimate)	206,743

Note: Breakdowns of full- and pan-time centre-based child care are not available by age.

Children receiving special needs resourcing in regulated child care

Note: Figures comparable to the other provinces/territories—that is the number of children at a given point in time—are not available.

A cumulative total of 21,305 children were served throughout the fiscal year.

Number of children in regulated child care receiving subsidies	
Regular fee subsidies:	89,787
	(Cumulative total throughout the fiscal year)
Ontario Works funding for licensed care	14,033
	(Cumulative total throughout the fiscal year)
Total	103,820
	(Cumulative total throughout the fiscal year)

[3] Please note that in the previous version of this publication, ECEC in Canada 2001 (2002), the number of on-reserve child care centres was reported as 86 (September 2002). Updated information from Ontario is that at December 31, 2002, there were 67 licensed First Nations child care centres on-reserve with a licensed capacity of 2,722 spaces and two licensed private home day care agencies with 36 homes.

Note: Figures comparable to the other provinces/territories—that is the number of children at a given point in time—are not available.

An additional 712 school-age children received regular fee subsidies for approved (unregulated) school-age recreation programs and an additional 11,387 received Ontario Works funding for unregulated care.

Number of centres and homes

Number of child care centres:	3,874
— Full day	2,321
— Part-day nursery schools/preschools	1,825
— Stand-alone school-age programs	1,582

Note: Child care centres may be licensed to offer more than one program (e.g., a before-and after school program for school-age children and a full-day program for preschool-age children). As a result, a number of individual centres will appear in more than one category above. As well, there may be overlap between the age groups served in the various program types. This means that before-and-after-school programs may serve children other than school-age children (e.g., JK, SK, preschool). It also means that programs exclusively serving school-age children may be listed as full-day, half-day or before-and-after-school.

Number of family child care providers	7,765
Number of family child care agencies	140

Openings and Closings

New child care centre licenses issued	349
Number of child care centre closures	256
Number of new licenses issued to family child care agencies	8
Number of family child care agencies who ceased providing care	5

Sponsorship of regulated centre spaces

Not-for-profit*	146,786
For-profit	40,345

*This includes municipally-operated centres. Current figures are not available for the number of municipally-operated child care spaces. In 1998, however, 18,143 of the non-profit spaces were municipal.

Sponsorship of regulated private-home day care agencies

	Agencies	Homes
Non-profit	123	7,343
For-profit	17	422
Total	140	7,765

This includes municipally-operated family child care agencies and homes. See previous note.

Standards and Regulations

Regulated Centres

STAFF QUALIFICATION REQUIREMENTS Centre supervisors must have a two year diploma in early childhood education from an approved College of Applied Arts and Technology (CAAT) or the equivalent and at least two years experience working in a day nursery with children who are of the same age and developmental level as the children in the day nursery where the supervisor is employed.

One staff person with each group of children must have a two year early childhood education diploma from a CAAT or the equivalent.

A Ministry Director has the authority to waive the educational requirements for directors and other staff in a specific program.

PARENT INVOLVEMENT Each centre and family child care agency must have a written statement regarding parent involvement. The type of parental involvement is not specified.

LICENSING, MONITORING AND ENFORCEMENT Ministry Program Advisors based in Regional Offices license, monitor and enforce the Day Nurseries Act and its Regulations.

Program Advisors are not required to have training in early childhood education.

The annual license renewal process includes an inspection of the child care facility to ensure compliance with the regulatory standards. Unannounced drop-in visits are also conducted. Noncompliance with the legislation that does not pose an immediate threat to the children's wellbeing may result in a provisional license with a time frame in which the operator is required to correct the noncompliance. Repeated noncompliance of a serious nature or noncompliance that poses a likely danger to the children may result in a refusal to renew or a revocation of the license. However, the provincial Director of the child care branch must give notice of intent to close the centre to the operator who then has the right to appeal to the License Appeal Tribunal. The legislation provides the authority for immediate closure in the situation of immediate danger to the children's well-being.

Regulated Family Child Care

In Ontario, family child care has historically been referred to as "private home day care" in provincial legislation. The terms "home child care" or "family child care" are also used.

REGULATION The Ministry licenses family child care agencies which then enter into agreements with caregivers to provide child care. The agencies provide supervision as specified in the regulations.

MAXIMUM CAPACITY Care for up to five children from 0-12 years. Not more than two of the children may be under two years, and not more than three of the children may be under three years, including the caregiver's own children less than six years. Not more than two may be children with special needs. Only one child with special needs may be cared for if there is one other child under two years of age or two children over two years of age.

If the caregiver's own children are under six years, then she/he may care for two children age 6-12 years. For example, if a caregiver's children are ages three and four, then she/he may provide care for up to two more children between the ages of 6 and 12.

PROVIDER QUALIFICATION REQUIREMENTS No caregiver training qualifications are specified in provincial regulations. Regulation requires caregivers to be older than 18 years and, if working with children with special needs, to hold a standard first-aid certificate. Many agencies provide training for caregivers.

Caregivers are supervised by agency staff, called home visitors, who are required to have completed a post-secondary program in child development or family studies, and to have at least two years experience working with children who are of the same age and developmental levels as the children cared for by the agency where the person is employed.

LICENSING, MONITORING AND ENFORCEMENT The agency home visitor is required to conduct quarterly in-home supervisory visits. The agency is responsible for ensuring that legislated requirements are met.

As part of agency licensing inspection, provincial program advisors may inspect homes to ensure that the agency is in compliance with the Day Nurseries Act and Regulations.

Special needs resourcing is split 80/20 between the province and municipalities. The province does not require that parents of children with special needs be needs tested for fee subsidy eligibility but some municipalities have imposed a needs test.

Municipal or Other Local Government Role

Responsibility for managing delivery of child care services lies with 47 Consolidated Municipal Service Managers (CMSMs) or District Social Services Administration Boards (DSSABs). (These are usually municipal or regional governments.)

The transfer of responsibility was completed on January 1, 2000 and was authorized by amendments to the *Day Nurseries Act*.

This change meant that 20% of funding for wage subsidies, resource centres and special needs resourcing is paid by local governments, whereas 100% of these funds were previously paid by the provincial government.

In addition, Ontario municipal governments operate regulated child care, a role they have played since the time of World War II.

Beginning in 1992, school boards also were authorized to operate child care services; however, very few do so.

The Ontario Municipal Social Services Association (OMSSA), in operation since 1950, works to "build members' (municipal governments and non-profit social service organizations) capacity to plan, manage and deliver quality human services in their communities".

Child Care Planning and Development

Beginning in 2000, the provincial government requires local governments to develop local service plans, including service targets and levels, according to provincial guidelines on local service planning. Although these are three year service plans, Regional Offices review them on an annual basis.

Other ECEC Services

Early Years Centres

The Ontario Early Years Centres were implemented in two phases: 42 Centres opened in 2002 (Phase 1), and 61 Centres opened in 2003 (Phase 2), for a total of 103 Centres (one in each provincial riding).

They offer a common set of programs and services for children and parents/caregivers including:

- Early learning activities for children, such as literacy and numeracy;
- Parent resources, information and training on topics such as healthy child development;
- Pre- and post-natal resources, information and training;
- Outreach to encourage parent participation;
- Volunteer co-ordination and speakers bureau;
- Monitoring program effectiveness and tracking community progress in improving child development outcomes; and
- Information about and linkages to services external to the Centre.

Ontario Works child care

Ontario Works child care funds maybe used to cover the cost of regulated child care as a transition measure where participants are in employment assistance activities or are entering the paid labour market; or payment for unregulated child care arrangements or alternatives to child care (e.g., summer camp, supervised homework programs, recreation programs) up to established maximums.

Whether the payment goes to the parent or to a service provider is determined by each CMSM/DSSAB.

Key Provincial ECEC Organizations

Ontario Coalition for Better Child Care
726 Bloor Street West, Suite 209
Toronto, ON M6G 4A1
Telephone: 416-538-0628
Facsimile: 4t6-538-6737
Website: www.childcareontario.org

Association of Early Childhood Educators, Ontario
40 Orchard View Blvd., Suite 211
Toronto, ON M4R 2G1
Telephone: 416-487-3157
Facsimile: 416-487-3758
Website: http:www.cfc_efc.ca/aeceo/index.html

Association of Day Care Operators of Ontario
Administrative Office
331 Dufferin Avenue
Belleville, ON K8N 3X6
Telephone: 705-733-2052 or 1-800-567-7075
Facsimile: 1-800-567-7075

Teachers' Organizations And Associations

Elementary Teachers' Federation of Ontario
480 University Ave., Ste.1000
Toronto, ON MSG lV2
Telephone: 416-962-3836
Facsimile: 416-642-2424
Website: www.etfo.ca

Ontario English Catholic Teachers' Association
65 St. Clair Ave. E., Suite 400
Toronto, ON M4T 2Y8
Telephone: 416-925-2493
Facsimile: 416-925-7764
Website: www.oecta.on.ca

Ontario Teachers' Federation
1300 Yonge Street, Suite 200
Toronto, ON M4T 1X3
Telephone: 416-966-3424
Facsimile: 416-966-5450
Website: www.otffeo.on.ca

People for Education
RO Box 64 Station B
Toronto, ON M5S 2S6
Telephone: 416-410-3571
Facsimile: 416-461-4107
Website: www.peoplforeducation.com

Manitoba

Kindergarten

Legislation

Manitoba. Legislative Assembly. *Public Schools Act.* 1987, C.S.M, c. P250. Amended 1992, 1996, 1997, 2001, 2002.

Children with Special Needs

There is a policy of inclusion of children with special needs in regular kindergarten. There is both block funding to school divisions and funding allocated to identified child needs determined on a case by case basis.

The number of kindergarten children with special needs is not available.

Regulated Child Care

Children With Special Needs

The Manitoba Children with Liabilities Program integrates children with special needs into mainstream child care. Support is available to non-profit child care centres, nursery schools and family and group child care homes. To receive additional supports, children must have an eligible cognitive, developmental or physical disability. The Child Care Program will also cover a child with "behavioural" problems as well as nursing support for medically fragile children. Services are not an entitlement but there is usually no waiting list once a diagnosis has been made. Parents pay the same basic cost of child care as other families, but regardless of family income parents do not pay the cost of the additional resources to support the child's participation in a child care program. Funding for the additional supports is paid to the program. Non-profit child care centres and regulated family day care homes are eligible for funding. Approximately 10% of the child care budget is allocated for supports for children with special needs.

Most of the special needs funding is for staff. There are also grants for necessary renovations, equipment and educational materials, training or professional services.

Children's Special Services staff work with the Child Care Program and the Departments of Education and Training and Health to coordinate and place children with special needs into child care programs. Children's Special Services also provides consultation and funding to non-government agencies that deliver therapy, respite and family support services.

There are no special training requirements for staff working with children with disabilities in child care.

Aboriginal Child Care

Manitoba does not license or fund child care programs on-reserve but the Child Care Branch assists facilities on-reserve to meet requirements equivalent to licensing. Sixty-two child care facilities have been established in First Nations communities under the federal government's First Nations/Inuit Child Care Initiative. A First Nations ECE training program has been developed in Opaskawayak-Keewatin Community College. A certificate program in Aboriginal child care is offered through Red River College. There are approximately 50 Aboriginal Head Start programs in Manitoba; they are not required to be regulated but many choose to become regulated.

Space Statistics (2003/04) (April 2004)

Number of regulated child care spaces		
Centre-based	Full-day	Part-time
Infants/toddler	1,367	*24
Preschool	9,859	4,049
School-age	—	6,126
Family child care	4,209	
Total regulated spaces	25,634	
*This represents children under two years attending a nursery school.		

Children with special needs in regulated child care	1,341

Children receiving subsidies	11,568

Number of centres and homes	
Number of child care centres:	567
— Full day	250
— Part-day nursery schools/preschools	193
— Stand-alone after school programs	124
Number of family child care providers	591

Sponsorship of regulated centre spaces	
Non-profit	19,678
For-profit	1,747

Openings and closings (2003/04)	
New child care centre licenses issued	23
Number of child care centre closures	10
Number of new licenses issued to individual family child care providers	95
Number of family child care providers who ceased providing care	101

Standards and Regulations

Regulated Centres

STAFF QUALIFICATION REQUIREMENTS Manitoba has three qualification levels:

Early Childhood Educator (ECE) III: An approved ECE II program and a recognized certificate program or an approved degree program from a recognized university.

Early Childhood Educator (ECE) II: An approved diploma in child care services from a recognized community college or satisfactory completion of the Child Care Program Competency-based Assessment (CBA) Program.

Child Care Assistant (CCA): Not eligible on the basis of educational requirements for classification at the ECE II or III level; employee in a child care centre.

Two-thirds of a full-time centres staff for 0-6 year olds must be classified as ECE II or III and 1/2 of staff employed in school-age centres and nursery schools must he classified as ECE II or III.

A director in a full-time preschool centre must be classified as an ECE III and have one year of experience in working with children in child care or in a related field. A director in a school-age centre or nursery school must be classified as an ECE II and have one year of experience in child care or in a related setting.

All staff must be 18 years of age and have completed a first-aid course that includes CPR training relevant to the age group. All staff must give permission to release information from the Child Care Program to a prospective employer about any criminal record or child abuse registry record.

PARENT INVOLVEMENT All licensed non-profit centres are required to have boards of directors where parents constitute a minimum of 20% of the board members. For-profit centres are required to have parent advisory committees.

LICENSING, MONITORING AND ENFORCEMENT There are 24.5 Child Care Coordinators. They conduct a minimum of three monitoring visits of each centre each year, one of which is a re-licensing visit. A fourth contact with the facility during the year is also required. Child Care Coordinators must be certified as ECE IIIs and have a minimum of five years supervisory experience in child care.

Provisional licenses may be issued if the facility does not meet all of the requirements of the regulations or if time is required to bring the centre into compliance.

A licensing order may be issued when a severe violation of the Act or Regulations occurs. The order requires immediate correction of the areas listed and is posted in the centre. Failure to comply may result in suspension or revocation of the license.

A license may be revoked if there is continued noncompliance with licensing requirements and the facility is deemed hazardous to the health, safety and well-being of the children.

Regulated Family Child Care

REGULATION Individually licensed

MAXIMUM CAPACITY Family child care homes (one provider): Eight children under 12 years (including the provider's own children under 12 years). No more than five children may be under six years, of whom no more than three children may be under two years.

Group child care homes (two providers): Twelve children under 12 years (including the provider's own children under 12 years). No more than three children may be under two years.

PROVIDER QUALIFICATION REQUIREMENTS New family child care providers are required to complete an approved 40-hour course from a community college in family child care or early childhood education within their first year of operating.

If a provider is classified as an ECE II or III, that provider may charge a higher maximum daily fee equivalent to the fees charged in child care centres.

Providers must be at least 18 years of age and have a valid first-aid certificate that includes CPR training relevant to the age group being cared for. Providers are assessed by the Child Care Program for their suitability to provide care based on recognized family child care competencies.

Providers must give permission to release information about any criminal record or child abuse registry record or prior contact with a Child and Family Services Agency.

LICENSING, MONITORING AND ENFORCEMENT When an individual applies for a license, provincial Child Care Coordinators complete safety inspection reports of the applicant's home. Three drop-in visits per year and one scheduled re-licensing visit per year are conducted.

Municipal or Other Local Government Role

There is no legislated municipal or other local government role in the delivery or operation of child care.

Child Care Planning and Development

In April 2002, Manitoba released its Five Year Plan for child care. The plan is intended to maintain and improve quality, accessibility and affordability. It sets out targets for funding new spaces, increasing wages and the number of trained ECEs. (See History section for details.)

CHILD CARE IN SCHOOLS There is a child care in schools policy that must be considered in all new, renovating or replacement schools. The capital funding comes through the Public Schools Finance Board. Community members work with the Child Care Program office to conduct a needs survey and help determine numbers. The school retains ownership of space and has a partnership agreement as long as there is a need for child care. Centres pay rent according to board policy for exclusive space and are expected to share common space. Twenty-nine centres have been built under this policy. Many other centres rent surplus school space.

Key Provincial ECEC Organizations

Manitoba Child Care Association
2350 McPhillips Street, 2nd Floor
Winnipeg, MB, R2V 4J6
Telephone: 204-586-8587 or 1-888-323-4676
Facsimile: 204-589-5613
Email: info@mccahouse.org
Website: www.mccahouse.org

Child Care Coalition of Manitoba
1376 Grant Ave., 2nd Floor
Winnipeg, MB, R3M 3Y4
Telephone: 204-489-0355
Facsimile: 204-487-2201
Website: www.childcaremanitoba.ca

Manitoba Government and General Employees' Union
601–275 Broadway
Winnipeg, MB, R3C 4M6
Telephone: (204) 982-6585
Facsimile: (204) 942-2146
Website: www.mgeu.mb.ca

Teachers' Organizations and Associations

The Manitoba Teachers' Society
191 Harcourt Street
Winnipeg, MB, R3J 3H2
Telephone: 204-888-7961
Facsimile: 204-831-0877
Website: www.mbteach.org

Saskatchewan

Kindergarten

Legislation

Saskatchewan. Legislative Assembly. *Education Act,* 1995. E-02. Amended 1996, 1997, 1998, 1999, 2000, 2001 and 2002.

Under the *Education Act,* 1995, independent schools must be registered with the Department of Learning in order to operate legally. *The Independent Schools Regulations* set out the criteria with which independent schools are required to comply.

Saskatchewan funds and delivers denominational education. Both "public" and Catholic school boards are publicly funded.

Children With Special Needs

Children's Services Policy Framework (2002) outlines policy and procedures for Early Childhood Education for children with disabilities within the school system. Children who are three years of age or older and meet the criteria for designation are eligible for early entrance programs. Funding is provided to school divisions to support programming needs.

During the 2003/04 school year, funding was provided for more than 500 children between the ages of three and five years who were designated as special needs. Approximately 300 of these children were three and four year olds. Personal Program Plans for these children may take the form of involvement with a community preschool program, child care centre or early kindergarten entrance.

There were 200 designated special needs children of kindergarten age; each designated child has a Personal Program Plan.

Regulated Child Care

Children With Special Needs

The Child Care Inclusion Program provides three types of grants to child care facilities to include children with special needs. First, individual inclusion grants are available to licensed centres and family child care homes to include children experiencing a delay or a condition of risk that may result in a delay. For this a referral is needed but not necessarily a diagnosis, and the child must attend the program a minimum of 20 hours per month. The amount of the grant varies from $200 to $300 per month depending on the need within three defined levels. This grant is an entitlement for eligible children.

Second, an enhanced accessibility grant of up to $1,500/month may be paid to assist with the additional cost of including a child with exceptionally high needs. For this grant, the child must have a diagnosis and require significant additional support, and the parents must be enrolled in an education program or employed.

There may be waiting lists for enhanced accessibility grants if the budget is fully expended.

A third kind of grant for the centres are training and resource grants of $100 ($200 for exceptional needs) per child with special needs as well as a grant of up to $600 ($1,200 for exceptional needs) for adapted equipment required to meet the needs of the child.

Inclusion grants are approved for a one year period and then are reviewed; enhanced accessibility grants are approved for a maximum of six months, after which time the facility must reapply for funding.

Funding for inclusive child care is intended to support the centre as a whole and not to provide a worker allocated to a specific child. Parents of children with special needs pay for the space but not the additional supports.

Aboriginal Child Care

Saskatchewan does not regulate child care programs on-reserve.

The First Nations/Inuit Child Care Initiative has resulted in the development of approximately 45 on-reserve child care centres.

Approximately 15% of all regulated child care programs not on-reserve have an Aboriginal program component.

Space Statistics (2003/04) (March 2004)

Number of regulated child care spaces	
Centre-based spaces	
Infants	452
Toddlers	1,129
Preschool	3,085
School-age	874
Total centre-based spaces	5,540
Family child care	2,370
Total regulated spaces	7,910
Children with special needs in regulated child care	360
Note: This includes an unspecified number of children in four centres receiving pilot funding of $75 per licensed space.	
Children receiving subsidies	3,716

Number of centres and homes	
Number of child care centres	153
Full day	153
Part-day	0
Number of family child care providers	291

Sponsorship of regulated full-time centre spaces	
Non-profit	5,540
For-profit	3

Openings and closings (2003/04)	
New child care centre licenses issued	16
Number of child care centre closures	1
Number of new licenses issued to individual family child care providers	51
Number of family child care providers who ceased providing care	37

Standards and Regulations

Regulated Centres

STAFF QUALIFICATION REQUIREMENTS Saskatchewan has three levels of certification:

ECF I—120-hour child care orientation course or equivalent provided through regional community colleges

ECE II—One year certificate in child care or equivalent

ECE III—Two year diploma In child care or equivalent

Centre directors hired after July 2001 must have at least a two year diploma in child care or equivalent (ECE III). Directors appointed to a centre director position prior to July 2001 must meet or exceed the qualifications of an ECE II (one year certificate or equivalent) but must upgrade to a two year diploma if they accept employment with another centre.

Effective January 2002, all staff employed in a centre for at least 65 hours per month had to meet the qualifications of an ECE I (120 hour child care orientation course or equivalent provided through regional community colleges). By January 2005, 30% of staff must have a one year certificate in child care or equivalent. By January 2007, a further 20% of staff must have a two year diploma or equivalent.

Individuals must apply to the Child Day Care Branch for certification. Child Day Care sets out the requirements for classification, and the courses required to achieve equivalency status,

All staff members in each centre must have completed a first-aid and CPR course.

PARENT INVOLVEMENT Non-profit child care centres are administered by parent boards; 51 % of the board members must be parents who are using the program. For-profit child care centres are required to have parent advisory committees.

LICENSING, MONITORING AND ENFORCEMENT Twenty-two provincial program consultants develop, license, monitor and consult with both centres and family child care homes and conduct two visits annually. A provincial program consultant is not required to have a background in early childhood education.

A facility may be issued a provisional license to remedy any unmet requirements as long as the health and safety of children is not at risk. If the non-compliance is not corrected within the specified period (to a maximum of six months) the license will be revoked. There is no appeal board or formal appeal mechanism but the facility may appeal directly to the Minister of Community Resources and Employment.

Regulated Family Child Care

REGULATION Individually licensed

MAXIMUM CAPACITY Family child care homes

Up to eight children (including the provider's own children under 13 years) between six weeks and 12 years. Of the eight children, only five may be younger than six years; of these five, only two may be younger than 30 months.

Group family child care homes

Up to 12 children (including the provider's and assistant's own children under 13 years). Of the 12 children, only 10 may be younger than six years, of these 10 only five maybe younger than 30 months and only three younger than 18 months.

Teen student support family child care homes. Up to six children (including the provider's own children under 13 years). Of these six children, no more than four maybe younger than six years; of these four, only two may be younger than 30 months.

PROVIDER QUALIFICATION REQUIREMENTS Must be 18 years old. All require an orientation session with a program consultant and first-aid/CPR training, plus six hours of professional development workshops each licensing year.

Providers whose homes are licensed after July 2001 must have a 40 hour introductory early childhood education course within the first year of licensing.

Providers in group family child care homes have three years to complete the 120 hour orientation course (ECE I). Assistants require first-aid and CPR training, plus six hours of professional development each licensing year.

LICENSING, MONITORING AND ENFORCEMENT Program consultants conduct annual visits to renew licenses in addition to periodic drop-in visits throughout the year.

Municipal and Other Local Government Roles

Saskatchewan legislation provides for child care centres administered by municipalities. As of 2003, there was only one centre licensed under this provision.

Child Care Planning and Development

A government-appointed Early Learning and Care Advisory Board advises on early learning and child care issues and may assist in the establishment of long-term program directions.

In 2003/04 the government announced Child Care Saskatchewan, a plan to develop 1,200 new regulated child care spaces over four years to support labour market attachment, taking advantage of federal Early Learning and Child Care funding.

Key Provincial ECEC Organizations

Saskatchewan Early Childhood Association
510 Cynthia Street
Saskatoon, SK 57L 7K7
Telephone: 306-975-0875
Facsimile: 306-975-0879

Teachers' Organizations and Associations

Saskatchewan Teachers' Federation
2317 Arlington Ave.
Saskatoon, SK 57J 2H8
Telephone: 306-373-1660 or 1-800-667-7762
Facsimile: 306-374-1122
Email: stf@stf.sk.ca
Website: www.stf.sk.ca

Alberta
Kindergarten
Legislation

Government of Alberta. Legislative Assembly. *School Act.* 2000. Early Childhood Services Policy (ECS) 1.13

Early Childhood Services Regulation 3 1/2002

Private Schools Regulation 190/2000 (under revision)

Private School Policy 3.6.1

Alberta funds and delivers denominational education. Both "public" and Catholic school boards are publicly funded.

Children with Special Needs

Integration to the fullest extent possible is recommended by Alberta Education's Inclusion Policy. Extra supports are available; appropriate funding may be allocated to specialists.

Number of children with special needs in kindergarten: Information not available.

Regulated Child Care
Children With Special Needs

The Inclusive Child Care Program in Alberta provides for inclusion of children with special needs. Funding varies depending on the special needs of the child, the type of service required and the region. Funds are paid to contracted operators on behalf of eligible children. Additional training for staff working with children with special needs is not required in legislation; however, staff typically have an ECE credential. Children with special needs may receive ECS funding (see Kindergarten section) and may receive care and education in a child care centre or a nursery school/preschool.

Aboriginal Child Care

Child care centres on-reserve are not licensed. However, under an agreement between Alberta and the federal government, on-reserve child care centres are eligible for federal government funding equivalent to parent subsidies when provincial licensing standards are met and centres are approved. As of March 2004, there were 24 approved child care centres on-reserve with a capacity of 1,114 spaces.

Space Statistics (March 2004)

Number of regulated child care spaces

Day care spaces*	26,574
Part-day nursery schools	14,831
Out-of-school care	*17,767
Total centre-based spaces	59,172
Family day home spaces**	6,554
Total regulated spaces***	65,726

* Includes children up to six and under seven years of age and not in Grade 1. Age breakdown not available.

** Enrolled spaces; total number of approved spaces not available. ***Total includes regulated centre-based spaces and enrolled family day home spaces.

Children with special needs in regulated child care

Information not available

Children receiving provincial subsidies*   10,614

*Alberta Children's Services does not provide subsidies for school-age care. Many municipalities receive Family and Community Support Services (FCSS) funding from the province that they direct towards the prevention needs of the municipality. They may choose to use a portion of these funds for school-age child care. Five of the 227 municipalities provide subsidies to eligible parents. In other locations, out-of-school care programs are offered through the municipalities, but a grant is provided. Of the 227 municipalities, 42 redirect FCSS funding for out-of-school care and, of these, five provide direct subsidies.

Number of centres and homes

Full-day day care centres	541
Part-day nursery schools/preschools	637
Stand-alone after-school programs	523
Number of family child care providers	1,741
Number of family child care agencies	88

Sponsorship of day care centres and nursery schools

	Full day		Part day		Total	
	Centres	Spaces	Centres	Spaces	Centres	Spaces
Non-profit	182	8,773	454	10,970	636	18,843
For-profit	359	17,801	183	4,761	542	22,562

Sponsorship of family day home agencies

Non-profit	45
For-profit	43

Openings and closings

Information not available

Standards and Regulations

Regulated Centres

STAFF QUALIFICATION REQUIREMENTS Alberta has three qualification levels:

Level 3 requires completion of a two year ECE diploma from an Alberta public college or an equivalent level of training, or a four year Bachelor of Education degree with a major in ECE.

Level 2 requires completion of a one year ECE certificate from an Alberta public college or an equivalent level of training, or a four year Bachelor of Elementary Education from a recognized post-secondary institution.

Level I requires completion of the government's orientation course or equivalent course work equivalent of at least 45 hours related to ECE.

Between the hours of 8:15 a.m. and 4:30 p.m., programs must have a director with a Level Three certificate or exemption. One in four staff in each centre is required to hold a Level Two certificate or exemption. All other staff are required to hold a Level One certificate or exemption.

Certification is the process used by Alberta Children's Services to review training and determine eligibility for one of the three levels of certification. To be eligible to work in a child care centre in Alberta, all staff must apply for certification to the Day Care Staff Qualification Office. The Day Care Staff Qualification Office is also responsible for the delivery of the Level One orientation course, which is contracted out to public colleges, private vocational schools, individual instructors, and is taught in some high schools for credit. Funding is provided to the institutions to deliver the course at no cost to the participant.

Numbers of staff by certification levels (March 2004)*

Level I (and exempt)	2,575
Level 2 (and exempt)	858
Level 3 (and exempt)	1,242

★ This number does not include staff in school-age programs as there are no training requirements.

PARENT INVOLVEMENT Not specified

LICENSING, MONITORING AND ENFORCEMENT Alberta regional child care specialists conduct a minimum of quarterly licensing inspections. Child care specialists currently operate under a Human Service Worker classification and come from a variety of backgrounds, including family studies and early childhood education.

If a centre is not in compliance with the regulations, a series of enforcement actions may occur depending upon the severity of the non-compliance, including a formal written order directing the centre to comply within a specific time frame to the specified regulation, cancellation of the license, or refusal to renew the license. There is a formal appeal board set up by the minister to hear appeals if a license is cancelled or refused. The legislation allows the decision of the appeal panel to be appealed through the Court of Queen's Bench. Its decision is binding.

Regulated Family Child Care (Approved Family Day Homes)

REGULATION Family day homes are approved under contract with family day care home agencies that approve and monitor providers according to provincial standards. Agencies contract with individual care providers.

MAXIMUM CAPACITY Up to six children under 11 years (including the provider's own children under 11 years) with a maximum of three children under three years old and no more than two children under two years old.

PROVIDER QUALIFICATION REQUIREMENTS Provincial Safety Standard #10 requires that direct care providers receive training in such areas as child development, child guidance and employing appropriate culturally sensitive strategies. Family day home agencies are required to develop appropriate training based on the needs of their providers and families.

LICENSING, MONITORING AND ENFORCEMENT Agency staff (home visitors) visit family day homes to ensure providers are operating according to provincial standards. Provincial staff monitor agencies and homes on a regular basis. The minimum ministry-wide requirement is four times per year.

Municipal or Other Local Government Role

The provincial government allocates funds to municipalities and Metis settlements for preventive social service needs through the Family and Community Support Services (FCSS) program. Ninety-nine percent of the provincial population resides in communities receiving services provided by local FCSS programs. Funding for some preschool programs is currently available to municipalities and Metis settlements through the FCSS Program.

One of the key principles of the FCSS Program is local autonomy in priority setting and resource allocation. Each municipality or Metis settlement receiving FCSS funding determines how the dollars should be allocated to best meet the needs of their community. Out-of-school care is the responsibility of municipal authorities; 42 FCSS-funded municipalities allocate a portion of their FCSS funds to provide out-of-school care programs. Of these, five municipalities provide subsidies and the remainder provide grants.

The municipalities of Jasper and Beaumont operate the two remaining municipal centres in the province. Staff in the programs are municipal employees and salaries are 2-3 times the provincial average. These municipalities provide additional funding to reduce the operating costs.

Child Care Planning and Development

There is no provincial plan for the development of child care.

Key Provincial ECEC Organizations

Alberta Child Care Network Association
Contact: Sherrill Brown, Chairperson
Email: browns@macewan.ca

Early Childhood Professional Association of Alberta
Co-Chair Email: carolrob@tdusplanet.net

Alberta Family Child Care Association
Contact: Susan Elson (403) 250-5795
E-mail: susan@davarchildcare.org

Teachers' Organizations and Associations

Alberta Teachers' Association
11010–142 St. NW
Edmonton, AB T5N 2R1
Telephone: 780-447-9400
Facsimile: 780-445-6481
Website: www.teachers.ab.ca

British Columbia

Kindergarten

Legislation

British Columbia. legislative Assembly. *School Act,* 1996. [R.S.B.C. c.412]

Independent School Act, 1989

Children With Special Needs

There is a policy manual regarding educational services for children with special needs. School boards are responsible for providing facilities which allow equality of access to educational programs. Some students who are identified as having special education needs are eligible for 950 hours of instruction in kindergarten (full-day). Districts are advised to co-ordinate the entry of the child to school and the planning of the kindergarten program with programs which have been offered in the preschool years. In some cases, school districts may elect to contract for services through a preschool or child development centre for some portion of the child's educational program in the kindergarten year.

Children with special needs are typically included in regular kindergarten. Learning Assistance Teachers typically provide the major link with support services available at the district level. Some schools combine learning assistance with other special education services to create a "Resource Teacher" model.

Ministries of Education and Children and Family Development (Supported Child Care Program) share a protocol agreement with respect to shared funding responsibility for children who have delayed kindergarten entry.

In 2003/04 there were 904 kindergarten children (752 part-day, 152 full-day) with identified special needs in public schools only (includes severe handicap, severe behaviour, moderate handicap, and gifted).

Regulated Child Care

Children With Special Needs

The Supported Child Care Program is intended for children who require extra staffing and other supports to be included in a child care or other community setting because they have a developmental delay or disability in physical, cognitive, communicative or social/emotional/behavioural areas. Families participate on a voluntary basis. It is not income tested. The funds designated for these supports are referred to as the range payment.

Supported Child Care (SCC) community agencies provide both SCC Consultant Services for families and SCC Support Workers to families and child care and community settings. In addition, the Ministry of Children and Family Development (MCFD), provides a Special Needs Supplement of up to $107 to assist families eligible for the Child Care Subsidy Program with the costs of child care (see Recent Developments for announced change in amount). Supported Child Care is currently in transition.

Aboriginal Child Care

B.C. funds and licenses Aboriginal on-reserve and off-reserve child care through the same programs available to other (non-Aboriginal) facilities, parents and providers. There are 65 First Nations communities that have licensed child care facilities and approximately 800 licensed child care spaces are located on-reserve. Child care centres run by Band and Tribal Councils became eligible to apply for provincial funding as of October 1994.

A number of educational institutions have developed training for First Nations early childhood educators. British Columbia Aboriginal Child Care Society is funded by government to provide resource and referral services to Aboriginal child care providers. A number of Aboriginal communities are working with the Supported Child Care program to improve access to the program and to build capacity for SCC programs administered by Aboriginal communities.

Space Statistics (2002/03)

Number of regulated child care spaces		
Centre-based	Full-time	Part-time
Group child care (under 3 yrs)	4,511	—
Group child care (over 30 mths)	14,847	—
Preschool (nursery school)	—	17,728
Out-of-school	—	23,089
Child minding	—	1,972
Occasional child care/other	—	391
Special needs	320	—
Total centre-based spaces	62,858	
Regulated family child care	17,372	
Total regulated spaces	80,230	
Other: Registered (Licence-Not-Required)		*1,600

Registered LNRs are not licensed by the province nor are they regulated. They are expected to meet the requirements set by their Child Care Resource and Referral Program.

Average number of children with special needs in child care	5,000

This includes children in some unregulated settings. The number in regulated care is not available.

Estimated number of children in regulated child care receiving subsidies	11,000

Note: British Columbia provides fee subsidies for children in both regulated and unregulated child care. Actual numbers are not available.

Number of centres and homes

Number of child care centres:

— Full day	1,011
— Part-day nursery schools/preschools	982
— Stand-alone after school programs	969
— Other (child minding, emergency, occasional, specialized)	171
Number of licensed family child care providers	2,525

Sponsorship of regulated centre spaces (2003/04)

Information no longer available

Openings and closings

New child cart centre licenses issued	183
Number of child care centre closures	110
Number of new licenses issued to individual family child care providers	266
Number of family child care providers who ceased providing care	256

Note: In addition, 24 new licenses were issued to unknown facility types and 12 unknowns closed. Source: Information on numbers of new facility licenses issued and facilities closed comes from a 45% response rate of Health Authorities reporting to MCFD.

Standards and Regulations

Regulated Centre

STAFF QUALIFICATIONS REQUIREMENTS These are three levels of staff: Early Childhood Educators, Assistant Early Childhood Educators and Responsible Adults. The training requirements for each arc as follows:

Early Childhood Educator—There are three categories of Early Childhood Educators, each with specific training requirements:

- *Early childhood educator* requires completion of a basic one year early childhood education training program from an approved training institution and 500 hours of supervised work experience.
- *Infant/toddler educator* requires completion of the basic early childhood education program plus specialized training related to infant/toddler care and education.
- *Special needs educator* requires completion of the basic early childhood education program plus specialized training related to children with special needs.

Assistant Early Childhood Educators—This category includes those who are in the process of qualifying for an ECE certificate or who have completed a training program that the director recognizes as at least equivalent to one course of a basic early childhood education program.

Responsible Adults—These staff must have completed a course on the care of young children or have relevant work experience.

Staffing requirements vary by the type of care provider and the age of the children as follows:

- *Group child care, under 36 months:* Each group of four or fewer children requires one Infant/Toddler Educator. Each group of five to eight children requires one Infant/Toddler Educator and one Early Childhood Educator. Each group of nine to twelve children requires one Infant/Toddler Educator, one Early Childhood Educator and one Assistant. The same staffing requirements apply in emergency care for children in this age group.★
- *Group day care, 30 months to school-age:* Each group requires one early childhood educator plus Assistant Early Childhood Educators. The same staffing requirements apply in emergency care for children in this age group.★

★For children three years of age or more, the same staffing requirements apply for emergency care.

- *Out-of-school, child-minding, and occasional or ski resort care:* Staff must be older than 19 years and have taken a course on the care of young children or have relevant work experience. There are no specific early childhood training requirements (see above Responsible Adults).
- *Special needs facilities:* Special needs facilities (group care facilities where at least 25% of the children have special needs) require one Special Needs Educator for every group of four or fewer children. Larger groups require one Special Needs Educator plus Early Childhood Educators.

PARENT INVOLVEMENT Not specified

LICENSING, MONITORING AND ENFORCEMENT The Ministry of Health Services through the *Community Care and Assisted Living Act* is responsible for licensing and monitoring child care facilities as well as developing policies and procedures specific to program licensing. The functions are carried out by the local Health Authorities through the Medical Health Officers.

The local Medical Health Officer, through licensing officers, issues interim permits and licenses, amends, suspends or cancels licenses, investigates complaints about programs, and conducts inspections and ongoing monitoring of programs.

There is no legislated frequency for monitoring inspections. Generally, most facilities have an annual licensing visit.

If a centre is not in compliance, conditions can be placed on the license and the operator given a time frame in which to comply. If the situation is considered to be a danger to the children, the license can be suspended or cancelled. The operator can request a hearing and then, if not satisfied, can go to the Community Care and Assisted Living Appeal Board, composed of non-government members, including people from the child care field.

Regulated Family Child Care

REGULATION Individually licensed

MAXIMUM CAPACITY Up to seven children under 13 years (including children living in the home). Of the seven children, there may be no more than five preschoolers, no more than three children under three years of age, and no more than one child under one year. Children 12 years or older and who are related to the caregiver are not included.

PROVIDER QUALIFICATION REQUIREMENTS Must be over 19 years and have a first-aid certificate, be able to provide care and mature guidance to children, and have either completed a course on the care of young children or have relevant work experience. There are no early childhood training requirements.

LICENSING, MONITORING AND ENFORCEMENT Most facilities have an annual licensing visit. An initial inspection by the Fire Marshall's office may be required when a new house opens.

Municipal And Other Local Government Role

There is no legislated municipal or other local government role. The City of Vancouver and several other municipalities play a role in planning and developing child care.

Child Care Planning and Development

A Provincial Child Care Council of 14 members appointed by the Minister responsible for child care addresses policy matters and priorities in an advisory capacity.

There are no provincial target levels of service nor a long-term planning process.

Key Provincial ECEC Organizations

Provincial Child Care Council
2925 Meadowvista Pl
Coquitlam BC V3E 2P5
Phone: 604 941-0359
604-944-0101
Fax: 604-944-6166
Website: http://www.mcaws.gov.lx.ca/thildcare/index.htm

BC Aboriginal Child Care Society
209-1999 Marine Dr
Vancouver BC V7P 3J3
Phone: 604-990-9939
Fax: 604-990-9457
Website: http://www.acc-society.bc.ca/

BC Association of Child Care Employers
210W Broadway 3rd Fl
Vancouver BC VSY 3W2
Phone: 604-944-0101
Fax: 604-944-6166

Child Care Advocacy Forum
300W Broadway 3rd Fl
Vancouver, BC V5Y 3W2
Phone: 604-515-6257
Fax: 604-709-5662
Website: http://www.cccabc.bc.ca/forum/

Coalition of Child Care Advocates of BC
210W Broadway 3rd Fl
Vancouver BC V5Y 3W2
Phone: 604-888-8786
604-222-2290
Fax: 604-888-8729
Website: http://www.cccabc.bc.ca/

Early Childhood Educators of BC
210W Broadway, 3rd Fl
Vancouver BC V5Y 3W2
Phone: 604-709-6063
Fax; 604-709-5662
Website: http://www.cfc-efc.ca/ecebc/

School-Age Child Care Association of BC
210W Broadway 3rd Fl
Vancouver BC VSY 3W2
Phone: 604-325-1010
Fax: 604-325-1039

Westcoast Child Care Resource Centre
210 W Broadway, 3rd Fl
Vancouver BC VSY 3W2
Phone: 604-709-5661
Fax: 604-709-5662
Website: http://www.wstcoast.org

Western Canada Family Child Care Association of BC
210W Broadway 3rd Fl
Vancouver BC V5Y 3W2
Phone: 604-594-1146
Fax: 604-594-1146
Website: http://www.cfc-efc.ca/wcfcca/

Teachers' Organizations and Associations

British Columbia Teachers' Federation
100-550 West 6th Avenue
Vancouver, BC V5Z 4P2
Phone: 604-871-2283
1-800-663-9163
Fax: 604-871-2290
Website: http://www.bctf.ca/home.shtml

Northwest Territories

Kindergarten

Legislation

Northwest Territories. Legislative Assembly. *Education Act,* R.S.N.W.T. 1995, c. 28.
    The legislation applies to public and private schools.
    There is a departmental directive that provides additional guidelines (funding and reporting, administration, monitoring and education program) for private schools.

Children With Special Needs

There is a policy of inclusion of children with special needs. Children have access to the education program in a regular instructional classroom setting. Boards are required to provide support to make this possible through School Support funding. There is an exemption from inclusion for children with extreme needs; the child may be in a treatment centre instead of classroom.
    The number of kindergarten children with identified special needs is not available.

Regulated Child Care

Children With Special Needs

There are no segregated child care programs for children with special needs.
    Care providers are funded to provide extra support to children with special needs, through higher operating grants, funded at the infant rate. Parents may be eligible for fee subsidies for their children with special needs even if they are not employed or at school. They must meet the same financial eligibility requirements as other parents receiving subsidy, and have a medical referral from a recognized health care official for the child to be in developmental care.

Aboriginal Child Care

The Northwest Territories is comprised of Inuit and Dene communities outside the capital City of Yellowknife. The majority of community-based programs are equally available to all children. The Aboriginal Head Start programs are the only programs targeted specifically towards Aboriginal children. However, they may include non-Aboriginal children if their capacity allows.

Space Statistics (2003/04)

Number of regulated child care spaces

Centre spaces

Infant (0-2 years)	81
Preschool (2-5 years)	721
After-school (6-12 years)	161

Family child care spaces

Infant (0-2 years)	64
Preschool (2-5 years)	128
After-school (6-12 years)	64
Total regulated spaces	1,219

Note: All centres are licensed for full-time spaces even though many operate as part-day nursery schools/playschools.

Numbers of centres and homes

Number of child care centres	49
— Number of full-day child care centres	19
— Number of part-day nursery schools/preschools	21
— Number of stand-alone school age centres	9
Number of licensed family child care providers	32

Number of children with special needs in regulated child care

Information not available

Number of children receiving subsidies

Information not available

Sponsorship of regulated centre spaces

Currently all centres are non-profit and family day homes are considered to be non-profit.

Openings and closings

New centre licenses issued	1
Number of centre closures	4
Number of new family child care licenses issued 2003/04	7
Number of family child care homes that closed in 2003/04	2

Standards and Regulations

Regulated Centres

STAFF QUALIFICATION REQUIREMENTS Must be at least 19 years of age and have a first-aid certificate and a clear criminal record with regard to offences respecting a child.

There are no early childhood training requirements.

PARENT INVOLVEMENT The legislation requires non-profit programs to have boards of directors with at least 51% parent members. For-profit programs are required to establish and confirm in writing with the Director of Early Childhood and School Services a plan for involving the parents or guardians of children attending the centre in the operation of the program.

LICENSING, MONITORING AND ENFORCEMENT Licenses may be granted for 3-5 years, often issued in conjunction with annual inspections. All licensed child care centres are inspected by an Early Childhood Consultant from the Early Childhood Program, the Public Health Department, and Fire Marshall's office. The Early Childhood Consultant is required to have a background in early childhood education, either an ECE credential and four years experience at the supervisory level in a child care centre, or a teaching credential and six years front-line child care experience.

Regulated Family Child Care

REGULATION Individually licensed

MAXIMUM CAPACITY Maximum of eight children under 12 years (including the provider's own children). No more than six of the eight children maybe five years or under, no more than three children may be under three years, and no more than two children maybe under two years.

PROVIDER QUALIFICATION REQUIREMENTS A provider must be a minimum of 19 years of age and have a first-aid certificate and a clear criminal record with regard to offences respecting a child.

There are no early childhood training requirements.

LICENSING, MONITORING AND ENFORCEMENT Homes are visited at least once a year by staff from the Early Childhood Program and a representative from each of the Public Health Department and the Fire Marshall's office. Licenses are usually issued in conjunction with annual inspections.

Municipal or Other Local Government Role

There is no local government role.

Child Care Planning and Development

There is no territorial plan for the development of child care. New centres must complete a needs assessment before they are eligible to apply for start-up funding.

Related Programs

The Territorial Government provides communities with funding through the Healthy Children Initiative to enhance existing early childhood programs and services. This funding is provided to each community using a population formula and interested non-profit groups may submit proposals to regional management committees for review.

Key Territorial ECEC Organizations

There is no territorial child care organization.

Teachers' Organizations and Associations

Northwest Territories Teachers' Association
5018-48th Street
P.O. Box 2340
Yellowknife, NT X1A 2P7
Telephone: 867-873-8501
Facsimile: 867-873-2366
Email: nwta@nwtta.nt.ca
Website: www.nwtta.nt.ca

Nunavut

Kindergarten

Legislation

Northwest Territories. Legislative Assembly. Education Act. 1995, R.S.N.W.T. c.28.★

★ *The Nunavut Legislative Assembly Bill 1. Education Act 2002 was introduced but did not pass.*

★ *The Nunavut Act, S.C. 1993, c.28 as amended brought Nunavut into being on April 1, 1999. Laws passed by the Government of the Northwest Territories during this period were inherited by the Government of Nunavut upon its creation. The Government of Nunavut is in the process of developing its own education legislation.*

Children With Special Needs

There is a policy of inclusion; children with special needs have the right to be in a regular class with children their own age and in their own community. Extra supports such as student support assistants, Individual Education Plans, and specialists provided through Health are available.

Number of kindergarten children with identified special needs 2003/04: Information not available

Regulated Child Care

Children With Special Needs

There are no segregated child care programs for children with special needs.

Care providers are funded to provide extra support for children with special needs through the daily operating grants which are based on the age of the child and the area in which the centre is located. The operating grant for a preschool child is increased by approximately 50% for a child with an identified special need and is an entitlement.

In order for the centre to receive the additional funding for a child, a letter from a recognized health care professional is required. In addition, centres may apply for funding to the Healthy Children's Initiative for adaptive equipment or for a one-on-one worker if necessary.

Parents are eligible for fee subsidy for their children with special needs even if they are not employed or at school. This subsidy eligibility requires a financial needs assessment to be applied and parents must have a medical referral from a recognized health care professional for the child to be in developmental care.

Aboriginal Child Care

Since 1996, the First Nations and Inuit Child Care Initiative (FNICCI) has provided funding for the development of approximately 20 centres in what is now Nunavut. There is an Aboriginal Human Resource Development Strategy (AHRDS) regional office in each of Nunavut's three regions.* Each regional AHRDS office took on the responsibility for the delivery and administration of the Inuit Childcare Program in their Region, established with FNICCI funding.

In addition to providing capital funding for new child care centres, all child care centres receive block funding from their AHRDS office which may also provide one-time funding for repairs and renovations, and for developing or acquiring culturally relevant program materials. In addition, the AHRDS may provide wage subsidies based on the number of Inuit staff in a centre and fee subsidies to Land-Claim Beneficiary parents that is in addition to the regular fee subsidy funded through Early Childhood Services. AHRDS offices have also provided funding for training in each region, including the delivery of ECE training through Arctic College.

The federal Inuit Childcare Program spends approximately $3 million/year on child care in Nunavut.

* *In April 1999, the federal government launched the Aboriginal Human Resources Development Strategy (AHRDS) within Human Resources Development Canada (HRDC). Each of the HRDC regions entered into an Aboriginal Human Resources Development Agreement with various Aboriginal organizations across Canada.*

Space Statistics

Number of regulated child care spaces (March 2004)		
Centres	Full-time	Part-time
Infants (under two years)	158	—
Preschoolers	547	214
After-school	—	95
Family child care	0	0
Total regulated spaces	1,014	

Facilities and homes	
Number of child care centres (March 2004):	46
— Full-day	30
— Part-day nursery schools/preschools	11
— Stand-alone after-school programs	5
— Number of family child care providers	0

Children with special needs in regulated child care

Information not available

Number of children in regulated child care receiving subsidies:

Information not available; however, the number of families receiving subsidies was 263. There is no information available on the numbers using regulated or unregulated care.

Sponsorship of regulated centre spaces as of March 31, 2004

Non-profit	1,014

Note: All child care centres in Nunavut are non-profit. Family day homes are considered to be non-profit.

Openings and closings (2003/04)

New child care centre licenses issued	1
Number of child care centre closures	*3
Number of new licenses issued to individual family child care providers	0
Number of Family child care agencies/individual providers who ceased providing care	**1

*It is anticipated that the three centres that closed will re-open in 2004/05

**A family day home was licensed in 2002 and closed in 2004

Standards And Regulations

Regulated Centres

STAFF QUALIFICATION REQUIREMENTS Must be at least 19 years of age, have a first-aid certificate and represent the cultural background of the children. There are no early childhood training requirements.

PARENT INVOLVEMENT The legislation requires non-profit programs whose boards of directors do not have a minimum of 51% parent members to have a parent committee with a minimum of 51% parent members.

LICENSING, MONITORING AND ENFORCEMENT Licenses are granted for one year. Annual inspections of all regulated child care centres are conducted by an Early Childhood Officer from the Department of Education, the Public Health Department, and the Fire Marshall's office. It is recommended that the Early Childhood Officer have a background in early childhood education.

Regulated Family Child Care

REGULATION Individually licensed

MAXIMUM CAPACITY Maximum of eight children under 12 years (including the provider's children). No more than six of the eight children may be five years or under, no more than three children may be under three years, and no more than two children may be under two years.

PROVIDER QUALIFICATION REQUIREMENTS A provider must be a minimum of 19 years of age and have a first-aid certificate. There are no early childhood training requirements.

LICENSING, MONITORING AND ENFORCEMENT Homes are visited at least once a year by staff from the Early Childhood Program and a representative from each of the Public Health Department and the Fire Marshall's office.

Municipal And Other Local Government Role

Child care programs may be under the auspice of District Education Authorities who may hold the license.

Child Care Planning and Development

There is no territorial plan for the development of child care. New centres must complete a needs assessment before they are eligible to apply for start-up funding.

Key Territorial ECEC Organizations

Nunavut Inuit Childcare Association
Box 459
Pond Inlet, NU X0A 0S0

Yukon

Kindergarten

Legislation

Yukon Territory. Legislative Assembly. *Education Act,* 1990. S.Y. c.25.

Yukon funds and delivers denominational education. Both "public" and Catholic school boards are publicly funded.

There are no private schools in Yukon.

Children With Special Needs

There is a policy guideline for children with special needs. Children are included in regular kindergarten unless they have severe, multiple special needs. Extra support is available; the Department of Education assigns Educational Assistants. Services such as speech and language, physical and occupational therapies and psychological services for testing are provided.

The number of children with special needs in 2003/04:48

Regulated Child Care

Children With Special Needs

Child care regulations state that children with special needs in mainstream child care programs must be integrated to the fullest extent possible. A child is designated special needs on the assessment of a child care professional. An Individual Program Plan must be developed for the child in consultation with staff, parents and professionals in the community that outlines goals and objectives for the child.

There are no segregated child care programs. The Whitehorse Child Development Centre provides special needs programming and supports across the Yukon. It operates an integrated preschool program licensed for 25 children as well as unlicensed preschool programs. It provides early intervention supports and resources to families of children with special needs. It operates a mobile outreach unit that serves every community in the territory for support and resource provision.

Funding is also available for centres and family day homes through a Supported Child Care fund and is based on the individual need of the child. Funding may be provided for adaptive equipment, transportation, programming support and additional staff.

Parents who meet the financial eligibility criteria receive a fee subsidy for their child with special needs to attend a child care program whether or not the parent is its the paid labour force. Parents who are not eligible for a subsidy pay for the child care space but not for the additional supports.

Aboriginal Child Care

There are no reserves for First Nations people in the Yukon. First Nations receive the same start-up and operating grants from the Yukon government as other licensed child care centres and family day homes. They also receive funding from the federal First Nations and Inuit Child Care Initiative which is administered by the Council for Yukon First Nations. The Council for Yukon First Nations also provides financial support to one additional child care centre operated by a child care society and a number of family day homes that serve First Nations children.

In total there are approximately 225 regulated spaces operated or supported by First Nations in seven centres. There are three Aboriginal Head Start programs, two as part of regulated First Nations child care centres, and one stand-alone unlicensed preschool. Parents who use the regulated centres and family child care homes are eligible for fee subsidies.

Space Statistics (2003/04)

Number of regulated child care spaces	
Centre-based	
Infants/toddlers	345
Preschool	398
School-age	243
Family child care	383
Total regulated spaces	1,369
Note: All spaces are considered to be full-time.	

Children with special needs in regulated child care	(approximately) 45

Children receiving subsidies	786

Number of facilities and homes	
Number of child care centres	37
— Full day	31
— Stand-alone after school programs	6
Number of individual family child care providers	43

Sponsorship of regulated centre spaces	
Non-profit	729
For-profit	257

Openings and closings	
New child care centre licenses issued	6
Number of child care centre closures	2
Number of new licenses issued to individual family child care providers	6
Number of family child care providers who ceased providing care	2

Standards and Regulations

Regulated Centres

STAFF QUALIFICATION REQUIREMENTS As of 2000, 20% of staff must meet or exceed the Child Care Worker III qualifications, 30% must meet or exceed the Child Care Worker II qualifications and the rest must meet or exceed Child Care Worker I qualifications.

Levels

Child Care Worker III: Two or more years of training in early childhood development (ECD) or equivalent from a recognized college or university.

Child Car Worker II: One year training in ECD or equivalent from a recognized college or university.

Child Care Worker I: 60 hour introduction to early childhood development course (ECD) or equivalent.

PARENT INVOLVEMENT The operator of the centre must ensure that open communication is maintained with parents and guardians on all matters affecting their child. Parents and guardians must also have reasonable access to the program, inspection reports, written policies, menus, log of injuries, The Child Care Act, and the Regulation and Guidelines, and the Child Care Subsidy Regulation.

LICENSING, MONITORING AND ENFORCEMENT A government Child Care inspector is required to conduct an annual inspection and two to four unannounced visits per year to each child care centre. Centres are also required to have an annual fire and environmental health inspection.

Child Care Inspectors are required to have a background in early childhood education.

If a centre is not in compliance with the regulation., it is given an order to comply. If the centre does not come into compliance within the stated timeframe allowed by the order, the license may be suspended or revoked, or the Direct Operating Grant may be frozen. If a license is suspended or revoked the centre can appeal to the Yukon Child Care Board, composed of community members appointed by the Minister for a two-year term. Its decision is binding.

Regulated Family Day Care

REGULATION Individually licensed

MAXIMUM CAPACITY Up to eight children (including the provider's own preschool but not school-aged children). There may be no more than three infants if there are also three children who are preschoolers or school-age already enrolled. If there is an additional caregiver, there maybe four additional school-age children.

PROVIDER QUALIFICATION REQUIREMENTS Caregivers must complete a 60 hour introductory early childhood development course, a specific family day home course, or equivalent within the first year they provide care for children. Caregivers must be 18 years of age and have a first-aid certificate.

LICENSING, MONITORING AND ENFORCEMENT Family day care homes are regulated by the same legislation as child care centres. They receive one annual inspection and two to four unannounced spot checks per year by a government Child Care Coordinator to monitor for compliance with the regulations.

Municipal and Other Local Government Role

Legislation permits municipalities to hold licenses to directly operate child care programs although none do so.

Child Care Planning and Development

In 2003 the Minister of Health and Social Services appointed a time-limited child care working group tasked with developing recommendations for a four-year plan to address issues identified by child care stakeholders. In the fall 2003 a four-year plan was submitted to the Minister for consideration. In response to the plan additional funding was allocated to child care, with increases for subsequent years, to be split between wages and centre operating funds. (See Recent Developments for further detail).

Key Territorial ECEC Organizations

Yukon Child Care Association
P.O. Box 31710, Main Street
Whitehorse, YT Y1A 6L3
Telephone: 867-668-2485 or 867-667-4013
Facsimile: 867-668-3831

Society of Yukon Family Day Homes
12 Tutshi Road
Whitehorse, YT Y1A 3R3
Telephone: 867-668-6349
Facsimile: 867-393-3902

Teachers' Organizailons And Associations

Yukon Teachers' Association
2064-2nd Avenue
Whitehorse, YT Y1A 1A9
Telephone: 867-668-6777 or 1-866-668-2097
Facsimile: 867-667-4324
Website: www.yta.yk.ca

Index

"AS IS" LICENSE AGREEMENT AND LIMITED WARRANTY